MENNONITES IN ILLINOIS

MENNONITES IN ILLINOIS

Willard H. Smith

Foreword by Peter G. Schultz

Wipf and Stock Publishers
150 West Broadway • Eugene OR 97401
2001

Mennonites in Illinois

By Smith, Willard H.
Copyright©1983 by Herald Press
ISBN: 1-57910-771-0

Reprinted by *Wipf and Stock Publishers*
150 West Broadway • Eugene OR 97401

Previously published by Herald Press, 1983.

Dedicated to our Amish and Mennonite forebears in Illinois who labored diligently to pass on to their children a heritage that is worth perpetuating.

Contents

Foreword by Peter G. Schultz 13
Editor's Introduction by Theron F. Schlabach..................15
Author's Preface 19

1. Illinois When the Mennonites Came 25
2. The Mennonite Settlements in Illinois
   to the 1870s 34
3. The Amish Mennonite Settlements in
   Illinois to About 1878...................................55
4. The Central Conference Mennonites in Illinois to 1957......88
5. The Evangelical Mennonite Church (Defenseless Mennonites)
   in Illinois...111
6. The Old Order Amish in Illinois 132
7. Smaller Mennonite and Related Groups in Illinois 145

   Reformed Mennonites, General Conference to 1957, Conservative Amish Mennonites, Krimmer Mennonite Brethren (now merged with Mennonite Brethren), Defenseless Mennonite Brethren in Christ (now Evangelical Mennonite Brethren), Beachy Amish, and similar non-Mennonite groups—Brethren in Christ, Missionary Church Association, Apostolic Christian

8. Illinois Amish Mennonite Congregations and the Western
   District Amish Mennonite Conference.....................168
9. The So-Called "Old" Mennonites and the Development of
   the Illinois Mennonite Conference........................189
10. The "Awakening" Among Illinois Mennonites: Publication,
    New Agencies, Organizations 223

    Meaning and Sources
    Change to English Language
    Publication Interests

Sunday Schools and Sunday School Conferences
Revivals and Evangelism
Bible Conferences
Young People's Meetings, Bible Meetings,
  Christian Endeavor, etc.
Daily Vacation Bible Schools or
  Summer Bible Schools

11. The "Awakening" Among Illinois Mennonites: Education, Missions, Service 248
    Education
    Missions
    Service
        —*Orphanages and Old People's Homes*
        —*Hospitals*
        —*Ladies' Aid Societies, Sewing Circles*
        —*Others: Mutual Aid, Relief Work, etc.*
12. Strain, Stress, Liberalism, Fundamentalism 303
13. Illinois Mennonites and War 345
14. Illinois Mennonites and Social Issues...................375
15. Illinois Hispanic American and
    Afro-American Mennonites: The New Urban Challenge.....420
16. Other Developments and Trends in Recent Decades 436
17. Toward Mennonite Cooperation and Unity................459
18. American Acculturation and Keeping the Faith 484

Notes..493
Appendixes
    A. Survey of Occupations, Income, and Education Among
       Illinois Mennonites..................................527
    B. Illinois Mennonite Congregations and Leaders 531
    C. Maps:
        Illinois Mennonite and Related Churches
           and Institutions..................................558
        Amish-Mennonite Settlements, 1830-1850 559

Bibliography 560
Index 581
The Author 115
Chart: Origins of Illinois Amish and Mennonites ...... *Inside Back*
                                                              Cover

Foreword

In 1931, publication of Harry F. Weber's *Centennial History of the Mennonites in Illinois, 1829-1929*, led to a deepening interest in the lives and affairs of the Mennonites of that state. Organization of the Illinois Mennonite Historical and Genealogical Society in 1969 gave further impetus to study, research, and record-keeping. An abundance of new information indicates that Mennonite groups and individuals in Illinois had a profound effect on Mennonites generally. They were in the forefront when Mennonites dealt with issues concerning missions, education, and service programs. Some were prominent in the resolution of controversies that arose during the "Awakening" of the late nineteenth and early twentieth centuries.

Realizing that the newly uncovered information should be available in an organized form, our society began to consider a new history of Illinois Mennonites. In 1976 it formed a history project committee, to explore the possibility of a current, scholarly publication. The project became a reality when Dr. Willard H. Smith of Goshen, Indiana, consented to refine and organize the material, and to write the book. He has given generously of his knowledge, experience, and time to make this publication possible.

Smith is uniquely qualified to be author of this book. He is a native of Illinois and has a thorough knowledge and understanding of the customs and beliefs of Illinois Mennonites. His family was among the early Mennonite settlers in the state, and active in the spiritual life of their community. Smith himself has studied and taught history for many years, has written many historical articles, and is the author of several books. As a professor at Goshen College, he had the support of other Mennonite historians and ready access to library and archival materials relating to Illinois Mennonites. He has devoted many hours to the research and writing of this book—donating all of his time and effort and generously contributing to the cost of research and clerical assistance. Truly Willard H. Smith has given his readers and the society a "labor of love." We are deeply indebted to him.

Mennonites were not latecomers to Illinois. The first ones arrived about 1830—just twelve years after statehood. Some acquired farms by patents direct from the federal government. Mennonites came from eastern states and directly from Europe. They settled first in the timberlands, then subsequently were among the first to settle on the open prairies. In general the early Mennonites were grouped with "Germans."

While Mennonites lived within the culture of the times, they were a somewhat separate people with distinctive religious beliefs. The distinctives were the principal motivation for their individual and group existence. Much of history deals with politics and war, but those are processes which are not so fundamental in shaping the lives of Mennonites. Mennonites find their sources not in military chronicles or in political trends but in biblical perceptions and in the lives of individuals and the group. In this book, the author discusses and interprets those perceptions and events.

As the reader will notice, Illinois Mennonites did not live in isolation. They were influenced by internal and external religious, cultural, and economic forces to which they responded in various ways. Willard H. Smith has made every effort to present a true and correct story of what occurred and how Illinois Mennonites moved through the events of their history. They did not move as a uniform group because, as Smith points out, Mennonites "are quite individualistic." He also states, however, that "in recent decades there has been a remarkable growth toward inter-Mennonite cooperation and unity." It is our hope that this trend will continue, and with it a deeper awareness and appreciation of our spiritual and cultural heritage. We want this book to contribute to the Anabaptist-Mennonite testimony.

Peter G. Schultz, President
Illinois Mennonite Historical
and Genealogical Society

Editor's Introduction

For putting together the story of Mennonites in the United States and Canada, nothing can quite take the place of solid, competent, well-researched regional histories. In 1931 Illinois Mennonites had their story told quite well by scholar Harry F. Weber, in a book he published in that year. But as Willard H. Smith explains in his preface, the time has come for bringing Illinois Mennonite history up-to-date. We are fortunate that there is in the state an "Illinois Mennonite Historical and Genealogical Society" with strong leadership perspicacious enough to see the need for the new history, determined enough to sponsor and support it, and able to attract a mature, trained scholar to do the job. Willard H. Smith has done the job.

The Mennonite Historical Society is gratified to include Smith's book in its Studies in Anabaptist and Mennonite History series, as it included Weber's book fifty years ago. For the book is a strong one. One of its strengths is that the author has put his heart very much in this work. Although it was in neighboring Indiana that Smith taught history throughout his life, he is a son of Illinois and its Mennonite communities, in close touch with the state and its Mennonite and Amish people ever since he grew up and lived there until the early 1920s. Thus to all the benefits of historical training and a lifetime of scholarship he adds personal acquaintance and interest, with a spark that academic writing often lacks.

Another strength is simply the vast amount of information Smith has brought together. Any good local or regional church history should provide all the basic facts about congregations and their origins, about outstanding religious leaders of the area, about regional church institutions, and about how the groups covered have fit themselves to local geography, history, and community development. Smith's research and reporting are massive and comprehensive.

Yet Smith did not stop there. Many local and regional histories only catalog facts, and are very dull. Or they go on to unverifiable statements of chauvinistic praise for the locality and its people, and thus degenerate into hagiography. Smith's way, by contrast, is to move on from basic facts to interesting themes, such as how Mennonites fit into the frontier process, how they experienced religious awakenings, how they interacted with the political system (especially in wartime), how they reached out in mission and institution-building, and their patterns of cultural borrowing. He has developed his themes responsibly, as a professional. Especially in the second half of the book, the reader will find such themes unfolding.

Finally, a very great strength of the book is its inter-Mennonite approach. Over the years the Mennonite story in North America has become a kind of triangle—a triangle rather than, as often presented, some sort of straight line running from, say, traditionalism to progressivism or Anabaptism to Fundamentalism. And to understand the triangle—to understand Mennonitism in the American context—one must look at the various Mennonite groups together as Smith and as Weber before him have done.

At one point of the triangle is an in-group-oriented traditionalism. Old Order groups, Mennonite or Amish or Hutterite, demonstrate such traditionalism most starkly. In some sense fundamentalist (with small "f"), groups who hover near this point see themselves as living by a body of basic principles coming to them through their own life and history and not from surrounding culture. To protect the body of principles (in German the *Ordnung*, in English the "Order") they have surrounded their basic beliefs with various cultural traditions that have tended in turn to become part of the "Order." At another point of the triangle is a self-conscious progressivism and open acceptance of much surrounding culture. Those near that point participate avidly in North American life and North American institutions, in higher education, in denominationalism, in American skepticism about unchecked authority, and in faith that change usually brings improvement. Such people, found most notably perhaps among the General Conference Mennonites, tend to believe that it is best to adapt to surrounding cultural change if Mennonites are to preserve what is truly essential in their faith, and witness effectively to it.

At the third point is conservative American evangelicalism or, at the extreme tip, Fundamentalism. The individuals and occasionally groups that have clustered near this point are, like the in-group traditionalists, quite preoccupied with defense of traditions and fundamentals. But unlike at the first point, the traditions and fundamentals they defend come quite largely and quite openly from outside the streams of Amish and Mennonite history. In fact, they borrow culture

Editor's Introduction

quite as avidly as do those near the progressive point of the triangle—religious culture most directly, but also much of American lifestyle and social values. On the other hand they are much more cautious than are the progressives about accepting certain parts of a culturally modern outlook, especially those parts that might lead to religious or social liberalism.

Implicitly, Smith's presentation of Illinois Mennonite history develops quite a clear picture of that triangle. Not many Illinois Mennonites or Amish, it would seem, took positions precisely at the tips; and a few were drawn to still other positions precisely at the tips; and a few were drawn to still other positions, not covered by the triangle. But most individual Mennonites were at points well within the triangle's area, not even far out along one of the triangle's sides. As for groups, some covered rather large portions of the area, while others clustered more tightly around one position or another. Reading Smith's work gives strong impressions of how Mennonites not only in Illinois but across North America have been pushed or pulled toward the different positions. For in fact the Illinois Mennonites make a pretty good case study of forces that have impinged upon Mennonites throughout the United States, and to a degree in Canada. Indeed, they make a case study for a broader history of religion in North America: their stories tell much about how small groups in America have felt drawn to modify their own traditions and enter one or another stream of Protestant religion and Protestant culture. Despite American religious pluralism, the study of Illinois Mennonites tells much of Protestantism's cultural dominance and power.

Theron F. Schlabach
Coeditor-in-Chief
Studies in Anabaptist and
Mennonite History

Goshen College
August 25, 1981

Author's Preface

Spring of 1983, when this volume is to appear, is a good time to publish a history of Mennonites in Illinois. The time is approximately the sesquicentennial of the first substantial Amish migration to the state—the first two Amish families, of whom there is record, came in 1830. Nineteen eighty-three is precisely one hundred and fifty years after the Amish organized their first Illinois congregation, Partridge, near the present town of Metamora. For Mennonites also (as contrasted to the Amish), the year falls exactly a century and a half after their first settlement in Illinois. And since the first permanent Mennonite settlement anywhere in North America got underway at Germantown in Pennsylvania in 1683, 1983 marks a tricentennial for the whole North American Mennonite story.

No one should have to defend the writing and reading of history. One should not—but it seems that one must. Someone has well said that a group that forgets its past will soon have no future. Or, as the philosopher Santayana has warned: "When experience is not retained, as among savages, infancy is perpetual. Those who cannot remember the past are condemned to repeat it [with all its mistakes]."*

Among a number of vigorous Mennonite institutions in Illinois is a very active Illinois Mennonite Historical and Genealogical Society. It has, in effect, heeded Santayana's advice and sponsored this history. In 1976 officials of the society wrote to Dr. Leonard Gross, archivist and executive secretary of the Historical Committee of the Mennonite Church, Goshen, Indiana, asking if he knew of anyone who might be able and willing to head the project. He suggested my name, and the officals immediately approached me. I had just completed another research project and was ready to help them.

---

*Quoted in Wood Gray, *Historian's Handbook*, 6.

At the outset there was some discussion as to whether I should write a completely new book or merely update a comprehensive *Centennial History of the Mennonites of Illinois 1829-1929* that Dr. Harry F. Weber researched and wrote in the 1920s, and published in 1931. Because much new material has become available since Weber's time, the IMHGS decided that I should cover all of Illinois Mennonite history, in a complete, new volume. Yet I have not supplanted Weber's book; rather, I have supplemented it, for I have made much use of his good work.

In trying to cover all branches of Mennonites in Illinois, I have proceeded first with the origins of the Mennonites and Amish in Europe. This I did briefly, since numerous accounts are readily available. Then I recounted the beginning and early development of the Mennonites and Amish in Illinois up to the 1860s. After that the story became more complicated because of divisions among the Amish.

A complicating factor is writing the state history of a group that extends beyond the borders of the state. It would be much easier to write a conference history of one body. But this book is more than a conference history; it includes all branches of Illinois Mennonites. Moreover, I have attempted to write of the Illinois Mennonites in the larger national setting, emphasizing influences from outside forces. So there are fairly frequent references to individuals and forces from outside the state.

Since Weber gave considerable attention to details of the various church organizations, I have felt justified in paying less attention to them. Instead, I have emphasized more the thought and culture of the Illinois Mennonites and have offered a certain amount of interpretation. Similarly, I have not attempted to mention in the text the names of all the ministers in the state. Steven R. Estes kindly consented to make such a list for an appendix.

The first part of the book is a chronological treatment of the rise and development of the various bodies. Then, beginning with chapter 10, the organization is more topical and inter-Mennonite.

In the post-Civil War era—with the rise of more branches of Mennonites—the problem of terminology became greater. A group at Summerfield became known as General Conference Mennonites when they helped form a general conference in 1860. Those Mennonites who came to northern Illinois (except the Reformed at Sterling) and to Washington and Cullom continued the name "Mennonite," with the adjective "Old" sometimes used by others. Among those who came from the Amish, followers of Henry Egly first became known as the Defenseless Mennonite Church and then in 1948 as the Evangelical Mennonite Church. And followers of Amish leader Joseph Stuckey eventually organized the Central Conference of Mennonites, and in

1957 merged with the General Conference Mennonites. The largest Amish group became known as Amish Mennonites; but in 1920 (in Illinois) they dropped the name "Amish," for they merged with the (Old) Mennonite Church conference. Those Amish who wished to retain the old ways—the old order—became known as the Old Order Amish. However, this group did not come to Illinois until 1865 and later, settling around Arthur. The biggest problem in terminology arises in connection with the Mennonite Church, which officially has no distinguishing adjective. Some refer to its members as (Old) Mennonites, with or without parentheses; others may call them old-line Mennonites, or American Mennonites. In this work I use either "(Old) Mennonites" or "Mennonite Church" (with "Church" capitalized when it is meant as part of the name).

Abbreviations. To conserve space and avoid needless repetition of long titles, I at times use the following:

CIM—Congo Inland Mission
CO—Conscientious objector
CPS—Civilian Public Service
EMC—Evangelical Mennonite Church
GC—General Conference Mennonite Church
IMHGS—Illinois Mennonite Historical and Genealogical Society

MB—Mennonite Brethren
MCC—Mennonite Central Committee
MC—Mennonite Church
VS—Voluntary Service

Also in the interest of brevity, I have followed my own form for footnotes. In citing material in magazines I have used the dates and have used page numbers only if it seemed necessary. The reader can check the bibliography for fuller information about footnoted items.

As text and footnotes indicate, my obligations arising from the writing of this history are many. Therefore, in mentioning names, I fear I will omit some I should have included. Many in Illinois took Mrs. Smith (who usually assisted me on my research trips) and me from place to place in search of information, and entertained us in their homes. A large number (mentioned in the notes) responded to my requests for material by sending it to Goshen and generously permitted me to retain it for some time.

Staffs at the various libraries and archives where I have worked have been most helpful. These include those of the IMHGS library at Normal, Illinois; the EMC archives at Ft. Wayne, Indiana; Delbert Gratz and his assistants at the Bluffton College Mennonite Historical Library and Archives, Bluffton, Ohio; Paul Roten and his assistants at Associated Mennonite Biblical Seminaries Library, Elkhart, Indiana; Leonard Gross and his assistants at the Archives of the Mennonite Church, Goshen, Indiana; and John Oyer (director), Nelson Springer (curator), and Lena Lehman (assistant curator), of the Mennonite Historical Library, Goshen College, Goshen, Indiana. Mary Amstutz, who worked in both the Historical Library and Archives at Goshen, was also very helpful. For the untiring assistance of all these people I extend my heartfelt thanks and gratitude.

I am indebted also to the IMGHS executive committee and particularly to the History Project Committee, which was appointed to oversee this research. All of its members—Rachel Hassan, Gerlof Homan, Myrna Park, Peter G. Schultz, Edwin J. Stalter—and especially its chairman, Thomas Yoder, have taken time from busy schedules, and have been helpful in many ways, including reading the manuscript.

The following also have read the manuscript in whole or in part: Elizabeth H. Bender, Harvey Driver, Cornelius Dyck, Steven R. Estes, Delbert Gratz, Leonard Gross, Raymond L. Hartzler, H. Richard Hassan, James C. Juhnke, D. Paul Miller, Milo Nussbaum, Daniel Otto, John S. Oyer, Verle and Margaret Oyer, Theron Schlabach, Tilman R. Smith, Nelson Springer, J. C. Wenger, and Ellrose Zook. Ervin Beck, professor of English at Goshen College, has been very helpful as a copy editor. All of these have made useful corrections and suggestions, many of which I have gladly incorporated. I am grateful to all these people for their help in making this a better book. I accept responsibility for any errors or inadequacies.

I have been fortunate in having had able assistants as researchers and/or typists. Those working for me for more than very brief periods were Joseph C. Liechty, David Gingerich, Tina Hartzler, Terri Enns, Jeannie Stutzman, and Miriam Voran. In addition to typing the final draft of the manuscript, Miriam Voran has done valuable checking. Ellrose Zook, for many years book editor at the Mennonite Publishing House and who now resides in Goshen, has generously shared his expert advice and help in proofreading. As in previous research projects, my wife, Verna, has been my helpful colaborer in this venturesome journey.

Finally, I wish to thank the board of editors of the Studies in Anabaptist and Mennonite History (SAMH) series for including this work in its prestigious list. I am especially in debt to Theron F. Schlabach, coeditor-in-chief, whose careful scholarship and persistent labor have helped make this a better book. I have appreciated also his editorial generosity in accepting viewpoints and interpretations that did not always agree with his own. For me, as author, the relationship with the SAMH series and its editors has been a most fortunate one.

Willard H. Smith
Professor Emeritus of History
Goshen College Goshen, Indiana
September 1981

Mennonites in Illinois

CHAPTER 1

Illinois When the Mennonites Came

No one challenged the Indians' long and sole possession of the Illinois country until the seventeenth century, when the French, in rivalry with the British, came in search of a "northwest passage," furs, and the souls of natives. In 1673 Frenchmen Louis Joliet and Father Jacques Marquette became the first white men on record to see the Illinois country. A few years later, Robert Cavalier, Sieur de la Salle, coming likewise from New France, went as far as the present Peoria, in which vicinity in 1680 he built Fort Crevecoeur. On a later expedition (1681-82) he returned to the Illinois, reached the Mississippi River, and descended to its mouth. In the name of Louis XIV, king of France, he claimed possession of all the territory the Mississippi drained.

Within a few years, English colonists came through mountain passes into the Mississippi Valley, which they too claimed as their own. Rivalry between the French and the English for control of the Mississippi Valley and Canada became part of a larger world struggle, yet the conflict in America was no less intense because of that. From 1689 to 1763 the two world powers carried on the second Hundred Years' War. In 1763 France ceded Canada and the territory east of the Mississippi, except New Orleans, to England.

The Illinois country now passed to the British. Soon, however, some of Britain's American colonies sought French aid to carry on a War of Independence. The temptation of France to humiliate her ancient rival was too great for her to resist. As a result the British suffered the same humiliation at the Peace of Paris in 1783 that the French had experienced twenty years before. In the new peace treaty England gave the newly independent United States the Illinois country and all the territory east of the Mississippi except Florida. Aside from the land, the Illinois legacy from the French and English consisted of a few forts such as Crevecoeur and a few hundred French settlers in the southwestern part of what is now the state.

The United States now inherited problems of empire that the British had failed to solve, one of which was how to govern the territory west of the Alleghenies. This problem was resolved when the Confederation Congress passed the Ordinance of 1785 and the Ordinance of 1787. Perhaps the two most important pieces of legislation enacted under the Articles of Confederation, both these laws had important consequences for Illinois and other states. The Ordinance of 1785 provided for the rectangular land survey system with the township of six square miles (thirty-six sections) as the unit. It included the famous provision that section 16 of each township was to be set aside for the support of public schools.

The Ordinance of 1787 (often referred to as the Northwest Ordinance since it was passed for the Northwest Territory[1]) provided for the governmental organization of the area in the various stages from territory to statehood. There were to be at least three states and not more than five, with boundary lines designated for either eventuality. As soon as a given territory had 60,000 free inhabitants the area could organize a government and be admitted to the Union "on an equal footing with the original states in all respects whatever." The ordinance also contained guarantees of certain important civil liberties, including a famous provision against slavery in the Northwest Territory.[2]

These two Acts functioned so successfully that they became basic guidelines for all future territories added to continental United States. Perhaps the greatest significance of the 1787 Act is that there was now a policy for the old imperial problem, the relations of the parts of the empire to the center. The United States would have no permanent territories on its own continent.

The entire Northwest Territory, the area north of the Ohio River and east of the Mississippi to Pennsylvania, was at first governed by Congress as one territory. In 1800 Congress divided the area into a much smaller Northwest Territory and the Indiana Territory, and made Illinois a part of the latter. Then in 1809 it created Illinois Territory, which included the present state of Wisconsin. After the War of 1812, which had greatly decreased the likelihood of further Indian resistance, movement of population westward was so great that in 1816 Indiana became a state, Illinois in 1818, and Missouri in 1821.

Not many years before the Illinois country became a state, James Monroe, who investigated the area in 1786, wrote to Thomas Jefferson: "A great part of the territory is miserably poor, especially that near Lakes Michigan and Erie, and that upon the Mississippi and the Illinois consists of extensive plains which have not had from appearances, and will not have, a single bush on them for ages. The districts, therefore, within which these fall can never contain a sufficient number of inhabitants to entitle them to membership in the confederacy."[3] This, of course, sounds exceedingly strange to Illinois Mennonites and others who saw their land sell for $500 to $700 per acre in 1920 and seven to eight times that amount in 1980.

Illinois has become one of the wealthiest states in the union. An area of 56,400 square miles, its greatest length is 385 miles and its greatest width 218. The area is larger than Belgium, Switzerland, and Holland combined. Illinois is one of the most level of states: its greatest elevation is 1235 feet above sea level in the northwest, its lowest point 279 feet in the southwest, and its mean elevation is approximately 600 feet. Most of its area consists of almost level or slightly undulating prairies, though hills and bluffs rise along rivers and their tributaries, and in the northwest and the extreme south. With much rich, black soil, Illinois became one of the most prosperous of agricultural states, not only in the fertile Mississippi Valley but also in the entire nation. It possesses mineral wealth (especially coal), a good transportation system, and a central location that have enabled it also to become a leading manufacturing state. The state's rather extended length from north to south has brought variety not only in climate and crops but also in politics and other respects. For instance, Chicago and Rockford are farther north than is New York City and Cairo is farther south than is Richmond, Virginia. In fact, "Illinois ranges in latitude from that of Portsmouth, New Hampshire, to that of Portsmouth, Virginia."[4]

The state is surrounded mostly by water boundaries. In addition to Lake Michigan on the northeast, the state shares the Wabash River with southern Indiana, the Ohio with Kentucky, and the Mississippi with Missouri and Iowa. Geographic features were important in the settlement of the state. The fact that the Ohio River—one of the most important routes of travel to the West for many years—and other rivers like the Tennessee and Cumberland all led to southern Illinois explains in part why that area of the state was settled first. Furthermore, the government extinguished Indian titles to the land first in that area. When Illinois became a state in 1818, the Indians still possessed most of the land. However, in 1819 one of the most important cessions ever made in the state occurred when the Kickapoos ceded a large tract in the central part, constituting approximately a third of the state. A study of land cession maps suggests that the "westward" movement into Illinois was quite as much toward the north as toward the west. The last cessions were made in the extreme northern section of the state in 1829, although not until in 1833, following the Black Hawk War, was Illinois effectively free from all Indian claims.[5]

After the War of 1812 many factors combined to cause the westward movement into Illinois and other states to reach flood tide.

The so-called "Indian menace" was at least temporarily decreased, and British reluctance to give up the land ceded in 1783 now disappeared. In addition, the Ordinance of 1787 provided stable and attractive governmental organization. From time to time, Congress passed favorable land legislation, lowering the price of land and making it easier to secure. In 1820, for example, the price was lowered to $1.25 an acre, and the amount that could be bought was reduced to 80 acres. Thus it was possible to buy a farm for $100.

Postwar propaganda and advertising also increased migration. Whether this came from settlers in Illinois writing to home folks in the eastern states or in Europe, or whether it came from land agents and promoters, the effect was the same. The propaganda caused unrest among the people back home who wanted to go "west" and join their relatives and friends in the land pictured as the "new Canaan" flowing with milk and honey. Let one typical example suffice. J. M. Peck, minister, traveler, and author of several emigrant guides and gazetteers of Illinois, wrote as follows about Illinois in 1837:

> ... we would say, for the benefit of those who have determined on coming to the west, that the state of Illinois offers every inducement to emigrants. The state is advancing rapidly in population, and when her public works which are progressing are completed, and in successful operation, she will be the admiration of the "far west." It being by far the richest state in soil in the Union of course it holds out the greatest prospect of advantage to farmers. Here, too, there is plenty of room for farmers, there being vast quantities of first rate land lying in every direction uncultivated, which may be had very cheap, and one acre of it will produce at least three times as much as the same amount of land in most of the eastern states!
>
> If rural occupations are pleasant and profitable anywhere in our country, they must be peculiarly so in Illinois, for here, the produce of the farmers springs up almost spontaneously, less than one-third of the labor being necessary on the farms here that is required on the farms in the east. Indeed Illinois may with propriety be called the 'Canaan' of America!... We know of no better place west for a permanent location; and we hope that some of those who have been so unfortunate at the east, will come and mend their broken fortunes in a state where enterprise and industry meet with a sure reward.[6]

Such accounts were surely romantic, yet they made an impact among people in the eastern states and in Europe. Beginning in the decade following the War of 1812, they contributed significantly to the settlement of Illinois and other parts of the Mississippi Valley. The reports, of course, affected Mennonites as well as others.

However romanticized the boosters' accounts, there was real and substantial economic development in Illinois during these early years. To be sure, in keeping with the ruling laissez-faire philosophy of the nineteenth century, this growth had its ups and downs, its boom and bust cycles. Panics occurred in 1819, 1837, 1857, and less major ones in between. Census figures show large population increases from decade to decade: 2,458 in 1800; 12,282 in 1810; 55,211 in 1820; 157,445 in 1830; 476,183 in 1840; 851,470 in 1850; 1,711,951 in 1860.[7] Similarly large increases continued after the Civil War. Population expansion was largely from south to north. After the completion of the Erie Canal in 1825, northern Illinois filled more rapidly. The Erie was a popular route westward, and one that many Mennonites used.

In the 1820s and 1830s the air was full of talk about "internal improvements." In addition to being surrounded by 850 miles of navigable water[8] (out of a total boundary mileage of 1160 miles), Illinois has important intrastate navigable streams. The most important is the Illinois River. The state's greatest canal project was the building of the Illinois and Michigan Canal to connect Lake Michigan and the Mississippi by a channel from Chicago to La Salle on the Illinois River. Begun in 1836, the work was slowed down and then abandoned in 1842 as a result of the state's virtual bankruptcy because of the panic of 1837 and the years of depression that followed. Construction was resumed later and completed in 1848. Immediately profitable, the canal exerted such great influence on the development of the area that in North America only the Erie Canal was more important.[9]

During the period of the coming of the Mennonites, railroads were also introduced into Illinois and played a still greater part than canals in the state's economic growth. One of the more significant was the Illinois Central Railroad. Originally projected to connect Galena in the northwest with Cairo in the south, with a branch-line running to Chicago, it became part of a state-wide program of internal improvements. Since the cost was beyond the means of the state to finance, in 1850 Stephen A. Douglas and others sought and secured from Congress a grant of 2,595,000 acres of public lands to aid in its construction. With this aid, plus generous amounts of private domestic and foreign capital, the road was completed in 1856. With much of its track spanning the undeveloped prairies, the road contributed greatly to the settling of these areas. Mennonites, as well as others, took advantage of the new transportation opportunities. As a result of tremendous Illinois Central advertising, aimed at the East and Europe, the population flow to the state of Illinois increased remarkably.[10]

Other railroads also appeared, especially in the 1850s: among others the Chicago and Alton, the Chicago and Northwestern, the Chicago and Rock Island, and the Chicago, Burlington, and Quincy. Meanwhile, railroads were being constructed from eastern states, in some cases extending across the state to the Mississippi and beyond, and in many cases to Chicago, where they connected with other lines.

The effect of these internal improvements on the history of Illinois and of the nation were immeasurable. Soon after the Civil War, Chicago became the world's greatest railroad center because of its favorable location at the head of Lake Michigan and in the heart of a rich agricultural area. The Illinois and Michigan Canal and the Illinois railroads brought the products of farms, mines, and factories to the city and made it a great emporium of commerce. Cities like Alton or St. Louis, which had visions of becoming that great emporium, now had to yield to the growing giant on Lake Michigan. Of even greater significance was the part played by the railroads in holding Illinois and the remainder of the Northwest loyal to the Union during the Civil War, and in bringing about a situation where wheat rather than cotton proved to be "king," and helped the North to defeat the South in that war. Before 1860 the Mississippi Valley tended to be an economic unit whose trade followed the line of the Mississippi. But by 1860, thanks to the Erie Canal, the Illinois and Michigan Canal, and especially the railroads which extended from the East into the Northwest, this area felt bound to the North and remained loyal to the Union.

The Northwest needed the manufactured products of the Northeast, and the latter needed the agricultural products of the Northwest. In addition, in the early years of the war, England needed northern wheat more than she needed southern cotton. Thus England refrained from recognizing the Confederacy, which she had considered doing. Thanks to the invention of the reaper and some other farm implements, the western farmers, diminished in number by army service, could produce enough wheat to supply their own needs, those of the Northeast, and those of hungry England as well.[11] Illinois became one of the most important suppliers of this grain, and Chicago soon became the largest primary grain depot in the world. First in both corn and wheat production in 1860, Illinois was also a leader in oats and rye.[12] In the early 1830s, when the first Mennonites were coming to Illinois, a young Virginian, Cyrus McCormick, was playing around with some gadgets. Yet McCormick probably did not realize the importance of his invention, the reaper.

In Illinois, as elsewhere, grain-growing led to livestock production, which also became a most profitable business. One of the largest cattle raisers was Isaac Funk of Bloomington, who in 1854 "sold in a single lot 1,400 head of cattle averaging 700 pounds for $64,000." Pork production was likewise a thriving industry and Chicago soon became the "hog butcher of the world."[13]

Although Illinois now had the benefits of such internal improvements as waterways and railroads, the frontier problem of poor roads continued for many years. As late as 1892 the *Herald of Truth*, a Mennonite paper published by John F. Funk of Elkhart, Indiana, noted a general movement to provide better roads throughout the country. A. B. Kolb, assistant editor, listed among the advantages: cheaper, year-round transportation for farmers; an increase in land prices; better church attendance; and "last but not least ... good solid roads would stop a great deal of profanity among drivers, and consequent cruelty to our dumb animal friend, the horse. Bad roads help to make balky horses, angry drivers, broken harness, broken wagons, small profits on farm produce, and many other things which may be looked upon as evils."[14]

Another frontier problem in Illinois as elsewhere, which land promoters of course did not care to advertise, was disease and the scarcity of competent doctors. So-called doctors, along with quacks, folk medicine, and superstition filled the vacuum. In the 1830s one T. J. Luster of Springfield offered numerous favorable testimonials regarding his success in curing "sciatia, weak lungs, fits, inward weakness and nervous affections, liver complaints, fever and ague, pleurisy, asthma, coughs, colds, dyspepsia, rheumatism, cancers, rickets, fever sores, piles, worms and tape worms, and many other diseases that affect the human system." His claims were typical. No wonder the book in which this is quoted—*The Midwest Pioneer: His Ills, Cures & Doctors*—is dedicated "To the Pioneer Doctor who boldly faced the wilderness; and to the Pioneer who bravely faced the Doctor."[15]

On the frontier, death was frequent and children often were the victims. In 1871, in the Waldo Amish Mennonite Church in Livingston County, a variety of illnesses claimed the lives of eight children in a little over two months, three of the eight being from one family. About the same time Christian Schertz, of McLean County, was reported as having died of "old age." He was 48 years old! Relatively speaking, he was "old" for that time.[16]

Asiatic cholera also scourged the people of Illinois, including the Mennonites. It is hard to get the facts about this plague, partly because of the strenuous efforts by local businessmen to suppress all news of deaths from Asiatic cholera, through "fear that the spread of such information would ruin their interest." The present writer, through the closeness of his family to the tragedy and through stories handed down, can understand this fear. In the summer of 1855, near the present Congerville, two of his great-grandparents, Mr. and Mrs. Christian Schmidt (Smith), and three of their children died from the disease within a few days. Among scores who died in July and August 1855 were a number bearing other such Mennonite names as Lantz, Kauffman, McCullough, Bowman, Orendorff, Summers, and Zehr.[17]

Whether they all realized it or not, Mennonites came to Illinois during exciting times. They were close enough to the Indian problem or "menace" to make it a concern, or at least a matter of discussion, especially during and following the Black Hawk War in 1832 in northern Illinois and southern Wisconsin. The Mormons, too, must have been a topic of discussion during the period they were in Illinois, from about 1840-46. They had built Nauvoo into the state's largest city of perhaps 20,000. When rumors began to emanate from Nauvoo that Joseph Smith's strange religious group was practicing polygamy, and when Smith announced himself as a presidential candidate in the election of 1844, feeling among the anti-Mormons ran so high that it defied law and order. Charged with riot and lodged in jail in Carthage, both Joseph and his brother Hyrum were murdered by a mob on June 27, 1844. In 1846 the main body of Mormons under the leadership of Brigham Young was forced out of the community. So while the Mennonites were coming to Illinois in search of (among other things) peace and religious freedom, another group was leaving because of failure to find them.[18]

Slavery, another issue during the coming of the Mennonites, dominated Illinois politics for a much longer time. Although the Ordinance of 1787 forbade the further introduction of slaves into the Northwest Territory, it did not free the slaves already there, held by the French and a very few others. Furthermore, since the early settlers were largely from the South, there was strong agitation to draw up a constitution in 1818 which would permit slavery. That drive failed, but again in 1822-1824 came a strong movement to amend the constitution to permit the "peculiar institution."

Coincidentally, three important Illinois men played significant parts in the slavery controversy. Senator Jesse B. Thomas introduced the main element in the Missouri Compromise of 1820—that Missouri be allowed to come into the union as a slave state, provided that the rest of the Louisiana Purchase north of 36° 30' north latitude be free territory. Stephen A. Douglas helped bring about the Compromise of 1850 and then took the lead in putting through the Kansas-Nebraska Act in 1854, which repealed the Missouri Compromise. "No law ever passed by Congress," one historian has said, "produced such momentous consequences as the Kansas-Nebraska Act."[19] Abraham Lincoln, of course, contributed the most to end the slavery issue by his leadership during the Civil War.

Illinois had its more radical, fire-eating anti-slavery leaders, also. Presbyterian minister Elijah P. Lovejoy, publisher of the abolitionist *Alton Observer*, was harassed by threats of violence and finally became a martyr to the cause on November 7, 1837. His brother Owen, likewise a minister, knelt by Elijah's dead body and vowed "never to forsake the cause that had been sprinkled with his brother's blood." He kept the faith. He spoke for freedom's cause wherever he could get a hearing, and he continued in the same course after his election to Congress in 1856. He did not enter the promised land made free by the thirteenth amendment, but he saw it from a distance. "To him fell the honor of proposing the bill by which slavery in all territories in the United States was abolished forever. He heard at last the Emancipation Proclamation and died the next year."[20]

Benjamin Lundy was another to carry the antislavery standard that passed from the fallen Elijah Lovejoy. This roving, veteran abolitionist spent the last year of his life in Putnam County, Illinois. Here he reestablished his *The Genius of Universal Emancipation*, twelve issues of which appeared before his death in August 1839.

There is little direct evidence of how the Mennonites of Illinois reacted to these and other stirring events of 1830-60. Decidedly different from the Quakers, who with more sensitive social consciences witnessed more actively to society and government, the Mennonites were more the apolitical "quiet in the land." They had been so ever since their days of persecution in the sixteenth and seventeenth centuries. Yet the work of a few, such as John F. Funk, a young Mennonite activist in Chicago in the fifties and sixties, was an exception to the rule.[21]

Contrary to James Monroe's gloomy report to Thomas Jefferson in 1786, the Illinois country turned out to be one of the most prosperous areas in the new world in which the Mennonites have settled. Although facing the hardships of a pioneer economy along with their neighbors, even the apolitical Mennonites soon reaped the advantages of the economic, political, and social advances which the state experienced in the years 1830-60.

CHAPTER 2

The Mennonite Settlements in Illinois to the 1870s

The Mennonites are children of the left wing of the Reformation. In the sixteenth century their spiritual forebears, the "Anabaptists," agreed with much of what Martin Luther stood for but felt that he did not go far enough in his break with Rome. One region where Mennonites originated was Switzerland. In Zurich Anabaptists were happy to see Protestant Reformer Ulrich Zwingli go further than Luther but felt that he also stopped too soon. They were inclined to agree with Zwingli's view of the sacraments: that they were symbols of grace, and not the transubstantiation of the Catholic position, nor the "real presence" of the Lutheran view. But they were disappointed that Zwingli did not go all the way toward the Anabaptist position of voluntary membership, upon confession of faith as an adult, in a free church that was wholly separate from the state. The Mennonites, or Swiss Brethren as they were called in Switzerland, renounced the baptism of infants and insisted that those baptized as infants must receive the rite again when they accepted Christ as believers; hence the name "Anabaptist" (rebaptizer), a nickname often applied to them in reproach. Of the several kinds of Anabaptists on the left-wing fringe of the Reformation, the Mennonites stem from moderate ones who rejected the use of the sword.

Conrad Grebel was the chief leader of the new movement in Switzerland. A follower of Zwingli at first, Grebel was pleased with the way the Swiss Reformer was leading the Reformation movement, especially in 1523 when he considered abolishing infant baptism.[1] But since Zwingli did not follow through with this proposed reform, and after he resorted to using civil force to crush the new movement, Grebel and his followers had to break with the Swiss leader. On the next day after a debate between Zwingli and Grebel, January 18, 1525, the City Council announced that parents not baptizing their infants within eight days would be exiled. A few days later the Council ordered Grebel,

Felix Mantz, and their associates to cease their activities completely, especially the holding of Bible study meetings. Grebel and his followers met in Zurich to discuss what they should do in the face of the serious crisis.

After counsel and prayer, probably on January 21, 1525, "an astonishing event transpired." George Blaurock, a priest, went to Conrad Grebel, the acknowledged leader of the group, and asked to be baptized upon confession of faith. Grebel complied; then he and the others asked Blaurock to baptize them also. In the words of Mennonite historian J. C. Wenger: "This was an irony of history. The state decree which was supposed to suppress all sentiment for a free church and believer's baptism turned out to be the very event which occasioned the founding of the first modern free church!" Thus came the birth of Anabaptism.[2]

Unlike Zwingli and his followers, the Anabaptists wanted the complete separation of church and state; a free church of adult believers who joined voluntarily by being baptized upon confession of faith, with no infant baptism; a disciplined church in which members would be excommunicated if they did not live up to New Testament standards; no swearing of the oath; the promotion of peace and opposition to all warfare; a commitment to discipleship; and separation from the world. In short, the Anabaptists tried to recreate the simple life and faith of the New Testament church.[3] On one important issue, communion, the Swiss Brethren agreed with Zwingli—that both the bread and wine should be served and that the ceremony was a symbolic memorial of Christ's death.

Since the early Anabaptists were missionary-minded, the movement, despite legal prohibitions, began to spread rapidly in Switzerland and other countries such as France, Germany, the Lowlands and Austria. Anabaptism not only spread from Switzerland; it sprang up almost simultaneously and seemingly independently in some other parts of Europe. Some authorities say that even in Switzerland it had another origin, in Canton Bern, separate from that in Zurich.[4] The Netherlands were another important source of Anabaptism. Under the leadership of Melchior Hofmann, a stormy and somewhat unbalanced character, of Obbe and Dirk Philips, and of Menno Simons, from whom the Mennonites got their name, the new movement arose in the Netherlands a few years later than in Switzerland and began to spread rapidly.

With the rise and rapid expansion of such a movement, and with various leaders and would-be leaders arising here and there, European Anabaptism, understandably, did not speak with one united voice. Scholars have discovered that the voices were disparate, with some bordering on fanaticism. They have also discovered that the places of origin, and the social forces out of which Anabaptism sprang, were greater and more complex than formerly thought.[5] The Mennonites of today claim to have descended from the peaceful Anabaptists of the sixteenth century—not from the more militant wing who were ready to use force to accomplish their ends. They certainly do not claim descent from the violent Münsterites in Germany and the Netherlands.

Nevertheless, even the peaceful Anabaptists were considered too radical by the religious and civil leaders of that time. Their doctrines were so outlandish that the authorities could not tolerate such subversive ideas and actions. The result was persecution, by Protestant and Catholic civil authorities, on such a scale that the survival of the Anabaptist group at all seems miraculous. Thousands suffered torture and imprisonment; probably at least 5,000 paid the supreme penalty by drowning, burning at the stake, hanging, beheading, and other means of execution. Persecutions were more severe and continued longer in some areas and in some countries than in others. Often, instead of stamping out the new faith, persecution helped spread it far beyond the borders of Switzerland and the Netherlands, the chief early centers of Anabaptism. No Mennonite was put to death in the Netherlands after Calvinism largely replaced Roman Catholicism. In the southern Netherlands (Belgium) executions ceased by 1600 "because Mennonitism had been nearly extirpated." In Zurich, the last Mennonite martyr was one Hans Landis, who died on September 20, 1614.[6]

Despite severe persecution and the disparate voices among them, Anabaptists survived. One event which no doubt helped save the movement was the meeting of a number of leaders at Schleitheim on February 24, 1527.[7] Here the brethren agreed on seven foundational statements of belief, which gave direction to the group and saved it from the influences of the more radical faction: (1) Baptism is to be administered not to infants but to believers upon confession of faith. (2) Members who sin will be disciplined by means of the ban; those who refuse to turn from their error will be excommunicated. (3) The communion service is a memorial of Christ's death, to be partaken of only by those who are members of Christ's body. (4) Faithful Christians will separate themselves from all evil in the world. (5) The sword was "ordained of God outside the perfection of Christ" and is therefore not to be used by Christians in the magistracy or in war. (6) Christians are not to swear oaths. (7) In addition, the Schleitheim Confession specified the character and duties of pastors.[8] The most serious and only major schism among the South German Anabaptist-Mennonites did not occur until the Amish division in the 1690s, which will be discussed in chapter 3.

Even after the last Anabaptist execution, toleration and complete religious liberty were still remote goals. The spread of Anabaptism, often with the aid of persecution, continued for several centuries. During this period the new faith spread to Alsace and Lorraine, various parts of Germany, Poland, Austria, Moravia, Slovakia, Hungary, Russia, and then North America. In Moravia, under the leadership of Jacob Hutter and others, some Anabaptists developed a communal society, which remains a distinguishing characteristic of Hutterites even today.

In addition to legal discriminations against the Anabaptists, which varied greatly from country to country, another factor in the uneven enforcement of penalties on them was that Mennonites were very knowledgeable in the use of the soil. Thus Protestant and Catholic noblemen sought them out to farm their lands. With help and connivance of powerful noblemen, Mennonites often avoided the more severe restrictions.[9]

Mennonites have been known throughout their history as wanderers over the face of the globe "for conscience' sake." This pattern extends even to the so-called enlightened twentieth century. The search for greater religious liberty has been an important goal in the coming of many Mennonites to America. When the first Mennonites came to Germantown in colonial Pennsylvania in 1683—and even a few earlier elsewhere—they started a movement of tremendous significance in Mennonite history—a movement that was to eventuate in the United States becoming the center of the greatest Mennonite population in the world. Among the various reasons for this, not the least important, despite its too frequent failures and mistakes, has been the great emphasis which the United States, beginning in the colonial period, has placed on human freedom, including religious liberty. Regardless of the place of their origin, the long, bloody trail of the Mennonites to freedom in the new world followed different routes—one from Switzerland and South Germany to America; one from Switzerland and Central Europe via Russia; and one from the Netherlands and North Germany via Russia. One variation from this pattern was the coming of the first Mennonites to Germantown from the Low Countries in 1683 and the years following. In the eighteenth century, influenced in part by the invitation of William Penn, perhaps some 3,000 Mennonites found their way to the "Paradise of Pennsylvania." A number of their descendants played important roles in the founding of the Mennonite settlements in Illinois in the nineteenth century.[10]

Of course, not until the nineteenth century was Illinois ready under its new political organization to receive immigrants, and not until after the War of 1812 did the westward movement grow large. Illinois was directly in the movement's path. Conditions in Europe as well as in the United States combined to promote a new wave of immigration. Just as the close of the War of 1812 was a signal for a new unprecedented westward movement in the United States, so the close of the Napoleonic Wars in Europe in 1815 prompted a new interest in emigration from the Old World to the New. This element from abroad helped swell the American westward movement, with Mennonites, both from Eastern United States and from Europe, contributing to the tide. Many of these found their way to Illinois during the nineteenth century.

Some of the reasons for Mennonite emigration in the nineteenth century were peculiar to the Mennonites; others were not. Many people, whether Mennonite or not, were eager to improve their economic position in the new El Dorado of America. For over a century much of Western Europe, where many Mennonites lived, was periodically fought over and devastated by England and France and their allies, especially the stronger German states such as Prussia and Austria. Distressing economic conditions overtook many Europeans— Lutherans, Reformed, Catholics, and Mennonites, as well as others.

The causes for immigration in the 1820s under the new United States constitution were not too different from those that obtained in the 1770s. In 1773 Pennsylvania Mennonites had declared in a letter to some Dutch brethren that:

> The reasons that have induced so many of our fellow believers to come to us are various. It can be given as one reason that William Penn, the lord of this land, having received great freedom from the king of Great Britain, made it known to people everywhere. Now in many places in Europe, the inhabitants were not only hard pressed by being compelled to pay heavy taxes, but also they did not enjoy sufficient freedom to serve God according to the considerations of their conscience, and so many preferred to undertake the difficult and long journey to come to us.[11] Upon coming into this country, they not only enjoy great freedom, but also find that the land is fruitful and that everything of which a farmer has need it produces to overflowing if he will only work. We have no want of food or raiment, and there are among us even people who are rich. Some, in writing these things to their friends in Europe, and others who have made a journey to Germany for merchandise, have much, yes, too much extolled the country and given such inducement that many have come here for worldly profit. Other reasons we pass by.[12]

After 1773 the scourge of war and its devastation certainly did not decrease the problems of the Mennonites and Amish. The war of France against England in the 1770s and 1780s, and especially the French Revolutionary and Napoleonic Wars from 1792 to 1815, created horrors for all people of the middle areas and especially for pacifists. The national conscription policy of France in the 1790s was copied by her enemies on the continent in the name of survival. Despite pacifist principles, some Mennonites were forced into the army and some even accompanied Napoleon on the disastrous journey to Moscow. A few lived to tell the tale, even in Illinois; some did not. According to one detailed chronicle, these events, coming in the wake of many similar ones during the previous century, made a tremendous impression on Mennonites. No doubt it helped many to decide for the New World. Jacob Krehbiel (1781-1860), of the well-known Krehbiel family of the Pfrimmerhof and Weierhof area in the Palatinate, wrote page after page of details describing how people suffered as the French, Prussian, and Austrian armies swept back and forth over the lands of the Mennonites, taking virtually everything of value—livestock, grain and other produce, and money. In addition, the armies were often quartered in the community, bringing many moral hazards.[13]

Religious changes occurring among the Mennonites from about 1789 to 1830 probably also helped some to decide to emigrate to America. Mennonite beliefs and practices were in a state of flux, changing from the rigidly traditional to more progressive forms. By 1830, according to one authority, the Mennonites put less emphasis on being a closed society than formerly, softened a bit their position on separation from the world and maintenance of social boundaries, and began to talk more about the new birth and an experience of salvation. Some were even relaxing their position regarding war. Evangelically minded Mennonites developed new interest in missions. To be sure, these changes did not affect all Mennonite communities to the same degree; and even within the same community people reacted differently. Some believed that too much change was going on; others thought things were changing too slowly. In any case these conditions added to the discontent of many Mennonites and no doubt helped them to decide for America.[14]

Of course, propagandistic advertising by land promoters helped attract emigrants. Letters from the new settlers to family members and friends in the old world—letters extolling the virtues of Illinois—reinforced such advertising. And although war diminished in Europe following 1815, revolutions in 1820, 1830, and 1848 added to the unrest of the times. After 1815 there was more religious toleration. Yet for the Mennonites one basic concern still remained: compulsory military service and the danger of losing their nonresistance. Quite a few had been pressed into military service during the Napoleonic Wars, and a number of Mennonite churches were giving up the nonresistant principle. Many concerned Mennonites therefore opted for the New World.[15]

The first Mennonites known to enter Illinois were Benjamin Kindig and his family, who in 1833 went by covered wagon from Augusta County, Virginia to Tazewell County. Many years later (1893), a son, David, in an interesting account of the journey, indicated how soon after the retreat of the Indians the Mennonites came:

> We started for Hollands Grove, Tazewell County, Illinois. Traveling west we passed through the Worm [Warm?] and White Sulphur Springs, crossed the Allegheny Mountains to the Ohio River 225 miles. Crossing the Big Sandy river at its mouth over into Kentucky, passing through Lexington, Frankfort, and on to Louisville on the Ohio River. Crossed the river into New Albany, Indiana, thence to Vincennes on the Wabash, thence to Vandalia, Illinois, thence to Springfield, Illinois, then a small village, it being the last one we saw until we came to Peoria. We inquired for the Fort Clark road and as we came on we inquired for Hollands Grove.
>
> We landed on the farm where Christian Engle now lives (1893) (near Union Cemetery) on the 22 of Oct. 1833, a distance of 800 miles, being on the road seven weeks, camping in our tent and wagons.
>
> When we came to this state in 1833 there were no Indians here, but there were many signs of where they had their wigwams, also many ladders setting up against trees where they had cut holes in trees to catch coons and get honey. . . .
>
> In speaking of Indians, when we came to Illinois, I never saw any here nor was I in the Black Hawk war. But I saw the old Indian Chief Black Hawk in Richmond, Virginia, when they were on their way to Washington, D.C. That was in the summer of 1833. He was tall with a sharp, keen eye, had rings in his ears, and one in his nose, and had a blanket around his shoulders and was a fair representation of his picture.[16]

Although Kindig's account is illustrative of the mode of land travel and typical also in that Peoria was the usual center through which the Mennonites radiated to the surrounding communities, most Mennonites traveled west on a more northerly route through Pennsylvania and Ohio. It seems a bit strange also that David Kindig remembered seeing no villages between Springfield and Peoria as late as 1833. Be that as it may, the Kindigs were the first settlers in what became the Union congregation a few miles northwest of Washington. As will be seen in chapter 3, this was the same area to which some Amish had started to come, in much larger numbers, about 1830.

Soon after the Kindigs, other Mennonites came to the Washington settlement. In 1837 Peter Hartman came from Bavaria, Germany, by way of Lancaster County, Pennsylvania; Benjamin Kauffman, also from Lancaster, arrived in 1842; and in 1851 Benjamin Brubaker arrived from Richland County, Ohio. Other names of early settlers were Bally, Althaus, Hirstein, Baer, and Brownfield. Apparently the congregation was organized in the 1840s. As elsewhere among the Mennonites and Amish, church services, in the absence of meetinghouses, were at first held in homes and/or barns of members. In 1856, a mile northwest of Washington on land donated by Benjamin Kindig,, the first church building was erected. Ironically, the Kindig heirs, who were not Mennonite, eventually objected to having the church building on their land. It was then relocated a few miles farther northwest on land donated by Christian Engle. The congregation took its name from the Union Cemetery next to which it was located. Perhaps an additional reason for the name "Union" was that, since this Mennonite congregation was located among the Amish Mennonites, there was hope of union between the two groups. Although no union occurred, the two groups cooperated closely, and increasingly so in later years.

In 1795 Jost Bally, the congregation's first minister and bishop— also the first (Old) Mennonite bishop in Illinois—had been born in Bavaria, Germany. He settled in Woodford County, Illinois, in 1847 after a few years' sojourn in Lancaster County, Pennsylvania, and Richland County, Ohio. Ordained in the early 1850s as minister in the Union congregation and a few years later as bishop, he had charge of, in addition to his home church, the Cullom and Gardner congregations. According to the *Herald of Truth* Bally was active in the work of the Mennonite Church, not only in Illinois but also in other states. Despite poor health at times, including eye trouble, he reached the age of nearly 83, dying in 1878 at his home near Roanoke. Bally preached in German, the usual language for both Mennonites and Amish in this period, yet saw the need for more preaching in English. Already in 1869 he wrote to John F. Funk, the *Herald* publisher, asking for more bilingual preachers to visit and settle in his region. Union was one of the first Mennonite or Amish churches in Illinois to have a Sunday school (1866), a fact that Funk enthusiastically reported when visiting the congregation in November of that year. Unlike those in many other places, from the beginning this Sunday school was held on Sunday mornings prior to and in connection with the regular church services.[17]

While the Union Mennonite Church was developing near Washington, most other Mennonites were settling in the northern part of the state. The next Mennonite congregation was the Freeport church, located about seven and a half miles northeast of Freeport in Stephenson County. Either in 1840 or 1841 two brothers, Martin and Samuel Lapp, arrived with their wives as the first Mennonites to settle northeast of the city. The Lapps came from Ontario but had originally been from Clarence Center, New York. In 1844 the Godfrey Groffs and John Brubakers arrived directly from Clarence Center. Many early Mennonite settlers arrived at Freeport from Pennsylvania. One of the first was Jacob Mayer (Moyer) who came from Lancaster County in 1847 with his wife and family. The Rudolph K. Brubaker family, accompanied by Matthias Eby, who had been born at Dammhof, near Sinsheim, Baden, Germany, left Lancaster County in 1853 and traveled by rail to Rockford and by stagecoach from there to Freeport. Others from the Keystone State were the Christian Snyder family, the

Source: Mennonite Historical Library, Goshen, Ind.

This is a reproduction of the first church service drawn by Roy Vallartia

Sketch of interior of original Freeport Mennonite Church, near Freeport, Illinois, built in 1863.

The Mennonite Settlements   43

Joseph Shellenberger family, David Ebersole, and Jeffrey McConnell.

Some came directly, while others, like many other Americans, moved west by stages. This was the pattern, for instance, of the Benjamin Shoemaker family. Born in Montgomery County, Pennsylvania, in 1825, Benjamin married Veronica Shellenberger, born in 1830 in Juniata County, Pennsylvania. After their marriage in 1853 the couple lived in Philadelphia, where Benjamin worked principally as a cobbler and broommaker. In 1856 they moved to Covington, Ohio, and some six years later to Randolph County, Indiana. In 1863 they sold a small farm they had acquired and settled six miles northeast of Freeport. This was the family of Joseph S. Shoemaker, who was to become one of the outstanding leaders of Illinois Mennonites and also of the entire (Old) Mennonite Church.[18]

Apparently the Freeport church was organized sometime in the mid-1840s, possibly 1845.[19] As usual the first settlers met for worship in private homes, every second Sunday. This arrangement served the congregation well so long as the membership was small. But since the area had prairie land excellent for farming, new families continued to move in. Soon it was necessary to construct a building for church worship. In 1862 or 1863 the congregation erected its first meetinghouse on land donated by Samuel Lapp seven and one half miles northeast of Freeport. It was a white frame building, thirty by forty feet, with a feature in the sanctuary that was unusual for Illinois but borrowed from Lancaster County: a long table in the middle with the men and women seated on opposite sides and the ministers standing at the front end.[20] A unique feature of the congregation itself was that for many years it had no board of trustees. Martin Lapp was probably the first minister to serve the congregation. John Brubaker, who some say was the first, also was selected at an early date.[21] Others who served as ministers in the early period were Matthias Eby, Christian Snyder and Christian Snavely. Snavely lived at Shannon, southwest of Freeport, about twenty miles from the church. For a number of years he and the small settlement of Mennonites there had services in their homes every four weeks, although they were an integral part of the Freeport congregation and attended there as often as possible. Driving to church twenty miles by horse and buggy over unimproved roads required dedication of a high order.

Another area in northern Illinois that began to attract Mennonites almost as early as the Freeport district was Sterling, about forty miles south in Whiteside County. Members of the Reformed Mennonite branch came first, as will be discussed in a later chapter. The first members of the Mennonite Church to settle were Benjamin Stauffer and his wife, from Lancaster County, Pennsylvania, who arrived in 1852. Henry Kauffman and wife came in the same year. The soil of this area, a rich black loam, was excellent for farming and in the early period continued to attract others with such names as Kreider, Hendricks, Heckler, Detweiler, Snavely, Moyer, Book, Myers, Millhouse, Weaver, Hershey, Lapp, Ebersole, Rutt, Allebaugh, Mellinger and Reitzel, among others. These families located a few miles north and east of Sterling in a district called Science Ridge, the name assumed by the congregation when it organized in the late 1850s.

For those who migrated to northern Illinois the usual route was through Chicago, by either water or rail. As the railroad pushed westward from that city the first Mennonite settlers went part of the way by rail and completed the journey by wagon. By the summer of 1855, however, the railroad was built to Sterling, bringing mainly settlers from Pennsylvania. In 1865, according to Harry F. Weber, a large group of 55, "traveling on the same train, mostly from Chambersburg, Pennsylvania, came to Sterling." Later some visitors from Pennsylvania reported on a visit to Sterling where they said they met "quite a number of Pennsylvanians."[22] *Herald of Truth* obituary notices from Sterling confirm that a large majority of the early settlers were from the Keystone State.

The growth of the Sterling Mennonite settlement was impressive. Even a cholera epidemic in 1854, which took a number of Mennonites, especially the Reformed, did not discourage development. No doubt excellent potential for producing grain and livestock particularly attracted the Mennonites, a rural people. The present writer has heard his uncle, C. Henry Smith, a well-trained Mennonite historian, say more than once that the Mennonites had a "nose for good land."

The growing settlement at Sterling soon needed to organize its church life. Having services at first in private homes every two weeks, the congregation built its first church building in 1858, although it did not formally organize until January 16, 1859, when three trustees were elected. For some years all of the preaching was in German. Because of opposition no Sunday school was organized until 1882. Benjamin Hershey, ordained in Canada and moving to Sterling in 1860, became the first minister to serve the congregation for any length of time. For some years in the 1860s, Abraham E. Detweiler also served at Sterling. In 1862, in correspondence with John F. Funk, who then lived in Chicago, Detweiler reported a lack of harmony and fellowship in the congregation because of dissatisfaction with his (Detweiler's) beard, the way he cut and combed his hair, his dress, and his preaching. Funk had asked about taking communion with the Sterling congregation; Detweiler stated that because of the disunity at the time they were not able to have communion. He advised Funk to go to the Yellow Creek congregation near Elkhart, Indiana, for that purpose, which Funk did. The advice may have changed the course of Men-

The Mennonite Settlements

nonite history, for soon Funk moved to Elkhart and began making it an important center for Mennonite church life. What might have happened had Funk taken communion at Sterling?

Whatever its troubles, within a few years Detweiler's "Science Ridge" congregation became the largest Mennonite congregation in the state, maintaining that position until the merger with the state's Western District Amish Mennonites in 1920. With its growth the congregation enlarged its worship facilities a number of times, first in 1871. In 1872 the Illinois Mennonite Conference was organized with the first session held at Sterling in the same year.[23]

A second Mennonite church in Whiteside County was established about four miles northwest of Morrison, and some seventeen or eighteen miles west (and a bit north) of Science Ridge. Although this Morrison congregation has usually been a small church struggling persistently to "keep the faith," it has seen some prosperous days. Its history goes back to 1864 when William Gsell of Franklin County, Pennsylvania, bought a farm three miles north of Morrison. His family moved out in the spring of 1865. Adam Steiner of Orrville, Ohio, came to Morrison in 1869, purchasing 200 acres of land at forty dollars per acre. At first the newcomers drove the long distance to Science Ridge to attend church services, but after a few more families came they decided to organize a separate congregation. With the encouragement and help of Henry Nice, Sr., and Benjamin Hershey from

Source: Hazel Nice Hassan, Rockford, Ill.

Morrison Mennonite Church, also called the "Red Brick Church," built near Morrison, Illinois, in 1872.

Sterling, William Gsell and the other local Mennonites held an organizational meeting in the West Clyde schoolhouse in 1868. With a charter membership of less than a dozen, the congregation was known as "The Morrison Mennonite Church." Seven members of the group had been baptized just the year before. Since they desired to be baptized by pouring "in the water," the congregation walked three quarters of a mile to a stream for the ceremony. Meeting at first in Gsell's barn or in various homes for services, the members grappled with the problem of building a meetinghouse, which was not easy because of serious differences of opinion as to location. The building was finally constructed in 1872 with opening services on January 1, 1873. Because of its unusual construction in brick, it was locally referred to as the "Red Brick Church"[24] and became a landmark in the community. It shared the distinction of being one of the three Illinois Mennonite brick meetinghouses in that period, preceded only by the Partridge Amish structure in 1854 and Summerfield Mennonite meetinghouse in 1858.

According to one account, Morrison had thirty members when the meetinghouse was built. Among those interested in the development of this young congregation was Funk, publisher of the *Herald*. On several occasions he visited the community, worshiped with them in Gsell's barn, and through the *Herald* encouraged ministers to stop there, especially if they were able to speak in English. The ministerial problem was solved when Bishop Henry Nice moved from Sterling to Morrison in 1869. An able leader who left his imprint on the congregation and the church at large, he and his work will be discussed more fully in chapter 9.[25]

For its beginning, the Cullom Mennonite community goes back to the late 1850s. This rich prairie area in eastern Illinois, some of it swampy, was the last in the state to be settled and could be purchased at very reasonable prices. Among the first Mennonites to arrive were some named Graybill, Heckleman, Harshbarger, Herner, Shantz, and Baer. Some came from surrounding counties—Woodford and Grundy, for example—while others came from Pennsylvania or from Waterloo County, Ontario. Among the Canadians was the Isaac Shantz family. Isaac had married Elizabeth Snyder of Waterloo and, years later, came to Gardner in Grundy County in 1858 and to Cullom 1860. This family is a good example of pioneers who suffered hardships as they moved west. As they traveled by covered wagon, one of their mules died, and, unable to purchase another mule or horse, they bought an ox and completed the journey with the mixed team. But a tragedy struck as a result of fording a stream in cold weather. While trying to help a fellow traveler who was fording the stream with a casket on his wagon, Schantz' oldest son, Daniel, waded into the cold water to try to keep the casket from floating away. He continued the journey in his wet clothes and soon developed pneumonia, which so impaired his health that he never fully recovered. He died in 1863.

Isaac Herner typifies the many footloose migrants, including a good many at Cullom, who did not remain settled very long in any one place. He was born and reared in Waterloo County, Ontario, migrated to the lumber country in Michigan in 1853, thence to Carroll County, Illinois, in 1859, and returned to Canada later that year. In 1865 he moved to the oil fields of Pennsylvania where "work was plentiful and wages good." Shortly thereafter, he traveled to New York City, Philadelphia, Baltimore, Washington, D.C., and then to Cullom. At Cullom, in 1866, he bought a farm. He remained there until 1895, for him a relatively long time, whereupon he and his family moved to Jackson, Minnesota. Six years later he looked for another "new country" where land would be cheaper, and found it near Carstairs, Alberta, Canada. He died there in 1907.[26]

The Cullom congregation, organized about 1860, was never very large, and the shifting nature of its population presented problems. Since its members were quite scattered, the first church services were conducted biweekly in various schoolhouses in the community. Henry Baer, the first minister, was ordained in the Union Church at Washington, at least by 1864, for the *Herald of Truth* states that "Minister Baer" from Cullom, along with Jost Bally, visited the Gardner congregation in that year. Baer died in 1870. In 1873 Daniel Brenneman and J. A. Beutler of Elkhart County, Indiana, visited three days at Cullom and more briefly at Gardner. At Cullom they visited in many homes, had six services, took seven people into the church—five by baptism—and held the rites of communion and foot washing. Abraham Blosser was also chosen by lot as deacon. Brenneman reported that they were generally well pleased with their visit. Without being specific, however, he reported that "we noticed something we would rather not have seen"—adding that he did not want to be judgmental because if "we look into our own hearts, and consider our own past conduct . . . no doubt we will find many imperfections."[27]

An interesting sidelight on the Cullom community comes from a letter written in May 1869 by a member to a relative in Mahoning County, Ohio. Besides the usual talk about health, weather, and visiting, the writer reported that he thought the "place a little lonesome at first but it's settling up very fast now and everything seems lively and gay." The Mennonites still had no church building but were holding religious services in a schoolhouse. "There is mostly a pretty good turnout, though there are but about two dozen church members." At that time he was living with the John Zenst family, who had come from the East that spring and were farming his place. But he still farmed a few acres for himself. He stated he was going to put out about eight acres of corn and then added: "I am going to put out eight or ten acres of osage orange hedge seed though Brother David is with me on that. I expect to start to Warren county [Illinois] next week after hedge seed. I was there last fall and gathered it."[28] In the frontier era and well into the twentieth century, osage hedge had great economic significance for use as fencing and for durable fenceposts.

Of the congregations discussed above, two no longer exist. Union closed as a separate congregation in 1929, merging with the nearby Metamora congregation, and Cullom gradually terminated its activities in the 1960s. Several other early Mennonite congregations had even shorter existences.

In the early 1840s a few Mennonite families from Germany, mostly from Bavaria and Saxony, settled near Scales Mound in Jo Daviess County in northwestern Illinois. Bordered by the Mississippi River on the west and by Wisconsin on the north, the area was hilly and covered by timber. Galena, the largest city in the county, was famous as a lead-mining center and later as one of the homes of General Ulysses S. Grant. Land was inexpensive. In the late 1840s Mennonites were among the first to buy land from the Illinois Central Railroad. In 1848 Christian Herr bought eighty acres for $100 and in 1850 bought an additional 160 acres for $5 an acre. Among the first Mennonites to settle here were John Gustave and Louis Duerrstein (or Durrstein), Jacob Heer, Henry Heer, Henry Musselman, Peter Neuenschwander (or Neuschwanger), and, later, John Rudolph Hammer. Perhaps some Albrechts also settled here. Johannes Baehr (Bahr), a minister, died in 1863. A son, Heinrich Baehr, his wife, Lovina, and their first two children migrated from Bavaria to Lancaster County, Pennsylvania, and then on to Jo Daviess County.

It has not been possible to pinpoint the exact places of origin of many of the European emigrants. For example, the record states that Mrs. (Catherine) Jacob Bernhard Hammer was born in Mosbach, Germany, but there were a half-dozen "Mosbachs." Conrad Winter was born in Württemberg, but one wonders where in that state.[29]

Following the usual pattern, these Mennonites at first held worship services in their homes. Soon they built a log schoolhouse for an English public school and for church services. Very possibly a German school, which had been conducted in the homes, was also transferred to the building. When the log schoolhouse became too small, a larger stone building was erected, a building still standing, though no longer in use. Michael Musselman was the last Mennonite minister. Born in Bavaria in 1829, he came to the United States in 1846, lived two years in Lancaster County, Pennsylvania, and came to Jo Daviess County in 1848. A minister and a prosperous farmer, he was active in community affairs, serving nine years as school director, one term as trustee, and twelve years as road commissioner. In politics he was a Democrat. The last baptism Musselman performed was about 1878, and the congregation did not continue long beyond that date. After worship services ceased, and even before in some cases, the few remaining members began to affiliate with other groups, especially Presbyterian. David Heer, the last Mennonite, died on November 17, 1923. He had become a member of the Freeport Mennonite Church some forty miles away. In 1870 the John Neuschwanger family moved about thirty miles away to Carroll County. They then drove the sixteen miles to services at Morrison.

The Scales Mound congregation, never large, apparently was too small as a religious and social unit to endure for the long pull. Perhaps weak leadership and few religious and social activities were also discouraging factors. The few who remained and wished to retain the Mennonite connection did so through the *Herald of Truth*. In 1878 Heinrich Baehr, for example, wrote to John F. Funk to let him know how important the periodical was to him, especially since his church was closed. The *Herald* "encourages me to remain steadfast on the old foundations of truth," said he.[30]

Another Mennonite congregation, now extinct, existed for a few years near Gardner in Grundy County. Apparently, Mennonites from Pennsylvania and Ohio began to move to this area in the late 1850s and early 1860s. Good land could be bought for nine or ten dollars an acre. Aaron Scoggin, born in Hamilton County, Ohio, moved there in 1856 and married Anna Weaver from Pennsylvania the following year. At the age of 13 Lewis Kulp, born in Holmes County, Ohio, moved with his parents to Gardner about 1854 or 1855. Residing here for thirty-eight years, he and his family moved in 1892 to Elkhart, Indiana. He married Nancy Tinsman in 1863, to which union were born five daughters and two sons. In his later years Kulp became a leader in the Mennonite Church. Kulp Hall at Goshen College was named for him. Among the other family names at Gardner were Buckwalter, Showalter, Tinsman, Shelly, Bixler, Whitmore, and Bachman. Coming from Ontario in 1858, the Isaac Shantz family lived at Gardner for some years before moving to Cullom.

The Mennonites at Gardner, meeting at first in a schoolhouse, were having church services at least by the early 1860s. When John F. Funk was in Chicago, he had close connections with this congregation and in 1862 gave a few words of testimony in one of its services. His words so impressed one young man and his wife that they came forward and applied to become members of the church. According to one report, twenty-one people were served communion at a service in June 1864. John M. Brenneman of Elida, Ohio, a traveling shepherd to scattered Mennonites, included Gardner and other Illinois groups in his ministrations. He seemed not very optimistic about conditions at Gardner, apparently feeling that the aged minister, John Bachman, was not the man for the place. Probably the recent marriage of Bachman, at sixty-four, to a twenty-five-year-old Dunkard girl by a "J. H. Coles Esq." did not increase Brenneman's confidence. Believing, however, that if "these people were frequently visited ... by God's blessing good might be done there," he encouraged ministers to visit and serve them.

Brenneman probably also encouraged his friend John F. Funk to assist in ministering to the Gardner congregation. In any case, on May 28, 1865, the congregation selected Funk and Henry Shelly to serve as additional ministers—Funk to preach mainly in English and Shelly mostly in German. Bishop John M. Brenneman ordained them. A few years later the congregation built its own place of worship two miles west of Gardner. Though Funk, in Chicago, lived some fifty miles northeast, once a month he rode in the caboose of a freight train to Gardner to perform his ministerial duties. In a sermon at Elkhart in 1922 when he was eighty-seven years old Funk stated that fifty-seven years ago "today" he preached his first sermon "in a little frame schoolhouse, near Gardner, Grundy County."

Despite new ministers and its own meetinghouse, the congregation continued a struggling existence. It was still small in the 1870s when again it was without a leader. By the time of the death of Preacher Bachman in 1870, Funk had moved to Elkhart, Indiana, and Shelly had moved to Reading in Kankakee County. As so often happened in similar situations, some members began to move to other places while a few joined other churches. The last remaining Mennonite family was the Lewis Kulps, who, as noted, moved to Elkhart, Indiana, in 1892. The church building was sold shortly after.[31]

It is not well known that there was a Mennonite church in Chicago for a few years in the 1860s and early 1870s. Its origin came from an amazing coincidence. John F. Funk started publishing the *Herold der Wahrheit* and *Herald of Truth* in Chicago in 1864. Among the German immigrants coming to Chicago in mid-century were a few Mennonites, including Peter Neff. In 1865 Neff returned to Baden, Germany, to visit his old home. While there his friends showed him copies of the *Herold der Wahrheit*, which Funk had sent to Germany and elsewhere, and asked him what he knew about the paper and its editor. Neff had to confess that he knew nothing about either. He was still more amazed to discover that the periodical was published a few blocks from his own Chicago home! When Neff returned to Chicago he sought out Funk and the two discovered they had much in common. Since both were interested in the welfare of the Mennonite Church,

The Mennonite Settlements

they decided to start a Mennonite congregation for the benefit of those Mennonites scattered throughout this growing city. In 1866 they organized the first Mennonite congregation in Chicago, providing a place of worship by spending about $800 to add space to Neff's home. The location was on the north side, not far from the present Moody Memorial Church. During its first years the congregation had about twenty members plus children; some members were probably added later. Unfortunately, Neff's home and the church facility were destroyed by the great Chicago fire of 1871, and services were not continued afterward. Meanwhile, Funk had moved to Elkhart, Indiana.[32]

In addition to the Mennonite congregations already discussed, many Mennonites came to various parts of Illinois but never developed into groups large enough to organize congregations. Often Mennonites moved into an Illinois community that looked attractive, without thinking of their families' future church relations. Some of these remained Mennonite, while others eventually joined other denominations. One of the important services performed by the *Herald of Truth* was to serve as a link by which many of these scattered (Old) Mennonites retained some connection with the Mennonite Church. This they did by receiving the *Herald* and especially by correspondence through its columns. Considerable information is thus available about these isolated Mennonites, even though many others went unrecorded. A few examples may suffice.

Ivan Brunk, who has done considerable research on the history of the Brunk family, states that Brunks who "were probably descendants of Mennonites" came to Illinois before the Mennonites did. The earliest ones came in the 'teens and the early 1820s. Others came in the 1830s and 1840s. These Brunks, coming from Pennsylvania by various circuitous routes—through Virginia and/or Maryland, the Carolinas and Kentucky—were to be found at various times in the following Illinois counties: Madison, Menard, Sangamon, Morgan, Schuyler, Hancock, Jo Daviess, and Tazewell. Some Mennonite Brunks from Virginia migrated to La Salle and Henry counties in the 1850s and 1860s. Noah Brunk came from Rockingham County to Ottawa, Illinois, in 1855. Here he married Amanda E. Parr in 1857, to which union were born three children. In addition to farming Noah Brunk became a manufacturer of horse collars. His wife was, and remained, a Methodist. Although Brunk is listed in one place as a Universalist, John S. Coffman, who visited the Brunks in 1895 and preached a well-received sermon in the local Methodist church, states that Brunk remained a Mennonite.[33]

Another group of Mennonite settlers in Illinois who never developed into an organized congregation were from the Shenandoah

Valley of Virginia. In addition to some Brunks, who in this case definitely were Mennonites, the migrants included families named Rodgers, Funk, Driver, Heatwole, and Parret. Their motive for migrating was quite unusual—dissatisfaction with the way the Confederacy was handling the matter of conscientious objection to war. During the Civil War a number of Mennonite young men were virtually forced into the Confederate Army. As a result, some became deserters and hideaways, or fled to the North. Most or all of the above group were in this category. Coming at various times during the war, they settled in Henry County near Atkinson and Geneseo. At least Reuben J. Heatwole and the Brunk and Rodgers families came by train. Most of them were farmers; a few were plasterers. Some apparently intended to return to Virginia after the war, some later migrated farther west, and others remained in the area. George R. Brunk, who later became a prominent leader in the Mennonite Church, was born at Geneseo on December 31, 1871. Heatwole, brother of George R.'s mother, apparently expected at first to return to Virginia after the war but later decided to move to Kansas. There, although he was never selected as minister in spite of having been in the lot eleven times, he became an outstanding lay leader in the church.

  The Brunk family also decided to migrate to Kansas. Already having had its share of difficulties in Virginia due to the war, this family suffered additional tragedies seldom equaled by other pioneers. Making the trek by covered wagon in the fall of 1873, they found traveling difficult, especially in Missouri. "People remembered the Mormons," says Mennonite writer Paul Erb, "and were unfriendly to the wagon train. The Missourians, who had lost their contest with the Free Staters in the Civil War, were prejudiced against anyone going to Kansas. They refused even drinking water, and the Brunks had to drink from roadside ponds and streams. And so when they pulled off the Santa Fe Trail [near Marion, Kansas] to reach their farm a few miles to the south, the whole family was ill—big, strong Henry desperately so." Within less than two months the father and two children died from typhoid, and three months later the baby, Henry G., Jr., died of lung fever. "So instead of the beginning of a happy farmstead, this lonely widow had a row of four graves on her farm." Four years later her older son, Joseph, twelve years of age, lost his arm in a cane mill accident. It was not easy for the mother and the one-armed son to manage the farm operations.[34]

  A few scattered Mennonites settled in Warren County near Monmouth. In 1867 Jacob M. Hershey asked through the *Herald* for ministers to visit them and for other Mennonites to settle there. A few months later John M. Brenneman stopped there to minister to them. He encouraged others also to visit them and observed that the

Hersheys seemed "as lost as sheep that have no shepherd." Another couple, from Ipava, Fulton County, also reported that they felt like shepherdless sheep. James and Susan Boyer moved from Pennsylvania to Illinois in about 1865. In an 1878 letter they stated that there were four other Mennonites in the area and that another family would be moving there shortly. They much appreciated the *Herald of Truth*, to which they had been subscribers for a long time, but they had not heard Mennonite preaching for at least eight years. Whether or not due in part to this plea, John S. Coffman from Virginia, about to become a pioneer Mennonite evangelist, did visit them a few months later. Through him they "earnestly" begged for visitors and, if possible, for a resident minister to serve them.[35] This continued to be a problem for the Boyers, who had a large family. Although they worshiped in other churches, they were not satisfied with this arrangement. For this reason, they again reported a few years later, they were thankful to the *Herald* for providing them with some Mennonite teaching.

The visit of Henry B. Brenneman of Elkhart, Indiana, brother of John M., to scattered Mennonites is quite typical. Adam Winger of Crawford County, Illinois, had asked Brenneman for a minister to visit them, since they had not heard Mennonite preaching for seven or eight years. Winger was also concerned about his seven grown children, none of whom was Mennonite. Complying with the request, Brenneman visited Mennonites not only in Crawford County but also in nearby Piatt and Edgar counties. In cases where children had grown up and were either members of other churches or were not members of any, a number stated that had there been a Mennonite Church in their communities they would have been Mennonites. In 1884 one report stated that a Sunday school in Edgar County, presumably run by Mennonites, had an attendance of from eighty to ninety in the summer. Why this did not develop into a church is not clear. In an article, "The Scattered of the Flock," Abraham H. Kauffman of Edgar County, a frequent contributor to the *Herald*, told scattered Mennonites that they should not become discouraged and lax because of infrequent contact with other Mennonites. Nor should they join fashionable churches that are disobedient to Christ. Instead they should be as salt and light by showing the love of Christ. To help achieve these objectives Kauffman advised them to read the *Herald of Truth*.[36]

Such examples illustrate the spiritual problems of Mennonites who migrated west to areas where there were no Mennonite churches and little or no prospect of organizing them. Both in and outside Illinois many were concerned about the problem. That is why John F. Funk, Henry Yother, John S. Coffman, John M. Brenneman, and others traveled much among them. Some of the settlers themselves saw the problem, but often after it was too late. Adam Winger in Crawford County, for example, said after some years of experience that Mennonites should think long and hard before moving to a place where there was no church of their own. Some, no doubt, thought that a church would develop where they were moving. Too many, however, attracted by good, cheap land, failed to consider the spiritual consequences of such migration. The result was large losses to the Mennonite groups.

CHAPTER 3

The Amish Mennonite Settlements in Illinois to About 1878

This chapter will deal with Mennonite followers of Jakob Ammann, especially those who migrated to central Illinois in the second and third quarters of the nineteenth century. The Amish Mennonites came to Illinois a few years earlier than the Mennonites and came in larger numbers. As Harold S. Bender said: "The proper name of the followers of Jakob Ammann is 'Amish Mennonite' although frequently they are referred to simply as Amish. Not all the descendants have retained the name and the principles of the original group—none at all in Europe—most of them having reunited with the main body." But in the United States and Canada, thousands have retained the name, and also the characteristic principles—the Old Order Amish rigorously, the more progressive Amish groups less rigidly. Other descendants have dropped the name, and perhaps most of the principles.

The "most serious and only major schism" which occurred in the South German-Swiss Mennonite groups was the Amish division. In 1693-97 Elder Jakob Ammann, who had moved to Alsace from Erlenbach, Canton of Bern, Switzerland, separated from the Mennonites and took with him a substantial minority of followers. Ammann was a stern disciplinarian and rather dictatorial. The chief cause of the division was his interpretation of the article in the Schleitheim Confession having to do with the ban, that is, the shunning of a person excommunicated from church as suggested by 1 Corinthians 5:6. The main body of Swiss and South German Mennonites held that the commandment not to eat with a sinning brother applied only to the communion table; Ammann and his followers believed that it also applied literally to the regular tables from which church members ate their daily food. The latter went to the extreme of saying that even husband and wife should not share the same table and bed, if one was declared under the ban by the church. The controversy also involved other differences. One was whether a person who spoke a falsehood should be excommunicated. Another was whether truehearted persons—those Christians who did good works, such as helping out persecuted Mennonites, but had not become Mennonites—could be saved. Ammann seems to have held that no one outside the Mennonite fold could be saved. He also held strict views on uniformity of dress—including the style of hats, garments for the body, shoes and stockings—and the untrimmed beard. And he proscribed attendance at services of the state church. Ammann introduced the ordinance of foot washing, which had been practiced in Holland but not among the Swiss and South German Mennonites. He freely used the power of excommunicating those who disagreed with him. There were several attempts at reconciliation, and Ammann did offer to make some concession—but perhaps not enough. He was a headstrong man, and the division became permanent.[1]

Some Amish, like the Mennonites, had already come to Pennsylvania in the eighteenth century. After the Napoleonic Wars, many more were ready to take their chances in the New World, following the general reasons for leaving the homelands discussed in chapter 2. Although better economic opportunity in the New World was important to them, the few, brief records that have survived suggest also a longing to get to a land of freedom and away from war and conscription.

C. Henry Smith wrote that "nearly all the Amish immigrants to Illinois, as well as those to other states, during this period, came from Alsace-Lorraine."[2] But this statement needs modification. Large numbers also came from the Palatinate, Bavaria, and other central and South German states, according to histories of the central Illinois counties where the Amish settled and, more particularly, family histories and obituary records. The obituary records in the *Herald of Truth*, for example, indicate that the number coming from the French provinces of Alsace and Lorraine was not greatly different from that of the South German provinces. Of course, because of persecution the Amish, like the Mennonites, had moved from place to place a great deal; hence, some in the German areas, or their ancestors, had been in Alsace and Lorraine at one time or another. But whether the line went through France or Germany, their earlier ancestors were from Switzerland, most of them probably from Canton Bern.[3]

Coming to the United States was far from easy in those days. Long into the nineteenth century, crossing the Atlantic was quite an ordeal. Although the steamship was invented in 1806, its practical use on the ocean was long in coming, which means that before the Civil War the Amish and others used the sailing vessel when coming to Illinois. They endured long ocean voyages, often requiring fifty, sixty, or even seventy days. Providing for families for such a long journey required extraordinary management.

Although New York was a chief port of entry for many immigrants, others, such as Philadelphia and Baltimore, were also used. The immigrants soon used New Orleans heavily when they discovered the more direct, all-water route to Illinois by way of the Mississippi and Illinois Rivers. From the east coast there were various routes to Illinois. One was by way of the Hudson River, the Erie Canal and the Great Lakes. Another led through Pennsylvania, either by wagon or canal boat, to Pittsburgh, where the immigrants took river boats to Cincinnati and Butler County, Ohio, or all the way down the Ohio, then up the Mississippi and Illinois to Peoria and vicinity. Some came all the way from the East over land, but this was less common—at least until the coming of the railroads. Another route by which Mennonites and Amish came to Illinois was by way of Ontario, Canada, some of them directly, others by way of Butler County, Ohio.

An example of those taking this last route was the family of Christian Ropp, who became an important leader of the Amish in Illinois. The son of Andreas and Elizabeth Eiman Ropp, Christian lived with his parents in upper Alsace on a small farm called Barthelhütte about a six-hour walk from Basel, five hours from Belfort, and about two from both Altkirch and Dammerkirch. Having heard many favorable reports about America and noting the large emigration to it, Christian's father decided in 1826 to emigrate "rather than allow his [six] sons to be drafted into the army...." Having been born in 1812, Christian was fourteen years of age at the time. Going by horse and wagon through Belfort and Paris to Havre, the family sold the horse there but took the wagon along. The crossing—in this case to Philadelphia—encountered "some stormy weather and all became seasick, my mother being sick most of the time." It required forty-six days.

A grandson of Christian Ropp has allowed his imagination to reconstruct the landing of his forebears at Philadelphia about two weeks after the celebration of the fiftieth anniversary of signing the Declaration of Independence:

> ... it would be a wonderfully interesting scene if each one of us could stand where they landed and see a father, a mother, and six boys, eight green back country foreigners, their plain hand-woven hand-cut clothes so outlandish and illshapen, the garments of the boys handed down, with patches a plenty, and not so clean after forty days aboard and mother not so well; barefoot or in rough heavy shoes; without stockings; their hair uncut and unkempt; strangers all, unfamiliar with our speech, coming awkward and bewildered down the gangplank carrying every imaginable kind of a pack; this would be a most interesting sight and honestly, how many of us would walk up to great-grandpappy Ropp with his hook and eye clothes, his queer hat and funny beard, slap him on the back and take his hand say, "My, but I'm glad to see you. Come all of you and stay with us tonight."[4]

In Philadelphia Andreas Ropp hired a team to take the family to Lancaster. En route they visited a few days in the home of an Amishman named Zuck. Here Andreas bought a horse to pull the wagon brought from Alsace and started out for Butler County, Ohio. Near Lancaster the party met a Mennonite named King, plowing in his field, who knew by Ropp's dress and beard that he was Amish. King invited them to his home for the night and, after hearing about so many Mennonites going to Ontario, Andreas changed his plans. Instead of going to Butler County, the Ropps joined some others and went to what became Berlin, now Kitchener, Ontario. ". . . It was a hard journey lasting over three weeks." Here Andreas received fifty acres from the government, but the family had to work hard to clear the land.

In 1832 the Ropp family decided to join some others who were moving to Butler County, Ohio, because "it was too cold for them in Canada." In order to collect the money from the public sale of their goods, Christian and his brother Jacob had to remain in Canada until the following year. Then, taking with them about $1,100, they endured a "tedious trip of seventeen days, at one point of which we were in great danger of being robbed, but through the providence of God we happily escaped." So wrote Christian in his autobiography. To the providence of God he could have added that some fake guns, which they had made out of walnut timber, also gave the robbers pause! In any case they arrived safely in Butler County and had a joyous family reunion, the only disturbing news being the high price of land. At the same time they heard of greener pastures in Illinois. After a scouting trip, Christian's brother Andrew returned with a favorable report. In another family consultation they decided that Christian and Andrew should leave in January 1834 by horseback, and the rest of the family should come the following spring. However, the plan could not be carried out completely. The boys went, but just as the others were ready to leave in the spring their mother died and was buried in Butler County. Going by wagon, they stopped first at mother's grave. Gathering around the fresh mound of earth they worshiped in silence and tears. Finally the father, wiping a tear from his eyes, said, "Now we can go." They journeyed westward with a heartbreaking absence in the family circle. In due time they arrived in the Mackinaw River area of Woodford County, Illinois, where they joined Andrew and Christian.[5]

Butler County, Ohio, site of the first European Amish settlement (1819) in America following the Napoleonic Wars, was important in the origins of the Amish Mennonite settlements of central Illinois. Some immigrants, like the Ropps, came through Butler County by way of Canada. Larger numbers came through that area directly from Europe, or after a brief stay in Pennsylvania. Still others came through

Butler County even by way of New Orleans and the Mississippi and Ohio rivers. Probably the chief reason for the close ties between many Amish settlers in Illinois and this Ohio area was that Butler County had been settled by Amish earlier than was Illinois but recently enough that many Europeans who wished to emigrate in the 1820s and 1830s had relatives and acquaintances in the county who could help them get oriented in the New World. These Butler County settlers had also come from Alsace and South Germany. Among later Amish leaders who stopped for a time in this county were Christian Ropp, Peter Naffziger, Joseph Stuckey, Christian Reeser, all of Illinois, and Joseph Goldschmidt of Iowa.[6]

The more northerly sections of Illinois, the ones to which the Amish and Mennonites came in the 1830s and 1840s, were open to settlement shortly before they arrived. This came primarily through the United States government's policy of negotiating treaties with the Indians who claimed the territories, before allowing whites to settle. Unfortunately, whites have always tended to press illegally upon that Indian frontier line. This pressure of settlement in the northern third of the state helped bring on the Black Hawk War in 1832. But already in 1829 the Indians had been removed from the area where the Amish settled. This removal increased the rush of settlers to McLean and probably the other nearby counties, a rush that had already begun in 1827.[7]

As one Mennonite sociologist, Leo Driedger, has pointed out, "Mennonites, although historically suspicious of governments, have on numerous occasions reaped settlement benefits from government eviction of minority groups." Driedger was referring especially to the Russian Mennonites who settled in the Canadian West and who accepted land from the government, which had evicted Indians and Japanese. He claimed that these Mennonites compromised their "principle of love of neighbor" and their "principle of nonresistance by accepting land and protection from a government which used violence to get them these advantages." He continued: "This is perhaps one of the reasons why research of the Mennonites has focused more on their in-group community building than their out-group relations, because the latter raises many questions of conflict rather than equilibrium. It is these conflict relationships which need further study."[8] No doubt the history of Mennonites and Amish in Illinois and other parts of the United States also raises the awkward issue Driedger posed. U.S. Mennonites and Amish have also—perhaps more unconsciously than consciously—enjoyed the use of land which in too many cases has been secured by means that violated the rights of those forcibly dispossessed. Indeed, Paul Erb, in his *South Central Frontiers*, partly at the suggestion of the late Melvin Gingerich, has also raised this embarrassing question. "There is nowhere in the Mennonite records," he writes, "any hint that Mennonite settlers, from Germantown to this ... last stand of the Indians in the West, had any feeling that they were doing wrong in acquiring deeds of ownership for land that the Indians claimed as theirs. ... As we see it now, Mennonites do share a collective guilt for violating the tribal ownership of land, for killing the buffalo upon which Indian life depended, and for breaking the treaties which were given to protect Indian rights."[9] But when the Amish and Mennonites came to Illinois their consciences apparently were not bothered by this ethical question.

Just when the first Amish or Mennonite appeared in Illinois has been something of a puzzle, although it is clear that people of Mennonite ancestry, as pointed out earlier, came before the Mennonites themselves. For a long time 1829 was accepted as the first year of immigration. Harry F. Weber, in his *Centennial History of the Mennonites of Illinois 1829-1929*, stated that Peter Maurer was the first of whom there is any record and that he arrived in that year. This conflicts, however, with material in Appendix I in his book, and it also contradicts what appeared in Maurer's obituary in the *Herald of Truth* in February 1873, which stated that Maurer came with his family from France to Butler County, Ohio, in 1830, and to Illinois in 1837. The 1830 United States census figures for Illinois do not list him. That 1837, or possibly 1838, was correct is further corroborated by an account in a McLean County history. This is also the understanding of some descendants. Thus it seems that the 1829 date must be discarded.[10]

Substantial numbers of Amish began to come from the early 1830s onward and settled in what are now the counties of Peoria, Tazewell, Woodford, McLean, Putnam, Bureau, Livingston, and Champaign. Although there is some contradictory evidence, it is said that John Strubhar and Nicholas Maurer, walked from Butler County, Ohio, to McLean County in 1830.[11] In the spring of 1831 a group of Amish settlers, having come from Alsace and Lorraine the year before, came by way of Pennsylvania, and the Ohio and Illinois rivers, and located along the Illinois near Wesley City, a few miles south of the present East Peoria. Founders of what were called the "Creek Settlements," the early Amish, like other pioneers, preferred locations in the timbered areas along rivers and creeks. In fact, they actually avoided the prairies until they discovered in the 1850s that prairies were the more desirable for farming. They preferred the timbered areas because such areas provided fuel and did not present the drainage problem that the prairies did. They looked upon the prairies as disease-laden, not knowing about the germ theory of disease, or that certain mosquitoes which bred in prairie swamps carried germs which caused

The Amish Mennonite Settlements 61

malaria and other diseases. In addition, before the steel plow they found it very difficult to break or plow the tough prairie sod. Thus Peoria became the center near which the early Amish settled along the Illinois River and its tributaries—Partridge, Ten Mile, and Bureau creeks—and the Mackinaw River and its branches—the Little Mackinaw, Dillon, and Rock creeks.

Wesley City was the first Amish community west of Ohio. Jacob Auer and family, Peter Beck, Christian Roggi with three daughters, Joseph Rusche and two sisters, and David Schertz and family were in this group. Peter Guth, John Sweitzer and family, and Joseph Summer arrived in this settlement later in the year, and others came in the following years.

In the early 1830s other immigrants from Alsace and Lorraine also began settling about ten miles farther up the Illinois River along Partridge Creek between Spring Bay and what is now Metamora, in what shortly was to become Woodford County. At that time "Red" Joe Belsley bought a farm near Spring Bay, and John Engle located about a mile west of Metamora. Engle's obituary states that he too walked from Butler County, Ohio, to Illinois. In 1833 John's father, Christian, a bishop ordained in Alsace, arrived with several of his other children. In addition to those at Wesley City mentioned above, the Amish pioneers located in these settlements included (besides the Engles) Joseph and John Verkler in the Metamora area; and "Black" Joe Belsley, Christian Smith, John Kennel, and Peter Noffziger farther west along Partridge Creek.[12]

Amish immigration into Illinois continued for some decades. Most of it was in 1830-60 and followed traditional patterns as to routes and age of the immigrants. Most of the immigrants remained in Illinois, but there were interesting exceptions. One of the most extraordinary was the case of Andrew Baechler, born in 1828 in Lorraine, apparently near Nancy and/or Sarrebourg. About 1851 he left Illinois for England and from there sailed for the gold fields of Australia, arriving after a voyage of ninety-four days. Remaining there about eight years, he found some gold and then decided to try elsewhere. After a voyage of ninety-three days he arrived in San Francisco and spent a year in the California gold mines. He spent the next eight years in the mining districts of Idaho, British Columbia, and Montana, returning to McLean County, Illinois, in 1867 or 1868. But his wanderings were still not ended. He married Mary Habecker in 1869, and then the couple moved to a farm in McLean County in 1874; finally, in 1899, it appears, they moved to a farm in Kankakee County![13]

Other deviations from the usual patterns of immigration were less dramatic. Although most of the Amish immigrants were young or middle-aged, Nicholas Claudon was different. Born in 1800 in northern Lorraine, he married Barbara Baechler in 1836. Later he and his wife sent their five sons to America as they grew to military age. Finally, in 1889, nineteen years after his wife had died, his son Joseph persuaded his father to return with him to the United States. At the time Nicholas was thought to have been the oldest man ever to have crossed the Atlantic. He lived with his daughter, Mary Claudon King, at Flanagan, Illinois.[14] Maria Dellenbach was also quite old when she came, but not as old as Claudon. A widow, she came from France to Woodford County in 1842 at the age of 67. After leaving the Old World, most of the immigrants never saw it again. But again there were occasional exceptions. John and Mary Baechler Rupp, for example, migrated to Tazewell County in 1855 and then moved to McLean County. In 1874 they returned to visit their childhood home at Sarrebourg, Lorraine, and then took an extensive tour of Europe.[15]

Another deviant from the main pattern of immigration was Henry Bohn. He arrived in about 1885, not only after the main thrust of immigration was over, but as a Lutheran. The Bohn family, though not pacifist in the Mennonite sense, came partly because they also disliked the conscription system of Europe. Born in 1866 at Bischtroff, Alsace, not far from Strasbourg, he migrated to Woodford County in 1885 and found employment among the Amish Mennonites. Here he met his future wife, Rosina Zoss, a Lutheran immigrant from Switzerland. Both joined the Amish Mennonite Church.[16]

The Amish immigrants coming to Illinois by way of New Orleans usually remained in the port city only long enough to make the transfer to a Mississippi riverboat. However, for one reason or another, some remained longer. One who did was Christian Oswald, who probably came from Alsace. The Oswald family "came across with just enough money to land in New Orleans," where they remained seven or eight years, trying to make enough money to complete the journey to Illinois. In the words of a grandson: "My grandmother would bake fancy cookies, cakes, and bread, then sell them to the people around New Orleans in the French Quarter." In about 1860 the Oswalds completed the journey, settling in the Hopedale area. Apparently there was an Amish church in New Orleans for some years; very likely the Oswalds and others who remained there for some time were connected with it.[17]

Most but not all Amish immigrants who came to Illinois remained there. Like other settlers they reserved the right to move on when the pastures looked greener in other states. Some moved for health reasons. In those days tuberculosis—"consumption" they called it—was the disease causing the most deaths, and doctors thought that the climate of the states farther west was better for recovery. Joseph Schrock and his wife represent those who moved for this reason.

Joseph, born in Alsace-Lorraine in 1852, migrated to the United States with his parents and other relatives in 1855. His parents, Christian and Elizabeth Zentner Schrock, settled on a farm half a mile east of the present Roanoke Mennonite Church in which community the Schrocks were pioneers. In 1887 at the age of thirty-four, Joseph married Lizzie Bachman, who soon developed tuberculosis. They moved to Colorado in 1888, first to Manitou and then to Thurman, where she died in 1893.[18]

No doubt more people moved on for economic than for health reasons. Love of adventure probably also influenced a few. For instance, several Illinois Amish were caught up in the spirit of the 1849 gold rush. Two of these had the same name: Andrew Schertz. One of the two returned to Illinois and one did not. Many more Amish moved on farther west to newly developing farm communities in Iowa, Missouri, Nebraska, Kansas, and other Western states. For example, the Illinois contingent in the Mennonite settlement at Manson, Iowa, was very important.[19] An individual example was Nicholas Martin, who had been born in Sarrebourg, Lorraine, and emigrated to Tazewell County, Illinois, about 1854. Here he married Katherine Litwiller in 1855, moved to Decatur County, Kansas, in 1887, and made his last move to Beemer, Cumming County, Nebraska, in 1894. Jacob Beller, born in Saales, Alsace, in 1857, came to Chenoa, Illinois, at age eighteen. After marrying Anna Zimmerman in 1882, he with his wife moved to Milford, Nebraska, in 1885, and to Hesston, Kansas, in 1918.[20] The pattern of such persons, of course, is typical of all Amish and Mennonite groups. Christian Krehbiel (1832-1909), to be discussed later, is a good example of one who was involved in what became the General Conference Mennonite Church. As elsewhere, such migration by Illinois residents continued into the twentieth century, and not everyone moved west. The membership of the new Mennonite Church at Kouts, Indiana, founded in 1916, was composed largely of migrants from Illinois. Illinois also contributed a substantial part of the membership to the new congregation organized in 1920 at Ashley, Michigan.[21]

Organized church life for Illinois Amish became possible with the coming of Christian Engle, a bishop ordained in Alsace and the first Amish bishop in America west of Ohio. Organized in 1833, the Partridge congregation became not only the first among the Amish in Illinois but also the first German church in the state and the second church of any denomination organized in Woodford County.[22] This historic Partridge congregation, which today continues as the Metamora church, was at the time intended to serve all the Amish immigrants. However, as their number increased and they became more scattered, additional congregations were organized. Before they had

Source: Archives of the Mennonite Church.

Partridge Creek meetinghouse from 1854-1889 used by the Partridge Creek church, first organized Illinois Amish congregation.

additional congregations—and even after—many people often had to drive or walk long distances to attend church services. For that reason and also because of long services that often extended into Sunday afternoon, it was the custom to serve a simple noon lunch of coffee, bread, butter, apple butter or jam, pickles, and possibly pie or cookies. These services were held only every other week, or less often. Before the use of church buildings they were held in homes, sometimes in a house and sometimes in a barn.

In Europe neither the Mennonites nor the Amish were accustomed to using church buildings for worship services, partly because of earlier governmental proscriptions against them. In free America the Mennonites apparently built meetinghouses as soon as the size of the congregation made it desirable and as soon as economic conditions permitted. Many Amish, however, elevated the practice of not using meetinghouses into a principle, although there were differences of opinion as to the rigidity of application. The Partridge congregation built its first meetinghouse, a brick structure, a few miles west of Metamora in 1854. This was preceded by the Rock Creek Amish meetinghouse built in 1853 near Danvers and by a few farther east.[23]

This Partridge settlement grew rapidly, soon covering the western and southern areas of Woodford County, the northern part of Tazewell County, and the northwestern section of McLean County. Increasing numbers of immigrants continued to come from Alsace and Lorraine in France and from the Palatinate, Bavaria, Baden, and Hesse in Germany. By the early 1840s settlement extended along Black Partridge Creek from Spring Bay to Metamora, along Ten Mile Creek from Peoria to Washington, along Dillon Creek in Tazewell County, along the Mackinaw River in Woodford County, and, shortly, along Rock Creek in McLean County. By the 1840s additional congregations were also organized to serve the several centers of the growing settlement. About 1837 Wesley City and Dillon Creek were organized into two separate congregations, with Michael Mosimann ordained for the former and Andrew Ropp for the latter. Both were ordained bishops a few years later. Similarly the settlement on the Mackinaw, the "Mackinaw Meeting," was given its own organization with Christian Ropp, ordained minister in 1840 and bishop about 1846, in charge.[24]

Representative names of Amish immigrants from Europe in the pioneer period were Albrecht, Auer (Oyer), Augsburger, Augstein (Eigsti), Bachman, Baechler, Beller, Belsley, Brenneman, Burkey, Camp, Donner, Egli, Erismann, Engle, Esch, Farni, Garber, Gerber, Gingerich, Guth, Hieser (Heiser), Holly (Hooley), Imhoff, Ioder (Yoder), Jutzi, Kennel, King, Kinsinger, Kistler, Klophenstein, Leman, Litwiller, Martin, Maurer, Mosimann, Nafziger, Neuhauser, Orendorff, Oswald, Rediger, Ringenberg (Rinkenberger), Risser (Reeser), Roggy (Rocke), Ropp (Rupp), Roth, Schantz, Schertz, Schrock, Slagel, Smith, Sommer (Summer), Springer, Stuckey, Sutter, Sweitzer, Ulrich, Unsicker, Virkler, Wagler (Wagner), Yordy, Zehr, Zimmerman, and others. The variations in spelling of these names are not limited to those in parentheses.[25]

In addition to the Amish immigrants from Europe to Central Illinois, several early Amish families came to McLean County from Mifflin County, Pennsylvania. Some names in this group were Lantz, Troyer, Yoder, Zook, Plank, and Kauffman. One of these was Jonathan Yoder, who had been ordained bishop in Pennsylvania. He became one of the outstanding leaders among the Amish in Illinois and served as the first bishop of the Rock Creek (or Yoder) congregation organized in 1851 near Danvers.[26]

From this cluster of Amish settlements in Central Illinois emerged thirteen congregations in the period covered in this chapter—i.e., to about 1878. Since Harry F. Weber has discussed the organizational phases of these congregations in some detail, only brief treatment of these features will be given here, with some discussion of leading personalities. As noted, Partridge a few miles west of Metamora was the first to be organized and continued to be a prominent congregation from then to the present. The Amish highly revered their ordained men, selected usually by lot. As the Lord's anointed, they were almost clothed with the "indelible character" granted the priesthood by the Catholics. A minister or bishop was thought to retain his office, no matter where he went. Thus a congregation frequently had more ministers and even bishops than it needed. Tradition says that at one time Partridge "was blessed with four immigrant bishops, all with equal power, and thirteen ministers, but with what degree of harmony we are not told."[27] Such a situation makes it impossible, even if it were desirable, to name and discuss all of the ministers. Among the early bishops serving the Partridge congregation, besides Christian Engle, were Joseph Engle, John Nafziger, Andrew Bachman, John Gingerich, Peter Beller, Christian Esch, Joseph Maurer, and Joseph Bachman.[28]

The Wesley City group, given its own organization separate from Partridge in 1837, was known as the "Busche Gemein" (Bush congregation), and later as Groveland. Michael Mosimann, ordained about 1837, was in charge of the congregation. Appointed bishop a few years later, he remained in charge until 1868, when he joined a persuasion known as the Egly movement, taking with him nearly all of the congregation.[29]

The Dillon Creek settlement, which, as noted, was also given its separate organization about 1837, was led by Andrew Ropp, who was ordained minister some time before 1840 and bishop about that year. He faithfully served his church for over fifty years, not only his own congregation but also others, such as the Tiskilwa group. Dillon Creek became known as the Pleasant Grove congregation and was often referred to as the Tremont church because of its location near that town. It was a small church that never exceeded some 150 members, and, according to one writer, the members seemed susceptible to outside movements. The group lost members to the Egly and Stuckey divisions, and later to the Apostolic Christian and "sleeping preacher" groups and even to John Alexander Dowie, a prominent preacher of divine healing. Among those joining the Egly faction was Peter Hochstettler, who became one of the Egly group's leading ministers for fifty-four years. Among those defecting to the Dowie movement were a minister, Peter W. Ropp, and some members with considerable wealth. Peter W. Ropp himself gave his life savings of $75,000 to Dowie, and Andrew Ropp gave $65,000. Pleasant Grove had no meetinghouse until 1879 and no Sunday school until about 1880.[30]

The "Mackinaw Meeting" which, as noted, had its own organization since about 1840, did not result in a permanent congregation but rather developed into three or four congregations under other names. But until this separation occurred some twenty or thirty years later, Mackinaw continued as an active, influential Amish congregation. This strength was due partly to its strong leadership, especially that of Christian Ropp, one of the more important Amish bishops in Illinois. Associated with him for a short time was Jonathan Yoder, until Yoder organized Rock Creek (or Yoder) congregation in 1851.

Christian Ropp performed most of his major work in the period under consideration in this chapter. Ropp left a brief sketch of his life written in 1892 for his children and grandchildren;[31] and several of his grandchildren, particularly Edwin O. Ropp, collected or wrote some miscellaneous papers concerning him. These add considerably to our information about this remarkable man. After he arrived in Illinois by way of Ontario and Butler County, Ohio, he lived for short periods of time in Woodford and Tazewell counties. Then he married Magdalena Schertz in 1836 and settled on an eighty-acre farm in the Mackinaw River area, about two miles north of what is now Mackinaw Dells— then known as Slabtown or Farniville. Both Ropp and his wife worked for Christian Farni, who also had immigrated from Europe by way of Ontario and Butler County. Ropp, a farmer, also did the blacksmith work on a sawmill which Farni built. Magdalena worked in the household of Farni, she and her husband together receiving $20 a month.[32]

With such wages, however meager they seem now, the young couple was able within five or six months to purchase eighty acres from the federal government for the prevailing price of $1.25 per acre. On this farm they erected a log cabin that remained their home for a number of years, and in which the first five children—four sons and one daughter—were born. There the family lived for twenty-two years. Then, partly at the urging and foresight of Mrs. Ropp, they moved a few miles east and south to the prairie lands of McLean County. Here they succeeded in plowing under the tough prairie grass, tilling the swamps and other poorly drained areas, and prospering even more than formerly. Ropp was able to give each of his seven children who grew to maturity 160 acres of good McLean County land.[33]

Ropp and his wife accomplished all of this while he also carried out his church work. Besides his work in the Mackinaw Meeting he was involved in the leadership of other congregations, particularly the daughter congregations of Rock Creek, Roanoke, Goodfield, and also Waldo. As a farmer, Ropp was progressive in adopting new methods and new machinery. During his lifetime more progress was made in the scientific and technological development of agriculture than in all the previous centuries of history. Unlike many of his fellow Amishmen, especially those who became known as the Old Order, he did not oppose these changes.

In religious beliefs and customs, however, he remained conservative. Christian Erismann, a roving Amish schoolteacher who kept a diary, reported that on one wedding occasion Ropp, before performing the ceremony, required a confession from the groom because he parted his hair. (Incidentally, Erismann wondered when this thing about the "hair, clothes, and buttons" would end among the Mennonites.)[34] Ropp seemed strict to most of his children and grandchildren. One grandson, Edwin O. Ropp, reported that Christian regarded pictures on the wall, carpets on the floor, the wearing of jewelry and buttons, and the use of top buggies as worldly and out of place for the Christian. "As a result of such stringency," continued Edwin, "not a single son continued in the church of his father, though father and sons continued to love each other dearly." This statement is true only if by the "church of his father" is meant the Amish church. Another report states that "John was the only one of the family who remained a Mennonite." Among John's many contributions to the church were $180,000 to Bluffton College (Ropp Hall was named for him) and $53,000 to Goshen College. Actually, at least one of the two daughters also remained a Mennonite. One son, Christian, Jr., disavowed belief in eternal punishment and was banned from his church. He became a spiritualist and also believed in "universal peace." He also gained fame as the inventor of Ropp's calculator.

Despite differences the Ropps had with their father and grandfather over religious belief, they had a genuine respect and love for him and tried to understand him in the light of his position as a leader of his church. "Was he not bishop and one of the highest officers of his church?" asked a grandson. "If the shepherd is unwatchful, alas, what will become of the sheep?" The Ropp papers indicate that the family had a normal, happy home life full of love and understanding—understanding even of the pranks that mischievous children sometimes played. On behalf of children, grandchildren, and others, Edwin O. Ropp declared that his "own reverential love for the many sterling qualities of my grandfather would be difficult to describe. He was everywhere known to be honest and generous, endowed with a tender heart which his rigid religion too often had a tendency to render stern in appearance." To understand him, continued the grandson, "it is necessary to know that to achieve an abode in the Heavenly Temple was to him by far the most important part of our earthly existence."[35] Christian Ropp attempted to carry on his labors in that spirit.

Before discussing other congregations whose beginnings are related to Ropp's work, we must go back to the 1830s and note the begin-

The Amish Mennonite Settlements 69

nings of the Willow Springs congregation in Bureau County. Chronologically, this was the next area to be settled after Mackinaw. Most of these settlers came from the Palatinate, and especially Bavaria, in Germany. As was often the case, some came by way of Butler County, Ohio. The first families, arriving in 1835, settled in the Hennepin and Granville neighborhoods east of the Illinois River in Putnam County, among them being the Burkeys, Hollys, and Brennemans. In 1836 Christian Albrecht and family from the Palatinate and Bavaria made an important contribution to the settlement of the new community. With five sons and four daughters, Albrecht faced the problem of compulsory military training. The oldest son was excused on the ground that he was needed on the farm to help take care of such a large family. Even the second son was exempted by doing a good job of faking, before the authorities, that he was mentally deficient. But no strategy seemed to work on the third, who was inducted into the army. Christian and wife, Elizabeth, and the entire family, therefore, decided to migrate to the United States. Since one son and three daughters were already married and had seven children, the entire party consisted of twenty-three persons. They knew the John Burkey family at Hennepin, so they decided to go there. Arriving by way of New York City, they went up the Hudson River, then by way of the Erie Canal and the Great Lakes to Chicago. From here a hired freight wagon hauled their possessions while the family walked.[36]

In the fall of 1836 son Joseph, hearing of cheaper land, crossed to the west side of the Illinois River in search of a home. Heavy rains fell and flooded the area, making it impossible for him to return home for about six weeks. Thrown on his own resources, he subsisted on wild berries and wild game cooked over an open fire. When he did return safely he persuaded others to move to the west side and reside in Bureau County. Some family names among these settlers were Albrecht, Burkey, Ioder, Zierlein, Rocke, Gingery, Nafziger, and Shetler. Others came later, and the permanent congregation developed in the Tiskilwa area rather than at Hennepin. Hennepin, however, continued to be an important trading center for the community until the Rock Island Railroad was built through Tiskilwa in 1852. Other railroads were also built through the county, all of which greatly aided the settlers in marketing. In these early days land could be bought from the government for $1.25 and from private parties for $5.00 per acre. As time went on quite a few of these Amish settlers became fairly wealthy. For example, Jacob Albrecht, son of Christian and Elizabeth mentioned above, at one time owned 1,570 acres in Bureau County and 320 acres in adjoining Lee County.[37]

Church services were held from the beginnings of the settlement at Hennepin. The first minister was Jacob Burkey, a native of Hesse,

Germany, who was followed by Daniel Holly from the same place. Peter Naffziger—known as the "Apostle" because of his preaching among widely scattered groups—preached for a short time and was followed by Michael Kistler, a minister from the South Danvers Hessian congregation in McLean County. The settlers had problems with some of these ministers, particularly Holly, who was influenced by some Brennemans who did not believe in future punishment. Holly followed that unorthodox persuasion, withdrew from his group, and left them shepherdless. Kistler, like most of his fellow Hessians in McLean County and in Butler County, Ohio, proved too liberal for most of his parishioners. He relaxed the strict Amish rules and permitted members to do pretty much as they pleased. Later he left the Amish church. Some stricter men then led, especially Bishop Andrew Ropp from Dillon Creek, and Joseph Burkey, who was ordained bishop in 1869. But they displeased the more liberal element, and eventually some of the liberals organized a Central Conference Church. Long before that occurred, however, the congregation had erected its first church building near Tiskilwa in 1873 and soon after organized a Sunday school.[38]

The Amish next organized the Rock Creek, or Yoder, church. It grew out of the Mackinaw Meeting because of the large area over which that congregation spread. As the Amish population began to increase in the 1840s and 1850s southeast of the Mackinaw congregation, the settlers there found it more convenient to meet among themselves for worship services. That was particularly true after Bishop Jonathan Yoder and family came from Pennsylvania to the area in 1851, at which time the group was organized as a separate congregation. Continuing its rapid growth, the congregation erected in 1853 a meetinghouse on land donated by Joseph Gerber near Rock Creek, some five miles north of Danvers. As noted earlier, this was the first Amish meetinghouse in Illinois. It served the congregation until 1872, when the members, now numbering 400, decided to build a new structure on the prairie at the site of the present North Danvers Church. Needing ministerial assistance, Bishop Yoder ordained Joseph Stuckey and John Strubhar as ministers in 1860 and Stuckey as bishop in 1864.

Until his death in 1869, Yoder was an outstanding Amish leader, not only in his Rock Creek congregation but also among his people throughout the state and nation. He had a friendly disposition and was a man of intelligence and good judgment. One writer has said: "He was a typical Amishman from Pennsylvania and was conservative in his views. He believed in the conventional form of Amish dress, bonnets and veils for women, hooks and eyes and long hair for men. Yet he was progressive when compared with the other Amish bishops of his day. He very often showed a liberal attitude toward new things that came up." The story is told that on one occasion, when some Amish bishops had come together to discuss whether young men should be allowed to wear neckties, some bishops got out their tobacco and pipes and handed one to Yoder. He took it, looked at it a moment, and then threw it down, exclaiming: "We have met to consider whether the young men can wear neckties and yet we engage in this filthy habit of smoking." The meeting, according to the story, "adjourned without discussing the question of neckties."[39]

Down to about 1872 Joseph Stuckey, who followed Yoder as leader in the Rock Creek and then North Danvers churches, played an even greater role among the Amish than had his predecessor. Born in Alsace in 1826, he came with his parents by way of New Orleans to Butler County, Ohio, in 1830. Here he received his limited formal education—about three months—was baptized into the Amish church at the age of eighteen, married Barbara Roth in 1844, moved to the Rock Creek area in McLean County in 1851, and was ordained bishop in 1864. At the ordination Bishop Yoder was assisted by Bishops Jacob Zehr and Christian Ropp, with whom Stuckey was later to have serious differences. Like other Amish ministers, he was a farmer. Despite his limited formal education, he studied hard and was well informed. And although he preached mostly in German, he learned English, according to his daughter, by reading the Bloomington *Pantagraph*. Both before and after his termination of fellowship with the Amish Conference in 1872 he was much in demand as a preacher in Illinois and other states. He was a fluent speaker and few Amish preachers were able to attract as large crowds as he. Becoming an early subscriber to the *Herald of Truth,* first published in 1864, he wrote many reports and articles for the paper, and his wide travels, especially in the 1860s and 1870s, can be traced through its columns.[40]

The Hessians who settled near Danvers in 1837 and the years following had a connection with the Rock Creek church. They came from Butler County, Ohio, and the same differences that existed between them and the other Amish there were to reappear in McLean County. That is, the Hessians who had come to Butler County were more liberal than the other Amish there and were less inclined to retain the traditional customs and ways of thinking. Michael Kistler, who had been ordained minister by his father-in-law, Peter Naffziger, in Butler County, was their leader. Worshiping first in their homes, they united with the other Amish in the community after the Rock Creek church was built in 1853. But Kistler could not agree with the conservative leadership of Jonathan Yoder and the old practices which he tried to maintain, such as the wearing of hooks and eyes and the prohibition against the use of musical instruments. A strict disciplinarian, Yoder refused Kistler communion, after which (about 1859) the Hessians again worshiped in their homes until they built a meetinghouse in 1864 about two miles south of Danvers. In 1863, because of his view on baptism, Kistler left the old church and joined the Christian denomination. Before he left, however, the congregation elected as ministers Christian Gingerich and Michael Kinsinger, both of whom had likewise come from Butler County, Ohio. There is a striking similarity in this relationship that existed between the Hessians and the other Amish in Butler County, Ohio.[41]

Known originally as the "Delavan Prairie Church," the Hopedale church grew out of the Partridge and Dillon Creek colonies. This was the first Amish settlement on the prairies. Among the early settlers were the families of Christian and John Sutter, Christian and Peter Nafziger, Christian Slagel, Simon Bechler, Christian Birkey, Joseph Birkey, George Zehr, David Springer, Christian Schertz, Noah Augsburger, Christian and Nicholas Martin, Joseph Litwiller and Daniel Brenneman. A larger proportion of these immigrants came from South Germany than was the case of the Amish settlers in Woodford and McLean counties. Christian Nafziger, the first bishop at Hopedale, came from the Castle Weilbach estate in Hesse not far from Frankfurt, where he held an important financial position as "curator of funds," or treasurer. A "Certificate of Domicile," dated August 10, 1840, and an accompanying testimonial dated in 1848 testify to Nafziger's faithfulness, diligence, and good ethical conduct in carrying out the duties of this position. His successful experience in the use and care of finances in Hesse indicated an ability which stood him in good stead in his new home in Illinois. In 1854 he purchased for $350 eighty acres of land one mile south of Hopedale, which became known as the Nafziger home place. Nafziger soon became known as a good administrator and accumulated a large estate, while at the same time giving freely to good causes and to those less fortunate.[42]

As elsewhere, at the outset church services were not held every Sunday. Since some of the settlers came from Dillon Creek, services were rotated with the Amish at that place, perhaps every four weeks at Hopedale at first and later every two weeks. Though the exact date is uncertain, it was probably in 1854 that the Hopedale congregation was organized in a barn on the farm of Joseph Birkey. The congregation ordained Christian Nafziger minister in 1856 and bishop in 1860 or 1861. Among the other early ministers here were Joseph Litwiller, Noah Augsburger, Daniel Grieser, William Unzicker, and John Egly. Meeting in homes at first for their services, the congregation did not erect a meetinghouse until 1875, when they built a frame structure two miles southeast of Hopedale at a cost of $1,800.[43]

The Waldo congregation in Livingston County is another illustration of the movement to the prairies. The building of the railroads into these areas, together with the discovery that the prairie land was potentially valuable, began to draw the people from the timbered lands along the streams. The first Amish began to settle in Waldo Township in the late 1850s and early 1860s. Continuing the movement in the following years, they came from nearby counties, especially Woodford, Tazewell, and McLean, as well as directly from Europe. Some representative names of early settlers were Rediger, Stalter, Slagel, Oyer, Steinmann, Schmitt, Albrecht, and Wagler. In 1860 when it was thought the number was large enough, Bishop Christian Ropp of Mackinaw took the initiative in organizing the group into a congregation. The first minister, Jacob Rediger, soon died. John P. Schmitt, another early minister, served for more than forty years. Other early ministers were Joseph Rediger, Jacob Wagler, and Christian Slagel. In 1867 the group erected its first church house and in 1868 it started a Sunday school. After first meeting in Sunday school on alternate Sundays when it held no church services, the congregation decided in 1875 to join the two services. In all of Illinois, Waldo was one of the first congregations to take this step.[44]

Another congregation resulting from the movement of the Illinois Amish from the timbered tracts to the more fertile prairies was Roanoke, located in the township for which it is named. The migrants to Roanoke came from surrounding congregations, especially Partridge and Mackinaw. In fact, before Roanoke had its separate organization it was considered a part of the sprawling Mackinaw congregation. When the Rock Creek congregation built a new meetinghouse in 1872 north of Danvers, the southern portion of the Mackinaw Meeting used the old building for some time while the northern part continued to meet in houses. Soon after this, however, at a meeting in a grove on the farm of David Schertz across the road from the site of the present church, Bishop Christian Ropp proposed the building of a meetinghouse for the convenience of the northern part of the Mackinaw Meeting. The proposal was well received, only one person opposing, and the first church building was erected and dedicated in 1875. Christian S. Schertz donated an acre of land on the northeast corner of his farm for this purpose. Before the church was built, the first minister to serve the congregation, in addition to Bishops Ropp and Jacob Zehr, was David Schertz. In 1867 Joseph Wagner and Christian Reeser, Sr., also were ordained ministers. Joseph Rediger, likewise ordained minister, later moved to Nebraska. Joseph Schrock, son of deacon Christian Schrock, moved to Colorado, then to Nebraska, and finally to Oregon in 1909.[45]

Christian Reeser was an unusual person. He was born in Alsace in 1819 while Napoleon was still living and James Monroe was president of the United States; in 1923, at Eureka, Illinois, at age 103, he died when Warren G. Harding was president. He arrived in the United States in 1839 by way of New Orleans, and located first in Butler County, Ohio. About 1847 he joined his brother John near Muncie, Indiana, and in 1852 he married Barbara Zimmerman. The wife had a good education for her day and complemented her husband well, for he had wide experience and much common sense but very little formal training. In 1857, at that time with three children, the couple moved to Woodford County, Illinois, and settled on the Mackinaw River a few miles north of Congerville. The decision to locate in this area came largely because Reeser's friend Nicholas Maurer was there and gave the new arrivals a hearty welcome. The Reeser farm on the Mackinaw remained the home of the family for many decades and became a historic landmark. For the fifty-six years of his ministry Christian Reeser served in the Roanoke congregation and community, except for 1903-07 when he lived with a daughter in Missouri.[46]

The remnant of the Mackinaw Meeting that remained after the formation of the Rock Creek and Roanoke congregations came to be known as the Goodfield congregation. Its meetinghouse is closest to the sites of old Slabtown and Farniville. Wanting to meet more centrally than in the old abandoned Rock Creek church, which they had begun to use after 1872, the members decided to erect a building just a bit south of the present Goodfield. The first ministers of the congregation were Bishop Jacob Zehr, Bishop Christian Ropp, and Christian Reeser. All natives of the original Mackinaw Meeting, they were also among the first ministers at Roanoke. However, as time went on Ropp and Reeser became more associated with Roanoke and Zehr with Goodfield. In fact, the Zehr family was very important in the life and history of the Goodfield congregation. Jacob Zehr was only one of the Zehrs who lived in and served this church and community. Originally from Switzerland, the Zehrs lived in both Alsace, France, and Bavaria, Germany, and most of them came to this country from the latter. Some of them migrated to Illinois by way of Butler County, Ohio, while others traveled directly. Jacob, one of the latter, arrived in 1848 and settled in the Mackinaw area. Married to Elizabeth Ehrisman in 1850, he was ordained minister for the Mackinaw congregation in 1859 and bishop in 1863. He labored under the handicap of a "nervousness or sick-headache" for nearly forty years and was unable to preach the last few years of his life. The family produced a number of preachers. For example, a brother of Jacob, Peter Zehr, had four sons grow to maturity, all of whom became ordained. Some were fairly wealthy. Christian, another brother of Jacob, built a fine brick house overlooking the Mackinaw Valley and accumulated 900 acres of land.[47]

A few more Amish congregations emerged before 1878, such as

Source: Mennonite Historical Library, Goshen, Ind.

Bishop Jacob Zehr (1825-1898) and Elizabeth Ehrisman Zehr (1830-1902) by gate, with their family at the family homestead in the Mackinaw Valley near the Zimmerman Ford of the Mackinaw River in Woodford County; an example of a timber-area home.

Salem in Livingston County and East Washington and Groveland in Tazewell, but since these became members of other branches they can best be discussed in Chapters 4 and 5.

Life on the frontier, sometimes idealized by the romancers, was not easy. Amish life in Illinois about mid-nineteenth century and the years following was no exception. Nearly all of the Amish and Mennonites were farmers, and farming methods before mid-century were primitive, having changed little for many centuries. Farm "machinery" was very simple, generally made of wood. Plows pulled by oxen and later by horses did little more than stir the ground. To prepare a seedbed the farmer might drag a pile of brush weighted with some logs or stones over the ground. Yet the Amish and Mennonites came at a time in the nineteenth century when technology was beginning to change. From the invention of the reaper in the 1830s onward, development of farm machines was increasingly rapid. Sometimes the Amish and Mennonites aided the process. Christian Ropp, Jr., invented a "wind engine" in 1857 and a corn planter in 1859. He even manufactured the planters, although apparently not many.[48] The work of Wood, Deere, and Oliver to develop and improve the steel plow was very significant, since it greatly aided in the conquest of the fertile prairies as the settlers attempted to plow down the tall, tough prairie grass. Dozens of other inventions made farming easier and more profitable.

By the 1850s marketing was becoming easier. The coming of canals in the 1830s and 1840s and the development of steamboat navigation had helped somewhat, but the coming of railroads in the 1850s helped much more. Before the arrival of the railroads, Amish and Mennonites often had to go fifteen, twenty, thirty, or more miles to sell their produce and buy goods. For example, in Hopedale prior to the coming of the railroad in 1868 farmers had to haul grain some fifteen or twenty miles to Peoria or Atlanta. For a load of corn and the two days of travel John Sutter of Hopedale received a barrel of salt. So farmers tried to make their operations very self-subsistent. The George Sommer family on Partridge Creek was typical. They produced virtually all their food at home. Cloth they wove from their own sheep's wool. An itinerant tailor came once a year to make clothing. An itinerant cobbler came to make the footwear from their leather and wood. For light they used tallow candles made at home. They laundered their clothes in a stream. Berries and other wild fruits supplemented the food they grew on the farm and in their garden. The boys were herdsmen and woodchoppers. In winter the men cut down trees and hauled in the wood.[49] But with the coming of the railroad this simple, self-subsistence gave way to a market economy. The change brought advantages, but did not solve all problems, as the agrarian unrest

Source: Thomas Yoder, Normal, Ill.

Threshing at Louis C. Brinkman farm, Livingston County, with equipment of Daniel B. King, 1895. Note crew members' wives.

manifested by Granger, Greenback, and Populist movements in the post-Civil War period attests. The Amish and other farmers were now at the mercy of widely fluctuating markets which, so far as the sale of farm products was concerned, were in a state of depression for much of this period.

Despite economic hardships and problems on the Illinois frontier, hard work was well rewarded. Thanks to the productivity of most of the soil, most of the Amish made good livelihoods; some became quite prosperous, and a few grew quite wealthy. One early report from Bureau County, which could be duplicated elsewhere, tells about the abundance of wildlife, such as hens, ducks, geese, and deer. "Cattle you can have as many as you want. They have an abundance to eat here. On a small piece of land you make a great deal of hay. You can live a great del more comfortable herr [sic] than in Germany. The land is much more productive."[50] To be able to secure a few hundred acres of land over a period of years was not unusual. Peter Kennel in Woodford County had 1200 acres of good farmland and 160 of timber. Jacob Zehr accumulated 900 acres. Andrew Bachman in Woodford County secured 480 acres of good farmland and fifty-eight acres of timber. It is said that Peter R. Engle of Metamora had real estate valued at $40,000, a good sum for those days. There are many stories of farmers starting with virtually nothing and securing hundreds of acres of good land. Very wealthy was a family bearing the "Mennonite" name of Funk in McLean County, the forerunners of the present Funk Seed Company. But that family was not Mennonite or Amish, although their ancestors had been.[51]

A hardship on the frontier was the problem of health, which was compounded by the shortage of and distance from doctors and by the low state of medical knowledge. The germ theory of disease was still unknown in mid-century, and even after the discoveries were made it would take additional decades for this knowledge to filter down to the people. Peter Smith (Schmidt), near the present Congerville, lost his parents, Christian and Magdalena, and two sisters and a brother in the cholera epidemic in July or August 1855. As an orphan in his later teens he had to hire himself out to others. It is said that while working in the field one day he went to a nearby neighbor and asked for a drink of water. The lady, knowing his background, gave him a drink but would not permit him in the house, but instead opened the door only the few inches necessary to pass out the cup and then to receive it back. She knew nothing about possible germs on the cup but did know that people caught cholera from others! Such behavior added to the difficulties and loneliness of those suspected of being bearers of the dreaded disease.[52] Another serious disease, more widespread than Asiatic cholera, was tuberculosis. Known as the "white man's plague," it was the leading cause of death in the nineteenth century. Obituary notices in the *Herald of Truth* suggest how widespread it was. Still more prevalent but less fatal was malaria or the ague. As has been noted, the settlers avoided the prairies for a long time because prairies seemed unhealthful. They were more swampy, had more mosquitoes, and therefore more malaria. Of course, the connection between malaria-bearing mosquitoes and the disease was then unknown.

High mortality among children was another cross that Amish pioneers, like others, had to bear. Many families suffered multiple losses of children. For instance, Peter Zehr and wife of the Mackinaw area had thirteen babies. Of the first nine "six never lived to be over two years old. In the year 1860 two small sons died within 3 months." Although this, no doubt, was higher than average, it does point to a common problem.[53]

Intellectually and educationally, the tastes of the Amish were simple and, with some exceptions, easily satisfied. During the winter months, when there was less need for their labor on the farms, children profited by some study of the three R's in public elementary schools. Not starting to school until the farm work was completed in late fall, the pupils ended their "academic endeavors" with the resumption of farm work early the next spring. Frequently the Amish supplemented public school by attending private German schools to study German and some Bible. Historically, Amish and Mennonites have had a tendency to think of German as the mother tongue, if not indeed the language of God—hence the tendency to give it up reluctantly and never without a struggle.

Few Amish asked for much education, but an exception was Christian Erismann from Hesse, Germany. Erismann was born in 1835 and arrived in Illinois in 1857. A schoolteacher and one of the more progressive members of his group, he thought that the Amish (or Amish Mennonites, or just Mennonites, as he sometimes called them), especially the minister, should have had more education. He left a valuable manuscript, "Biography and Journal of Christian Erismann" (discovered in the attic of the former Mennonite Old People's Home at Rittman, Ohio, some twenty years ago). In an entry of August 9, 1868, he wrote: "Oh! would to God that we Mennonites would support our brothers in the faith in Ohio at the Educational Institute in Wadsworth with united strength and willing hearts." Erismann's belief in more education came through conviction, not simply because he was a schoolteacher.[54]

Religiously the Illinois Amish were still considered one church or denomination in the 1850s, though organizational changes were not far away. The more or less typical church service had a long period of worship, in German, of course, continuing from nine o'clock or nine-thirty in the morning until one or two o'clock in the afternoon. Attendance often meant traveling long distances over poor roads, with some people even walking fifteen or twenty miles.[55] Before the building of meetinghouses the Amish of course worshiped in their homes—in their houses or barns or outdoors. Because of the long distances, and the long services, they served a simple noon meal in the home where the meeting was held. At times they stopped the services for the noon meal and had another session in the afternoon. In the usual order of services the ministers, including the bishops, of course, would meet by themselves at the outset—in a room upstairs in the home, or in a small "anteroom" (the *Kämmerle*) near the entrance to the church building. Here they would discuss any problem that had arisen and would decide (presumably it was not known until then) who should preach the sermon and who should take the other assignments. Every minister was expected to participate, either reading scripture or leading in prayer or at least giving a testimony on the sermon. Since congregations nearly always had a multiple ministry—Partridge, it will be remembered, at one time had four bishops and thirteen ministers—one can easily understand why the service was long! According to Christian Erismann, J. P. Schmitt at Waldo once preached nearly six hours. Erismann said it was a good sermon but added that he and others thought it was "fast zu lang" (almost too long)! He wisely observed that people don't listen when the sermon is too long.[56]

Such circumstances made the maintenance of order and decorum in the worship services a problem, especially among the young, but even among others. C. Henry Smith has left us an interesting record of his youthful experiences in the Partridge congregation:

> Of course, we were not expected to sit quietly through four long hours of preaching without at least one prolonged visit during that time to the horsesheds in the churchyard. Beginning about twelve o'clock, and lasting to the close, there developed a restlessness among both the boys and older men, which ended in a continuous stream passing in and out of the church door during that time. Outside we clustered about in groups in the horsesheds in winter, or out on the grass in summer, listening to our elders exchanging views on the best methods of carrying on farm operations or swapping news items of the week's happenings throughout the community; for this was still the day before the advent of the telephone, rural delivery, or the automobile. We always aimed to return inside for the closing exercises, preferably for the last song.
> Through long experience we learned to sense quite accurately the best time to enter the church in order to be present at the close without sacrificing more of the pleasant associations outside than absolutely necessary. Sometimes we were kept informed by late arrivals from the inside. If Elder Bachman had reached the story of Tobit in his sermon, we knew he was nearly through with the main discourse. If old man Güngerich had just begun his testimony, we still had some time to spare,

for he was proverbially long-winded, having been known to pray for twenty minutes at a funeral in the presence of a bareheaded audience before an open grave, in a cold wind. But if Chris Schertz was the last man in the pulpit, we had little time to lose, for Chris never succeeded in adding many words to the few set lines he had memorized for such occasions in the early years of his ministry.[57]

Though all the Amish in central Illinois were considered to belong to the same denomination, there were differences among them. Diversity had developed between those in the East and those in the West, and especially between those who had come to America in the colonial period and those who came in the nineteenth century. Of course there were not only differences between groups but also within a given group, as is well illustrated by the fact that the Rock Creek congregation, which followed the progressive Alsatian Joseph Stuckey, included a number from Pennsylvania although the Pennsylvania Amish were generally the most conservative. Furthermore, the Alsatian Stuckey and his followers were more ready to change than were the Alsatian Christian Ropp and his followers. In addition, new influences which made divergent views more likely at this time were "the coming of modern transportation, the invention of new farm machinery, and hundreds of other innovations, [with which] changes were bound to come. This brought to the surface, and into direct conflict, old ways with new. The time had come to face the challenges of an entirely new and strange culture, in contrast to a traditional . . . way of life."[58]

A tendency of many Amish to be suspicious of anything new, regardless of what others might consider to be the merits, compounded the problem. In addition, since the Amish emphasized congregational control and had no centralized authority to give direction, and since they were quite widely scattered and even in many cases isolated, it is remarkable that the differences were not greater than they were. These differences, however, were great enough to cause concern, which led to a series of Amish conferences from 1862 to 1878, in which the Illinois Amish took a prominent part. It was hoped these conferences, called the *Diener-Versammlungen*, would reconcile the differences in practice that had arisen. The Amish in Pennsylvania who had come in the colonial period were inclined to hold to the old ways more than those who had moved west. Whether this was a case of the applicability of Frederick Jackson Turner's theory of the liberalizing influence of the frontier is an interesting question. However, when one considers that the Amish who came from Europe in the nineteenth century were generally more liberal than both the Eastern and Western Amish, Turner's theory hardly seems to explain the Amish case.

The conferences were primarily for ministers, but lay people attended. It is said that as many as from 1,200 to 1,500 people attended some of the meetings. Participants raised many questions, such as whether baptism should be done by affusion in a stream or at the usual place of worship. Other topics discussed were dress (especially hooks and eyes), meetinghouses, function of deacons, the use of the ban (shunning or avoidance), musical instruments, insurance, picture-taking, lightning rods, office-holding in government, and divorce. The delegates were more adept at raising questions than in answering them. But most, if not all, of the ministers seem to have been sincere and humble in desiring to follow the will of God in arriving at decisions. They unanimously decided, for instance, that their discussions should be based completely on the Word of God. They also emphasized at the first conference and later that delegates should be free to express their own ideas on the problems raised. In addition, individual speakers, such as John K. Yoder of Wayne County, Ohio, strongly urged those who did not agree to be free to state their views. Frequently also the delegates pleaded for tolerance, patience, and charity where their views might differ. Fortunately, the leaders of the conferences, following the example of Christ who did nothing in secret, made the meetings and minutes open and public.[59]

Others have discussed these conferences quite fully;[60] at points the proceedings touched the Illinois Amish. Four of the conferences took place in Illinois, one in Iowa, two in Indiana, seven in Ohio, and two in Pennsylvania. At the first meeting in 1862, held in Jonathan Schrock's barn in Wayne County, Ohio, Bishop Solomon Yoder of Long Green, Maryland, was nominated for moderator but declined. Jonathan Yoder of McLean County, Illinois, was then unanimously elected. He stated the purpose of the meeting and urged that the work be carried on in a spirit of love, peace, harmony, and good will. Occasionally when debate became too heated he asked for restraint and moderation. The usual method of operation was to refer a problem or a dispute to a committee for study and report. Michael Mosimann from Wesley City and Joseph Stuckey from Rock Creek Church, McLean County, served on a committee to settle differences among Amish from Elkhart County and Lagrange County, Indiana. Regarding the ban, some thought that the biblical injunction of not eating with a backslider applied only to the communion table. But Andrew Ropp from Pekin, a brother of Christian Ropp, thought it should apply also in more everyday situations. As to the problem of whether baptism should be in a stream, which was discussed considerably in the first conference, the Illinois Amish apparently were not disturbed as much by this as were those of Ohio and Pennsylvania. In addition to those already mentioned from Illinois, Jacob Unzicker from Pekin also attended the conference.[61]

At the second conference, held in 1863 in Mifflin County, Pennsylvania, only Joseph Stuckey and Jonathan Yoder attended from Illinois. Yoder was elected assistant moderator, and Stuckey was placed on an important committee to help decide a problem between two factions in Pennsylvania concerning the old question of place of baptism. Again Yoder urged that the meetings and the minutes be open. Very likely Stuckey was on the side of those who favored compromise on the question of baptism by permitting the candidate to have baptism in a stream or in the house. Jonathan Yoder raised the question as to whether a member who was put under the ban for marrying outside the church could be taken back into the church, without his wife, if he repented. Stuckey, who was on the committee to study this issue, saw nothing unscriptural in such a person being received without his spouse. The question of meetinghouses also came up. Jonathan Yoder, from the Rock Creek congregation, which already had a meetinghouse, defended their use by saying that homes were not large enough, the congregation had better order in a meetinghouse, and could better teach candidates for baptism with the new facility. Another question concerned holding political office. Apparently quite a few Amish were holding some kind of local government offices. Stuckey said he had been made road commissioner without his knowledge and that if he did not serve he would be fined. The conference decided that a member should not hold an office having to do with criminals or the military or with the use of force. On another issue, both Yoder and Stuckey spoke up against the taking of photographs.[62]

Ten brethren from Illinois attended the third conference, held near Goshen, Indiana, in 1864: Joseph Stuckey, Jonathan Yoder, Christian Ropp of McLean County, Andrew Ropp, John Birky, Christian Nafziger, Jacob Unzicker, Andrew Bechler of Tazewell County, Christian Forney of Woodford County and Andrew Zimmerman of La Salle County. The conference apparently was called to do something about the differences of opinion among the Amish of northern Indiana. Other than that, with a few minor exceptions, nothing new was brought up. Apparently the conferences did not come to any positive conclusions.[63]

Only Joseph Stuckey and Jonathan Yoder from Illinois attended the conference held in 1865 in Wayne County, Ohio. That conference decided that if a member refused to keep the ordinances of the church and dressed lavishly and adorned himself like those of the world he was to be warned. If he paid no attention to the warning, he was to be cut off like the unfruitful vine. A document signed by various brethren from McLean County, Illinois, plus a letter from a brother in the same place, were laid before the assembly for consideration. Unfortunately,

Source: Mennonite Historical Library, Goshen, Ind.

Barn built by Christian Sutter near Hopedale in 1868 as it appeared ca. 1900. Site of the *Diener Versammlung* of 1875; this barn, dismantled and moved, will be re-erected at the IMGHS headquarters.

the record does not describe the contents. The conference unanimously decided not to make any decision in the matter, except to point out that such matters should be handled as Paul advised in Titus 3:10.[64]

The fifth Amish conference was held in 1866, in the home of John Strubhar (Strupbar) near Danvers, Illinois. Forty-five Illinois ministers attended—many more than from all the other states combined. Christian Erismann, who also attended, thought nearly 1200 people were present on Sunday. Aside from listening to addresses and noting considerable diversity of opinion in the church, the conference did not take much specific action. On whether a person in the liquor business could be a useful member of the church, the consensus seemed to be that it was better to stay away from drinking places. One of the more significant occurrences at this conference was an announcement by Joseph Stuckey calling attention to a significant article by John M. Brenneman of Elida, Ohio, in the March 1866 issue of the *Herald of Truth*. There Brenneman made a strong plea for unity of the Mennonites and Amish and suggested calling a conference for that purpose.[65]

Seven Illinois delegates attended the sixth conference, held at West Liberty, Ohio, in 1867. Little that was new came up for discussion. Again the conference tried to help local congregations where there was some dissension, notably this time in Johnson County, Iowa. On one new question, whether members should contribute toward monuments honoring soldiers, the conference voted "no." The 1868 conference in Mifflin County, Pennsylvania, dealt with similar military problems, apparently growing out of the late Civil War. Only Jonathan Yoder attended from Illinois. The question was whether a former member who had served in the war, was wounded, and was now receiving a pension from the government could be reunited with the church and still receive his pension. The conferees decided that if he severed all his connections with the military, including the pension, he could be reinstated. If he was poor the church was to help him.[66]

A conference held in Holmes County, Ohio, in 1869 was poorly attended. But one in Fulton County, Ohio, in 1870 had more delegates, including ten from Illinois, and dealt with more important issues. One wonders to what extent the recent movement initiated by Henry Egly of Berne, Indiana, with its emphasis on regeneration and being born again, had to do with one question raised in this session. The question was: "Is a person who does not know through feeling and perception that he is God's son through Jesus Christ worthy of baptism?" The answer, unanimously accepted, was that a person to be baptized must have a living hope and show through fruits of true repentance that he has obtained God's grace through Jesus Christ. Another important issue, to have important repercussions on the Illinois Amish in the next few years, was universalism. The Amish leaders asked how one should deal with those who insist that there is no eternal punishment, that each receives his punishment in this world, and that all people will be saved. They decided that this universalist position was unscriptural.[67]

In 1871 the conference again convened in Illinois, this time in the Waldo meetinghouse in Livingston County. The attendance was fairly large, with the Illinois brethren outnumbering others by forty-two to fifteen. In this and the remaining sessions of the Amish conferences (1872-76 and 1878), few new items were brought up, other than how to deal with Joseph Stuckey and his followers. Otherwise, discussion had to do mainly with nonconformity and other questions discussed earlier. Among such were two questions discussed at Hopedale in 1875: Can members of the church belong to the Grange, a farmers' organization at the peak of its strength in 1875? The answer was "no." The other question was whether a minister or a lay member might take out a patent on a machine and receive a lot of money from the "world." The somewhat curious answer was that a lay member could, but not a minister; he had to give himself to his ministerial duties.[68]

The conference showed increasing concern over the unrest and dissension in the church, and heard many pleas for tolerance and understanding. Was there no longer any balm in Gilead? asked concerned people. One more session was to be held in Illinois—the final one, at Roanoke in 1878. The really important problem that these conferences dealt with in the early 1870s was in regard to Joseph Stuckey and his followers. This problem will be dealt with in the next chapter. Incidentally, the Illinois Mennonite Historical and Genealogical Society now owns the Christian Sutter barn in which the 1875 *Diener-Versammlung* was held at Hopedale. The society has dismantled it and is in the process of reassembling it west of Metamora on a site near the old Partridge church area, which is to serve as a Mennonite historical complex.

These Amish conferences between 1862 and 1878 started with the high purpose of reconciling differences in the brotherhood. Unfortunately, they failed in that purpose. They had barely started when Henry Egly withdrew and started another branch, which included many from Illinois. And before the conferences ended Joseph Stuckey severed his connection, which resulted in another division. The conferences were a watershed. With a few very minor exceptions, the Amish were officially united up to this point. But the differences that led to the conferences persisted and became even greater during and following these meetings. Those Amish insisting on maintaining the old ways became known as the Old Order Amish. The more progressive

Amish became followers of Joseph Stuckey and eventually formed the Central (Illinois) Conference of Mennonites. The Butler County, Ohio, Amish and the more liberal elements in Iowa and a few other places, such as Summerfield, joined the new General Conference Mennonite Church, as did eventually the Central Conference Mennonites. Most of the Amish, in Illinois as elsewhere, were in between the conservative Old Order and the more progressive elements and became known as the Amish Mennonites. They soon formed Amish Mennonite district conferences, the Illinois Amish Mennonites becoming a part of the Western District Amish Mennonite Conference.[69]

David Luthy, an Amish scholar of non-Amish background, admits that it was David Beiler from Pennsylvania, leader of the Old Order persuasion, who suggested the conferences, and that some other strict Amish attended. Nevertheless, Luthy states that it is "obvious from studying in which communities the meetings were held and who the chairmen were that from the beginning the meetings were under the control of the progressive Amish, not the stricter ones." In a very recent study James N. Gingerich confirms this view and also states that the break between the progressive and more conservative (Old Order) Amish groups had largely occurred before the *Diener-Versammlungen*. By 1865, he says, the split between them "was nearly complete."[70]

CHAPTER 4

The Central Conference Mennonites in Illinois to 1957

Joseph Stuckey, head of the group that became the Central Conference Mennonites, was an important Illinois Amish leader. He wrote articles and reports for the *Herald of Truth* and often appeared in its news items, even after he eventually broke with the old church. Although other questions were involved in the controversy, such as dress, adornment, and transfer of membership from one congregation to another without a church letter, the question that more than any other brought matters to a crisis was universalism, a doctrine that was influencing other denominations at that time, even some Amish and Mennonites. The question was brought into the Amish conferences first in 1870, and more seriously in 1872. As Samuel F. Pannabecker has said: "It is interesting that such an unacceptable doctrine, which incidentally was current in other Christian circles, should have filtered through into the Amish fellowship."[1]

Joseph Joder, brother of Bishop Jonathan Yoder, was a charter member of the Rock Creek Amish Church (1853) and was still a member when Joseph Stuckey assumed leadership following the Bishop Yoder's death in 1869. Something of a teacher, poet, and linguist, Joder began to spell his name the German way, Joder. As he studied the Bible, Joder came to emphasize the love of God and to play down his wrath and judgment. This became increasingly evident in some poems that he wrote in the 1850s and 1860s. In fact, he came to embrace the idea that God's love was so great that through Christ's death all would be saved and no one would suffer eternal punishment in hell. Since the poems were written in English, they did not immediately attract the attention of the Amish leaders. A few years later Joder wrote his poems in German also. One especially, *Die Frohe Botschaft* ("Glad Tidings"), not only attracted attention but blew up a storm. It was written and publicized in 1869, the year the poet's brother, Bishop Jonathan Yoder, died and Joseph Stuckey took over the leadership of the Rock Creek congregation. The poem was addressed to the Amish and seemed to be advocating pure universalism.[2] Thereupon the 1870 conference made that decision to pronounce universal salvation unscriptural. In 1872 the conference raised the issue again and specifically mentioned Joseph Joder and Joseph Stuckey. Joder's poem was circulated among the delegates, and it became known that Stuckey was his minister.

Apparently part of the trouble at this time was some misunderstandings between Joseph Stuckey and Christian Ropp, due to overlapping responsibilities and the fact of Stuckey's greater liberalism. A committee of the 1872 Amish conference noted that the chief trouble in Illinois lay between these two brethren and urged Stuckey, with God's help, to be more patient and careful. As to the central message of the poem, that all men would be saved and none would suffer everlasting punishment, the conference decided that a member still holding such views after counseling should be put under the ban. At the 1873 conference a committee reported on visiting Stuckey and asking him whether he continued to claim the author of the poem as his brother. Stuckey said he did and added that he had gone to communion with him. Because of the importance of the phrase and because it has been interpreted in several different ways, Stuckey's recorded reply in German should be given: "J. Stuckey erklärte sich, dass er ihn als Bruder hält, und auch mit zur Einigkeit gegangen sei." In his excellent work, *Faith in Ferment: A History of the Central District Conference*, Samuel F. Pannabecker translated the phrase "und auch mit zur Einigkeit gegangen sei" as "and would be in accord with him." True, the Amish held strongly to the view that brethren taking communion together should be basically in accord with each other. But the above phrase quite definitely meant taking communion together, and it is probably too precise to say that it invariably meant, including Stuckey and Joder's case, that the participants always agreed in details. Stuckey's writings and expressions make it clear that he did not believe in universalism, and later he did refuse Joder communion. Nevertheless, whatever the meaning of Stuckey's reply, he was not ready to move as rapidly as the conference desired. Being more liberal, Stuckey was less inclined to put people out of church than were most of his brethren. And so the conference withdrew from him "in the matter of the kiss and spiritual fellowship."[3]

This marks Stuckey's break with the Amish conferences and with the church in which he had been a member and leader for many years. It also marks the break with his old colleague and fellow bishop, Christian Ropp. Yet the severance of relations was neither sudden nor complete, which is explained in part probably by the congregationalism of the Amish. For years his followers were known as the

Source: Illinois Mennonite Historical and Genealogical Society Archives, Metamora, Ill.

Joseph Stuckey (1826-1902), minister at North Danvers Mennonite Church, 1860-1902, and father of the Central Conference Mennonite Church; photo taken Dec., 1901.

Stuckey Amish, and their organization into a new conference was a long time coming. Relations with the old group, even with Christian Ropp, continued in various ways. John Stahly, Stuckey's associate bishop at Rock Creek, attended the Amish conference in 1873 and seems to have maintained good relations with the ministers of the Mackinaw Meeting.[4] On a number of occasions in the 1870s and 1880s these ministers and Stuckey's congregation, North Danvers, worked together on a number of assignments. In May 1881, for example, Ropp and Jacob Zehr, another bishop at Mackinaw, assisted at the funeral of Christian Imhoff, a deacon in Stuckey's church. Ropp was present with Stuckey at the latter's church when John K. Yoder of Wayne County, Ohio, preached there in 1889. Peter Schantz, a young minister ordained in Stuckey's congregation in 1882, was Christian Ropp's friend, had extensive business dealings with him, and preached at his funeral in 1896. These and other occasions seem to indicate, as one authority has said, "that the hard feelings were at a minimum among the ministers of the congregations."[5]

The same can be said elsewhere. Ministerial visits, though fewer than before, continued between the Stuckey churches and the other Amish Mennonites for years to come. The best example of this is reported by G. Z. Boller in the *Herald of Truth*, June 15 and July 1,

1882. For "several weeks" in June of that year Stuckey visited Amish churches in Indiana and Ohio preaching and assisting in baptismal, communion, and ordination services. At a service at the Clinton Church in Elkhart County, Daniel Johns (written Tschantz by the reporter) was ordained to the ministry, and a few days later Jonathan Kurtz was ordained at Haw Patch. On returning from Ohio Stuckey preached in Lagrange County, Indiana, and "to a large congregation at Clinton [again], where he bade them farewell. On Friday morning he and his wife started for home. We hope much good may result from . . . his earnest preaching." As late as December 15, 1895, the *Herald* reported that on October 20 the "aged Bishop Stuckey of Danvers, Ill.," conducted the funeral services of Joseph Albrecht, a deacon at the Willow Springs congregation in Tiskilwa. These do not sound like the reports of a person who had severed all contacts with his former brethren.

Would the break between Stuckey and his Amish brethren have come had it not been for the Joseph Joder problem? Quite possibly so, for the differences which had led to the calling of the Amish conferences were quite different from universalism. The conferences failed to do away with unrest, misunderstanding, and dissension. William B. Weaver has well summarized this point:

> There was considerable difference between the congregations of the East and those of . . . [the West], particularly in relation to customs in dress and various religious practices. The Amish Church of the West in which this difference was marked was the one under the leadership of Rev. Joseph Stuckey. The Amish men of the East still wore hooks and eyes on their coats and vests and did not "shingle" their hair nor did they wear neckties. In some of the western congregations, especially in the Stuckey Church, men began to wear buttons, shingle their hair, and the younger men began to wear neckties. These were some general causes for the separation of Rev. Stuckey's congregation from the Amish conferences.

Weaver concedes, however, that the real crisis came over Joseph Joder and the problem associated with his poem.[6] Perhaps the Joder incident was the occasion for the break, but not the real cause.

If Bishop Jonathan Yoder, who was more conservative than Stuckey, had still been living, would the separation have occurred? If the Illinois Amish had been permitted to settle the controversy themselves without the intervention of the more conservative easterners, especially Pennsylvanians, would they have succeeded in preventing the break? These questions cannot be finally answered. But one authority has stated: "Had the Illinois congregations been permitted to settle the controversy in their own way it is altogether probable that there would have been no division."[7]

Only a few Amish congregations followed Stuckey out of the conference[8] at the time of the break in 1872-73—namely, North Danvers, Washington, and a small group at Weston. South Danvers, more inclined to be independent, came along more slowly to the Stuckey side. However, individuals from some of the other congregations followed him, and within a few years additional Stuckey churches were organized. These were usually in the old, settled Amish communities and were composed largely of people dissatisfied with the old church. Stuckey was sometimes blamed for splitting churches, a feeling that lingered long in the minds of many who remained in the old church. More likely, however, as Weaver points out, "he was only trying to care for those who had left the old church and were without a leader."[9]

North Danvers, Stuckey's home congregation, became known as the "Mother Church," and the leader was often admiringly referred to as "Father Stuckey." The General Conference *Mennonite Year Book and Almanac* for 1919 states that this congregation was "the mother church of the present congregations of East White Oak, Congerville, Normal, Carlock, and Danvers [formerly South Danvers]." Its membership grew substantially, reaching 400 by 1872 and 425 by 1890. Its growth by the new century would have been still greater had some members not left to help organize the surrounding daughter congregations.[10]

Under the leadership and influence of Stuckey, North Danvers inaugurated various progressive measures, such as the Sunday school in 1867, Christian Endeavor in 1892, and a Ladies' Aid Society in 1892. Several ministers, including Peter Schantz, Joash Stutzman, Joseph H. King, and John Kohler, were ordained to assist Stuckey, thus enabling him to spend more time traveling and looking after the growing number of congregations under his care. After the leader's death in 1902 the church, despite some opposition, purchased a reed organ and then a piano in 1907. The church building, constructed on its present site in 1872, underwent remodeling on several occasions. In a major renovation in 1917 the long the long minister's bench was done away with, the partition between men and women was eliminated, a full basement was constructed and the entire structure was covered with brick veneer. The congregation also installed stained-glass windows, one of them in honor of Stuckey and his wife.[11]

A new era in the life of North Danvers was introduced when William B. Weaver became minister on July 1, 1922. His coming "marked a decided departure from much that was formerly practiced." This was the first time that the congregation secured a trained minister from the outside and supported him with a fixed salary. The congregation organized a church board, began to have weddings in the church, elected its first deaconesses in 1944 and built a parsonage in Danvers. In addition to his preaching, Weaver organized and taught

The Central Conference Mennonites

a popular men's Bible class from 1925 to 1950, composed of those from high school age to the elderly. For a number of years Weaver was also the editor of the conference organ, *The Christian Evangel.* Somehow or other he also found time during his ministry here to author two books, *History of the Central Conference Mennonite Church* and *Thirty-five Years in the Congo,* a history of the Congo Inland Mission.[12]

While all this marked a transition for North Danvers, it was also something of a transition for Weaver. Born at Nappanee, Indiana, in 1887 and reared in the vicinity of Shipshewana, he was a member of the (Old) Mennonite Church until he went to North Danvers in 1922. He taught for six years in public schools and for eight years at Goshen College, from which he had graduated in 1914. Licensed to preach in 1913, he was ordained in 1914 and served the Prairie Street Mennonite Church until 1920. One bit of evidence that the shift to the Central Conference marked something of a change for Weaver is an old "Record Book" that he kept and that is in the archives of the North Danvers church. One item for July 17, 1915, while he was still preaching at Elkhart, records this financial transaction: "For Two Bonnets, G. L. Bender, $1.50." Weaver did not need these items for his family in his new, more liberal conference! Weaver served as pastor in the old church at a difficult time of growing tension and unrest, especially in the Indiana-Michigan Conference, over what some interpreted as modernistic influences appearing in Mennonite circles, including

Source: Archives of the Mennonite Church.

Central Conference Mennonite and Illinois Mennonite Conference women gathered at Hopedale for shower of Vinora Weaver, who married Earl Salzman (1895-1961) in 1927. Vinora Weaver was lay minister of Danvers Mennonite Church, Danvers, Jan.-Aug., 1927.

Goshen College. Because of misunderstanding over this question and others, and probably also because of a lack of statesmanship among Mennonite leaders, a number of ministers left the (Old) Mennonite Church and served elsewhere, including some eight or nine who served the Central Conference in Illinois at some time or other. Weaver served North Danvers until he retired in 1952, by which time a retirement or pension plan—something new for North Danvers—had been worked out. Weaver was succeeded by Hugo Mireau who served from 1952 to 1955, and by Arnold E. Funk who was pastor from 1956 to 1962.[13]

The South Danvers church also existed when Stuckey broke away from the Amish in 1872-73. The Hessians in McLean County then worshiped among themselves from 1841 to 1853, but with the building of the Rock Creek Church they became a part of its group. Later they again had their own separate congregation, and still later (1943) they again united with the North Danvers. In the meantime, as the South Danvers church, they experienced a normal development, although they were usually a small congregation. Leading ministers included Christian Gingerich, his son John, Michael Kinsinger, John Kinsinger, and Harvey E. Nunemaker. In his later years Bishop Peter Naffziger, father-in-law of Michael Kinsinger, probably worshiped and occasionally preached at South Danvers. Already a minister and bishop in his native Hesse, Germany, he had come to the New World in 1826 and served successively in Ontario, Canada, Butler County, Ohio, and finally in Illinois. Because he often served scattered areas of Amish settlers, and frequently traveled on foot, he was affectionately known as "Apostle" Peter Naffziger. In 1915 the congregation began having its worship services in Danvers, where a number of members had moved, first renting and then building a meetinghouse. In 1943, with only thirty-four members left, it merged with North Danvers.[14]

Dating back to 1866, the East Washington Amish congregation became one of the largest and most important in the Central Conference. The congregation worshiped in a frame building a few miles east of Washington until 1925, when it built a brick church in Washington, at which time the name was changed to Calvary. Among its ministers were Peter Stuckey, brother of Joseph, Peter Guengerich, Michael Kinsinger, Valentine Strubhar, Ben Esch, and Harry Yoder.

Strubhar, minister from 1893 to 1935, was an outstanding leader not only in his congregation but also in the "Central Conference" that the Stuckey group organized. In about 1893, through the death of one minister and the removal of another to Nebraska, Michael Kinsinger was left alone as bishop and minister and felt the need for assistance. Although he urged Strubhar to accept this assignment, Strubhar was reluctant to accept because he felt the congregation was

The Central Conference Mennonites 95

not united in feeling the need for additional ministerial help. But when the congregation called him unanimously, he overcame his reluctance and accepted the call.

Strubhar began to enjoy his ministry, and everything seemed to be going along well and harmoniously under the leadership of Bishop Kinsinger. But then in 1894 arose a well-nigh universal problem among Amish and Mennonite churches—whether English should be introduced into the services. Up to this time all the services were held in German. In 1894 a number of young people asked to have a Sunday school class in English. The congregation granted the privilege, but the decision hurt the feelings of a number of older people, including Bishop Kinsinger. For a short time the trouble worsened, and finally on June 24, 1894, Strubhar reported that "one of the saddest events took place in the history of our church. One Sunday morning . . . our bishop with a large number of the members secceeded [sic] from the church" and formed what became known as the "South Washington Mennonite Church." "To me," continued Strubhar, "this was by far the saddest experience in all of my ministerial work." The next service

Source: Ralph A. Forney, Graymont, Ill.

Left: Johannes Unsicker (1815-1888), member of East Washington Mennonite Church, 1866-1888; ca. 1875.

Right: Katharina (Kennel) Unsicker (1824-1909), member of East Washington Mennonite Church 1866-1894, and founding member of South Washington Mennonite Church, 1894-1909, ca. 1875; wife of Johannes Unsicker.

following the separation, he said, "was one of the gloomiest Sundays of my experience throughout my ministry." After much prayer he preached a powerful sermon on "Love," which is what the members badly needed. The congregation survived and began to grow, reaching a membership of nearly 400 by the time of Strubhar's retirement in 1935.

This growth continued under the leadership of Ben Esch, Strubhar's assistant and successor. While still an assistant pastor in the 1920s, Esch pointed out the difficulties of the ministry. To try to do some ministerial work at the end of a week of hard farm work—six days of fifteen hours each—was discouraging. "I often feel," he added, "my live [life] work is all one big mistake." But he must have overcome this discouragement, for his later ministry was long and fruitful. By 1952 the Calvary membership was 540. In 1966, at the time of the centennial celebration, seven members who had been baptized in the church more than seventy years earlier were still attending services regularly. Meanwhile in 1937 the South Washington congregation of some seventy-five members had voted to disband, with most of the members joining the Calvary church.[15]

The Flanagan Mennonite Church was the first new church to be organized by the Stuckey group. Many of the charter members had been a part of the Waldo Amish congregation earlier, and subsequently a part of the more progressive Amish group worshiping at Weston. Organized by Amish from Tazewell County in 1866, the Weston congregation survived for only some twenty years. The Flanagan Sunday school began in 1876 and the church was organized in 1878, when the congregation ordained as minister Christian Rediger, who had arrived from Germany in 1867. The members met in homes until 1882, when they built their first meetinghouse two and a half miles southwest of Flanagan. Others who served as ministers included Stephen Stahly (1882-1916), Joseph B. Zehr, William Engle, Emanuel Ulrich (1918-58), Robert Coon, Earl Salzman, Don Nester, and Lotus Troyer. The membership has never been large, but a good many workers have gone elsewhere into full-time Christian service.[16]

Another church under Stuckey's leadership was Meadows Mennonite. This congregation also grew out of the work started near Weston, and likewise out of the Flanagan congregation. Since the Weston congregation had become so widely scattered, both Flanagan and Meadows became more convenient centers for meetings. In addition, other Amish and Mennonites were moving into these areas. The Flanagan church had started Sunday school in the Meadows area in 1889 and in 1890 the group organized as the Meadows congregation. In 1891 the congregation built its first meetinghouse three quarters of a mile north of Meadows, at a cost of $1,379.25 for the building and its furniture. Within a week after dedication the church was debt-free. In 1908 the church was moved to its present location in Meadows and remodeled. It was again remodeled and enlarged in 1953. As one of the more active and influential congregations in the Central Conference, by 1954 its membership, mostly rural, reached 248. Long before, Bishop Stuckey conducted the first communion service in the new building in 1891; in the same year he ordained Andrew Vercler and Joseph Kinsinger as ministers and, in 1897, as elders. Others included in the ministry between the 1890s and the 1950s were Aaron Roszhart, George Gundy, and Lotus E. Troyer. Gundy's ministry lasted from 1925 to his death in 1951. For twenty-two of those years he was also superintendent of the Meadows Mennonite Old People's Home.[17]

East White Oak Church was an outgrowth of the North Danvers members who had moved too far east for convenient attendance at the old congregation. These members started a Sunday school in their community in 1892, later in the year organized a church and then began building a meetinghouse that was dedicated in February 1893. Under the leadership of Peter Schantz the congregation grew rapidly. In 1899 the church chose and ordained assistant pastor Emanuel Troyer, who was destined to become a leading figure in the Central Conference. In 1910, when Schantz left to lead in a new work in Normal, Troyer became pastor and then bishop in 1911. In addition to serving as pastor at East White Oak until 1928 and at Normal from 1928-36, he served for many years as president of the conference, as its field secretary from 1936-42, frequently as evangelist, as president of the Mennonite Hospital Board in Bloomington from its beginning, as a member of the Bluffton College Board, and as a leading committee and board member of the foreign mission work of the conference. He married Ida Horst on January 23, 1895. Their son, Maurice Troyer, was vice-president of International Christian University, Tokyo, Japan, for nearly twenty years. In a tribute to Troyer on the occasion of his death in 1942, William B. Weaver said, "... the history of our Conference can be written in the biographies of four men,—Rev. Jonathan Yoder, Rev. Joseph Stuckey, Rev. Peter Schantz, and Rev. Emanuel Troyer."[18]

Earl Salzman served as assistant pastor at East White Oak from 1921-27. A few years after Troyer left as pastor in 1928 the history of East White Oak took a turn that was unusual for Central Conference churches. Reuben J. Zehr, who followed Troyer, started auspiciously and seemed to be a talented, popular, young minister. But by 1934 he and a majority of his members had come to a parting of the ways with the conference. Zehr, asked by the conference to resign, was supported by a majority of his congregation. They then severed their conference relations and since then have continued independently as the "East White Oak Bible Church," as will be discussed in Chapter 12.

In eastern McLean County, Anchor Mennonite Church was started as a Sunday school five miles south of Anchor by about fourteen families who had moved from the North Danvers area in the early 1880s. Joseph Stuckey, who frequently preached for the group, organized them as a congregation in 1894. Aaron Augspurger, grandson of Stuckey, was selected and ordained as their pastor and in 1900 as their bishop. In 1910 the congregation built a meetinghouse six miles southeast of Anchor. Augspurger gave several reasons for the problematic future growth of the congregation: its "itinerant membership," its "location in a strong Lutheran community," and the scattered character of the Mennonite community. In time the church lost some of its already small membership and about 1953 it became extinct.[19]

Congerville Mennonite Church was also an outgrowth of North Danvers. When the Lake Erie and Western Railroad was built from Bloomington to Peoria in the 1880s, towns such as Carlock, Congerville, and Goodfield sprang up, while those like Slabtown and Farniville not on the line became extinct. Various dates have been given for the organizing of the Congerville congregation: Harry Weber (p. 473) says 1898, William Weaver (p. 90) says 1896, Frank Irons (*MH*, Sept. 1975) says 1899, and *The Mennonite* (Aug. 11, 1964) says 1889. S. F. Pannabecker and *The Mennonite Encyclopedia* follow Weaver. Apparently the first regular pastor was Lee Lantz, elected in 1898. Included among those who served here in subsequent years were George I. Gundy, Reuben Zehr, Paul Tschetter, Raymond Yoder, and Joe Atherton. In 1956 the membership was 100.[20] Yoder's ministry (1945-57) followed a difficult period in the life of the congregation when, for a number of years, due in part to the small size of the group, the congregation was unable to secure a regular pastor. Yoder, who had served as pastor in the Chicago Home Mission congregation, now transferred his membership from the Mennonite Church to the Central Conference Mennonites and threw himself enthusiastically into a rural work quite different from that of the big city. The congregation responded accordingly. There were many signs of new vitality and activity, including greatly increased giving. The pastor reported that contributions increased five times in four years. In 1950 he also reported that the "minister received more financial support in the past two years than all the ministers received in the previous forty-eight years." The membership more than doubled and began to include quite a few of non-Mennonite background.[21]

The next "Stuckey Church" to be established was Bethel, a few miles east of Pekin. After some attempts had been made to hold a local union Sunday school under the leadership of D. D. Augspurger, members from East Washington started holding services in the area in the

1890s. The church was organized about 1905 with Allen Miller as minister. The congregation worshiped in a schoolhouse until 1910 when it constructed a meetinghouse three miles east of Pekin. Allen Miller, also an outstanding conference leader, is reported to have "energetically and faithfully served for twenty-three years." His term as minister was longer than that of any other at Bethel. Reported to have had forty-seven members in 1907, the congregation grew under Miller's leadership. By 1919 Bethel felt able to host the annual church conference. It was one of the best attended in the history of the conference, with 1900 people reportedly fed during one of the days of the session. Among those who succeeded Miller were E. A. Sommer, Frank Mitchell, Lloyd W. Gundy, William B. Weaver, Milo Miller, Samuel Ummel, and Roy W. Henry. Never a large congregation, the membership was sixty-nine in 1956.[22]

All of the congregations mentioned above became charter members of the Central Illinois Mennonite Conference when it was formed in 1908. In subsequent years the establishing of new churches continued, of course, as before. The Boynton congregation near Hopedale was the first to enter the conference in this period. Because of cultural differences, the Hessians in the community, like their counterparts in Butler County, Ohio, and at Danvers in McLean County, found it difficult to worship with their Amish neighbors, now Amish Mennonites. In addition, a few members of the local Hopedale Amish Mennonite Church were dissatisfied and ready to join a less conservative group. These parties combined to organize the Boynton Mennonite Church in 1901 under the leadership of Peter Schantz of Danvers. In 1899, while Schantz was holding evangelistic meetings in Wayland, Iowa, Mrs. Wittrig, who had several married children in the Hopedale area, asked Schantz to do something for these people. This led to holding the first service in Boynton Township in 1900. Included in the ministry through the 1950s were John Litwiller, Lester Bixel, Frank Mitchell, Ernest Hostetler, Maynard Shelly, Melvin Funk, Paul Dyck, and William B. Weaver.[23]

One remarkable lay member of the Boynton congregation was Jacobine Iutzi (Mrs. Jacob) Brenneman who was born in Hesse, Germany, in 1828 and came with other Amish Hessians to America in 1832. After a brief sojourn in Maryland, her family settled in Butler County, Ohio. After marrying Jacob Brenneman in 1853, she migrated with him to Tazewell County in 1854, settling south of Hopedale. She died in 1926 at the age of 97, outliving her husband by many years. When she was 94, a correspondent of the Bloomington *Pantagraph* interviewed her and reported, among other things, that the Brenneman home "was never without a musical instrument." "She learned to play the piano when young and during the long years of toil in helping to make a home for her family she did not forget her music, and a few days ago when the writer called on her ... she sat down at the piano and played one of her old time selections which the *Pantagraph* correspondent enjoyed to the fullest." The correspondent also reported that the Hessians with whom she came to the United States had with them two pianos, a strange importation indeed for an Amish group! This simply highlights, however, the cultural differences that had developed between the Hessians and the other Amish. It would indicate, too, why "Grandma" Brenneman would not feel at home with the conservative Hopedale Amish and then Amish Mennonites. She and her children played an important part in starting the Boynton congregation, especially in the holding of a Sunday school in the 1890s and in the promoting of social activities for children and young people.[24]

The church in Normal was the outgrowth of mission activities started by Peter Schantz of East White Oak that also attracted from Normal and Bloomington members of surrounding Mennonite churches who were interested in joining a church nearby. Under Schantz's leadership, these two elements worked together to build a church in Normal, and managed to dedicate it in 1911 free of debt. At first operated as a mission by East White Oak, the congregation was fully organized the following year as a separate unit with thirty-five members. Lee Lantz, the first minister, was followed by, among others, W. H. Grubb, Emmanuel Troyer, Alvin J. Beachy, Leonard Metzler, and H. N. Harder. Membership in 1957 was 218.[25]

The Central Conference Mennonite Church in Tiskilwa grew out of the Willow Springs Amish Mennonite congregation in that community. Almost from the beginning in the 1830s the old church had trouble with those who complained about Amish strictness. They objected, among other things, to wearing hooks and eyes or the bonnet or the prayer head covering. Since a few settlers, including some early ministers, were Hessians, it is possible that they, as elsewhere, were a liberalizing influence in the congregation. Occasionally Joseph Stuckey would preach for these people, as would also the very liberal-minded Michael Kistler. As a result, some young people joined other churches in the community, some did not join any, while others went farther south to join one of the Stuckey churches. Long before it occurred, a number had hoped that a less strict Mennonite church would be organized in the Tiskilwa area. Finally in 1911 the long-awaited organization took place. After the organizing of a Sunday school, and following some evangelistic meetings held by Lee Lantz, the church was organized with a membership of some twenty or thirty.[26] Ministers who served in this church included Eugene Augsburger, Ernest Bohn, Harvey E. Nunemaker, Henry Toews, L. R.

Amstutz, Emil Sommer, and Ben Esch. Never large, the congregation reached a membership peak of 102 in 1931 under the leadership of Ernest Bohn. The figure of sixty-two has been given for 1957. After a long term of service at Calvary in Washington, Ben Esch resigned there and served an additional fifteen years at Tiskilwa.[27]

As in some other places, Mennonites were living in Carlock before a Mennonite church was located there. For the most part, these people were members of North Danvers. According to the *Central Conference Yearbook* for 1922, the North Danvers women living in Carlock organized a branch of the Ladies' Aid Society in 1911, and in 1913 also helped organize a Christian Endeavor Society. Together with some Sunday school work, and also with preaching services conducted by J. H. King of North Danvers, who had moved to Carlock in 1911, these activities were the prelude to organizing a Mennonite church in 1914. Among the twenty-three Mennonite families in Carlock at this time, a number thought of joining another local church if the Mennonites did not build. On the other hand, the other local church, United Presbyterian, disbanded, and some of its members expressed interest in joining the Mennonites. William B. Weaver, long before he was called to serve in the Central Conference, delivered addresses morning and evening at the organization meeting. J. H. King was the first minister. The members enthusiastically raised the necessary funds for a house of worship, which they dedicated on January 2, 1916. Before this, the congregation had used the town hall for services. The charter membership of 103 grew to 151 in 1957. In addition to King, the ministry included W. S. Shelly, Raymond L. Hartzler, Harry Yoder, Lotus E. Troyer, David Habegger, Paul Roth and James Dunn.

The few city mission congregations which the conference organized will be discussed in chapter 11.

Although originally called the "Central Illinois Mennonite Conference," the organization soon included congregations outside Illinois, located in Nebraska, Indiana, Idaho, Kansas, and Michigan. For this reason the conference dropped "Illinois" from its title in 1914, subsequently being called the "Central Conference Mennonite Church."[28]

Until his death in 1902, Joseph Stuckey was of course the central figure of this emerging branch of the church. Even though he hesitated to give his assent for the organizing of a new conference—perhaps because of his experience with the old Amish conferences from 1862-78—thousands of his followers affectionately looked upon him as "Father" Stuckey. An energetic man of strong physique, he possessed little formal education, but worked hard farming, studying, traveling, and preaching among the brotherhood and writing articles and reports for various church periodicals, especially for the *Herald of*

Truth and the *Christlicher Bundesbote*. According to his records he officiated at 255 weddings, baptized 1328 new believers, and ordained eighteen bishops and many more ministers. One admirer has said that Stuckey had a greater "concern for what people have in their heads and hearts—rather than for what they have on their heads," and that he put a greater "emphasis on heart attitudes—rather than on outward forms." Those who followed him in separating from the old church naturally had different views from those who remained, as is well illustrated in the division that occurred in the Clinton Frame congregation near Goshen, Indiana, in 1892. Later when William B. Weaver was gathering material for his history of the Central Conference Mennonites, he wrote to J. C. Mehl and D. J. Johns of Goshen, among others, for their views of Stuckey. Mehl, a follower, replied that Stuckey was "a very large man physically and to me he seemed even larger morally, mentally and spiritually. As an organizer, without any training in that line, he had very few equals. He was a clear clean thinker, and his delivery was excellent. I do not think," Mehl concluded, "that I have known any one of Rev. Stuckey's limited educational opportunities and of his environment who was able to draw so large crowds as he."

On the other hand, Johns, who remained with the old church, wrote: "I consider myself the wrong person to give you information on [the split at Clinton Frame, near Goshen, in Indiana]." Johns thought the matter would not have "gone so far if it had not been for [Stuckey]," who organized the new group into the Silver Street Church. Samuel F. Pannabecker has stated that "first his own [Stuckey's] church, then the founding and care of new churches and the providing of pastors: these were the great concerns and the contribution of Joseph Stuckey to the Central Conference," even though the formation of the conference itself was not his idea.

However people may differ in their views of Stuckey, William B. Weaver was probably correct in concluding that "Stuckey's outstanding qualities were his natural ability for leadership, his pulpit powers, his positive convictions, his great organizing ability and his sympathetic attitude towards people and towards the problems that the church was facing."[29]

The following story told of Stuckey illustrates his forceful and independent spirit and his practical turn of mind. One day in church, while still adhering to Amish dress, his hooks and eyes somehow got caught in a woman's hair. The embarrassing episode caused him to remark that these things were no good, and he proceeded to get rid of them! "Away with this nonsense!" he is reported to have said.[30]

Even though Stuckey was sometimes referred to as the "Father of our conference," the organization itself did not come about as a result of his planning. Near the end of his life, however, the pressure for a conference from his fellow ministers, especially the younger ones, became so great that he finally acquiesced. A ministers' conference met in 1898 or, probably, 1899. Stuckey had ordained many of the men who attended, among them being his grandson, Aaron Augspurger, who was quite influential in calling the meeting. They met largely for Bible study, inspiration, fellowship and discussion of common problems and concerns, not intending that the body should be legislative. Stuckey was made president of the meeting.

This conference proved so helpful that the ministers decided unanimously to call another one for the following year. The first conference had met in the home of Stuckey's assistant, Joseph H. King. The second, which included some lay delegates, met in Stuckey's home church, North Danvers. Thereafter the group usually met annually, and it decided in 1907 to effect a more permanent organization. A committee drew up a constitution later in the year and presented it to the congregations for acceptance, rejection, or modification. The twelve existing churches accepted and became charter members of the conference, which was officially promulgated at the session in North Danvers in 1908. Although "Father" Stuckey died six years earlier, it was fitting that the Central Illinois Conference of Mennonites should have been organized in the "Mother Church," North Danvers.[31]

While this new organization pleased most of the members, some had questions. Feeling that the new conference was born "out of necessity," Aaron Augspurger nevertheless added that the severing of old ties and the "dissipation of our Christian forces" were to be deeply deplored. He firmly believed that the church should be composed "of one great army," divided into regiments, of course, but "all in perfect harmony and cooperation, with the spirit of Christ prevailing everywhere." Prophetically, Augspurger was of the strong opinion that the conference, though born out of the spirit of the age—"the spirit of disintegration [rather] than of unity"—would in time, after its mission was fulfilled, be reabsorbed into the great body of Jesus Christ and ... loose [lose] its identity." If he could view the scene in the 1980s he no doubt would be happy with the growing number of cooperative activities among Illinois Mennonites.[32]

Doctrinally, though giving up the "Amish distinctives," the Central Conference continued to take a "conservative and orthodox position." Even on the so-called Mennonite distinctives, such as marriage and divorce, nonresistance, washing of feet, communion, and others, the group was still conservative, as is well illustrated by the new constitution drawn up by the Ministerial Association of the Conference in 1912 and discussed in the *Christian Evangel* (Feb. 1912). The editor commented as follows:

Rev. Aaron Augspurger of Saybrook, Ill., drafted the constitution and with but few exceptions it was adopted as drafted. After the adoption of the constitution a number of questions were raised with reference to points of doctrine. To many of us it was an encouraging sign to note the emphasis the ministerial association is placing on the importance of thoroughly doctrinating all those adhering to the conference. On the following points the association takes a conservative and orthodox position. Remarriage only permissible in the case of death of one of the parties. Does not recognize divorce but allows that husband and wife may be separated on scriptural ground in the case of adultery and fornication but in such cases neither party has the right to remarry. No minister or bishop belonging to the above conference shall officiate in any case where one party is a disciple of Christ and other not, nor in any case where both parties are non-professing Christians. Marriage in the Lord is a scriptural injunction to all ministers. The sacred ordinance of communion is to be administered to those of like faith. This is not to be construed to mean that all others outside of our particular denomination are excluded, but in any case where the doctrines of the church are accepted and where for reason of convenience, or expediency a transfer of membership is not deemed advisable, to all such persons the communion shall be administered providing they so desire. It is the duty of every minister to so doctrinate his people in the faith that there shall be no laxity in the faithful observance of every command of Christ. The sacred ordinance of washing the saints' feet is obligatory and, since it is thus, ministers should realize the embarrassing position they will be placed in where there is any laxity on the part of any of their members in the observance of this sacred ordinance. The constitution of the Central Illinois conference is plain and pointed in this respect and the ministerial association likewise is sounding forth no uncertain notes. If Mennonites are to retain their identity they must stand as courageously for those parts of their faith and doctrine that make them unlike other Protestant churches as they do for the points wherein they agree with orthodox Protestant churches.

For the lack of time many other points of doctrine were not taken up. For the benefit of any reader who may not be acquainted with the leading doctrines of the church, the writer makes the following statements. We believe in the inspiration of the holy scripture, in justification by faith, in the deity of Christ, in adult baptism, in the sacred ordinance of communion and washing of the saints' feet, in the affirmation and not the oath, in non-resistant Christianity, in the doctrine of the trinity, the virgin birth of Christ, the doctrine of the atonement, the resurrection and second coming of Christ. We teach separation from the world. The church does not fellowship with any of the many oath bound secret societies but at all times and everywhere exhorts the people of God not to become entangled in these secret orders since the very spirit of these organizations is anti-Christian.

The ministerial association further urged that we strive after conformity and uniformity in the work of our churches throughout the conference, and that in this as in all other work of the conference we exercise love, forbearance and patience.

A few months later, in another article in the *Christian Evangel* (Aug. 1912), Augspurger wrote on "The Future of the Central Illinois

Conference of Mennonites." He covered similar ground and spoke of these doctrines as doctrines of the conference. He did add two points, however, which make one wonder whether the conference had in mind the old trouble over universalism and the Henry Egly defection. The one doctrinal statement emphasized belief in everlasting life in heaven and "everlasting death and hell for the wicked," which of course is the opposite of universalism. The other point emphasized belief "in experi-

Source: Ralph A. Forney, Graymont, Ill

Aaron and Mary B. (King) Forney of Flanagan, married by Joseph Stuckey on Jan. 22, 1889, in Danvers. Note dress and hairstyles.

mental [experiential] religion" and stated that everyone has the privilege of knowing "they are saved in Jesus Christ by faith through grace," a major point advocated by Henry Egly. In most other ways, this statement simply reinforced the earlier one of the Ministerial Association.

Even on the matter of dress, which the Stuckey people claimed the old church overemphasized, the Central Conference could not remain wholly silent. In 1912, to cite but one example, the editor of *Christian Evangel* (Aug. 1912), had an editorial entitled "Needed—Dress Reform." On this subject, said the editor, Albert Rutt, seldom do we say anything, but the "present craze for dress, especially among women" led him to insert an item from the Bloomington *Pantagraph* about servitude to dame fashion from Paris. Rutt then added: "When will Christian men and women, especially women, take dame fashion into their own hands and dress with the propriety becoming the followers of the lowly Nazarene? . . . Let your women adorn themselves in modest apparel."

In practice the Central Conference apparently took a middle road between extreme emphases on faith and doctrine on the one hand and works and ethics on the other as the proper road to salvation. No doubt the position that Raymond L. Hartzler took in an article, "The Essence of Christianity," represents the balance that the rank and file endeavored to maintain. Both faith and works were necessary, he said. Although the transformation known as conversion or regeneration was the necessary beginning experience, it must be followed by the fruit of the Spirit. Hence, the essence of Christianity "is a spiritual experience wrought in one's inmost self by the Spirit of God, by virtue of which one believes," and then produces the fruit of the Spirit—"love, joy, peace, longsuffering, gentleness, goodness, faithfulness, meekness, purity. . . . By their fruits ye shall know them."[33]

The Central Conference Mennonites, like others, were influenced by the "Great Awakening" in the latter part of the nineteenth century and the first part of the twentieth. In fact, the new church activities that then arose were another compelling factor in the creation of a conference. Although these will be discussed in chapters 10 and 11, suffice it to say here that the conference became very busy with the promotion of publication, Sunday schools and Sunday school conferences, revivals and evangelism, Bible conferences, young people's meetings or Christian Endeavor Societies, education, missions, orphanages, old people's homes, hospitals, sewing circles or ladies' aid societies, relief work, and other projects. To properly plan and promote such activities the congregations had to work together through a conference to coordinate and enlist the full support of the entire church body.

Source: North Danvers Mennonite Church Historical Collection.

Central Conference Mennonite Church Ministers attending 1934 Conference in Danvers. Standing: Allen Yoder (Goshen, Ind.), William B. Weaver (Danvers), Aaron D. Eglii (Kouts, Ind.), Aaron Augspurger (Saybrook), Lee Lantz (Chicago), Benjamin Esch (Washington), Irvin R. Detweiler (Bluffton, Ohio), Jacob Sommer (Peoria), Emanuel Troyer (Carlock), Joseph H. King (Carlock), Emanuel Ulrich (Panola). Sitting: Emil A. Sommer (Normal), Amos M. Eash (Chicago), Simon S. Yoder (Middlebury, Ind.), Roy Unzicker (Foosland), Harvey E. Nunemaker (Tiskilwa), Raymond L. Hartzler (Carlock), and George I. Gundy (Meadows).

In time this vision of increasing the potential strength of the church by working together in larger units led many conference leaders to think in terms of union with other Mennonite conferences. Since the steps taken first toward affiliation and then merger with the General Conference Mennonite Church have been traced by S. F. Pannabecker in his *Faith in Ferment*, only a brief resumé is necessary here.[34] Raymond L. Hartzler in historical editorials and articles in the *Christian Evangel*, in the *Central District Reporter* and in *The Mennonite* has also traced the development toward affiliation and merger. It was not the General Conference Church, with its historic emphasis on unity, which delayed the merger between two bodies with very similar beliefs. Rather it was the Central Conference group, under the influence of its organizer and leader, Joseph Stuckey, who demurred. Even though Stuckey's home church, North Danvers, served as host to the General Conference group's Middle District Conference in 1898, whose leaders encouraged Stuckey and his churches to unite with them, nothing happened. Hartzler thinks that, had Stuckey agreed, union would have occurred at that time and that "it would have been far simpler then."[35]

Following Stuckey's death in 1902, and as the conference went through one crisis after another—World War I, the Great Depression and World War II—more and more leaders began to realize that their branch could not meet the emergencies alone and that they had to cooperate more closely with the larger Mennonite fellowship. In fact, said Hartzler, "We ... began to question whether the isolation as a distinct entity, which we had held and cherished through the years, could be justified in the future as it had been in the past." The General Conference branch and the Central Conference each set up a unity committee to study the problems connected with working more closely together. By the end of World War II in 1945, these committees, which had been joined by the two executive committees, concluded a series of conversations and studies that recommended affiliation of the Central Conference with the General Conference Mennonites—which then occurred in 1946. The psychological effect on the smaller Central Conference was significant. To quote Raymond Hartzler again: "Our group's sense of Mennonite geography, our circle of acquaintance, our knowledge of Mennonite missions and other kingdom service, have all been enlarged; and we have found it to be for our good."[36]

Another effect of the new relationship was to think of the next logical step. Affiliation provided for the Central Conference to come into the General Conference along side of the Middle District Conference, which covered similar territory, although each carried on its separate functions for a few years, just as before. Leaders and other members soon began to ask, however, why just an affiliation? Why not a complete merger? New committees from the Central and Middle District conferences were appointed to study such areas as faith and practice, organizational structures, and activity and service programs. No hindrances surfaced involving these points. They began to visit each other's conference sessions and then agreed to draw up a new constitution providing for merger. This effort came to fruition in 1957 at Normal, where both conferences met simultaneously. Erland Waltner, president of the General Conference, assisted in the process. Both adopted the new constitution, elected new officers, and the new Central District Conference replaced the two old ones. Among the new officers were Lotus Troyer, Meadows, president; Theodore Sommers, Pekin, treasurer; and Raymond L. Hartzler, Bloomington, field secretary. If at the affiliation meeting in 1946 those assembled were thrilled with the "new meaning" that the reading of Christ's prayer for unity in John 17 and the singing of the old hymn, "In Christ There Is No East or West," "seemed to take on ... at this memorable occasion," it is easy to imagine the still greater inspiration and excitement that must have come with the merger eleven years later.[37] This union was similar to that between the (Old) Mennonites and the Western District Amish Mennonites in Illinois in 1920, particularly in that it represented the joining of two groups committed to virtually the same beliefs and practices.

The rise and development of the Central Conference from 1908 onward corresponded with new growth and expansion of church work. A revised constitution in 1915 called for a full set of conference officers, a board of home and foreign missions and seven standing committees, with provision for others as needed in the future. Mission work began in Chicago in 1909 and in Peoria in 1914. In 1923 the conference took over the Twenty-Sixth Street Mission in Chicago from the (Old) Mennonites. The Congo Inland Mission Board was founded and its work begun in 1911 in cooperation with the Defenseless Mennonites; publication work was started in 1910; and the Bloomington Mennonite Hospital and the Meadows Mennonite Home, both cooperative ventures with the Defenseless group, were begun in 1919. In addition, the conference actively supported such institutions as the Mennonite Central Committee, Bluffton College, Witmarsum and Mennonite Biblical seminaries, and others. To this expanded work, said Editor Hartzler, "let us set ourselves with resolution and humility; but, above all, let us do it *together.*"[38]

Meanwhile, the growing conference had increasing resources with which to carry on its expanded activity. Central Conference Mennonites, like others, were blessed with increasing wealth. Many farmers became prosperous and an increasing number of Mennonites took up related or other lines of economic activity, and also prospered.

This trend, already noted in the nineteenth century, continued even more in the twentieth. William H. Springer, for example, a member at North Danvers, became president of the Stanford State Bank and manager of the Stanford Grain Company. Early in the twentieth century during the corn-husking season Oscar J. Sommer of Pekin began laying aside the best ears of corn to use as seed. By 1910 he was selling seed at special prices. Oscar studied seed corn in special courses at the University of Illinois and elsewhere. In 1917 he constructed a seed house—back from the road so that in case of failure the building would not be seen as a mark of folly! Gradually the enterprise grew into a great business and was extended to other kinds of seed. Other sources, especially county and local histories, give many additional examples of prosperity among Mennonites, not only in farming but in business enterprises as well.[39]

Some, however, saw this growing Mennonite prosperity as a mixed blessing. Writing in 1912 on "The Future of the Central Illinois Conference of Mennonites," Aaron A. Augspurger noted that conditions today "are wonderfully changed." The simple life of our forefathers and church were challenged and threatened. The conference had become "highly prosperous financially," a condition the leaders were "having a hard time to keep pace with spiritually." Prosperity, he continued, was good only if used as the "handmaid of the church." When not so used, spiritual life became atrophied. Could the leaders meet these new conditions? he asked. Raymond L. Hartzler, who came from Indiana in the 1920s to serve in Illinois, also noted the materialistic spirit of many. They had worked hard for what they got, the property was theirs and they were not to be told how to use it. To many, status depended on wealth; even some marriages were arranged with this end in view. But in the fifty years Hartzler served in Illinois he saw a growing sense of stewardship. Heinz Janzen, who came later and was pastor at Calvary in Washington for some years, observed a similar problem in his service.[40] Materialism, however, was a common problem among all groups of Mennonites and Amish in Illinois and elsewhere. Nevertheless, because of the prosperous conditions in which most Illinois Mennonites found themselves, perhaps their temptations in this regard were greater than in some other areas. In spite of high idealism, strong doctrinal statements, and commendable ethical assertions, materialism was a plague that continually had to be guarded against. But it was also a problem that Illinois Central Conference Mennonites could and did address.

CHAPTER 5

The Evangelical Mennonite Church (Defenseless Mennonites) in Illinois

Unlike the Central Conference of Mennonites, which originated in Illinois, the Defenseless Mennonite Church of North America, renamed the Evangelical Mennonite Church in 1948, originated in Indiana. Although it never had many congregations in Illinois, it has played an important role in the state. For, as Stan Nussbaum, at present a leader of the group, has pointed out, the group's Illinois membership included some of the most influential congregations and leaders in the denomination. In the latter part of the nineteenth century and in the first part of the twentieth, there was a surge of organizational activity in the denomination. Nussbaum has said it is difficult to say precisely what caused that surge, but that clearly,

> the geographical hot-house for these new ideas and programs was central Illinois. With only one exception, Brotherhood Insurance, every project we have discussed—Salem Home, Meadows Home, Mennonite Hospital, Salem Gospel Mission, and the English and German periodicals—was founded in Illinois primarily by Illinois men such as D. N. Claudon (Henry Egly's son-in-law), C. R. Egle, and Benjamin Rupp, all members of the Salem Church. When applying for a deed to the church property on July 23, 1898, the Salem Church apparently coined the name 'Defenseless Mennonite,' which became the official name of the 'Egly Amish.' The Conference was chartered as a corporation in the State of Illinois in 1908, and listed Flanagan, near the rural Salem Church, as 'its principal place of business.' But we have not yet discussed a project these men helped found which may have had more impact on EMC than all the others combined—an overseas mission work.[1]

The Defenseless Mennonites began about 1865 in Adams County, Indiana, where Henry Egly, the founder, lived. Egly was an Amish immigrant, who in 1839 as a boy of fifteen had arrived with his father in Butler County, Ohio. Married to Katherine Goldsmith in 1849, he moved with her in 1850 to a farm near Geneva, Indiana, where they lived the remainder of their lives. After becoming a member of the church at the age of seventeen, he was called within a few years to serve in various responsible positions. In 1850 he was ordained a deacon, in 1854 a minister, and in 1858 a bishop. Apparently for several years in the early 1850s, Egly was in failing health. Then through prayer and a rededication of his life to God "he was restored to health and led to a deeper experience of the peace of God and an assurance of salvation by faith in the finished work of Jesus Christ through His atonement on the Cross of Calvary."

As minister and bishop, Egly began to emphasize regeneration and rebirth and the necessity of Christians manifesting a conversion experience before being baptized as members of the church. While about one half of his own congregation agreed with him, many other staid Amishmen thought he was putting too much emphasis on this aspect. Egly also felt that the Amish were becoming too loose and liberal in some of their ways, including dress. Some of the older preachers, disturbed by this Egly emphasis, called in three Amish preachers from Holmes County, Ohio, to examine him. According to Nussbaum, the strategy backfired; the visitors concluded their investigation by laying hands on Egly and ordaining him bishop. Differences and misunderstanding continued, however, and the break came when Egly began to rebaptize those members who could not claim they had had a conversion experience when first baptized. In 1865 he became the head of a new movement that spread to other congregations and other states. As Nussbaum has stated, Egly probably was encouraged in some respects by the work of John Oberholtzer, who had separated from the Franconia Conference in Pennsylvania in 1847 and in 1860 had helped found the General Conference Mennonite Church.[2]

Egly's group took the name "Defenseless Mennonites of North America," which did not mean too much because all branches of Mennonites and Amish emphasized *Wehrlosigkeit*, that is, defenselessness, or nonresistance. Just as the followers of Joseph Stuckey for years were often called "Stuckey Amish," so the followers of Henry Egly were frequently called "Egly Amish." Aside from greater emphasis upon experiencing the new birth before baptism, doctrinally they were little different from other Amish. The new group continued to emphasize separation from the world. Women wore the prayer veiling, a practice that the Salem congregation in Illinois continued until 1917, when it voted to permit hats as a substitute. The wearing of jewelry was still proscribed, as was the use of musical instruments in churches and homes. Egly wrote that on February 6, 1887, his congregation "had an important council meeting about having organs in our houses. We were decided against it and God gave us the victory. Also other things wanted to creep in."[3]

The Evangelical Mennonite Church 113

In Illinois the new movement did not affect many Amish areas. But a few were affected deeply. Almost the entire Wesley City Amish congregation near Groveland, for instance, under the leadership of Michael Mosimann and Minister Nicholas Roth, went over to the Egly camp. Those who remained, too few to continue a separate organization, joined neighboring congregations. In Livingston County, also, the new movement had important results. Joseph Rediger, ordained minister in the Waldo Amish Church in 1863, agreed with Egly regarding lack of adequate teaching about the new birth. Hearing of the new movement in Indiana in the mid-sixties, Rediger visited Egly and had a similar experience of the forgiveness of sins. When Egly visited the Gridley-Flanagan area in 1866, many who claimed to have had similar experiences of regeneration joined the new church. No doubt, a good many Amish felt a void in their spiritual lives at this point, and it also seems clear that the leaders should have been more sensitive about their members' needs. In any case, to one viewing the past from the perspective of the 1980s, it appears a tragedy that a split in the church should have occurred over this point. Christian R. Egle, himself a leader in the new movement, stated in 1925: "Joseph Rediger and

Source: Nelson Springer, Goshen, Ind.

Barbara Naffziger Springer (ca. 1840-1921) of Hopedale, showing early plain dress of the Defenseless Mennonite Church (now Evangelical Mennonite Church); photo taken in 1917.

Source: Ella Ruth Rousselle, Meadows, Ill.

Christian R. Egle (1858-1926) and Jacobina (Bena) Angermeier Egle (1869-1954). He was a minister of Salem Evangelical Mennonite Church, 1883-1926, and an outstanding leader of the Defenseless Mennonite Church in Illinois, in the early twentieth century.

Henry Egly too, often said afterward that had they not received so much opposition concerning the spiritual life and had they themselves been riper in experience and exercised more forbearance with the brethren, the outcome might have been different."[4]

Be that as it may, two Egly churches developed in Illinois in the later 1860s when the movement entered the state, and more originated later.

The important Salem church was begun between Gridley and Flanagan not far from the Waldo Amish Mennonite congregation, which supplied a number of members. This was about 1865, according to C. R. Egle, or 1866, according to Edwin Stalter. Like the Amish, the new group continued to hold worship services in homes until it constructed its first meetinghouse in 1875 one mile southeast of the Amish church, erected in 1867. Both congregations continued to use the Waldo cemetery, located midway between their meetinghouses. Upon the death of Joseph R. Rediger of Salem in 1904, Christian R. Egle became elder. He was active as conference chairman, conference secretary for twelve years, served on various boards and committees, and edited the group's magazine, *Heilsbote*, from 1898 to 1917. Salem built up a notable record of supplying church leaders, missionaries, and other Christian workers, such as Joseph Rediger, Christian R. Egle, Ben Rupp, D. M. Zimmerman, Harry E. Bertsche, Eli J. Oyer, Chris Rediger, B. E. Rediger, I. R. Calhoun, D. N. Claudon, J. M. Gerig, James E. Bertsche, E. E. Zimmerman and E. M. Rocke—a few of these not being natives of the Salem community. Missionaries who were either members of Salem or largely supported by it were Mathilda Kohn (later Stevenson), Alma E. Doering, Amos Oyer, Julia Oyer, and Anna Zimmerman. The church always had a strong emphasis on evangelism and mission work and its members backed their programs with their pocketbooks. In a Thanksgiving offering in 1949, for example, Salem raised $4,347.92.[5]

Donald W. Roth, a younger worker from Salem, paid Harry E. Bertsche, his first pastor, high tribute, saying that "possibly no adult [was] more influential in a young life than his first pastor." Roth also said that many thought Pastor Bertsche "the prince of preachers." He had an eloquence and dynamic that made even sinners "sit up and at least respect the person of Jesus." Bertsche taught Roth to love the Bible, the church, and the worship services.[6]

In many ways Salem, like other Egly churches, did not represent a strong break with its cultural past. In dress, for example, it continued for many years to follow Egly's conservative pattern of separation from the world. "The sisters wore the bonnet, very plain clothes and the veil as a head covering in private prayer and in public meetings. No ornaments or gold or silver were worn. The men wore plain clothes but no special cut, and wore some form of beard but no mustache. The church stood against the use of tobacco and soon against frequenting the saloon and use of strong drink. But there were always backsliders that fell ... back into these habits for a time." And later, according to the author of those words, "the dress question has taken a great change." Indeed it had. In 1917 the Salem sisters gave up the prayer veiling and by this time the dress of both men and women was more in accord with that of the general populace. The changes occurring at Salem were also transpiring in the other Defenseless churches in Illinois and elsewhere.[7]

In other ways also the cultural break with Amish and even Mennonite origins became greater as time went on. As in some of the other Amish and Mennonite churches, English began to replace German in the church services, Sunday schools came into use, and musical instruments were introduced into the homes and churches. Missions, revivalism, evangelism and evangelicalism came to be emphasized more and more.

The social life of young people also changed. According to C. R. Egle, to whom we are indebted for a "Brief History of Salem Mennonite Church," the conduct of the young people was "very exemplary. They came together to sing, had testimony, Bible reading, and prayer, without parties, games or such life [like?]." Egle adds:

> There was not much of courtship. When the time came that a young brother thought it time to get married he sought the Lord in prayer for guidance to show him what sister He has for him as a life companion, also praying that the Lord might reveal this desire to the sister. After believing that the Lord showed him the particular sister and consulting with his parents about it he generally sent the minister or deacon to the parents of the sister to ask them if they and especially the sister had anything from the Lord concerning this matter, and in most cases they were successful.

One wonders what happened in those cases where the brother and the sister received different signals from the Lord! But courtship methods also changed with time, as Egle somewhat pessimistically concluded: "In the last years the social life and way of courtship have taken a decided change and as I believe not to the better, but as a detriment of the deeper spiritual life."[8]

The matter of having church services in the home or in church buildings was never a divisive issue in Central Illinois as it was in some states. The Salem Defenseless congregation built its first meetinghouse in 1875, but the Waldo Amish, as noted, had constructed theirs already in 1867 and Rock Creek and Partridge still earlier.

Similarly, Salem and other Defenseless churches faced the issue of the use of the German language in about the same way as the other branches. They continued to use German in their church services down into the twentieth century and, also like the others, made efforts to provide teaching and religious training in the language. This continued down to World War I when hostile elements in the community painted the Salem meetinghouse yellow with the demand written on the side that preaching in German be stopped.[9]

In line with its concern for conversion, the Salem church placed considerable emphasis on praise and testimony by the members. Of course, preaching stressed the new birth, repentance, and the forgiveness of sin "as a personal definite experience which was first generally expressed in regular and special meetings by simply rising sometimes amidst the preaching and asking the church mostly with tears for their prayers, asking forgiveness of parents and friends and making wrong[s] right and holding on in prayer until they received through faith in Jesus' atoning blood the evidence that their sins were forgiven." This was the kind of assured experience the candidate for church membership was to have before receiving baptism. The same emphasis and freedom to give testimony also pervaded all other religious services—prayer meetings (usually held on Wednesday evenings), Sunday schools, young people's meetings, revival meetings, missionary meetings, conferences and others. And that pious, evangelistic spirit characterized written reports of such meetings. In 1940, for example, the Salem church correspondent, reporting on the annual church conference held at that place, wrote that God did "many things for us and answered our prayers. The best of all was for salvation and help for souls. He still saves and fills with his spirit, praise His name."[10]

As in many other places, there was opposition when, in the 1870s, Sunday schools were first introduced and held in several public schools in the community. By 1880 when the first Sunday school was held in the meetinghouse, the opposition had disappeared. Since religious services at first were quite lengthy and included a noon lunch, the Sunday school was held in the afternoon. Sunday school offerings went for supplies, mission and relief work, the Salem Orphanage, the Meadows Old People's Home, publication, and other charities. The Salem and other Defenseless Sunday schools met together in annual Sunday school conferences. Other typical auxiliary church services that Salem organized included young people's meetings, a Christian Workers Band and a Sisters' Sewing Circle, which had ample opportunity to make and distribute garments and bedding for the poor, the local orphanage, the Meadows Old People's Home, the Mennonite Hospital in Bloomington and home and foreign missions.[11]

The Salem congregation was important also in the publishing work of the Defenseless Church. Henry Egly wrote in his diary in 1889: "Nov. 20. This evening at 3 o'clock went to Elkhart. Nov. 21. This morning at 3:30 I got there and at 6 o'clock I came to John Funk, there I met bro. Chris R. Egle from Salem, were together til 10 o'clock. We ordered to have the books printed by April 1, 2000 books for $1000. At 10 o'clock took the train came to Waterloo then to Ft. Wayne arrived there at 4 o'clock, stayed overnight."[12] Egle explains this item more fully in his "Brief History" by saying that the first publication in the Defenseless church was a German songbook in which the selection of songs was made by Joseph Rediger and Egle, both of Salem, and prepared by Egle for the printer. "Some of the songs were original by some of the members but mostly selected from other German song books. The name of the book was *Glaubens Lieder* [Songs of Faith] and consisted of 600 German hymns with an appendix of 50 English hymns ... bound in leather and published by the Mennonite Publishing Company of Elkhart, Ind. But as there were no notes in it and had to be learned and used with melodies from the Philharmonia it soon no longer filled the need of the people."[13]

In 1895 C. R. Egle bought a printing plant in Flanagan, where he printed the constitution and bylaws of the Salem Orphanage and some conference reports. When in 1898 the conference passed a resolution to start a German paper under the name of *Der Heilsbote*, Egle was made editor, with Joseph Rediger and Peter Hochstettler as assistants and D. N. Claudon as business manager. All of these were from Salem except Hochstettler, who was from Groveland, Illinois. Egle served as editor until the journal ceased publication in 1917. He also printed it, except during its later years when the work was done by the Berne (Ind.) Witness Company. An English paper, *Zion's Call*, also started in 1898, was edited and printed by D. N. Claudon in the interests of the Salem Orphanage. In 1913 the conference adopted *Zion's Call*, as its official paper. In 1919 the Defenseless Mennonite Brethren Conference began publishing *Good Tidings*. George P. Schultz of Chicago was editor. In 1921 these two papers were merged under the title *Zion's Tidings* with Amos Oyer as editor and Schultz as assistant. Shortly thereafter, Schultz became editor. After 1953 the name was changed to *Evangelical Mennonite*, in line with the new name of the Defenseless body.[14]

Higher education was not a problem for Salem in the nineteenth century, since very few of its youth attended high school, let alone college. But in the twentieth century it did become a problem for the Defenseless Mennonites as for others. Since the Defenseless people never had their own college or seminary, they supported and attended other institutions, generally of the more conservative and evangelical type. In 1905 a conference-appointed committee, most of whom were from Illinois, investigated colleges that the church could recommend to its young people. After spending two days at Goshen College visiting the various departments and "looking into its facilities for Bible study and preparations for mission work," the group "unanimously" recommended Goshen. Some members were already attending at that time and others came later. For a while the group supported Bluffton College and Witmarsum Seminary, but the liaison was a bit uneasy. Egle thought that "these schools are not in good favor with the local church as they have not influenced the local church in the best way."[15]

From an early date Salem was a strong supporter of missions. In 1892 it began to support the work of John A. Sprunger, a General Conference Mennonite and free-lancer who was engaged in mission work in Chicago. From 1896 on, partly through the efforts of Elder Joseph Rediger of Salem, enthusiastic advocate of missions, the conference began to support Mathilda Kohn (later Stevenson) as its first foreign missionary. Born a Roman Catholic in Germany, she became a Methodist in the United States and later joined the Salem church. While serving in the Congo, she was joined by Alma E. Doering of Chicago who did not join the Defenseless Mennonites but was supported by them. In the years following 1906, in cooperation with the Africa Inland Mission, the conference sent out additional missionaries to British East Africa. As noted earlier, three of these—Amos Oyer, Julia Oyer, and Anna F. Zimmerman—were from Salem. But because this territory was claimed by other mission groups, the Defenseless missionaries were recalled. The Central Conference Mennonites, who had also sent missionaries to this area, recalled theirs about the same time. Since both conferences were interested in finding a new, unworked field in Africa, they decided to work together in this part of their foreign mission program. In 1911 the two groups organized the "Congo Inland Mission, Incorporated," with headquarters at Bloomington, Illinois. This fine work was a splendid example of what can be done through inter-Mennonite cooperation.[16] Other cooperative ventures, such as the Meadows Mennonite Home and the Bloomington Mennonite Hospital, will also be discussed later, as will the Salem Children's Home at Flanagan, with which the Salem church has had more to do than any other congregation.

The importance of the Salem congregation is not measured by the size of its membership. There are larger congregations. In 1925 Salem's membership was 190; in 1957, 196; and in 1977, 250. Lack of any notable expansion might be due at least in part to the fact of three other Mennonite churches within six miles. Also, many members moved to other localities and helped start other churches. In one way Salem is unique. It is the only congregation, according to Egle, that did not experience a division over and lose members to the Missionary Church Association movement that struck the conference at the turn of the century.[17]

It was in 1868 that the Wesley City (later Groveland) Amish congregation went over almost as a body to the new Henry Egly movement. Since then its development as a Defenseless Mennonite congregation has been much like that of Salem. Like Salem, Groveland has had a strong program of evangelism and outreach and produced a number of ministers, missionaries and other Christian workers. It has invited Christian workers from elsewhere to come to Groveland and lead revival and missionary efforts. George P. Schultz of Chicago, for example, held meetings many times in this church. Ministers who have served the congregation include Peter Hochstettler, Benjamin Birkey, Joseph Rediger (who later moved to Nebraska), Joseph Springer, Moses Ropp, Christian Oyer, Amos Oyer, E. M. Rocke, Paul W. Rupp, Milo Nussbaum, Walter McDowell, and Thomas Taylor. E. E. Zimmerman, a deacon, was one of their most active and influential persons and one of their leading historians. Benjamin Birkey, who died in 1939, served as minister for about fifty-one years. Peter Hochstettler, who was born in Bavaria, Germany, and came to this country in 1849, was nearly ninety when he died in 1924. Ordained minister in 1870, he served many years also as bishop. The pioneer (Old) Mennonite evangelist, John S. Coffman, who preached in the Morton and Groveland area in 1893, has some interesting entries in his diary for February of that year. For February 25 he noted: "There is some interest in the good work here, but there is a great mixture of the Mennonite family—Egli, Stuckeys, old [not Old Order] Amish, comeouters." Invited to preach at Groveland on February 26, he recorded briefly (Feb. 27) his visit with Bishop Hochstettler, who "asked me hard questions to put me to test, but I had a pleasant and profitable time with him. Their hobby is that we know the time and place that we were converted."[18]

As elsewhere, the members at first held their worship service in their homes. It was not until 1878 that they built their first meetinghouse, a frame building located one-half mile east of Groveland. Its capacity, originally 200, but increased to 300 in 1935, was ample because Groveland's growth was never large. Unlike Salem, Groveland was seriously affected by the Missionary Church Association movement led by one Joseph E. Ramseyer. After the death of Henry Egly in 1890 Ramseyer, Defenseless minister of Elkton, Michigan, appeared on the scene as a new leader. A dynamic personality, powerful preacher, and man of apparently deep and sincere convictions, Ramseyer in the 1890s began to hold doctrinal positions considerably beyond those of Henry Egly and most of his followers. According to Nussbaum's analysis,

> Egly had led a conservative revolution in which he tried to take the church back to the doctrines of Scripture and the Anabaptist reforma-

tion. He charged that the Amish church of his day had fallen away from truths formerly held by Mennonites, specifically the ... [truth] of the necessity of the new birth for salvation.

Ramseyer, on the other hand, had virtually no Mennonite precedent for any of his three major points of contention: a distinct experience of the baptism of the Holy Spirit, pre-millennialism, and baptism by immersion. His quarrel therefore was not simply with error in his particular branch of the contemporary Mennonite church, but with some basic inadequacies in the whole Mennonite tradition. Egly led his people back to pure Mennonitism—Ramseyer led his outside of it. This was new territory for EMC people, and a good many of them equated novelty with error. They concluded the first chapter of EMC history by refusing to add new doctrines to Egly's essential teaching, even though it cost them the unity of the church.[19]

Nussbaum stated that every Defenseless church then in existence, except Salem, "suffered a major schism during the next ten years." Groveland, of course, was one of these. Its membership was slightly over 100 in 1926; 134 in 1937; 149 in 1954; and 104 in 1977. Probably the chief reason for the decline in membership after 1954 was the starting of new churches—Oak Grove in East Peoria and Grace in Morton—which some of the Groveland members joined. This caused some bruised feelings at Groveland, especially when pastor Milo Nussbaum left Groveland to become pastor at Grace. The present pastor (1980) is Emil J. Krahn.[20]

Other Defenseless Mennonite congregations were not formed in Illinois until after the turn of the century. The next one grew out of an interest in city missions that developed among various groups of Mennonites in the 1890s and following. After some early support of other denominational mission work in Chicago, the conference in 1907 passed a resolution to open its own mission in that city, a decision it carried out in 1908 by starting the Salem Gospel Mission at 249 Root Street, in the famous South Side stockyards district. The conference appointed Joseph K. Gerig of Woodburn, Indiana, as superintendent and his wife as matron. Other workers, of course, were added, the first being Mary Rediger from the Salem congregation. In 1912 the mission secured a better and larger building across the street. The work of course had its failures and successes. One sign on the church read, "The weak and the poor always welcome." Another read, "Hope for all who enter in." One of the more sensational successes was that of a woman with teenage children who had become very discouraged and despondent—so much so that she decided to go to Lake Michigan and end it all. Her route providentially led her past the mission. Observing the sign, "Hope for all who enter in," she decided to enter and see what it was all about. The mission workers kindly received her and showed her the way of salvation through Christ, whom she accepted as her savior. Leaving the mission with joy, she "went to her home looking at her troubles in a different light. As a result, two of her daughters were saved and one later became a [foreign] missionary."[21]

This mission changed locations several times, and finally became the present Calvary Memorial congregation. In 1929 the Root Street mission property was sold, and after several temporary locations for services, the conference decided to build the Southwest Gospel Tabernacle at 1221 W. 72nd Street in the southwestern part of the city. In 1944 the group organized as a congregation and changed its name to Calvary Memorial Church. In 1964 the group again relocated, selecting a site at 111th Street and Roberts Road in Palos Hills. Partly because of racial changes in the old area, many of the parishioners moved farther out. Also in 1964, but before the move to Palos Hills, a fire damaged the church building to the extent of about $20,000. Set by an arsonist who was mentally ill, the fire apparently had nothing to do with race or community relations. Most of the loss was covered by insurance.[22]

In addition to J. K. Gerig, the founder, Amos Oyer was among the pastors who served this congregation. Oyer headed the work some three years from 1928-31, when he came to an untimely end by being killed by crossfire during a drugstore robbery. Some have wondered whether the death was accidental, as usually assumed, or whether Oyer was the victim of foul play by someone opposed to the mission work. At least one authority claims that the question has never received a clear answer. Born in Livingston County in 1882, Oyer was converted at age 23 and gave his life to Christian service. His training included work at Goshen College, Moody Bible Institute, and Northern Baptist Theological Seminary. Before going to Chicago he served from 1907 to 1911 in British East Africa, and then as pastor at the Groveland Defenseless Mennonite Church.[23] Other pastors who have served in this work include Ivan Calhoun, C. E. Rediger, Richard Rupp, Clarence Fast, William Pauley, Tillman Amstutz, James Glenn, and Arthur Enns.

Calhoun, who later served at Salem near Flanagan, had difficulty in adjusting to a conservative rural community and made his greatest contribution in Chicago. He and Mrs. Calhoun provide a realistic picture of the conditions of many with whom the mission worked near the end of the Great Depression. Apparently many took seriously the above-mentioned sign, "The weak and the poor always welcome." In their report of the needy families helped at Christmas 1938 the Calhouns list case after case such as the following: "Young married couple ... unemployed"; "family of five, unemployed"; "widow ... family of three, no support"; "an afflicted unemployed minister and his wife"; "family of eight ... in great need"; "widow with invalid son, no support"; "widow with four children, very discouraged"; "maiden lady of 86 years living alone, no support"; "family of nine, unemployed";

"family of five, father afflicted, in real need"; "family of five with sickness and reverses"; and so the distressing list continues.[24] Economic conditions probably improved in the 1940s, although one may wonder to what extent the congregation's moving farther into the suburbs changed these conditions.

Membership at the Salem Gospel Mission, the Southwest Gospel Tabernacle, or the Calvary Memorial Church has never been large. Although it was fifty-three in 1977, it had reached some fifty earlier as a mission station. Attendance at church and Sunday school services, however, has been larger, often averaging about ninety. Moreover, the congregation faces the future with courage and optimism. Said Pastor Arthur Enns on a recent occasion: "God is building His Church and we are seeing it happen here at Calvary Memorial."[25] One of the active and influential lay members of this congregation is Peter G. Schultz. Born in Chicago, son of the well-known missionary and evangelist, George P. Schultz, Peter trained as a lawyer at a time when few Mennonites took up this profession. He had earlier been a member of the Brighton Mennonite Church, of which his father was pastor for many years, and transferred to the Calvary Mennonite Church in the 1960s. Here, as in his earlier membership, he provided a significant service to the spiritual and material strength of the congregation in its new home in Palos Hills. As a matter of fact, Attorney Schultz was well acquainted with all Mennonite groups in Chicago and frequently provided legal and other services to many of them. In November 1966, editor Harvey Driver of the *Evangelical Mennonite* paid tribute to him as "Layman of the Month": "salute Attorney Peter Schultz for his significant service to Calvary Memorial Church, his many professional services to the Evangelical Mennonite Church Conference and to the Congo Inland Mission over a longer span of years."[26]

The Oak Grove Bible Church in East Peoria, the next Defenseless church to be organized in Illinois, goes back to 1955, by which time the denomination had changed its name to Evangelical Mennonite Church. Like Calvary Memorial, this congregation is composed mostly of people who do not have a Mennonite background. Paul W. Rupp, pastor of the Groveland Church, had much to do with Oak Grove's beginnings. In 1946 he invited a number of children from the Oak Grove area to participate in a joint daily vacation Bible school. Nineteen children responded and the number increased in ensuing years. These became the nucleus of the new church. Evangelistic meetings were held in 1950, a Sunday school was started, and Rupp became full-time pastor in 1954. The church was organized the following year with eighteen charter members. Purchasing a schoolhouse for worship in 1956, the group later built a new meetinghouse, which was dedicated May 15, 1966. In the meantime the congregation publicized its work and outreach in the community. Among its aggressive methods was sending tracts to every home in Peoria with a telephone. In 1970 church membership reached fifty-five and Sunday school attendance 250. Also in 1970 the group started a new station in East Peoria, with a Sunday school attendance of sixty-four. With Paul's son, Jerald, assisting in this work, services were possible in both places. Paul W. Rupp has led the Oak Grove work from the beginning. In 1977 the number of members was seventy-two; the Sunday school enrollment runs three times that high.[27]

Another recently organized Evangelical Mennonite church in Illinois is Grace at Morton, which has the distinction of being not only the second youngest but also the largest, with a 1977 membership of 344 and a Sunday school enrollment of 602. It is the fastest-growing congregation. Grace was organized in 1958 after considerable thought and some hesitancy. For years various members had been thinking of starting a church in Morton. Milo Nussbaum and others felt that in 1957 and 1958 a new opportunity was presenting itself. A new Caterpillar plant in Morton had brought many people into the city, just as the Morton Bible Church was closing its doors. So there was "urgent need and plenty of room for a good Gospel church." But when Nussbaum, who then was pastor of the nearby Groveland Church, mentioned the possibility to his congregation, many did not share his enthusiasm for the new step. Perhaps they sensed the loss of some members and possibly even of their pastor to the new venture—which in the end happened, causing misunderstanding and tension for several years. Working closely with and receiving helpful counsel from Reuben Short, the head of the denomination, Nussbaum was able to work through this difficult and delicate problem in a positive manner. The new Grace congregation met for services in a temporary location until 1961, when it dedicated its own meetinghouse. The seating capacity of 250 was soon too small and the facilities were enlarged. In fact, a second expansion was soon necessary, and the new facility was dedicated on April 4, 1976. From its beginning the congregation has strongly emphasized evangelism at home and abroad, and its record of growth is truly remarkable.

Milo Nussbaum—Grace's first and only pastor until Bryce Winteregg was called in January 1973 to be his assistant, followed by Stephen Ford in 1976—would be the first to insist that an active laity deserves much credit for the healthy growth of the congregation. But an objective analysis also indicates that Nussbaum himself contributed much to the congregation's progress. A few years earlier J. F. Gerig, another church leader, had reported to the annual conference that their church was not winning souls as it should have, that it was winning only 20 percent of those enrolled in its Sunday schools, thus losing 80 percent "of those entrusted to us. And 40% of the 20% we lose within five years."[28] A dynamic personality and an aggressive leader, Nussbaum was not satisfied with such meager results. "The Evangelical Mennonite Church," he told the annual conference in 1964, "must refocus her vision and recapture the zeal of her founder and use all the resources entrusted to her to accomplish that which is her work for this day." In 1966, at the beginning of the church's second century, Nussbaum wrote an appropriate article for the church paper in which he emphasized "VICTORY, VISION, and VITALITY." He thought: "Our present stature is not one of refreshing victory. When the average age of ten of our smaller churches is over thirty years and the average membership is about 40 members, one might conclude that victory is not the chief characteristic of this fellowship. But we must find victory. If victorious living is not possible where we are, let's go where it is possible. We must do whatever is necessary to achieve personal and group victory." Then, citing the sense of Deuteronomy 20:8, Nussbaum put forth a ringing call to march forward and added, "Let all the fearful go home."[29]

No doubt this spirit, plus the record of accomplishment at Morton, caused Harvey A. Driver, then conference executive secretary, to refer to Nussbaum as an outstanding leader in the Evangelical Mennonite Church, domestically and internationally. After pointing out the important positions he had held, including the presidency of the church for a number of years, Driver added this tribute: "During his busy presidency, Brother Nussbaum also has been the dynamic leader and effective pastor of Grace Congregation in Morton, Illinois, which in about every department has been the pilot congregation for Evangelical Mennonites." Always a strong believer in the Sunday school and other Christian education agencies, Nussbaum emphasized that the church must be ready to change not the message but its methods and must have more effective teachers in its teaching agencies. "There is no room for the untrained teacher in Sunday School anymore than there is room for an untrained person in the public school." Perhaps the church will have to establish its own weekday schools, at least in some areas. "The philosophy of the public school," thought Nussbaum, "may become totally unacceptable to the Church within the next years," and that institution may have to educate its own young people.[30]

In 1979 the youngest Evangelical Mennonite congregation in Illinois was the one at Eureka. After two years of preliminary work in temporary facilities, the group held ground-breaking ceremonies for a new edifice on July 8. LaVerne Fauber, a graduate of Eureka College, had been "praying for many years that a fundamental Bible-believing church would be established" in Eureka. "She faithfully drove the distance from Morton to Eureka for 2 years, to help get the church started." At the morning service on July 8 ninety-three people attended, with ninety-eight in attendance at the ground-breaking ceremony in the afternoon. Jerry Spencer, a conservative Southern Baptist leader, led in a series of evangelistic meetings in November, 1979. Gary Hedrick, the pastor, reported that the work in Eureka was "thriving."[31] Before long, however, Hedrick had some misunderstanding with the congregation, and left.

These Illinois congregations never have had their own district conference but have constituted an important minority in a larger organization. Following some earlier ministers' meetings, the denomination held its first convention in Berne, Indiana, in October 1883. The next one did not occur until 1895; but thereafter the conferences have met annually. At first they were not legislative bodies. Instead, delegates, some of them ministers and some laity, discussed doctrinal matters, listened to inspirational messages given in German and English, and participated in praise and testimony services. Not until 1908 was the conference officially organized as a corporation under the laws of Illinois, with the name "The Conference of the Defenseless Mennonite Church of North America." In 1945 the conference instructed the executive committee to work on a new name for the denomination and also on a new plan of government to eliminate overlapping and inefficiency. Accordingly, in 1947 the executive committee proposed a new constitution, which the conference considered and adopted. The proposed new name, Evangelical Mennonite Church, was adopted in 1948. In reviewing the new constitution, Reuben D. Short, an important leader, said that doctrinally the constitution made no changes in principle and thought, and that the new document was simply a restatement of "the same basic beliefs that have been historic with us." He stated also that the new name "retains our Mennonite identity and the prefix Evangelical suggests our evangelistic emphasis." Harvey A. Driver characterized this period in the life of the denomination under Short's leadership as a "renewal of the church," resulting in the revitalization of the older congregations and the founding of a number of vigorous new ones.[32]

Not only has the Evangelical Mennonite Church brought about changes in its conference structure, but it has also sought affiliation and merger, without much success so far, with other bodies of similar beliefs. According to a historian of the group, the "merger issue is the most comprehensive problem ever faced by the EMC," and the two reasons for desiring union had to do with its small size (2,103 members in 1954): "(1) missions could be more effectively done in cooperation with other groups, and (2) doctrine could be standardized and protected only if there were a Bible college and/or seminary controlled at least in part by the conference." The church constitution itself says, "We are prepared to study sympathetically plans for closer affiliation with groups of like faith and emphasis." Already in 1921 the church considered joint missionary work and merger with the Mennonite Brethren in Christ. In 1948 the Unity Committee of the conference recommended that "aggressive efforts" be made to bring about closer cooperation and possible union with the Missionary Church Association and the Evangelical Mennonite Brethren "for the purpose of hastening the day when the Gospel shall be brought to all peoples and nations." Since the Missionary Church Association was already operating Ft. Wayne Bible College, the connection with the group would provide the desired church college.[33]

The group with which the Evangelical Mennonites came closest to union was the Evangelical Mennonite Brethren, located largely in the Western United States and Canada. In 1953 one writer stated that close friendships between the two groups had begun over thirty years earlier through the evangelistic ministries of George P. Schultz and C. R. Egle. Both groups emphasized a definite personal experience of salvation, nonconformity to the world, and missionary outreach. From 1947 on, serious discussions about affiliation were held between the two conferences. In a joint meeting of the two at Grace Bible Institute in Omaha in 1950 a board of eight men—four from each group—was appointed to work out a proposal and arrange for the next meeting. The conference closed in high hopes and noble talk about how wonderful it was "to see brethren dwell together in unity."[34] Reuben D. Short used similar words to characterize the joint conference that met at the same place in 1951: "The spiritual tide ran high. There was a beautiful scene of brethren from across the states and Canada sitting together in harmony and unity. There was warmth of fellowship with the grass roots of love firmly taking root." But the very cautious and lengthy procedure used to bring about even a loose affiliation, to say nothing about a real merger, suggests that some had their doubts. The proposals drawn up by the eight-man board and submitted to the joint conference in 1951 were unanimously adopted, but merely "for our study and prayer. These will be submitted to our next annual conference for ratification." The joint conference in 1952 did accept the proposals.

The groups met in high hopes in 1953 for the "Inaugural Conference" of what was to be called the "Conference of Evangelical Mennonites." Harry E. Bertsche, veteran Illinois Evangelical Mennonite Church worker, gave an impressive "Inaugural Sermon" stressing Christian unity as portrayed in John 17. Pointing out the similarities of the two groups, he had "a strong conviction ... and I believe it's God-given, that these two organizations have been led together by

God." His plea for Christian unity was tremendously powerful. "There is nothing in the ministry or the life of the Lord Jesus Christ," he said, "that would even intimate any other thing than that it was His will that His followers should be united. There is nothing on record in divine holy writ that would suggest anything else was uppermost in His thinking." The reason for this was "that the world may believe." Bertsche believed that the closer union about to "transpire in this auditorium will stimulate faith in many who are looking on."

But the union was an affiliation rather than a true merger. Under the new arrangement, although the joint conference was to be called "The Conference of Evangelical Mennonites," the former conferences continued as separate, independent organizations with little control from the center. The central supervision provided was to come from a general board and several commissions. The two groups were to continue their former missionary affiliations and later unite these as "time and opportunity permit." Perhaps one of the more important results of this affiliation was the exchange of ministers between the two bodies.[35] Another result was the appearance of the *Evangelical Mennonite*, the new organ of the affiliated conferences. This periodical replaced *Zion's Tidings* and *Gospel Tidings* published by the two conferences prior to the affiliation.

The development of this union during the next ten years reveals two separate, parallel lines of thought. The one stressed unity, harmony, similarity of belief, good conferences, and so on. The other indicated some questions, doubts, problems, and failure to go on to a true merger.[36]

In any case, the union was not permanent. In 1962, after ten years of affiliation, the two groups dissolved their union. In the language of the resolution, the two bodies proposed "that in the finest spirit of spiritual fellowship and by unanimous agreement we release each other from organizational responsibility one to the other but resolve to remain of kindred mind and spirit in the Lord and pray for each other so that the building of the Church of Jesus Christ might continue to be built as rapidly as possible looking forward to His imminent return." John R. Dick, an EMB leader in the unity movement, has given some plausible explanations. The foremost difficulty was geographical, the congregations being too far away from each other. With a combined affiliated membership of only some five or six thousand, the geographical spread supposedly increased operational costs. On the other hand it could be argued that the savings from less duplication by affiliating or merging would more than offset the costs of geography. Dick also cited different methods in missionary work as a reason for the union's failure. For example, it was common practice for Evangelical Mennonite Brethren missionaries to find their own support from individual donors. In the Evangelical Mennonite Church the conference assumed this responsibility. Also, said Dick, affiliation did not solve the problem of higher education.[37]

However, other efforts of the Evangelical Mennonite Church to unite with groups of similar beliefs, where geography was not a factor, suggest other reasons for failure. When the Missionary Church Association broke away from the Defenseless Mennonites in 1898 there was hard feeling, which later gave way to friendlier attitudes and even to thought of reunion. By the 1940s the differences that had brought separation in 1898—immersion, premillennialism, and a separate and distinct experience of the baptism of the Holy Spirit—were more acceptable to the Defenseless people. In that decade the Unity Committee of the Defenseless Mennonite Conference and the Missionary Church Association drew up a proposed constitution "as a basis for consideration of union of the two societies." Again, nothing came from the move, but the idea was not forgotten. At the time of the Evangelical Mennonite centennial in 1965 there were renewed efforts to unite. In fact, on this occasion the church considered uniting not only with the Missionary Church Association but also with the United Missionary Church. However, this attempt likewise was to no avail.[38]

It is very difficult to say precisely why these efforts to affiliate or merge have thus far failed, especially in cases where geography was not a problem. Dick likened the merger problem to a lonely old man and a kindly old woman who had become very fond of each other but also agreed that they were "too old to marry" because they had become too set in their ways. Perhaps historian Stan Nussbaum has come closest to the mark. The church, he says, "has always taken the pragmatic approach to merger, and the advantages of merger have never seemed to outweigh the practical difficulties of organizational amalgamation and the intangible but very real hesitation of EMC people to trust other churches, especially when they know that their voting strength in any merged denomination would be negligible. That is the dilemma—EMC seems too small to work efficiently alone and too small to have much influence on any group it joins."[39]

Be that as it may, the number of Illinois churches involved in the first affiliation was very small. In fact the Evangelical Mennonite Brethren had only one church in the state—Brighton in Chicago—and that ceased to exist in 1976. As to the Missionary Church Association, now a part of the Missionary Church, the case was different. It had about a dozen congregations in the state at the time of the attempted merger.[40]

A related problem facing the Evangelical Mennonite Church has been its search for identity. After pointing out how this branch has made great changes since Egly's day and has "undergone the most adaptation to the American environment," the scholarly study by Kauffman and Harder states: "The most distinctive mark of the EMC is its long search for denominational identity in the face of such overwhelming transition." In the first generation following the Egly schism "during which it clung to cultural traditions more conservative than its roots, it borrowed church-work methods from the Sunday school movement, the revivalist movement, the holiness movement, and the fundamentalist movement. Its ethic was thoroughly nonresistant ... but today barely one-fifth of its members hold to a pacifist position."[41]

Historian Stan Nussbaum says that Kauffman and Harder are right. "In a little over a century the EMC has moved from the most traditional and most closely knot [sic] end of the Mennonite spectrum all the way to the most progressive and cosmopolitan end."[42] By the 1970s the group was increasingly questioning the validity of its Anabaptist-Mennonite roots. To be sure, there were differences of opinion among its members, some wanting to continue to stress at least some Mennonite ties and values while others were ready if not eager to eliminate the word "Mennonite" altogether.

These differences appear among the Illinois members of this body. There is a tendency in some congregations, in Illinois as elsewhere, to drop the word "Mennonite" from their names. This is probably truer of younger congregations such as Oak Grove and Eureka, where most of the members do not have a Mennonite background, than of older ones. The question arose in connection with the new congregation at Morton. E. E. Zimmerman, veteran worker from Groveland, wrote to Reuben Short, the conference president, that "many others with me feel that the name Mennonite should be left in addition with any other name that may be adopted. I think it is just good judgment to do that.... Is there any reason why we should be ashamed of that name?" Zimmerman added: "We already have perhaps two or more in our conference in which the name Mennonite is dropped.... If new churches continue to be formed," as is our vision, and we "leave off the name Mennonite there will undoubtedly not be much use if any to have that name at all for our conference. I think you as conference president and others of the highest officials should have that much authority in the naming of any new church." The new congregation retained the word "Mennonite," now being known as the "Grace Evangelical Mennonite Church." The problem is also illustrated in a local conference that included Oak Grove. One leader raised a question about the appropriateness of a proposed topic, "Anabaptist Encounter." He wondered whether "since the name Mennonite is not too popular at Oakgrove might it not be to[o] much of a thrust all at once?" However, this same leader, E. M. Rocke, suggested that Kenneth Good, pastor of the (Old) Mennonite Church in Morton, speak at their conference. He was, said Rocke, evangelical, popular in the community and "diplomatic enough to fit into most [sic] any situation." He "never wears his cut collar coat not even sometimes in his own service," and he would thus be able to handle the topic satisfactorily.

The Evangelical Mennonites have been wrestling with a problem that applies more or less to all Mennonite groups. As a group stresses evangelicalism and evangelism more and more, can it also emphasize and maintain the Mennonite distinctives? Or will these increasingly be looked upon as impediments to spreading the gospel? Apparently the majority in the Evangelical Mennonite Church now look upon these distinctives as impediments, and believe that it is better to be "right than Mennonite." During the last fifty years, says Nussbaum, "the distinctive marks of Mennonites have faded on the visage of EMC," and it "now refuses to emphasize Mennonite doctrinal distinctives." At present, the strong prevailing tendency in the Evangelical Mennonite Church is to stress "Evangelical" more and more and "Mennonite" less and less. A growing number, perhaps a majority, feel more comfortable with the evangelicals than with the Mennonites. Harvey A. Driver, however, thinks that a larger percentage of the members in Illinois still want to work with other Mennonites. This desire may draw strength from cooperation in such ventures as Meadows Mennonite Home, Bloomington Hospital, and the African Inter-Mennonite Mission. While the identity problem for the EMC is probably less in Illinois than in the denomination as a whole, it is still a problem.[43]

CHAPTER 6

The Old Order Amish in Illinois

The Old Order Amish settlement around Arthur, Illinois, is located between Champaign-Urbana and Mattoon in the southwest portion of Douglas County, the northwest part of Coles County, and the east-central area of Moultrie County. It extends about twelve miles north and south and thirteen miles east and west of Arthur. The land is fertile but flat, and drainage was a problem. One Amish writer stated that he could not "think of another Amish community where the ground lies so low and level as it does around here." He adds that it "took a large amount of tile, time, and patience to drain this low flat area."[1] It also required much patience on the part of those who suffered from drowned crops, malaria and other diseases, and poor roads.

The history of this Amish community, which goes back to the 1860s, has no connection with the Amish who settled in the Bloomington-Peoria area. In 1864 Joel Beachy of Grantsville, Maryland, and Moses Yoder of Summit Mills, Pennsylvania, traveled to the Middle West in search of good land that they could farm without using as much limestone as they had found necessary on their Eastern farms. After investigating in Wisconsin and Missouri, they stopped on their return trip at Pana, Illinois. Their first impressions were good, and they investigated further in the direction of nearby Mattoon, Arcola, and Arthur. They completed their homeward journey, reported favorably what they had seen, and with Daniel Miller and Daniel Otto returned later in the year to purchase land. Yoder, Miller, Otto and their families from Summit Mills, were the first Amish settlers, arriving on March 3, 1865. Others from that state as well as from Ohio, Indiana, and Iowa followed them shortly. The price of land, if Moses Yoder's purchase of a section of railroad land in the later 1860s was typical, was scarcely more than $8.00 per acre.[2]

Joseph N. Keim from Goshen, Indiana, was the first minister and bishop in the new settlement. The first minister to be ordained in the new community was Jonas J. Kauffman. Selected in 1865, he became bishop in 1873. Like the Amish farther north in the early years, the Arthur Amish met in their homes for worship. Unlike the Bloomington-Peoria Amish, however, who by the 1850s and 1860s were using meetinghouses, the Arthur group chose the "old order" and have continued to meet in their homes to this day. Accommodating people in their homes for worship services made it necessary to have districts limited to from about fifty to slightly over 100 members. Growth by natural increase and by immigration made it necessary in 1888 to divide the Arthur church into two districts. The Moultrie-Douglas county line, which runs through the village of Arthur, became the dividing line. Daniel J. Beachy was bishop in Moultrie County and David J. Plank in Douglas County. By 1922 there were five districts, and in 1980 there were thirteen.

Sources (such as the *Mennonite Yearbook and Directory*) do not seem to give precise figures of Amish membership. Since the same number (300) is listed for the Arthur Amish for quite a few consecutive years, it cannot be accurate. *The Mennonite Encyclopedia* gave the membership in about 1955 as 800 in nine congregations or districts. An authoritative article written in 1975 says there is no accurate census of the Amish population in the area, but estimated it to be 1500. This seems conservative, since there are thirteen districts and since the membership was already listed as 800 in 1955. Another study gives the population as 1491 already in 1930.[3] The membership from the *Mennonite Yearbook* for selected years is as follows: 1917, 300; 1927, 375; 1937, 466; 1947, 567; 1957, 772; 1967, 791. In 1937 Cadwell was listed but not the membership. The most recent and most authoritative work on the Arthur Old Order Amish has been done by D. Paul Miller, professor of sociology at Illinois Wesleyan University, Bloomington, Illinois. He listed thirteen districts with 430 families, 1014 church members, and 1991 total Old Order population.[4]

In 1872, some twenty miles southwest of Arthur, a small Old Order Amish community was started in Shelby County. Seventeen families are known to have resided here, most of them from Indiana. In the 1880s they moved away, mostly to Reno County, Kansas. Church disunity was no doubt one reason, but one authority thinks the high price of land was probably also a factor. A similar result followed an effort to establish another Amish community in Fayette County just south of Shelby County near Brownstown and Vandalia. The first families came from Arthur in 1893, but a larger number came shortly thereafter from Elkhart County, Indiana, and other places. By 1896, thirty-two families—about 181 persons—were there. However, discouraged by drought, late spring frosts, and chinch bugs, as well as by illness from smallpox, malaria, typhoid, and scarlet fever, the people moved away a few years later, the last family leaving in 1906.⁵

Hence, Arthur is the only Old Order Amish settlement in Illinois. While older Amish communities farther north were gradually changing, the Arthur Amish maintained the old ways with a dogged persistence. This meant maintaining the very conservative lifestyle of the Old Order throughout the country. This did not mean there were absolutely no changes, but rather a very simple and strict life pattern was maintained in order to carry out the Old Order interpretation of separation from the world. Forms of dress continued to be very simple and plain. Most of the clothing for men and women was made in the home, using hooks and eyes instead of buttons. Houses, generally two-story frame buildings, were adequate but also plain with simple furnishings—no wall-to-wall carpeting, plain blue curtains but no drapes on the windows, no electric lights or appliances and no lightning rods. Since church services are still held in the homes, houses were and still are built with this in mind. Rooms downstairs are fairly large, with the floor plan so arranged that the speaker at a door near the center of the house can be seen, or certainly heard, in at least three rooms.

Sometimes in summer the service is held in the barn or in a shed. Services are not as long as where congregations had six or eight or more ministers, as earlier in some Amish congregations farther north. But they are still long, making it desirable to continue the practice of having a lunch at late noon, provided by the host in whose home the congregation is meeting. A bishop, a minister, and a deacon serve in each of the districts into which the Arthur group is divided. The deacon has charge of the alms money and often participates in the worship services by reading the Scriptures in the opening. In each district the services are held on alternate Sundays, but not on the same Sundays in all congregations.

In the selection of a minister each member in good standing may nominate one man. All nominees who have at least two votes then submit themselves to the lot in which, it is believed, the Lord will select the proper person. The bishop, selected by the same method, is a powerful leader among the Arthur group as elsewhere among the Amish. Theoretically, the Amish congregation is the autonomous decision-making unit. Also, theoretically, decisions should come in the form of recommendations from the *Abrath*, or ministers' council, to the congregation. Although actual practice varies in different districts, the bishop, usually in consultation with his ministers and with his congregation, and often with other districts' bishops, makes the final decision on many issues. In addition, he takes his turn in preaching and also has charge of such special events as weddings and baptismal and communion services.⁶

Although there is not complete agreement on education, in general the Arthur Amish object to centralized schools and to letting their children go beyond the eighth grade. This did not become a serious problem until well into the twentieth century when the state began to require a minimum number of years in school. The Amish do not want acculturation and strongly feel that public high schools, especially centralized ones, will bring it. The Conservative Mennonite Church near Arthur operates a Christian day school with ten grades, which has been a solution for a few. The educational authorities also have attempted to make some accommodation to Amish opinion. In 1962 they still maintained a number of one-room schools for the group. Had they preferred, the Amish could have operated their own parochial schools. There have been differences of opinion among them as to whether they should have or not, but until recently the majority seemed satisfied to send their children to the public schools through the eighth grade. In addition some Amish schools have been established in the settlement to teach children to read and write German and sing German songs. During the winter months young people past the eighth grade attended these schools. Also during the summer months the Amish had Sunday schools, for the same purpose, on those Sundays when there were no services in the districts. Some Amish parents favor more education for their children than what they are getting at present.[7]

Despite past indifference to parochial schools, Amish opinion has shifted considerably in recent years. The shift has come because of conflicts between the school authorities and the Amish, not only over raising the minimum age requirements for school attendance but also over consolidation of school districts. As a result of struggles in various states—Pennsylvania, Michigan, Ohio, Wisconsin, Iowa, and others—the parochial school movement has gown by leaps and bounds. *Wisconsin v. Yoder*, a Supreme Court decision of May 1972, upheld the right of the Amish to operate their own schools, and became an important factor in this development. In 1977-78 the Old Order Amish had 426 schools in the United States and Canada, with 519 teachers and 12,545 pupils. The great majority of these schools were started in the 1960s and 1970s, including six schools in the Arthur area with eleven teachers and 196 students. About 160 Old Order Amish students at Arthur still attend the public schools. After the Amish began serious efforts to establish parochial schools, the public school officals made still further concessions to the Amish to retain their children in the public schools, partly in order to secure larger amounts of state aid, which is based on enrollment figures. These officials made conscious efforts "to respect the beliefs and wishes of the Amish." Consequently communication between the

Arthur Amish and public school officials is good.[8]

The reading habits of the Arthur Amish, as reflected by reading materials in the homes, indicate a strong interest in, besides the Bible, the *Martyrs Mirror*, the writings of Menno Simons and other early leaders, *Herold der Wahrheit*, *Sugar Creek* (Ohio) *Budget*, local weekly newspapers (especially the *Arthur Graphic Clarion*), and farm papers such as the *Prairie Farmer*. Some, and this is probably a growing number, take daily papers. Radios and television are not permitted. In 1964 a group of Amish founded the Pathway Publishing Company at Aylmer, Ontario, Canada. The company publishes three monthly periodicals *(Blackboard Bulletin, Family Life,* and *Young Companion)*, textbooks for their schools, and books of general interest to Amish readers. The Amish in Pennsylvania recently began publishing another monthly, *The Diary*. Thus the Amish, including those at Arthur, have a wider selection than formerly of reading material produced and distributed under their own auspices.

One Amishman, L. A. Miller, also operated a religious bookstore at Arthur for some years. Some of his advertising seemed a bit unusual, not to say strange, for an Old Order Amish member. The books he sold were mostly by non-Amish and non-Mennonite authors. "It is our desire," he said in a 1946 catalog, "to circulate only those books with a distinctly evangelical flavor," some of which were "heart warming volumes on prayer and the deeper life." More unusual were the advertisements supporting the war effort. One said, "Send the Christian Digest To Boys In Service." "It will aid the moral and spiritual *Defense* of our country in time of crisis." Those "serving Uncle Sam ... will deeply appreciate the Christian Digest coming as a gift from you." He also advertised "Patriotic Christian" wall plaques, such as, "We Must Win," "The Price of Liberty is Eternal Vigilance," "Let Freedom Ring"— all wrapped in language of Scripture! "These plaques," Miller's catalog added, "will witness to your patriotism and inspire all who see them."

The economy of the Arthur Amish continues to be agricultural. But by the second half of the twentieth century, and especially by the fourth quarter, remaining agricultural has become exceedingly complex, if not impossible, due to growing Amish population and scarcity of land. The group has thus been forced to adapt in order to survive. Located between two nearby state universities, and not far from others, the Arthur Amish have been the prey of sociologists and other scholars. The products of these scholars vary in quality, of course, but we are greatly indebted to some for useful information about the history and social, economic, and religious conditions of the community, including the changes which do occur from time to time. One authority, writing in the late 1960s, points out why the Amish farmer has become more visible in the twentieth century: "It was only with the general introduction of tractor-farming, the increasing adoption of automobiles and trucks and the advent of rural electricity . . . that the exclusiveness of the Amish became highly visible. . . . The Amish also lagged behind other farmers in their refusal to adopt other amenities. It is only in the last ten years that running water, bathrooms, storm windows, gas stoves and refrigerators have appeared in Amish houses in east central Illinois."[9]

Another study made in the early 1960s identifies the Amish farm

> by its small size, well-fenced fields, comparatively large percentage of land in crops other than corn, omission of soy beans from the crop rotation, small grain cut with a binder, shocked and threshed, straw stacks, presence of large numbers of livestock, particularly dairy cows, and unique draft horses. The farmstead has most or all of these features: a large barn, a large house with a slate roof and windows curtained with a single straight full-length piece of plain material, grandpa house, many smaller buildings, windmill, large garden, fruit trees, and absence of lightning rods, electric wiring and telephone lines.[10]

Some of these studies have dealt with the Amish demographic problem. Since keeping their young people on the farm is a highly cherished objective, the Amish have done everything possible to secure farms for their children in the community. Countering the national trend toward larger farms, the Arthur Amish have made more farms available by making them smaller and engaging more in intensive agriculture than is common among their non-Amish neighbors. A study by Judith A. Nagata shows that the average size of these farms has decreased from 141 acres in 1896 to 77 in 1965. Lois Fleming's figure for the average-size farm in 1962 is a little higher—101 acres—as compared with a state average of 201. This average-size farm is very likely still smaller as of 1981.[11]

Whatever the precise figure, Amish farms are becoming smaller. "Small farms and dense population are the most important characteristics of the Amish settlement," says Fleming. Another difference is that these farms have more livestock and more buildings, some of which are used by older people who retire in *Grossdawdy* (grandfather) houses. The *Grossdawdy* house stands on the farm, next to the home of one of the children. Another reason for more buildings is more livestock. Not only the horses that the Amish use for draft power instead of tractors but also other animals, especially dairy cattle, require more buildings. Though living in a cash-grain area, the Amish do considerable dairying as a part of their intensive farm operations in order to make more jobs available at home for their families. Having more livestock also benefits these people by providing a larger supply of manure, which they prefer over commercial fertilizer. In fact one authority states that they "have not used any commercial fertilizer" and "have some of the most extensive tracts of land that would be regarded as 'clean' by the organic purist." So for various reasons, "Intensification of livestock enterprises is the favored Amish adaptive device."[12]

Another mark of the Amish intensive, livestock farming is greater use of fencing than in the case of their neighbors. The typically current view of vast expanses of Illinois farmland without fencing is foreign to the Arthur Amish. Much of the fencing is "hog-tight, horse-high, and bull-strong." They also use some battery-powered electric fence.[13]

Another interesting development has occurred in the Arthur community. Victor Stoltzfus, until 1981 a sociologist at Eastern Illinois University, has observed that acculturation to livestock enterprises is occurring more rapidly than in the case of crop-farming. In Stoltzfus' words:

> Modern hog farrowing equipment and especially dairy equipment contrast sharply with the Amish, horse-drawn grain binders and threshing rigs. There also seems to be no hesitation to draw on the services of veterinary medicine.... Artificial insemination is frequently utilized for dairy herds and sometimes for swine. The mixer-grinder unit for livestock feed processing is usually the single most expensive piece of equipment on the Amish farm. Tractors are permitted in limited ways to assist in the livestock enterprise with belt power, manure forklift, and as power units for feed grinding. They are not permitted as a general rule in the field.

The writer then gives a possible explanation as to why acculturation is occurring more rapidly in the livestock enterprises. These livestock enterprise innovations, being newer, "are less likely to run afoul of morally sanctified past agricultural precedents. Cage layer operations [chicken raising] and specialized calf raising are relatively new in conventional agriculture. There is therefore less of a past Amish heritage that change would 'violate.'" Stoltzfus then goes on to give this significant example of accommodation:

> In 1970, the most important single innovation in livestock technology was the experimental adoption of bulk milk tanks. The "experiment" was made to satisfy both secular and sacred [church] authorities. The Illinois state health department had to be satisfied that a bulk milk tank could function correctly without electrical power or controls. Amish adaptive skills were equal to the task of using diesel cooling power and an air motor for agitation to the bulk units to satisfy the state. The church issue was more complicated since neither the church members nor the bishops were unified in their understanding on community life. After the year's experimental period elapsed in January, 1972, an informal agreement emerged among the bishops not to formally oppose or endorse the bulk tank innovation. In the absence of a specific prohibition, Amish dairymen are now installing bulk tanks.[14]

Another adaptive device that modern agriculture has forced upon the Arthur Amish is the increased use of commercial credit. Depending on one's kinfolk and the church community for this kind of help was common in earlier days, but the present high costs of building materials, land, farm equipment, and livestock have changed this picture. In August 1971 one bank in the area had loaned $1,300,000 to 135 Old Order Amish customers, representing fourteen percent of the bank's total loans. With debts reaching as high as $50,000 on some Amish farms it is apparent that this new type of aid has become necessary. None of the loans has been written off as a loss. Even though they are not able to produce these amounts of capital among themselves, the Amish do continue their spirit of mutual aid by helping each other pay off loans in cases of necessity. This use of outside capital has made it possible for more young Amishmen to remain on the land, although a growing number of these are tenant farmers. In 1968, according to Nagata, 29 percent of the Amish farmers in that area were tenant farmers of non-Amish landowners.[15]

While these adaptive devices have helped considerably they have not completely solved the problem. The demographic pressure, due in part to the Amish birth rate, has been too great, causing some out-migration to other Amish communities or to areas where new settlements may be started. Since land at Arthur has become very expensive it is often possible to sell a small farm there and buy a larger one in another state for the same or less money. Another adaptive strategy for survival has been to engage in other economic activities in the community, activities in most cases still closely connected with their agricultural way of life. Or the Amish find employment in various capacities among the non-Amish either on farms or in towns. An estimated 50 percent of the young married men who remain in agriculture were, in 1968, employed by non-Amish farmers. This trend is common in other Amish communities as well as at Arthur. Some Amish young men leave Arthur to go to other Amish communities in search of work, such as in the trailer factories of northern Indiana. This may be a temporary move or it might prove to be permanent.

In addition to cultivation, agriculture-related activities vary widely. D. Paul Miller recently identified ninety-four Amish businesses or shops in the Arthur community. Amish operate a few retail stores, and some engage in turkey and chicken raising; a few do custom slaughtering and processing of meat, including freezer and locker service. The power for such machines comes from tractor motors or stationary diesel engines, while the refrigerators are gas-powered. A few Amish operate feed mills. Those who need transportation in their business either employ Mennonites who own trucks or—more likely in recent years—hire those who do custom trucking.

A few operate cider and sorghum mills, the products of which are used also as components of cattle feed. Others engage in welding and blacksmithing, tiling, shoe-repairing, carpet-weaving, harness-making, carpentry and cabinetmaking, coffin- and tombstone-making, and repairing and partial manufacturing of buggies. At times Amish have operated canneries and cheese factories. A few have engaged in logging and one or two have worked at horse-breaking—even of race horses! According to Daniel Otto, a recent development has been the establishment by Amish of several grocery stores throughout the community. Some of these, known as "salvage" stores, handle damaged items and odd lots bought from wholesalers in St. Louis or Chicago. The Arthur Auction Company is not owned by the Amish but is much patronized by them, especially on the days when horses are sold. Says Fleming: "Anyone who wishes to observe the Amish men and boys in a spontaneous public situation should attend the horse auction."[16]

In view of demographic pressure on the land and objections on religious grounds, one can understand that the Amish do not participate in crop reduction programs of the government.[17]

Compared, for example, to the Old Colony Mennonites of Mexico, the Amish from Arthur and elsewhere have not moved as much from country to country to "get away from the world." Most have chosen to face the problem of change right on their home territory, which does involve at times some tension and accommodation, if not compromise. While it is true that some Old Order Amish tend to resist the new simply because it is new, some others' rationale is deeper. They object to too much technology if the technology is not good for the whole group or if it means changing their religious way of life, particularly when the change means putting their people out of work or out of the community.[18]

Nagata is probably correct in saying that the greatest changes among the Arthur Amish are in the economic area. D. Paul Miller, a more recent authority, agrees. For one thing, the detailed rules on the use of technology have never been the same in all Amish districts, whether at Arthur or elsewhere. "A number of Amish communities, for example, now permit the use of tractors for cultivation in limited circumstances; some allow them for all phases of the agricultural cycle; others hardly at all." The same is true of electricity. The Arthur community has seen considerable increase in the use of tractors since World War II. Though they are still prohibited for the major work of disking, plowing, and harvesting, they are used quite universally in the operation of threshing and baling machines, freezers, power saws, welders, feed grinders, mixers and feed dispensers in large chicken and turkey sheds. Those renting from non-Amish landlords may freely use tractors, as well as electricity, trucks, cars, and telephones—on the ground that if this is the only way young people can get started, the concession should be made. Dispensations are now also made in connection with the harvesting of such special crops as soybeans, which the Amish concede can be done more efficiently by the use of power other than horsepower. But even in the harvesting of the traditional wheat and oats, tractors are permitted, says Nagata, "in an excessively wet season when the crop is late and must be cut with all possible speed.... The definition of 'too wet,' however, becomes more flexible as the years go on."[19]

As another symbol for boundary maintenance, the ownership of automobiles is still prohibited at Arthur, although here, too, compromises are made. Amish do not object to riding in the automobiles of others, nor to riding in buses or taxis. In fact, the taxi business in Arthur flourishes. A few Amish may own automobiles under certain conditions: for example, if it is necessary to have one as a condition of tenancy or employment. In a few cases young men, with no economic justification, may manage to own and drive a car but ingeniously refrain from bringing it into the home community. Many I-W boys who served their alternate service in city hospitals or elsewhere had automobiles during that period. How long the Old Order will be able to maintain their determination to use slow-moving buggies in the face of the growing hazard of their appearance on today's highways remains to be seen. Some eighteen years ago already one writer reported that there were many accidents in the Arthur community.[20]

Quite understandably, the changes discussed above have brought tension among the Old Order Amish. For some the changes were too great and too rapid, while for others they were not great enough and came too slowly. This has caused considerable defection from the Old Order in the twentieth century, which has increased the tension, at least temporarily. Even before the appearance of other Mennonite churches in the Arthur area in recent decades, there was some defection. Already in the mid-1890s some dissatisfied members had joined with a few Amish Mennonites from other states in forming an Amish Mennonite congregation, which became a part of the Western District Amish Mennonite Conference. But it became extinct at least by 1915. With the appearance of a Mennonite church in the area in 1936, an even larger number left the Old Order group. In 1945 the Conservative Mennonites organized a congregation near Arthur. A few years later the so-called Beachy Amish Mennonites also started a church. So today the Arthur area is served by three kinds of Mennonites in addition to the Old Order Amish.

These defections have added to the tension brought about by the changes discussed above, which is understandable when one notes the source of membership of the new churches. A table in Nagata, which lists the members as of 1967-68, shows that the Mennonite church had a membership of 212, with 90 percent from the Old Order; the Conservative Mennonites had 173 members, with 99 percent from the Old Order; and the Beachy Amish had 49 members, all of them from the Old Order.[21]

In 1936 when the Mennonite church was started, the tension and the feeling against the new congregation were rather strong. In fact the entire new church was shunned at first. But the effect of the ban was different from what the Amish had planned. The unexpected effect of the shunning was to increase the defection since "some family members followed defected kin into the Mennonite Church merely to avoid loss of social contact with them. Today this is no longer necessary, and most intra-Mennonite evangelism has now disappeared." Shunning declined soon after the Mennonite schism, partly also because of economic factors. The Amish with Mennonite relatives soon became aware that they could benefit from the use of the relatives' automobiles, trucks, telephones, and other machines, but not while a ban was in effect. One observer noted that present-day shunning is usually harder on the Amish than on the defectors. Family reunions have also contributed to the decline of shunning. Reunions between the Amish and their kin in other Mennonite churches, common today, were almost impossible twenty-five years ago. A reunion today, "with its strong emphasis on both commensality and common participation in prayers and hymns of each other's churches, has become a form of ritual activity in itself, with the *Freundschaft* as the unit of reference instead of the cult group." Few Amish families in the Arthur area today refuse full commensality to defected members, publicly or privately. Very likely the decline in shunning is also due in part to the "spirit of the age": less respect for authority, more tolerance, less inter-sect hostility, and more ecumenism.[22]

As to the future of the Old Order Amish at Arthur, these concessions to change certainly do not mean that these people have given up the idea of what sociologists call cultural barriers or boundary maintenance. Far from it. It simply means that the boundaries are being somewhat modified. Quite possibly, as one authority has stated, modification in dress and grooming habits "will be among the last cultural features to change ... as they have enormous boundary-preserving value and in no way impede economic success." This same authority thinks that the Old Order will continue, but that they will be forced to make further accommodations, economically, and that ultimately they "may be indistinguishable technologically from their cash grain, or at least more mechanized non-Amish neighbors." But "it is to be expected that, like the Hutterites in their form of 'controlled acculturation' ..., the Amish will always be able to create sufficient boundaries to assert a certain cultural and social autonomy." He speculates that within a generation possession of automobiles, telephones, and electricity will be permitted, while cultural barriers will be maintained by dress, grooming, language, and "possibly the ritual use of the buggy for church going." They have a future, this same writer predicts, by reason not only of continuing to make economic concessions, but also by continuing to have defections of the more liberal, thus leaving a conservative hard-core to resist extreme changes. The high birth rate of the Amish can counterbalance defections. These are interesting projections and perhaps valid. At least so far they seem to be working out as projected, for, despite defections, the Old Order Amish are still growing in numbers.[23]

In democratic America the Amish have come a long way, at Arthur and elsewhere, since the days of their founder, Jakob Ammann. Though still regarded by some as a public spectacle, the nature of the spectacle has changed from public drownings, hangings, burnings, and beatings in the public arena in the sixteenth century to one that includes being unwilling tourist attractions in their own communities. Says sociologist John A. Hostetler, the Amish near Lancaster in Pennsylvania, "have become the unwilling attraction of a tourist industry that yields over $170,000,000 in Lancaster County." Now often regarded as "objects of merchandise, and theater," touristic "enterprises offer the Amish to travellers as a scarce commodity, a living museum, a quaint sideshow and something worth seeing." The Arthur community has not escaped this commercialism. From 1952-58 the Mennonite Church's mission board operated a place near Arthur called Rockome Gardens, donated by Arthur Martin, as a retirement home for missionaries and other church workers. Unsuccessful in serving this purpose, the place was then sold and the funds used by the Board elsewhere for similar purposes. Elvan Yoder, a Mennonite who had been reared Amish, bought the land and at first intended to farm it. But he soon developed it into a tourist attraction purporting to show the Amish way of life. Taking over and developing further one of the largest private rock and flower gardens in the nation, Yoder and his family have added one attraction after another—some Amish and some not so Amish. The enterprise has become gigantic, with, it is said, hundreds of thousands visiting Rockome Gardens annually.[24]

Many Americans, from the Supreme Court on down, look beyond the quaintness and exoticism to see and appreciate the Amish as a sincere, solid people making up a part of the American mosaic and exemplifying the freedom and liberty which democratic America grants its religious minorities.[25] In all probability the Arthur Amish share the sentiments of a Pennsylvania brother, who wrote about *Wisconsin v. Yoder* as follows:

> It made us humble to read through Chief Justice Burger's opinion. We were made to realize that our way of life is being looked upon and is better known to the outside world than we had ever thought likely. The principles stated, the ideals set forth, and the humble God-fearing people described by the judge in the opinion handed down caused us to reexamine ourselves and wonder if we are really living up to these standards.
>
> Of all the court decisions over the past years, this was the first decision handed down that fully upheld our way of life.[26]

Appreciation for free America has also been shown in a poem written by Amos J. Stoltzfus, which Menno A. Diener from Arthur includes in his book, *History of the Diener Family*. Written before *Wisconsin v. Yoder*, the poem expresses sentiments that would be strengthened by that decision. The latter part goes as follows:

> The undertaking of this voyage we cannot express,
> Over the waves of the sea in hope of success,
> For their children and children, how many they be,
> To live their religion with conscience free.
>   The State Book shows the government agreed
>   For Christians to live as their conscience decreed,
>   So many true Christians left friends and left home
>   And came to America, through woods they did roam,
> To search a good place for their children to live,
> Commune with the brethren in faith, and to give
> Thanks to the good Lord, for answering their plea
> To live with the noble in the land of the free.[27]

Although they have disappeared in Europe, where they originated nearly three centuries ago, the Old Order Amish are still growing and flourishing in the United States and Canada. This is due partly to the religious freedom in these countries. It is due also to land being more available than in Europe, thus allowing the Amish to live in compact settlements where the advantages of community life are more effective in maintaining the Amish faith.[28]

CHAPTER 7

Smaller Mennonite and Related Groups in Illinois

This chapter will discuss the smaller Mennonite groups in Illinois, as well as the General Conference Mennonites, who were a small group in the state until 1957 when they merged with the Central Conference Mennonites. Brief mention will also be made of three similar non-Mennonite bodies—the Missionary Church, the Apostolic Christian, and the Brethren in Christ.

The oldest of these is also the smallest. The Reformed Mennonite Church, sometimes called the "New Mennonites" or "Herrites," has only one congregation, located at Sterling. Its beginnings in Illinois were in 1847, when the first representatives of this branch settled in Whiteside County. Their history goes back to John Herr of Strassburg, Lancaster County, Pennsylvania, who founded the church in 1812. Herr's reasons are not entirely clear. One view is that his father, Francis Herr, was expelled from the Mennonite Church for dishonesty in the sale of a horse. The Reformed view is that Francis, feeling that the old church had departed from the principles of Menno Simons and had become corrupt and spiritually dead, left the church when it refused to reform. In any event, the controversy developed into a polemic in which a clash of personalities, as in too many other cases, helped bring about schism. Daniel Musser, a nineteenth-century Reformed Mennonite historian, recorded a bleak picture of the Mennonites as a dead church and his own group as the one and only true church of Jesus Christ. The members of the old church, he insisted, were "unconverted, carnal people of the world, as all non-professors are." They were lax in maintaining nonresistance, the holy kiss, foot washing and the ban; they engaged in politics, they attended fairs, the young people had their sports on Sunday afternoons (with the older people including ministers as spectators), they drank intoxicating beverages and "often became partially intoxicated, and sometimes considerably more than partially." "The members of the church were," charged Musser, "in regard to inward or spiritual life, as ignorant, cold and dead as any carnal, unconverted person could be." So the old church had become "unbelieving and disobedient, the Holy Spirit no longer dwelt in it, and it became a dead body, nothing different from any other human organization...."[1]

In a book he called *The Mennonite Church and Her Accusers*, John F. Funk vigorously denied Musser's charges. He conceded that some members in the old church were not the moral lights they should have been, and also that some ministers and bishops were less rigid in their administration of church affairs than the gospel required. But he added that if the old church had and has "weaknesses in this direction, the Reformed Mennonite Church had a greater weakness, by endeavoring to display, adorn, and beautify her own perfections by pointing out the imperfections of the Old Church, and basely falsifying and misrepresenting her." "If our light is so dim," Funk continued, "that it will not shine unless we first extinguish our neighbor's, we ought to gather more oil and put it in better trim." And "if a church cannot stand on its own merits, and prove a power and exert an influence on the world without stooping to degrade its neighbors, it proves that the church is not the church of God...."[2]

Soon after Francis Herr left the old church, in about 1800, he began to conduct religious services in his home as a layman. After Francis' death in 1812 his son John was asked to lead the meetings. He was elected pastor and bishop, even though he was not yet baptized. The group elected Abraham Landis to baptize Herr, who in turn administered the rite to Landis and Abraham Groff, as well as to others soon thereafter. They dedicated their first meetinghouse on November 7, 1812. Herr traveled considerably in Pennsylvania and also in western New York and Ontario, where he founded some congregations, mostly of former Mennonites.

As one would expect from the charges they made against the old church, the Reformed Mennonites have been very strict and conservative in their interpretation of nonconformity to the world. They still wear plain clothes, the women wear a head covering at all times, they do not vote in political elections, and they do not attend places of worldly amusements. They also believe that they cannot consistently participate in any form of worship that is not in harmony "with the principles, purity, and simplicity, of the doctrine of Christ." Being interpreted, this means that they cannot attend religious services other than their own. In explaining why they could not worship with others their periodical, *Good Tidings*, stated that they claim that the church is a united body and that divisions are condemned in the Bible. "If they would worship with bodies that sanction divisions they would not bear out this claim, but would by their actions sanction a divided

Church."[3] They do, however, invite others to worship with them. According to their belief, the pure church, meaning their own, is "a city that is set upon a hill which cannot be hid" to which the sin-sick soul may flee as a refuge from earth's vanities. The "poor penitent should have no difficulty in deciding who God's people are, or where the spiritual ark of safety is, in which alone is security against the day when the elements will melt with fervent heat and a fiery wave shall usher in the closing scene."[4]

However, the problem of seeing the city "set upon a hill" and the difficulty of deciding "where the spiritual ark of safety is" must have been greater than what the writer of the above anticipated; for the number of those who have found this city of refuge has been very small. The membership of the entire church, probably never exceeding 2500, has steadily declined during the last seventy years. In 1948 there were twenty-four congregations in the United States with 733 members, and six congregations in Canada with 217 members—a total of 950. In 1958 the membership in the United States was 616, and in Canada 211. Pennsylvania, with ten, had the most congregations; Ohio had five; Indiana, Michigan, Illinois, and New York had one each; and Canada had six. Incidentally, Milton S. Hershey, the Pennsylvania chocolate king, came from Reformed Mennonite ranks. Though never a member himself, his mother was, and his grandfather, Abram Snavely, was a bishop.[5]

In some of their ways like the Old Order Amish, the Reformed Mennonites have confined their religious services largely to Sunday morning meetings. They have no Sunday schools, young people's work, revival meetings, or missions. According to them Sunday schools use questionable methods; children or young people who attend might have a feeling of righteousness that could easily make them less open to conversion. The only paper the Reformed Mennonites ever published was *Good Tidings*, a quarterly printed from 1922 to 1932 at Lancaster, Pennsylvania. Unlike the Old Order Amish, however, they have church houses and such modern conveniences as electricity, telephones, automobiles, trucks, and tractors.[6]

The first of the Reformed Mennonites came to Sterling in the late 1840s. Among the early settlers were such names as Baer, Beiler, Buhler, Delp, Henricks, Kratz, Landis, Reinhart, Shultz, and Watson. A fair number were already there by the time of the dreadful cholera epidemic in 1854. Jacob and John Landis, sons of Abraham Landis, of Lancaster County, Pennsylvania, who helped organize the Reformed Mennonite Church, were among those struck, and probably no other family suffered as much as this Landis family. According to a story in the Sterling *Daily Gazette*, Jacob Landis contracted the disease in July 1854 while on a trip to Rockford to purchase a reaper. He recovered but remained an invalid until his death in 1857. The blow was made heavier by the death of his wife, six children, his brother John, and some other relatives.[7]

No respecter of persons, the plague struck the entire community, Mennonite and non-Mennonite. At first the diminished Reformed Mennonites held services in their homes, and in the 1860s they organized as a congregation. In 1867, for $1200, they built a small, plain, frame church building, which somewhat remodeled is still used today. According to several authorities, the membership, never large, was sixty-five around 1870, about forty in the 1920s, fifty-two in 1958 and between thirty-five and forty-five as of 1980. Clearly, most young people do not become members. In this the congregation is typical of other Reformed Mennonites. So long as the children and young people are not members they are permitted and probably are expected to live like other young people, and so are allowed social and cultural contacts with the rest of the community.

"The radical transformation from this free and easy way of life," says one authority, "to the rather rigid regulations of membership no doubt accounts partially for the fact that so few of the children of Reformed Mennonite parentage join the church of their fathers."[8]

Like other Reformed Mennonites, the Sterling congregation

Source: Mennonite Historical Library, Goshen, Ind.

Reformed Mennonite Church, built in 1867, in Sterling, Illinois, ca. 1929. A good example of classic Mennonite church architecture.

selects its ministers from its own ranks by majority vote. They serve unsalaried and with no special training. These ministers—in 1979 Elmer Sedig and Wilmer Schwank—do not prepare sermons; instead, they do extensive reading from the Bible and from inspirational literature, and meditate and reflect in the time available. When called upon to speak they believe that God will give them "the gift of expression." Though the pastors are not salaried, the "congregation should always be concerned so that the pastor should not be in need." The bishop with oversight over Sterling resides in Shelby, Michigan. The congregation practices the ban and shunning. Minister Sedig summed up the work of the Sterling church as follows:

> The church must be the light to the world. This is the highest calling that the church as an organization can present to the world. I believe that this is the position that the church has taken down through all the ages. I like to think that the church in Sterling has continued to this day to display that purpose as an organization before its fellow man and the world.[9]

As Reformed Mennonites settled at Sterling, other Mennonites, who would eventually join the General Conference branch, migrated just a few miles east of St. Louis to the area of Summerfield in St. Clair County, Illinois. In 1842 the Conrad Schrag and John Wittmer families moved on farms northwest of Summerfield near O'Fallon. Others soon came, including some from the Palatinate in Germany. Some of the Germans came directly; others sojourned briefly in Lee County, Iowa. Because of the large number from Lee County in the 1850s and 1860s, the Summerfield church had much in common with the Iowa churches and cooperated with them in conference work. Among early settlers who were to become important as workers and leaders in the General Conference Mennonite Church were Daniel Hege, the Ruths, Jacob and Christian Krehbiel, Michael Eicher, Daniel Hirschler, S. S. Haury, David Goerz, Bernhard Warkentin, and others.[10]

The Ruths, Krehbiels, and Haurys came by way of Iowa. A detailed graphic account survives of the hardships and anxieties they endured in coming from the German Palatinate and Bavaria to the Midwest in 1852. The long monotonous sea journey by sailing ship required fifty-two days. Twelve deaths en route included one of the Mennonite party. Other tragedies and near-tragedies followed. In New York Susan Ruth, later the wife of Christian Krehbiel, "would have been kidnapped, had it not been prevented by the watchful eye of the hotel keeper." From New York City the party went to Albany by boat and from Albany to Buffalo by train. At Buffalo, upon hearing the terrible word "cholera," they left as soon as possible by ship on Lake Erie for Toledo. But their leaving was not soon enough. A Mr. Lehman, who was already ill with the disease, boarded the ship and died within ten hours. The body was taken ashore in a rude box "and the boat continued the trip with the family." From Toledo they continued the journey by train to Chicago: The group had to travel part of the way in freight cars, and "once the train stood from morning to evening on the main track, and once all night on a side track." After a stopover in Chicago long enough for the women to wash "the most necessary things" in Lake Michigan, the journey continued on the Illinois-Michigan Canal and the Illinois River to Peoria. Originally the party intended to go on to Summerfield, Illinois, by way of St. Louis.[11] But when they heard that cholera was prevalent there, they went to southeastern Iowa instead. Widow Lehman and her children went to Ft. Madison by carriage and en route suffered more tragedy—the death and burial of her youngest son. In addition, the group at times felt the indignities meted out to foreigners by members of the American Nativist movement then on the rise. As the writer of the article, Jacob Ernest Ruth, has well said, "What a journey like this must have meant for the mother to lose her husband and youngest child on the way and to have to leave them behind in unknown graves," and facing alone an unknown future in an unknown land, "one can hardly imagine without having experienced it oneself!" Ruth has also said that at West Point, Iowa, his own grandfather and two-year old sister died, "both from the consequences of the hardships of the journey, which took three months." Whatever the truth of this last statement, the facts are clear that uprooting from the old homeland, saying good-bye to loved ones and friends whom the emigrants would likely not see again, and facing the hardships of a three-month journey on land and sea to a new and unknown country required the highest kind of courage and resolution.[12]

The group held its first preaching service at Summerfield in 1856, in the home of Christian Baer. The first church building was completed in 1859, at which time Daniel Hege was called from Iowa to be the first minister. In the 1860s and 1870s Hege and his successors, Jacob and Christian Krehbiel and other members, made Summerfield a focal point in General Conference history. Hege, nudged a bit by Christian Krehbiel, made some history in his own congregation. Krehbiel, who moved to Summerfield from West Point, Iowa, in 1860, states in his autobiography that the Summerfield Mennonites, from different congregations in Europe, "had not yet established a definite church organization. A feeble church union resulted, with no church role and no rules." He decided not to join the church "until some stable arrangement had been made by Daniel Hege." A resolution was then put to a vote by all those who wished to become members. "It affirmed that any Mennonite man or woman who signed would be a member, regardless of previous home or past record. But only those who signed would be members." As was often the case at that time, women could not sign, "but a minister could sign for them upon their request. This served," concluded Krehbiel, "to give the church a firm foundation. Our family now became members of the Summerfield Mennonite Church."[13]

Under Hege's leadership the congregation aligned itself with the new General Conference of Mennonites of North America, which was organized at West Point, Iowa in 1860. This organization developed partly from a conflict among the Mennonites in eastern Pennsylvania in which one of the ministers, John H. Oberholtzer, found himself dissatisfied with many customs and methods of the Mennonite church of his time and place. Among these were the requirement to wear the ministerial collarless coat, and especially the lack of a written constitution and keeping of minutes in the conference. Thinking that a constitution and minutes were necessary to prevent arbitrary action by a few, Oberholtzer proposed them to the conference but was turned down. By October 1847 this refusal led to the division. Oberholtzer led in the formation of a new conference in the East; then in 1860 he was one who helped organize the General Conference at West Point.[14]

In 1861 Hege was sent as a delegate to the second meeting of the conference, at Wadsworth, Ohio, and was elected conference secretary. Even more important was his work as apologist for three causes: missions, Christian higher education, and unity. If Mennonites are not to increase their guilt, he said at the conference, they must no longer neglect "the duty of missions as commanded by the Lord." But if we undertake mission work, he continued, "we first need Christian educational institutions." And that requires money—"much money, and for that churchwide participation and unremitting sacrifice is required as well as unity." To best provide for this, Hege proposed the appointment of a *Reiseprediger*, an itinerant preacher, to travel among the churches promoting these causes. The conference adopted his suggestion and could think of no better candidate for the position than Hege himself. He was selected unanimously.[15]

In 1862, speaking in the churches from Pennsylvania to Iowa, Hege successfully advanced the three causes. He spoke effectively for the union of Mennonites as provided in the new General Conference plan and tied it to higher education and missions in these words: ". . . above all things we need for the beginning at least one Christian Mennonite educational institution both as a foundation of union among our Mennonite divisions and also for the spreading of the kingdom of God which was commanded us as the last will of our Savior."[16] Unfortunately, Hege contracted typhoid fever near the end of his tour, returned home seriously ill, and died on November 30. But he had accomplished much. According to the leading conference historian it is "hard to overestimate the value of Hege's services" for the three causes. John H. Oberholtzer testified that "if the aims of the general conference ... are ever accomplished, then Brother Hege stands forever as one of the first men who helped break through the opposition. Through his tour as well as through the written plans for developing this Mennonite project, he will always remain in the thoughts of the Mennonite denomination in America."[17]

Though influential in bringing about Wadsworth Institute, Hege did not live to see the rise of this pioneer Mennonite college. Another member from Summerfield who worked for a church school and helped locate it at Wadsworth in Ohio was Christian Krehbiel. The General Conference session of 1863, held at Summerfield, discussed and decided the location. Though not a delegate to the conference, Krehbiel attended as a visitor and added his bit. During a pause in the discussion he politely asked whether those not delegates might also speak to the question. Chairman John H. Oberholtzer readily consented. Krehbiel then spoke, as he says, in his deep bass voice, "The school should be built in the center of the Mennonite population. Today Ohio is the center.... I propose Wadsworth." And Wadsworth it was. Since a building had to be constructed and a faculty secured, the school did not open until January 2, 1868. Because of various problems it operated for only ten years. Apparently not all the congrega-

Source: Krehbiel, Prairie Pioneer.

First Mennonite Church, near Summerfield, Ill., used by the Summerfield congregation 1859-1911, and shown as it appeared in 1864.

tions supported it as fully as did Summerfield, which provided students and more than its share of money.[18]

Because of the absence of Hege from Summerfield on long trips, followed by his death, there was a need for new ministers in his congregation. Daniel Hirschler was selected and shortly thereafter Jacob Krehbiel. But Krehbiel's eyesight soon began to fail and he returned to Iowa. The lot fell next on Christian, Jacob's brother, who a little later also became elder. From the time that Christian Krehbiel became minister in 1864 until he moved to Kansas in 1879 his leadership, according to one writer, "overshadowed or dominated the many activities of his church. He was active in the Conference, [and] in the Wadsworth school." And he "was foremost in the expediting of the Russian migration to Kansas from 1873 through 1877," working closely with John F. Funk in this labor of love.[19]

Krehbiel became a top leader not only in his congregation, but in the entire church. He and his wife, Susanna (Ruth), had sixteen children, twelve of whom grew to adulthood, with three sons becoming ministers. In 1868 while still at Summerfield he helped found the Western District Conference (now the Middle District) and in 1877 he helped organize what became the Western District. Under his guidance S. S. Haury from Summerfield became the first missionary sent out by General Conference Mennonites. Although Haury had offered his services earlier to go abroad, an opening for that did not occur, so he later went to work among the Indians in Indian Territory (Oklahoma). This missionary interest had already led in 1872 to the organization of the Foreign Mission Board, of which Krehbiel served as president for twenty-four years. An ardent believer in education, he supported not only Wadsworth Institute, but after he moved to Kansas in 1879 he also promoted plans which brought about Halstead Seminary and Bethel College.

While still at Summerfield, Krehbiel became deeply involved in the settling of Russian Mennonites, and a few from other countries, in America in the 1870s. Through visits from and correspondence with Russian Mennonites prior to the migration, he was familiar with the changing conditions in Russia and with the Mennonite reaction to new orders from the Russian government concerning military duty. Earlier Krehbiel had replied to a letter written by Cornelius Jansen from Russia, which inquired about conditions in America. Jansen's letter had actually been sent to Daniel Hege, but arrived after the pastor's death. As a matter of fact Jansen had been corresponding with several leaders in America, including John F. Funk, who was known in Russia through his *Herold der Wahrheit*. Krehbiel, to whom Jansen's letter to Hege had been given, decided it had to be answered. He stated later: "Out of that decision there grew my extensive participation in the immigration of European Mennonites to America."

The effect was to make Summerfield, along with Elkhart, Indiana, one of the important stations on the route of Russian Mennonite migration to the Western states. Krehbiel and his congregation helped the wayfarers immensely, and he also went with early deputations to Kansas and other states to spy out the land. To aid the Russian Mennonites, various organizations were formed, including the Mennonite Board of Guardians. Of that board Krehbiel was chairman; John F. Funk, treasurer; David Goerz, secretary; and Bernhard Warkentin, traveling agent. Both Goertz and Warkentin were Russian Mennonites who lived for some time at Summerfield. Goertz, as well as Krehbiel, operated from there during the main migrations in 1874.[20]

Even before the coming of the Russian Mennonites, Krehbiel had advocated Mennonite colonization farther west. The coming of the Russians and his aid in their search for land increased his interest, especially in Kansas. He recorded that he had "noticed the good land in

Source: Elinor Krehbiel Kreider, Goshen, Ind., and Robert Krehbiel, Hutchinson, Kan.

Christian Krehbiel (1832-1909), a minister of the Summerfield congregation from 1864 to 1879; photo taken in 1861, about a year after he moved from Iowa to Illinois.

the vicinity of Halstead, Kansas," and that a later journey confirmed his favorable impression. The upshot was that a number of Mennonites from Summerfield moved to Kansas. Bernhard Warkentin was the first, in 1873, followed by others, including David Goerz in 1875 and Krehbiel in 1879. The removal of a substantial number of members together with these enthusiastic, able leaders was a serious loss for Summerfield. It never recovered. From "its early place as one of the largest congregations in the conference, it became smaller and eventually weak, but its vitality was transferred to a most strategic place for future growth."[21]

Despite the loss, the congregation continued to be a viable, effective organization for many years. In addition to the Sunday school which had been started already in 1865—probably the first Mennonite one in Illinois—the women organized a Mission Society in 1877, and the pastor, C. H. A. van der Smissen, took the initiative in founding a Christian Endeavor Society in 1890. The congregation built a parsonage in 1906 and purchased a larger meetinghouse from the Methodists in 1910. Unfortunately, this parsonage, along with the valuable church records and historical documents, was destroyed by fire in 1928. Despite vicissitudes the membership has held up fairly well until recently. According to the *General Conference Mennonite Handbook of Information*, the membership was 140 in 1898, the same in 1931, 156 in 1940, 96 in 1952, 112 in 1960 and 1965. Since 1969, when it was 109, the membership has declined rapidly to fewer than thirty. The congregation is now without a locally resident minister. George Dick of Bloomington preaches for the group.[22]

The only other General Conference Mennonite activity in Illinois prior to the merger with the Central Conference Mennonites grew out of mission and seminary work in Chicago. What became the First Mennonite Church of Chicago was started as a mission in 1914, with W. W. Miller, pastor from Pulaski, Iowa, as its first leader. Beginning as a rescue mission on Sixty-third Street near Halstead, in 1915 it was moved in search of more adequate quarters. In 1918 it moved to Seventy-third and Laflin, where a church building was constructed. But no formal organization of the congregation occurred until December 1921 when twenty-two people became charter members. In his *Seventy-third and Laflin* Leland Harder provides a brief but insightful history of the success and severe problems of the church. It appears that the problems were the greatest and the survival of the church most questionable in the early 1930s when William C. Rhea was minister. Since he was inclined to be dictatorial, misunderstandings and internal disharmony increased for several years. Matters reached a crisis when Rhea "with a large per cent of the congregation withdrew and started their own congregation and ... Rhea and his family left the city." The General Conference Board was successful in getting the veteran mission worker, A. Hershey Leaman, to come in and put the pieces together again. Leaman had earlier been superintendent of the Mennonite Home Mission (MC) for over twenty years. His success was amazing. Under him the membership grew in a few years from "probably less than 50" to 147.

But by 1940 the General Conference Mission Board felt that Leaman was not able to give its cause as much time as they had hoped. In that year, at their request, he resigned at the end of his first term. Then after a term served by Ervin A. Albrecht, Leaman was asked to return as pastor in 1946. This remarkable servant continued until illness forced him to resign in 1949. He died in 1950.[23]

Although slow in reaching independence, eventually the congregation took on more of the character of a city church and less of a mission, especially under the ministry of Leland Harder in the 1950s. Harder was the first full-time pastor. Partly as a result of this experience he, with Peter Ediger, prepared some guidelines on "Church Extension Policies" for the General Conference Mennonite Church. The guidelines emphasized that no matter where it was located every congregation, new or old, was a "home mission" congregation "sharing in the privilege and responsibility of ministering for Christ in its particular area." Also the guidelines considered every pastor a "home mission" pastor, "sharing the same responsibility of the pastoral ministry, whether serving a new church partially dependent on the Conference for support or whether serving an older established congregation." Thus the distinction between "churches" and "missions" was quite properly diminished if not wholly done away with.[24]

A second work in Chicago to come under the administration of the General Conference was a Mennonite Bible Mission opened by Abraham F. Wiens in 1917, in the 4200 block of South Rockwell Street. It later became the Grace Mennonite Church. As frequently happened in such outreach efforts, services, especially evening services, "were often disturbed by the loud pounding on the door and noises outside. Sometimes the noisy group came inside and it was then quite a problem to keep order." For a people from peaceful rural areas, unacquainted with the city and its people of completely different social and religious backgrounds, such experiences were "interesting" and challenging, to say the least. But persistence and patience paid off. John T. Neufeld arrived from Kansas to study in Chicago in the early twenties and assisted in the work. He married a daughter of Wiens, became Wiens' successor, and for forty years "was the best-known pastor in the community." In 1939 he proposed that the General Conference take over the responsibility for the mission through its Home

Smaller Mennonite and Related Groups 157

Missions Board, and the Board accepted. Though like First Mennonite the congregation has never been large, and though it is still not fully self-supporting, its contribution to the community through its various services is unquestionable. At one time twenty nationalities were represented in its daily vacation Bible school.[25]

A third General Conference church in Chicago, Woodlawn, grew out of seminary work carried on in the city in affiliation with Bethany Biblical Seminary, an institution of the Church of the Brethren. This was another chapter in the seminary training program begun at Bluffton College in the 1910s and carried on by Witmarsum Theological Seminary from 1921-1931. Under the leadership of Abraham Warkentin and other General Conference and Central Conference leaders the Mennonite Biblical Seminary opened its doors in Chicago in September 1945. After one year on the Bethany campus the Mennonite seminary established its own quarters in the 4600 block of South Woodlawn Avenue, but students commuted to Bethany for classes. Students and staff of the seminary operated a Sunday school. After several years the work evolved into the Woodlawn Mennonite Church, organized as a congregation in 1951. It was located at 1143 East Forty-Sixth Street, where the seminary had been able to buy a church building from another denomination. J. N. Smucker was the first pastor. In 1959 the congregation had fifty-one members, with Delton Franz as pastor and Vincent G. Harding as associate pastor. After some years of promise and prosperity, the church's history was marked by vicissitudes which will be discussed in a later chapter.[26]

Another small Mennonite group in Illinois is the Conservative Mennonites, or Conservative Amish Mennonites, as they were called prior to 1954. This group was organized in 1910 at Pigeon, Michigan, with a position between the more progressive Amish Mennonites on the one hand and the more conservative Old Order Amish on the other. The middle group, while retaining a conservative position on dress and some other matters, was more ready to use modern technology than were the Old Order Amish. Moreover, they were developing convictions for missions, evangelism, Sunday schools, church buildings, publication, education, and other agencies or institutions that might help advance the cause of Christianity. The Conservative Mennonite Conference has grown from less than 500 in 1910 to 4259 in 1954 and 7225 in 1978.[27]

In Illinois the congregations affiliated with this conference are of fairly recent origin. They are in the vicinity of Arthur, where they have stemmed pretty largely from the Old Order Amish. A few of its members belonged to the local Mennonite church for a time. Apparently the Mennonite congregation became too progressive for those who left; in the words of a few, the Arthur Mennonites became lax on Mennonite doctrines and threw them "out of the door."[28] One study of the late 1960s shows that 99 percent of the Conservative Mennonites at Arthur came from the Old Order Amish.[29] The first congregation was organized in 1945 with a membership of eight. Shem Peachey of Springs, Pennsylvania, had ministerial charge for a short time, followed by Eli Swartzentruber of Greenwood, Delaware. In 1947 a local man, Levi M. Miller, was ordained for that position. The membership was 45 in 1953, and in 1978 there were two congregations—Sunnyside with 91 and Quinn with 52.[30]

Another group of Illinois churches sometimes associated with the Conservative (Amish) Mennonites, but really unaffiliated, is the Kauffman or "Sleeping Preacher" group. These originated about 1907 under the influence and leadership of John D. Kauffman, who was noted for his preaching while apparently in a trance. Born in Logan County, Ohio, in 1847, Kauffman lived most of his life in Elkhart County, Indiana, but moved to Shelbyville, Illinois, where he lived until he died in 1913. He was an unordained and self-appointed "preacher" for years until he was finally ordained at Shelbyville in 1911 by Peter Zimmerman of Linn Township Amish Mennonite Church near Roanoke. Kauffman was a controversial figure not only because of his trance preaching but because of some of his views and practices. His biographer, Pius Hostetler, has conceded he had his weaknesses. In fact, Hostetler thought he "may have been one of the weaker ones," although adding that "God hath chosen the weak things ... that he might confound the mighty." Hostetler defends Kauffman against the charge of drinking by saying he used strong drink for his health's sake on the advice of his doctor. He smoked tobacco for the same reason. "The Lord's ways are not our ways and He no doubt so ordered these things," adds the biographer.[31]

Kauffman's controversial trance preaching was an awe-inspiring phenomenon that attracted large, curious crowds of believers and doubters. The present writer remembers when he, as a child of perhaps six or eight in his home congregation (Roanoke), heard Kauffman on one of these occasions. Too young to be a believer or doubter, the child was struck only with the novelty of the situation and the large, curious crowd. Kauffman would preach in the evenings in his sleep, and his messages were regarded by his followers as coming from the Holy Spirit, hence the term "Spirit preaching." After his ordination, according to a follower named Adam Schrock, Kauffman preached "to us every two weeks in day time (with eyes open) with the same power that he does after night, having no respect of persons, but cuts right through with the Sword of the Spirit."[32]

Long before Kauffman moved to Illinois, two able Mennonite leaders heard and commented on the preaching of Kauffman and of another sleeping preacher, Noah Troyer, from Iowa. On several occasions John F. Funk wrote about them in his *Herald of Truth.* On March 2, 1882, Funk went to see and hear Kauffman, who was then living near Goshen, Indiana. In his detailed report in the *Herald* of March 15, 1882, Funk stated that Kauffman was "highly respected both as a Christian and as a man." When Funk arrived there at about six-thirty in the evening, Kauffman was already "under the power of the spasm as it must properly be designated." These spasms, states the report, came on him regularly every Wednesday evening, although when he was away from home they might come on other evenings. At first lying rigid on the floor, Kauffman would relax somewhat when the audience started singing. He then prayed and, after being helped to his feet, he started preaching in German, telling the story of salvation beginning with creation. After speaking quite a while he stopped, prayed in a low voice, and then began speaking in English, repeating mainly what he had said in German, with further elaboration on some points and even switching back sometimes to German. Several times he stopped and gave signs which his attendants understood to mean that he wanted water. In the traditional Amish way he even asked the ministers present to give testimony to his remarks, which some did. After the service Kauffman's attendants carried him to his bed, where he slept until morning, knowing or remembering "nothing of what he did or said." Funk concluded, "There are a great many singular things that men do while in a somnambulistic condition, but for a man to have a recurrence of such spasm regularly each week, upon a certain night and under its influence to preach the word of God, and warn sinners to flee from the wrath to come, and to keep himself within the range of propriety and a certain creed or doctrine, is certainly one of the remarkable things of the age." And so it was![33]

Historian J. C. Wenger has stated that Kauffman, like Troyer, had some source of information beyond the five senses. When preaching in 1886 "at the very moment when a gun exploded for Noah Troyer in Iowa as he was trying to shoot a chicken," Kauffman "interrupted his discourse to announce the death of Troyer, who was for him a brother beloved." A few days later word came verifying Troyer's accidental death. Wenger cited another occasion in which Kauffman is supposed to have received a supersensory message. While preaching at Hopedale he suddenly interrupted his sermon to remark that Bishop John Smith had just driven onto the church grounds. A few minutes later Smith opened the church door and walked in![34]

John S. Coffman, associated with Funk in the work at Elkhart, heard Noah Troyer preach at the Prairie Street Church in Elkhart on August 25, 1880. After going to the church about five o'clock in the evening, Troyer lay and slept on a bed for some time. Then after praying in German and English he stood up with assistance and began to preach in his sleep, first in German for twenty minutes and then in English for thirty-seven minutes. Following his sermon, in which he spoke on various incidents in Christ's life and made applications, he was laid on his bed from which he was taken on a cot to a nearby home, where he slept soundly until four o'clock the next morning. Some thought Troyer was an impostor. But Coffman disagreed and thought no one "would fail to be convinced of his honesty, if he were present and would carefully watch him from the beginning of the strange phenomena, but for one night."[35]

In Illinois Kauffman was more influential than was Troyer, but this influence extended only among his rather small following. Among the Amish Mennonites in general his influence decreased as time went on. A small group followed him from Indiana to Shelbyville in 1907, where they started the Mt. Hermon Amish Mennonite Church, and where he was ordained bishop in 1911. Even the bishop who ordained him was a controversial character, having had his troubles with his own Roanoke congregation. Feeling called to the office of bishop and not being given it at Roanoke, he went to Shelbyville to be ordained by Bishop John R. Zook, who came from Pennsylvania for the occasion.

In addition to those who followed him from Indiana, a few other like-minded individuals from other areas joined Kauffman's movement at Shelbyville. Never large, the Mt. Hermon congregation reached a peak membership of 85 in 1930. In 1954 the membership was 45 and in 1977, it was 41. Joseph Reber was chosen minister in 1912 to assist Kauffman and was ordained bishop in 1914, following Kauffman's death the previous year. Under Reber's leadership the church progressed harmoniously until about 1933. Though the church followed a conservative line, differences over the particulars of nonconformity arose at that time, resulting in a division.[36]

The Fairfield Amish Mennonite Church near Tampico came into existence as a result of this Mt. Hermon division. Levi C. Hostetler, a minister and leader of a more conservative faction, led his group out of the Mt. Hermon Church. At first the new group established its own fellowship in the same community, meeting for a short time in homes for services and then remodeling a building for that purpose. But in 1937 three families of the Levi C. Hostetler group moved to Henry County in northwestern Illinois, where they rented farms from a large landowner, Joseph Gingerich of Kalona, Iowa. In 1938 the remainder of Hostetler's fellowship followed. After again meeting initially in homes for services, the congregation erected a meetinghouse in 1940 at Anawan. In 1944 they dismantled the building and reerected and enlarged it at its present site in Bureau County, not far south of Tampico.

Located in the tri-county area which includes parts of Henry, Bureau, and Whiteside, the Fairfield congregation has flourished despite some divisions. The Levi C. Hostetler family has provided most of the leadership. In 1964 the church divided over the perennial issue of application of the ban, about half of the group then moving to Buffalo, Missouri. In 1975 twenty-two families moved to Nashville, Arkansas. This removal was not because of differences in faith or practice but for economic reasons. In spite of these withdrawals the membership as of 1978 was about 135, with weekly church attendance close to 200. Although the Hostetlers continued to be important leaders in the congregation—Herman as bishop and Ova as minister—Raymond Kauffman and William Schrock shared in the ministry, with Joseph Kropf as a deacon. While the Fairfield church "holds to the basic precepts of all Mennonites," it is "more conservative in forms of worship, education, attire, lack of Sunday school, and usage of the German language in services."[37]

A third unaffiliated Amish Mennonite church in Illinois, often associated with Mt. Hermon and Fairfield, is the Linn Township Church located about six miles northwest of Roanoke. Locally, it is sometimes called the "Kennell" church, after several Kennell families who supplied much of the leadership and membership. It was organized about 1910. Shortly before that, Peter Zimmerman, a minister, and forty members had withdrawn from the Roanoke congregation because they wished to adhere more rigidly than the congregation desired to the old practice of shunning members under the ban. Another factor was that Roanoke failed to recognize or accept Zimmerman's ordination to the office of bishop, which had occurred at Shelbyville in 1909. After first meeting for services in a remodeled farm home, the congregation built a meetinghouse in 1916. The group is often associated with the "Sleeping Preacher" churches because Zimmerman and others had come under the influence of John D. Kauffman.

Those serving as ministers in the Linn Township Church, in addition to Zimmerman, include John W. Kennell, Joseph J. Kennell (bishop), D. M. Hostetler (bishop), John E. Hostetler (bishop), Harold D. Hostetler, and Ervin Hostetler.

In recent decades a considerable number from this congregation have rejoined the Mennonite churches in the area. According to the 1980 *Mennonite Yearbook* the membership was 123. Like Mt. Hermon and Fairfield, Linn is independent or congregational in church government. Though unaffiliated with any conference, the three congregations "hold fairly well to the same nature or order of practice in church life." Linn, like the others, cooperates to a degree with other Mennonite churches in such services as relief and disaster work. But they still do not have Sunday schools or mission work. Hence, though formerly closely associated with the Conservative Amish Mennonites, the latter have advanced much further in aggressive Christian service. For example, Milton Otto, from one of the Conservative Mennonite congregations at Arthur, spent four months visiting churches throughout the conference in promoting the cause of missions. Unlike Fairfield, which is the most conservative of the three, Linn gave up the use of the German language in their services some years ago.[38]

The Krimmer Mennonite Brethren Church is another small group in Illinois. It started mission work in Chicago in 1914 when D. M. and Mrs. Hofer and Joseph W. and Mrs. Tschetter opened the Lincoln Avenue Gospel Mission. The Krimmer Mennonite Brethren church had its origin in the Crimea, South Russia, in 1869. During a religious revival these Mennonites sought a deeper experience in conversion and emphasized triune immersion forward as the proper form of baptism. They were called *Krimmer* (Crimean) to distinguish them from the Mennonite Brethren founded in Russia in 1860. But like the Mennonite Brethren they emphasized conversion, assurance, and Christian experience. The Krimmer have probably been more conservative. Always a small group, virtually all of them followed their

Source: Archives of the Mennonite Church.   Source: Oyer, *What Hath God Wrought?*

Left: David M. Hofer (1869-1944), superintendent of the Lincoln Avenue Gospel Mission (now Lakeview Mennonite Brethren Church) of the Krimmer Mennonite Brethren, 1915-1944.

Right: George P. Schultz (1880-1957), superintendent of Happy Hour Mission, 1908-1916, and of Hoyne Avenue Mission, 1916-1951.

Smaller Mennonite and Related Groups 163

leader, Jacob A. Wiebe, to Kansas in 1874. As time went on they worked more and more closely with the Mennonite Brethren and the two groups finally merged in 1957.

Despite their conservatism, the group had a missionary spirit. They were the first Mennonites to open mission work among black Americans—in North Carolina in 1886. This same spirit led to the work in Chicago. Hofer was a student at Moody Bible Institute when he saw in the city a need for work. Tschetter, a brother-in-law who had been doing mission work in North Carolina, came to join him. In 1915 these two men also became joint founders of *Der Wahrheitsfreund*, published in Chicago. This periodical served as the conference paper until 1947, when the *Christian Witness* became the conference organ. Thus missionary and publishing work were carried on together in two adjoining buildings, and the mission workers, including Hofer as editor, helped in the printing and mailing of the paper. As of 1953 the mission was not an organized congregation, although several families made it their regular church home. Hofer apparently did not keep careful, accurate records of attendance and membership. Said Hofer: "It is very hard to keep records in the city. Anyway the Lord knows it all. It will come out in eternity." In the late 1930s he gave the figure of 150 for the membership, but one authority thought that a high estimate. The theological orientation of the mission has been toward Moody evangelicalism. But the missionaries have also cooperated in a number of activities with other Mennonites in the city.[39]

The Defenseless Mennonite Brethren of Christ in North America, since 1937 called the Evangelical Mennonite Brethren, had one mission church in Illinois. This was the Brighton Mennonite Church in Chicago, started in 1907 by Abraham F. Wiens and his wife, Katherine, at Hoyne Avenue and Thirty-third Street. Since then it has been located at several different places and under several different names, the mission eventually moved to Thirty-fourth Place and Wolcott Avenue, where in 1919 the conference had purchased a formerly Congregational Church building. In 1916 Wiens terminated his connection with the mission and the conference appointed George P. Schultz as pastor. Wiens then established the Grace Mennonite Church at 4221 South Rockwell Street, where he continued to serve as one of the outstanding Mennonite mission and church workers of Chicago.

With the change in administration from Wiens to Schultz, the earlier Wiens mission changed its name to Brighton Mission Chapel. Later, it changed to Brighton Mission Church, and finally to Brighton Mennonite Church. It experienced good growth, making it necessary to secure larger facilities. George P. Schultz and other members of his family became outstanding Mennonite leaders in Chicago and the state, as well as elsewhere. After moving to Chicago in 1907 from

Saskatchewan, Canada, to attend Moody Bible Institute, he became superintendent of the Happy Hour Mission in 1908, a position he held until 1914. During this time he studied also at the Chicago Theological Seminary and Northern Baptist Theological Seminary. In addition, he assisted at the Salem Gospel Mission and the Mennonite Home Mission, which was indeed a training school for many mission and church workers.

At the new location the Brighton church expanded its ministry and added many new members to the church roll. A report for 1938 indicates 160 members, and a later report says that the Sunday school enrollment was over 300. Included among its members was Dr. Arnold C. Schultz, son of the pastor, who became a specialist in Near Eastern studies and taught, among other places, at Bluffton College, Northern Baptist Theological Seminary, Winona Lake School of Theology, and Roosevelt University.

Recent decades have seen a marked decline in the attendance and membership of the church. In the 1950s George P. Schultz stated that "the shifting of population and changes in religious trends of the newcomers caused a 50 per cent decrease in the Sunday-school attendance and church membership."[40] Since that report, church statistics indicate a still greater decline. Following Schultz's retirement in 1951, a number of pastors served the church for much shorter periods until it closed in 1976.[41]

A Mennonite group appearing recently in Illinois on a small scale is the Beachy Amish Mennonite, a branch with origins in a division among the Old Order Amish in the 1920s in Salisbury, Pennsylvania. Bishop Moses M. Beachy refused to observe the Old Order rule to ban and avoid those members who had left his congregation to join the Conservative Amish Mennonite church near Grantsville, Maryland. By 1927 Sunday school, electricity, and automobiles had also become issues. The Beachy Amish permit electricity, automobiles, tractors, meetinghouses, and Sunday schools. In general, they are still quite "Amish" or conservative in dress, and until recently they used German in their worship. They are increasingly missionary-minded.[42]

According to Lois Fleming, the Beachy Amish organized a congregation at Arthur in 1957. She says that if a person there is dressed like an Amishman and driving a car he is probably of the Beachy group. They prefer black automobiles, but, she adds, "it is not always practical to insist on that detail." Their meetinghouse is located about five-and-one-half miles southeast of Arthur. In 1961 they had 40 members; by 1980 they could report 150. These members have come almost wholly from the Old Order Amish, although recently a few left the local Mennonites to join them. Now faced with a greater choice, those contemplating leaving the Old Order at Arthur are more likely to join either the Conservative Mennonites or Beachy Amish than to join the Mennonites, because the break with their past is less sharp. As of 1980, Sam Petersheim is bishop and Dannie Diener is minister of the Arthur Beachy Amish.[43]

The Brethren in Christ originated in Pennsylvania in the latter part of the colonial period. Although they do not bear the name Mennonite, many of their religious ideas are similar, many of their founders were former Mennonites, and they have worked closely with the Mennonites.

This group has had a very limited amount of work in Illinois. In 1894 it established a mission in Chicago, just one year after the founding of the Mennonite Home Mission (MC), but four years after the initial decision of the Brethren to start such a work. Abram Meyers, Benjamin and Elizabeth Bert Brubaker, Sarah Bert, and Anna Bert were among the early leaders. According to John T. Neufeld, Carl J. Carlson served as pastor and leader from 1917 to the 1960s. The ministry terminated in 1968 when the mission building burned and was not rebuilt.[44]

Another work of the Brethren in Christ in Illinois, Mt. Carmel Home and Orphanage, opened her doors "to needy children" at Franklin Corners near Morrison in 1900. Providing a home and educational opportunities for those living there, the institution served twenty-two children in 1939. In 1949 the institution served an average of eighteen. It closed in 1968 because of soaring costs of meeting state fire and safety codes. But a Brethren in Christ church in Morrison which grew out of the orphanage still continues. In the latter part of the nineteenth century Brethren in Christ work had also started at Albany, Freeport, Shannon, and Polo. But the church in Morrison is the only one left.[45]

Another similar, non-Mennonite group in Illinois is the Missionary Church, formerly the Missionary Church Association. Its doctrinal emphases and its origin as a split from the Defenseless Mennonites have been noted in chapter 5. The historians of the church have stated that it "stems from a Mennonite source and without doubt has been influenced by Mennonite character and tradition." For some years after its founding by Joseph E. Ramseyer in 1898, most of the congregations established "had some Mennonite background." But after 1908 "the church grew largely through other influences and sources which have weakened the Mennonite character of the church."[46]

Already in 1898, the year of its origin, the new movement divided the Defenseless Mennonite congregation near Groveland. Those members who withdrew started a Missionary church in Groveland, meeting first in the town hall, then in a small building which they erected, and finally in a meetinghouse bought from the Methodists and renovated. John C. Birkey was the first pastor. In the next twenty-five or thirty years the only additional congregation founded in the state was Mt. Olive Missionary Church in Peoria. But as of 1957 there were nine congregations in Illinois, and since that time the number has grown to twenty-six. They are now a part of the Missionary Church.[47]

The Apostolic Christian Church in Illinois is another group that is non-Mennonite but similar in many respects. It had its origin in or near a Mennonite community in Switzerland, where it drew Mennonites into its membership. In America it has also done considerable proselytizing among them, especially among Amish Mennonites. Hence, it was often referred to as "New Amish," although there was never an organic connection. Some similarity in doctrinal belief, however, comes in part from this Mennonite and Amish influence.

Samuel Fröhlich, a Reformed minister in Switzerland, left the Swiss Reformed Church about 1832 and founded what eventually became known in America as the "Apostolic Christian Church of America." Migration of these people to America began in the 1840s and increased in succeeding years. Appearing first in New York and Ohio, they started settling in the Amish areas in Illinois in the 1850s. Benedict Weyeneth from Switzerland, one of their important leaders in Illinois, arrived in Peoria in 1853. It appears, however, that Joseph Grabill and Peter Virkler (or Verkler), both formerly Amish Mennonites, held the first religious services in Peoria, in 1852.[48]

Eventually some eighteen Apostolic Christian churches were established in Illinois, all but three or four of them in or near Amish or Mennonite communities. The tendency of the Apostolic group to proselytize among the Amish and Mennonites and the Apostolic belief that one could not attain salvation outside their church did not make for the friendliest of relations between the two bodies. But in recent years this church has also experienced something of an "awakening" or "quickening." The Illinois Apostolic people have become interested in publication, in mission and relief work (they cooperate with MCC), and in operating homes for children, the elderly, and the handicapped. They do not have educational institutions of their own, but many of their young people attend colleges and universities, and nurses' training schools such as the one at Mennonite Hospital in Bloomington.[49]

With few exceptions, these smaller groups have remained small in Illinois. One exception is the General Conference Mennonites who became the second largest Mennonite group after absorbing with the Central Conference Mennonites in 1957. Among the related non-Mennonite groups the Apostolic Christian and the Missionary Church Association (now Missionary Church) have grown sufficiently to have a noticeable impact on the religious life of the state.

CHAPTER 8

Illinois Amish Mennonite Congregations and the Western District Amish Mennonite Conference

After the Amish general conferences *(Diener-Versammlungen)* from 1862 to 1878 failed to bring about a reconciliation of differences, Amish history took several different directions. The more conservative party, insisting on the old, traditional policies and ways, became known as the Old Order Amish. In Illinois the more liberal faction became followers of Joseph Stuckey and were known at first as "Stuckey Amish" and later as Central Conference Mennonites. The middle group became known as Amish Mennonites and shortly organized themselves into three conferences: the Eastern Amish Mennonite (1893-1925), the Indiana-Michigan Amish Mennonite (1888-1915), and the Western Amish Mennonite, generally called the Western District A. M. Conference (1890-1920). The Western District included Illinois, along with Iowa, Missouri, Arkansas, Kansas, Oklahoma, Nebraska, Colorado, and Oregon. This chapter will note briefly the development of this middle group of Illinois Amish Mennonites following the *Diener-Versammlungen*. Many of the organizational aspects and the people involved in them can be dealt with briefly or omitted altogether, since Harry F. Weber has covered them into the 1920s.

A congregation that developed in this period and became quite important in the life of the conference and denomination was the East Bend church near Fisher in Champaign County. The name came from the congregation's location in East Bend Township and from a turn in the Sangamon River, from a southeasterly direction toward the southwest. Amish Mennonite settlers started coming to this area in the 1880s from Dillon Creek, Goodfield, and Hopedale, and other Illinois communities. The settlement illustrates the point that the large prairie areas of east central Illinois were the last parts of the state to be settled. No doubt relatively cheap, fertile land was an attraction. The first Amish Mennonite settler, Charles Stormer, who came in 1882, paid only $27.50 per acre. Samuel S. Zehr paid less than $20, buying eighty acres in 1891 for $1500.[1]

Beginning in 1889 the group held religious services first in a schoolhouse and then in a rented Methodist meetinghouse. In either 1889 or 1890, the congregation was organized.[2] Its first minister was Peter Zehr, who had moved from Deer Creek. Zehr had been ordained minister in 1883 at Goodfield and was ordained bishop ten years later at East Bend. He was a sincere, kindly man with a motto which he had printed on cards to hand out to his friends declaring: "I expect to travel through this world but once. Any good therefore that I can do, or any kindness I may be able to show any one, let me do it now. I shall not pass this way again." Others who served in the East Bend ministry included Daniel Greaser, Joseph Baecher, Bishop George Gingerich, Bishop Joseph A. Heiser, Harold A. Zehr, Dr. George Troyer, Bishop Howard J. Zehr, J. Alton Horst, Irvin Nussbaum, and Wilbur Nachtigal. The only deacon the congregation ever had was Samuel S. Zehr, who was ordained in 1906. He regularly took his turn at preaching.[3] In addition to Peter Zehr, J. A. Heiser, and others, Harold A. Zehr and Howard J. Zehr became important leaders not only at East Bend but also in the church at large.

In 1895 the congregation erected its own house of worship. In 1902 and in 1907 the building was badly damaged or destroyed by storms, but in each case it was promptly replaced. On several occasions the congregation's substantial growth required remodeling and enlargement of the facilities. In 1948 the congregation erected a new brick church adjoining the old structure, which was remodeled in brick veneer. It has a seating capacity of 750. Unfortunately, the fine growth of the congregation, which had reached a membership of 579 in 1950, suffered a setback in the early 1950s through a church division. Under the leadership of Bishop J. A. Heiser, about 130 members left the East Bend congregation and established the Gibson City Bible Church. A complicated set of factors having to do with faith healing, evangelicalism, and Mennonite practices seem to have caused the misunderstanding. These will be discussed in chapter 12.[4]

Otherwise, East Bend experienced a normal growth similar to the other Amish Mennonite congregations during that period. Sunday schools were already accepted by the time this congregation was founded. Although evening services were few before 1906, they were held regularly after that. The struggle around the turn of the century to make the transition from the use of German to English in the church services was similar here as elsewhere. In 1917 Mrs. Lydia Smith from Waldo helped organize the first Ladies' Sewing Circle. A literary society which later became a part of Mennonite Youth Fellowship was organized in 1920. Revival meetings and missionary outreach also became important activities at East Bend. J. A. Heiser was widely used as an evangelist among the Illinois churches and elsewhere. The first summer Bible school was held in 1936 and continues as an annual event to the present. In 1938 the congregation organized the Christian Workers' Band to encourage young people to witness for Christ. Through this band the congregation has sponsored a number of extension projects, some of which have resulted in separate churches "such as Dewey Mennonite, Arthur Mennonite, Gibson City AME, and Lake City Bible Church." The East Bend membership, listed as 320 in 1978, would be higher were it not that some placed their membership with one or two of these other groups in order to help along with extension work. The congregation's missionary outreach extended of course to supporting the general Mission Board at Elkhart. One field of special interest to East Bend was Puerto Rico, where a number of its members, including Dr. and Mrs. George Troyer, have served.[5] The Arthur congregation of today exists partly as a result of East Bend extension work.

Another Arthur Amish Mennonite church existed from the 1890s to about 1915. It was begun by dissatisfied members of the Old Order Amish community and a few Amish Mennonites from other states. Serving as ministers were Seth P. Hershberger, Moses J. Helmuth, and Isaac A. Miller. Included among those performing bishop services in the congregation were Peter Zehr from East Bend and John Smith from the Roanoke church. In December 1914 the last members moved away and the church building, erected in 1897, was sold.[6]

Another congregation now extinct, the Harmony Church between Eureka and Washburn, was never really organized separately but was a part of the Roanoke and Metamora congregations. The custom in the earlier days for congregations to meet only on alternate Sundays provided an opportunity to have services on the odd Sundays in a community northeast of Metamora and northwest of Roanoke. Quite a few members of each congregation resided there, and thought it more convenient, in the days of the horse and buggy and poor roads, to attend church meetings nearer home.

Roanoke apparently took the initiative. A Harmony church record book states that the Harmony church house was built by the Baptists and Methodists in 1865. It adds, in curious spelling, that in 1902 "the A. M. Brethren of the Ronoak Church begain to hold services in it and in Nineteen Hundred and Three the A. M. Brethren of the Ronoak church Bought the Harmony Church house of the Babtis association for Three Hundred Dollars."[7] Apparently Metamora was not involved until four years after that 1902 beginning, for another contemporary document reads: "This [March 4, 1906] was the first Sunday the Metamora and Roanoke congregations met together at the Harmony Church."[8]

Thereafter both congregations actively promoted the work at Harmony. But by 1920 Roanoke, now with a fine new church building, had bowed out of the work at Harmony. Metamora continued it until 1929. For a number of years Metamora and the Union Mennonite congregation near Washington also had a similar arrangement for meetings on alternate Sundays. When church services were held at Metamora, the Union people met there; and on alternate Sundays when services were held at Union, the Metamora members living in that area attended there rather than travel the greater distance to Harmony. The work at Harmony came to a close in 1929; since then Metamora, like Roanoke, has had services every Sunday. The small Union Church was also dissolved in 1929 and became a part of the Metamora congregation.[9]

All of the Amish Mennonite churches in Illinois that joined the Western A. M. Conference[10] had a rather similar development in the latter part of the nineteenth century and the first part of the twentieth. Of course there were differences in congregations and in leadership, but by and large they were affected by the same forces and their responses were similar. Some, such as Willow Springs at Tiskilwa, might have been a bit more liberal and progressive, while others, for instance, Hopedale and Goodfield, might have been a little more conservative. But although emphases on simplicity and separation from the world were still strong in all the congregations, hooks and eyes as a symbol of these were gone. *Meidung*, or shunning and social ostracism, had also largely disappeared. On the other hand, the "awakening" or "quickening" of this period stimulated more or less all the congregations into a new dynamic spiritual activity. Due to the movement the Amish Mennonites, like most Mennonites, were embracing and supporting church publications, Sunday schools and Sunday school conferences, revivals and evangelism, missions, young people's meetings, Bible conferences, Christian educational institutions, and other projects such as orphanages, old people's homes, and hospitals.

Church life and administration, which later would become more complex, were still simple and inexpensive in the early part of the twentieth century. The Pleasant Grove congregation between Morton and Pekin illustrated the simpler and less costly times. In 1906 its financial record reports, for example, "To D. D. Miller from Indiana

5.00." Daniel D. Miller was a prominent Indiana Amish Mennonite bishop. Very likely this was a contribution to his traveling expense for a speaking engagement. Another item is $1.00 for "one Dozzon [sic] A. B. C. Books"—no doubt German materials for Sunday school. In 1908 the Sunday school "Lesson Quarterlies" for this congregation of a few less than 100 members cost $4.97, $4.22, $4.40, and $4.24 for the respective quarters. In the same year the church treasurer, starting out the year with a balance of $223.76, ended it with total receipts of $521.16 and expenses of $326.68. In 1910 the total receipts were $404.29 and total expenses were $236.37. The comparable figures for 1912 were $478.07 receipts and $272.69 expenses. For a conference held at Pleasant Grove in 1899 the treasurer paid $17.50 for 250 pounds of sausages and $22.50 for 250 pounds of wieners—500 pounds of meat for $40.00! This of course was in a period when the expression "sound as a dollar" really meant something. Even in 1922 the treasurer paid only $13.80 for three dozen copies of *Life Songs*.

Except some very modest payments to missionaries, possibly for speaking engagements, offerings for missions are not included in these reports until about the time of World War I. The records do not clarify whether or not there were any such offerings. However, in 1918, probably due to World War I, a radical change took place. Local expenses were only $236.05, but, according to Elva May Roth, church historian, the money the congregation sent to outside causes that year, including relief, was $2282.10.[11]

In 1904 a reporter from the Bloomington *Pantagraph* covered some sessions of a Western A. M. Conference held at Hopedale. He stated that some 800 to 1000 people attended, over 800 being served meals at 11:30 and 5:30. "In the rear of the church is a kitchen," he wrote, "and here coffee is made and the viands made ready for the table."[12] The group had over 600 new tin cups for the serving of coffee. The menu, the reporter added, included "ham, hot sausage, bread, dried beef, butter, pickles, cheese, cookies and mustard, served on wooden plates." The food was served in a dining tent, where people stood at tables, with others eating on the lawn in picnic style. The report continued:

> During lunch time the scene is a picturesque one. The women in prime [sic] caps and plain garb flit about waiting on the tables, or caring for the little ones, of whom there is a plentiful supply, for none of the Amish Mennonites, seemingly, believe in race suicide. The boys and young men first feed the horses and then take plates of food, sit by themselves and eat, for there is no mixing of the sexes, the females sitting on one side of the church or tent and males occupying the other. The food is the best and in great abundance. Everyone, whether member or not, is urged to eat.

The reporter commented further that an older woman typically wore a "cap of black silk, much like a hood, but many of the younger ones appear in smart caps of filmy lace. Dresses are plain, but generally of excellent material, as nearly all of these people are well off financially."[13]

Samuel Gerber of Pleasant Grove was one of a number of capable leaders in the Western A. M. Conference. In 1940 Melvin Gingerich published an article in the *Mennonite Historical Bulletin* (October, 1940) on "Ten Leaders of the Western District Amish Mennonite Conference." Of the ten discussed from this large territory—which in 1914 had thirty-three congregations as compared with nine from Illinois—six were from Illinois. They were selected on the basis of regularity in conference attendance, number of conference sermons preached, election to offices, and appointments to committees. Gerber is included in Gingerich's list.

Born in 1863, Gerber was ordained minister at Pleasant Grove in 1897 and bishop in 1911. Like many other leaders of the time he was, as C. L. Graber has put it, "educated beyond his formal training." Possessing good judgment and tact, he was often asked to help adjust church problems and misunderstandings. He served as secretary or assistant secretary of the conference from 1902-05 and again in 1908. He was also assistant moderator in 1911, 1912, and 1920, and moderator from 1913-19. According to church leader Sanford C. Yoder, who knew him well, Gerber was not too interested in merger with the Mennonite conference in 1920; but "when it got so far he went along cheerfully." In fact, Gerber was on the merger committee that brought about the union of the two conferences, thus terminating the Western A. M. Conference. He continued to fill important positions in the merged Illinois Mennonite Conference, and died in 1929.[14]

Another leader with similar characteristics was John Smith (1843-1906), bishop of the Roanoke congregation. Since he was the only son in a family of six children he was needed badly to help with farm work; so he was able to spend only a few short winters in school. But he too was "educated beyond his formal training." With a friendly, peaceful disposition and good judgment and tact, he also was frequently asked to help settle church problems. Indeed, his services in this respect were sometimes extended to secular community matters. Smith attended fourteen of the first sixteen sessions of the Western A. M. Conference. He served as moderator or assistant moderator three times and as secretary six times. Ordained minister in 1887 and bishop in either 1891 or 1892, he served not only his home congregation but also others when needed. Some years before his sudden death in 1906 the conference had asked him to have bishop oversight of all the Illinois Amish Mennonite congregations that did not have a resident bishop. That he was not opposed to education, despite his own limited schooling, is evident in that he helped his son, C. Henry, to secure not only a college education but also graduate training. That son became the first (Old) Mennonite to earn the PhD degree and remain a Mennonite.[15]

Source: Smith, *Mennonite Country Boy*.

John Smith (1843-1906), prominent Illinois Amish Mennonite bishop and minister of the Roanoke Amish Mennonite Church, 1887-1906; photo taken in his twenties, i.e., probably in the 1860s.

John C. Birky (1849-1920), another conference leader from Illinois, attended at least twenty-seven sessions of the Western A. M. Conference. He was assistant moderator in 1909, was moderator in 1911, and on three occasions preached the conference sermon. Ordained minister in 1877 and bishop in 1890, he moved in 1896 from Kansas to Hopedale, where he served as bishop until his death. After John Smith's death, the conference appointed Birky bishop of those Illinois congregations that had no resident bishop. Reserved in manner, he was respected wherever he labored. Daniel Orendorff (1848-1918), minister at Waldo congregation, was conference treasurer for several years, and attended at least twenty meetings. Andrew Schrock (1863-1949), minister and then bishop from Metamora, served as either moderator or assistant moderator six times and attended at least twenty-one sessions. The sixth conference leader from Illinois was Chauncy A. Hartzler (1867-1947) from the Willow Springs congregation at Tiskilwa. Ordained minister in Cass County, Missouri, in 1906, he served for a time as worker and superintendent of the Kansas City Mennonite Mission, from where he moved to Tiskilwa in 1913. Here he was ordained bishop in 1914. He attended all sessions of the conference from 1907-20 and served eleven times as secretary.[16]

As Gingerich conceded, "Many other bishops and ministers were influential in the work of the Western District Amish Mennonite Conference." Among these Illinois leaders were Joseph Burcky of Tiskilwa, John P. Schmidt of the Waldo congregation, Peter D. Schertz of Roanoke congregation, and Peter Zehr of East Bend.[17] Still others to mention might be younger men such as Clayton F. Derstine, Ezra Yordy, Henry R. Schertz, and Joseph A. Heiser. These attended some of the later Amish Mennonite conference sessions but their main impact on church life came after the merger with the Mennonites in 1920.

Apparently the Western A. M. Conference was not formally and completely organized until 1890. Before that time, however, the more progressive Amish Mennonite leaders had met occasionally for fellowship and counsel. They held one such informal meeting in Illinois about 1882, and some additional ones in other states soon after. In a meeting in Henry County, Iowa, in 1884, these Western Amish Mennonite leaders decided to hold annual conferences, "a plan which was followed from that date on." Whatever the nature of these conferences, official reports are not available for any conference before 1890.[18]

Official reports of these conferences, in which apparently only ordained men served as delegates, are composed mostly of questions raised and the answers given.[19] Although brief, they are the best sources for portraying Western Amish Mennonite thought, at least of the ministry, during the latter part of the nineteenth and the first part of the twentieth centuries. The men who participated have been referred to as the "more progressive Amish Mennonite leaders."[20] Yet many of the resolutions they passed, especially those on nonconformity or separation from the world, would not seem very progressive or liberal today.

Occasionally the delegates dealt somewhat ambivalently with the question of the relation of the conference to the local congregations. This was a concern because the Amish always rather strongly emphasized congregational control. After passing some resolutions at the 1890 session the delegates agreed that the "above resolutions were not ... made obligatory for the churches, since it was not considered in order to make binding laws and rules for the churches, but they are only an expression of the opinion of the ministers, as to the meaning of God's Word, and their instructions for the churches." The 1891 conference, however, agreed that "these resolutions were given as the sense of the conference, to be considered as advice *and rules* by which the congregations should be conducted."[21] This ambiguity continued through the 1905, 1913, and 1916 conferences. The 1905 conference said that "every individual church should likewise be subject to the counsel of the conference." The 1913 conference said that "according to the Word (Acts 15 and 16:4) the Conference resolutions were binding, hence when a conference passes a resolution based upon God's Word, members who continuously disregard such resolutions cannot be considered as being in harmony with the Church." In 1916, when the question involved a minister or a few members thwarting a majority in a congregation, the conference said that though the majority can be wrong "we believe the Bible upholds congregational government."

On the question of the relative authority of a minister and his congregation, Bishop John C. Birky of Hopedale took a middle position. In a meeting of Illinois A. M. ministers he warned against two extremes—namely, where the minister (or bishop) assumes sole authority, or where a congregation assumes all power "without a minister or divinely appointed overseer and leader."[22]

In the resolutions having to do with nonconformity and separation from the world, the Western A. M. Conference remained conservative. For instance, it saw in Populism the threat of secret societies. The conference of 1890 met in Cass County, Missouri, and the next met in Seward County, Nebraska. Both of these states were hotbeds of Populism, which developed from various organizations such as the Farmers Alliances. Because of economic difficulties, Amish Mennonite farmers were inclined to join these organizations. But the conference said "no" in 1890 and gave a fuller explanation the following year: "After extended deliberation, it was decided that it was not permissible [to join], since such secret societies are incompatible with the nonresistant principle [and] ... their object is only worldly gain and they are consequently not conducive to piety." Similarly, it was "contrary to evangelical doctrine to belong to secret societies" (1898).[23]

Worldly amusements and other activities leading away from nonconformity were to be avoided. The 1890 conference declared that "worldly amusements, such as parties, the dance, etc., are injurious to the body as well as the soul, and are to be shunned," and "to frequent places where strong drink is sold, is equally injurious." The delegates in 1896 held that since "birthday parties, surprise parties and similar gatherings are not held to the glory of God, we consider them as injury to the cause of Christ, and advise our members not to ... participate in them." It was not "appropriate that Christians frequent shows, fairs, soldiers reunions, etc.," since "these places have influences that are misleading and ruinous" (1900, 1905). In 1909 the conference said Christians should not "take part in pound and basket suppers, surprise parties, ball games, etc.," since such "tend to the gratifying of the lusts of the flesh and are destructive to spiritual life." It was "not advisable" for brethren to take part in horse races, nor was it proper to take part in "any game of chance, or hazard, such as are offered by the 'board of trade,' 'lotteries,' etc." (1894, 1902). The Amish Mennonites, of course, were not the only people at that time who believed that buying on the Board of Trade was like other forms of gambling.

In business relationships with nonmembers, the conference frequently cited the argument of the unequal yoke between believers and unbelievers (2 Cor. 6:14), as well as the argument that many business relationships might be inconsistent with nonresistance. For these reasons the conference thought it advisable for members not to own stock in corporations along with non-Mennonites, partly to avoid taking part in lawsuits "and using violence, as is so often done" (1893). This applied even to telephone companies or farmers' elevator companies "that are not non-resistant" (1904). On the question of "life insurance, so-called" the answer in 1893 was: "It is not believed to be evangelical. The best insurance is that of the soul, by faith, in accordance with God's Word." This argument was extended to property insurance and lightning rods. Since these, said the conference in 1909, "have a tendency to weaken our trust in God and the money spent for them could be used for better purposes we deem" them "inconsistent with true Christian living." On being a real-estate agent the same conference said: "Since a Christian truly converted will be honest with his fellowmen, and in such business there are many temptations to receive undeserved wages we deem it not advisable" to be a land or real-estate agent.

In the effort to maintain the nonconformed life, dress also received considerable discussion. Hooks and eyes were no longer an issue—at least so far as conference resolutions were concerned. So in Amish terms, the Western A. M. Conference was liberal enough. But plain and modest dress was an issue (1892, 1894, 1898, 1901, 1907), as was a prohibition against wearing jewelry. The question was repeatedly raised as to how to deal with those members who violated rules of attire. If after public teaching and personal dealing in the light

Source: Nelson Springer, Goshen, Ind

Simon Litwiller of Hopedale and Katy Ehrisman of Flanagan, married on February 7, 1905. Compare their costume to that in their picture on the following page, taken in 1954.

of 1 Timothy 2:9-10 and 1 Peter 3:3-5 such members still persisted in their course, they could not "be considered in full fellowship with the Church" (1913, 1915).

This dress problem seemed to increase as 1920 and merger with the (Old) Mennonites approached. In 1919 the conference expressed the hope that the time would speedily come when the church could be "entirely free from such violations of scripture as the wearing of jewelry, costly array, fashionable clothing, low-necked dresses and other immodest apparel and both brethren and sisters show by their appearance that they are a people who believe in the Bible doctrine of nonconformity to the world." A committee appointed to study the question and report to the next conference was composed of A. G. Yoder, I. G. Hartzler, Simon Gingerich, Joseph Zimmerman, and Ezra Yordy. Their report, accepted by the 1920 conference, advocated:

> That the ministry set the example by wearing plain clothing, allowing nothing on their person that bears the marks of vanity, as neckties, gold, buttons for display, and such like. 1 Pet. 5:3. That their hats be plain without crimps, dents, etc., and that they encourage the wearing of the regulation coat both among themselves and among the brethren.
>
> That the brotherhood support the ministry by conforming to the above standard, and by using their influence in the home and the church.

Bishop Simon and Katy Ehrisman Litwiller of Hopedale Mennonite Church, 1954.

That sisters wear a plain bonnet or hood, conforming to the shape of the head, without trimming or ornamentation, sufficiently large for protection and wearing of the devotional covering, and made to be consistenty [sic] tied. That costly array, laces, embroideries, low cut or unbecoming short dresses, short sleeves, transparent fabrics that give an immodest appearance, jewelry, such as pearls, rings, bracelets, broaches [sic], chains, wrist watches, and all other outward ornamentation and display be avoided. 1 Thes. 5:22.

That brethren avoid cutting or combing the hair in the ever changing styles and fashions. That sisters part their hair in the middle and arrange it in a modest and becoming way, so that the devotional covering may be consistently worn. II Cor. 1:1-16.

That parents co-operate with the ministry by teaching their children the scriptures and the position of the church. Prov. 22:6; Deut. 6:6, 7.

With the hope that all of our Bishops, Ministers, and Deacons will put forth special and untiring efforts to explain to their members these regulations, in order to stem the tide of worldliness, and that they endeavor by the grace and help of God, to lead the entire membership to the standard herein set forth, we remain

Your Brethren,
Signed, Committee.

The report begs several questions. Along with some other reports, it shows the rising influence of conference, even among the Amish Mennonites who traditionally had emphasized congregational control. Also, to what extent if any were the Amish Mennonites influenced by the Mennonites in view of the coming merger? For example, the plain coat had not earlier been an issue among the Amish. Finally, to what extent if any was the conference influenced by the current controversy between so-called liberals and Fundamentalists, which touched Mennonites and Amish Mennonites also? Although these influences probably were important, how important is uncertain.

The Western A. M. Conference attempted to maintain its traditional position on use of musical instruments. Use of instruments in the church was not an issue down to the merger, but use in homes was controversial. The conference of 1893 answered the question by saying that even home use "is not believed to be edifying, since it is not possible to glorify God by playing on a dead instrument." Some delegates brought up the question again in 1902 and 1913. On the latter occasion conference urged "a more decided stand against them." But conference was losing the battle. By that time many homes, even ministers' homes, had pianos or organs, and more were on the way. In some cases lay members were more conservative on this issue than were the ministers. Ezra Yordy, bishop of Roanoke, has told the story of Clayton F. Derstine who became minister at Roanoke in 1915. Soon thereafter Derstine was being considered for bishop, and one conservative member of the congregation came to Yordy, then minister, to object about a piano in Derstine's home. At Yordy's suggestion the two went to Derstine to discuss the matter. After some discussion and prayer the one who objected said to Derstine: "You get that piano out of the house and I'll listen to you as bishop. Otherwise, I won't." "To this Derstine replied, 'You throw your cigars away and I'll listen to you.' Following the confrontation,... [the conservative layman] replied, 'Brother Yordy, I guess we'd better go.' "[24]

In their conference resolutions the Western Amish Mennonites also commented on the Christian's relation to government. Church members were not to "accept worldly offices, except school director, road master and post master." On this the conference was unanimous because holding such offices involved the administration of the oath and the exercise of authority based on the sword which "is not permitted us" (1891). Later the brethren were advised against holding offices even "such as assessor, tax collector, etc." Though the conference recognized that the governmental powers were ordained of God and that Christians must be subject to them, insofar as the Bible permitted, yet members were not to take part in elections or in political meetings, "for the reason that we believe it leads away from nonresistance" (1893, 1900, 1902, 1907). Likewise members were not to serve as jurymen; they were not to accept pensions from the government for war services or for injuries received "although at the time they were not members"; and they were not to use the government to collect wages or other debts, or threaten people "with the law" or take the "difficulty into court" (1890, 1893, 1894, 1895).[25]

The above discussion reflects the negative rather than the positive aspects of Amish Mennonite thought and policy. In the past the Amish and many Mennonites have been justly criticized for overemphasis on the negative—nonresistance, nonconformity, non this and non that. Actually even in such "nons" there was a positive concern for being practical about an ethic of love and about purity of life. And the Western A. M. *Conference Reports* frequently show great concern for the deepening of spiritual life: "That we all—beginning with the ministers—have need of more pure spiritual life, and that our conversation should be of heavenly things, that our walk also may be pure and holy" (1890). Many "meetings were held which were well attended," continues this 1890 report—meaning, of course, that many laymen were present. "We were richly and earnestly admonished by the brethren regarding our duties. Through these earnest sermons a number of persons were moved to renounce sin and to consecrate themselves to the service of the living God." In 1892 the conferees asked what could be done to "awaken more spiritual life" in the congregations, and in 1908 they discussed the evidences of, and the means of growth in, the spiritual life. In the same meeting (1908) the delegates were concerned with the preparation that "is necessary for engaging in the work of the Lord." Again in 1914 they addressed themselves to the need for awakening more spiritual activity among the members.

On other occasions the delegates discussed the purposes of the conferences in positive terms. One purpose was to spread the gospel and win more souls for Christ. Also through conferences the Amish Mennonites became better acquainted with one another and "more united in faith, love and mind." And they were "encouraged, strengthened, and built up, so as to do more work for the Master" (1903). This concern that conference would make the members better workers in Christ's kingdom was reiterated various times (1908, for example). Other basic concerns the conference seriously discussed included the aim and purpose of the church, avenues of Christian service, creating a greater zeal for the unsaved, the greatest needs of the churches, the call to do mission work, the inspiration of the Bible, the mission of the church, and the glory of the church (1915, 1916, 1918, 1919, 1920). On divine healing the conference took a position that would probably still satisfy most Mennonites today—that all healing comes from God and that in addition to prayer and commending themselves to his will Christians "should also do their part in the application of proper remedies" (1897). On still another point the delegates sounded very much like Mennonites today: The conference decided that members ought to "counsel more with their congregations before they allow themselves to go into so many temporal vocations" (1904).

In the 1890s the (Old) Mennonites and the Amish Mennonites discussed the issue of having a "general" conference. In 1894 the question came up in the Western A. M. Conference. Several addresses pointing out the advantages of such a meeting "if held in the right way and with right intentions were earnestly presented." By unanimous vote the conference then supported such a meeting. At the 1896 session John Smith of Metamora, Illinois, and Joseph Schlegel of Milford, Nebraska, were appointed as Western A. M. representatives to serve on a committee to arrange for such a "General Conference."[26]

Meanwhile, the Mennonite awakening—to be discussed in chapters 10 and 11—was also occurring; and the various phases of it, of course, came up for discussion and support during the life of this Western A. M. Conference. The positive side of conference deliberations can be further seen in the ultimate concern underlying the doctrine of nonconformity—namely, a deep concern for real spiritual life in the members. In 1901, in addressing the question, "How can our members become stronger in the doctrine[s] of nonresistance, and nonconformity to the world?" the conference answered: "First, by examining themselves as to whether they are truly born again of the Spirit of God." As this indicates, the Amish Mennonites believed basically that if a person were truly born again he would be nonresistant and nonconformed to the world. Evidence is clear that Western Amish Mennonite thought, including in Illinois, had its positive aspects and a concern for real spiritual life, even as reflected in conference resolutions.

Of the thirty-one annual sessions of the Western A. M. Conference, twelve were held in Illinois. That this was more than in any other state of the district was only natural, since Illinois had the largest number of Amish Mennonite congregations. Roanoke hosted the conference three times; Hopedale, Willow Springs, Waldo, and Pleasant Grove, twice each; and East Bend, once. At the Roanoke conference in 1906 the ushers, who counted the people as well as "they could while in the tent," calculated that about 1200 people were present.[27] Goodfield, a small congregation, never hosted the conference, and Metamora, although one of the larger and older congregations, likewise did not.

Other records of Western Amish Mennonite religious thought can be found especially in church periodicals. Whereas only a few people wrote books, hundreds of members wrote articles—lay people as well as ministers. Sometimes lay opinion was more liberal than that of the ministry, but not always. Not in an article but in a letter one young sister from Illinois, a daughter of Bishop John Smith, stated in 1899 that her father had "put in a question for the Conference to decide; what the Conference thinks about the sisters wearing . . . plain hats. I hope the answer will be that we can wear them."[28]

On the other hand, Christian Neuhauser from Eureka, Illinois, showed himself more conservative than at least a number of the ministers. He felt that Christians should not attend Chautauqua programs, as many Illinois Mennonites were doing, because the programs were a seductive mixture of questionable religious and secular entertainment. On weekdays the programs were "all worldly." Neuhauser also said that Christians could not engage in banking because to do so would lead inevitably to breaking Christ's commandments about giving to the poor and about getting involved in lawsuits. Celebrating so-called church holidays such as Thanksgiving and Christmas likewise received his disapproval. He pointed out the pagan origins of the Christmas celebrations, and added that "the sports usually connected with a Christmas tree are un-Christian." Picnics, he contended, were mostly if not altogether to gratify the lusts of the flesh and "are of the world and belong to the world." Attending Fourth of July celebrations was inconsistent for nonresistant Christians because of the day's association with war. It would be better, he urged, to hold religious services on that day to explain Mennonite principles.[29]

Illinois Amish Mennonites discussed a wide range of subjects, including the so-called "peculiar" doctrines of the church as well as the "fundamentals." Clayton F. Derstine, who as noted earlier became a minister at Roanoke in 1915, himself spoke on a diversity of topics, ranging from "Salvation" to "A Glimpse at the Bonnet Question." His comments on the bonnet were typical in the large number of points he used to cover his subject, whether in speaking or writing. In this case he used twenty-one points, some of them repetitive, to cover the "Glimpse." Among them were that: "the Bonnet [sic] is safe"; "it is reasonable"; "it is modest"; "it is beautiful"; "it is woman's apparel"; "it is scriptural"; "it denotes obedience"; "it has a good history"; "churches that gave it up never remained plain"; "the bonnet settles the question for all time"; "Godly women always dressed differently from worldlings"; "the bonnet safeguards from evil men"; "it points the observer to Christianity"; "the wholly surrendered woman is glad to wear it"; "most opposition comes from the worldly-minded"; "some once plain churches that discarded the bonnet are losing out terribly"; "the surrendered life is called for by Christ"; "there is ... respect for those who wear it"; and, "the devotional covering ... goes with the bonnet."[30] Was there a connection between the conservative-liberal controversy over theology in the church and the conservative-liberal controversy over dress and nonconformity? In the same article Derstine concluded that many trends in the church were encouraging, "if conservative members stay reasonable and those inclined toward liberalism open their eyes to the facts of Scripture and of the Church's highest interest."

Derstine had come from Pennsylvania, and expressed some interesting opinions about the Illinois churches:

> We have been at all of the Amish and Mennonite churches in Illinois except one. While one sometimes finds a little gap between the east and the west in certain matters, I am sure that if they were together for a time, they would find the same interests ruling the lives of each. I must say that while I was in Illinois I have found a ministry deeply interested in giving to the world a Gospel unadulterated in life and creed. The "mighty dollar" is a hindrance to the best spiritual interest of some, but many use their money to help in laying up treasure for "the times that are to come."
>
> A very hopeful indication is the craving after the truth. While it is often said that "the farmer is too busy in summer to go to church every evening," yet for ten weeks there have been well-filled houses even on very hot days and evenings.
>
> If I were to offer a criticism on the methods in these parts, I would suggest a more rigid exercise of church discipline. Too often the evan-

gelist is expected to correct errors in worldliness that should be checked when they make their first appearance. Such things, if allowed to go on for a time, are beyond our reach and it is almost impossible to exterminate them.[31]

Was Derstine saying or implying by this that the Illinois Mennonites were a bit more lax than others?

In addition to articles, Derstine published a number of pamphlets and books, and the lines of his thinking can be seen in the following titles: *Ancient and Modern Idolatry: Fashionable Attire; The Church Age in Prophetic Limelight: Revelation 2 and 3; Forty Principles in Bible and Sunday School Lesson Study; The Great Apostasy: Or Departing from God and the Living Word; Hell's Playground: Theater and Movies; The Home from Four Angles; The Last Message of Jesus Christ: What Primitive Christians Believed—Practiced—Taught...; A Lighthouse for Young Believers; Manual of Sex Education for Parents, Teachers, and Students; The Path to Beautiful Womanhood: A Book for Parents, Women, and Girls on Sex Life; Right Knowledge—Right Proportion—Right Time; The Path to Noble Manhood: A Book for Parents, Men, and Boys on Sex Life; Paul—A Pattern for Them Who Should Hereafter Believe on Him to Life Eternal: Guide to 20th Century Christians; The Sheet Music of Heaven: The Mighty Triumphs of Sacred Songs; Signs of the Times; Six Rooms in the House of Life;* and *The Yawning Pit of Lodgery.* Derstine will be discussed further in connection with Fundamentalist influences in Illinois.

Illinois Amish Mennonite thought was influenced by forces from outside as well as from within. Although Illinois had the largest membership of any state in the Western District, the Illinois people naturally were somewhat influenced by their fellow laborers from other states. Of still greater consequence, no doubt, was the influence of the two major (Old) Mennonite periodicals, the *Herald of Truth* and the *Gospel Herald* which took its place in 1908. Both were published by able, vigorous editors and both circulated widely in Illinois. The *Herald of Truth* was started in Chicago in 1864 and then moved to nearby Elkhart, Indiana, in 1867. Its editor, John F. Funk, a minister for a few years at Gardner, always retained a lively interest in and contact with the state. For many years (1908-43) Daniel Kauffman, originally from Missouri, edited the *Gospel Herald.*

Partly because of its crossroads position, Illinois was blessed with many visiting ministers. They too, of course, were an outside source of thought and opinion. For instance, one Sunday in November 1892 Deacon N. Stuckey of Flanagan spoke at the Willow Springs church at Tiskilwa. Following his visit D. Z. Yoder from Wayne County, Ohio, held several meetings at Willow Springs. In December J. P. Smucker of Nappanee and Daniel J. Johns of Goshen, Indiana, came and held a number of meetings for over a week in the vicinity. They were joined by John Smith of Metamora, Daniel Orendorf of Flanagan, and a Nafzinger from Kansas. A report indicates that these meetings were successful in strengthening church members and in winning converts to Christianity. Another example is of John C. Lugibill of Leo, Indiana, who left his home on December 7, 1893, and preached the following Sunday at East Bend near Fisher. He went to Eureka on December 11, attended a funeral at Metamora on the following day, held a meeting at the Roanoke meetinghouse on the thirteenth, and that evening held services in the home of a Brother Kennel who had a sick daughter. On December 14 he preached at the Metamora church. Two days later he went with Peter Summer to Minier and met with the Hopedale congregation on December 17. J. Litwiller and Joseph Egly accompanied him to Tremont, where he preached on December 18. Following the engagement, he had a fine visit with the aged bishop, Christian Ropp, near Hudson. From here he went to Waldo near Flanagan, where he held two more meetings before returning home. In 1895 S. B. Miller from Pekin reported that Menno S. Steiner from Ohio delivered a sermon apparently at Pleasant Grove near Tremont on August 2. A few days later Jonas S. Hartzler from Indiana preached twice. On August 9 Daniel D. Miller of Indiana delivered a series of five sermons. Several important out-of-state ministers who visited frequently were the Mennonites J. S. Coffman from Indiana and M. S. Steiner from Ohio, and the Amish Mennonites Daniel J. Johns and Daniel D. Miller from Indiana.[32]

Perhaps no two Mennonite groups were ever more ready for merger than were the so-called "Old" and the Amish Mennonites of Illinois in 1920. Long before that date the two groups had been working together increasingly. Since Harry Weber has ably discussed this in his work, a mere summary of such activities should be sufficient here, with perhaps a bit more emphasis on one or two of the points.

1. The *Herald of Truth, Gospel Witness,* and *Gospel Herald*—which both groups read and supported and to which both contributed articles—were of tremendous influence in growth toward unity.

2. The Mennonite Publication Board was organized in 1908 for both bodies.

3. Both worked together in mission work, such as the Home Mission in Chicago and the work in India. The Mennonite Mission Board was organized under various names long before 1920.

4. They worked together in education even before the founding of the Mennonite Board of Education in 1905.

5. As already noted, there was a great deal of pulpit interchange by both groups.

6. There was also much interchange in revival meetings, as represented especially by Coffman and Steiner.

7. There was much conference interchange of both speakers and attendants. As early as 1893, for example, Amish Mennonite Bishop John Smith spoke at the Illinois Mennonite Conference and, among other points, said: "It matters not what we are called, Amish or Mennonites or any other name. Let the heart be right so that we may work to the upbuilding of the church in a way that will stand before God."[33] Joseph S. Shoemaker, Mennonite bishop at Freeport, spoke often in Amish Mennonite conferences and other meetings. This interchange applied to Bible conferences, mission conferences, and Sunday school conferences, as well as to church conferences.

8. The Illinois Sunday School Conference in both branches worked together for many years before 1920. Already in 1899 J. S. Coffman, who attended this conference at Freeport, recorded in his diary (May 25) that the "sentiment is decidedly growing that the S. S. Conf. is a strong factor in gaining acquaintance and building up unity between the Men. and Amish members."

9. The Illinois District Mission Board preceded merger.

10. The Women's District Missionary Society was started in 1917 and included both branches.

11. Already in the 1890s both branches helped organize the Mennonite General Conference and, by becoming members, indicated common beliefs.

12. Apparently because of the convenience of shorter distances the Western Amish Mennonite ministers of Illinois began to meet in annual conferences about 1909. This too can be thought of as a step toward merger with the Illinois Mennonites, for it indicated the inconvenience of holding meetings over such a large area as the Western District and thus helped to bring about reorganization of the Western District into smaller areas merged with the Mennonites in those states.[34]

Such evidence shows that long before 1920 the two branches were united in thought, spirit, and practical concerns. Even the old question, shunning, which was the most important one in causing the original division in the 1690s, was now a matter of the past. The logical next step was the merger of the conferences. In 1919 and 1920 the Western A. M. Conference and the Illinois Mennonite Conference worked out the merger. The proceedings can be easily followed in Weber, in the *Reports* of the Western A. M. Conference for 1919 and 1920, and in Daniel Kauffman (and others), "Report of Conference Merger Committee," *GH*, Oct. 28, 1920. Kauffman was chairman of the merger committee. In giving a report of the first merged conference in 1921, the secretary, A. L. Buzzard, referred to it as the "Illinois Conference: Report of the First United Mennonite Church Conference for the State of Illinois." Editor Daniel Kauffman commented that the merged conference "was a union in a common faith and not the union of compromise." Weber also states it was a "true merging." Both groups made a few adjustments in practice and administrative patterns of working. Among such adjustments the Mennonite congregations gave up lay representation in the conference, and the Amish Mennonite ministers accepted the clerical or "plain" coat, which was new to them. The name Amish was dropped.[35]

Thus by 1920 another large segment of Mennonites of Amish background had given up the Amish name, as had the "Egly Amish" and the "Stuckey Amish" before them. In their development in the years after the *Diener-Versammlungen*, these Amish Mennonites, the largest Mennonite group in Illinois, followed a middle course between the Central Conference Mennonites and those wishing to maintain the old order. The history of their thought shows that they were conservative. But they were willing to make cultural adjustments. In fact, they were on the eve of making still greater ones.

CHAPTER 9

The So-Called "Old" Mennonites and the Development of the Illinois Mennonite Conference

The origin and growth of Mennonite settlements in Illinois to about the 1870s was treated in chapter 2. The congregations then in existence were Union, Freeport, Science Ridge, Morrison, Gardner, and Cullom. Scales Mound had already disappeared, and the small congregation founded by Funk and Neff in Chicago did not survive the great fire of 1871. Since the Gardner church also died out in the 1880s, it did not play a significant part in the new Illinois Mennonite Conference. Union terminated its existence in 1929 and Cullom more recently. The others have continued a more or less active existence and growth.

Union, near Washington, was the oldest of the Mennonite churches in Illinois, with beginnings in 1833. In the 1870s it was still a small, struggling congregation. In 1886 its bishop, Emanuel M. Hartman, writing in the *Herald of Truth*, noted that it was small, and invited anyone who could to worship in its biweekly services.[1] The congregation's aged bishop, Jost Bally, died in 1878. A few years earlier he had become involved in an unfortunate dispute with a few fellow members. Bishop Henry Nice of Morrison, asked to help settle the matter, felt that Bally was less conciliatory than those who differed with him. Possibly the one who wrote Bally's obituary (probably Bishop Hartman) had these troubles in mind, for he stated: "He desired to be released from this life to try the realities of the future, with a readiness to leave all in the hands of a just God."[2] In 1876 Bally had already been succeeded as bishop by Hartman, who had been ordained a minister at Cullom in 1873 and had returned to Washington, his birthplace, in

1874. One of the most active leaders in the Mennonite Church, he served his congregation and denomination faithfully until he joined the Apostolic Christian Church in 1897.[3]

Although it got the name "Union" from its location next to Union Cemetery, the congregation also served to link Mennonites and Amish Mennonites, in a community where the latter predominated. Both groups attended each other's services more and more, long before the merger in 1920. For example, when the Union Sunday school was reorganized in 1904 its superintendent, George I. Sommer, and assistant superintendent, J. J. Summer, were both Amish Mennonites. One leader in this era was Union's minister, A. L. Buzzard, who was ordained minister in 1906 by his father-in-law, Joseph S. Shoemaker. Buzzard served through the merger until 1929 when the congregation merged with the nearby Metamora church. He then moved to Goshen, Indiana, where he had been born.[4]

The second oldest Mennonite congregation, Freeport, experienced several ministerial changes soon after the Mennonite conference was organized in 1872. Christian Snyder died within a week after the first meeting of conference, and Martin Lapp died suddenly in March of 1875. In that same year Christian Snavely was ordained minister. It has been said of him that though he was "comparatively well to do financially, he had all his possessions on the altar of the Lord." Ephraim M. Shellenberger, ordained in 1878, and Christian Snyder, ordained in 1864, were two of the first to preach in English. In 1878 Bishop Matthias Eby was relieved of his office because of personal difficulties. Another change occurred when Joseph S. Lehman was ordained minister in 1887 to fill a vacancy left when Shellenberger moved to Kansas. But in 1892 Lehman moved to Elkhart, Indiana, to become business manager of the Mennonite Publishing Company. In addition to these fairly frequent changes in the ministry, an unusual and tragic event in the congregation occurred in 1899. Deacon David Ebersole, "in a season of mental derangement," took his own life. A reporter stated: "We have never seen the sympathies of everyone in the church and community more deeply stirred than on this occasion."[5]

Normally, everyday life among the rank and file in this rural community was more humdrum than exciting. Ida Beidler (later Mrs. Samuel Kniss) kept a diary in 1898 while working as a hired girl in the farm home of a Mennonite, Ben Brubaker, brother-in-law of J. S. Shoemaker. In addition to the usual accounts of cleaning, cooking, churchgoing, and the weather, she recorded such items as: "Dug garden," "white wash[ed] cellar," "white wash[ed] fence," "papered," "laid kitchen carpet & oilcloth [linoleum]," "cleaned up woodshed," "scoured tinware," "fetched cows," "white washed & mended gates," "helped milk," "milked 14 cows," "unpitched 2 loads of oats," "canned pie plant," "made shirts," "Tramps" and "salve peddlers."

In 1891 membership in the Freeport congregation was about 55, but with the turn of the century came more prosperous and stabler times. As noted earlier, Joseph S. Shoemaker moved into this community in 1863 and lived here until his death in 1936. He was ordained minister by a unanimous vote in 1892 and bishop in 1902, again unanimously. In 1892, because the church was having difficulties, the bishop had refrained for a while from holding the communion service. But Shoemaker's kindly and peaceable disposition made him respected by all who knew him and exerted a settling and healing influence. Under his leadership the congregation began again to make progress.

Shoemaker's methods of working are shown by how he dealt with one of his members who was an unusual character. A man from Europe, L. H. Ledochowiski, had been a Benedictine monk and was known as Father Hillary. Soon after 1900 he claimed to have found new light at the Chicago Home Mission and wanted to join the Mennonite Church. After careful questioning on the Christian faith as understood by the Mennonites, Bishop Shoemaker, whom A. H. Leaman had called to Chicago, was satisfied and received him as a

Source: Oyer, What Hath God Wrought?

Joseph S. Shoemaker (1854-1936) and Elizabeth S. Brubaker Shoemaker. He was a minister of the Freeport Mennonite Church, 1892-1936; a prominent (Old) Mennonite bishop; president of the Mennonite Board of Missions and Charities, 1906-1920; and president of the Mennonite Publication Board, 1908-1933.

member. Later Shoemaker received him as a member at Freeport. A gifted speaker, Hillary seemed to be a true and sincere convert to the new faith and displayed a readiness to work for the church. As news about him spread throughout the church he was much in demand as a speaker. Before long, however, various kinds of reports of him and his work began to circulate. Some thought he was doing a good work while others thought he was a fraud. Some of these reports "reflected seriously on his character." In a letter to the *Herald of Truth*, Shoemaker felt compelled to explain "What We Have Seen and Heard of Hillary," and said if the charges against him were true "his connection with the church would be forfeited and he could not be recognized as a brother." Shoemaker said that Hillary had become a "puzzle" and a "mysterious character" to him, and that perhaps he was mentally unbalanced. In the meantime Hillary tried to get people to believe he had returned to his home in Bohemia, and the bishop encouraged people to remember the good he had said and done and to forgive and forget that which was not good.[6]

Shoemaker virtually "made" the Freeport church, and he also was very important in molding the Mennonite Church as a whole. In order partly that he might be freer to help serve in the wider church, Shoemaker was given a faithful assistant: Simon Graybill was ordained minister in 1903.[7]

Following its beginning in the 1850s the Sterling congregation experienced a substantial if uneven growth. An 1890 report indicated that for some years the church had not been very active, but it added that recently the members had become more zealous. Jonas Nice had been ordained minister that spring. Young people had expressed interest in Sunday school work. On August 16 a harvest Thanksgiving service had been held which a number of visiting ministers, including John S. Coffman, had attended, and on the following Sunday nine persons had been baptized. One year later the reporter stated that both the church and Sunday school were making progress. The congregation had recently begun to hold services every Sunday; it also hoped to keep the Sunday school open every Sunday of the year, instead of closing for the winter months, as was the general custom. In January of 1892 Coffman, of Elkhart, Indiana, was asked to come to Sterling to preach at the funeral of Abram Ebersole. The Sterling church, "thinking that under the condition of things existing in their midst it was urgently necessary that some meetings be held, prevailed upon Bro. Coffman" to remain for a week of evangelistic meetings. Earlier Coffman must have made a good impression on the congregation, for one member wrote to him in 1890: "I think it was well that you did not preach church ordinances that last Sunday[;] it would have been a disapointment [sic] for we have had restriction ordinances and

Mennonitism preached to us until we are soul sick and outsiders gospel hardened[;] it seems to me our Mennonite preachers are to [sic] apt [to] preach on these points and forget other important points."[8]

The 1892 meetings must have been successful. In May of the same year the reporter stated that as the result in the past two years of a "considerable direct effort ... in the church for the ingathering of souls," fifty-three new members had been added.[9]

In the growth of the Sterling congregation in the following years, the Good family from Virginia was important. Around the turn of the century, three brothers—Solomon, Samuel, and Aaron—migrated to Sterling, where they were to live the rest of their lives. Eventually Samuel was ordained minister; Aaron, minister and bishop; and Solomon, deacon. Another brother, Daniel, came later, and the father, Christian, also lived at Sterling for a short time in 1904 and 1905, helping in the ministry.

Solomon had been first to leave the parental home in Virginia, coming to Ottawa, Illinois, in 1893 to work for his father's uncle, Noah Brunk. During the four years Solomon was there he had occasion, both at Elkhart and at Ottawa, to visit John S. Coffman, who was his uncle. Coffman asked his nephew what he was doing at Ottawa, where there was no Mennonite church, and urged him to go to Sterling, where the church could use his services. He told Solomon of a "fine young school teacher up there that he might be interested in." This started a correspondence and visits. In 1897 Solomon moved to Sterling and on January 27, 1898, Coffman recorded in his diary: "Arrived at Sterling at 7:35 P.M. I went at once to the house of Bro. John R. Ebersole where all was in readiness, and Solomon R. Good and Martha E. Burkholder were married at 8 P.M. A nice quiet wedding. God bless them." On the following day Coffman added: "It is strange what a little incident will lead to." Solomon was an active worker in his congregation and denomination. In addition to being deacon, he served as Sunday school teacher and superintendent, chorister, member of the Church Hymnal Committee, president of the Illinois District Mission Board, and treasurer of the Mennonite Board of Education.[10]

Unfortunately, Samuel, who was ordained in 1904, was able to serve as minister only one short year before he died. This was a severe blow, for Sterling was again without a minister. Aaron said of his brother: "He was one of the finest Christians that I have ever known." As it turned out Aaron became Samuel's successor in 1906, although that was not in accord with Aaron's plans at the time. He was then serving at the Home Mission in Chicago and was planning the following year to enroll in Goshen College, where he had attended a six-week Bible term the winter before his brother's death. But the call from Sterling became increasingly strong. Bishops J. S. Shoemaker from

Freeport and John Nice from Morrison were called in for consultation. After further deliberation the bishops and the congregation decided not to use the lot if the congregation could unite on one man. Except for one vote, the call to have Aaron return to Sterling as pastor was unanimous. After counseling with friends, Good, who had long before felt a call to special Christian work, was confident that this was a call from God that he could not turn down. He was ordained on February 25, 1906. Of the more than a score of ministers that Science Ridge has had, Good's tenure, which stretched from 1906 to 1951, was by far the longest. "What a challenge," he observed, for a "boy of twenty-five with very little experience for such a large task." The task was large indeed! Science Ridge was the largest congregation in the Mennonite conference before the merger in 1920, and in terms of progressive work it was a leader both before and after that event.[11]

The Morrison congregation, organized in the 1860s, was one of the younger charter members of the Illinois Mennonite Conference when the conference was organized in 1872. Always a small congregation, Morrison has actually decreased in membership, having only fourteen members in 1980. Many Mennonites, like others, had a tendency to move west in the nineteenth century, as is illustrated by a visit that Preacher John Kornhaus from Morrison made to Nebraska in 1878. A Mennonite community near Juniata, Adams County, Nebraska, which he visited, was composed of ten families, with fourteen of these people having come from Whiteside County, Illinois. Kornhaus himself moved to Kansas in 1887. Such movement caused a greater out-migration than in-migration. Additional reasons for the failure of Morrison to grow have been summarized by a well-informed daughter of the congregation. One reason has been the people's "dislike for the hilly country." In addition, the "conference rules were very strict; Grandfather [Bishop John] Nice tried to abide by the rules but the people rebelled." Then, too, some people came to help out temporarily and then returned to their communities. "The people who were more adventurous went west as homesteaders; large plots of ground could be purchased for less than a small plot at Morrison." The social aspect must also be emphasized. Since the congregation was small and composed mostly of relatives, parents tended to move to communities with more Mennonite young people.[12]

From the beginning to the present the Nice family has been very important in the history of the congregation. Henry Nice, Sr., had been minister at Sterling since 1865, the year he arrived from Ohio. In 1868 he moved to Morrison and served as the first minister and later as bishop until his death in 1892. Henry Nice, Jr., was ordained deacon in that same year. John Nice, son of Henry Nice, Sr., was ordained minister in 1887 and bishop in 1895. He died in 1931. Daniel H. Deter, a relative, served as deacon a number of years. Aaron D. Nice, grandson of Bishop John Nice and great-grandson of Henry, Sr., was ordained minister in 1938 and has served to the present. Hazel Nice Hassan, writing in 1952, stated that the membership of only sixteen at that time consisted "of Deters and Nices and all are closely related. My family of my parents, my four brothers and sisters, my two sisters-in-law, and myself, constitute nine members." Hazel also stated how happy the group became in 1933 when a new minister, J. Kore Zook, his wife, and six children moved from Roseland, Nebraska, to Morrison. Before the Zooks came there "were only half a dozen young folks in the church and we were all cousins. We had many pleasant times during the next four years. Then the Zook family felt that more associates of like faith were essential for their children's good and they moved to Ashley, Michigan . . . [in] 1937."[13]

Henry Nice, Sr., was not only a pillar in the Morrison congregation, but also an able leader in the early days of the Illinois Mennonite Conference. In fact, J. S. Shoemaker has stated that Nice was "the prime factor" in organizing the conference. Characterized as "widely known and highly esteemed and respected," Nice had a significant past. Born in Montgomery County, Pennsylvania, in 1822, he and his family moved to Medina County, Ohio, in 1850, with a brother and a sister and their families accompanying him. Though later considered quite conservative, he was in some ways quite liberal for his time. At Wadsworth, instead of joining the Mennonite group already there, he helped form an Oberholtzer congregation, which later joined the General Conference. One reason for leaving Pennsylvania had been the refusal of the Mennonite leaders there to permit Sunday schools. Nice and the group's minister, Ephraim Hunsberger, organized the first Mennonite Sunday school in Ohio. Nice continued this interest in Sunday schools in Illinois, even in the face of opposition from some of his own congregation. In 1853 Nice had been ordained assistant minister at Wadsworth, a function he carried out until he moved to Illinois in 1865, where he continued as minister and then as bishop until his death in 1892. When the General Conference Mennonites met at Wadsworth in 1861 for their second session, to complete their conference organization that they had begun a year earlier at West Point, Iowa, Nice was a delegate and one of the signers of the "articles of constitution [on which] we the undersigned declare ourselves as united." Whatever the explanation for this apparent difference between his earlier and later positions, there is no question about his leadership ability, his patience, and his great usefulness in helping settle church difficulties.[14]

Another charter member of the Illinois Mennonite Conference was Cullom. Although it usually had a larger membership than Morrison, Cullom struggled more, probably because of a greater problem in leadership. Seldom did ministers remain long enough to give stability to the congregation. The turnover of lay members in Cullom also seemed more marked than in most Mennonite communities. One member commented that "Cullom had the biggest turnover of people of any [Mennonite community]." Using items from the local *Cullom Chronicle*, as well as other sources, Thomas Yoder discusses this problem at some length in his history of *The Cullom Mennonite Church*.[15]

Church periodicals also indicate something of the problem. John F. Funk, editor of the *Herald of Truth*, continued his interest in Illinois after moving to Elkhart and seemed to have special concern for Cullom. For some reason he seemed to include more news about Cullom than about the other Mennonite and Amish Mennonite congregations, many of which were larger. These items are a mixture of stories of progress on the one hand and obstacles to progress on the other.

Emanuel M. Hartman of Washington was ordained minister at Cullom in 1873 but returned to his native community in 1874. In 1877 C. D. Beery from Indiana preached at Cullom, with seven people being baptized and three reclaimed. During the next few years Cullom almost persuaded John S. Coffman to come from Virginia and serve as minister. Noah Grabill at Cullom, Coffman's second cousin, took the initiative in this attempt. On December 19, 1877, Grabill wrote Coffman about the great need for a minister at Cullom and also said something about the good land available there. If Coffman could not sell his land and could not come permanently, Grabill urged him to come for at least a year. Very much interested, Coffman seriously considered the matter. On one occasion he recorded in his diary that he would go if his wife, Betty, "would consent to go with me." In January 1879 he recorded: "I have nearly made up my mind to emigrate to Illinois in the next summer."

But meanwhile John F. Funk, who had been corresponding with Coffman, urged him to come to Elkhart to help in the publication work there. These letters from Funk continued and insistently pointed out the great opportunity that the publishing work represented for service in the church. Finally, Coffman recorded in his diary on March 13, 1879: "I am now in a full notion to go to Indiana." Coffman informed Noah Grabill of his decision and realized his cousin would be "wonderfully disappointed." But Coffman could not "think it otherwise than [that] providence is directing me to another field of labor." He then added: "I have a great attachment to the people in Livingston County, Illinois, and I had a great desire to work among them." This interest continued to the end of Coffman's life. As the historian of the Cullom congregation has written, even though he did not move to Illinois probably no other church leader "gave as much impetus to the development of a church in Cullom as did J. S. Coffman."[16] One wonders what difference it would have made at Cullom and in Illinois had the evangelist made the other decision.

Cullom's quest for ministers continued, as did also requests that itinerant preachers stop there. In May 1882 Coffman, who was becoming the foremost of such itinerants, reported in the *Herald of Truth* on two recent trips to Cullom. His report encouraged readers to aid members there to build a house of worship. He believed that opportunities for evangelism were great in that area and said a meetinghouse would fill an important need. He urged people to send in contributions to raise the $1200 or $1300 necessary to erect the building. The appeal was successful, and a completed building was dedicated in the same year. Benjamin F. Hamilton was minister at the time. Along with Bishop Hartman from Washington and others, Coffman was back to participate in the dedication services on September 24, 1882. He spoke in the morning and the evening in English and Hartman spoke in the afternoon in German. In his diary Coffman recorded that "the house was crowded and some outside this a.m. and full at 3, and crowded again in the evening." The evangelist remained for a week of meetings well attended by Mennonites and others. There were seven candidates for baptism and others "were almost persuaded."[17]

About a month later John's father, Bishop Samuel Coffman of Virginia, and Noah Metzler of Indiana spent a week at Cullom holding meetings, including baptismal and communion services. During that time also the congregation ordained young Peter Unzicker as minister, to assist Benjamin Hamilton. The visitors were pleased that the meetings were well attended, the people manifested "much interest and zeal," and the church appeared to be "enjoying a season of prosperity." But an 1885 report was less optimistic. J. S. Coffman, it said, was again with the church in Livingston County, which probably meant Cullom. Then it added: "There is in this church like many others, a pressing need for more laborers." In 1889 Peter B. Snyder was chosen minister by "the united voice of the church"; the congregation had not had a resident minister for several years. But then in 1894 Snyder moved to Alpha, Minnesota.

There must have been some ups and downs in the meantime. Coffman was back to Cullom for more meetings in December 1890. On December 21 he optimistically recorded that the day was beautiful and the roads good: "Had the finest roads I ever had at Cullom when we had meetings, the finest moonlight, the best attendance, the greatest interest, the deepest spirituality, and the greatest number of conversions [19]." But soon difficulties arose. Charges were brought against Peter Snyder "for not heeding his bishop's advice and Bro. Hartman [bishop] for dealing unadvisedly with the case at the council meeting." "Also charges against others." One thing Snyder did that a number at Cullom did not like was to attend Moody Bible Institute for one term after his ordination. "They were utterly against it and never did cooperate after that," wrote one son. Yet a few months later, May 16, 1891, came good news of a highly successful baptismal service. Twenty-three new members, mostly young people, were taken into the church—a rather large number for a congregation of fewer than a hundred. The meetinghouse was filled to capacity.[18]

Again in the early 1890s the Cullom congregation attempted to carry on without an active resident minister. J. S. Coffman, along with others, continued to come from time to time to preach. He also worked to solve Cullom's problems. In May 1893 he reported that he had a long talk with Benjamin Herner "regarding the trouble in the ch." The church looked "very peaceable, but the feeling [was] not good among the members." Minister Shelly of Reddick, in the same county, Bishop Hartman of Washington, and John F. Funk of Elkhart were also there to help Coffman bring about a better understanding. After several church meetings Coffman recorded: "Nearly all expressed themselves satisfied. We hope that the few dissatisfied ones will be reconciled." One dissatisfied person, at least as of July 1892 when he wrote to Coffman, was a person from Cullom who signed himself as "P. B. S." This was probably Minister Peter B. Snyder, who wrote a critical letter to the evangelist in which he expressed utter disgust with the conditions in the congregation and said he was about ready to give up. He felt that Coffman had made matters worse by siding with Snyder's critics. And, he charged, "where serious things were brought to your notice no attention was given them."[19] The problem of ministerial leadership at Cullom continued into the twentieth century, as did also the misunderstandings between individuals and groups.[20]

Around the turn of the century a remarkable number of reports appeared in church papers of Mennonites, both lay and ordained, making exploratory trips to various parts of the United States in search of good land at cheaper prices, especially for group settlement. Minister Peter Unzicker of Cullom was especially interested in the South. Sometimes with other ministers such as M. S. Steiner, sometimes with laymen such as Lewis D. Appel or L. J. Lehman (later to become minister), he made various southern trips to check out climate and possible sites for colonization. Finally in 1905 Unzicker moved to Tuleta, Texas. There he lived for some years, and a Mennonite community developed. One wonders to what extent the published reports proclaiming the virtues of the new areas led such Mennonites to move to the new areas—especially in a case like this where an ordained person led the venture.[21]

Despite obstacles to growth, many faithful members remained at Cullom to carry on the work of the church. And, of course, those who left usually made important contributions in the many places to which they moved: Texas, Idaho, Iowa, Louisiana, Kansas, Alberta, Missouri, Michigan, Nebraska, Oklahoma, Ohio, Indiana, Minnesota, and elsewhere, including other communities in Illinois. Surely the contributions of Cullom included those made in these other communities. For example, as one person has put it, "Practically the whole foundation of the Alpha, Minnesota, church moved away from Cullom."[22]

Those who remained at Cullom continued normal congregational activities—under occasional difficulties to be sure. A number of able laymen were a distinct asset in carrying on the work. One of the most active was Benjamin Herner, a schoolteacher who served also for a number of years as secretary of the Illinois Mennonite Church and Sunday school conferences. A number of successful revival meetings have already been noted. A Sunday school was organized in the early 1880s and young people's meetings were started about 1884. The women started an active sewing circle in 1919. Partly through talks given at Cullom by Aaron Loucks, J. S. Coffman, Coffman's son S. F., and others, the congregation became quite a supporter of missions. Missionaries Elsie Drange Kaufman and Esther Ebersole Lapp (also claimed by Science Ridge) had lived at Cullom, a circumstance that further stimulated the missionary interest.[23]

After the turn of the century new ministers came to Cullom, but their pastorates likewise were not very long. Alvin Ropp was ordained in 1905 but moved to Indiana in 1908. Samuel Honderich, a graduate of Elkhart Institute, came to Cullom in 1909 and then moved to Filer, Idaho, in 1913. After another period without a minister, J. S. Shoemaker persuaded John W. McCulloch, minister at Morrison, to go to Cullom in December 1916. He served ably until his death in January 1923.[24]

Cullom and the other congregations discussed above—Union, Freeport, Science Ridge, and Morrison—constituted the charter members of the Illinois Mennonite Conference organized in 1872. Before that date the Mennonite churches in Illinois were considered a part of the Indiana Conference, although the connection was rather loose and tenuous. In 1871 the Illinois brethren asked to have their own conference, which request the Indiana Conference readily granted. Henry Nice of Morrison, described as "one of the moving factors in organizing the Illinois Conference," extended an invitation to the Illinois Mennonite bishops, ministers, deacons, and lay members to attend the conference and hoped that ministers from other states would also attend.[25]

This first Mennonite conference met for one day, May 24, 1872, at the church near Sterling, then met annually thereafter. The first conference was attended by "some eighteen bishops, ministers and deacons" from Illinois, Indiana, and Missouri. According to one report in the *Herald of Truth,* everything "was discussed with the greatest love and harmony.... This is indeed a subject of the greatest importance, that in all such meetings unanimity and harmony should prevail. To inculcate peace and love, gather souls to Christ, build Zion and glorify God, is the great work of all God's ministers, and to this end may we all labor and pray." Daniel Brundage of Missouri gave the opening message to the conference, offering appropriate remarks based on Menno Simons' motto, 1 Corinthians 3:11. Conference discussed specific issues and asked members not to take part in worldly gatherings such as places of amusement, fairs, shows, celebrations, political gatherings, and so forth. Nor were members to adorn themselves in fashionable attire, take the sword, or take the oath. They could hold only those political offices that did not involve "taking the oath or enforcing the law." Joining secret societies was also forbidden, and no brother was permitted to "transfer his property over to his wife to avoid payment of debts."[26]

The annual conferences rotated more or less among the five Mennonite churches. Cullom, however, hosted none until 1891, and Union none until 1893, so that Sterling, Morrison, and Freeport hosted all of the conferences in the early years. John F. Funk, who attended some of these early conferences, reported them in the *Herald of Truth.* Unfortunately, right after the 1873 conference, held at Morrison, he was so busy leading a Russian Mennonite delegation to investigate possible land purchases in the West that he did not have time to write the report until later. So he reported the proceedings as well as he could remember. Apparently he had notes to help him, for his report was quite full.

Bishop Benjamin Hershey from Missouri and Bishop Henry Nice from Morrison gave opening discourses. They emphasized that all religion must be based on Jesus Christ and the Word of God, and all of our actions must be governed thereby. As long as we so build we shall progress, but as soon as we build on the traditions of men we shall fail. These messages set a conservative tone that characterized the Illinois Mennonite Conference for many years. The proper application of the Word of God meant, among other things, separation from the world, no holding of offices where it was necessary to use force, and no serving as jurymen especially in criminal cases "and where capital crimes are to be tried." Building on the true foundation also meant working together in the power of God's love which "will bind us immovable in one common union."[27]

The conference also spent some time discussing what constituted a church council and what cases should come to it for consideration. Apparently no hard and fast rule was laid down. But ministers were strongly urged to be very careful to take adequate counsel from their congregations, in order to protect the "most precious possession of the church," that is, "union, peace, love and good feeling among the membership." In case of dissension in the church they were to follow strictly the rule laid down by Christ in Matthew 18:15-18.

The conference also asked every minister to "make a proper effort" to preserve good order in his church during services. One problem was a "great deal of going in and out," which disturbed the worship. Another was a habit of chewing tobacco during church services. The conference noted that tobacco users

> sometimes spit on the floor to such an extent that worshippers cannot kneel without kneeling into a pool of tobacco spittle, and that in this way the house of worship is put into a condition that makes it disgusting to those who are accustomed to habits of purity and cleanliness, and that the minds of the worshippers are often very much drawn away from thoughts of purity and holiness, with which they at these times should be filled, and that it is objectionable to many. It was therefore advised that ministers should admonish the members of their respective churches to desist from chewing tobacco during services, and in every way try to keep the house of worship in a clean and orderly condition at all times.[28]

In the main address in 1875, Matthias Eby of Freeport emphasized the love of God and the necessity of being born again, as well as showing love to all men and following a life of obedience to Christ's teachings. He also pointed out that Christians should be humble, meek, and plain in appearance and dress. And they should not sue at law, engage in warfare, swear oaths, or have lightning rods, "but trust in God for protection." Two years later, the 1877 conference advised members to "exert themselves to prevent, as much as possible, the vain display of personal adornment and pride." "German parents" were to try to teach their children the German language. At the conference in 1878 it was considered "not advisable" to vote, and "earnest testimony was given against it." The conferees also said members should not "use lightning rods, nor insure their property," nor go to shows and other "places of amusement and worldly folly."[29]

Succeeding conferences often repeated these requirements and occasionally added new ones. In 1882 members were asked not to use musical instruments "to make a show in the world," but were to "sing praises and make melody in the heart to God." A significant new item on the positive side was the adoption of a mutual aid plan, such as Indiana had, for sharing losses due to natural disasters. In 1887 an "earnest protest" was made against "the taking of likenesses." Also, in case a member was sued in court it was deemed proper for him to present the facts of the case and accept the decision without appeal. In 1889 the subject of prohibition was discussed, but no action was taken. Conference action in the following year stated that members should refrain from attending "fairs, picnics, political rallies and celebrations, etc." Sending exhibits to these fairs was also proscribed. Again on the tobacco question, an "able argument" that someone presented at this conference and that was not refuted was that its use was "altogether as much conformity to the world as fashionable dress."[30]

One new question that the 1892 conference raised was whether ministers should be allowed to attend theological institutions. It decided that such attendance was not scriptural. Whether Moody Bible Institute was regarded as a "theological institution" is not clear, for shortly thereafter a number of Mennonite young men began attending this school. Another significant action at this conference was the resolution to make a great effort to instruct new converts so that they would be "thoroughly converted" when they came into the church. Was this an influence of the Mennonite awakening or of the Defenseless Mennonites, who had stressed this point a great deal? In 1893 the conference again emphasized this matter. New also was the advice of conference that women members should not vote in school elections, even though Illinois law permitted it. Nor should Mennonites join the Christian Endeavor Society and similar organizations, since many of the society's members conform to the world "in its vanities, customs and practices." Another resolution favored supporting the new Chicago Mission, provided it was operated according to gospel principles. Bishop Emanuel Hartman, who was asked in 1894 to investigate the mission, gave a favorable report at the next conference. The conference then heartily approved all mission work, both home and foreign.[31]

For some decades conference thought and development continued along similar lines, emphasizing nonresistance and nonconformity on the one hand and regeneration on the other. As one conference speaker put it in 1897, the church could stand only if it is composed of regenerated and consecrated believers. Church ordinances, though necessary, are not sufficient for salvation. Another said we must lay aside all formalism and "churchism" to attain the perfect liberty in Christ. Still another stated that sermons to the unsaved should begin and end with repentance and conversion, "laying special stress on true conviction of sin, faith in the Lord Jesus Christ, forgiveness of sins through faith in the atoning blood, and a thorough change of heart and mind...." The ideal church, said the 1900 report, was a group of members who had experienced evangelical conversion, were well acquainted with the Bible, were bound together by love, cooperated with each other, and were eager to bring salvation to the lost.[32] Both nonconformity/nonresistance and repentance/conversion were considered important. They were parts of the "whole gospel" as the (Old) Mennonites and Amish Mennonites were wont to say.

Though the conference became more powerful after the merger in 1920, some increase in power is noticeable even before that date. In 1899, for example, the conference report stated that "our form of church government is congregational." However, it also stated that some members who objected to conference decisions were "not in harmony with the church."[33]

In view of the conservatism of the conference, an action taken in 1904 with regard to marriage might be surprising. The question arose as to whether bishops and ministers could marry couples who were not church members. Since there was no specific command against this, the answer was affirmative, provided the parties, "so far as we know," were of good moral character. Another seemingly liberal action was taken in 1911. Heretofore the conference had not permitted the use of lightning rods, but now the action was different: "Since the Bible does not oppose the idea of protecting our lives and property against the elements, and since many of our brethren are protecting their property along other lines, be it resolved that the conference repeal all previous rulings on the use of lightning rods" and leave the matter up to the individual. Finally, in the more liberal vein, in 1918 the conference took a very small first step toward a paid ministry. It discussed the problem of the minister serving his congregation and church as he should when at the same time he had to make a living for a growing family. The delegates then decided to ask the newly organized District Mission Board to set up a fund from which a minister could draw to defray expenses that he was not personally in a position to meet.[34]

A new day dawned for these Illinois Mennonites when the new conference, the result of the merger of Illinois' (Old) Mennonites and its Amish Mennonites, met in 1921. The Amish Mennonites had greatly outnumbered the (Old) Mennonites, and now, with the dropping of the name "Amish," the Illinois Mennonite Conference membership jumped from 516 to 1,958.

In terms of theological position and observance of the ordinances, the union meant no change. The first new conference in 1921 made that fact clear. As before, the church continued to emphasize the new birth along with nonresistance and nonconformity. The 1920s in American history was a conservative period, and the Illinois Mennonite Conference shared the mood. Nonconformity was still construed very narrowly. There was to be no wearing of gold "for display" or jewelry of any kind. "Worldly amusements," that is, "theatres, circuses, horse races, fairs, moving picture shows, dances, Sunday baseball games, and all other places of questionable amusements," were not to be patronized. In the 1923 conference the report of a committee appointed earlier to draw up a "permanent resolution upon Nonconformity to the World and Separation in Attire" was discussed and accepted. The women were required to wear bonnets or hoods or "such forms of headdress consistent with the Devotional Covering, without any resemblance to the form of hats." Those who refused to respect the requirements were to be held under church censure and not considered communicant members until willing to conform. In 1924 the conference requested General Conference to establish a "place where our people can purchase clothing that are [sic] in line with Bible teaching on the doctrine of simplicity."[35] Possibly this strictness was in part a result of the tension caused by the controversy in the Mennonite Church which led to the temporary closing of Goshen College in 1923-24.

Conservatism also prevailed in the 1920s, when the conference turned down the request of the young people to organize a state literary society. Having no objection to local societies, the conference leaders thought the young people had sufficient outlet through Sunday school conference programs, missionary and young people's meetings and others, and that a state organization was therefore superfluous. In 1933, however, the conference rescinded this action, explaining that the state meetings could be profitable if conducted according to high literary and social standards and in cooperation with the conference Young People's Problems Committee.[36] In 1927 the conference considered the question of appointing lay delegates to its sessions; however, "after some deliberation [the question] was tabled."[37]

In 1924 the conference encouraged Illinois Mennonites to support the church schools (including the recently reorganized Goshen College) by prayer, financial contributions, and the sending of students. A few years later the conference expressed confidence in the Mennonite Board of Education and pledged its support and cooperation in the Board's program to increase the endowment fund of the college. In fact, throughout the succeeding decades the conference, while reserving the right to raise questions, loyally supported Goshen College. No doubt the fact that Noah Oyer, a native of Illinois, was dean at Goshen for some years until his death in 1931 helped bring about this support. Among others, Henry R. Schertz, respected leader from Illinois connected with the Mennonite Board of Education for many years, also made it easier for the support to develop. In 1931, Harold S.

Bender, who had succeeded Noah Oyer as dean of Goshen College, made an effective appeal to the Illinois conference for continued support. After pointing out how our schools had contributed to evangelism and missions, he emphasized that "compulsory military training, moral habits, social life, modernism, and ridicule of [the] faith of our Fathers in other school systems make church schools have an important place." To be sure, there were later occasions when Illinois questioned Goshen. One of these was in 1958, when the conference executive committee expressed concern about the influence of the college "upon the life and thought of our students." President Paul Mininger gladly invited a full discussion of the matter.[38]

In the period since the merger in 1920 the conference also took a number of steps that indicated its growing sense of the importance of Mennonite history. In addition to promoting Harry F. Weber's *Centennial History of the Mennonites of Illinois*, it agreed (in 1938) to take offerings in the congregations to help construct a building in Goshen for the housing of the archives of the Mennonite Church. In 1944 the conference decided to keep its records in these archives. When the new archives building was constructed in Goshen in 1959, the Illinois conference raised $1000 to be used in the building as a memorial to John Smith of Metamora and Joseph S. Shoemaker of Dakota. Their names appear on a plaque, along with those of pioneer leaders from other states. About the same time Arthur W. Nafziger (Hopedale) was appointed as the first official conference historian. Nafziger, in turn, encouraged each congregation to appoint its own historian, whose responsibility was to "preserve the items and records of value for the future." Since the Mennonites and the Amish had been notoriously lax and unsystematic in this regard, these moves represented notable steps forward.[39]

Conference action indicated other changes also. By the 1940s the conference was under increasing pressure to do something about ministerial support. So in 1946 the Illinois District Mission Board recommended the establishing of a fund to help support ministers who were not already receiving aid as missionaries under some mission board. A committee appointed to study the problem recommended in 1947 that Illinois start a definite program of teaching on the subject; that each congregation inaugurate its own program so that its minister would "live on a standard comparable to that of his laymen"; that conference set up a fund to help smaller congregations, when necessary, give special aid to ministers in time of emergency and provide for a retirement plan. The conference asked the committee to implement their recommendations. By this time the ministers were unanimous, according to the conference report, in feeling that they should receive support in order to carry on their work more effectively.

Apparently this program went into operation gradually over a period of years. For in 1954 the committee which had said, "The time is here for a program of ministerial support," was still pointing out the many problems in its implementation.[40]

One problem was that with the coming of a supported ministry, ministers moved more from place to place. Since pastors had to be better trained, especially in the face of contemporary tensions and challenges, this resulted in a shortage of qualified ministers. Another problem was that small congregations could not make offers as attractive to pastoral candidates as could the larger congregations. Consequently, the conference minister, Edwin Stalter, reported in 1973 that "one of the current frustrations is the lack of ministers for various conference churches."[41]

By the 1940s the pressure for the use of lay delegates in conference was increasing. The Amish Mennonites had used them earlier, but apparently the Mennonites had not. In 1949 the conference authorized the executive committee to appoint a committee to study the problem. In the following year the conference voted in favor of the principle of lay representation, and shortly thereafter each minister in charge of a congregation was authorized to bring to the business session one layman for each fifty members. In 1953 the conference also gave strong encouragement to a still wider use of the laity, including women. It had in mind the various auxiliary agencies and programs such as the District Mission Board, Christian Education Cabinet, Mennonite Youth Fellowship, camp activities, relief and service activities, and others.[42]

Other changes in emphasis in the second and third quarters of the twentieth century had to do with the various aspects of nonconformity. Conference topics and resolutions, as well as the newer constitutions and disciplines, indicate a declining concern for nonconformity, or at least a broader definition of the term.

By the 1940s and 1950s, and especially by the 1960s and 1970s, one can detect quite a difference. The newer documents put more emphasis on the positive and less on the negative aspects of Christian doctrine and belief. Here are the topics of a few conference programs to illustrate the point: "The Place of the Church in the Community," "The Church, the Pillar and Ground of the Truth," "Evidences of the Spirit-Filled Life," "Shepherding the Flock," "Ye Are Our Glory and Joy," "The Greatest Need of Our Conference" (love of God in our hearts), "Spiritual Food for Spiritual Hunger," "The Testimony of Radiant Victorious Living," "Sermon on the Mount," "Conserving our Resources," "The Missionary Message of the Cross," "The Place of the Bible in a World of Confusion," "Our United Effort in Presenting a Full Gospel Message."[43] A document entitled "Some Suggested Areas of Work for

Ministerial Committee of Illinois Mennonite Conference" lists the following: Tenure of Pastors and Transfer Implications, Ministerial Support Problems, Pastor Congregational Relationships, Spiritual Development, Recruitment of Workers, How Can We Serve Pastors In Their Current Assignments.[44]

This is not to say, of course, that the Illinois Mennonite Conference was no longer interested in nonconformity and simplicity. The new constitution of 1962 states the broadened concept and positive emphasis very well: "We believe that simplicity as a principle in living is taught in Word and example by Christ and His apostles. All Christians should seek to follow this principle in personal appearance, home, business, church, and social activities. The Christian life," continues the statement, "is one of genuine and lasting beauty if adorned with modesty, sobriety, and good works. A Christian should be clean and neat, practice economy, and possess only the wholesome, essential and utilitarian materials of life that are in harmony with his commitment to Christ. The best adornment is that of a meek and quiet spirit that does not call attention to self. The Christian life," the statement concludes, "is to be free from a love for money and anxiety about things, so that Christ may be served without hindrances." The committee that drafted the constitution and the conference that accepted it recognized that while God's Word and the gospel message do not change, the church, if it is to have a message that is meaningful to itself and the world, must endeavor to define how the Word of God and these unchanging principles are related to the contemporary situation, which changes from time to time. Hence the need for restatements or new constitutions.

Probably not all members in the conference, and certainly not all outside the state, were satisfied with such changes. Already in the late 1930s the Mennonite General Conference, through its General Problems Committee, expressed its concern and offered its services on several occasions by sending communications and goodwill representatives to speak at the state conference. The Illinois officials acknowledged receipt of the communications and thanked the general conference for having sent the men and for the messages they had brought. These officials also gave assurances that they would do their best to teach the Bible standards and counteract any wrong tendency in their own ranks.[45]

In the meantime, however, some rather serious misunderstandings had arisen between Illinois and the general conference officials. Apparently some Mennonites outside Illinois were critical of the Illinois Mennonite Conference and complained to the general conference officials. Some of these complaints came from the Indiana-Michigan Conference, which had very conservative leaders at this time. These brethren apparently had Illinois in mind when they complained that members in some districts were "openly known not to adhere to the faith and practice of some teachings of the Church" and that sisters were "wearing hats instead of the time honored bonnets." The Indiana-Michigan officials wanted the general conference to act.

The Illinois people became concerned about the "rumours, reports and conversations that the Illinois District Conference is not in good books with the Mennonite General Conference," as the state conference wrote to the general conference executive committee in 1939. The statement added that adverse reports about the Illinois conference have been circulating for some years—reports that "have a partial basis in fact" but that were greatly exaggerated. "In common with other conferences we have our serious problems," "including the style of headgear for sisters," many of whom had discarded the bonnet and were wearing hats. But the writers did not think the case was hopeless, and they wanted to be sure that Illinois would not be put out of general conference without an adequate hearing. They said that they were working on their problem, and that they believed in "scriptural separation from the world." The statement concluded, "Let us have faith in God and in one another."[46]

The reply of the general conference executive committee relieved the situation considerably, by making it clear that they had no conference on the "prohibited list and never contemplated nor planned anything of this nature regarding the Illinois Conference." They also stated that there had been no planned exclusion of Illinois names from the general conference program. Having cleared up the misunderstanding, the executive committee was pleased to read the "note of optimism regarding the future" contained in the Illinois communication.[47]

In 1948, in response to another request from the general conference, the Illinois Conference decided to send its moderator and its secretary to a meeting of all such district officials to discuss nonconformity in dress. The effect of this meeting apparently was minimal.[48]

The so-called plain coat (without lapels, and buttoning to the top) for the laity never was an issue in the Illinois Mennonite Conference. But its use by the ministry, as a clerical garb, was an issue—especially following the merger in 1920, which was a period of reaction in the larger Mennonite Church against some allegedly liberal tendencies. Although the Illinois Amish Mennonites had never required the plain coat, even of their ministers, they did accept it after the merger as a requirement for ministers. They never fully enforced the rule. This apparently never became a great problem. In 1948 the conference executive committee surveyed the ministers to ascertain their thinking about the requirement. By this time a few of the younger men were no longer wearing the garb, while a few others still wore it but thought it not necessary. As a result of the survey and of other developments, the conference in 1949 recommended the continued use of the regulation coat but decided no longer to require it: "its use will be optional with each minister." Gradually thereafter, the clerical coat disappeared. Some argued against its use on the grounds that they did not want to be called "Father," while others claimed that it interfered with their Christian witness among the unsaved. But the cause was probably deeper. One conference official thought the action was taken "because a number used the 'coat' as a scapegoat for their non-cooperation. When that was taken away the majority [of those opposed] still could not work with conference."[49]

Another question bound to face conference sooner or later was the use of musical instruments. Among both the Amish Mennonites and the (Old) Mennonites their use had been forbidden for many years in the home and church. After the turn of the century their use in the home began and was soon widespread. Their use in the church, however, did not become a pressing problem until the 1950s. More and more members began to ask why they could not use them, at least in a limited way, in church services. In 1958 conference appointed a committee headed by Oscar Roth of Flanagan to study the music practices in the Mennonite churches in Illinois and, to some extent, elsewhere. The committee was asked to study the problem from various angles: history, Scripture, value of the instrument in witnessing, experience of others, the effect on the unity of the church, and especially the effect on congregational singing. The committee produced an excellent report, not necessarily favoring or opposing the use of the instrument, but laying down important guidelines for its use if and when a congregation decided to use it. One of these strongly emphasized the importance of maintaining strong congregational singing by using the instrument only in a limited, subordinated manner.[50] Since that time, using musical instruments in church services in this limited manner has become widespread.

Important changes involving the ministry came in 1961-62, when the old time-honored order of bishop, minister, and deacon was eliminated. At that time the conference put into effect a system that recognized "a single ordination to the full ministry which carries the responsibility for this oversight of the congregation in which the minister serves as pastor." This meant that no more bishops would be ordained and that the full minister would assume the bishop's functions. Deacons or deaconesses could still be ordained, but in 1964 the secretary of the conference wrote that so far as he knew none were any longer. About this time congregations began to set up church councils or boards of elders to assist the pastor.[51]

In the 1950s the prayer veiling for women, an issue long thought to have been permanently settled, came up for new consideration in the Illinois Mennonite Conference. Responding to questions arising in the new congregation at Lombard, the conference in 1957 recommended "cooperation with conference practice in observing the ordinance" as "a means of establishing confidence within our constituency" toward the Lombard work. After some discussion the motion was tabled. The delegates then expressed appreciation for the work Lombard was doing in its community, acknowledged that "unique problems" existed in such urban areas, accepted their problems "as our mutual concern," and expressed desire to unite with them in finding solutions.[52] The conference constitution of 1962 still states that the Bible teaches that "women should have a symbolic veiling in praying and prophesying," but the statement says "should" rather than "must." In the mid-sixties the conference studied the topic in greater depth, using as its chief consultant and resource person Clayton Beyler of Hesston College. His position on the covering, which of course influenced the results of the study, was that the regulation came late in the Mennonite Church and evolved from a sort of cultural practice and symbol, more or less common earlier, into a crystalized ordinance by the use of 1 Corinthians 11:2-16. As the result of this study and of the conference action with regard to Lombard, the covering has declined in use since that time—as is also true, of course, in a number of other Mennonite Church conferences.[53]

Divorce and remarriage was another difficult problem that could no longer be settled by the old, simplistic solution of refusing church membership for divorced and remarried persons so long as both parties to the original contract were still living. In the 1950s the Illinois Mennonite Conference struggled hard with the problem, first and most insistently in the city mission churches. An increasing number of ministers could not believe that the redemption offered by the church through Christ did not cover all sins, including those that might have been committed through divorce and remarriage. These ministers did not feel that they should have to say to these people, "You can be saved in another church," or that the Great Commission meant that they should "not preach the gospel where there are divorces." To make a long story short, new statements emphasized as before the permanence of Christian marriage and put still more emphasis on the necessity of more training on this point. They stated that the breaking of marriage by divorce and remarriage was a sin for which Christians must repent. Each case had to be considered separately. When breaking the existing union does "not seem advisable or right," the persons involved could be considered for church membership "on such a basis as gives to the persons involved peace with God and the foundation for a growing experience with Christ." Such individuals should confess their sin and promise that "in Christ they now pledge lifelong faithfulness to their spouse." The congregation should agree to "receive them warmly"—probably with a 75 percent vote. The statement added that usually such persons "will not be considered as candidates for the ministry."[54]

Within the Mennonite Church conference the resolution of these problems has been accompanied, since the merger, by an impressive program of outreach—particularly as compared with other periods. Of course, this new period of activity came at the peak of the movement called the awakening or the quickening of the Mennonite Church, which affected Illinois as it did other states. This new emphasis on outreach took various forms, including the volunteering of many individuals for mission and relief work at home and abroad; the continuation of evangelism, with some experimenting with mass evangelism such as the Howard Hammer campaigns in the 1950s; letter-writing evangelism; roadside evangelism as conducted by John Harnish; radio messages such as those given by Howard J. Zehr, Lester Hershey, the Calvary Hour, the Mennonite Hour and others; summer Bible schools; voluntary service units; installation (in the home of C. Warren Long of Tiskilwa) of a telephone dial-a-number to receive a one-minute devotional message, for which an average of ninety people a day called during the first three months; the better training of Sunday school teachers through the promotion of Sunday school normals or institutes; better church and Sunday school literature and libraries as promoted by Ruth C. Roth and others; the establishment of the Mennonite bookstore in Bloomington; the work of the Illinois District Women's Sewing Circle as promoted by Lydia H. Smith and others; and, finally, the work of Mennonite Youth Fellowship. In 1949, for example, the Willow Springs MYF decided that they "would again pick up corn out of husked fields, sell it, and use the money for some missionary purpose," thus antedating the widely advertised work of Eureka College students in this same activity just a few years ago.[55]

In addition to the above methods of outreach, Illinois Mennonites also emphasized the necessity of planting new Sunday schools and congregations. The Illinois District Mission Board, organized in 1917, provided effective leadership in this work, its chief purpose being as stated in its constitution, to "create and promote missionary interest and work." One important means of carrying forward this effort was the publishing of a new periodical, the *Missionary Guide*, founded by the board in 1944.

Although there were some efforts to form extension Sunday schools before 1920, most of this type of activity has come since that date. Over and over the board and/or congregations and individuals emphasized the necessity of more aggressive outreach. For example, in 1937 J. N. Kaufman, veteran missionary to India then living and working in Illinois, reported as field-worker for the district mission board that he thought it would be better and more fruitful if congregations rather than the board would start branch Sunday schools. The secretary of the board said that each church in the conference was "responsible for evangelizing the local community." Henry R. Schertz of Metamora agreed that extension Sunday schools were a "very practical phase of any congregation's program." But the board reported later that it too had to become more active "if it is to fulfill its assigned evangelistic task." In 1961 it announced an aggressive program, including a "Conference-Wide Program for Church Expansion."

About the same time, Ivan Kauffmann, president of the Illinois Mennonite Mission Board, in announcing a "Missions Week," said that the purpose was to enlist the whole church in mission, whether at home, in the city or abroad. In an article in the *Gospel Herald* Edwin J. Stalter, later the conference minister, emphasized the same theme under the title "The Hour of Urgency" (Aug. 23, 1960). Richard Yordy, looking at the congregational level again, stressed that individual initiative alone would not fill the need. The church also should hear the "call," discover persons with gifts and abilities, and then train them for service. The aggressive outreach is well illustrated by the Sterling sister, Pauline Lehman, who felt the church was strong in theorizing but weak in action. Using Exodus 14:15, "Why do you cry to me? Tell the people . . . to go forward," she wrote: "Read the Bible to see what it says and then go forward." Jonathan J. Hostetler, who had already had many years of experience in the promotion of Sunday school work when he came to Illinois from Ohio in 1952, continued the same interest in his new field of labor. Thus, the influence of many people was felt in this new impact. Among the many Illinois laymen, the lifelong work of John Roth of Morton, Chris E. Martin of Hopedale, and John D. Conrad of Sterling could be given as examples. The new emphasis said that all Christians should engage in full-time service, whether or not they were engaged in church work full time.[56]

This outreach in the Illinois Conference has resulted in persistent although hardly phenomenal growth. At times some people thought they ought to do better, which led occasionally to discussion of the need to reevaluate "our evangelistic and soul-winning function," and to more self-searching and emphasis on an every-member evangelism. But the growth was clearly greater than before.

Outside of Chicago the oldest Mennonite Church extension work was the Garden Street Mission in Peoria begun in 1919. In 1921 the Illinois District Mission Board, which started the mission, turned it over to the Mennonite Board of Missions and Charities; still later it became known as the Ann Street Mennonite Church. In 1938 the congregation opened a branch Sunday school in Bellevue, just west of the city. This work was organized, under the leadership of Orie A. Miller, "into an indigenous and later unaffiliated congregation, known as the Bellevue Bible Church." Among the leaders at Peoria were John Roth, John Harnish, Earl Miller, C. Warren Long, Howard J. Zehr, and Jonathan J. Hostetler.[57]

At Pleasant Hill, located between East Peoria and Morton, the Mennonites started services in 1920, although John Roth had done some planning for it years earlier. It was organized as a congregation in 1924. Among the many who served here were John D. Conrad, veteran missionary J. N. Kaufman and Roy Roth, who left in 1951 to become president of Hesston College.[58]

Jonas Baer, a Lutheran, started the mission project at West Sterling in 1928. Before his death in 1933 he had asked A. C. Good whether Science Ridge would not take it over. Science Ridge agreed to do so. Fanny Gish, also a Lutheran, had assisted Baer and continued to help after the Mennonites took over. Daniel G. Lapp, veteran church worker from Roseland, Nebraska, concluded his long career by serving as pastor at West Sterling from 1940-46. On at least three or four occasions the meetinghouse facilities have been enlarged. At the fiftieth anniversary program in May 1978 all of the former pastors except Lapp, who had died, were present: Robert Keller, Paul Friesen, Vernon Schertz, Melvin Hamilton, Ron Schraeder, and Harley Stauffer.[59]

The next point of outreach was at Arthur in the 1930s, the result of an active interest in mission at East Bend. Bishop Joseph A. Heiser of Fisher, about forty miles north, kept in touch with the situation in Arthur, particularly so after some Mennonites began to move to Arthur and after some from there began to attend church at East Bend. In 1936 the Obie Bontrager family in Arthur opened their home for church services every other Sunday, the people going to East Bend on the alternate Sundays. In 1938 Henry J. King, from Harper, Kansas, was called to be pastor at Arthur, and in 1940 the group was organized as a separate congregation with fifty-seven charter members. Through revival meetings and other means the congregation grew rapidly, drawing largely, as noted previously, from the Old Order Amish community. At the dedication in 1949 of a new church edifice, 550 people were present. The membership in 1953 was 241. Soon after, however, some problems arose in the congregation, leading to the withdrawal of some thirty-five or forty members. The problems were complicated, among them being differences over a Christian day school in the community, the bringing in of an assistant pastor (Theodore Wentland) and his support, and, especially, questions of how to preach and apply nonconformity in the congregation. A dissatisfied group, thinking the church had become too liberal and worldly, withdrew and joined the newly organized Conservative Mennonite congregations in the area. The membership in 1980 was 234. Richard Yordy and Paul Sieber also served as pastors at Arthur; Wayne Hochstetler serves at present (1981).[60]

One church venture at Arthur was not successful. In 1951 the Mennonite Board of Missions and Charities and the Illinois Mennonite Mission Board joined to establish near Arthur the institution called "Rockome," intended as a home for retired or furloughed missionaries, and other church workers. It was also to serve as a possible center for church conferences, retreats, and other activities. As stated earlier, Arthur Martin of Arthur donated the land to the church-wide mission board for these purposes. But only one retired missionary, Mary Good, lived here, for only two years or less. The place was too far from any town and from major centers of Mennonite life.[61]

The Mennonite work at Highway Village in East Peoria also goes back to the 1930s. Pleasant Hill started a Sunday school there in 1937. C. A. Magnuson and wife headed the work until 1945, when Wilfred Ulrich came from Roanoke. After Ulrich left in 1947 to take up the work in Peoria, Paul Friesen became the minister until 1951, when he left for West Sterling. At that point the Illinois Mennonite Mission Board assumed responsibility at Highway Village and secured Robert Harnish of Roanoke to serve as pastor. The church prospered, became an independent congregation and soon had a larger membership (103 in 1978) than its parent-sponsor, Pleasant Hill. After Harnish's fairly long period of service Clarence Sutter became pastor.[62]

Before the Pleasant Grove and Goodfield congregations united in Morton in 1941, the former sponsored an extension Sunday school there for a short time, beginning in January 1939. Preaching services also were held twice a month, besides some Sunday evening services and women's meetings. Interest in this ministry was strong from the beginning. Mahlon Eigsti was superintendent and John Roth, assistant. This merging of Pleasant Grove and Goodfield into one congregation could be interpreted as contraction but it really was not. The new united congregation grew in giving as well as in membership. It reported in 1958 that in the previous five years its giving had more than quadrupled.[63]

Like its sister congregations, the Metamora congregation was also influenced by the new emphasis on evangelism. In 1939 E. H. Oyer and others started an extension Sunday school at Richland near Spring Bay. Richland became an example of a work that resulted in no permanent congregation, yet continued for some fifteen or more years and did much good for the cause of Christianity. Many renewed their

Christian commitment, while others found Christ for the first time and joined churches already established in the community. The work at Germantown between Metamora and Peoria that Metamora started in 1949 and was carried on into the 1960s likewise did not become permanent. In 1949 Metamora also took over a ministry in Cazenovia, which did result in a separate congregation. Mrs. Isa Stivers had continued Sunday school services there after her denomination, the Christian Church, had closed its work. After some years she asked H. R. Schertz whether Metamora would continue the ministry, and it did. Vernon Schertz and others assumed leadership until Melvin Hamilton, who had come into the Mennonite Church from an Evangelical United Brethren background, became their minister. Wayne King, minister in 1965 (also of Germantown), reported the Cazenovia membership as 44. The figure was 54 in 1980.[64]

Another point of outreach was Newcastle, between Deer Creek and Mackinaw. Sponsored by Goodfield, with some help from Hopedale, the ministry became Morton's responsibility after Goodfield merged with Pleasant Grove in 1941. Although a summer Bible school had been held there as early as 1936, the Sunday school work was not organized until 1940. Robert Zehr was the leader. This ministry prospered but did not long remain in the Mennonite Church.[65]

Work was started in 1941 at Dewey, an outpost of East Bend, with Joseph C. Good as superintendent. In 1955 it became a separate congregation with Ivan Birkey as minister. It had a membership in 1980 of seventy-four. The East Bend congregation reopened a closed church in Lake City in 1948 and operated it for several years.[66] And East Bend started a work at Gibson City, which since the 1950s had been carried on under other auspices.

The Rockwell congregation near Sheffield, also started in this period, represents a slightly different kind of outreach—at least after its beginnings. Beginning in 1942 as a mission Sunday school operated by the Willow Springs congregation at Tiskilwa, the work soon included preaching and evangelistic services by various visiting ministers. One chief purpose of the congregation, after its organization in 1945, was to serve as a place of worship for Mennonites who had recently moved into the community. Joseph M. Gingerich, a Mennonite from Ohio and Iowa, had bought farms in the area and had encouraged Mennonites to move onto them. The congregation asked John Detweiler of New Wilmington, Pennsylvania, a recent Goshen College graduate, to serve as their minister.[67]

Unfortunately, for various reasons the project did not work out as planned, and in 1950 it ended. Probably the chief reason was the death of Joseph Gingerich in March 1946, followed by the death of his wife, Fidella, the next year. The long, involved settling of the estate jeopardized the hopes of the Mennonite settlers to continue renting and eventually to buy the Gingerich farms. John Detweiler resigned as pastor in 1948. His successor, John I. Byler of the singing Byler family, could not forestall the inevitable. In addition to the deaths of the Gingerichs, other discouraging factors were the small number of members, their being scattered over a wide area, and the failure of the church to make an impact on the predominantly Catholic community.[68]

Extension work at Hopedale is a good example of how outreach increased the witness for the gospel. In 1945 at Dillon about twelve miles southwest of the church, the congregation started a Sunday school, which became a separate congregation in 1952, with John Troyer ordained as minister. In 1950 Hopedale also began a Sunday school at Midway south of Pekin. This, too, became a separate congregation, with Howard Wittrig ordained as minister in 1955. In 1959 Dillon, Midway, and Hopedale joined to begin a work in the town of South Pekin. As a result, reported Boyd Nelson in 1960 in an article "Outreach in Illinois," the "combined attendance of 500 or 600 people touching four communities reaches many more persons than the single congregation at Hopedale could." Joe W. Davis became the pastor at South Pekin. The ministries at all three of these places became separate congregations and members of the Illinois (MC) conference.[69]

In 1950 Roanoke established an outpost at Robein, a locality then between Washington and East Peoria but now a part of the latter. After continuing for a quarter of a century the work terminated for various reasons. Among them was difference of opinion arising over the appearance of some Fundamentalistic tendencies, which to an older nucleus seemed to downgrade Anabaptist-Mennonite principles, thus causing much confusion and lack of clear direction. A tragic experience for this congregation was the drowning in 1960 of their young pastor, Eldon Kortemeier, in a lake in Minnesota. Norman Kauffmann was pastor from 1962-69.[70]

The outpost at Amity Chapel near Sumner, quite distant from any Mennonite community, apparently developed because it was in the home territory of Howard Hammer, who had come into the Mennonite Church from another background as an evangelist and missionary. After Harold Zehr and I. Mark Ross made the initial survey, the Illinois Mennonite Mission Board sponsored the development of the work under the leadership of Joe I. Kauffman, Kenneth Good, and J. Alton Horst, among others. At the end of the 1950s the Amity Chapel group released the Board of its responsibility, and no permanent Mennonite church developed at Amity.[71]

The work at Lombard also began in the 1950s, from several groups and interests: Mennonites living in the western suburbs of

Chicago who felt too far away from the Union Avenue Mennonite Church (Home Mission); Mennonite Voluntary Service people and I-W men and their families; some General Conference Mennonites in the area; and encouragement from the Mennonite Church's Mission Board and from C. Warren Long, bishop of the Union Avenue Mennonite Church. These Mennonites first organized the Western Suburban Mennonite Fellowship, which began to meet in homes in December 1952. In September 1954 they decided to organize a church and affiliate with the Illinois Mennonite Conference.

As noted earlier, some problems arose in this congregation over the use of the prayer veiling in church services, but were eventually resolved. LeRoy Kennel, the first pastor, served for a number of years and was then followed by Joe Richards, former missionary in Japan. In the 1970s a new problem faced the conference when the congregation wanted to ordain Emma (Mrs. Joe) Richards to the ministry in order to serve with her husband. This caused considerably more than mere raising of eyebrows. But in 1973, after further study, the conference allowed "the Lombard congregation to go ahead and ordain Emma Richards in this specific case," apparently taking into account her special gift for speaking and preaching.[72] Emma has the distinction of being the first ordained woman in the (Old) Mennonite Church. The congregation has been well pleased with the arrangement and continues to flourish. In 1980 its membership was 151, nearly half of whom were of non-Mennonite background. The Mennonite General Board and the Mennonite World Conference have their headquarters on the Lombard church grounds.[73]

In 1956 the Illinois Mennonite Mission Board started church services in Bloomington with the dual purpose of beginning a mission outreach and serving as a church home for the large number of (Old) Mennonites living there. This work progressed for some years under the pastorates of Joe Kauffman, H. J. King, Harold Zehr, and Carl Newswanger. In 1976 it and the larger General Conference congregation at Normal merged.[74]

An outreach of a different nature began in Evanston about 1957. Started by John Miller, Virgil Vogt, and others who desired to live in Christian community, the project grew out of discussion in the early 1950s by a group of seminary students and relief workers who "were deeply challenged by the rediscovery of ancient Anabaptist thought which was taking place at Goshen College.... An exciting vision of the church took shape—a concept of the church as a disciplined brotherhood, determined to be radically obedient to Christ whatever the cost, and intensely evangelistic through the witness of its life." In 1957 John Miller bought a house at 727 Reba Place in Evanston, which gave the group its name: "Reba Place Fellowship." As its numbers increased, the fellowship, as a commune, bought additional housing nearby. The philosophy was that it was more important for members to be near each other than near their jobs. Living within walking distance of each other made possible frequent group meetings for shared decision-making, and allowed more helpfulness to each other. The group holds possessions in common "because we see the needs of our brothers and sisters as our own." Coming from many backgrounds, the fellowship numbered about 250 adults and children by the mid-1970s. It has affiliated both with the Illinois Mennonite Conference (MC), though not until 1976, and with the Church of the Brethren. Membership in 1979 was 148.[75]

In 1953, Freeport began an extension work at Lancaster Heights, a housing development located between the church and the city of Freeport. It started as a Sunday school, but in 1958 Paul Sieber was installed as a licensed minister. He moved away in 1965 to become pastor at Arthur, and his brother Floyd served the congregation for one year. Melvin Hamilton succeeded him. Because of declining membership and attendance—due in part to the removal of several families active in the church—the work closed about 1972.[76]

The unique work at Norwood, a suburb of Peoria, is the product of several former outreach posts: Ann Street Mennonite Church and Pleasant Hill, plus a bit of assistance from Highway Village. The Norwood work began in 1959, following a survey that showed need for a spiritual ministry and interest of many community people. Another significant element in Norwood's development was that, aside from the leadership of Lester Sutter, who was called in to serve here, the work was carried on almost wholly by those from the community, rather than by assistance of Mennonites from the outside. At first the people met in the basement of Sutter's home, but from the beginning crowds were larger than expected. They rallied round their pastor in the building of a church, with one man giving $3,000 for the purpose. Such a situation, where so many were of non-Mennonite background, presented problems as well as opportunities. Norwood as well as many other outreach congregations required a great deal of teaching on such principles as nonresistance.[77]

Several groups converged at Evanston in 1959 and 1960 to form a congregation in that city: Mennonite families in the area; Mennonite students at Garrett, Northwestern, and other institutions; I-W men and their families; persons from Reba Place; Mennonite college girls working in the northside communities in the summer; and interested non-Mennonites from the area. Representatives formed a planning committee for the organization of a church, Dr. Ernest and Mary Smucker and others already having started a Mennonite Fellowship in 1958. The result of this committee's work was a decision to go ahead with the organization of a church to be affiliated with the Illinois Mennonite Conference. Services marking the organization and dedication were held February 26, 1961. Ron Goetz served as pastor on an interim basis until Laurence Horst came in 1963. Since the I-Ws have been phased out, the membership is less now than a few years ago. Recently it has become a "house church."[78]

Outreach in Urbana-Champaign, which grew out of a Mennonite fellowship started in the late 1950s, will be discussed in chapter 17.

Partly, if not largely, as a result of the new emphasis on outreach, statistics show church growth. Its pattern, however, was "persistent rather than phenomenal." Arthur W. Nafziger and Thomas Yoder have constructed tables that show this growth. The Yoder table appeared in the *Missionary Guide* of August 1973.[79]

Year	No. of Organized Congregations	Membership
1920	7	516
1925	16	2106
1930	16	2156
1935	15	2359
1940	15	2675
1945	17	2985
1950	20	3355
1955	22	3086
1960	27 organized 8 unorganized	3356
1965	33 organized 4 unorganized	3680
1970	36	3946

Yoder's figures for 1920 include only (Old) Mennonites. From 1925 they include the merged Amish Mennonites. The decrease between 1950 and 1955 reflects the loss of members in the early 1950s discussed in chapter 12. Membership figures, of course, do not tell the whole story. Many attended who became members elsewhere, and the number attending the Sunday schools was several thousand greater than the membership.[80]

Not everyone was satisfied with this record, especially with the figures for 1960. Ivan Kauffmann, president of the Illinois Mission Board, wrote in 1961: "We ought to be ashamed of our record." "It took 10 years for 3,355 Mennonite Christians to win 1 convert to Christ and the Church." Although Kauffmann thought there was something wrong with such church life, he added: "But God is granting us time and opportunity to do better in the next 10 years." As the figures indicate, they did.[81]

Camping has also been an important ministry of spiritual outreach in the Illinois (Old) Mennonite church. One Illinois leader called Christian camping "another effective tool of Christian education" and a "strong arm of evangelization and nurture for the church." Another called it an "extension of the Christian education program of the local churches." Camping programs began in the 1940s when Orie A. Miller from Peoria, Lester Hershey and James Lark from Chicago, and others took boys, especially from the cities, to camps for brief periods in summer for various Christian-directed activities. At first they used the camps of other groups, until the Mennonites formed a Camp Association in 1957 and bought land near Tiskilwa in 1958. This was the beginning of Camp Menno Haven. Since then both the acreage and the facilities have been increased. Consisting of some 233 acres of wooded terrain and farmland, the camp contains a small lake formed by a government dam and has excellent facilities for both youths and adults. Vernon Schertz was the first director.[82]

The emphasis on outreach after the merger in 1920 also affected the conference's older, established congregations. With a few exceptions such congregations experienced a steady but not phenomenal growth. As already noted, Harmony, which was not a separate congregation, closed in 1929. In the same year Union merged with Metamora. Cullom continued to have its ups and downs, especially the problem of retaining a minister long enough to provide stability. In 1952 the pastor reported that "God's candle" at Cullom was "flickering." He pleaded for Mennonites to move there to help fan the little "choking wick" into full flame. The same pastor had reported in 1949 that a religious survey showed that more than twoscore Mennonites and their descendants had been lost to the Cullom church in the previous twenty years, and that more of these had joined the local Catholic church than any other. Even before that, one reliable source had stated in 1947 that the membership was then "only 17, and about 5 of those inactive." The misunderstandings and factionalism in the congregation noted earlier, and especially the fact that young people often had to seek economic opportunity elsewhere, were also important reasons for the decline. Church services diminished in number and finally ended in the early 1960s. The other exception to the general rule of growth was Morrison. Here, unlike Cullom, the problem was not lack of a stable ministry but other complex factors. In fact, the persistence of the ministerial and lay leadership at Morrison was probably the main reason the work continued. In 1980 the membership was fourteen.[83]

One big change in the Illinois Conference which came by the midfifties, probably largely as a result of a supported ministry, was that the pastorates became single rather than multiple and the ministers began to move from one congregation to another. If congregations were to support pastors adequately, one congregation was not inclined to support several of them, except that a large congregation might at least partially support a second one. The tendency toward more mobility also meant that the long pastorate of a J. S. Shoemaker at Freeport, an A. C. Good at Sterling, an H. R. Schertz at Metamora, an Ezra Yordy at Roanoke, or of others, were now gone. Congregations also began to insist more and more on an educated ministry, with at least some training in college and seminary. This, of course, does not mean that older ministers were not educated. By dint of hard study many were educated far beyond their formal training. Indeed, in view of their accomplishments, one wonders what leaders like Shoemaker and Good, for example, could have done further had they had college and seminary training. Schertz did have some training at Moody Bible Institute and Bethany Bible School in Chicago and put it to good use in his leadership. But Shoemaker had very little formal training and yet became one of the outstanding leaders in the Mennonite Church.

Many examples of the changing trends could be given, but the four congregations mentioned above, two formerly Amish Mennonite and two Mennonite, are typical. At Roanoke Ezra Yordy served from 1917 to his retirement in the 1950s. For most of this period John Harnish was also one of the ministers. Since 1957 the terms have been quite different. Wesley Jantz served about four years; Norman Derstine, seven years; Percy Gerig, eight years; and Norman Yutzy, from January 1978 to January 1981. At Metamora, following H. R. Schertz's sudden death in 1954, LeRoy Kennel (who actually began as assistant minister shortly before Schertz's death), Roy Bucher, and James Detweiler served as pastors. In 1979 while the congregation was seeking a pastor, LeRoy Kennel again preached for the group on a temporary basis. In the summer of 1979, Larry Augsburger, who had just graduated from Goshen Biblical Seminary at Elkhart, accepted a call to serve as minister. At Freeport, following Shoemaker's death in 1936 and Simon Graybill's in 1941, Howard J. Zehr, Richard Yordy, Don Blosser, and Paul O. King have served as pastors. Following A. C. Good's long ministry at Sterling, from 1906-51, Robert Keller, Frederick Erb, Edwin Stalter, and Mark N. Lehman have served as pastors. Phil Helmuth is the present minister. Thus, though the periods at present still vary in length, the trend is strikingly toward much shorter pastoral terms.[84]

Apparently this trend was a matter partly of philosophy on the part of the younger pastors. Howard J. Zehr probably was typical. With regard to his ministry at East Bend, he wrote that he and his wife never considered it permanent. They wanted to "maintain a pilgrim stranger attitude toward life" and wanted to consider their place of service in that light. "One cannot do his best work by staying in one locality," he continued. "All of us have limitations.... This is my conviction."[85]

Thus developed the non-Amish settlements and congregations of the Illinois Mennonite Conference. Most were in the northern part of the state. These congregations—Union, Freeport, Science Ridge (Sterling), Morrison, and Cullom—organized the conference in 1872, which was greatly enlarged when the much larger group of Illinois Amish Mennonites merged with it in 1920. In the newly merged body there developed outreach which brought new congregations into the conference and new members into most of the older ones. Perhaps more important than growth in numbers were changes in thought patterns that overtook the Mennonite Church by the 1950s and since, through new interpretation and application of nonconformity, divorce, women's prayer veiling, the role of women, support of ministers, and other beliefs and practices.

CHAPTER 10

The "Awakening" Among Illinois Mennonites: Publication, New Agencies, Organizations

Awakening" is the term often used to describe a new spirit of activism that came over American Mennonites in the latter part of the nineteenth and the first part of the twentieth centuries. Originally the Anabaptists in Europe were "intensely evangelistic." But long-continued persecution and martyrdom finally took their toll and the Anabaptists' spiritual descendants became the *Stillen im Lande* (quiet in the land), thankful finally to have found freedom and peace but not aggressive in spreading their gospel message. The Mennonite and Amish immigrants to America in the colonial period and in the nineteenth century brought with them this quiet spirit. In fact, this attitude so prevailed that when more courageous spirits felt led to be more aggressive, they were sometimes ostracized or even excommunicated from the brotherhood.[1]

Not all authorities are satisfied with the term "Awakening." Some prefer "Quickening."[2] But whatever term is used, it refers to a revived and growing sense of mission that characterized most of the Mennonite brotherhood in the last third of the nineteenth century and into the twentieth. In place of the meek, humble, passive attitude of the past, the new movement revealed a more aggressive spirit of attacking the forces of evil. Declared a report of an Illinois Sunday school conference at Freeport in May 1899: "We are entering a new field of labor in the history of our church. We need to cut loose from all moorings that hinder spiritual advancement and enter on an era of more aggressive work in all departments of the work of the church."[3] A spirit of enthusiasm, hope, and faith also characterized awakened Mennonites.

"The wonderful awakening among the Mennonite people during the last fifteen years," said N. S. Gingerich of Elkhart Institute (Ind.) in 1900, "was only a revival of that ... enthusiasm ... zeal ... eagerness to know ... and spread the truth, which was the chief characteristic of our ancestors...." S. D. Ebersole of Sterling had stated earlier that this "hope opens a new world to us; the world grows beautiful and duty becomes a privilege." Ebersole thought that the Christian should have faith in himself as one "created in the image of God and only a little lower than the angels, and God makes no mistakes." One should also have faith in humanity "because it is God's instrument for spreading the Gospel and redeeming the world." Finally, one must have faith in God the Creator and Redeemer.[4] To be sure, the Awakening came to some groups earlier than to others and affected some more than others. Indeed, a few segments here and there have hardly been affected at all even to this day. Of course, some knowledgeable authorities questioned whether the mainline Mennonite Church was as decadent spiritually as some of its critics stated. John Horsch was one of these. But even he conceded there was room for considerable improvement.[5]

In any case, a number of influences combined in the latter part of the nineteenth century to bring about a new sense of mission. Technological changes in transportation and communication that brought Mennonites closer to a needy world no doubt influenced them, as it also did others. Certainly, developments in mainline Protestantism with regard to missions and evangelism, revivals, Sunday schools, education, and other movements affected Mennonites considerably. Harold S. Bender, one of the leading authorities on the Mennonite renewal, has stated that the outside influences came "largely through the aggressive work of the American Sunday School Union and the frontier evangelism of the Methodists, Baptists, United Brethren, and similar groups, with whom they [the Mennonites] often came into close contact. The evangelistic revivalism of Charles G. Finney ... and more especially of D. L. Moody, 1870-90, and his successors had probably still greater influence." In still stronger terms, Theron Schlabach has asserted that this Protestant influence affected Mennonites "so much so that sometimes the most 'awakened' groups soon lost such marks of Mennonitism as nonconformity, nonresistance, and a holistic approach to faith and obedience."[6] At any rate, old inhibitions were still powerful and the transition to the new and more active order brought some schisms such as those creating the Evangelical Mennonites, the Oberholtzer movement, the Wisler division, and the Mennonite Brethren in Christ (under the leadership of Daniel Brenneman and others). Illinois, although influenced by these forces, was spared some of these divisions. Nevertheless, it was affected by the Egly division and especially the Stuckey separation, in which movements were many who thought that the Amish Mennonites and Mennonites were deficient in vitality and aggressiveness.

The Civil War probably also had an awakening effect on the rather complacent, nonresistant Mennonites. Since Mennonites had experienced no war since Revolutionary days in which they themselves were involved to any great extent, the new conflict made them rethink their position, especially after the draft was introduced in 1863. At least two important booklets on their peace position appeared as a result of the coming of the war—one by John F. Funk, *Warfare. Its Evils, Our Duty* . . . and one by John M. Brenneman, *Christianity and War*. Both appeared in 1863 and were widely read. Both writers felt the Mennonites needed more teaching on peace and nonresistance.[7]

Another event or movement that increased the vision of the Mennonites was the coming of the Russian Mennonites to the United States and Canada in the 1870s. About a century earlier Catherine the Great had invited the ancestors of these Mennonites to come to Russia from Northern Europe, where they had recently lost exemption from military service. About 1870 the Russian government announced that the privileges that Catherine had granted the Mennonites, including military exemption, would be terminated or considerably curtailed. Primarily out of concern caused by this turn of events, thousands of Mennonites migrated to the United States and Canada, principally in the 1870s. Mennonites in North America were concerned and stirred by this development, and did much to aid the immigrants.[8]

Few if any in North America assisted the Russian brethren in their migration more than did John F. Funk of Elkhart, Indiana. Through the columns of the English and German editions of his *Herald of Truth*, he not only kept North American Mennonites well informed of the progress of the various migrations to the new world, but also made them sensitive to the needs of the brethren. The many reports in these and other periodicals of financial contributions to the cause attest the widespread response of the Mennonites and others. The *Herald* listed contributions usually by congregations, at times by individuals. A letter from someone in northern Illinois, apparently not a Mennonite, said:

> I have been laboring for your people, in my circle, among a community that knows but little of the Mennonites, indeed my own personal acquaintance among your people is very limited, but they have always been represented to me as an honorable people, and because of that and your noncombatant principles, which we likewise hold sacred, and because I felt myself called upon, by you and your people in their oppressed circumstances, I canvassed and obtained (mostly in quarters, halves, and dollars, also a few V's), $32.75. Some Catholics, even, gave some.[9]

Thirty-two and a fraction dollars may not seem impressive; however, given in a time of great economic depression, and coming from non-Mennonites, they were.

The coming of the Russian Mennonites created a stir among the Mennonites in North America, including those in Illinois. Mennonites at Summerfield especially influenced this migration, and made their community a stopping place for many of the Russian immigrants. Here, under the leadership of Christian Krehbiel and David Goerz, the immigrants received hospitality, counsel, and assistance in moving to homes farther west. Elkhart, Indiana, was also an important stopping place. There, under the leadership of John F. Funk, the immigrants received the same type of assistance. Krehbiel, Funk and Goerz served on the Mennonite Board of Guardians, Krehbiel as president, Funk as treasurer, and Goerz as secretary. This was the chief agency in the Middle West and West channeling aid to the immigrants. Goerz also served as editor of *Zur Heimath* (1875-81), a periodical started at Summerfield particularly for the benefit of the immigrants. Since Funk, as noted, was the editor and publisher of the *Herald of Truth* (and the German edition), and since he used its columns to publicize widely the plight and the needs of the brethren and to report the funds contributed, the Illinois brethren learned more about the Russians by way of Elkhart than by way of Summerfield.[10]

One authority, William W. Dean, states that although it is difficult to estimate the influence of the coming of the Russian Mennonites on the Mennonite Awakening, "it is believed that as the American Mennonites aided their Russian brethren they developed certain attitudes which were of value in the other phrases [sic] of the Awakening. Some of these attitudes and abilities were: an interest in those outside their own communities and environment, a desire to contribute financially to a worthy cause, and the ability to work together in order to establish a common goal. It is believed," concludes Dean, "that the American Mennonites were influenced in their thinking in a positive way concerning several important issues as they came in contact with the various elements represented among the Russian Mennonites. Among the most important of these issues were nonresistance, evangelism, missions, and abstinence from alcohol and tobacco."[11]

Of course partly because of contacts with non-Mennonites as well, many leaders within the Mennonite and Amish Mennonite groups were important individual influences for bringing about renewal in the church during this period. John H. Oberholtzer and John F. Funk were two examples from the ministry. Christian Erismann of Illinois can be taken as a lay example of one influenced from the outside and thus ahead of the times in his Amish Mennonite circles. Born in 1835 in Germany, he migrated in 1857 to Putnam

County, Illinois, where some relatives resided. After losing his left hand in a threshing accident he became a schoolteacher, studying in a district school in Granville and then in a sem'nary in nearby Henry.

At the seminary Erismann had a deepening Christian experience under the influence of a Methodist minister, a Mr. Barnes, whose church Erismann attended. He thereafter taught private school in various Illinois Amish Mennonite communities and his diary or journal indicates that for him to attend other churches was not unusual. In his contacts with many people in these communities he no doubt served as an instrument for the promotion of new ideas and change. Attending their Sunday schools also, he became an early advocate of Mennonite Sunday schools. While enrolled at normal school in Normal in 1869 Erismann attended church services and Sunday school in the Baptist, Methodist, and Congregational churches. Influenced by missionaries he heard speak in these churches, he thought the Mennonites should have mission work. He likewise advocated the school started at Wadsworth, Ohio, by the General Conference Mennonites, and felt strongly that Amish Mennonites should have similar institutions. In his forward-looking position, Erismann typifies a number of Mennonites and Amish Mennonites who were an indigenous force for renewal and who were also influenced by mainstream Protestant forces.[12]

A factor bearing upon the Mennonite Awakening was language. Both the Amish and the Mennonites in America continued to use the German that they brought with them. All groups held onto their native tongue with great persistence. Using German was looked upon as a cultural barrier against becoming too closely associated with the "world." To many, giving up German meant giving up an important part of one's religion. But by the latter part of the nineteenth century more and more young people, educated in public schools, could communicate better in English than in German. Hence the battle over language in the church services and the rising Sunday schools.

No doubt exclusive use of German helped maintain a community closed to outside influences. The Amish Mennonite congregation at Hopedale was an example. When M. S. Steiner visited it in 1889 he noted the group's complacency and self-satisfied condition: "They seem to be satisfied and in want of nothing." He claimed to have heard the following in a sermon: "We have been blessed abundantly in the past; we have all that we desire to eat, drink and wear; have good health and all the temporal blessings we can enjoy. In spiritual things likewise we are in want of nothing. We can go to church every two weeks, hear the word preached, and this is enough; we lack nothing of either temporal or spiritual things, for which we ought to thank God." The church services, said Steiner, were conducted entirely in German, and the Sunday school, begun in 1886 and held on Sundays when there were no church services, devoted most of the two-hour sessions to studying the German language. The congregation, according to Steiner, held closely to Amish customs and principles.[13]

This, of course, was only one man's observation and he was quoting only from one sermon. But Steiner clearly suggested that German helped maintain a closed community. What a growing number especially of younger people wanted in the latter part of the nineteenth century was not closed communities but more open ones, that partook more of the American mood and that could feel the pulsebeat of a needy world. As time went on this became a larger problem, not only so far as worship services were concerned but especially among those who were developing a conscience on the need for a wider evangelism. One Illinois Mennonite wrote in the *Herald of Truth* (Dec. 1881): "We have not had one communion service to my knowledge that the English part of the congregation had full satisfaction.... It seems to me much good might be done if we had more service[s] in the language which the people generally understand." The writer concluded that the ministers should not be concerned solely with the ninety and nine but should "go into the wilderness to search for the lost."[14]

During the period of transition from German to English various compromises were attempted, although not with full satisfaction to all concerned. Often part of the service was in one language and part in the other. Sometimes the same minister would preach partly in one and partly in the other. Some ministers would usually speak in the one language and others in the other. In any case there were growing protests against having all the services in German. There was also a growing number of requests for ministers who could stop off in the various communities and preach in English. One report of church services from northern Illinois in 1881 is typical. The sermons were excellent, said the report, but unfortunately the many English-speaking people in attendance could not understand what was going on. Probably no one tried more than did John F. Funk to remedy this situation. His *Herald of Truth* columns are full of exhortations to use language that the people understood. Seeing that many young people were being lost to the church, due in part to the language problem, he asked: "Shall we shut them out from our communion because they cannot understand our words, while we speak to them in an unknown tongue?" At the time of that question he had the Illinois congregation of Gardner in mind. Yet he could not be considered scornful of what many thought was the "Mennonite" language—German—for he published considerably in both languages.[15] In time, with increasing numbers of Mennonites securing more education in the public schools, and finally with the coming of World War I, when the German language became very unpopular, the problem of language in the church services in Illinois as in other states virtually solved itself. Actually in Illinois, except in a few communities, German had been largely dropped in church services before World War I. English won the battle, and Mennonites now had another window on the world.

Mennonite publishing was one of the most important factors in the Awakening. John H. Oberholtzer started *Der Religiöser Botschafter* in Milford Square, Pennsylvania, in 1852. This biweekly was the first Mennonite church paper in America. It changed its name several times in the next few decades and in 1881 was consolidated with *Zur Heimat* to become *Christlicher Bundesbote*.[16] Outside of the General Conference community at Summerfield, these papers probably had little circulation in Illinois.

Of greater consequence for the Illinois Mennonites and Amish Mennonites was John F. Funk's *Herald of Truth* and its German edition *Herold der Wahrheit.* Started in 1864, the *Herald of Truth* was the first (Old) Mennonite periodical and the first English Mennonite paper "ever published in the world." Funk wrote in his autobiography that since the Mennonites were nearly all German and their preaching and singing were all in German, many thought an English paper "quite out of place," "something the world had never heard of."[17] In light of Mennonites' schooling in English, of course the paper really was not out of place.

Funk was indeed a remarkable person. His great-great-grandfather, Heinrich Funck, an immigrant and bishop in the eighteenth century in eastern Pennsylvania, had written two books. Funk himself (1835-1930) was born and reared in Bucks County, Pennsylvania. In pursuit of higher education he studied two terms at Freeland Seminary (now Ursinus College) and took some business training later in Chicago. After teaching school two years, he accepted an invitation to join his brother-in-law in the lumber business in Chicago. Here he spent ten significant years (1857-67), which were important and decisive for the Mennonites, not only in Illinois but throughout North America.

Funk's liberalism apparently came from his parental home; from association with his brother-in-law, Jacob Beidler, who had become a Presbyterian; from his other business partners, one of whom was a "devout and faithful . . . Catholic" and from experiences in the city. A granddaughter later wrote that "he was about as much like any other Mennonite preacher as day is like night." The statement is an exaggeration. With greater accuracy she wrote of the Chicago years: "And what a terrific thirst for knowledge he had! Piles lumber, keeps the books, hauls lumber, feeds the horse, goes to business college, works in the garden, attends every lecture and political meeting, reads everything he can lay his hands on, including 'sentimental poetry'; even inspects the beer garden; goes to church 5 times a day, addresses prayer meetings, puts down carpet, teaches S. S. classes, and goes on S. S. excursions, distributes tracts, writes articles ... keeps his diary, writes many lectures—and has a little time left over to attend Strawberry Festivals!"[18]

In 1858 Funk became converted in a series of Presbyterian revival meetings. Unable to accept some of that church's doctrines on such matters as predestination, war and peace, and infant baptism, he promised God that if he were spared another year he would go to his home where he had been born and reared and "where I had for so long ... sat under the preaching of the Mennonite Church, and there I would unite with the old church of my fathers, and this is the way I became a Mennonite."[19] On February 13, 1859, Funk became a member of his home church at Line Lexington, Pennsylvania. This was a tremendously important decision, since probably no one had more to do with bringing about the Awakening or Quickening in the (Old) Mennonite Church than did Funk. Having earlier started teaching in a Baptist Sunday school near his home as early as 1853, in Chicago he soon met and engaged in Sunday school work with D. L. Moody, "to whom he attributed much of the influence which moved him into active service with progressive ideas in Sunday school, evangelism, and religious publication far in advance of the lethargic mid-century Mennonite (MC) Church of his fathers." In addition to being a pioneer in Mennonite publishing, Sunday school, and evangelistic work, Funk "played a major role in the immigration and colonization of the Russian Mennonites ... and in effect became the publisher for the Manitoba Mennonites." The authority here quoted, Harold S. Bender, concludes that "he was all by all odds the most influential leader for 30 years (1870-1900), shaping the course of the Mennonite Church."[20]

Funk never forgot his Moody connection. He referred to it in his writings and occasionally revisited the Chicago scene after he moved to Elkhart. In December 1876, for example, while on a trip west in the interests of the Russian Mennonites, he stopped in Chicago to attend a Moody and Sankey revival meeting. In the *Herald of Truth* report of the trip (Dec. 1876), Funk used nearly half of the article to describe the revival meeting and his early days in Chicago with Moody. On November 8, 1925, Funk, ninety years old, was invited to speak at the dedication of the Moody Memorial Church in Chicago. He was introduced as "one of the few persons left that had been a coworker with Moody at the Mission Sunday School."[21]

From the angle of the Mennonite Church the really important work that Funk performed in Chicago was starting the *Herald of Truth*. January, 1864, was a big month for him—when he married Salome Kratz of his home community and also the month in which the first issue of the *Herald* appeared. For some time he had thought about the merits of a church paper. From boyhood he had wondered how he could help his church. "I thought of Sunday School work and the subject that lay close to my heart was a religious paper." Other groups had theirs, he reasoned, and "why not the Mennonites...?" Funk knew of course about John H. Oberholtzer's paper, now called the *Christliche Volksblatt*. He was a subscriber to it, praised it very highly, and thought "every member of the Mennonite Church should not only be a subscriber ... but should make every effort to extend its circulation among his friends and neighbors."[22]

Although he was a pioneer, Funk was not the only one in the (Old) Mennonite Church who thought a periodical was needed. Some discussed the matter in other areas, especially Ontario and Virginia. But several brethren from Ohio and Pennsylvania were especially helpful and encouraged Funk to proceed: Bishop John M. Brenneman and his brother Daniel from Elida, Ohio, and Peter K. Nissley from Lancaster County, Pennsylvania. Nissley and John M. Brenneman, passing through Chicago in May of 1863, stopped off with Funk over a weekend. Brenneman went along with Funk to church on Sunday morning and both accompanied him to Sunday school in the afternoon. Funk discussed with them his ideas about Sunday school and a church paper by which Mennonites could be better taught and more fully informed "on Church Doctrine, Church History, Church Practice, etc." Both continued to encourage him after they returned home. Daniel Brenneman also agreed that Funk would be just the man to initiate a church periodical. Both Brennemans promised to help by writing articles.[23]

While others talked, Funk acted. In order to appeal broadly to the old and to the young, to the German-speaking and to the English-speaking, he decided to publish in both languages. The German edition had subscribers in Europe, and in that way too was important for the Russian Mennonites, both before they left Russia and after they came to North America. Funk was determined and persistent. He estimated that it would cost about $500 to issue the paper the first year. "I made up my mind," he wrote, "if I should not get a single subscriber, I could spare the $500 myself out of my own pocket and quit." He promised God that if he got 1000 subscribers by the end of the first year he would accept this as a sign that God was leading, and would continue. By the end of the year he had 1200 subscribers and thirty dollars above expenses! So the *Herald* continued—not only into a second and third year but through a long life to 1908. Published first as a monthly with a yearly subscription price of one dollar, it became a semimonthly in 1882 and a weekly in 1903.[24]

Funk knew there would be opposition to his paper, and there was. He anticipated it in the first issue. In fact, much of this issue is composed of articles that explain the need for and give a defense of a religious paper "devoted to the interests of the Denomination of Christians known as 'The Mennonites,' " as the subtitle states. With much logic and vigor Funk strongly stated that such a church paper would have definite benefits for the brotherhood: it would strengthen people in the Christian faith as understood by Mennonites; it would help the Mennonites become better acquainted with each other by knowing about differences that might exist; it would help bring about greater unity; it would encourage people; it would help scattered Mennonites in distant non-Mennonite communities keep in touch with the church and the old faith; it would provide good Christian reading material to help counteract the influence of "the great majority of these ... political newspapers" appearing in so many Mennonite homes, an influence "so great, so powerful ... so wicked and so corrupt and so detrimental, to a pure life, and a pure Christianity." An article by John M. Brenneman also buttressed the argument for a church paper.

Despite these good articles, quite a few Mennonites raised their eyebrows upon seeing the *Herald* in print. Many prejudices showed up, reported Funk, and all kinds of speculation, predictions, and conjectures came from those opposed to any innovation in doing church work. These were the people who were inclined to say: "Ah! That young fellow from Chicago was at work." Some people felt so strongly about this that they started an opposition paper, the *Watchful Pilgrim*, "to keep the church more closely upon the old track." Its editor, Abraham Blosser of Virginia, said that Funk was "inclined to follow the fast element favoring Sunday schools and other things inclined to bring our church into a closer friendship with the high and most popular and war-like Christian denominations of the present time."[25]

Despite this criticism the *Herald* continued to grow and flourish and increasingly to become an influence in the Mennonite church. Funk's work soon became too much for his strength, as he tried to do the bookkeeping for the lumber company during the day and edit the paper at night. So in 1866 he sold his interest in the lumber company and devoted all his time to publishing. Meanwhile he considered what was the best location for his enterprise. He had become acquainted with Elkhart County, Indiana, in 1862, when he attended a church conference at Yellow Creek, met many ministers (including John M. Brenneman), and found his visit there "a source of real spiritual profit."

In a recent study Joseph Liechty has shown the importance of this visit in Funk's life. It came about as a result of Funk's desire to take communion in a Mennonite congregation. First he wrote to Abraham Detweiler at Sterling about taking communion there. Detweiler replied that because of some difficulties at the moment the Science Ridge congregation was delaying its communion service, and he suggested that Funk write to the Yellow Creek congregation at Elkhart. Funk did so and had the good fortune not only to participate in a meaningful communion and foot washing service but also in a Mennonite conference held at the same time. Liechty thinks that this Elkhart experience was "momentous" for Funk in strengthening his peace convictions and other phases of his Mennonitism.[26] The experience also probably made it easier for Funk later to decide to relocate his printing business at Elkhart.

In any case, Funk decided that Elkhart should be the place and in 1867 he moved there, even though some questioned the wisdom of the move. One friend advised that it would have been better to "remain some distance from your church members lest they become too well acquainted with your progressiveness and [you] thereby lose influence.... You know a paper among that class of people is decidedly progressive." Because he gave aggressive leadership to the Mennonite Awakening, and because he attracted many able young Mennonites to his publishing enterprise, Funk soon made Elkhart a center of a Mennonite renaissance.[27]

Even though Funk and his *Herald* had now moved from Illinois, in terms of his influence on the Illinois Mennonites the move meant very little, except possibly for the Gardner congregation where Funk had been one of the ministers. The Illinois Mennonites continued to support the *Herald* as they had before, and Funk continued his interest in the church of that state. Mennonites and Amish Mennonites supported the paper. Two of the latter were Joseph and Peter Stuckey. Peter wrote Funk that he thought the paper was a good one and wanted to do all in his power to promote it. In the matter of faithful and loyal support of these church papers perhaps few could match the record of Christian H. Smith of Eureka. In 1955, in his nineties, he wrote to the *Gospel Herald* saying he had started reading the *Herold der Wahrheit* "some 70 years ago." He then added that the *Herald of Truth* and the *Gospel Herald* had "come to my address regularly for more than 60 years."[28]

Among the important services that the *Herald* provided in Illinois was to serve as a means of communication with the scattered Mennonites in the state. The paper contains many, many letters from areas where there were no Mennonite congregations. Correspondents wanted to maintain some connection with the church and asked for ministers and others to stop and visit them, which frequently happened. And even where the visits were infrequent, the *Herald*, as one scattered Mennonite wrote, was always a welcome visitor because it encouraged him "to remain steadfast on the old foundations of truth."[29]

By the turn of the new century an increasingly persistent question was whether the Mennonite Church ought not own and control its own publication company and paper. There was a growing dissatisfaction with the *Herald*, evidenced by another private paper, the *Gospel Witness*, out of Scottdale, Pennsylvania, beginning in 1905. The publication issue became rather divisive in the (Old) Mennonite Church during these years, with the movement for church ownership growing rapidly. District conferences and the newly organized General Conference began to take positions on the issue, generally in favor of church ownership. The Illinois Mennonite Conference, for example, took this position by 1907 and appointed J. S. Shoemaker of Freeport to a church committee to investigate the matter further. This, in fact, was the beginning of the long and significant role that Shoemaker played in the publishing interests of the church. Included was his important work in merging the *Herald of Truth* and the *Gospel Witness* in 1908 into a new church organ, the *Gospel Herald*. This meant also the formation in the same year of the Mennonite Publication Board and the organization of the Mennonite Publishing House at Scottdale, Pennsylvania, which purchased some of the publications of the Mennonite Publishing Company at Elkhart and bought out the Gospel Witness Company at Scottdale. Shoemaker was a good person to carry on these delicate negotiations with Funk, for C. C. Shoemaker, Joseph's brother, had served in recent years as assistant manager and board member of the Elkhart company.[30] J. S., as he was often called, served as president of the Mennonite Board of Publication from its beginning in 1908 to 1933. His son, C. B. Shoemaker, and a grandson, Joseph R. Buzzard, were also a part of the administration at Scottdale. The Shoemaker family thus was closely connected with the publishing house from its beginning until recently.

There were, of course, other Mennonite publishing ventures that influenced the Mennonite renewal, some with greater and some with lesser effect on Illinois. William B. Weaver wrote that the *Herald of Truth* as the first English-language Mennonite paper "undoubtedly encouraged the publishing of church papers by other Mennonite groups."[31] This was probably correct. *The Mennonite*, founded by an eastern wing of the General Conference Mennonites has had a growing impact in Illinois in the past half century. Maynard Shelly, writing in 1960, stated that General Conference life "has undergone a real revival.... Many factors have been at work to stimulate our Conference in its Christian witness, and *The Mennonite* has been one of the strong though quiet forces at work."[32]

Several periodicals originated in Illinois during the period of the

Awakening. From 1906 to 1908 A. H. Leaman and the Mennonite Home Mission (MC) in Chicago published *The Mission Worker,* a monthly. Even earlier, in 1898 C. R. Egle of Meadows, Defenseless Mennonite, was largely responsible for starting the *Heilsbote.* He printed it on his press in Flanagan and was editor until it was discontinued in 1917. Its purpose was especially to develop interest in mission work that had been started in Africa. D. N. Claudon, who was connected with the *Heilsbote,* started *Zion's Call* in 1898 in the interest of the Salem Children's Home at Flanagan. In 1913 it was adopted as the official church organ of the Defenseless Mennonites. In 1920 it became *Zion's Tidings,* merging with *Good Tidings,* which had been started by the Defenseless Mennonite Brethren Conference in 1919. In 1953 it became *The Evangelical Mennonite* and still later it assumed other titles. But whatever names these journals had, their purposes included the promotion of some or several phases of the Mennonite Awakening. Since several very active Defenseless churches were located in Illinois, the effect in the state was substantial.[33]

The *Christian Evangel* appeared in 1910. As the official monthly organ of the Central Conference of Mennonites, most of whom were in Illinois, it naturally had great influence on the state. As stated in the first issue, its purposes, as was usually the case, included unifying the church and encouraging mission and other forms of aggressive Christian work, education, and correct doctrine. Always published in Illinois, the *Evangel* is a good mirror or reflector of the many activities of this branch of the church. In 1934 the *Christian Evangel* and *The Mennonite* merged for a short period, largely because of the Depression, but went their separate ways again in 1936, with the hope that the time would still come when the two bodies, and the periodicals, could unite in "broader efforts." This union came in 1957. In 1937 the topic "What Our Publications Are Doing for Our Churches," was discussed in the Central Conference *Yearbook.* These functions were, said the writer, making the church conscious of world needs, stirring up enthusiasm and interest among the members, presenting the cause of missions and the program and doctrines of the church, promoting church unity, and providing a Christian interpretation of the news. The *Evangel,* under the capable leadership of Albert Rutt, William Weaver, Raymond L. Hartzler and others, made a good contribution to the Mennonite Awakening in Illinois.[34]

A *Herold der Wahrheit* appeared in 1912 (not to be confused with Funk's *Herold,* which terminated in 1901) and had readers in Illinois among the few independent conservative Amish congregations and among the Old Order Amish at Arthur. Because of its conservative character, however, it had little effect on the renewal. In fact, later on when the Awakening overtook the Conservative Amish in other states, they changed their name to Conservative Mennonite, moved beyond the position of the *Herold,* withdrew their support from it and started the *Missionary Bulletin* and *Brotherhood Beacon,* which did support the Awakening.[35]

Begun in 1929 with A. M. Eash as editor, the *Congo Missionary Messenger* was also published in Illinois (at Chicago) for a number of years, after which it moved to Elkhart, Indiana, where it continues as the *AIMM* (Africa Inter-Mennonite Mission) *Messenger.* The organ of the Congo Inland Mission, it promoted the work of that mission and the enlarged African work in more recent years.

Another element in the Mennonite Awakening was the rise of Sunday schools. Here, too, of course, the church was influenced from outside sources. John F. Funk had attended a Baptist Sunday School in Pennsylvania and was influenced by D. L. Moody and others in his Sunday school work in Chicago. He, of course, then became an early advocate in the Mennonite church of the advantages of the Sunday school ministry. John H. Oberholtzer of eastern Pennsylvania also spoke quite early of the beneficial results of the Sunday school. The slowness of the Mennonite Church to see the advantages of this and other new religious agencies and organizations was one of the reasons for the schism of his group. Jacob N. Brubacher, a Sunday school advocate and leader in Lancaster, Pennsylvania, received his inspiration from an Episcopalian Sunday school that he had attended in Philadelphia. We have already seen how Christian Erismann's attendance at non-Mennonite Sunday schools in Illinois made him an ardent advocate. These and others simply could not close their eyes to the advantages and benefits of the Sunday school.[36]

One authority has summarized the benefits of the Sunday school as follows: (1) "The Sunday school was an important factor in holding the young people for the church. Before the time of the Sunday school, large numbers of young people from Mennonite homes were attracted to other denominations, often through the influence of Sunday schools." (2) "The Sunday school has greatly increased Bible knowledge." (3) It "elevated the level of spiritual life." (4) It "raised the level of moral life in the church, especially through the teaching of temperance." (5) It "provided activity and expression and thus contributed to new life in the church." (6) It "created lay leadership." (7) It "was largely responsible for the missionary movement." These two elements in the Awakening—Sunday schools and missions—were almost inextricably related. An article by A. E. Kreider of Sterling, "The Sunday School and Missionary Interest" (*GH,* May 4, 1916), is typical of many that show this linkage. (8) "The Sunday school was a factor in the Great Awakening of the Mennonite Church...." (9) "The Sunday school helped to give the Mennonite Church a new vision."[37]

All of these beneficial results applied of course to all branches of Illinois Mennonites that adopted the Sunday school. One Illinois voice typical of the defenders of the Sunday school was that of Samuel Hirstein of Morton. When the Virginia Conference condemned Sunday schools, Hirstein replied that they were a necessary supplement to the education received in the home. We have already pointed out in chapter 9 the importance of the Sunday school in starting new congregations. And as to the Central Conference of Mennonites, both S. F. Pannabecker and William B. Weaver have shown this connection. Weaver was correct when he wrote that "the origin of the congregation can often be traced to the establishment of a Sunday School in the community." Evangelical Mennonites also emphasized this advantage of Sunday schools.[38]

In addition to the benefits mentioned above, one other advantage of Sunday schools influenced even some conservative doubting Thomases. This was the opportunity to use the Sunday school to teach something of the German language along with knowledge of the Bible. The present writer remembers how in his childhood days at Roanoke in the first decade of this century the older members made a noble effort to teach youngsters a minimum of German from old ABC books. This combination of the two purposes of the Sunday school is illustrated by a report from Washington, Illinois, in 1890. The reporter stated that the children were "making progress in reading (in German) and also in the knowledge of the Word of God...."[39]

In view of the many advantages of the Sunday school it may seem strange that there was opposition. But there was. Nor was the opposition limited to the Mennonites and the Amish Mennonites. For example, a Baptist Association in Illinois in 1830 stated: "We as an Association do not hesitate to say that we declare an unfellowship with Foreign and Domestic Mission and Bible Societies, Sunday Schools, and Quack Societies, and all other Missionary Institutions." The chief points of Mennonite opposition seem to have been that: no scripture permitted lay members, especially women, to teach in our churches; persons not members of our church were allowed to teach; Sunday schools were "in fashion among the highest, the proudest, and the dressiest classes of the country"; "there is a mixture of other books used along with" Scriptures, "made up of select matter from the Word of God in part and partly of tales by societies not opposed to war, bloodshed or ... suing at law"; "the spirit of pride and exaltedness is being cultivated by giving the most progressive scholars marks of honors"; "it is something new that has crept into our church"; "it is represented to our youth as something better than that practiced by our forefathers"; "the Mennonite Church was to be a people of God, separate from the world, having close communion," but the "Sunday-school system is a mixture with other societies and the world"; the Sunday school is "a nursery of pride ... and children taught in it become self-righteous"; "these English Sunday schools are all pride." This last statement emphasizes the German-speaking Mennonites' tendency to think of the English language as that of a "proud" and "worldly people." Since the Sunday school was of English origin, that made it suspect for some.[40]

Mennonite opposition to union Sunday schools was very probably stronger than to the type mentioned above. That Mennonites often participated in these union Sunday schools was, no doubt, one reason for opposing Sunday schools in general. Conferences took positions against the union schools. For example, the Western A. M. Conference in 1897 resolved that it was "not in accordance with the gospel that we as plain nonresistant followers of Jesus Christ" associate ourselves with popular Sunday schools and other Christian societies whose leaders are conformed to the world. The Illinois Mennonite Conference in 1907 stated that Mennonites should not use their churches for union Sunday school meetings because such meetings had questionable features. One Virginia Mennonite wrote in 1885: "I think there is no quicker way under heaven to exterminate a Non-resistant church than by its going into a union Sunday school with the high dressy fashionable warlike denominations of the present day by making them our equals in the eyes of our children." Although this Virginia writer accused Funk of leading the Mennonites in this direction, even Funk warned against the flag-waving union rallies of Sunday schools. In one union Rally Day for Sunday schools that he observed there were so many flags involved and so much militant music and marching that it looked "more like a great military pageant than a religious gathering ... to promote the cause of Christ." It was hard to decide, he added, whether the church was in the world or the world in the church.[41]

Considerable discussion and some controversy have arisen as to where and when the first Sunday schools appeared in the Mennonite churches. But it is clear that they appeared elsewhere earlier than in Illinois. Reportedly, the first one appeared in 1840 in Waterloo County, Ontario, and a second one in the same place in 1841. A third was probably one established at Masontown, Pennsylvania, in 1842. In 1847 or earlier John H. Oberholtzer introduced a Sunday school, apparently before the Oberholtzer schism, into the West Swamp congregation near Quakertown, although a regular, formal school was not organized there until 1858. The first Mennonite Church Sunday school in America to continue permanently was presumably one in the South Union church near West Liberty, Ohio, which was organized in 1863.[42]

Among Illinois congregations the Summerfield General Conference group probably organized the first Mennonite Sunday school. That was in 1865. In 1866 the Union congregation at Washington organized its Sunday school, the same year the Willow Springs congregation organized one at Tiskilwa. In 1867 the Yoder (Rock Creek) Amish Mennonite church in McLean County organized a fourth school. Others followed, although often not until the 1880s. Because of opposition it was common to start the Sunday schools in schoolhouses and then gradually move them into the meetinghouses after the novelty had worn off. With the church services held usually only every other week, Sunday school was ordinarily held on the alternate Sunday. Another common pattern, because of bad roads, was to close the Sunday schools for the winter months. In the 1890s the more venturesome began to operate their schools throughout the year, such schools being called "evergreen." By the turn of the century nearly all of the Sunday schools were meeting every Sunday throughout the year and were held in conjunction with the church services. The Science Ridge congregation at Sterling was a pioneer in holding its Sunday school on Sunday morning *after* the church service. It must have been something of a pioneer also in having a Sunday school teachers' meeting every Friday evening.[43]

The Union congregation near Washington must have been one of the more progressive ones with regard to the Sunday school. Established in 1866 as noted, the school apparently met from the beginning on Sunday mornings just prior to the church services. John F. Funk, an early and enthusiastic advocate of Sunday schools, has left us an impressive eyewitness account of this school. "It was truly encouraging to my heart," he reported, "as I sat there and saw children and young men and women sitting together there reading the Word of God and receiving instruction from its precious precepts." What a contrast, thought Funk, to the thousands who wasted their Sabbath hours in idleness, sin, and wickedness.[44]

Not long after Sunday schools came into the church, leaders began to organize Sunday school conferences—later sometimes called conventions, normals, or workshops—where those interested could exchange ideas on how to improve the schools and stimulate each other to become better Sunday school workers. Very early in the Sunday school movement a large number of women became active as teachers and speakers in the conferences, despite the Pauline injunction about women keeping silent in the churches. A sampling of topics discussed in these conferences, both before and after the turn of the century, indicates the concerns of the promoters: "How to Promote Spiritual Life in the Sunday School," "The Christian Culture of Childhood," "Humility," "Incentives to Bible Study," "Pride," "The Power of Influence,"

"Prayer," "Faith," "The Sunday School and Its Foundation," "Christian Unity," "What Should Be the Object of a S. S. Conference," "Qualifications of S. S. Superintendents and Teachers," "Duties of Superintendents and Teachers Towards Visitors and Strangers in S. S.," "Dangers That Threaten Our Young People," "The Ultimate Aim of S. S. Teaching," "Preparation for Christian Service," "Evangelism in the Sunday School," "Best Method of Teaching," "The Problem of Foreigners in Our Cities," "Is the S. S. a Part of the Church or a Distinct Organization?" "What Kind of Literature Should Parents Encourage their Children to Read?" "The Teacher's Duty Out of Sunday School," etc., etc.

A side effect of the Sunday school was that publishing Sunday school literature became a huge undertaking. Although the larger Mennonite bodies established their own presses (or at least had presses owned and operated by Mennonites such as Funk), in some cases the Sunday schools depended on non-Mennonite publishers. However, Mennonite publishers served most of the needs of the Illinois Mennonites.[45]

Many elements, no doubt, contributed to the Mennonite Awakening, such as the work of Evangelist John S. Coffman and publisher John F. Funk. But "it cannot be disputed," says one authority, "that underlying the whole movement was the Sunday school with all the manifold and powerful influences which it had set in motion and which were actively at work in the church preparing for the time.... The Sunday school made the Great Awakening possible."[46]

Revivalism and evangelism were also important in the Mennonite Awakening. Although the two words were often used interchangeably, technically there was and is a difference. Revival referred to the "reviving" of life in those who had made a profession of Christianity before but who had become indifferent, whereas evangelism had to do with reaching out to those who were not Christian. To have "revival" or "evangelistic meetings" meant having a protracted series of meetings in which special emphasis was put on the renewing of life in lethargic or indifferent members or on reaching out to non-Christians. The older acceptable way in the nineteenth century was the slower catechetical method of teaching the young the principles of Christianity and then having them decide about church membership and baptism at the age of accountability.

In the revival and evangelistic movement, also, forces from the outside influenced the Mennonite churches. Again John F. Funk is a good example. He was, of course, converted during Presbyterian revival meetings. Through his *Herald of Truth* and in other ways he became an aggressive advocate of evangelism. This influence extended to nearby Illinois, where the *Herald* circulated and where its editor continued to visit. At Elkhart on December 28, 1882, Funk, by then pastor of the Prairie Street congregation, was the leading spirit in organizing a Mennonite Evangelizing Committee. This was "the first organization for evangelistic and mission work in the Mennonite Church (MC)." A forerunner of the Mennonite Board of Missions, its purpose was to collect and distribute funds to defray "the expenses incurred in traveling to visit scattered members and churches," as well as "to preach the gospel where our church and doctrines are not known." The committee included Illinois in its ministry. When the committee was reorganized in 1892 and became the Mennonite Evangelizing Board of America, it included members from Illinois.[47]

Another person who like Funk settled at Elkhart and who also continued to cast a long shadow over Illinois was John S. Coffman. He was associated with Funk in publishing and interested in Illinois Mennonites, especially at Cullom. Participant in many of the activities of the Awakening, he probably made his greatest contribution as evangelist. His caution, tact, and winning personality were great assets in overcoming the opposition to this new type of outreach. Although he did not hold the first revival meeting in the (Old) Mennonite church in the United States—that was probably done by Funk and Daniel Brenneman at Masontown, Pennsylvania, in 1872—Coffman did become the "great carrier of revivalism into the church" from 1879, when he moved to Elkhart, until his death twenty years later.[48]

That revivals for Mennonites were something new was reason enough for some to be opposed. No doubt another reason for opposition was that in the earlier American revival movements many Mennonites were lost to such revivalistic groups as the Evangelical Church and the United Brethren—one of whose founders was a Mennonite, Martin Boehm. The later revivalism of D. L. Moody and others, however, had the indirect effect of starting revival fires in the church itself, thus saving the young people for the church. The loss of young people greatly disturbed Coffman and others. The Science Ridge congregation near Sterling is a good example. Mennonite young people refused to wear the strict, somber garb of their elders and united with the Lutheran congregation, making it the leading church in the city. Men such as Funk, Coffman, M. S. Steiner, J. S. Shoemaker, Joseph Stuckey, and many others deserve much credit for turning that pattern around. Valentine Strubhar thinks that in 1880 Joseph Stuckey held the "first genuine revival" meetings among the Illinois Amish and Mennonites, at the East Washington congregation, where Joseph's brother Peter was minister. There was still opposition, but it was more likely to be the kind that one Illinois brother wrote about when he complained that much modern evangelism was producing shallow converts because many of the evangelists, too much interested in mere numbers, did not follow up with sufficient concern and care for the converts. As a result, many were no better off than before.[49]

By 1900 revivals were widely accepted in the (Old) Mennonite Church, and by 1920 "it had become practically a universal custom for each congregation ... to have at least one series of revival meetings annually." Perhaps no one was more responsible for this acceptance than was Coffman. He became popular not because he believed in watering down Mennonite doctrine but because he successfully synthesized revivalism with Mennonitism. Moreover, with a friendly, gracious personality, he was able to present his messages in an appealing manner. At his meetings at Cullom in 1890, for example, a good many Methodists attended as well as "a number" of Lutherans and Catholics. A few months earlier, while he was preaching at the Metamora and Union congregations, the Stuckey people at Washington insisted on his "coming to them so that they would feel slighted if I did not visit them." Apparently he also visited Carlock and Danvers. The record in his diary a few days later (Feb. 23, 1890) indicates how he could get along with people even though he differed with them on some points. Referring to his meetings in the Stuckey church near Washington, he wrote: "There will come changes here some time, and our influence may do some of them good. Afternoon yesterday four preachers were with me at old bro. Strubhar's in W[ashington]. We talked over the situation here ... and the moustache and plain dress and some things came out. I had all against me at times. I think the Lord gave me grace to tell them much truth, and yet keep them in the best of feeling. I am sure I have many warm friends in this church. I am glad I came."[50]

The price Coffman paid for such devotion to evangelistic work was high. His diary entries record the trials he and his family suffered by his many absences from home. Compounding the problem was the fact that Coffman was a poor man financially. On a trip to Cullom in 1888 he worried and prayed about a note of his for $75 coming due within a few weeks. The answer to his prayer and the removal of his fear came sooner than expected, and in a surprising manner. At Cullom, while visiting along with minister Peter Unzicker and wife in the Samuel Shearer home, Unzicker handed Coffman a gift of $100 that a donor had contributed. The evangelist was speechless. Finally he said: "Brethren, you can't realize what this means to me." He then told them of his worry about the debt and how this was a direct answer to prayer.[51]

Coffman continued his active evangelism in Illinois and elsewhere until he died prematurely in 1899 at the age of fifty. Funk said he had few equals as a speaker, and referred to him as a "pioneer in evangelistic work" who had called hundreds to Christ. Funk modestly added that Coffman was "probably more widely known than any other minister in the Mennonite Church."[52]

While Coffman deserves much credit for popularizing evangelism in the Mennonite church during the Awakening, even before and especially after his passing, many others carried on the task. Nearly all of the Mennonite ministers in Illinois, except in the very conservative groups, did some revival and evangelistic work, some of course being gifted more than others. Among those who served in the latter part of the Awakening—the first third or so of this century—one might include such men as J. S. Shoemaker, M. S. Steiner, A. H. Leaman, George P. Schultz, Arnold Schultz, C. F. Derstine, Harry E. Bertsche, Emanuel Troyer, J. A. Heiser, A. C. Good, E. M. Rocke, Chancy A. Hartzler, C. R. Egle, all of whom lived at least a part of their lives in Illinois, plus D. D. Miller, D. J. Johns, S. E. Allgyer, J. E. Hartzler, A. D. Wenger, J. K. Gerig, E. M. Slagle, and others from elsewhere.

Bible conferences, occasionally called Bible normals, came into vogue around the turn of the century. These would continue for a few days and have morning, afternoon, and evening sessions. As in revivals, speakers were generally from outside the community or the state. Quite often the meetings would close with a revivalistic appeal. Although many of the topics discussed were similar to those discussed in the Sunday school conferences, the Bible conferences were more concerned with adult Bible study and inspiration and less with methods and problems in Sunday school work. The character of these meetings is suggested by the occasional "Children's Exercises," a sermon without an announced subject, and topics such as the following: "Plan of Salvation," "The Worker," "Church Government," "Christian Graces," "Ordinances," "Marriage," "Nonconformity," "Life Insurance," "Man—The Creation," "Man—The Fall," "Man—Redemption," "Secret Societies," "Dangers That Threaten the Church," "Baptism," "Sanctification," "Nonresistance," "Love," "Practical Piety in the Home," "Self-Denial," "Christian Giving," "Future Destiny of Man," "Prayer," "Holy Spirit," "Christian Business Relations," "Missions," "Humility," "Unity," "Prodigal Son," "Christian Home," "The Lord's Day," "Temperance," "Foot Washing," "Second Coming of Christ," "Evils of the Tongue," "The New Birth."[53]

Young People's Meetings—sometimes called Bible Meetings, Christian Endeavor or, still later, Mennonite Youth Fellowship—were another new institution that the Mennonites began to develop in the latter part of the nineteenth century. John H. Oberholtzer was one of the first Mennonites in North America to recognize the importance of young people's work. The General Conference Mennonites, which Oberholtzer helped organize, and the Central Conference Mennonites borrowed the term "Christian Endeavor" from the interdenominational organization founded in 1881. The first Christian Endeavor society in the General Conference church was organized in Philadelphia in 1886. In 1891 or 1892 the North Danvers, Illinois, congregation organized a Christian Endeavor society, said to be the first in the Central Conference. However, at least by 1891, the Central Conference church at Flanagan had evening meetings that resembled Christian Endeavor meetings but included younger married people.[54]

In addition to serving as social occasions for the young people, these meetings were to stimulate their interest in the work of the church and to provide them with opportunities for self-expression in speaking and working. The meetings stressed such matters as Bible study, spiritual growth, missions and peace. John L. Horst pointed out three needs that brought young people's meetings into existence: a means of giving expression and activity to Christian life, a way of providing Christian instruction (in which the young people instructed themselves), a means to train Christian workers. In order to carry out their functions better, the Central Conference in 1910 appointed Elizabeth Streid of Washington as field-worker to visit, encourage, and advise the societies in their work. Out of these efforts grew the practice of having annual conferences or "rallies" of all the societies in order to inform and stimulate those participating.[55]

In the (Old) Mennonite Church the Ontario Conference approved young people's meetings for the purpose of studying the Bible as early as 1877. J. F. Funk and Henry B. Brenneman supposedly started similar meetings in Indiana in the early 1870s. Apparently, however, these were more like children's meetings, with a great deal of singing prior to the evening preaching service, rather than like the young people's meetings that developed in the 1880s. From that time on the movement spread rapidly throughout the church. Since they began rather spontaneously, they went by different names in different places. District conferences, somewhat later in the states than in Canada, began to approve young people's meetings in the early 1890s. In 1894 the Western A. M. District Conference advocated these meetings, but asked that "due care be exercised that they are in charge of and conducted by the church, so that not the young people only, but the older members, also, can take part in them." Some participation by middle-aged members did become common practice among the (Old) Mennonites. In the same year the Illinois Mennonite Conference encouraged these meetings, but asked the young people not to join the Christian Endeavor Society, since many of its adherents conformed to the world "in its vanities, customs and practices." To join such would not be maintaining "the purity of the church." Apparently the appearance of young people's meetings was closely connected with the growth of evangelism. The more young people that came into the

Source: North Danvers Mennonite Church Historical Collection.

North Danvers Mennonite Church Young People's Society for Christian Endeavor in 1895, first permanent youth group in Illinois.

church as a result of evangelism, the greater was the demand for young people's meetings. Probably the same can be said about the connection with and the influence of the Sunday school. In fact, all of the elements in the Awakening had an influence upon each other.[56]

As in the case of the (Old) Mennonites, the Defenseless Mennonites had no standard name for young people's meetings. Terminology was determined locally, with some using "Christian Endeavor." The Central Conference used that term more often, but less after about 1943 when the name of the union of local societies was changed from "Christian Endeavor Union" to "Young People's Union."[57]

Just as the advocates of the Sunday school believed that holding Sunday school conferences or conventions occasionally would be profitable, so those who believed in young people's meetings felt the same for those organizations. Provision was made for conventions either separately or in connection with the annual church conferences. Persons closely connected with these young people's meetings seemed to agree on their value. In 1911 Elizabeth Streid, the above-mentioned Christian Endeavor field-worker for the Central Conference, gave an enthusiastic, glowing report of her work. She characterized the Christian Endeavor as a God-made movement, adding that "it is the training of the church of the future."[58]

The (Old) Mennonite Church had its first young people's conference in 1920 at West Liberty, Ohio. Because this was the beginning of a period of strain and stress in this branch, members viewed the conference with mixed feelings of interest and anxiety. The young people still were not fully trusted. Quite a few from Illinois, or those such as William B. Weaver and Raymond L. Hartzler who were shortly to come to Illinois, attended the West Liberty meeting and served on the program. The conference secretary reported that Samuel E. Allgyer, bishop at West Liberty, gave a masterful address on 1 Corinthians 13 in which he emphasized that "charity *never* faileth." The conference secretary closed his report with these words; " 'Charity never faileth'— never faileth." Words of irony indeed! While charity did not fail, some people did. In a few short years, because of a breakdown in charity and statesmanship, a number of fine, capable young people who participated in the West Liberty conference found themselves in other branches of the Mennonite church or in other denominations. But that is another story. Even so, all those who attended found it "an inspiring and helpful meeting." And as to the value of young people's meetings, one conservative authority later characterized them as one of the three great agencies for instruction and service in the church, along with the Sunday school and the church service.[59]

The first youth convention of the Defenseless Mennonites of Illinois was held at the Salem congregation in 1933. George P.

Schultz's church in Chicago (Defenseless Mennonite Brethren in Christ) was also included, and the Schultz family took a prominent part in the program. The report states that "all were greatly blessed and many benefits derived from this convention."[60]

These young people's meetings and organizations indicate that the Mennonites were making serious efforts to do something constructive for their young people and to improve the record in holding them for the church. As S. F. Pannabecker has stated: "The young people were becoming a real voice in the life of the church."[61]

Another new religious activity that came into wide acceptance a bit later involved children. This was the summer Bible school, or vacation Bible school. These were religious education schools operated for a few weeks in the summer for nursery, kindergarten, grade school, and high school students, including a few older people in some areas. Although this range in age of attendance varied from place to place, it is probably correct to say that high school students participated less than the younger ones.

Here again the Mennonites were influenced by outside sources—Presbyterians, Baptists, and others who started organizing vacation Bible schools around the turn of the century. The first strictly Mennonite summer Bible school, said Clayton F. Yake, a leading authority, was started in 1923 by Dean Noah Oyer of Hesston College, Hesston, Kansas. As noted earlier, Oyer was from Illinois. After 1923 the movement expanded rapidly.[62]

Yake, who was connected with the Mennonite Publishing House, Scottdale, Pennsylvania, was an outstanding promoter of this cause and the publishing house there was the leading producer of curriculum materials. Many of the various Mennonite groups have used these materials. The General Conference Mennonites had an official understanding with Scottdale that they would use the literature for the lower grades without change; they would use literature for the upper grades with some changes adapted to their own needs. Many non-Mennonites—including Catholics, Seventh-day Adventists, and Mormons—have also used the materials widely. In fact, probably through this movement the Mennonites have had their greatest outreach beyond their own circles—both in terms of the Scottdale summer Bible school literature used by others and in terms of non-Mennonites attending Mennonite vacation schools. Statistics from Illinois for 1945, applying only to the (Old) Mennonite Church, indicate that there were sixteen Bible schools, a total enrollment of 1738, an average attendance of 1419, 135 teachers, expenses of $1078.87, missionary offerings of $608.91, and a range of pupils' ages from 3 to 70. Fifteen schools ran for two weeks and one for one week. The following data from the same record lend credence to the above statement on outreach: 539 pupils were from Mennonite homes, 930 were from non-Mennonite homes, and eighteen denominations were represented! Except among some smaller, very conservative groups, summer Bible schools had become a major feature of the Christian education program among the Illinois Mennonites.[63]

CHAPTER 11

The "Awakening" Among Illinois Mennonites: Education, Missions, Service

One of the most important elements in the Mennonite Awakening was education. In 1900 one writer stated: "The wonderful awakening among the Mennonite people during the last fifteen years is only a revival of that intense enthusiasm, that untiring zeal, that eagerness to know ... and spread the truth, which was the chief characteristic of our ancestors in the Old World." Although true in part, it is an overstatement. Many Anabaptist leaders were educated, but for various reasons the followers seem soon to have developed a distrust of education, partly because theologians used their training to explain away Scriptures, and because leading opponents who were responsible for the severe persecution and suffering inflicted on the dissenters were often educated men.[1]

Although, there was not much done about education during the persecution and the long night that followed when sheer survival was the problem, some did keep learning alive. In Europe the Russian Mennonites did so in the nineteenth and early twentieth centuries. In America men such as Christopher Dock in Pennsylvania in the eighteenth century and Christian Erismann in Illinois in the nineteenth century are notable examples. No doubt frontier conditions in Illinois, as elsewhere, militated against extended education. But the persistence of the Mennonite philosophy since persecution days summed up in the phrase, *"Die Stillen im Lande,"* (the quiet in the land) probably better explains the low level of interest.

In any case, a new educational outlook began slowly to emerge in the latter part of the nineteenth century. To be sure, this element of the renewal, like the others, affected the various Mennonite bodies differently, some feeling its impulses much earlier than did others. The General Conference Mennonites took the lead in emphasizing the need for higher education, the Wadsworth school being the result of this early interest. But as to Illinois, the school's impact was very small except at Summerfield.

The Summerfield involvement was important, however, for notable people from the congregation had connections at some time or other with the school. Pastors Hege and Krehbiel and others played important roles in founding and supporting the institution. Upon the opening of the school in 1866 Krehbiel gave the dedicatory address, calling vigorously for more activism on the part of the Mennonites. The Lord, he said, had never spoken so emphatically to Mennonites as now. "Break the chains which through years of tribulation have been so tightly forged that you have hardly been aware of them. Bring me your sacrifices," he added, "and pledge me your talents, which I have not given you to bury but to put out to interest." Though because of persecution our forefathers could not be blamed for being content with "ordinary education," he said, we now face "new conditions," "new times," in a land of freedom, prosperity, and new opportunities. Krehbiel noted that too many Mennonites had joined other denominations because they wanted more education and better-educated ministers. He concluded his stirring appeal with a strong plea to enter the new door of opportunity that Wadsworth symbolized, believing that the work was from the Lord and that he would carry on.[2]

As to Wadsworth's impact on the church, one authority has stated that it "had a profound influence on the churches and especially those of the Middle District area.... It marked the end of the untrained ministry in [the] General Conference...."[3] That was true, even though in 1878 the school closed, partly because the constituency was not ready to support higher education.[4]

The (Old) Mennonites and those stemming from the Amish developed their interest in education, especially the higher levels, a bit later. One person critical of the *Herald of Truth* apparently was opposed in part because of the editor's education. Writing to a church brother, he stated: "I have understood by a brother that John F. Funk went three years to the High School. If you know about this please let us know." That his opposition was not an isolated case is evident from an earlier letter that Bishop John M. Brenneman wrote to Funk in 1867: "Brother I feel very much interested for you, for I know that many jealous eyes are watching your movements with regard to the Herald and also with regard to your Ministry, because you are a little better educated than the generality of our Ministers, to which som [sic] are greatly opposed. The education in our church, or among our

Ministry has become so Low, that a great many of them cannot know any more how little they do know. O! Brother be watchful, 'be wise as a serpent, But harmless as a dove.' "⁵

Some Illinois Mennonites also indicated a rather low level of education. One person wrote an article on novel-reading, which contained some truths, some half-truths, and some errors. He weakened his good points by making extreme statements about others. Assuming that fiction was ipso facto opposed to Christian truth, he concluded that novel-reading led to insanity: "If we visit the Insane Asylum we can there find cases of hopeless insanity—the fruits of reading novels."⁶ In the 1890s a brother from Cullom, where J. S. Coffman was highly regarded, wrote to the evangelist saying that he was not in favor of the school (Elkhart Institute) for which Coffman was soliciting money. The Cullom brother thought a grade school education was sufficient for Mennonites. If we were to educate our boys, he said, then they would want to fill "the worldly offices" and that would not be right. "We do not want to educate our boys for preachers," he continued, because "if we have manufactured preachers they would soon want salery [sic] for preaching and that we can't acknowledge as right. I believe as soon as a man hiers [sic] himself out to preach for a certain amount of money he preaches more for money than to save souls." "What will become of our church," he concluded, "when we get all our young people high school educated? There will be nothing left then but to have educated preachers also."⁷

Another 1890s letter from Illinois to Coffman furnishes stronger evidence of the need for more education. The author wrote:

> Ditend harley know wat to write. I can tell you one thing thad I cand help you on money matters. I don't think it is write for our members to bild a high school. Our children wond to go to hirer school. We wouldn't let them. The get good enough edukasion in comen school. Would it be ride to pay for others. I say no.... And another thing, I always thoud if any thing to be don in church maters it habt to be brout before the counfrence. Why is it thad you go a hed of the counfrence. Wat is the youse to hold counfrence if we don won to live so by. Thad is my opinen, if I am rong correct me.⁸

Letters from such people made Coffman determined to go on and do all he could "to help them in spite of themselves."

Conference support for higher education in the (Old) Mennonite Church came slowly. In the Illinois Mennonite Conference in 1892 a delegate raised the question whether ministers were allowed to attend theological institutions. The answer was, "We believe that it is neither proper nor scriptural for a Mennonite minister to attend a theological institution." In 1894 M. S. Steiner, then in charge of the new Chicago

Home Mission, attended the conference at Freeport. He had hoped the Mennonite Church would establish a Bible training school that would grow into a Bible college or Bible institute similar to Moody's in Chicago. He presented his plan to the Illinois Conference, but the delegates turned it down, partly, it seems, because of opposition from the Indiana ministers in attendance. Steiner and his friend J. S. Coffman were disappointed in this outcome. Coffman wrote to him: "I was glad to hear from your experience in the Ill. conference. I wish those dear people could see the need of schooling for themselves. But they will likely learn even if they learn slowly. They have *had* to learn on the Evangelizing work, and their eyes will open on the school question. *But* here comes a caution again, we will have to work carefully that the results will commend themselves to the brotherhood at large."[9]

In 1895 the Western District A. M. Conference raised the question whether the church should establish and support high schools "in which both theology and the spiritless sciences of the world are taught." It decided that it was not "edifying" to have such schools "where the wisdom of God is intermingled with worldly wisdom." Four years later this conference decided it was all right to have Bible schools if conducted "under the direction and with the counsel of the church where they are held."[10]

One of the Illinois voices in the wilderness crying for more education was of course the itinerant German schoolteacher Christian Erismann. He had hoped and planned to go to the dedication of the Wadsworth school in 1866 but could not. He prayed that the Mennonites with united strength and willing hearts would support "our brethren" in the work at Wadsworth. Attending the Amish Versammlung in Livingston County in 1871, he disagreed with a speaker who said that high school was not necessary because grade school was sufficient. The ministers especially needed more education, he said, because they had no religious training in the common schools. The argument often used, that the disciples were not educated, was irrelevant, he explained, since they had had intensive training for three years from the master teacher himself. And, Erismann added, the Apostle Paul was highly educated.[11]

Others also secured more education than was common among the Amish. Christian Ropp, Jr., after attending a German school in the 1840s, enrolled in Walnut Grove Academy in Eureka, attending seven weeks in 1851 and four weeks in 1858. "He was there when the name was changed to Eureka College, starting to school on Monday; the following Tuesday he marched in the procession from one building to another, a distance of about two blocks, in homespun, hooks and eyes, the first clothes bought for him being an overcoat purchased ... for four dollars." And William Albrecht (1850-77) from Tiskilwa graduated from Lombard University at Galesburg and studied medicine at Long Island College in Brooklyn, where he died.[12]

Progress had been made by 1899 when the Illinois Sunday School Conference met at Freeport. Christian education was clearly necessary, said its report, in order to carry out the work of the church. "A boy or girl who goes through college without being converted is hard to reach afterward, hence the importance of supporting and attending schools where an earnest effort is made to bring the students to Christ." The report favored the "movement toward establishing a school [at Elkhart] for our people." In 1903 the report of a Bible conference at Cullom stated that if church schools had Spirit-filled instructors they would tend to unify the church, save the young people for the church, and promote the mission spirit.[13]

Another early Illinois Amish Mennonite who advocated higher education was C. Henry Smith of the Partridge-Metamora congregation. Although he did not appear on the scene as early as Erismann, he was able to go much further academically. Born in 1875, Henry attended the community grade schools, just as other farm boys did. But, as he aptly put it, country boys of working age in Illinois in the 1880s and 1890s "were not expected to waste much time in school, except during a few winter months when there was nothing else to do on the farm." During his first few years in school there was no promise that he would go far in education. "A decent regard for the truth," he said, constrained him to confess that for some years he "hated school and everything connected with it."[14] But in his later elementary school years the story was different. He began to develop a thirst for knowledge that characterized him throughout life. One man above all others was responsible for this turn of events. Smith has paid a high tribute to this person—"the most inspiring teacher I ever knew, and who did more to arouse my life ambitions at a most critical time in my boyhood days than any one else I have ever known since in high school, college or university—Willy Whitmore.... He inspired me to launch out on a course from which I have never wavered since, and for this he has my eternal gratitude."[15]

With his horizon thus enlarged, Smith decided to go to high school, something unheard of in his Amish Mennonite community. Thus he set out on a lifetime educational trail; the trail did not end until he secured a doctorate in history at the University of Chicago in 1907. In the meantime he did some teaching at Elkhart Institute and Goshen College, to which he returned in 1908. He continued at Goshen until 1913, when he along with President N. E. Byers moved to Bluffton College, Bluffton, Ohio. There he labored almost to the end of his career in 1948. In all of these institutions he had numerous students from Illinois in his classes.

C. Henry's father, Bishop John Smith, the only son in a family of six children, did not have the opportunity to secure much formal training, but gladly helped his son with his education. No doubt as C. Henry's educational trail became longer and longer, the good Amish Mennonite bishop wondered at times what would become of the son. On one occasion Paul E. Whitmer, who knew C. Henry well, was visiting in the parental home when the son was nearing the end of his doctoral study. The bishop drew Whitmer aside and asked frankly: "Do you think Henry will ever amount to anything?" Whitmer replied: "O, give him a little more time. I think he will."[16]

In addition to his teaching in the above-mentioned institutions, Smith did pioneer work in the writing of articles and books in Mennonite history, and also lectured widely on the subject. He treated not only the history of the Mennonites but also the Mennonites in history, showing the important contributions they had made in the development of free institutions. In fact, while Smith was working on his master's degree at the University of Chicago, he discovered the importance of the Mennonites. It was a discovery that helped him to decide his life work. To quote from another work of the present writer:

> One day while casually leafing through a library book on Baptist history he [C. Henry Smith] ran across the name of Menno Simons. Upon further reading he found to his surprise that the Baptists claimed a common origin with the Mennonites in the Anabaptist movement of the sixteenth century. Still further reading during the year brought the information that even the Separatists of England and the Congregationalists were indebted to some extent to the influence of the Anabaptist movement. To Smith, who had not known much about Mennonite origins, this was a startling and interesting discovery. He had always thought of Mennonites as an obscure and peculiar people, with strange unpopular practices, and with little influence on the currents of history. He had never expected to find their deeds recorded in either secular or religious history books. To discover, therefore, that they were pioneers in the rise of religious toleration, and that, in a sense, they were the spiritual forefathers of the Baptists and the Congregationalists was a revelation to this young Mennonite as surprising as it was pleasing. "The real contribution of the Mennonites to the great cause of religious toleration and world peace ought to be given wider publicity, I thought. Before I left the university I had decided to make a thorough investigation of their history and if possible write a comprehensive treatise on the subject for publication." And so there, at the University of Chicago, began a task that did not end until a few weeks before his death in October, 1948.[17]

For much too long, Smith felt, Mennonites had been shortchanged at the hands of historians, and he was going to try to do his part in correcting the imbalance. No doubt one of his greatest contributions was to change the attitude of Mennonites, especially young people, toward the place of Mennonites in history. This is well illustrated by an address to a Mennonite young people's conference at Sterling in 1922. After stating that the Mennonites had "always stood for religious toleration and the regenerated life," he continued: "The only colonies in America practicing those principles were Rhode Island and Pennsylvania. These were founded respectively by Baptists and Quakers, both of whom had come under Mennonite influence. One historian has said that in certain principles Mennonites were three hundred years ahead of the times. A sane knowledge of Mennonite history should transform completely the attitude of Mennonite Young People toward their church."[18] This was accomplished not only by Smith himself but also through a large number of younger historians whom he inspired and who recognized him as "the master."[19]

John S. Coffman deserves part of the credit for Smith's educational contribution. Smith has recorded how that, dissatisfied with the preaching in his home church (Partridge and then Metamora), he was pleased to hear Coffman preach an English sermon in which "he showed himself thoroughly at home in ... literature and history and other subjects which I had been studying in school. He seemed a kindred spirit, so different from our own uneducated preachers. Riding home with us, he told me ... interesting things about the stars which I had been reading about. If we only had a preacher like Coffman...." Smith was so impressed with Coffman that he readily embraced the opportunity to live in his home during the two years that the younger man taught at Elkhart Institute, 1898-1900. The fine Christian devotion and the high tone of refinement and culture he experienced in this home made these years "perhaps the most pleasant of my whole educational career."[20]

Another Illinois Mennonite educator was Noah E. Byers from Sterling. About the same age, Byers and Smith worked together many years in the promotion of Mennonite education—at Elkhart Institute, Goshen College, and Bluffton College. Byers was principal at Elkhart, president at Goshen, and dean at Bluffton. Smith was dean at Goshen. Both of them grew up during the Awakening. Byers has stated that in his youth the church at Sterling was "formal and lifeless." "The first outside help that came to this dying church," he adds, "was due to the work of John F. Funk" whose *Herald of Truth* "advocated a more spiritual life and promoted a more active church work. He visited the church ... and preached good sermons in the English language." While some members objected to helping Funk pay his travel expenses, "others were awakened to the necessity of a more active church life."

Byers also credits J. S. Coffman as having been influential in his own life as well as in his congregation. When he was assistant editor of the *Herald of Truth* Coffman came to Sterling in 1891 to hold evangelistic meetings which proved very successful. Byers was among the more than forty converts, and, like Smith, was very much impressed with the character and personality of the evangelist and with the way in which he conducted his meetings. Byers was the first in his congregation to go to high school and also the first to go to college. After two years of teaching school and after graduating from Northwestern University in 1898, he accepted Coffman's invitation to become principal of Elkhart Institute. "So this prophet who led me into the Christian life and the Mennonite church now gave me the opportunity of starting on my career not as a missionary but as a teacher of missionaries."[21] Byers was, of course, a strong believer in church schools. He appreciated what the public schools were doing and said Mennonites should be thankful for them. But, seeing the necessity and desirability of the separation of church and state, he believed that the church must provide religious training through its own services and institutions.[22]

Smith and Byers came to Elkhart at the same time, with 1898 marking the beginning of a long educational trail that these two Illinois Mennonite educators traveled together. While at Goshen both men were responsible for founding the Intercollegiate Peace Association, which is still functioning. They also became increasingly interested in closer inter-Mennonite cooperation, particularly in the operation of an inter-Mennonite theological seminary. Thinking they could more easily carry out these purposes at Bluffton, they transferred to that institution in 1913. Since quite a large number of students from Illinois attended Elkhart, Goshen, and Bluffton, these two men had a tremendous educational impact in Illinois as elsewhere.[23]

Noah Oyer, younger than Smith but also from Metamora, took a slightly different route in making a contribution to Mennonite higher education. Spending his early life at home on the farm, he enrolled at Hesston College and Bible School in 1912, where he was graduated from the academy and in 1919 from the college. After graduate work at Princeton Theological Seminary and Franklin and Marshall College (Pennsylvania), he returned to Hesston in 1922 to teach. Following the death of John D. Charles in 1923, Oyer became dean. In 1924 he moved to Goshen, where he served as dean of the college and pastor of the College Mennonite Church. Unfortunately in December 1930 he became ill with typhoid fever and died on February 25, 1931. Though cut off before reaching forty, his life had already produced much fruit. One of Oyer's visions, unfulfilled in his lifetime, was for a three-year Mennonite graduate biblical institute or seminary, a vision later realized in Goshen Biblical Seminary. He was a recognized and widely respected leader who did much to bridge the gap at a time of strain and stress in the life of Goshen College.[24]

Illinois supplied not only many Mennonite educators but also a number of college administrators. Some of these served during the Awakening and some later. Among these, in addition to Smith, Byers and Oyer, were Amos E. Kreider, Lloyd Ramseyer, Gordon Zimmerman, Roy Roth and Tilman Smith. Irvin R. Detweiler of Goshen also lived in the state for some time. Lloyd L. Ramseyer of McLean County was president of Bluffton College from 1938-65. After graduating from Bluffton in 1924 he was teacher and administrator in Illinois until 1936, when he gave full time to graduate study at Ohio State University, to receive the PhD degree in education in 1938. Ramseyer's term as president at Bluffton was "marked by solid progress and the attainment of goals that had long been held before the college, especially a debt-free accredited institution." In 1953 after much preparation and hard labor the college became a member of the North Central Association.[25]

Once their denominational schools were established, the Illinois Mennonites slowly gave them increasing support. Bishop John Smith of Metamora served on the Elkhart Institute and Goshen College Boards from 1902 until his death in 1906. His son J. D. Smith then served a few years in addition. L. J. Lehman of Cullom and J. S. Shoemaker of Freeport were among the ministers attending the four-week Bible term at Elkhart in 1900. In 1903 Shoemaker, then bishop, helped arrange for the transfer of the school from Elkhart to Goshen. He was also one of those responsible for changing the board of control from private hands to church control under the new Mennonite Board of Education. Announcing this change in a constructive article in the *Herald of Truth*, he commented that some had been more liberal with their criticism than with their means and counsel. His basic attitude was that if Goshen College had faults, the answer was for all to "put our shoulders to the wheel" and make the necessary changes, but not to do away with the college.[26]

Having no college of their own, the Central Conference Mennonites in the earlier years supported others' institutions, especially Goshen. This support remained strong into the administration of J. E. Hartzler, president from 1913-1918. With Illinois Mennonites Hartzler carried on extensive correspondence, indicating that Goshen looked considerably to Illinois for support, both to the Central Conference and to the (Old) Mennonites. Hartzler vigorously and sometimes successfully solicited money in Illinois. The largest Illinois donor in that period was John Ropp of Bloomington. In November 1914 Hartzler advised him that he had "given to the extent that you have become our leading doner [sic]; and for this you will always be remembered in connection with Goshen College.... You are ... the man who has largely made Goshen College what she is. We appreciate it." Ropp and his wife's mother, Mary Rupp, gave substantial additional amounts later.[27]

At about the same time and also later the Ropp family was giving still larger amounts to Bluffton College. In 1913 and the years following, Ropp was much interested in the movement to establish a central Mennonite college or university and seminary, operated and supported by the several Mennonite branches. Had the old church been more receptive and cooperative, quite possibly Goshen could have become this central institution. But since the Mennonite Church controlling board was not interested, Bluffton became the center of this new united effort. President Byers and Dean C. Henry Smith of Goshen were interested in the movement and moved to Bluffton to join it. The old Central Mennonite College, founded in 1898, was reorganized in 1913 and became a four-year institution named Bluffton College.

When Bluffton President S. K. Mosiman visited John Ropp of Bloomington and told him of the new plans for inter-Mennonite cooperation at Bluffton, Ropp enthusiastically replied: "If you will succeed in working out such a plan you will do more for the Mennonite Church than any one has done in the last hundred years. I am greatly interested in it. This does not mean in words only, for John Ropp is known to be as good as his word." Ropp was indeed that and more! On a number of occasions he gave generously as also did his wife and her mother. Altogether, the Ropp family gave Bluffton College some $180,000, and gave it when the school needed it badly. Others from Illinois also gave substantially to the institution. One of them was Gerhard Vogt from Summerfield, who for some years served on the Board of Trustees of Central Mennonite College. But the largest donors in the early years were the Ropps, for whom Ropp Hall was named.[28]

Even though support for church schools increased after the turn of the century, the struggle continued. The Central Illinois Conference, 1914-16, approved supporting Bluffton College and Mennonite Seminary and authorized a financial campaign in the churches. In 1921 the conference accepted Witmarsum Seminary as "our Seminary." Central Conference leader Emanuel Troyer was elected vice-president of the Bluffton board in 1913, and J. H. King of Carlock and A. B. Rutt of Chicago were elected board members. But some conference leaders had their doubts about this venture in Mennonite educational cooperation. Aaron Augspurger, for example, said he was "thoroughly convinced that the time is not ripe for the Central Illinois Conference to enter into any movement of that nature.... Not until we are ready to make compromise, are we ready to enter into a united school movement."[29] In a letter to J. E. Hartzler of Goshen he wrote that he saw two possible dangers: "too extreme progressiveness, or too extreme conservatism." He thought Mennonites needed to look for a middle way between the two. If they could find that happy medium, then he could see a "possibility of building up a school that will prove of the greatest benefit to the majority of the Mennonite people.... I fear that the hast[e] of the progressive element will rather retard than advance the spirit of closer cooperation between the different branches."[30]

But by 1916 Augspurger had changed his mind. After a visit to Bluffton in that year he reported good impressions: "Great possibilities are open to us in this school, and we need not hesitate to embrace them and give it our earnest and hearty support of which it is certainly deserving." The number of students from Illinois at Bluffton increased each year. In 1920 Illinois sent the largest number of any state except Ohio.[31]

Yet in 1923 William B. Weaver, the pastor at North Danvers, was disappointed with the support coming from his congregation. To J. E. Hartzler, now president of Witmarsum Seminary, he wrote about the small financial contribution his group had made to the seminary: "They're not enthusiasts in my church for education either High School, college, or seminary. It sometimes disgusts me. You'll have to wake them up when you come on Education." There must have been some awakening, since the treasurer of Bluffton College reported that Illinois contributed nearly $40,000 to the college endowment drive that ended in September of 1929. Illinois was fourth in the amount contributed—after Ohio, Pennsylvania and Iowa.[32]

During the troubled 1920s when Goshen was closed during the school year 1923-24, about forty former Goshen students boosted the Bluffton enrollment by transferring to that institution.[33] Only a few returned to Goshen after it reopened in 1924. But Illinois as well as other regions gave reasonably good support to the new Goshen administration under the leadership of President Sanford C. Yoder and Dean Noah Oyer, and within a few years the enrollment reached and surpassed the former figures. Thus the cooperative educational venture at Bluffton did not succeed in one sense: the colleges of the various branches continued their separate courses as before. Likewise, the cooperative effort in seminary training attained only minimal success. Significant developments in this area had to await a later day.

But Mennonite schools had proved their value. Writing in 1937 on "What Our Schools Are Doing for Our Churches," Minister Harry Yoder, later associated for many years with Bluffton, was convinced of their value in unifying the churches, providing leadership, leading the churches and communities to higher levels of thinking and living, helping members to live more effectively in and better understand "the social order as it is today," and doing much "for the educational evangelism of our mission stations." Missionaries, he said, must have more than Bible training.[34]

No element of the Mennonite Awakening was emphasized more

than the missionary movement. In fact, it was closely connected with education. Over and over the awakened leaders emphasized that it was necessary to have educational institutions in order to train church workers, especially missionaries. Even more than the Oberholtzer group, Daniel Hege from Summerfield and other immigrants from South Germany who became a part of the General Conference Mennonites took the lead in missionary activity. The General Conference school at Wadsworth is a good example of the close tie between education and missions. Founded to train missionaries, ministers, and other church workers, the school included in its first graduating class in 1871 Samuel S. Haury from Summerfield. Haury became "the first missionary sent out by the General Conference." After investigating several fields, including Java and Alaska, the mission board sent him to Indian Territory (Oklahoma) to open work among American Indians there. Daniel Hege himself did much to promote education and missions. And in 1885 J. B. Baer from Summerfield accepted a call to become the "home missionary for the General Conference." Baer traveled widely among the churches until 1899, promoting the mission cause as well as education and union.[35]

General Conference interest in foreign missions also goes back to its founding in the 1860s, though the actual sending of overseas missionaries did not occur until the turn of the century. In 1899 General Conference Mennonites arranged for the opening of work in India, the first missionaries arriving in 1900. Work in China began in 1909 and was taken over by the church's Foreign Mission Board in 1914. This Board also cooperated with the Congo Inland Mission; which carried on work in Africa and with which many Illinois people were more directly involved.[36]

Though the mission interest developed more slowly among the (Old) Mennonites, the cause found a growing number of powerful advocates late in the nineteenth century, and even more in the twentieth. Many ministers and lay people were deeply affected by the new currents and were stirred to strong support of the mission movement. In 1892 Abram Burkhart from Sterling lamented that many areas were being evangelized by Christians who "glory in war and bloodshed and the awful suffering it brings," while Mennonites were withholding from the unsaved "the true nonresistant doctrine of Jesus." He proposed that American Mennonites raise a large sum every year for missionary work and believed the missionaries would be forthcoming. Mennonites could succeed in mission "if we loved Christ more than our money." One sister from Cullom, warning that Mennonites cannot hide behind the excuse that following the popular churches into mission work might lead to worldliness, asked pointedly: "Can you sit at your own table (own church) and enjoy this great feast while many souls are standing outside, starving, famishing, for food? i.e., for the want of being taught?" The souls of men, she added, were worth vastly more than worldly possessions.[37]

John F. Funk offered one of the most powerful voices among the (Old) Mennonites for missions, and because of his *Herald of Truth*, one of the most influential. Referring in 1892 to a powerful appeal for missions that Solomon D. Ebersole of Sterling and temporarily of Chicago had made, Funk stated in an unsigned editorial: "It is our firm conviction that if we had a suitable place in Chicago to conduct Sunday-school and other gospel services, a glorious work could, by the grace of God, and with efficient help, be done among the spiritually destitute of Chicago." A few years earlier another statement in the *Herald*, very probably by Funk, referred to the purported fact that only 10 percent of the people in Chicago belonged to any church. Gravely concerned, the writer added: "Should not living Christians be up and doing something for the Lord and for spreading the Gospel?"[38] Funk's pleas, which continued for years, no doubt bore much fruit in the end.

Closely associated with Funk in pushing the mission phase of the Awakening was of course John S. Coffman. As one writer has well stated, both of these men "had an uncommon ability to retain the confidence of conservatives while introducing progressive ideas." Their mission interest, both home and foreign, entered center stage and "became fruitful in the closing years of the century." This occurred partly through organization of the Mennonite Evangelizing Committee (1882), with which Funk and Coffman were closely connected, and the Mennonite Evangelizing and Benevolent Board (1896), both of which were among the predecessors of the Mennonite Board of Missions and Charities (now "Mennonite Board of Missions"). M. S. Steiner, founder of the Chicago Home Mission, was president of the latter board from its founding in 1906 until his death in 1911.[39]

Another such powerful voice was J. S. Shoemaker from Freeport. Secretary of the Mission Board from 1906-21 and widely respected and loved as a leader in Illinois and elsewhere, he was tremendously important in pushing interest in missions to a new high among Mennonites. In 1910 and 1911 he and J. S. Hartzler of Goshen, Indiana, visited the mission field in India, and in 1912 published an account of their trip under the title *Among Missions in the Orient and Observations by the Way*. This report of 467 pages, including over 100 illustrations, was widely distributed and greatly enhanced Shoemaker's influence as an advocate of missions. En route they had attended a historic World Missionary Conference at Edinburgh in Scotland, June 14-24. The conference was indeed a stimulating and educational experience for both men—for Hartzler, who was a teacher at Goshen and also member and treasurer of Mennonite Board of Education at the time, and especially for Shoemaker, as Mission Board secretary.

This journey no doubt also made Shoemaker an abler secretary. In that role he became an early advocate for work in South America. Throughout his life the mission program of the church "dominated his thinking and was one of his primary aims." His strong endorsement of missions was bound to have an effect on the Mennonites of his home state. In any case, by the second decade of the new century there was probably very little opposition to missions in Illinois. Three statements illustrate many of the things written about missions at that time: Ruth E. Buckwalter, a Chicago Home Mission worker, said: "No Christian church worthy of the name, ever existed, no matter how poor, that was not a missionary church." Walter A. Zook, a farmer from the Roanoke congregation, wrote: "No one can read the New Testament without seeing that the uppermost thing in the mind of Christ was the evangelization of the world. He came into the world to save it. He spoke in world terms.... When Christ ascended it did not change His attitude toward His program. He is the same yesterday, today, and forever. He knew no distinction of race or caste for His interests are world wide." A. E. Kreider from Sterling, later a well-known Bible teacher, considered missions "the central theme of the New Testament." He then made the statement stronger by saying the theme of both Testaments was of "a missionary nature." "The Bible abounds with illustrations of how individuals were seized with an unquenchable desire to make known to others the joys of forgiveness, and the peace of fellowship with God."[40]

Meanwhile the growing missionary impulse had begun to bear much fruit. The first mission efforts of the (Old) Mennonite Church, except for the rural missions of the Virginia Mennonites in West Virginia, centered in Chicago. The remarkable story of the Mennonites in Chicago is best appreciated in the Home Mission enterprise. For an unprepared rural people to thrust themselves into the midst of a large city to carry on mission work was a stupendous task that required courage as well as commitment. Very likely, as some workers soon discovered, better educated laborers with more knowledge of urban problems would have been better for the cause. But Mennonites learned the hard way.[41]

After the John F. Funk period, Mennonites had become seriously interested in Chicago as a mission field in the early 1890s. After a short period in missionary work in Switzerland, John A. Sprunger and wife from Berne, Indiana, became interested in the work of deaconesses, and in 1892 started a Deaconess Training School in Chicago. Here, for a few years and with the help of others, he combined deaconess, orphanage, hospital, and mission work. Later Berne, Indiana, and then Cleveland, Ohio, became the centers of his activities. While

Sprunger's work in Chicago remained private, he received aid from the churches, especially Salem near Flanagan.[42]

At about the same time, the (Old) Mennonites became interested in Chicago. Their story usually begins with S. D. Ebersole and the Mennonite Sunday school conferences of 1892 and 1893. Ebersole from Sterling was studying medicine at Northwestern University and had become deeply concerned about the missionary needs in the city. Already in December 1890 he had written to M. S. Steiner, stating that a number of people in Chicago were eager to discuss with him the possibility of starting mission work. Ebersole expressed his concern in an address at an important Mennonite Church general Sunday school conference at the Clinton Frame congregation near Goshen, Indiana, in 1892. His subject was "Relation of Sunday Schools to Missions, Or Missions and Their Value." Quoting various biblical passages that laid a great responsibility on Christians to proclaim the good news, he warned that if they failed they were *"trifling with the solemn words of a great God."*[43]

In terms of action the next Sunday school conference—held at Zion, M. S. Steiner's congregation near Bluffton, Ohio, in 1893—was more fruitful. Steiner was a leader in this one as he also had been in the one at Goshen. Once more, S. D. Ebersole addressed this conference. Focusing this time more on Chicago, he gave information about its population and its evils: its "some 7,000" flourishing saloons, its drug addicts, its "about 100,000" illegal abortions, and its homeless vagabonds. "Yet," he stated, "these poor creatures are human beings, our brothers, possessed of souls with eternal possibilities." He quoted Spurgeon's reply to the question as to whether the heathen would be saved without the gospel: ". . . . it is not so much whether the heathen will be saved as whether you will be saved if you don't do your part to spread the Gospel." The secretaries reported that it was a "telling address" that caused much discussion. According to Ebersole, an interested group in Chicago plus Steiner, calling themselves the "Mennonite Mission Committee," had already selected a site and were making some plans for the operation of the mission. Apparently a group of the most interested people at the conference met informally and appointed Steiner as superintendent of the new Chicago venture.[44]

Ordained to the ministry a few months earlier by John F. Funk, Steiner moved to Chicago in November 1893 to assume his new responsibilities. One is impressed with the zeal of these awakened, young Mennonite activists behind the Chicago undertaking. The new superintendent was only twenty-seven years old and unmarried, and S. F. Coffman, who succeeded him in 1894, was only twenty-two. Three of them—S. D. Ebersole, William B. Page, and DeWitt Good—were doctors either in or recently graduated from medical school. Their youth, together with the fact that the mission's founding hardly rested on a full-blown, official mandate from the church, soon brought mixed reactions. Many were happy with this new step forward and sent in words of encouragement and financial support to back up their words. Others were cautious. Still others were critical and opposed the work. Ebersole had been selected as treasurer, and his confused mission accounts did not help matters. Failing to keep the mission "Mennonite" would be a criticism that many would be ready to offer. A number of critics had already said that rural Mennonites should not try to operate city missions.[45]

Some Illinois Mennonites were among those who had questions. The Illinois Mennonite Conference in May, 1894, passed a resolution on the Chicago Mission, stating that the conference would "stand by them with prayer and offering, providing [sic] they teach the word, and conduct the same according to the Gospel which we believe and practice." The conference also asked Bishop E. M. Hartman to visit the mission and report the following year. Hartman did investigate and report; S. F. Coffman, the new superintendent at Chicago, also reported. As a result the conference resolved to encourage and support the mission, "suggesting, however, that the workers shall be diligent to conform their work to the commonly accepted usages of the church." Hartman and J. S. Shoemaker were to investigate again during the ensuing year, but the 1896 minutes offer no account of any report.[46]

As the first superintendent, Steiner was a very busy man. In addition to getting the new mission equipped and going in the last months of 1893, he was also editor of a new periodical published at Elkhart, the *Young People's Paper*, the first issue of which he sent to the printer on December 4, 1893. He was also secretary of the Mennonite Book and Tract Society, founded in 1889 to help awaken interest in and supply good literature. In addition he had to attend many church meetings, a necessary part of his labors. Because of his heavy work load he was forced to resign as secretary in February, 1894. Of course, his romance with Clara Eby of Pandora, Ohio, whom he would marry in April of 1894, also required attention.[47]

One of his closest friends and supporters, J. S. Coffman, gave Steiner good advice and encouragement from time to time. "If you take up the work and carry it forward in the order of the church and teach and maintain the principles of the Bible as held of our people," wrote Coffman just before the mission opened, "you will have the support of a great part of the church and the inactive and the opposers will eventually fall into line.... But any mistake that you might make would go far to defeat the very end you aim at. Remember ... that I expect to stand by you with my prayers, and all the influence I have with our people. My heart is in it. But I see many chances for defeat." In

March of 1894, a few months after the mission opened, Coffman again wrote: "Now Bro. be careful in pushing along that mission work. See that you stay fully in the church order. If you do not it will prove your defeat." A few days later: "My heart is truly glad that you wish to push your work in a way that will meet the sanction of the conferences.... The church, I find all along, will stand by you if you stand by the church."[48]

Steiner's bringing a wife to Chicago after his marriage in April put him in a better position to face problems, but the problems did not diminish. Reports were mixed. In January, 1894, Steiner wrote that the "churches are contributing more than our most sanguine expectations dared to anticipate." On various occasions he wrote that meetings were being blessed with conversions.[49] Unfortunately, some reports were less optimistic. And Mrs. Steiner's health was not good in Chicago. As a result, during the summer of 1894 the Steiners began to consider other possible fields of labor. Steiner's correspondence makes it clear that he was concerned about his wife's health and wishes. It is also clear that his wife's decision was important in determining to go to Canton, Ohio, where he would pastor a small, struggling church. Steiner was aware of some criticisms leveled at the Chicago work. In one letter to his wife he warned that they could not expect an easy time at Canton either: "We will have to settle down to solid work or there will be much more talk out on us about being ambitious and stuckup [and] too lazy to work, etc." (The present writer has not gotten that kind of picture of Steiner from Steiner's correspondence.)[50]

On October 1, 1894, at the close of his active service in Chicago, Steiner issued a report of his work as superintendent. He felt that "judging from the support that the mission has received, the efforts put forth have been heartily approved." He thought the great interest of the brotherhood at large in city missions was clear and that the movement would continue until all the large cities had the opportunity to hear the message "as practiced by our people." He believed that Mennonite "oddities and peculiarities," including the simple lifestyle and "plainness of dress," would not be a hindrance but would "fit us to do first-class mission work." But the advisory committee (J. S. Coffman, A. R. Zook, D. S. Yoder, Abraham Metzler, Jr.) was not quite so optimistic. It cited such problems as opposition of Catholics (especially clergy), general distrust in the community toward workers (some workers were arrested and imprisoned for short periods), suspicion, and lack of support of "some of our people." But the committee made suggestions and provisions for the continuation of the work.[51]

The advisory committee appointed Samuel F. Coffman, son of the evangelist, as manager of the Chicago mission, although Steiner apparently continued to have some administrative connection for a year or two longer. E. J. Berkey of Middlebury, Indiana, replaced S. D. Ebersole as secretary-treasurer. In these early years Indiana apparently had closer ties with the mission than did Illinois, at least organizationally. In 1894 the Elkhart-based Mennonite Evangelizing Board of America recognized the mission and promised to cooperate with and support it. But that did not prevent the partial closing of the mission for a few months in 1895-96. A special conference of interested people met on July 25, 1895, at the mission to consider its problems and its future. The group included Steiner, now from Canton; E. M. Hartman, Joseph Buerckey, J. S. Shoemaker, John Nice, and Philip Nice from Illinois; John Shenk from Ohio; John F. Funk, J. S. Coffman, J. S. Lehman, and G. L. Bender from Elkhart; plus the mission workers. They decided to close "the Home [where the workers lived] of the Chicago Home Mission," "but also recommend that the mission work be continued by members residing in the city, who support themselves by attending to other duties. This work should be continued in this manner until the church shall make provision for a mission under her charge in the city." In March of 1896 the workers sorrowfully announced that the "Mission has been closed." E. J. Berkey reported that Steiner, who himself "thought it advisable to have it close," preached the last sermon on March 5. Berkey also reported that a bright boy of about five, who had recently started attending Sunday school, came up at the close of the service and asked, "Is it all done now?" These words pierced the hearts of the workers "like arrows" and made them more determined than ever that somehow the work must go on.[52] The whole matter of "closing" and "reopening" the mission—who did what and who was responsible—is confusing. Interested readers can probably follow the tangled story best in chapter 2 of Theron Schlabach's recent book, *Gospel Versus Gospel*.

In any case, the mission soon resumed its ministry. In the latter part of 1896 the newly constituted Mennonite Evangelizing and Benevolent Board (MEBB) took over and reopened the mission at a new location. It now became more of a denominational institution and enjoyed a gradual but not outstanding growth and operation for many years. The medical dispensary, a part of the work from the beginning, was also reopened. Since the doctors operating the dispensary were part-time helpers at the mission, and since they also had some beds for patients and had to secure a license from the city, one writer has referred to this as the first Mennonite hospital in the United States.[53] The dispensary was important in the work of the mission. J. S. Shoemaker said it was a means of gaining the trust and respect of the poor. Many who attended the meetings had first been influenced through receiving medical help and had then been invited to come to the meetings. One worker reported that the service reached people who could not have been reached in any other way. The doctors also made house calls in needy homes. By 1902 when the dispensary closed it had served its purpose. By that time numerous free clinics had opened.[54]

More stable times for the mission began in 1897 with the appointment of A. Hershey Leaman as superintendent. Determined to devote his life to missions, Leaman, from Lancaster County, Pennsylvania, was only nineteen in 1897 and the youngest head ever to be appointed at the mission. Thereafter he had the longest

Source: Oyer, *What Hath God Wrought?*

A. Hershey Leaman (1878-1950) and Amanda Eby Leaman. He was superintendent of the Mennonite Home Mission, 1897-1920.

superintendency—twenty-three years. Since the Home Mission was the oldest Mennonite mission in Chicago (not including John F. Funk's church), and because of Leaman's emphasis on and experience in inter-Mennonite activity, perhaps his mission's development can be looked on as more or less illustrative of all of them. Although other Mennonite missions in Chicago varied somewhat, basically programs and problems were similar. Even the greater emphasis of the (Old) Mennonites on nonconformity, which caused some problems in adjusting to city life in the earlier years, was a difference only in degree.

Apparently Leaman himself was able to adjust to and work with other groups without much difficulty. He labored not only with several different Mennonite groups but with some non-Mennonite ones as well, and later worked at Moody Bible Institute after he left the Home Mission in 1920. In some cases leaders in other Mennonite missions had some apprentice work with Leaman at the Home Mission before beginning on their own. Such cases included prominent missionaries such as A. F. Wiens, G. P. Schultz, Amos Eash, and A. B. Rutt. Close relations between the missions continued. The history of the Hoyne Avenue Mission, founded in 1907 by A. F. Wiens and later placed in charge of G. P. Schultz, is a good example.[55]

Leaman, understandably, was a believer in the various phases of the Mennonite Awakening. He had been converted in one of J. S. Coffman's evangelistic meetings in Lancaster County and in 1902 had married Amanda Eby, a worker at the mission and a sister of Clara (Mrs. M. S.) Steiner. In the same year he was ordained minister by Bishop John Nice of Morrison. He was much better educated than the average Mennonite minister of his day. He had attended Millersville State Normal in Pennsylvania one year before coming to Chicago, and then he studied one year at Moody Bible Institute before his ordination. After that he studied at Chicago Theological Seminary, securing the BD degree in 1915. This latter part of his education was delayed somewhat because of opposition, for one reason or another, from his bishop.[56]

Under Leaman's leadership the Home Mission work continued to grow. One activity, common among city missions, was the so-called "fresh air" program. Leaman took over this project and greatly expanded it. He did the same with dispensary work, but the fresh air program continued in operation much longer. Under this program children attending the mission had the privilege in summer of spending about two weeks in the homes of Mennonite farmers in Illinois and other nearby states, a privilege to which the youngsters eagerly looked forward. The Mennonite farmers accepted them without charge, of course, and railroads also cooperated by providing free transportation. These experiences were very valuable, physically, educationally, and spiritually, to the children and to the mothers who occasionally accompanied them. The program flourished for many years until wide use of the automobile made contact with the rural areas easy. It was especially meaningful to children in congested areas like that around the Home Mission, where virtually the only playgrounds available were the streets and the alleys.

The largest number going out in one season from the Home Mission was about 300. One beneficiary later said: "Don't stop the Fresh Air Program. I believe this is what has helped to keep me from the wrong road." Another (Mrs. Ralph King) said the Mennonite homes in which she lived in the country gave her ideas as to how to build a Christian home. One Home Mission worker considered fresh air contacts most successful ways of doing mission work with boys and girls. He added: "I believe two weeks in a home where Christ is lived is worth more to the child than a whole year in the Sunday school." Other mission workers were also convinced that this phase of the work "has been one of the most fruitful in reaching children and young people for Christ and very helpful in seeing them through hard places and experiences in their early Christian life." Beyond such testimonies, it seems that Leaman had an additional value in mind: that of developing better understanding between rural and city Mennonites, and a better understanding of the place of city missions. To these ends he encouraged correspondence between the two groups by providing addresses. In 1951 the fresh air program was still serving a useful purpose. Many testimonies, said a report, "ring with praise for this service. This is practical Christianity."[57] As a matter of fact, this program was still continuing at least as late as 1979. Sadie Oswald of the Mennonite Community Chapel was chiefly responsible for its operation.[58]

Serving an annual Christmas dinner at the Home Mission was another service that Leaman inherited and expanded. Apparently primarily for children at first, the dinner grew and included adults, both members of the congregation and visitors. Rural Mennonite communities annually sent in provisions, which the workers prepared for the meal served in late afternoon a few days before Christmas. Emma Oyer, who participated in dozens of these dinners, has described them in detail. Usually Superintendent Leaman, "who kept things moving at top notch," gave the welcome and then called for the singing of several hymns. Following the invocation some 300 to 400 people or more partook of the bounteous meal. An inspiring part of the celebration following the dinner was a praise and testimony service. A number testified how they were gloriously saved and helped through the work of the mission. Those who heard testimonies from people such as Hans Dahlgren, David Stork, and Ole Martensen would never forget them. The whole service contributed to meeting spiritual and social needs, as well as physical. It helped the mission's work and its services to grow, including Sunday school and church.[59]

Emma Oyer who as a worker knew Leaman well described him as "the man with ideas and visions, with the desire and ability to make reality of them." One can see this in his administration of the mission. There were many facets to his program, although one should not credit them to him alone for he had able assistants. A. C. Schultz has also pointed out Leaman's broad vision and versatility in the operation of a varied program. "The Home Mission carried on the usual church program of a Sunday school, Sunday worship, and midweek services, but expanded this into a variety of other activities." There were in addition, says Schultz, "young people's meetings, cottage prayer meetings, mothers' meetings, meetings in German, sewing classes for girls, a ministry to the shut-ins and the aged." The fresh air program was expanded to include "an annual Sunday school picnic in a city park, and preaching the Gospel out on the streets." To help carry out this phase Leaman used a unique "gospel wagon." This was "merely a platform on wheels with a railing around it and drawn by a horse. Ten or twelve men could stand on this wagon and conduct a gospel service. A favorite trip on this wagon was to Skid Row, and frequently trips were made to the city's main business district, 'the Loop.' " In 1908, to follow up with this type of work, Leaman opened a rescue mission at 437 South State Street. Calling it the Happy Hour Mission, he arranged for George P. Schultz of Saskatchewan, Canada, to serve as superintendent. Leaman was interested in inter-Mennonite cooperation in Chicago. He had already taken a step in this direction in 1907 by organizing the first quarterly Sunday school meeting, in order to get the various Mennonite churches to work together in the promotion of Sunday school and mission work. The Happy Hour Mission was another inter-Mennonite effort.[60]

Leaman and all the workers believed in the philosophy that they should not only preach the gospel directly to sinners but that they were to provide for material needs also. That is well illustrated by A. M. Eash, a laborer at the Home Mission who later became superintendent of another Mennonite effort, the Twenty-sixth Street Mission. In reporting about a carload of goods received from the country churches to be distributed to the poor, Eash stated: "We believe this is one way—and a very good way, too—of doing missionary work. Many of the people cannot be reached with the gospel until they are supplied with that which they need to satisfy their hunger. You may say to a man, 'My God will supply all your needs,' but unless you are able to prove what you say to him by helping to fulfill the promise, his faith in your teaching is small."[61]

Near the end of Leaman's administration he provided able

Meeting at Happy Hour Mission, an inter-Mennonite rescue mission in Chicago from 1908-1916.

Source: Peter Schultz, Justice, Ill.

Education, Missions, Service 271

leadership in raising funds for a new mission building. The work of the mission, which had been organized by J. S. Shoemaker as a congregation in the Illinois Mennonite Conference in 1903, had long outgrown its facilities at 639 West 18th Street. Authorized by the mission board at Elkhart, Leaman, who had been very successful as a fundraiser earlier, secured the money in a comparatively short time. In fact, he had secured more funds than necessary for the building itself. Built at a new location at 1907 South Union Avenue, the structure was begun in July 1918 and completed in December. What one writer has described as one "of the outstanding events in the history of the congregation" was a "combined missionary meeting, dedication service, and twenty-fifth anniversary celebration [of the mission] which lasted four days in January, 1919." The workers were delighted to have enlarged facilities for living quarters and for carrying on the work, and the congregation was happy for a new auditorium where, farther removed from the noise and the rowdies of the street, it could worship in greater peace. Earlier the workers had at times asked some of the noiser Sunday school pupils to leave the room or "help them to leave." A few times they had even called in police officers. One time while the Sunday school was singing "Bring Them In," "Brother Steiner, who insisted on order was very busily putting them out." With the new facilities and with the mission better established, such incidents were now pretty largely in the past.[62] Because of the adequacy of the new building, the Home Mission served as a center or meeting place for church committees and for Mennonites who were working or visiting in Chicago. The annual meetings of the Mennonite Central Committee are a good example. This was true until the mission had to close at this location in the late 1950s because of being in the path of a new expressway.[63]

Soon after the new building was completed, and at the peak of what seemed like a very successful Leaman administration, an incident occurred that brought regrets to some of the mission family. Leaman's friendly, outgoing personality was apparently misinterpreted some years earlier by one of the female workers, who for some strange reason started talking about it only in 1919—not with the Leamans and/or the mission board but with some members of the Home Mission congregation. Differences in personality, lifestyle, and philosophical outlook added to the misunderstanding. An investigating committee from the mission board, including two representatives from the district Illinois Home Mission Board, utilized many witnesses in investigating the matter, and concluded that the parties, in view of their positions as mission workers, had in some instances been indiscreet. They felt that the woman had been indiscreet in some other cases also. Both were invited to remain as workers, but neither did.[64]

Much disturbed by the new turn of events, Leaman resigned at the Home Mission in 1920 to accept an invitation to join the staff of Moody Bible Institute. Here he was Assistant and later Director of the Practical Work Department and taught courses in Personal Evangelism. In 1932 he resigned at Moody's to devote himself to several other projects, one of these being the formation of the Christian Business Men's Committee. This group, with Leaman as its head during the first year, organized noonday religious meetings held in a large Loop theater. Since the meetings were addressed by well-known speakers, were evangelistic in nature and were broadcast over the radio, they were well attended and resulted in conversions and the strengthening of spiritual life. The idea spread to other cities in this land and in foreign countries. Another of Leaman's projects was organization of the annual Easter sunrise services, which met for the first time in 1933 in Soldiers Field attended by about 20,000 people.[65]

Though Leaman left the Home Mission in 1920 he remained a Mennonite to the end of his life in 1950. He retained his connection with the Illinois Mennonite Church Conference and continued to be used in its circles. An early advocate of inter-Mennonite cooperation, he also served on two occasions in the 1930s and 1940s as pastor of the General Conference Mennonite Church in Chicago at 73rd and Laflin streets. In November 1946, on the fiftieth anniversary of his coming to Chicago, some 450 of his friends, many of whom Leaman had helped personally, met to honor him for his fifty years of missionary service in the city. Commenting on the event, Raymond Yoder, superintendent of the mission from 1938 to 1945, stated: "Brother Leaman has been criticized ... just as Christ was, and Christian workers often are.... But he has a big string of fish. After all, how good a 'Fisher of men' one is determines the reality of divine love within, and not the mistakes." In the present writer's judgment this is a good evaluation of Leaman's contribution in Chicago.[66]

None of Leaman's successors served as long as he. Henry R. Schertz was superintendent from 1920 to 1923. A farmer from Metamora who had been ordained minister in 1917, he with his family moved to Chicago in 1919, where he enrolled in Bethany Biblical Seminary for more training. He accepted the superintendency of the mission reluctantly, feeling the limits of his experience in city mission work. Later he reported these years as the "most blessed" in his life, yet "perhaps the most trying years as well." It was not easy to follow the long ministry of a Hershey Leaman.[67]

Simon M. Kanagy served from 1923 to 1932, in the longest administration in the post-Leaman period. He arrived with considerable Bible training, experience in mission work in Toronto, and teaching experience at Hesston College in Kansas, and was well

Source: Oyer, *What Hath God Wrought?*

Mennonite Home Mission (founded 1893), located at 1907 South Union Avenue, Chicago, 1919-1957.

fitted for his new position. No doubt many could share the testimony that one convert has given of this kindly, dedicated Christian worker: "Brother Kanagy was my pastor and friend, my spiritual father. I am deeply grateful for his sincere and earnest ministry." After nine years the Kanagys left the mission because of Mrs. Kanagy's health.[68]

In succeeding years the mission had problems getting and keeping superintendents. The turnover was too rapid for the good of the cause. Frequently missionaries on furlough, or others, including relief workers, waiting to go to the field, consented to take charge for short periods. They did as well as possible under the circumstances, but their terms were usually too short to do effective work. Between 1932 and 1938 P. A. and Florence Friesen, J. W. and Salena Gamber Shank, Edwin and Irene Weaver, and Levi C. Hartzler served. Raymond and Frances Yoder served a little longer—1938 to 1945. From 1945 to the mission's close at 1907 South Union Avenue, the following, with their wives, served: G. Irvin Lehman (four months), Earl S. Lehman, John I. Byler, J. Otis Yoder, Don Driver (four months), and Laurence Horst. Included among those who served as assistant pastors were James Christophel and Wayne D. King.[69]

While superintendents came and went, the longer terms of some of the workers provided more continuity, as did also the faithful assistance of local members. Such longtime workers as Emma Oyer and Anna Yordy and others, together with experienced lay members of the congregation, such as Fred Burkey and Frank D. King, provided able assistance. But a program of longtime workers and short-term superintendents had weaknesses as well as strengths. Some leaders felt so inexperienced that they sought and welcomed the counsel of the workers, while others felt that some workers were too free with advice as to how things were run in the past and thus inhibited the new leaders' own ideas.[70]

Elements of drama attended the closing of the Home Mission at its old location. In 1957 the congregation decided to move to the Englewood section, where it became the Englewood Mennonite Church. However, since the building of the expressway was delayed, part of the congregation continued to worship at the old location until 1959. At a significant anniversary service in 1957, memorializing the many years of mission work that were about to close, among the attendants was Lizzie Lehner, the only living charter member from 1902. She had to be carried to her seat by members of her family. Mrs. Lehner had been outstanding in her service at the Home Mission from A. H. Leaman to Laurence Horst. In 1959 she died on the day that the wrecker started razing the mission building and was buried on the day that the wrecker completed the job. Because of this coincidence people said: "Mrs. Lehner and the Home Mission went down together." Yet the drama was not ended. A few, led by Sadie Oswald, felt so strongly that the work should go on that they rented new quarters nearby and, to make a long story short, are continuing the work to this day (1981) as the Mennonite Community Chapel![71]

It may be putting it too strongly to say that starting the Chicago Home Mission was opening the floodgates to home missions. But Mennonite interest certainly mounted significantly in the next few years, and no place illustrates this better than Chicago. The Brethren in Christ started a Chicago work in 1894. Most other Mennonite missions in Chicago were probably influenced more by the Home Mission precedent. One of these, the Twenty-sixth Street Mission, sometimes called the Mennonite Gospel Mission, was to a certain extent an outgrowth of the Home Mission. Sponsored by the same Mennonite group, the mission had as its first leaders Mr. and Mrs. Amos Eash, both former workers at the Home Mission. In fact Mrs. Eash, formerly Anna Annacker, had been converted there. Eash was from Middlebury and later Lagrange County, Indiana. Educated in the local public schools, he also attended two Indiana colleges, what became Tri-State University at Angola and Huntington College, plus two years at Bethany Biblical Seminary in Chicago. The Home Mission Board of the Illinois (MC) conference opened the new mission in 1906. After renting several buildings for a few years, the conference erected a new building at 720 West Twenty-sixth Street and dedicated it in December 1910.

The mission's history was somewhat checkered although in its weekly routine it resembled the Home Mission. Among the reasons the local board selected its location was that there were "not many saloons." Superintendent Eash later reported they must not have investigated very thoroughly! Eash also pointed out an inaccuracy in the report of the first meeting, where the report indicated good attendance and "good attention." A large attendance they had, said Eash, but the order left much to be desired: the overflow crowd of children raised so much noise and commotion that even a thirty-minute effort of "songs, prayer and talks failed completely to quell the uproar." In this way, too, the mission resembled others in the city.[72]

Like the workers at the Home Mission, Eash was an enthusiastic believer in the fresh air program. In July, 1912, he reported that already that summer his mission had sent about 250 children out to Mennonite homes in Illinois, Iowa, and Indiana, and hoped to send 100 more. This "particular activity," he stated, "in proportion to the time and money expended has been more fruitful in adding to and holding to the Sunday school than any other single activity in the mission."[73]

The Home and other missions also shared many problems, including: the shortage of workers and a too rapid turnover, the cramped quarters, the changing ethnic composition of the community, and the difficulty of building up an (Old) Mennonite church in the city. On this last point the fairly frequent reports from the mission indicate that Sunday school attendance was large and that the number of conversions at evangelistic and other meetings was also large as compared with the number who actually joined the mission congregation. In the evangelistic meetings in 1906, for example, there were nineteen confessions; in 1910, fifty; and in 1912, thirty-six. But in 1910 there were only twenty-nine members in the church besides the workers. Eash reported that many hesitated because of fear of estrangement from relatives and doubts about specific Mennonite issues such as life insurance, membership in labor unions, lodge membership, and the bonnet. The total membership never reached 100.[74]

Although in 1916 Eash faced the future "with a confidence and expectations which banish all thought of failure," the mission fell on difficult times in the early 1920s. After doing two years of relief work in the Near East (Syria) 1919-21, Eash returned to the mission and upon further consideration decided to change his conference affiliation to that of the Central Conference of Mennonites. In 1923 he informed the Mennonite Board of Missions and Charities that he no longer considered it possible to labor at the mission "with a view of building up a congregation under the policy of the Board and the regulations of the [Illinois] Conference in which the Mission is located." The Board accepted his proposal to leave the work, asking only that he give due notice of his departure. Since the Board for some time had been considering terminating the work at Twenty-sixth Street, it decided that now was the time to do so and asked Eash for aid in disposing of the property. To assist him Eash then appointed a committee from the mission congregation, which decided that the congregation should apply for membership in the Central Conference. The Central Conference accepted the group, decided in 1923 to take over and continue the mission, and began negotiations with the Board to buy the mission building. Since there were differences of opinion between the parties as to what was a fair price for the mission property, the Central Conference at first operated the mission under a rental agreement with the Board.[75]

The Central Conference asked Eash to continue as the leader and pastor of the mission. Church membership at the mission had fallen from a high of sixty-eight in 1916 to a low of seventeen in 1923. Eash slowly built this up again to a high of seventy-two—with over 300 in Sunday school—in 1935. In view of this apparent success, to many it came as a surprise that Eash resigned in 1936. The work was not progressing as much as it appeared to be; some workers were resigning; and Eash's health was not good. Discouraged with all of these, he pleaded with the Central Conference Mission Board for help. The Board replied that in view of all the circumstances they felt he was wise in resigning. Accepting his resignation, they expressed appreciation for his "faithful and sacrificial service," and assured him of their "interest and prayers for his future work." Eash's son Harold, Carl Landes of Bluffton, Ohio, and others continued the mission work for short periods. But again population shifts, increasing indebtedness, and decreasing attendance plagued the mission. The mission was closed about 1944 and the building was sold to a Baptist group. In 1958 it was bought by the Knights of Columbus. The experience of the mission under the Central Conference indicated that it took more than the easing of Mennonite restrictions on dress and other Mennonite distinctives to make a mission succeed.[76]

Long before taking over the Twenty-sixth Street Mission, the Central Conference had in 1909 established its own mission in Chicago. Albert B. Rutt from the (Old) Mennonites, among the many who received his apprentice training at the Home Mission, transferred his membership to the Central Conference and became superintendent of the new work, called the Home Chapel. The Central Conference members, partly no doubt because they lived close to the work, took a lively interest in the mission and supplied funds and gifts in kind as well as workers. John and Mary Rupp of Bloomington, generous contributors to Christian education, gave substantially to this cause also. By 1909 there was a more united support for home missions among the Central Conference people than among the (Old) Mennonites in 1893 when they started the Home Mission.

The Home Chapel, located on the south side on Sixty-third Street and then nearby at 6201 Carpenter Street, experienced good growth for some years. In addition to Rutt, E. T. Rowe and Lee Lantz served as leaders. Then changing ethnic, economic, and religious patterns caused new conditions with which the mission seemed unable to cope. Membership began to fall from its high point of seventy-three—with a considerably higher attendance. Members moved out of the neighborhood. In 1948 the conference closed the work and sold the property.[77]

In 1907 Abraham F. Wiens and wife opened a mission at Hoyne Avenue and Thirty-third Street. About 1910 the Defenseless Mennonite Brethren, now Evangelical Mennonite Brethren, took over the work. Other workers were soon added to assist the Wienses. Wiens had been born in Russia and had come to Richmond, Texas, in 1897. After a hurricane demolished his home in 1900—apparently the same storm that destroyed Galveston—he and his wife moved to Kansas. Having convictions that they ought to be missionaries, they moved to Chicago in 1906. Like so many others he studied at Moody's and was an apprentice of A. H. Leaman at the Home Mission. After changing its name and location several times, the mission finally located at Thirty-fourth Place and Walcott Street, and eventually became known as Brighton Mennonite Church.

According to a daughter, a bit of tension later developed when some members wanted George P. Schultz as pastor, while others wanted Wiens to continue. The conference stepped in and asked Schultz to take charge. Schultz, born in Mountain Lake, Minnesota, attended Moody Bible Institute and held degrees from Northern Baptist and Chicago Theological seminaries. He had had experience at the Home Mission and as superintendent of the Happy Hour Mission. Under Schultz's leadership Brighton grew to a membership of 160 and a weekly attendance of 450 to 500 in all meetings. But soon the church suffered from "suburbanism." Nearly all of its supporting members moved to suburban areas.[78]

In the meantime Wiens, who still strongly felt called to mission work in Chicago, moved a mile west of Brighton Mennonite Church and started the Mennonite Bible Mission in 1917. It was not easy. The conference wished him God's blessing but did not promise any support. However, with the help of seven daughters, one of whom married missionary John T. Neufeld, he succeeded and the work developed into Grace Mennonite Church, a member of the General Conference Mennonites. Some workers from Moody Bible Institute also assisted. When Wiens died in 1937 Neufeld succeeded as pastor. The membership was sixty-eight in 1955, but with higher attendance, especially in the Sunday school. In 1940 the work began to receive financial support from its conference. As was true with other Mennonite city missions, the ethnic composition of the community was subject to constant change. Said Neufeld: "This church must serve the people of this community as 'a house by the side of the road where the races of men go by.'"[79]

The other earlier Chicago Mennonite missions have been discussed in connection with church outreach under the several Mennonite branches.[80]

Other than the later Spanish work, the only other Illinois city in which Mennonite missions were founded was Peoria. We have already mentioned the (Old) Mennonite work there in connection with church outreach discussed in chapter 9. Suffice it to say here that the dedicated leaders, well typified by John Harnish, the first superintendent, and by his wife, Viola, were all good examples of the Mennonite Awakening in Illinois. While the mission had its successes and failures, on the whole it experienced a good growth in what Harnish characterized as the "wettest city in the country." Among the women workers, Elizabeth Schrock was honored in 1952 for twenty-five years of service to the mission. Already in 1914, five years before the (Old)

Mennonites started their work, the Central Conference had established on North Adams Street the first Mennonite mission in Peoria. Jacob Sommer, who had had mission experience in Chicago, was the first leader and carried on for almost twenty-five years. Frank McNutt and Frank Mitchell followed Sommer. The highest point in membership was about 150 in 1940. Both of these missions became organized as church organizations. Also, because of changing conditions, they found it desirable to merge in the early 1970s under the name United Mennonite Church.[81]

Some commentators have stated that Mennonites have not been very successful in establishing "strong 'indigenous' city congregations composed of non-Mennonite converts." One authority wrote: "The rural mind-set, frequent lack of trained workers, inability to adapt to new conditions, and similar facts have been handicaps." Others, too, had their doubts and wondered whether Mennonites could not be using their resources more effectively in other kinds of mission activity. J. Winfield Fretz, who made a study of the religious institutions in

Source: Melvin Norquist, Flanagan, Ill

Mennonite Gospel Mission in Peoria, founded by the Central Conference Mennonite Church in 1914. In 1971 it united with the Ann Street Mennonite Church (MC) to form the United Mennonite Church of Peoria.

Chicago about 1940, concluded that the city Mennonite missions and churches were not successful from the standpoint of their own objectives and that the communities in which they were located, with one or two exceptions, were not conducive to fellowship-building. He felt that the same funds could have been used more efficiently in rural areas where the Mennonites were "more familiar with the general conditions and the life of the people."[82]

One other approach to city mission, emphasized many years later, was suggested already in 1908 by John Roth of Morton: the establishment of reasonably priced Mennonite boarding and rooming houses in cities as one kind of mission outreach. Roth thought such places could be supplied with good reading material and that some religious meetings could be held in them. Only in recent years have Mennonites begun to carry out this proposal.[83]

As noted above, the General Conference Mennonites led the way in mission interest, although as it turned out, missionary Haury landed in the "foreign" country of Indian Territory, later called Oklahoma. (Actually, in that era the American Indians were considered foreigners.) A famine in India in the 1890s added to the forces that were causing Mennonites to be interested in outreach beyond their own borders.

Famines in India were of course not unusual. But the one of 1896-97 was exceptionally severe and led to an extensive relief project in which the Mennonites participated substantially. The Mennonite Evangelizing and Benevolent Board at Elkhart took the initiative to organize a "Home and Foreign Relief Commission" (HFRC). This relief agency appointed J. A. Sprunger of Chicago to superintend collection of grain in America. In 1897 a shipload of corn and beans, mostly from Mennonites, was sent to Calcutta. George Lambert of Elkhart, a Mennonite free-lance traveler, writer, and minister, was sent to supervise the distribution of the food. He also took along some $20,000 in cash for further purchases of food and services in India. "For a time the HFRC assumed a quasi inter-Mennonite character." Although this changed later, at first almost all Mennonite groups contributed. Lambert returned late in 1897 and aroused tremendous interest in India as he reported his observations in the Mennonite churches in Illinois and elsewhere. As a direct result of this relief effort, the Mennonite Church established a mission in the Central Provinces of India in 1899, having appointed and sent the first missionaries: Jacob A. Ressler, Mennonite minister of Pennsylvania, and Dr. and Mrs. William B. Page of Indiana, in 1898. In 1899 the General Conference Mennonites organized their own Emergency Relief Committee, in 1900 sent David Goerz of Kansas to India on a mission similar to Lambert's, and later in the year started their mission. Both of these missions continued famine relief at intervals through much of their history.

The Illinois Mennonites, much interested in this new outreach, contributed substantially—although, no doubt they like others could have done more. One couple from Cullom, for example, after contributing $500 to various benevolent purposes, gave $500 for the girls' orphanage in Dhamtari in 1902. About the same time the Mennonites in McLean County contributed $400 toward establishing a new station in India.[84] This support by the Illinois Mennonites grew in the twentieth century. In 1945 a report in the *Gospel Herald* stated that the Illinois (Old) Mennonite churches had given for missions during the previous year a total of $105,996.18, amounting to $35.90 per member. Donations from the state constituted almost one-tenth of the total receipts of the Board.[85]

The awakened interest in foreign missions was similar among the various Illinois groups except of course among the more conservative ones. The Central Conference and Defenseless Mennonites became intensely interested in Africa and decided to work together in that field in a fine example of early inter-Mennonite cooperation. The Defenseless group was the first to become interested. In 1896 it sent Mathilda Kohn to work in the Congo under the Christian and Missionary Alliance. In 1900 it sent Alma Doering to serve with the Swedish mission in the lower Congo. Active missionary work in the

Salem Orphanage (now Salem Children's Home) near Flanagan, organized in 1896; as building appeared in 1913.

Central Conference of Mennonites began at the annual conference held at Meadows in 1905. Miss Doering and Charles E. Hurlburt, Director of the African Inland Mission, spoke at this conference. The minutes state: "The addresses so stirred the conference that the sentiment . . . was that we ought to do something for dark Africa." A "hearty response" came from the churches when the matter was presented to them. In 1906 the Defenseless Church sent Miss Doering and five others to British East Africa to work in the area of the Africa Inland Mission. In the same year the Central Conference sent L. B. Haigh and his wife to the same area. But these workers soon concluded that this field was overly crowded with missions. Mr. and Mrs. Haigh and Miss Doering returned to the homeland in 1910 to make a plea to open their own Mennonite work in the Congo. Their stirring verbal and written appeals to Mennonites in Illinois and elsewhere were successful. The newly founded Central Conference periodical, *Christian Evangel*, was one important advocate of an independent Mennonite work in the Congo.[86]

In 1911 officers of the two conferences met in joint session at Meadows, Illinois, to form a committee of four men from each conference. "This committee," according to the minutes, "shall have charge of all joint foreign mission work, to examine candidates, and to appoint committees on the fields except that each board shall have full control of their own funds." The name of the group was at first "United Mennonite Board of Missions," but four months later they chose the name "The Congo Inland Mission," and became incorporated under the laws of Illinois. They used this name until fairly recently, when they changed to "Africa Inter-Mennonite Mission." Of the eight members of the group, seven were from Illinois: Valentine Strubhar, Aaron Augspurger, Joseph King, Peter Schantz, J. K. Gerig, C. R. Egle, and D. N. Claudon. Only Ben Rupp was not. All but one of these served until 1926; two continued until 1929. Later the controlling board was enlarged to include representatives from the Evangelical Mennonite Brethren Conference and the General Conference Mennonite Church.

In the meantime the Haighs left by way of London for the Congo to search out a suitable site, while Miss Doering did deputation work among the churches. Alvin J. Stevenson, former Baptist missionary with experience in the Congo, was asked to assist in the selection of the mission area. Miss Doering aroused considerable interest in the work, but seemed more successful in raising funds than in recruiting workers. As a result, some non-Mennonite recruits from America and from Europe were used, which caused tension because some were not very sympathetic with certain Mennonite beliefs. An effort to make CIM an interdenominational rather than a Mennonite organization drew a sharp rebuke from the home board. Another discouraging factor was the loss of $15,000 through the failure of the Meadows, Illinois, bank where the mission funds were kept. Though these funds were later recovered through friends, the mission experienced other serious financial difficulties during the depression of the 1930s.[87]

Despite these and other vicissitudes the CIM could record progress. Thousands of converts came to the faith—about 20,000 by 1957, some 35,000 by 1974, and additional thousands since. By 1950 the CIM received a subsidy, earlier limited to Catholics, from the Belgian government. By the 1970s five Mennonite branches instead of two were supporting the work: General Conference, Evangelical Mennonite Church, Evangelical Mennonite Brethren, Evangelical Mennonite Conference, and Mennonite Brethren. Illinois maintained its close association with the mission and continued its good support in terms of missionaries and finances—as typified by $10,000 pledged by the North Danvers Mennonite congregation in 1921. In 1957 the CIM Board sponsored some missionary meetings and rallies in central Illinois, which also symbolized this growth. At a missionary meeting at the Groveland church, with rallies at Washington and Flanagan, the Board arranged to have the first missionary, L. B. Haigh, and one of his first Congo converts, Kazadi Matthew, attend and address the meetings. Then past eighty and retired in North Carolina, Haigh was anxious to meet his African brother, who was the "first representative of the mission work in the Congo to visit the home churches." To be sure, very difficult days for the mission were just ahead with the coming of independence and tribal warfare and then the indigenization of the mission and church. After the turmoil had lifted, one veteran missionary who lived through it reported:

> God's bountiful blessings had prospered the CIM effort. Sixty years after a group of Christians, meeting in Illinois, decided to send missionaries to the Congo, a strong church of 30,000 members [as noted above this number is now larger] was on its own and expanding its outreach of evangelization. What did this mean for the Congo Inland Mission? Would the mission now retire to reflect on its successes or would it have the will and the vision to accept new challenges to preach the Good News of Salvation?

Under its new name, "Africa Inter-Mennonite Mission," the awakened Mennonites of Illinois chose the latter course.[88]

As elsewhere, the Mennonites of Illinois became awakened or quickened also in mission-related service activity, such as orphanages, old people's homes, and hospitals. In fact, orphanages were an important part of foreign missions. At home also the church constructed homes for orphans because of Christian compassion, hoping that loving care would provide an environment conducive to developing Christian faith in the children. One worker reported that children were not in her institution long "until they respond to the gospel and get saved." The first Mennonite orphanage in America was established in 1884 by a General Conference group near Halstead, Kansas. A few years later another one was established in Kansas near Hillsboro under predominantly Krimmer Mennonite Brethren auspices. In 1896 David Garber and Solomon K. Plank, members of the (Old) Mennonite Church, started a children's home near Orrville, Ohio. The Ohio home received some support from Illinois. One Illinois Amish Mennonite woman, for example, bequeathed $500 to it. The Mennonite Board of Charitable Homes assumed control in 1899 and moved the institution to West Liberty, Ohio, the following year.[89]

Illinois Mennonites became interested in orphanages fairly early. The Salem Children's Home near Flanagan began in 1896 when Mr. and Mrs. Daniel King gave a 100-acre farm for that purpose. Having no children of their own may have increased their concern for orphans and children from broken homes. The amount of land given by the Kings was added to by others until the Home soon had more than 300 acres. It also received much support in money and gifts in kind. The Salem Defenseless Mennonite Church took the initiative in forming the Salem Orphanage Association, which became an Illinois corporation in 1896. The Defenseless Mennonite Conference, now Evangelical Mennonite Church, operates the institution; for a few years, however, the Central Conference Mennonites and the Defenseless Mennonite Brethren in Christ had representatives on the board of the Orphanage Association. Various groups, including other Mennonites, contribute workers and finances.

The work has grown from small beginnings to a substantial size. The first building, with a capacity for about twenty-five children, was begun in 1898 and the home opened formally in 1900. The building was soon filled and a number of additions had to be made in succeeding years, beginning as early as 1904. By these additions the home's capacity was doubled, tripled, quadrupled, and more. Some two thousand youngsters found compassionate love in a Christian home, which they desperately needed. One resident who had never known love as a youngster in his own home wrote later as an adult: "When I knew that I was loved by the people at Salem Children's Home, from that moment on, despite ups and downs, it was home to me.... For a child to know that he is loved—makes his world. When that ingredient is missing for a child—he feels it. He feels the coldness of his world, the loneliness, the sadness."[90]

Illinois Mennonites also established old people's homes. But this developed later, due in part no doubt to the strong Mennonite tradition that taking care of the elderly was a function to be carried out in the family circle. The continuation of this traditional way is best illustrated by the Old Order Amish, including those at Arthur, Illinois, where the parents and grandparents retire to smaller homes built in the yards near the homes in which they reared their families. This proximity enables the children to look after the needs of their aging parents.

Eventually, however, other Mennonite groups saw a need to take care of some of the elderly in institutions. The Salem Home established at Hillsboro, Kansas, in 1894 by the Krimmer Mennonite Brethren was the first such Mennonite home in America. The General Conference Mennonites founded one in 1896 at Frederick, Pennsylvania, and another at Goessel, Kansas, in 1899. The Lancaster Conference (MC) started one in that county in 1899 and private individuals established another in Lancaster in 1903. This latter, plus two others, were the only ones established in the first two decades of the twentieth century. The upturn in opening homes for the aged came later, especially from the 1940s onward.[91]

In the meantime the Illinois Mennonites constructed two homes within twenty-five miles of each other, one at Meadows and one at Eureka—something that probably would not have occurred in the

Source: Thomas Yoder, Normal, Ill

Jacob Salzman homestead on the Gridley Prairie near Flanagan; note wooden windmill structure and "Grossvater Haus"; ca. 1900.

later period of inter-Mennonite cooperation. The Defenseless and Central Conferences, sponsors of the home at Meadows, apparently were the first to start planning, but the (Old) Mennonite Church people were the first to get their home at Eureka completed and in operation (in 1922). The one at Meadows opened in 1923. Duplication of facilities so near each other caused some misunderstanding, not to say ill feelings. According to Central Conference leader Aaron A. Augspurger, when their group discovered that the (Old) Mennonites were planning a home at Eureka they asked them about a united effort; but the (Old) Mennonites turned them down. Augspurger thought "it certainly does not look very Christ-like to have two such Mennonite homes in such close proximity, and where one could be conducted with half the expense. I consider this a sad reproach to mennoniteism [sic] and an offense to our critics...."

Augspurger added that they and the Defenseless people were working "unitedly" and "agreeably" in the work and thought there was no reason why they could not also so work with the (Old) Mennonites. "Again I say, *shame on such conditions.*" The reply of John Horsch, to whom Augspurger had written, is not available, but according to a later letter by Augspurger, Horsch must have pointed out that since the Central Conference people had found it necessary to build duplicate churches in (Old) Mennonite communities, it would be unwise to unite in such work as hospitals and old people's homes. Augspurger was not impressed. He thought surely there ought to be some point at which Mennonites could begin to work together. One thing was certain, he concluded, "I shall from now on do all that is in my God given power to break up this unchristian spirit between mennonites [sic]." Augspurger did add that he was in sympathy with Horsch's attack on liberalism.[92]

In a sense the Eureka home grew out of one that the Mennonites had established at Rittman, Ohio, in 1901 and that had burned in 1919. Illinois had connections with the Ohio institution. Two Illinois men, J. S. Shoemaker of Freeport and John Schertz of Metamora, were on the Mennonite Board of Charitable Homes which originally operated the Rittman home. M. S. Steiner, president of the Board, reported the Illinois churches had "contributed very liberally." When the building burned the Mennonite Board of Missions and Charities, which replaced the earlier Board after 1906, at first had planned to rebuild on the same site. But then it decided to build in Illinois, where there was considerable favorable sentiment and support. At Eureka, the site selected, and elsewhere in the state there was a "hearty request" for the home. Two brethren at Flanagan, for instance, each donated an eighty-acre farm as endowment for the institution.

In May 1921 the Board authorized the erection of the building,

Maple Lawn Home for the Aged, built in 1922, showing the workers there on May 14, 1946.

Source: Archives of the Mennonite Church.

Everything went well and the building was completed, with a capacity for some fifty residents, and dedicated on July 23, 1922. An imposing array of Mennonite Church talent was on hand for the service: among others, J. S. Shoemaker, D. D. Miller, S. C. Yoder, Samuel Gerber, and S. E. Allgyer, all leading bishops from Illinois and other parts of the Midwest. Part of the eighteen-acre tract on which the building was located was farmland. Joseph D. Smith, who served for twenty-five years as the first superintendent, had been a farmer and wanted to produce as much of the food needed as possible. Planting fruit trees was part of the project. Reporting to a later Board meeting, Smith stated that "aged people as well as young people enjoy fruit." He then added: ". . . I would be happy to see the day when the aged people who have outlived their usefulness sit under the apple or peach tree and say, 'Praise the Lord for the kindest hearted brotherhood who helped me to this,' and can eat to their heart's content, and at the same time there would be no expense to the church." Smith himself was as kindhearted as anyone. This attitude of Christian compassion well symbolizes the spirit that characterized not only the Eureka Home through its various stages of growth but also the Illinois Mennonites as a whole as they experienced the several phases of the Awakening.[93]

Interest in what became the Meadows Mennonite Home began about the turn of the century. In 1917 both the Central Conference of Mennonites and the Defenseless Mennonites appointed committees to investigate and explore the possibility of cooperating to found such a home. A joint meeting of the two mission boards at Meadows Mennonite Church in May 1919 elected a board of directors of five members, shortly increased to six—three from each conference. These directors created an organization called the "Mennonite Old People's Home," which became incorporated under the laws of Illinois. All of the directors on the first board were from Illinois: D. N. Claudon of Meadows, Joseph Rich of Washington, S. E. Baughman of Gridley, Daniel Augustine of Carlock, Moses Roth of Groveland, and C. R. Egle of Meadows. This board, together with a larger group of delegates, decided to locate the Home at Meadows. They started constructing a two-story brick-veneer building in April 1922 and completed it in March 1923. The total cost, including site purchase, was some $40,000. An estimated 2000 people attended the dedication services held on May 20, 1923, on the south side of the building. J. H. King, Joseph Kinsinger, J. K. Gerig, and G. P. Schultz took part in the program.

With an initial capacity of hardly more than a dozen residents, the Home soon outgrew its facilities. Financial problems prevented major expansion, however, until the early 1950s. Then capacity was virtually doubled. Operated of course on a nonprofit basis, the Home has been financed by payments from residents, income from the farm,

Source: Meadows Mennonite Home and Retirement Center, Chenoa, Ill.

Meadows Mennonite Home and Retirement Center in Meadows showing the original structure (center) dedicated in 1923, the nursing and self-care wing (right) dedicated in 1978, and the cottages (upper right) maintained on the site. Also, in background (center) is the Meadows Mennonite Church.

gifts from donors, plus any necessary support from the two conferences. The institution has served many non-Mennonites. In fact, at times fewer than half the residents have been Mennonites. But the purpose of the Home was and is to provide a Christian ministry of compassionate service through a caring community to the elderly needing such a ministry. In this it has been eminently successful.[94]

Hospitals came late into the thinking of awakened Mennonites. People earlier looked upon a hospital as a halfway station between one's home and the cemetery. So they tried to avoid hospitals. Furthermore, as W. S. Shelly, then of Bloomington, stated in 1922: "... for years we read our Bibles without seeing that the spirit of the Gospel taught hospitals." As late as 1921 one element among the (Old) Mennonites questioned the wisdom of the church carrying on hospital work at all: better to preach the gospel "to those who are dying in the spirit rather than to those who are dying naturally." But the majority saw the need to bring the whole gospel to the entire world, including carrying out Christ's injunction to "heal the sick."[95]

There were voices in the wilderness, however, including some in Illinois. The first Mennonite hospitals to appear anywhere were in Russia in the latter part of the nineteenth century. In the United States in 1900 General Conference Mennonites established the first Mennonite hospital, at Goessel, Kansas, with others following soon after. Already in 1893, John A. Sprunger, prominent leader from Berne, Indiana, had become interested in establishing a hospital in Illinois. He had but recently started mission work in Chicago with assistance from some deaconesses and from Joseph Rediger and others from the Salem Defenseless congregation. He now found some Illinois Mennonites interested in a hospital. With the help of a society he organized for the purpose, the interested group raised funds and took an option on a site. But the support was not sufficient and the project lapsed.

Yet the interest persisted. Local forces, especially the McLean County Medical Society, raised funds and secured those that Sprunger's society possessed. They recalled Sprunger from Chicago to secure his advice. This time the story was different. Under Sprunger's supervision, a twenty-bed hospital was erected and opened in Normal in 1896. Though he and his assisting deaconesses left in 1897, the hospital continued under different auspices and since 1901 has been known as the Brokaw Hospital. As the historian of the Bloomington Mennonite Hospital has stated: "While the work Sprunger did with the Deaconess Memorial Hospital [as it was first called] did not long remain connected with the Mennonites, he provided a vision which inspired the church with the idea of establishing hospital work in Illinois."[96]

The vision that Sprunger and others had in the 1890s did not entirely fade out. In the meantime the Central Conference of Mennonites had been organized. During the conference session held at Hopedale in 1917 a committee was appointed to study a question of having a Mennonite hospital. The committee's work included carrying on a program of education among the churches on the need of a church hospital. Dr. E. P. Sloan, who had practiced in nearby Mennonite communities and who had become head of the Sloan Clinic in Bloomington, accompanied the committee to the churches and encouraged the building of a Mennonite hospital. In 1919 the Central and Defenseless Conferences incorporated the Mennonite Sanitarium Association, later called the Mennonite Hospital Association. Membership in the Association consisted of delegates from the constituent churches. The Association chose a board of five directors, eventually enlarged to nine, of which Emanuel Troyer served as president until his death in 1942. After the Association purchased and remodeled a large residence on North Main Street, Bloomington, the hospital received its first patients in May 1919. Then within a few months, having learned that the Kelso Sanitarium a few blocks farther south was for sale for $75,000, the Association purchased the Kelso property for its purposes. Five men went to the bank and borrowed the money, making themselves personally responsible for the amount, "for which fact many of them paid heavily in later years." The institution was dedicated as the Mennonite Sanitarium in June 1920.[97]

This humble beginning resulted in a great and flourishing institution, now called Mennonite Hospital. But for the operators the trail from 1919 to the present has had some serious difficulties and discouragements, as well as bright spots. Fortunately, the hospital was inter-Mennonite in its operation, and had the support of at least two conferences rather than one. Either body alone would not have been able to carry it through. Having a close connection with Dr. E. P. Sloan, noted thyroid surgeon, and other well-known doctors, was a mixed blessing. Since adjacent Normal also had a group of ambitious doctors, some rivalry developed between them that often affected their decisions as to which hospital they would send their patients.

A problem that affected hospital finances still more adversely was the great economic depression of the 1930s. Under the leadership of Noble Hoover, who succeeded Benjamin Rupp as superintendent in 1927, the administration felt compelled to enlarge the hospital facilities. It put on a successful drive for funds, completing the campaign in August 1929. Most of the $192,000 raised was in the form of cash pledges, which were difficult to redeem after the panic in the fall of 1929 and during the long, serious depression that followed. Probably no one has had a longer connection with the hospital during its darker as well as brighter days than has Raymond L. Hartzler. Not long ago the hospital congratulated Hartzler, "who recently celebrated his 60th year of involvement with the Mennonite ministry, and who has been a good friend to the hospital for many years." The salute noted that "Rev. Hartzler served on many hospital committees and on the board for some 24 years. He was secretary from 1933 to 1941 and chairman from 1945 to 1960. Besides helping the hospital, he was active in many church-related involvements in the community. He was pastor of the Carlock Mennonite Church for 13 years and served on numerous church-related committees," also as field secretary for the Mennonite Central Conference from 1945-64. He was in addition editor of the *Christian Evangel* from 1938-57.[98]

In his published secretarial reports and in an unpublished history of the hospital, Hartzler has portrayed a poignant picture of a new Christian hospital desperately trying to meet its obligations and keep its doors open in a tragic decade. Quite a few bondholders, for example, were widows with little other income. "Many of their pleas for payment of the interest due them are truly pathetic," reported Hartzler. Creditors at times were none too cooperative but decided they did not want a hospital on their own hands. Through the sacrifices and cooperation of many people, the storm was weathered.[99]

The hospital succeeded. Occupancy of beds got so high in the 1940s that more space was needed and acquired. The nurses' training school begun soon after the hospital opened was growing and also in need of a larger home for the nurses. In one residence they had "17 girls in a 10-room house with one bathroom—believe it or not!" The state demanded better facilities, which came with the construction of a new nurses' home named in honor of the late Emanuel Troyer, prominent leader in the conference and friend of the hospital. By this time the federal government was interested in the expansion of nurses' training and in 1946 granted $53,000 to the cause. In the 1950s also bed capacity was increased. The hospital was growing in favor with the public and with the doctors. Despite ups and downs, Hartzler could state at various times in his annual reports that a given year "witnessed a continuation of the experience of preceding years in reaching ever higher levels in the amount of service rendered." Earlier, the institution had been known especially for goiter operations and treatment, and later for eye treatment and operations. The Watson Gailey Foundation-Mennonite Hospital Eye Bank was established there in 1951, with the doctors there performing the first corneal transplant in 1952.

One factor bearing on the Bloomington hospital was a decision in 1956 to close the (Old) Mennonite nurses' training school at La Junta, Colorado. Consequently Mrs. Maude Swartzendruber resigned as director of the La Junta school and was available for other service. She moved to Bloomington in 1957. While the Illinois (Old) Mennonites gave some support to the Bloomington hospital from the beginning and had representation on the board, their support increased after the La Junta closing. Raymond Hartzler has said "while La Junta was in operation we were always cognizant that there was a feeling of obligation on their part, that while most of them looked to area hospitals for service, they regarded their moral and presumably economic support as due to La Junta, so our approach was leavened accordingly. By that closing Harold Zehr, then editor of the *Missionary Guide*, felt more free to serve on the hospital board and encourage it through that organ." This Harold did. Hartzler then concluded: "The other factor was that due to the [La Junta] closing we were able to attract Mrs. Maude Swartzendruber to join our school staff in a leading capacity [director of education], and her coming was effective in drawing attention, interest and support in this direction, which has now become a real resource for the institution." Maude remained for six years.[100]

In addition to orphanages, old people's homes, and hospitals, awakened Illinois Mennonites also began to witness through such auxiliary service organizations as ladies' aid societies and sewing circles. They were closely tied first to city and foreign missions and then to relief work. Already in the 1880s Mennonite women in Kansas had such organizations. Mrs. Christian Krehbiel, formerly of Summerfield, was a member. By 1895 Mennonite women in eastern Pennsylvania were making clothing for the needy. A sewing circle in Paradise, Pennsylvania, was organized in 1897. The Illinois Mennonites were not far behind.

In 1900 the Science Ridge (Sterling) sisters organized the first Mennonite circle in the state. In October 1907 the correspondent from Sterling reported that for eight years the congregation had "Sisters' Meeting Day" on the first Thursday of each month when the women met to make things for "Church institutions and individuals" and to worship together. This was pretty much the pattern as circles developed in the various congregations. Later the local societies formed a state organization. Assisting in meeting needs in home and foreign missions and in other institutions such as orphanages, old people's homes, and hospitals was a high priority, but meeting local individual needs, Mennonite or non-Mennonite, also received much attention. During and after World War I the sisters sought to help war sufferers. In addition to clothing, the women liberally contributed cash offerings, food, and helped in housecleaning. Lydia Albrecht Smith, early Illinois leader in the movement, put it very modestly when she wrote years later: "We believe much good has been accomplished. We are only giving God a little of what belongs to Him."[101]

Apparently the Central Conference Mennonites organized their first sewing circle or Ladies' Aid Society in 1906. Missionaries Mr. and Mrs. Lawrence B. Haigh spoke at South Washington during the winter of 1905-06 and sparked the interest by asking for help in meeting clothing needs, especially for children in their Africa mission. Among the listeners was Bertha Kennel, the Dorcas of that time, who felt that the church could help the mission cause better by organizing a sewing circle. A seamstress, Miss Kennel asked the young women's classes of the church to meet in her home March 20, 1906, to make the clothes for which the Haighs had asked. Shortly thereafter the group drew up and signed a constitution. The preamble stated: "Whereas this is the age of social development and whereas the great doctrine of Christianity is to live for others we ... agree to form an association to be known as the Mennonite *Nähe Verein* [Sewing Circle], whose purpose shall be ... the helping of the poor and needy...." Twenty-two women became members the first year. Kennel has been honored as the founder of the first Ladies' Aid Society in the Central Conference.[102]

A. B. Rutt from the Central Conference mission in Chicago and other people reinforced the appeal for the kind of aid that the sisters could give. In order to carry on their work more effectively, the women organized in 1925 on a conference-wide basis. This organization met in Bloomington in 1929 to consider how to aid mission work in Africa. A. M. Eash, mission worker in Chicago who in the meantime had become involved with the Congo Inland Mission, addressed the Bloomington meeting. He asked the sisters to support the clothing needs of the African children connected with the mission stations. The Central Conference assumed responsibility for supplying three fourths of the clothing and hoped the Defenseless Conference would assume responsibility for the other part.[103]

Formally organized aid among Mennonites was also new in the Awakening period. Mennonites' attitude toward commercial insurance was quite negative. But from their earliest history the Mennonites have followed the practice of sharing their losses with each other as an integral part of Christian life. For many years this expression of bearing one another's burdens was informal, spontaneous, and unsystematic. Yet there are records of more organized sharing in Europe as early as the seventeenth century. Planned, systematic giving did not come in the United States and Canada until the latter part of the nineteenth and the first half of the twentieth centuries. The more organized plans of sharing came with the formation of Mennonite mutual aid societies, of which there were some seventy by the 1950s. By the twentieth century opposition to property insurance was less strong than against life insurance. Hence, most of the above societies protected only against losses from fire, storms, hail, and other natural disasters. But a few of these were death benefit or

Education, Missions, Service   295

"burial aid" societies, which the more conservative probably considered euphemisms for life insurance.

Many dragged their feet when it came to supporting planned, organized sharing. Records of opinions and actions show mixed attitudes. To the general principle of helping needy members, everyone agreed. The outpouring of aid by the many, many thousands to the Russian Mennonites in the 1870s attested to that fact. But how organized and systematic should aid to needy members be? That was a different question. As late as 1906, when the Western District A. M. Conference was considering whether it should have an aid plan to protect members against fire and storm losses, it decided that the church itself ought to be the Christian aid plan and thus disapproved of a formal plan. The same conference in 1898 had decided that a congregation was not obligated to assume the medical debt of a brother who was unable to pay it, yet should have paid it out of love for the church and for the individual. In 1892 this same body determined that more could and should be done "for our poor members . . . by giving them the preference in renting farms, etc. . . . and to the needy poor in general by appointing a committee of three brethren . . . to find out where there are really needy ones and make it known to the different congregations and receive alms and see that they are properly distributed." C. S. Schertz of Eureka was one of the members appointed to this committee.[104]

A more organized system was the Mennonite Aid Plan of Elkhart, Indiana. Although not a conference-controlled organization, it was authorized by the Indiana Mennonite Conference in 1882. It was a voluntary association of property owners that included members from other states and other Mennonite conferences. According to Harold S. Bender, this "was the first all-Mennonite organization." Illinois Mennonites became members and had representatives on the board of control. The *Herald of Truth* editor defended the plan, saying it was not an insurance company, "though some would construe it that way." It was simply a plan, he continued, to share losses from fire, lightning, and storms "in a systematic way, so that we may be able more fully to carry out the apostolic admonition to 'bear one another's burdens.'" He thought the arrangement was "entirely Scriptural." At the biennial conference of the Aid Plan in 1900 the delegates decided to pay crop losses by hail if the entire crop was destroyed. Unlike some states, for instance Indiana and Michigan, the Illinois Mennonite Conference did not have its own conference aid program before the 1940s, when a churchwide organization known as Mennonite Mutual Aid was set up. For many years, however, it had been urging the adoption of such a plan.[105]

One of the more notable and successful cases of organized

mutual aid is the Brotherhood Mutual Insurance Company, organized in 1917 under the name "Brotherhood Aid Association of the Defenseless Mennonite Conference." Its purpose was to aid members of the Defenseless body in cases of losses from fire or storm. The Association soon extended coverage to members of other Mennonite branches and later to other non-smoking Christians. Its central office was in Grabill, Indiana, until 1939, when it was moved to Ft. Wayne. Many of its policyholders have been and are in Illinois. By 1935 the organization was changed to a mutual insurance company and became independent of conference control. Even the matter of church membership in practice is apparently no longer completely decisive in the acceptance of applications. A separate company, Mutual Security Life Insurance Company, which grew out of the parent organization, offers health, accident, and life insurance. Though coverage has been greatly extended and the company has become large, it still has the basic Christian concern of its founder, Albert Neuenschwander, that Christians "bear one another's burdens and so fulfill the law of Christ."[106]

In an authoritative article on Mennonite mutual aid in *The Mennonite Encyclopedia*,[107] authors J. Winfield Fretz and Harold S. Bender have listed sixty-nine organizations that were operating in 1956, divided into the following categories: Property Insurance Societies; Automobile Aid Insurance; Burial Aid Societies; Medical, Surgical, and Hospital Aid Plans; and Loan Aid Organizations. Only one of these sixty-nine organizations is located in Illinois: the Illinois Old Order Amish Mutual Aid Plan at Arthur. This of course does not mean that the other Illinois Mennonites have not been interested in mutual aid. It simply means that they have worked through larger groups, often their churchwide agencies based elsewhere.

Relief work, closely related of course to mutual aid, has also been important in Mennonite history. Both it and mutual aid in fact go back to the founding of the church in the sixteenth century. Writing about the qualities of Christians, Menno Simons stated: "They show mercy and love.... They entertain those in distress. They take the stranger into their houses. They comfort the afflicted; clothe the naked; feed the hungry." History is filled with illustrations of this faith in action among the brotherhood. Guy F. Hershberger's article on "Relief Work" in *The Mennonite Encyclopedia* is a good summary. Mutual aid and relief work are similar. But the former can be thought of more as members aiding one another. Relief work, while certainly including mutual aid such as the helping of the Russian Mennonites in the 1870s, can be thought of as extending aid to anyone in need regardless of their religion.

No doubt some events before and after the turn of the century helped awaken Mennonites and restore their vision for mutual aid and relief. The epic of the Russian Mennonites during the 1870s was one such event. Illinois Mennonites made large contributions to the Russian brethren. The contributions were the heaviest for 1874, but there were some for later years also. Since helping the Russian Mennonites was an inter-Mennonite project, the contributions came from the various groups.[108] Another event that helped enlarge the vision of Mennonites in Illinois and elsewhere was that famine in India in 1896 and following.

An event that did still more to shake the Mennonites to action was World War I with its accompanying upheavals. Like their fellow Americans Mennonites were quite complacent in the decades prior to the war, with many of them deceived by the spirit of progress abroad in the land, including the supposed progress toward peace and a warless world. Mennonites were unprepared for what happened in 1914 and the years following. The Civil War generation was gone. The war with Spain in 1898 had scarcely touched the Mennonites since it was of short duration and there was no conscription. Still holding to nonresistance, the Mennonites had to work out a new modus vivendi with a government determined to win the war after the United States entered it in 1917. Whatever their motivation, Mennonites in Illinois and elsewhere were prompted by current forces to take a fresh look at old doctrines in a new setting. A world-shaking war had the effect of clearing the vistas and lengthening the horizons of the Mennonites, especially with regard to Christian service in a needy world.

As the devastation of war became known Mennonites thought more and more of relief work. Administratively, however, the Mennonites were not as prepared to take on war relief assignments as were the Quakers and others. So the Mennonites carried out their first war-relief efforts in conjunction with the American Quakers in Europe and with the Near East Relief organization in its area. From the beginning of World War I Mennonite periodicals had stressed the importance of relief as a part of the gospel message of love, and funds had started coming in for this purpose. Some of the branches organized relief agencies, such as the Mennonite Relief Commission for War Sufferers (MC), The Relief Commission of the Central Conference Mennonites and the Emergency Relief Commission of the General Conference. Their purpose was to solicit and distribute funds and supplies. They also supported the relief work in France and the Near East and helped coordinate the different Mennonite branches' efforts. The Mennonite Brethren Church, at least at the outset, channeled its relief aid through its mission board.

A new chapter in Mennonite relief work opened in 1920. Following the revolutions in Russia in 1917, which brought the collapse of the czar's regime and then also of the Kerensky government, news came slowly and unreliably of great suffering in that country. In South Russia, where some 100,000 Mennonites were living, famine conditions began to appear and become serious, induced by drought as well as by war. The continuation of war between communists and noncommunists plus the plundering, raping, and killing by bands of outlaws made the sufferings of the people intolerable. These conditions, reported by a committee of Russian Mennonite leaders, impelled the American Mennonites to send representatives from the various bodies to Elkhart, Indiana, in July 1920 to consider the problem. Out of this historic meeting in the Prairie Street Mennonite Church came the Mennonite Central Committee (MCC). Since that time MCC has served as the central relief agency for all the groups. Originally it was intended to serve only during the emergency that engulfed the Russian Mennonites in the late teens and early 1920s. But other emergencies arose, its mission became broader, and it has continued to play an increasingly important role to the present. The two best accounts of its founding and development are *Feeding the Hungry* by P. C. Hiebert and Orie O. Miller, and *In the Name of Christ* by John D.

Source: Hazel Nice Hassan, Rockford, Ill.

Workers ready to board the ship *Pensacola* for Beirut, Syria, to enter Near East Relief on January 25, 1919. Left to right: William Derstine (Pa.), Frank Stoltzfus (Ohio), Orie O. Miller (Pa.), Christian Graber (Iowa), Ezra S. Deter (Morrison, Ill.), Silas Hertzler (Va.). David Zimmerman (Pa.), Aaron Loucks (Pa.).

Unruh. In July 1970 the *Mennonite Quarterly Review*, in a fiftieth-anniversary issue, gave an excellent survey of the founding, development, and philosophy of the MCC.[109]

The Illinois Mennonites ably supported relief efforts, both before and after the formation of the Mennonite Central Committee. They have provided their quotas of funds, supplies, and relief workers. Among the early workers immediately after World War I were Walter Smith, Albert Sommer, Roy Buchanan, and George Springer of Metamora, Edward Drange of Cullom, Arthur Slagel of Flanagan, Ezra Deter of Morrison and A. M. Eash and D. M. Hofer, mission workers of Chicago. Eash went to the Near East in 1919 and took charge of the Syrian Orphanage in Jerusalem until 1921, when he returned to Chicago.

Arthur Slagel graduated from Goshen College in 1919 and taught the following year at Hesston College, Hesston, Kansas. In 1920 he became a member of the first unit sent to Russia, along with Orie O. Miller of Akron, Pennsylvania, and Clayton Kratz of Blooming Glen, Pennsylvania. They arrived in Constantinople on September 21. While Miller and Kratz continued on into South Russia, making contact with the Mennonites there, Slagel remained in Constantinople and began relief work among refugees from Russia, including Mennonites. In the meantime occurred a tragedy in South Russia that cost Kratz his life. General Wrangel's anticommunist army was defeated, Kratz was arrested, freed, and then rearrested, taken away, and never heard from again despite many efforts to find and save him. This upheaval delayed the entrance of the Mennonite relief unit into Russia. It also increased the flow of refugees into the Constantinople area and the need for relief work there. Among the additional workers appointed for service in Constantinople were the first women MCC appointed, Vinora Weaver and Vesta Zook from Indiana. Graduates of Goshen, Miss Weaver was a teacher in the public schools and Miss Zook was a teacher and dean of women at her alma mater. Both lived in Illinois for some years after their return to America. Vinora taught school there for four years, 1923-27, serving in addition as pastor of the Mennonite congregation in Danvers for one year. Later, as the wife of Earl Salzman, she lived at Flanagan, where her husband served as pastor. Vesta married Arthur Slagel and lived with him in Chicago.[110]

Two other workers from Illinois were Mr. and Mrs. David M. Hofer, founders of and workers at the Krimmer Mennonite Brethren mission in Chicago. They had founded and edited the KMB periodical, *Der Wahrheitsfreund.* Hofer had a special interest in Russia, since he had been born in Molotschna colony in 1869. After sailing to Bremen, Germany, in October 1922, the Hofers traveled from there by train to Moscow and then to the Molotschna district. Here they helped in a feeding program which, said Hofer, "reached far beyond the Mennonite circles and will go down as a milestone in Mennonite history for generations to come." As they returned to the United States in 1923 the Hofers took the long way around, going by way of Palestine, India, and Japan and arriving home in May 1924. Hofer wrote a book of more than 500 pages relating their experiences in Russia and during their trip around the world.[111]

Guy F. Hershberger has said that the "founding of the Mennonite Central Committee in 1920 represents an important milestone in the total sweep of Mennonite history, bearing a twofold symbolic significance. Looking backward from that date, we see that it symbolizes the recovery of the Anabaptist vision of mission and service; looking forward, it symbolizes the opening of the door to a greater world-wide Mennonite brotherhood united in that mission and service to the modern world." The Illinois Mennonites likewise have affirmed the work of MCC. The story of its founding to meet the needs of World War I sufferers, especially the desperate Russian brethren, continued for years to impress them. One example is an article on the twenty-fifth anniversary of MCC written by L. A. Miller, the Old Order Amish

Source: Walter Smith, Eureka, Ill., and Albert Sommer, Washington, Ill.

Albert Sommer of Metamora, one of relief workers in France after World War I, at Varennes with truck he used to carry provisions to refugees.

bookseller at Arthur. In December 1944 he heard J. S. Toews of Kansas tell an MCC meeting in Chicago how he as a seventeen-year-old boy at home with his parents in Russia had suffered the tribulation of war, pillage, and hunger. "Everything," said Toews, "looked dark before us; we were facing death and starvation; we had lost hope in God." Then one day "word came that food was coming from America, and what a great joy it was! . . . If it had not been for the Christian spirit of those that helped us as they did, we would not be here tonight to bring you this message, but would have starved to death."

Miller was also impressed, as were many others, by the story of the devoted Clayton Kratz who left his studies at Goshen College, where he was president of the Young People's Christian Association, to answer his church's call to do relief work in Russia. Wrote Miller:

> Twenty-five years have passed since Clayton Kratz disappeared, but his name has not been forgotten. The words of A. J. Miller (Russian Relief Commissioner then), written a few years later, remain fresh and applicable today: "Clayton Kratz will probably never come home; and his resting place probably never be known. No marble shaft marks the spot where his body returned to earth. But his name is graven on the hearts of thousands and thousands whom he came to help. Their children and children's children will repeat the story of the Mennonite youth who came from far away America to save their lives and gave his own."

(The present writer experienced the truth of this statement. In 1944-45 when he was in Paraguay as director of MCC work, a number of Mennonite refugees from Russia told him of Clayton Kratz who had come to help them and had given his life for the cause.)[112]

Not only in the early days of relief but throughout its development to the present, Illinois Mennonites have continued to support relief as represented by MCC. In recent years its contribution in funds has been significantly increased through annual relief sales.

One additional avenue of service in which Illinois Mennonites shared a pioneering role has been the work camp with its "voluntary service." In the summer of 1938 a group of Central Conference and General Conference young people under the leadership of Carl Landes did voluntary service at the Central Conference Gospel Mission in Chicago. Among other tasks, the work consisted of renovating the mission buildings, making surveys of the needs of the community, and preparing the ground for a successful two-week Bible school. In the summer of 1944 a similar type of voluntary service by the (Old) Mennonites in connection with their mission work in Chicago gave the idea a further boost. These Chicago efforts together with the Mennonite experience in World War II brought Voluntary Service to the fore as another part of the Christian peace witness.[113]

Although the impact is difficult to assess, obviously the Mennonite Great Awakening deeply affected church life. Harold S. Bender has said, "It was a remarkable awakening to new spirit and life internally, and to a new sense of mission and outreach to the world. The church was transformed, first in the Midwest and Ontario, then in the East as well." Many Illinois Mennonites have shared this sentiment. In 1912 Mamie C. Good from Sterling wrote an article for the *Gospel Herald* entitled "Privileges And Attainments." She characterized her age as one of organization, pointing out a number of church programs that had come during her lifetime. Of these she thought the opening and support of missions was "perhaps the greatest privilege we have." But all were important because they were bringing new life to the church and "were working for a fuller and deeper fulfillment of God's Word." Lewis D. Appel of Cullom also was pleased with the Awakening. Referring to (Old) Mennonite developments he was pleased to remember "the first series of midweek evening meetings that were conducted for evangelistic purposes, the first educational institution that was founded by the Mennonite Church and the first meeting that discussed the missionary movement. Today we have an organized mission board, an educational board, and a publishing board in the Mennonite Church. Without any reflection on our forefathers, we are not like we used to be and we hope as time goes on the next generation may progress and increase in scope and efficiency." The verdict was not unanimous but largely favorable.[114]

Recently, however, Theron Schlabach has presented a qualified view. He appreciates much about the Awakening, or "quickening" as he prefers to call it. Yet Schlabach believes that through the influences of Protestant revivalism and Fundamentalism in the nineteenth and twentieth centuries, Mennonites have lost something of an earlier sense that nonresistant love was at the very heart of the gospel. He has argued that the quickening introduced theology that relegated the peace message to being more and more marginal, an optional nonessential or at most a principle to observe rather legalistically.[115] Whatever weight one gives to that qualification, nobody can doubt that after the Awakening (or quickening) there came a time of theological and other stresses, with repercussions in Illinois.

CHAPTER 12

Strain, Stress, Liberalism, Fundamentalism

Illinois Mennonites have endured strains and stresses over such points as nonconformity, faith healing, conference authority, Liberalism and Fundamentalism. With regard to the last two especially, one is reminded of Stuart Chase's book, *The Tyranny of Words*. Even when these terms refer to *religious* "Liberalism" and "Fundamentalism," they are ambiguous and loosely used, and leave much to be desired in the way of clear meaning. Using "Modernism" instead of "Liberalism" and "Evangelicalism" in place of "Fundamentalism" does not clear up the confusion. Terms such as "conservative," "liberal," or "orthodox" are likewise far from precise. There was not a great deal of either theological "Liberalism" or "Fundamentalism" among Illinois Mennonites. But there has been some tension over Fundamentalist influences and over liberalistic tendencies. The "liberalism" has not been so much with regard to the "fundamentals" of the Bible, as with Mennonite "distinctives," and the interpretation of nonconformity.

American Mennonites have seen no contradiction between being descendants of the Anabaptist "left wing" of the Reformation, and being "fully evangelical and orthodox, and deeply loyal to the Bible." Their reaction to the rise of liberalism or modernism in the nineteenth century, especially after the publication of Charles Darwin's *Origin of Species* (1859) and *Descent of Man* (1871), was similar to that of theologically conservative Protestants: they opposed it. So they inclined to sympathize with movements and groups organized to defend orthodoxy. On that basis many leaned toward the Fundamentalist movement, which arose in the latter part of the nineteenth and the first part of the twentieth centuries and became highly vocal with the organization of the World's Christian Fundamentals Association in

Philadelphia in 1919. Key doctrines that the Association set out to defend were the Trinity, the virgin birth, Christ's substitutionary atonement, the verbal inspiration of the Bible and its inerrancy "in the original writings," original sin, regeneration through faith in Christ, the resurrection of Christ's body and the ascension, the premillennial and imminent return of Christ, the resurrection of all, with the "everlasting blessedness of the saved," and "the everlasting conscious punishment of the lost."[1]

Reaction among Mennonites, however, was not the same among all individuals and groups. There was some ambivalence. In 1937 Daniel Kauffman, editor of the *Mennonite Cyclopedic Dictionary* and influential (Old) Mennonite leader, declared in the article on "Fundamentalism" that "the Mennonite Church is firmly committed to the Fundamentalist faith; including some unpopular tenets of faith which many so-called Fundamentalists reject." On other occasions Kauffman said that Mennonites were fundamentalists, spelled with a little "f," meaning that they believed in the fundamentals, plus more of them, but did not believe in the organized movement that stood for some things—for example, militarism—which Mennonites could not accept. Harold S. Bender, a leading church historian and theologian, held a somewhat similar position. In 1955 he wrote that among "distintegrative and damaging outside influences" threatening Mennonites, "Fundamentalism is currently the greatest danger," especially to certain Mennonite groups. Yet he counted himself "as thoroughly fundamental (with a small 'f') 'evangelical,'" and he saw "no place for modernism or liberalism in any form, least of all in Mennonitism, which has historically been thoroughly Biblical in its foundation and more completely so than Fundamentalism ever was." In a *Mennonite Encyclopedia* article on "Fundamentalism," Bender wrote that "Mennonites, though generally continuing to insist upon a conservative evangelical theology and resisting Modernism in any form, see more clearly than before that they belong neither in the Modernist nor Fundamentalist camps, but have a satisfactory Biblicism and evangelicalism of their own with its unique Anabaptist heritage."[2]

The (Old) Mennonites were not alone in holding that so-called Mennonite doctrines should be considered as part of the fundamentals of the faith. In 1900 the Central Conference Mennonites held a conference at North Danvers to which leader Joseph Stuckey had invited other brethren and sisters to discuss fundamentals of the faith *(wichtige Glaubensgrundsätze)*—mentioning especially nonresistance, the oath, and temperance—and to ask whether more should not be said about these things from the pulpit. Stuckey thought that brethren and sisters should become better acquainted with these teachings.[3]

Outside forces clearly influenced many Mennonites on Fundamentalism, as on many other matters. Among these the Moody influence has been outstanding. According to J. C. Wenger, Illinois has been influenced more by Moody Fundamentalism than has any other MC district conference.[4] This began, as noted earlier, through John F. Funk's contacts with Moody in Chicago from 1857 to 1867. This was important because of Funk's later stature as a Mennonite leader and publisher of the influential *Herald of Truth*. Moody's influence increased as Mennonites sympathetically followed his world-renowned career as unordained preacher, evangelist, and founder of Moody Bible Institute in Chicago. Proximity made Moody even more important to the Illinois Mennonites after the coming of radio and the establishment of radio station WMBI. Even before it began radio broadcasting, Moody Bible Institute was influential as a publisher of Fundamentalist periodicals and books that Mennonites purchased. Many Mennonites have attended the Institute, which was formally opened in 1889. When studying the history of the Chicago Home Mission, one is impressed with the close connection, especially in the earlier years but also later, between the Mission and the Institute. Many young Mennonites came to Chicago to work at the Mission and attend Moody Bible Institute.

Other students at Moody's, including non-Mennonites, often aided in the work at the Mission. Among these two groups were A. D. Wenger, Aaron Loucks, E. J. Berkey, S. F. Coffman, A. I. Yoder, D. S. Oyer, A. H. Leaman, Levi Hartzler, Gilbert Johnstone, J. J. Hostetler, H. R. Schertz, Noah Roeschley, and G. P. Schultz. Other Illinois Mennonite leaders who attended Moody's included A. C. Schultz, D. M. Hofer, J. W. Tschetter, Emanuel Troyer, Lee Lantz, and P. B. Snyder. Few if any of these men were radical Fundamentalists; rather, they were theological conservatives who, like Emanuel Troyer, felt that Moody and Reuben A. Torrey had a needed breadth of Christian perspective. According to his son, Troyer was "disappointed that later Moody students 'built a fence around Moody and Torrey' when these two men would have 'reached out.'" The son apparently was referring to his father's feelings about later Mennonite Moody graduates "who were very [much] caught up in fundamentalism."[5] And indeed, theology at Moody Bible Institute in the early days of Mennonite mission had not yet become the twentieth century's Fundamentalism.

A number of Mennonite women as well as men attended Moody Bible Institute. In 1906 a correspondent from a congregation near Bloomington, apparently East White Oak, reported that "Sister Edna Patton and Maud Gundy are at present attending the Moody Bible Institute at Chicago preparing themselves to labor in the Lord's vineyard."[6] With regard to S. F. Coffman, M. S. Steiner wrote when trying to persuade him to come to the Mission: "We need a boy at the Home Mission about your makeup. How would it suit you to come soon. You can stay with us and attend the Moody Institute lectures every forenoon...."[7]

Moody's also was influential among Mennonites because of the large number attending its lectures and conferences. Because of J. S. Coffman's influence in Illinois, his case may well be cited. His diary and other accounts tell the story. As early as 1876 he had noted the good results flowing from Moody's evangelistic meetings. On July 25, 1893, he heard Moody speak at the Chicago World's Fair. The sermon was good, he recorded. On July 26 he reported that he stayed in Dr. Ebersole's "office last night with Wm. Page. Heard Dr. Gordon of Boston at Moody Bible Institute—excellent lecture on the human side of redemption." "They have fine singing here." At eleven o'clock he heard Mr. Pierson. "It was some satisfaction and quite instructive to be at these meetings in Chicago. I can make practical use of many things I have heard today." On August 15, 1893, Coffman went with J. F. Funk to Chicago to attend the World Peace Congress. They listened to papers and speeches, "but the exercises were rather tame." In the

Source: Peter G. Schultz, Justice, Ill.

Mennonite students attending Moody Bible Institute in 1912. Top row: _____ Groening (S.D.), David Schultz, George Thiessen, _____ Peters, Jacob Lutke, Frank Wiebe, _____ Boydson. Center row: Christian Bertsche, Peter Friesen (Neb.), Amos Oyer (Ill.), George P. Schultz (Ill.), Elmer Rupp (Ohio). Front row: Jacob N. Wall, Adam W. Sommer, John N. Wall, David A. Regier.

evening they attended an Alliance Convention at Moody Church. "Exercises excellent," Coffman recorded. On August 16 Funk went back to the Peace Congress, but Coffman went to Moody Church and put in a busy day listening to "some excellent lectures and sermons."

In view of C. I. Scofield's importance in the Fundamentalist movement, the following Coffman diary items are significant: "Heard a most excellent lecture on Revelation by Scofield." August 17—"I heard Scofield again on Rev. which gave me a better line of thought than I ever had of that book." In April, 1899, a few months before his death, Coffman went to Chicago to aid in the work at the Home Mission and to "hear Mr. Moody preach several sermons." For April 7 he recorded he had a good time with Hershey Leaman and the sisters. In the morning Leaman and he walked nearly four miles to Moody's, where they heard Moody preach a sermon on Acts. He held up Christ "in contrast with politics, education, talent, Higher criticism etc. declaring his conviction to stand by Christ and the old Book." Coffman took dinner at the Institute with Brethren E. C. Shank and Joe Hoover. Jonathan Kurtz (from Indiana) was also there. At 2:00 p.m. Coffman heard Moody deliver another sermon.[8]

This Mennonite interest in the old Moody's and in early so-called fundamentalism is understandable. As implied earlier, it was a continuation of the Mennonite concern for orthodoxy. The belief of the Illinois Mennonites in the so-called fundamentals was not so much argued as it was taken for granted. That does not mean that fundamentals were not discussed and emphasized. They were, both before and after the rise of the organized Fundamentalist movement. Sermons to the unsaved, said a typical Illinois Mennonite Church Conference report in 1898, should begin and end with repentance and conversion, "laying special stress on true conviction of sin, faith in the Lord Jesus Christ, forgiveness of sins through faith in the atoning blood, and a thorough change of heart and mind. . . ." The report then added that faith manifested itself in works. This is only typical of the large amount of evidence that the Illinois Mennonites emphasized such fundamentals as the inspiration and infallibility of the Bible, the virgin birth and deity of Christ, the incarnation, the Genesis account of creation as opposed to evolution, the new birth or regeneration, second coming of Christ, the bodily resurrection, the atonement, miracles, everlasting punishment for the unsaved, and glory for the righteous, plus the emphasis on the Mennonite distinctives and on holy living. E. William Heiser's comment that the East Bend Mennonites were "very fundamental in the basic doctrines of the Bible" could have been made about nearly all of those in the state. The great majority wanted to be orthodox and Anabaptist.[9]

Mennonites could be interested in the old Moody's in the earlier years because Moody and the Institute he founded were not militaristic. In fact Moody was something of a pacifist. Although he was strongly antislavery and although many of his Chicago and other friends were enlisting in the Civil War, he could not conscientiously do so himself. According to his son's biography: "There has never been a time in my life," said Moody, "when I felt I could take a gun and shoot a fellow-being. In this respect I am a Quaker."[10] Unfortunately, this passage about Moody's pacifism was deleted from his son's later edition of his father's biography. Especially during and after World War I the institution became more militant and militaristic.

Many Mennonites apparently did not perceive this change. Or if they did, they felt that the benefits they received from the institution greatly outweighed any negative influences. In any case the evidence clearly indicates that Mennonites continued to be influenced considerably by studying at Moody's, or attending meetings there, or reading its literature, or listening to its radio station. Emma Oyer from Metamora, worker at the Mission from 1907 to the late 1940s, kept a diary and frequently recorded visits to Moody's, by herself and with other workers and visitors. Some typical diary items follow. For 1924: Feb. 5—"Went to Moody's this morning—Founders Conference in Session." Feb. 7—"At Moody's all day ... Mrs. Sloan's address in defense of the faith was wonderful." For 1926: Feb. 4—"Went to Moody's all day. Missionary day. Certainly heard a good talk by Harry L. Strachan of S. A. and testimonies of missionaries in P.M." Feb. 18—"We went to hear Ensminger at Moody Church.... Very good. H. R. Schertz and D. G. Lapp were here and went with us." For 1928: Feb. 17—"Anna [probably Yordy] and I went to Moody's with Miss Moyer. Attended three classes." Feb. 6—"Went to Moody's tonight. Heard good talk by Mac Beath." Feb. 7—"Up to Moody's again tonight." Feb. 9—"Went to Moody's this afternoon. Had Eighty Missionaries present. Very good."

In the 1930s and 1940s Oyer's diary reporting was similar. Feb. 5, 1934: "Had to be real early in order to get a seat." Feb. 5, 1937: "This evening we all went to the Coliseum (Moody Day) 15,000 inside—5,000 turned away." Although Oyer was forced to slow down in the 1940s because of illness, she still attended Moody programs when she could. Then in the late 1940s when compelled to retire to her home near St. Johns, Michigan, she would listen to Moody programs by radio.[11]

Later S. F. Coffman, although he had attended Moody's while working at the Home Mission in the 1890s, suggested something of a negative Moody influence on Mennonites. He wrote: "When our preachers and workers are going about teaching and preaching with Schofield [sic] Bibles under their arms and Moody books in their libraries, and Los Angeles magazines in their hands and Toronto notes in their reference lists, it makes us wonder 'What is the Mennonite Church? and for what does she stand? and how has she existed? and how will she continue to exist?'"[12]

One of the Fundamentalistic beliefs that came into the Mennonite churches, including those in Illinois, was premillennialism—the belief that there will be a literal 1000-year reign of Christ (the millennium) on earth between the first and second resurrections. In general, all premillennialists were Fundamentalists, but not all Fundamentalists were premillennialists. Moody Bible Institute definitely was both. Apparently A. D. Wenger, one of the above-mentioned Moody students, was the first to preach premillennialism prominently among the (Old) Mennonites. He spoke at the first Bible conference ever held in the Mennonite Church, at Scottdale, Pennsylvania, in 1895, and also at the second, held at Johnstown, Pennsylvania, December 27, 1897 to January 7, 1898. John S. Coffman, also a speaker at Johnstown, reported that Wenger's treatment of unfulfilled prophecies "was something new" and was "by no means the generally accepted view of the Mennonite people," which was the amillennial view.[13] That Moody's was an important source of Fundamentalistic and premillennial influence among the Mennonites is indicated also by C. Henry Smith, Mennonite historian who came from Illinois. He wrote: "In recent years millennialism [and] loss of nonresistant doctrine both have been largely a result, I think, of the later Moody influence though not directly [due] to Moody personally."[14]

A Fundamentalistic doctrine that often accompanied premillennialism was dispensationalism. This was the belief, synthesized perhaps most effectively by C. I. Scofield, that salvation history could be divided into ages or dispensations and that in the present age, "Grace," the application of such portions of Scriptures as the Sermon on the Mount were postponed until the millennium in the age to follow.[15] At least as early as 1894 Mennonites were already listening to Scofield. In that year M. S. Steiner, superintendent at the Chicago Home Mission, went to Moody's "on my wheel" to hear the great dispensationalist. Scofield became still more famous and more influential with the publication in 1909 of his famous reference Bible, which was to be found in many Mennonite homes, including those in Illinois. The present writer went from Illinois in 1917 to attend Hesston Academy (later Hesston College) for four years and has vivid memories of the promotion and large sales of the Scofield Bible through the college bookstore. Many Illinois Mennonites no doubt purchased it also from the Mennonite Publishing House at Scottdale, which promoted and advertised the book in its catalogs from 1909 until 1944. At least one prominent Mennonite Fundamentalist evangelist was an agent for it for many years. Another indication of its popularity among Mennonites was that at the graduation in 1922 of the first class of nurses from the Bloomington Mennonite Nurses Training School each member was presented with a Scofield Bible.[16]

One of the persons most responsible for introducing premillennialism and dispensationalism along with other emphases of Fundamentalism into Illinois Mennonite circles was C. F. Derstine, evangelist and minister at Roanoke from 1915 to 1924. He brought a new, voluble manner of speaking as well as new, Fundamentalistic emphases to this staid Amish Mennonite community. With these he "awakened" people in more ways than one. He literally made the people who were accustomed to quite ordinary preaching "sit up and take notice." Derstine did a great deal of writing in addition to his preaching at home and elsewhere. A considerable amount of this writing as well as of his preaching had to do with Liberalism and Fundamentalism, or Evangelicalism, the term he no doubt would prefer to use if he were still living today. Much of this writing appeared in the 1920s, that time of growing concern among Mennonites that the Mennonite churches were threatened by Liberalism or Modernism.

Derstine was influenced considerably by Jacob B. Smith, John L. Stauffer, and others at Eastern Mennonite School, where he was graduated from the academy in 1919. He read and clipped from *Moody Monthly, Defender, Prophecy, Revelation,* and the *Plain Truth;* as well as from Mennonite papers, including the *Sword and Trumpet.* He also studied the writings of such Fundamentalists as William Evans, F. B. Meyers, D. L. Moody, G. Campbell Morgan, W. H. Griffith Thomas, R. A. Torrey, and others. Several times he spoke at Moody Founders' Week, and he gave the commencement address there in 1955. In 1951 he received an honorary D.D. from Bob Jones University, an institution even more rigorously Fundamentalist than Moody's. Derstine was editor of the *Christian Monitor* in the 1920s and for many additional years was editor of the *Monitor's* section on world news. Through his writings and evangelistic preaching Derstine continued to be an important influence in Illinois long after he moved to Ontario in 1925.[17]

Liberalism, Derstine wrote in 1920, "eats like ... a canker." It is to be feared because of its subtlety and "masked unbelief." The notorious skeptic, Robert G. Ingersoll (who, incidentally, was also from Illinois), had been open in his infidelity. "He promulgated his errors in error's clothes." But the liberal masquerades under the guise of truth and religion. Of all the tendencies in the church, Derstine feared "liberalism more than any. It is Satan as 'an angel of light,' not the 'roaring lion.' It is the ghost of Robert Ingersoll in religious garb, not lecturing in theaters, but in sound churches and conferences of God-fearing people." Derstine proceeded to define a liberal as one who privately questioned nearly all the fundamental Bible doctrines, such as verbal inspiration, the Genesis account of creation, the atonement, the deity of Christ, miracles, et cetera. In place of such doctrines the liberal put an undue emphasis on social service, personal righteousness, the man of Galilee, and world improvement.[18]

Along with Amos E. Kreider and Daniel Kauffman, Derstine served on the resolutions committee at the Illinois Mennonite Church Conference in 1922. One question assigned to Kreider was how to safeguard young people in high school and college days. The committee recommended, and the conference adopted, a resolution saying that no school was safe for young people if the teachers were not outspokenly in favor of the Christian fundamentals and that it was "always best to keep our children in schools where both the fundamentals of the faith and distinctive doctrines of the Church are faithfully exemplified in daily life." Since Kreider was a Goshen College professor whom some would have labeled "liberal" and Kauffman was the newly elected president who was really more just a conservative than a Fundamentalist, the composition of this resolutions committee is interesting. It is interesting also in view of what was to occur at Goshen College shortly.[19]

For years Derstine continued to be an important foe of Modernism in the church and a promoter of premillennialism. His influence became still greater with the publication in 1922 of his book, *The Church Age in Prophetic Limelight.* A premillennial interpretation of prophecy, this work sold widely in Mennonite circles. In 1919 Derstine had already published *The Great Apostasy,* a compilation of writings by himself and other premillennialists. Of course, his field of influence was still further enlarged when he became editor of the *Christian Monitor* in 1923, following editor Vernon Smucker's resignation as a result of differences during the conservative-progressive conflict in the 1920s.[20]

Derstine's positions brought criticism. Take, for example, his defense of Moody Bible Institute. On one occasion he had included the institution in his list of "safe" schools that Mennonite young people could attend. Professor Paul E. Whitmer of Bluffton College, Bluffton, Ohio, objected because of the Institute's position on war. He wrote to Derstine, saying that these schools "practically all believe in the efficacy of fight and contention as a method by which to rid this world of evil. Their dominant method is combative. They use it lavishly in speech, in writing, in Bible teaching and they do [it] to the extent that nations shall even appeal to the sword in helping God to bring in an era of peace and good will." Praising other parts of Derstine's article, Whitmer then added: "I am told that quite a few former (Mennonite) students of these schools are openly repudiationg [sic] the nonresistant position of the church, explaining the Sermon on the

Mount and Christ's whole program of peace and good will as having nothing to do with us and this present age. The whole Gospel (Evangel) is said to apply to a future age, leaving us nothing better than the militarism of paganism to live by."[21]

Derstine replied that he did not endorse "everything they do and teach" at Moody's. Nor did he endorse "entirely" what they taught at the other schools he mentioned, not even at the Church of the Brethren's "Bethany Bible School," the "best ... in my estimation. But I claim they do better work than the average Bible Seminaries do." He said they were "providing thousands of consecrated, sound theologically, and equipped workers." Derstine was less satisfactory in his defense of Scofield and his postponement theory. He thought the statement by critics that the "Sermon on the Mount, according to 'Scofield's Helps,' does *not* need to be obeyed by the Church" was not correct—that the "accusation is a straw man." According to Derstine, Scofield said, "These principles fundamentally reappear in the teachings of the Epistles." "There is a moral application to the Christian." Derstine then added: "The Scofield Bible with its footnotes has accomplished more to make Christians expectant of the Lord's return, than any other known agency."[22] Possibly Scofield has been somewhat misunderstood and misinterpreted in the matter of the postponement theory.[23]

Despite the criticism, many Mennonites shared Derstine's beliefs. It is impossible to say, of course, just how many Illinois Mennonites were influenced by Derstine's and Moody's premillennialism and by Derstine's qualified endorsement of Scofield's dispensationalism with its postponement theory. Clearly, more were influenced toward premillennialism than toward the postponement theory. Some accepted the latter, however. For example, one Illinois Mennonite, writing from Chicago where he then lived, criticized a fellow Mennonite for opposing the postponement theory. "If people could only see the simplicity of God's plan," stated the writer,

> I am sure there would be less divisions among Christians.... [They] fail to "rightly divide the word of truth." They get all confused by mixing up what was intended for Israel and what is intended for the church ... We have scripture to show us that the sermon on the mount was given to Israel and not to the church. God had a very definite purpose in bringing Paul to repentance. Paul is the apostle to the Gentiles and if people would only study the Pauline epistles more there certainly would be less controversy over the ten commandments, the sermon on the mount and various other portions given for the Jew.... Paul does not tell us to adhere to the sermon on the mount or the ten commandments. He does not tell us that the Lord's prayer is ours. He knew "thy kingdom come" is not what the church will be praying because we will come back with the Lord to set up that kingdom. Israel is looking for that kingdom and not we.[24]

To be sure, many voices in addition to Derstine's influenced Illinois Mennonites in a Fundamentalist direction in the 'teens and especially the 1920s. The Fundamentalist-Modernist controversy was in the air and Illinois Mennonites breathed it. Other voices in the state agreed with Derstine, and some from outside had a great impact through lectures and writings that circulated widely in the state. There was also controversy in the colleges, especially Goshen and Bluffton, which many Illinois Mennonites attended.

Concern about the fundamentals, Fundamentalism and Liberalism appeared more and more in conferences of various kinds. The Western A. M. Conference in 1919, for example, took a strong position supporting "the plenary and verbal inspiration" of the Bible. It also took a stand against "the present world-wide movement in favor of the federation of churches," a favorite target of the Fundamentalists. In September 1921 the Mennonite Church (MC) General Conference, clearly influenced by the spirit of the times, felt it expedient to accept a list of "Christian Fundamentals." The rationale was that "Particular doctrines of the Church have been attacked and there has been much compromising with the world on matters of Christian living." It claimed that its list did not supersede the Mennonites' ancient (1632) Dordrecht Confession but rather restated it "in the light of present religious contentions and teachings." Many of these doctrines recently had been "questioned or denied by many church organizations." In addition to doctrinal articles of faith with which the ordinary Fundamentalists agreed—such as the "plenary and verbal inspiration of the Bible," the historic and literal truth of the Genesis account of creation, the virgin birth of Christ and others—the statement went further and included as fundamentals such Mennonite distinctives as nonconformity and nonresistance.

This statement was influential in Illinois as elsewhere. National and local Mennonite "Fundamentals Conferences," or sessions on the fundamentals in connection with other conferences, were held frequently during the 1920s and later. At the Illinois Mennonite Conference in 1922, C. F. Derstine was asked to discuss "methods of disseminating the fundamental doctrines of Christianity throughout the state." In 1924 the conference resolved that it was definitely "against all forms of destructive modernism creeping into our beloved church." Such conference statements bore clear imprint of American Fundamentalism.

The 1924 conference had H. R. Schertz speak on "The Changing Modern Mind and the Unchanging Word of God." Following his address the conference stated that the Word of God was "Truth," "final, complete, infallible, unchangeable," and it resolved that "we . . . accept the inspired Word of God as our rule for life." Such biblicist language was not really much different than Mennonites might have expressed before American Fundamentalism began to influence them; yet the conference's desire to reiterate its biblicism may have come partly from Fundamentalism. And in the same year a "Fundamentals Session" was a part of the Illinois Mission Board program.[25]

In line with the times, the General Conference of the Mennonite Church asked in its 1923 session: "Since the Mennonite Church has been more or less disturbed by the world-wide menace of modernism as compared with the faith and practice of our forefathers, what has this conference to offer as an effectual remedy for stemming the tide of this destructive movement?" In response the delegates, conceding that Modernism had "become a menace to the Church, threatening its foundations," asked for the diligent and faithful study and teaching of the whole gospel; that all Christian workers take a definite, positive position in support of the entire Bible, not failing to warn against Modernism; that those in responsible church positions who were friendly toward modern Liberalism "should not be continued in their positions"; and that more literature upholding the fundamentals of Christian faith and showing the evils of Modernism be circulated among our people. S. M. Kanagy, speaking on "The Menace of Modernism," had opened up "this timely subject" for discussion.[26]

Of course, these conferences, including the General Conferences mentioned, influenced the church in Illinois. Especially was this true of the Mennonite Church General Conference held at Eureka in 1925. Early in the year an Illinois committee began making arrangements for a Fundamentals Conference to be held at Eureka just prior to the meeting of the General Conference in August. The committee wrote to the Illinois (Old) Mennonite ministers for their reaction to the proposal; of the fifteen who replied, all favored it except one. This was during the upheavals that closed Goshen College for 1923-1924 and that led some groups, mostly in Indiana and Ohio, to leave the (Old) Mennonite Church. In giving his opinion on the proposed conference A. C. Good, the lone dissenter, wrote: "We wonder as to the adviseability [sic] of discussing fundamentals just at this time. You know what is in the air. Now let us not start a fire in Illinois such as they have in Ohio and Ind. Fundamentals we have always believed, why discuss them. Under *Normal* conditions it would be alright [sic]. But we question the wisdom of the Fundamentalists 'Hammering' the Modernist at the conference." Despite this lone but perceptive voice, fundamentals meetings took place. The organizers, following a plan used at Waterloo, Ontario, two years before, held the conferences in twelve surrounding congregations on the Saturday and Sunday before the General Conference convened on Monday, August 24. In reporting "Nine Days at Eureka," the editor of the *Gospel Herald* wrote that these fundamentals conferences were "one of the most valuable features" of the meetings.²⁷

Various Illinois individuals were involved in the Fundamentalist controversy, usually on the conservative side. Less colorful and dramatic than Derstine, and usually less influenced by premillennialism, these people were deeply concerned lest the church lose its bearings. Among these was J. S. Shoemaker. More serene, peaceful, and less combative in his methods than the usual Fundamentalist, he nevertheless feared inroads of religious Modernism. "Repentance toward God and faith in the Lord Jesus Christ," he wrote in 1927, "are doctrines that need to be emphasized again and again as the fundamental means of salvation and reconciliation to God the Father, which, of course, is wrought through faith in the atoning merits of Christ's shed blood." He continued: "The doctrine of the Virgin Birth, the incarnation of Christ, and the doctrine of Atonement through His death on the cross, need to be especially emphasized in this age of modernism and fallacious teachings on the part of many who fill the pulpits of some of the more popular churches." Shoemaker subscribed to the other fundamentals, including the Mennonite distinctives, as indicated in a letter to J. E. Hartzler: "... I am especially concerned about the best welfare of the church and the inculcation and dissemination of Her peculiar doctrines, the doctrines of love, non-resistance, non-conformity and separation from the world."²⁸

Deacon David E. Plank from Roanoke was probably more of a Bible student than was the usual deacon. He may have been somewhat influenced by Derstine, who had been in the same congregation. Plank was "sure" that the sentiment in the Mennonite Church was "overwhelmingly in sympathy with Fundamentalism." He was no doubt correct if by "Fundamentalism" he meant concern for the fundamental doctrines, including those in which Mennonites were interested, rather than the militant, organized Fundamentalist movement. He was more sophisticated than some in trying to harmonize the Genesis account of creation and the findings of modern geology. He pointed out that many Bible students "make a marked distinction in time, between the first Scriptural statement, 'In the beginning God created the heavens and the earth,' and the subsequent work of construction ..." a distinction allowing for the beginning in an indefinitely earlier time period, which could account for the existence of fossils.²⁹

Aaron Augspurger, Central Conference minister at Saybrook, was another voice concerned with the religiously liberal trends in the period from the 'teens to the 1930s. But Augspurger and others showed that warning against Modernism did not necessarily mean adopting rigidly Fundamentalist positions. The grandson of Joseph Stuckey, he helped found the Central Conference Mennonite Church in 1908 and its periodical, *The Christian Evangel,* in 1910. As doctrinal editor of the *Evangel* he and editor Albert B. Rutt and others made the journal wary of "liberalism" or "modernism." In taking such a position, they thought they were voicing the "unanimous sentiments of their constituency." Among the points in the announced platform were the inspiration of the Bible; the Genesis account of creation, although they did not think that the purpose of the Bible was to "give us a scientific account of creation or natural law"; belief in God the Father and Creator, in Christ as Savior, in the Holy Spirit as guide and comforter; the visible organized church to evangelize the world; and God's people as a "distinctly separate people."[30] Their list showed a certain flexibility in its disclaimer concerning the Bible as science, and a Mennonite flavor in its reference to being a separate people.

In 1932, after the turmoil of the 1920s, Augspurger spoke at his conference on "What Is Modernism?" He had read books on both sides and tried, he said, to be fair. Some of his language was quite Fundamentalist. He warned against the Modernist denial of the fall of man, the virgin birth, the deity of Christ, the atonement, and the bodily resurrection, and against Modernists' characterization of all such as "mythical stories." But if Auspurger was rather Fundamentalist, he was also fairly moderate, for in the same address he expressed his appreciation "to our brother ministers who have come to us from the Old Mennonite Conference" which they had left in the 1920s, voluntarily or otherwise, because they were too "liberal."[31] In that reference he was clearly referring to nine or ten prominent individuals who had changed their conference affiliation. Incidentally, most of them were either from Illinois or served there or both: William B. Weaver, Raymond L. Hartzler, Ernest Bohn, Harvey Nunemaker, A. E. Kreider, I. R. Detweiler, and Amos Eash. Albert B. Rutt had changed earlier and Raymond Yoder changed later.

Another important figure from Illinois in this period was Noah Oyer. Since his adult life other than when he attended university and seminary in the East was spent largely as teacher and dean at Hesston and Goshen, his influence on Illinois was less direct. But it was still important. Oyer is a bit harder to categorize than some. He was quite Fundamentalistic in his Hesston years (the 'teens and early 1920s) and his early years at Goshen, to which he came in 1924. In an article in the *Gospel Herald* (Nov. 24, 1921), after expressing pleasure that General Conference had in that year endorsed the "plenary and verbal" inspiration of the Bible, he went on to make a brief, scholarly defense of the doctrine. Oyer believed that Mennonites had held this view throughout their history. Like many others at Hesston, he had some questions about Goshen and felt that "Hesston represents the church better than any other school." When he became dean at Goshen in 1924, the same year in which the *Christian Exponent* was started by an "old" Goshen group whom many considered quite liberal, Oyer felt that these people were "our most dangerous rivals as far as the college is concerned." Oyer had attended the conservative Princeton Seminary and favorably reviewed a notable book by one of its more Fundamentalistic professors, J. Gresham Machen's *Christianity and Liberalism*. He had had correspondence with Machen earlier, and after the publication of the review Machen wrote to him: "Of course I rejoice with all my heart in the unity of aims that prevails between us."[32]

As time went on and it became evident that the pendulum at Goshen was not going to swing as far toward conservatism as some had hoped, and criticism of the college by conservatives again became common, Oyer, never extreme, became still more moderate in his views. For a few years before his untimely passing in 1931, Dean Oyer, like President S. C. Yoder, became more and more a builder of bridges between disputing Mennonite groups who were at least partly misunderstanding each other. Especially interested in "Conserving Our Mennonite Young People," he noted the divisions of the time and said that in religion and theology we face the same question of conservation. "One camp is known as the conservative or fundamentalist group. The other," he continued:

> is known as the liberal or modernist group.... The ... question ... is not ... primarily the question of conserving our faith and ideals. Simply stated it is ... When we have conserved our faith and ideals, what will we have conserved in the way of individuals to keep the faith? The conservation of the human element is the problem. Faith is to be kept, not merely by being written in the form of creeds, but by being lived in the lives of individuals. This is the question of first importance. Shall we be successful in leading our youth to possess our faith and ideals as an experience in their own lives?[33]

After Dean Oyer's death a statement of faith written in the autumn of 1929 was found among his papers. After stating his belief in the usual fundamentals of the Christian faith, including the "historic principles and tenets of the Mennonite Church," he concluded with a significant paragraph that helps explain the philosophy and methods he followed:

> I do not profess to have a solution for the present mooted questions that are rife in our church at this time, but in the past years have endeavored to work for the peace, unity, and purity of the church. In working with young people it has been my policy to work for a better feeling on their part toward the church and its leaders. In my policy of Church work I do not find it possible to give myself any radical program.

> To me it seems that a conservative course which is free from radicalism, personal feeling, and is based upon deliberate sound judgment, seasoned with much prayer and fervent love of the brethren, has the greater promise of success.[34]

When Oyer died in 1931 the entire Mennonite brotherhood lost an important reconciling influence.

Church periodicals were one of many outside influences upon Illinois Mennonites in this controversial era. The *Gospel Herald* is a good example. Daniel Kauffman, from Missouri, edited the *Herald* from its founding in 1908 until his retirement in 1943. Although he was a strong personality and leader in his own right, as editor of the Mennonite Church organ he became an even more powerful influence in Illinois and wherever the periodical circulated.

In the liberal-conservative or Fundamentalist-Modernist controversy of the time Kauffman put his tremendous weight on the conservative side, claiming to be a "fundamentalist" with a small "f." He also made it clear, clearer than did some others, that his fundamentalism included the Mennonite fundamentals of nonresistance and nonconformity. The "whole Gospel," he often called it. The *Herald* carried many editorials and articles by Kauffman and others on the controversy. Like nearly all Mennonites Kauffman was strong for orthodoxy. In 1912, for example, in the earlier part of the controversy, he felt it necessary to "Speak Out." Under that heading he published an editorial on orthodoxy, or "fundamentalism." One must believe the Bible "from lid to lid," he wrote. One must "not question the truth of a single doctrine or historical fact recorded in the Bible" and must "regard as fake anything that may be brought against it."[35]

In 1920 Kauffman editorialized on "Two Kinds of Fundamentals," one list deriving from a "well-known federation society" which stresses the "Fatherhood of God," "The Brotherhood of Man," "Friendship," "Charity," "Civic Pride," "Honesty," "Tolerance," "Americanization," etc. D. K. (as he was often called) wondered about this list and asked "why not work along this [other] line of fundamentals": the absolute authority and reliability of Scripture, instant creation of man by God, fall and total depravity of man, deity and virgin birth of Christ, atonement through his blood, obedience to God, bodily resurrection, eternal punishment of the wicked and eternal glory of the righteous. In 1926 Kauffman asked in an editorial, "Are you a fundamentalist?" He said you may possibly not be known by that name but it was certain that:

> if you carry a consistent testimony for God and His righteousness; if you believe that the Bible is absolutely authoritative and reliable in all its teachings and show by your life and testimony that you have no other idea of the Bible; if you believe that Jesus was born of a virgin, that He

was and is both God and man and that all His commandments were given with the idea that they should be taken at their face value and literally obeyed by all believers; if you belong to an orthodox church and are loyal to it in fact as well as in theory, you will never be mistaken for a modernist; neither will you apologize for modernists and rap the church or the individual that opposes or exposes them.[36]

When one writer asked whether there might not be a third position between "the bold, rash" materialism and "unbelief espoused by Modernists" on the one hand, and the "spirit of bigotry and intolerance in the Fundamentalist camp" on the other, D. K. stated that this man was "making himself a lot of unnecessary trouble. With him it ought not to be a question of passing judgment upon any particular group of individuals but a matter of faith." If he believed the Bible to be "authentic and infallible," then "he accepts without question such fundamental Bible doctrines [as those mentioned above] ... which Modernists deny or call into question. This makes of him a Fundamentalist, as the word is now understood, no matter how 'bigoted' his fellow fundamentalists may appear to him. He talks like a man who is either confused in his vision of present day issues or leans toward Liberalism and tries to hide his leanings."[37]

In the battle against evolution and its teachings in the public schools, the battle led by William Jennings Bryan and others, D. K. solidly supported Bryan. Tennessee had the right to pass the law under which John T. Scopes was tried. No state, D. K. conceded, had the "right to dictate what a man shall or shall not believe," but neither did any man have "the right to interfere with the state in the exercise of its rights to self-government." To him atheists were less dangerous than those educators who claimed they could be believers and also evolutionists. If we did not stop the teaching of evolution in the public schools we would soon be a nation of unbelievers.[38] "Fundamentalists," he wrote at the conclusion of the Scopes trial, "have no choice in the matter, but to rally in defense of the orthodox faith or surrender to the army of unbelievers who have been and are overrunning our schools and churches."[39] In later years Kauffman like some others used the term "fundamentalism" less, and returned more to an earlier favorite term, "conservatism."

Harold S. Bender was another important person from outside the state who greatly influenced the thinking of Illinois Mennonites at this crucial time. Bender was of course Bible teacher and dean at Goshen College and Goshen Biblical Seminary. Many Illinois students, along with others, attended Goshen, sat in Bender's classes, and read his writings. During the stress of the 1920s Bender aligned himself with the moderate conservatives, and when Goshen reopened in 1924 he returned from study in Europe to rejoin the faculty. In an important address given at the Indiana-Michigan Sunday School Conference in 1925, and published in the *Gospel Herald* "by resolution of the Conference," Bender strongly urged that, in the words of the title, the "Fundamentals Should Be Taught These Days." There was no excuse for wavering or uncertainty, "and the Church has a right to ask of every one of its workers, and of every father and mother who teaches in the home, 'Where art thou?' on the great fundamentals of the faith." The Mennonite Church, he said, had always been one with definite faith and teachings, "not always perfect indeed," but a church which through four centuries "has given a clear and unmistakable testimony to a definite, certain unshakable faith in the great fundamentals. I hold this to be true beyond the shadow of a doubt in spite of the fact that some would-be historians of today would have us believe otherwise." These fundamentals, Bender thought, could be summed up in four cardinal points of Christian doctrine "about which everything revolve[s]": *"Christ, His Person and Work; The Holy Spirit; The Bible, the Word of God; and the Church."* Bender said his appeal could not "be made strong enough to the Mennonite Church of today, to every Christian worker, and father and mother, *that the fundamentals really be taught effectively and fruitfully....*"[40]

Bender gave this address in the 1920s at the height of the controversy over Modernism. Although he said that it was not his assignment in that speech to "describe in detail the fundamentals," he did stress that Christ's salvation required "absolutely consecrated personal discipleship and separation from the world"—more a Mennonite than a classical-Fundamentalist kind of phrase. As time went on he made it still clearer that most Mennonites were, as noted, lower-case fundamentalists who endorsed such fundamentals as nonconformity and nonresistance, to which the members of the Fundamentalist movement did not adhere. By the mid-1950s Bender had come to the place where he thought "Fundamentalism must be rejected as was Liberalism and Modernism." Conceding that Fundamentalism still had a strong hold on some Mennonite groups and individuals, he felt that most Mennonites, "though generally continuing to insist upon a conservative evangelical theology and resisting Modernism in any form, see more clearly than before that they belong neither in the Modernist nor Fundamentalist camps, but have a satisfactory Biblicism and evangelicalism of their own with its unique Anabaptist heritage."[41]

No doubt the most outspoken and outstanding Mennonite writer on religious liberalism and modernism was John Horsch. Horsch was a German immigrant who lived for some years at Elkhart, Indiana, and then at Scottdale, Pennsylvania, after the founding of the Mennonite Publishing House there, and in 1923 became Bender's father-in-law.

Even before moving to Scottdale, where he became famous as a defender of orthodoxy in the Modernist-Fundamentalist controversy, he manifested a conservative approach. For example, he enjoyed attending programs at Moody's and he also had some questions about Elkhart Institute. An article in the *Herald of Truth* in 1899 also indicated his thinking. "Beware," he said, "of popular liberalism which objects to the upholding of principles of faith, which objects to creed, claiming that it makes little difference what one may believe; it is spiritual anarchism, the liberalism of Satan."[42]

Through his work at Scottdale Horsch became quite influential in the controversy, not only among Mennonites in Illinois and elsewhere but also among Protestants in general. In 1920 he published a book, *Modern Religious Liberalism*, which according to Paul Erb in 1941 probably had a wider circulation "than any other book by a Mennonite author of our day." It was used as a textbook at Moody Bible Institute.[43] Affecting the Mennonites more directly were his *The Mennonite Church and Modernism* (1924) and *Is the Mennonite Church of America Free of Modernism?* (1926).

Horsch's books on liberalism, together with his articles and correspondence on the subject, caused a great stir among the Mennonites. Horsch thought he could sniff Modernism at a great distance. The controversy involved not only individuals and churches but also institutions such as Goshen College, Bluffton College, and Bluffton's Witmarsum Seminary. The strain and stress of the period led to the temporary closing of Goshen College in 1923 and played some part in the discontinuance of Witmarsum Seminary in 1931. Since a considerable number of students from Illinois attended these institutions, the Illinois Mennonites, of course, had a lively interest in them. In 1920, for example, Illinois stood next to Ohio in the number of its students attending Bluffton. Aaron Augspurger, Central Conference minister from Saybrook who gave that speech on fundamentals at the Central Conference, was one of the more articulate correspondents with Horsch. He often agreed—although not always fully—with Horsch on liberalism and Fundamentalism, but not on dress and nonconformity.

In a letter in 1920 Augspurger thanked Horsch for calling attention to conditions at Bluffton College. He and others were "acquainted with the situation" but at the time could do nothing about it. He said it was difficult to "keep college faculties free from the influence of higher criticism and liberalism," adding that the colleges could become more of a curse than a blessing. But he still hoped to have these conditions changed, "for the sentiment of the constituency is strongly against" liberalism and rationalism. A year later Augspurger wrote Horsch that he firmly believed the Mennonites could have colleges and seminaries that fully represented our faith and were "free from the taint of liberalism that reflect[s] on the fundamental doctrines of the Bible." He suggested that an "attempt be made to lead our erring brethren back into safe paths. We need them and need them badly." But, he added, we did "not need them so badly that [we] can afford to compromise with false theories and teaching...." If the "erring brethren" when appealed to failed to listen, then Augspurger was ready to "cast out the old leaven." "If cleaning is a necessity, then let us roll up our sleeves and go at it with our might."[44]

With his more flexible views Augspurger apparently was not quite as ready to "clean house" as was Horsch. In a letter in September, 1924, Augspurger stated that he appreciated Horsch's attack on liberalism but wanted more specific information on some of his charges. He had often heard J. E. Hartzler, president of Witmarsum, speak and had had him in his church at Saybrook. "I gave him the very closest attention at all times," said Augspurger, "knowing something of the adcerse [adverse] criticism made about his soundness, and never at any time have I detected a single word or statement that would afford me any reason for thinking that he was otherwise but loyal to evangelical teachings of the word of God." He then added: "I can say the same thing of Prof. Witmer [sic] and Byers. Of course I can not always concur with them in some of their interpretations of the scripture, but to say that they were fundamentally unsound I have no reasons to say or think."

As to the closing of Goshen College and the controversy "now existing in your conference," Augspurger felt that the issue was "not modernism and liberalism, but rather 'the dress question.' It is pretty much the same question," thought Augspurger, "that gave origin to the Central Conference of Mennonites ... some 50 years ago." Since then the dress question has "ceased to be a point of controversy in this division of Mennonites." But, emphasized Augspurger, "we do ... insist on the simple life, not only in one particular form, but in all life and conduct. I have observed that ... your members ... have just as elegant and up-to-date houses as are found anywhere else; drive just as fine ... [automobiles] ...; wear just as high priced clothing as any one else. Dear brother, I have come to the conclusion long since, that if undue pride exists in the human heart, it might just as well have the privilege to ... [advertise] the fact, as to seek cover under a pretended cloak of modesty." Augspurger thought the splendid opportunity of the (Old) Mennonites to build a strong institution at Goshen would slip away from them unless they ceased insisting on certain forms of dress. Somewhat simplistically he advised: "Remove this obstacle and you will receive patronage from other Mennonite groups and conferences, who thought favorably of Goshen" except on this point. He hoped the old conference would not fail to take advantage of this opportunity rather than "refuse and cause another serious rift in its ranks."[45]

Apparently this letter did not sit well with Horsch, who must have written a strong letter of dissent. In any case Augspurger replied in similar fashion, accusing Horsch of misinterpreting his motives and sincerity. "I have done my best to treat you with Christian courtesy. I have absolutely no apologies to make for anything that I have written.... I am sure that I can not appreciate your recent reply." Augspurger added that during his thirty years of Christian service he had observed that "about the last resort of those who differ with the views of others, is ridicule and sarcasm. Now if you find any enjoyment in such indulgence, you are ... [entitled] to it. My own mind happily does not chance to run in the same groove.... I accept no blame for your unhappy controversy with others," and "pray God that all might work together in the spirit and unity of the love of Christ."[46]

The correspondence between these men seems to have ceased or diminished, at least for some time. But in 1931 Horsch wrote him again about some problems at Bluffton. Augspurger replied that the Central Conference had been closely observing "our Bluffton Schools, ever since we have become interested in them." This was not the first time such reports had come from there, he added. But the reports "were bitterly denounced and denied by the accused. We as a conference are bitterly opposed to any form of curriculum that savors [of] modernism or rationalism, but stand firmly for the old time 'Faith once deliver[e]d to the saints....'" However, Augspurger advised caution, which Horsch could well have used with much profit. Augspurger said "we do not wish to be unfair" to the institutions or their teachers by making public charges before investigating and having in hand the true evidence. "Nothing will hurt our institutions so much as to make charges of unfaithfulness when it [is] perhaps only a teacher or two that have gone away on some fundamental principles or teaching of the true faith.... We should ... be extrem[e]ly cautious lest by public criticism or otherwise, we destroy their very purpose."[47]

Others also had exchanges with Horsch—some sympathetic and some otherwise. One was C. Henry Smith, the Mennonite historian who was born and reared in Illinois and then became a teacher at Goshen and at Bluffton. In 1924 Smith wrote to Horsch saying that when he ordered the book *The Mennonite Church and Modernism* he did not have "the least idea that you were classifying me with the modernists, and so you may imagine my surprise when I found that you had quoted me in connection with a number of others who were teaching dangerous doctrine for the Mennonite church." There was some misunderstanding about Horsch's use of a quotation from

Smith's writings. But even after that was cleared up, Smith thought Horsch used the term Modernist recklessly and indiscriminately and that the average reader would think of Smith as a Modernist in the worst sense. Smith also felt strongly that Horsch quoted out of context and made the author say something he did not say. "I most emphatically deny these imputations. I never held the view you say I do [with regard to church government and discipline], and . . . I . . . can't see by what twist of logic you can twist that meaning out of what I said if you read all of what I said instead of taking a few disconnected sentences." Smith, regarding this as an "unfair and unChristian procedure," then added: "This may seem a little harsh, but not more so than the language you use in your book against the men you name. . . ."[48] Indeed, many others whom Horsch described as liberals criticized him for the same errors.

A. S. Bechtel from Summerfield also corresponded with Horsch. In 1925 Horsch wrote him in regard to Professor Jacob Quiring's alleged teaching of Modernism at Bluffton College and Witmarsum Seminary. Bechtel replied that he had heard that Quiring had taught questionable views on Genesis, but also that Witmarsum president J. E. Hartzler and others had told him that such teaching must be stopped and that the seminary was to be "soundly orthodox according to the Bible." Bechtel then reminded Horsch that Quiring was only one member, and possibly soon leaving, "so why condemn the whole faculty and the College too. Brother Horsch my confidence in both Bluffton institutions is just as strong as ever." Bechtel thought they were "fundamentally sound." True, they did not agree with some of the particular teachings and practices of the (Old) Mennonites; "neither do I, but that does not make them unsound. *Fundamentally* we all agree in *Essentials*."[49]

In further exchanges Bechtel responded more directly to some of Horsch's writings such as *Worldly Conformity in Dress*, which the author had sent him, and *Is the Mennonite Church of America Free from Modernism?* Neither work impressed Bechtel. He was "still decidedly impersuaded to accept" the (Old) Mennonite view on dress regulations. He pointedly asked: "Do you really beli[e]ve that there is a deeper and more devout spiritual life in your branch of the Mennonite Church than in the General Conference branch to which I belong?" Although Bechtel was also opposed to the "ungodly manner of so much of the present day female mode of dress," he believed that the heart would "change the dress to what it should be" and not that the dress would "change the heart to what it should be." He also asked who "made the rule concerning women's dress in your Church, the women who are most affected by it, or the men?" As implied in this statement, Bechtel, like C. Henry Smith, challenged Horsch on the issue of church government, which he thought should be democratically controlled and not run by conferences dominated by the ministers, especially the bishops.

Finally, Bechtel suggested Horsch might be critical of men like N. E. Byers, Smith, P. E. Whitmer, J. E. Hartzler, A. E. Kreider, Lester Hostetler and others connected with Bluffton or Witmarsum or the *Christian Exponent* (the new periodical of the progressives) because they were formerly (Old) Mennonites who had withdrawn or been forced out of that branch and later wrote about conditions in the old church with which they were acquainted. "I can well see why the *Exponent* should not be well thot [sic] of by your branch.... Naturally your leaders do not take kindly to it." Rightly or wrongly, Bechtel agreed "with Brother [Lester] Hostetler and many others that there is nothing of a fundamental and essential character that separates the Mennonites. We all agree in the essentials of salvation, the Bible as God's inspired Word, the Atonement, bodily resurrection, Ascension and second coming, Christ the Son of God. Why continue to look daggers at each other. Possibly a good spanking all around would do good."[50]

A radically anti-Horsch letter came from Sterling, Illinois. Abram Burkhart, a member of the Science Ridge congregation, had earlier served many years as deacon. He apparently was deeply hurt by the current controversy over "liberalism" in the Mennonite churches, and, accustomed to speaking his mind forthrightly, he wrote a bitter letter to Horsch about his book *Modern Religious Liberalism*. He was upset that leaders such as N. E. Byers, A. E. Kreider, Harvey Nunemaker, I. R. Detweiler, and others who had come from Sterling or had had close connections with it were now all out of the old church. Burkhart had good things to say about the liberal Harry E. Fosdick but not about the Fundamentalists. "God has men in waiting like J. E. Hartzler and others," he wrote, "who will gather the remnant together again. When a good young man like A. E. Kreider is completely thrust out just because he would not forswear himself I do not hesitate to call that the work of hell. They let men dress in the h[e]ight of fash[i]on but will bar a woman if she wears a hat from Church fellowship. It strikes me its [sic] only a matter of time until they can be rightly called a stag Church. Those are my convictions; by them I stand or fall. I fear neither man nor the devil." Strong words for a Mennonite Church deacon![51]

A different kind of letter had come from J. S. Shoemaker to Horsch a few months earlier. Shoemaker, bishop at Freeport, had also served for years in that capacity in Burkhart's congregation at Sterling. Ironically, he was bishop at Science Ridge at the time Burkhart wrote his letter to Horsch! Shoemaker thanked Horsch for sending him a complimentary copy of *The Mennonite Church and Modernism*.

He praised Horsch for his work and ordered three more copies. "You certainly do not shield those who have been sowing the subtle seeds of modernism in the church. The same should be an eye opener to those who have been drifting toward Liberalism, and the deadly influences of Modernism. I trust that all such may be constrained to secure a copy of the book, and read the same with an unpredjudiced mind, and thus become better established in the Fundamental doctrines of God's Word."⁵²

Among those who earlier had had connections with the Sterling congregation and whom Horsch had attacked was Noah E. Byers. In a restrained reply through the columns of the *Christian Exponent*, Byers joined others in complaining that Horsch had taken his words out of context, making him say things he had not meant. Had he been a Modernist, Byers stated, he would hardly have been asked to remain at Goshen when he resigned in 1913, nor have been asked four years later to return.⁵³

The afore-mentioned *Christian Exponent* was a biweekly journal founded by a group dissatisfied with the closing of Goshen College in 1923. Published from January, 1924 to September, 1928, the paper attempted to serve the (Old) Mennonite Church's' more progressive element, whose interests, some felt, the *Gospel Herald* did not adequately represent. Quite a large number of subscribers in Illinois, both in the (Old) Mennonite and in the Central Conference groups, supported the enterprise. For instance, Walter E. Yoder, moderate Illinois supporter of the *Exponent*, thought that such a paper caused "the 'powers that be' to work more carefully."⁵⁴

Another aspect of the problem in Illinois was mentioned in a letter from H. S. Bender to Horsch in 1925. Bender, professor at Goshen, wrote in September that the new school year had started very well. "The students," he continued, "are on the whole a fine group of young people. We find that a number of the young girls, especially from Illinois, are quite 'dressy.' It is a problem to deal with them, but it is one that must be handled."⁵⁵ Once again, at least with the largest Mennonite body in Illinois, the matter of dress and cultural liberalism was a complicating element in the liberal-conservative controversy.

In the ensuing years Horsch's part in the controversy decreased, along with the diminution of the controversy itself. But he did not become silent. He began to step up warnings against communism as "A Deadly Foe to the Christian Faith" and tied it to religious Modernism. He also began to emphasize that much "of the pacifist anti-war propaganda in America is of a Communistic character." Among the Illinois Mennonites who were delighted with this enlargement of the war against Modernism was Lee Lantz, a Central Conference minister then in Chicago. In thanking Horsch for a new article on the subject, Lantz thought the warning was "more needed in the Central Conference of Mennonites than perhaps you may realize. It surely looks quite threatening when we know what a tremendous effort is being put forth to encourage so many of these peace movements which I am thoroughly convinced originate in Moscow." Although Lantz hoped the Mennonites would always believe in peace, he thought it "almost distressing that they should walk into the trap Moscow is setting to be sprung in the most furious war Moscow can possibly wage just as soon as they feel able." It was, he added, "almost unbelievable that Mennonites are such candidates for modernism within so short a time," and "even so recently from the more conservative branches.... I sincerely hope you sent your article to each of the ministers of the Central Conference of Mennonites and may God richly bless you for this action."[56]

Illinois Mennonites were also much concerned with the liberal-conservative controversy as it related to J. E. Hartzler, and especially his work at Goshen College and Witmarsum Seminary. Some of the letters from Illinois to Hartzler were quite unsophisticated. Andrew A. Schrock, bishop at Metamora, had been born in the German-speaking part of France (Alsace-Lorraine) and never had mastered English very well. Nor did he feel a need for much formal education. But he was a sincere, conscientious churchman. When Hartzler gave a commencement address at Metamora High School in 1916, Schrock, who did not hear the speech but heard rumors about it, was not very happy, even though the president of the school board who had invited Hartzler was a member of Schrock's congregation. The bishop wrote Hartzler saying that "there are things going on in that School that we dont [sic] approve off [sic]; therefore we believe it is necessary that you change your speaking, or Preaching, & Preach more a separation from the World, and Christ & crucified, instead of bringing to them comical illustrations ... which are not edifying." Schrock added that the church needed men who stood solidly on the Rock Christ Jesus who were not swayed by every wind of doctrine; "and especily [sic] with the doctrine of Education as it is running wild now days, with mixing good & bad together, which ... Gods word sais, you cant do [sic] ...." Quite clearly Schrock had misunderstood some of Hartzler's points and illustrations. The latter wrote the bishop asking his forgiveness and explaining his illustrations. Schrock, glad to forgive, added that what he had written was written in Christian love for the advancement of Christ's kingdom.[57]

Slightly different was a warning that Deacon Henry Albrecht of Tiskilwa sent Hartzler also in 1916. Bishop Elias L. Frey of Archbold, Ohio, had just completed a week of meetings at Tiskilwa. Frey had said he was afraid of Goshen College and continued: "If the teachers [of

Goshen] go to a place like Northwestern University of Chicago [sic], where the head of the Institution is an Infidel it is dangerous." Albrecht then added: "Bro. try and see that such things may be adjusted so people need not fear[.]" We "certainly do not want to send our Boys and girls to a place that we will have to fear they may be taught wrong...."⁵⁸

Illinois Mennonites were concerned in 1918 when J. E. Hartzler resigned as president of Goshen College. In fact, concern among the more conservative had existed for some time before this. When his administration began in 1913, Hartzler apparently was evangelical and desirous of working with the Mennonite Church by upholding its standards. Later some began to question this. In addition, a financial crisis in 1916-18 as a result of indebtedness due to the building of Science Hall and the purchase and equipment of the college farm added to the strain. J. S. Shoemaker illustrates those concerned over this new turn of events. "As a father in Israel" Shoemaker wrote Hartzler a pointed letter saying that the church "had lost confidence both in the management and policy of the School." Since the college could not exist without the support of the church, "it is absolutely necessary for the School to fall in line with the Church and her peculiar doctrines.... In some of these things the School has been 'weighed in the balances and found wanting.'" In this letter Shoemaker was more concerned about the Mennonite "peculiar doctrines" than about the so-called Fundamentals of the period. He thought that if Hartzler, who had asked for suggestions, went to the university for another year it would not improve his service to the church. "... it is my candid opinion that your life and labors would have meant much more good to the Church in the past if you would have had less University training, and would have clung more tenaciously to the anti-world principles for which the Church has been standing."⁵⁹

A. C. Good from Sterling was more sympathetic. "I know," he wrote to Hartzler, "you have had a hard pull, and not the sympathy from the heads of the Church that you ought to have had. If there was one man in the Church that I had sympathy for it was the President of Goshen College. I was in hopes that you could pull thru [sic]. What now?" A few days later Good wrote: "I hear there is a general uproar in the student body, and I do not wonder at it either." In 1921 when Hartzler was pushing an all-Mennonite seminary at Bluffton, Good had reservations. He thought Mennonites needed such a school but that it ought to be located at Goshen rather than at Bluffton. He thought, too, that Hartzler ought to have been connected again with Goshen College "in some way." Good and his brother Solomon, also from Sterling, encouraged this. "We believe," he wrote, "that you believe in the doctrine[s] of the Mennonite Church, and we believe that a strong school man will be a great help in defending those principals [sic]."60

These letters suggest the complexity and confusion of the period. Not by any stretch of the imagination could Good be considered a liberal or a Modernist. Yet he was sympathetic with a man such as J. E. Hartzler at a time when a substantial number did consider such a person liberal, if not modernistic.

A. E. Kreider, also from Sterling, and a son-in-law of J. S. Shoemaker, likewise responded to Hartzler's request for an opinion on the proposed all-Mennonite Seminary at Bluffton. He too saw the need for such an institution. "I see no future for the Mennonite Church unless she have [has] a trained ministry." But he thought the (Old) Mennonite Church would not support the proposition. It would be considered "a move in the direction of 'liberalism' (whatever that is). You may have the money.... And it will be possible to secure a faculty. But money and faculty without a steady inflow of strong young men from our [(Old) Mennonite] branch would quite defeat the purpose of the movement." When asked if he would consider a place on the faculty, Kreider replied that he as a young man was not quite ready to risk his future in a movement unless he was convinced it could be a success. "At the present stage in the development I am not ready" to consider a place on the faculty. But he was sufficiently interested that he wanted to be kept informed of the progress of the work. Incidentally, Kreider did join the Witmarsum faculty in 1923 and remain there until the institution closed in 1931.61

The varying fortunes of Goshen College during the 1910s and 1920s concerned many Illinois Mennonites, and not just the (Old) Mennonites. Because of "excellent support" from Central Conference Mennonites J. E. Hartzler tried hard to secure representation for that conference on Goshen's board of control. When this failed to develop, most of the Central Conference support from Illinois went to Bluffton, although some individuals continued an interest in Goshen.62 As noted earlier, some Defenseless Conference members also supported Goshen College.

The rapid succession of Goshen College presidents from 1918-23—six different ones in less than six years—indicates the deep trouble in which the institution found itself. It also indicates the deep confusion of the time over "liberalism," "Modernism," "conservatism," "Fundamentalism" and "orthodoxy." The "liberalism" that caused trouble at Goshen was both cultural and theological, although probably more of the former than the latter. And if any theological liberalism existed there, it was probably greater in the minds of conservative constituents than in fact. In other words, no doubt rumor and misunderstanding played a part in the unfortunate controversy that led to the closing of the school in 1923-24.⁶³

But J. E. Hartzler's troubles did not end with leaving Goshen and eventually going to Bluffton, where he became president of Witmarsum Seminary in 1921. When he and others were pushing hard for an all-Mennonite seminary at Witmarsum he wrote to C. R. Egle, Defenseless Conference leader in the Salem congregation near Gridley, about his disappointment that Egle's group was not going along with the new union seminary movement. Somewhat bitterly, he wrote that he thought they had met the criticism of Egle and others: "Now, in spite of the fact that we tried to meet every condition laid down, our work is getting no real consideration, our most conscientious efforts are ignored and out [our] reorganized Seminary is given no chance at all to prove itself. Is this right?" But Aaron Augspurger, the Central Conference leader from Saybrook, explained to Hartzler that "the Defenseless Conference is very suspicious of Modernism and liberalism at Bluffton and Witmarsum. This is what makes them so slow in giving them support. It is up to the officers of the institution to clear away any such Doubt [sic] in their minds. As a conference we are very closely associated with them, and if they should refuse to support the schools because of their suspicions, that would have a most serious effect upon our own conference."⁶⁴

Augspurger himself had some doubts about Bluffton and Witmarsum. Why invite speakers who unsettle the faith of students? he asked Hartzler. "Why not invite lecturers who stand four-square on the true faith, without doubt or wavering." Writing soon after Goshen closed temporarily in 1923, he told Hartzler he had "much sympathy for Goshen." He felt that the church "must regulate the school, and not the school the church," adding that he would like to see Bluffton College and Witmarsum "come out openly and publicly for conservatism and fundamentalism in faith and doctrine. This is what the Central Conference stands for and will stand by, and no other. Some things are causing doubt in our minds, and you know . . . brother J. E., that such doubt will not encourage hearty support." All that the Central Conference asked, he wrote in conclusion, was to "close your doors against rationalism and higher criticisms that would unsettle the faith of the student in his own church, and its teaching. Give us this assurance, and we are with you."⁶⁵

Also in 1923 another but quite different concern over Fundamentalism came to Hartzler. William B. Weaver, who had known Hartzler well at Goshen and who now was pastor at the North Danvers Central Conference congregation, wrote:

> Say, I'm a little bit disturbed since Sunday. You know Rev. Kensinger and wife returned missionaries (from Africa) and two candidates

(Beckers) gave us a missionary convention. They boosted Moody Bible Institute about as much as Africa. Every one connected Moody Bible Institute with their consecration for service. They always said if any young person volunteers for service then they should go to Moody's. I get tired of having missionaries sent to my church and then stuff my people with Moody Institute. I have hard enough sledding to get my people interested in Bluffton College and Seminary. Can't you people give candidates for the foreign field for this conference so that they can come to our churches and say that Bluffton gave them the vision? There have been seven missionaries in my church since I'm here[66] and everyone boosted Moody's. I'm tired of it. I'm not interested in this conference if that's going to be our program for the future. How does it look from out there?[67]

A still different communication came to Hartzler from A. M. Eash who with his Twenty-sixth Street Mission in Chicago left the (Old) Mennonite conference and joined the Central Conference in 1923. "Things have been going fine since we jumped overboard," he wrote to Hartzler, in words Hartzler could appreciate from his own experience. "Think of it—Over three months of comparative peace. Not a single delegation or committee has waited on me to investigate either character, faith or conduct. Frankly, I sometimes get a little lonesome for some of the oldtime confabs." Eash also asked Hartzler to come to the mission for a week of Bible lectures, not only for the good of his own people, but also for the Mennonites in Chicago, who were living as "sort of free lances." Nominally they were in the old church but not in sympathy with it. "The old conservatives," wrote Eash, were "chuckling up their sleeves because these liberals are sticking by their conservative mission here in Chicago instead of coming over and lining up with our group. The old conservatives wouldn't use these folks themselves but they do not want them to work for anyone else. I believe your presence here for a week would do some of those folks a world of good."[68]

For many conservatives, in Illinois as elsewhere, Hartzler's image was not helped when John Horsch's book on *The Mennonite Church and Modernism* appeared in 1924. In this work Horsch painted Hartzler and other Mennonites with a liberalistic brush. Hartzler reacted vigorously, like C. Henry Smith accusing Horsch of misquoting him or quoting out of context. In every case, Hartzler said, he "juggled my thought," using "decidedly unscientific, inaccurate, unfair, unreasonable and uncalled for" language to attack.[69]

Illinois Mennonites, of course, were much interested in the controversy over liberalism also at Bluffton College. Peter Stuckey, Joseph's brother, had been an early member of the board, and by 1913 Emanuel Troyer, J. H. King, and A. B. Rutt had become members of the newly elected board of the reorganized college. The controversy came to a head in the winter of 1928-29 when the Board of Deacons of the First Mennonite Church of Berne, Indiana, and their former pastor confronted the college with alleged evidence of Modernism in the institution. The charges had to do largely with the faculty's view of the Scriptures, the incarnation, the resurrection, and the atonement. About six months later the Bluffton faculty, through President S. K. Mosiman, sent a "Statement of Faith" in reply. The Board considered the statement unsatisfactory, a judgment that was strengthened when the Board received negative replies from leading Fundamentalists to whom it had sent the statement for comments. The Central Conference, however, whose leaders were much concerned in the controversy, did not take quite the same negative view of the Bluffton problem as did the Board of Deacons at Berne. In any case the issue was carried to the conferences, including the General Conference, which finally in 1933 drew up a compromise statement that warned that Modernism was "attempting to exert its influence." In the meantime, due to pressure, Professor Jacob Quiring resigned from the Bluffton faculty in 1930, and Witmarsum Theological Seminary closed in 1931. Although the reason given for closing the seminary was economic instability, theological controversy "was certainly in the background." Concerning the college, apparently some misunderstanding continued, for in 1934 President Mosiman sent form letters to ministers inviting them to a meeting "primarily for the discussion of College and church relations." He said he wanted to know the reason for a growing feeling that the college was not serving the church "as well as it ought."[70]

In this same period theological differences were also causing strain and stress in the East White Oak congregation near Normal, Illinois. A charter member of the Central Conference, the congregation prospered under the leadership of Peter Schantz and then Emanuel Troyer. In 1928 Reuben J. Zehr became pastor. Even more than some others Zehr seems to have been much influenced by Moody Bible Institute, and to have influenced many of his members in the same direction. Some of these attended the Institute, more attended various kinds of meetings there, and Moody students and teachers quite often spoke at East White Oak. On one of these occasions the reporter stated: "We always enjoy having anyone from Moody's with us as they always seem to manifest a wonderful spirit. This spirit is lacking in many of our churches today." Unfortunately, the zeal for correct doctrine began to produce tension and rigidity in the relations with the Conference, the result being a split and a separation in 1934. This occurred after various conference committees, at the urging of some fifty members of the congregation, had investigated Pastor Zehr's relation to the Central Conference and his failure to cooperate. The conference finally silenced and dismissed him until he would change his attitude and work harmoniously with the church body. A majority of the congregation supported Zehr and formed the East White Oak Bible Church. Those remaining loyal to the conference joined other congregations.[71]

At about the same time the Central Conference had a problem with one of its licensed pastors in Chicago. Walter Guth, a Moody graduate and pastor of the Sixty-second Street Mission, was so much imbued with Fundamentalism that he insisted on sole control of selecting speakers, rejecting supervision by the conference mission committee. He wanted to select speakers who were "absolutely sound" in doctrine, and also wanted to be ordained by a committee that was "one hundred percent sound and premillennial in their theology, and ... spirit filled. ..." He felt he did not have to support the church's mission program because he considered the conference postmillennial. In July, 1934, the conference quite understandably dismissed Guth for having demanded special privileges "detrimental to the best interests of the Conference and her institutions" and for "manifesting a spirit of disloyalty and insubordination."[72]

In the decades following the mid-1930s, by which time even leading liberals were conceding that the church had to "go beyond modernism,"[73] the strain and stress over liberalism among the Illinois Mennonites changed from time to time and from place to place but did not disappear. In time the term "Evangelicalism" was preferred over "Fundamentalism," but otherwise the vocabulary of the conservatives remained pretty much the same. In 1937 the Illinois Mennonite Conference, in "the light of [the] confusion of these last days," resolved "to unitedly dedicate ourselves to the work of presenting the full Gospel message of Christ's shed blood as an atonement for sin." Writers and speakers continued to emphasize—in addition to the atonement—repentance, the new birth, sanctification, separation from the world, inspiration of the Bible, the second coming of Christ, the incarnation and virgin birth, Christian service and the other fundamentals. Preaching the conference sermon for the (Old) Mennonites in 1941, Henry R. Schertz stated that the higher critics and modernists were "busy digging about and under this rock [Christ] with their spades and pickaxes, but the foundation is sure." The editor of the influential *Gospel Herald*, who by 1940 preferred the term "Christian Orthodoxy" to "Fundamentalism" but claimed that they meant "the same thing," wrote that "Christian orthodoxy is something that every Christian professor should espouse, defend, exemplify, and promulgate." He added that "Christian orthodoxy includes service as well as faith." Some continued the dispensationalist emphasis also. In November 1940, S. J. Miller of Pigeon, Michigan, held a series of evangelistic meetings at Hopedale, Illinois, in which he gave a chart lecture on the six dispensations covering the period from Creation to Christ's return.[74]

Fundamentalistic influences continued in other Illinois groups as well. Arnold Schultz, writing in the Defenseless Mennonite *Zion's Tidings*, emphasized the need to avoid modernistic literature in the Sunday school. Not having colleges of their own, Defenseless Mennonites strongly urged their young people to attend evangelical institutions such as Moody's, Ft. Wayne Bible College, Taylor University, Marion College, Wheaton College, Asbury College, Grace Bible Institute, and Bob Jones University. Taylor University, it seems, was most favored. "Many of our pastors and young people have been and are now at Taylor," reported H. A. Driver in 1944. In January of 1952 Evangelical Mennonite leader Reuben Short reported in *Zion's Tidings* (Jan. 15, 1952) that Dr. Milo A. Rediger, Evangelical Mennonite, had been appointed dean at Taylor, and added that the development was good for the University and for "our Conference." One of the advantages of this institution, he continued, was that it "contends for the faith which is so much needed in these apostate times."[75]

Evangelical Mennonites had problems with International Sunday School materials published by the International Council of Religious Education, which editor E. G. Steiner of *Zion's Tidings* said was "the tool of the Federal Council of Churches." Steiner objected to the International Sunday School Lesson Helps because of their Modernistic emphasis. Since about half of the church was already using the materials promoted by the National Association of Evangelicals, Steiner urged all to use them for the sake of a united witness against Modernism: "We are evangelicals, so let us be consistent and support the evangelical cause rather than lend encouragement to the enemy."[76]

When the EMC and the EMB began their temporary affiliation in 1953 the *Evangelical Mennonite* reported the "Impressive Inaugural Service Held at Omaha." The periodical stated that the affiliated group stood for the verbal inspiration of the Bible and all the other usual Fundamentals, including premillennialism. It added that the close friendship between the two groups began over thirty years before through the evangelistic ministry of George P. Schultz of Chicago and Elder C. R. Egle of Flanagan.[77]

Many Mennonite churches, especially in or near Chicago, continued to rely on Moody teachers and students for speaking assignments. One writer, making a survey of Mennonite religious institutions in Chicago, characterized a certain Central Conference minister as a Fundamentalist who had no social conscience: "Our work is to save souls.... All of this working for peace is useless." The same writer described another Chicago minister as a very evangelical person whose church had "no social service outlook . . . as it does not conceive that to be a part of the Christian Gospel." Some also complained that too many Mennonites were giving their money to such places as Moody Bible Institute rather than to causes of their own church—a situation that was to be true later also.[78]

In some areas of the state the (Old) Mennonites went through another period of strain and stress in the late 1940s and early 1950s due primarily to Fundamentalistic influences, faith-healing, and cultural (not theological) liberalism. One point of contention was the conference requirement that the ministers wear the collarless clerical garb, or "plain coat" as it was often called. Some ministers, usually younger ones, disliked this requirement and were not very strong on other Mennonite "distinctives." They did not like to be mistaken for Catholic "Fathers," as sometimes happened when they wore the garb, and they also felt that the Mennonite emphasis on nonconformity was a hindrance to evangelism, which they stressed a great deal.

Another factor was a feeling that the Mennonite Church was not supporting its ministers as it should have. After some years in the ministry Raymond M. Yoder struggled with the question of whether he "could afford to be a Mennonite preacher." "Shame on you big churches of our conference," he wrote frankly, "that send thousands of dollars to foreign mission work and have given your minister but a few cents for their work.... It's about time you take the muzzle off and give them their groceries at least." In 1946 Yoder, while still a member of the old conference, became a minister of the Central Conference church in Congerville, where he received support.[79] This raised eyebrows in the old conference. The critics did not lower their eyebrows when Yoder had some girls baptized and received as members without their wearing the covering. Nor did his editorials in the *Missionary Guide*, of which he continued to be the editor, help when they criticized the plain coat requirement for ministers and the power of bishops. The executive committee of the (Old) Mennonite conference met with Yoder to review their relations. Each side agreed that it had made some mistakes, including Yoder's use of some unfortunately strong language. After further attempts to clear up misunderstandings, the matter was settled by granting Yoder's request for a conference letter in order that he "might labor in another conference of his own choice." At the same time he was commended for his "fine spirit" in asking for a letter and thanked for his work, especially in missions.[80]

The problems and differences of opinion that arose around 1947 to 1952 were largely of the same pattern in the several places. A dissenting group of ministers, who of course had a following, included Orie A. Miller of Peoria, Robert Zehr of Newcastle, Harold Oyer of

Morton (formerly of Goodfield), Noah Roeschly of Morton, and J. A. Heiser of East Bend at Fisher. Raymond Yoder, and Wilfred Ulrich, who was for a short time at the Peoria Mission before moving to Canada, could also be considered in the group. Influenced by Fundamentalism, they stressed Anabaptism less and felt that the distinctive Mennonite doctrines and practices were a hindrance to evangelism, which they emphasized strongly.

The conference requirement that the ministers wear the "plain coat" or clerical garb was only one issue that brought matters to a head. When the conference dropped the requirement in 1949, dissatisfaction and defection continued. The dissenters emphasized that they had to follow their consciences as directed by the Spirit and Scripture, which they quoted copiously. Orie A. Miller's comment was typical: " 'He hath clothed me with the garments of salvation, He hath covered me with the robe of righteousness. . . .' I find also that Christ has appointed unto us the 'garment of praise for the spirit of heaviness' and he brought forth the best robe and put it on us taking away our filthy garments. So also I find myself well dressed in Him for the marriage supper of the Lamb."[81]

After considerable discussion and exchange of correspondence between the conference officials and these brethren the latter joined other conferences. Or, with their followers, they formed independent Bible churches, such as Bellevue under Orie A. Miller's leadership and Newcastle under Robert Zehr. Though differences and separation produced some strain, those involved attempted to manifest a Christian attitude. Harold Oyer, for instance, in severing his connection with the Mennonite Church, said he bore no ill will toward it and added that he was "indebted to the Mennonite Church for many God-given principles, which by God's grace I shall endeavor to maintain through life." In reply, the conference secretary regretted that Harold felt it necessary to leave and added: "We appreciate your method of withdrawal and we hold no ill will toward you."[82]

The withdrawal of Robert Zehr from the conference was doubly difficult. His brother Howard, whom Robert loved dearly, was an important leader in the Illinois conference and the entire church. Both were devoted evangelical Christians; both strongly supported evangelism. But Howard saw more value in the Mennonite heritage and remained a loyal member of the Mennonite Church, choosing to work for growth and improvement from within rather than without. Robert, after continuing some years with the independent Newcastle Bible Church, became a minister in the Evangelical Mennonite Church and now (1980) happily serves as a pastor in the Upland, Indiana, congregation.[83]

Developments at the East Bend congregation in this period were similar but a bit more complicated. Fundamentalistic tendencies were present, but charismatic emphases on baptism of the Spirit and on faith healing were greater. Bishop J. A. Heiser, an older and highly respected leader for decades, had much in common with the younger dissatisfied ministers discussed above. He too put more and more emphasis on evangelism and less and less on "Mennonite" doctrines and practices. In fact he too was now saying that the latter were hindrances to evangelism. To what extent personalities and differences between Heiser and his assistant pastor, Harold Zehr, entered into the picture is difficult to say. Accounts agree that their preaching differed, both in style and in content. Heiser, a more dynamic speaker, put much emphasis on prophecy. Some evidence indicates that in later years he put less emphasis on such things as nonconformity and nonresistance and was more favorable to congregational rather than conference control. Whatever the difference in style and content, clearly Zehr insisted more on continuing to work with the conference than did Heiser. Heiser, as bishop, was opposed to calling in the conference officials to help resolve the difficulty. But ultimately Zehr and the church council felt there was no other recourse.

To what length Heiser carried his belief in faith healing is difficult to say. Some sources indicate that he believed in it, as did most Mennonites, to the extent of James 5:14-15. Others say that he went further than that, or at least interpreted the James passage more extremely to say that healing was covered in the atonement. In any case apparently some of his followers were more extreme than their leader. Some cases of illness among local Mennonites entered into the controversy, one case in particular being the cause of much conversation and misunderstanding. Mrs. Elmer Schrock, sister of Pastor Harold Zehr, had cancer. She was anointed with oil and upheld in prayer, but got worse and died (April 13, 1951). After her death some reportedly prayed to bring her back to life. Allegedly, Heiser had earlier stated that disease such as cancer and tuberculosis were examples of demon possession. The allegation was probably incorrect, for on another occasion he said Christians could not be demon-possessed; these diseases were caused by demon *oppression*, not demon *possession*, Heiser thus making a distinction between the two. When Mrs. Schrock died, people tended to blame others, especially doubters in the group who, it was said, had not had sufficient faith that she would be healed.[84]

Unfortunately, the train of events leading to a division in the congregation did not end with the death of a few people in 1950 and 1951, for whose recovery many, including the strong believers in faith healing, had ardently prayed. Charges and countercharges and the manner of handling the growing factionalism in the church also helped exacerbate division. It is not necessary to recount all details. Suffice it to say that the majority, including associate pastor Harold Zehr, who wanted to remain in the conference, asked conference officials for advice and help. Under Bishop Heiser's leadership a minority seemed to resent intervention of the conference, which the majority felt was proper. After the congregation held many meetings and sought an understanding, the majority felt that the only practicable solution was to have the conference officials take the counsel of the congregation.

After Milo Kauffman of Hesston, Kansas, had held a successful series of meetings in the congregation, the East Bend Church Council along with conference officials decided to hold an election on February 3, 1952. The first question the members were to vote on was: "Are you willing to work with the East Bend Mennonite Church as a part of the Illinois Mennonite Conference?" Just before the meeting on that Sunday morning 120 members of the dissatisfied group handed a statement to the conference executive committee saying that they could not participate by their presence or their vote. So the vote of those participating was one hundred percent affirmative. This group then decided by slightly more than a 95 percent vote to call Howard J. Zehr from Peoria to be their bishop and pastor in charge and Harold Zehr to continue as their associate pastor.[85]

Heiser and his group then joined a Fundamentalistic Bible Church in Gibson City, which some East Bend members had been attending for some time. This church had been started a few years earlier by some members of the United Brethren Church together with the few remaining members of the Central Conference Mennonite Church at nearby Anchor. For a number of years Heiser served as minister of the new Gibson City group.

Like other church divisions, this one brought some bitterness. The group leaving felt that they and especially Heiser were ignored by the church council and by the conference officials who took the initiative in making the new arrangements. The conditions that the dissenting group laid down for reconciliation were quite rigid and apparently unacceptable to the majority. Those leaving also asked for a financial settlement for their contributions to a newly erected church building. Fortunately, the two groups worked out a satisfactory settlement of this problem.[86]

The brighter side of the East Bend picture is that time and the Holy Spirit have brought healing. In a perspicacious paper entitled "My Years at East Bend," Verle Oyer, local historian, has given a good summary. As one who from his youth on had admired Heiser's spiritual leadership but yet in the crisis remained at East Bend, he saw both Heiser's strengths and his weaknesses. "The division," he states, "made many bitter on both sides. Today the wounds have healed in many ways. I personally feel that at heart J. A. was a Mennonite and never felt a grudge against East Bend. He would attend on occasion in his later years. I personally still held him in high esteem although I think he made some mistakes as I also have made perhaps more mistakes."[87]

A very few of those involved may not be fully reconciled as yet, but the healing process has continued. Conference leader Ivan Kauffmann wrote in 1965: "Things are going fairly well at East Bend, the wounds are in process of healing, and some people (especially youth) are finding their way back in fellowship at East Bend again. Harold [Zehr] has had just recently some personal contacts with Joe Heiser and also some of the members of Joe's family. These contacts have been redemptive in nature and will be the means of further healing of some deep wounds. I would surely hesitate to do anything that would agitate and reopen any of these bygone events."[88] Visits and observations by the present writer, indicated in the above footnotes, provide additional evidence that the healing trend has continued.

Into and beyond mid-century, Illinois Mennonites continued for the most part to be theologically conservative and evangelical. Some Fundamentalistic influences have also continued although "evangelicalism" would probably be the preferable term. In 1959 in view of so much disbelief the Illinois Mennonite Conference reaffirmed its unflinching confidence in the Bible as God's inspired, written, and progressive revelation, its central theme being the ultimate living expression of himself, Jesus Christ, the Redeemer of and final authority for man. One writer from Tiskilwa, no doubt typical, characterized the virgin birth as one of the "cardinal doctrines" of the Bible, the foundation stone of Christianity.[89] In their Triennial General Conference in 1962 the General Conference Mennonites also adopted a statement reaffirming the authority and inspiration of the Scriptures.[90]

The "battle of the versions" of the Bible did not pass Illinois by. Heinz Janzen, pastor at Calvary in Washington, wrote an article in *The Mennonite* entitled "After Ten Years with the Revised Standard Version" (Sept. 25, 1962). What we want, he wrote, is better communication in order to understand God's Word more clearly. He believed the new version supplied this, and thought the King James Version should be discarded except by older people "who have learned to automatically translate the archaic phrases into sensible English." He added that it pained him to "see sincere but misguided parents buy a King James Version for young people. It immediately creates a stumbling block to understanding the message of God and of salvation." Janzen thought the positive features of the new translation clearly outweighed any alleged weaknesses.

The article caused much controversy. In the next five or six issues of *The Mennonite* numerous letters poured in pro and con, most of them favorable. But Professor William Klassen of the Mennonite Biblical Seminary in Elkhart, who thought the article was one of the best "you have printed," was shocked at the "vicious response" of some of those opposed. Several ministers from Illinois who knew Janzen to be a conservative came to his defense. Ben Esch, Heinz's predecessor at Calvary, praised him very highly and thought he was misunderstood. Paul N. Roth at Carlock was certain that if the critics had known Janzen "as I do they would have written in a different vein."[91]

Others had difficulty in replacing the familiar King James Version. In a Sunday school survey made in 1976 in the Illinois Mennonite Conference (MC), over 1,900 indicated that they attended Sunday school. Eighty-five percent of these carried their Bibles with them to services, mainly the King James or *The Living Bible, Paraphrased*. Only 1.8 percent used the *New English Bible*, although it was used as the text in the Sunday school quarterlies. Harley R. Stauffer, pastor at West Sterling, had his doubts about this version and asked Howard J. Zehr's opinion about it. Stauffer enclosed a booklet attacking the new version and wanted Zehr to "be more aware of the N. E. B." Zehr replied that no version was perfect, including the King James. He thought the Holy Spirit could guide the true seeker to the truth by means of various versions. He also felt that the author of the booklet that Stauffer had sent was extreme in his views and added: "I do hope you won't allow yourself to become too deeply involved with such radical personalities and views that would limit your usefulness and freedom in the Holy Spirit.... I deeply appreciate your dedication to Christ and the Church."[92]

Whether Fundamentalistic influences among the Illinois Mennonites have decreased or increased in recent years is difficult to say. Clearly they have not disappeared. One (Old) Mennonite Church pastor recently speculated that if Goshen College and Goshen Biblical Seminary would disagree with Fundamentalist Grace Presbyterian Church of Peoria, and the Mennonites of that area had to decide between them, Grace would win in most Mennonite minds. Apparently the decline and closing of the Robein congregation in the 1970s was due in part to Fundamentalistic influences that divided the group. In 1967, when the Congerville General Conference congregation was looking for a new minister, among the concerns members expressed was that their minister believe the Bible from "cover to cover" and that he emphasize the conservative fundamentals. Some conference leaders believed there was a Fundamentalistic group—"a definite Winona Lake faction," they called it—and feared that they might call a non-conference pastor, thereby beginning a separation from the conference. Fortunately, this did not occur.[93]

Strain, Stress, Liberalism, Fundamentalism 341

Opposition to the World Council of Churches, usually an indication of Fundamentalistic influences, has recently been heard in the Tiskilwa General Conference congregation. When Pastor J. C. Atherton heard in 1976 that the question of membership in and cooperation with the Council was to come up in a conference session, he stated that he wanted to express his and his congregation's strong opposition. Several members voiced similar views. One new member wrote that her "opposition to any dealing with W.C.C. or United Nations, etc. can scarcely be made strong enough on paper." She had been brought up as a Methodist, she added, and had seen the church lose out. "You cannot," she concluded, "legislate the Lord Jesus with socialism. You cannot compromise his Church with the world and get away with it." Other Illinois Mennonites also opposed the National Council and World Council of Churches, although probably few as vehemently as did this sister. Edwin Stalter explained that the (Old) Mennonites were members neither of the National (and World) Council nor of the National Association of Evangelicals.[94]

Some say that while the Moody influence has decreased, that of Fundamentalist Grace Presbyterian Church of Peoria has increased among Illinois Mennonites. Certainly, various radio and TV personalities such as Billy Graham, Oral Roberts, Bruce Dunn of Peoria, and other lesser lights vie with the several Mennonite broadcasts for the air-wave affections of the Mennonites. Bill Gothard's meetings, especially those having to do with strengthening family life, also attracted a considerable number of Mennonites. Pastor Percy Gerig from Roanoke arranged to take several busloads of his parishioners, and some from outside his congregation, to Gothard's meetings in Chicago. Pastor Ernest W. Neufeld of Chicago is typical of the many who seemed sure that Billy Graham was being used by God. Neufeld participated in several of his crusades.[95]

What one conference official said of the Roanoke congregation, in 1961 as it was looking for a minister, could no doubt be said of many others. He wrote: "The Roanoke Congregation would like a minister with a warm evangelical Spirit. They do not require a scholarly approach. Some of the people are Fundamentalistically inclined. The congregation has grown in unity and appreciation for Biblical preaching under the pastorate of Wesley Jantz."[96]

Desire for that kind of "warm evangelical spirit" was evident in a communication that the Illinois Conference Executive Committee sent to Goshen College in 1958. Expressing appreciation for the good relationship that existed between the college and the conference, and for "the contribution the College and Seminary have made to our ministerial life," the committee said: "We further appreciate the endeavor to maintain a conservative theological position in harmony with the life and practices of our congregations. We have confidence in the desire of the administration to maintain these good relationships." The committee then added:

> We do, however, have a few concerns relative to maintaining the historic foundations of our faith. We are concerned that our schools lead our youths to such a faith and commitment to Jesus Christ, as well as growth in understanding of the scriptures. We are also concerned that the classroom reflect more of the life and vitality of the church, and a closer relationship with its life and ministry.
> While the values of higher criticism may make a contribution in the experience of advanced students, we question the advisability and necessity of introducing this to younger students. We have a concern that guidance be given to the faculty in their higher education experiences.
> We are also concerned for a warm evangelical spirit in the student body.
> We appreciate the deep concern and sincere effort of the administration in encouraging and promoting growth in Christ, and loyalty to the church. We sense something of the difficulty of the task which you face and therefore pledge our prayer support.[97]

This group spoke as constructive friends of Goshen, most of the committee and at least half of the conference ministers having been students there.

Relations between the churches and their colleges probably always will and should be a recurring concern. Recently Goshen College has made a more conscious effort to have meetings with Illinois leaders and others to discuss matters that might cause strain and misunderstanding. College officials and Bible teachers have met occasionally for dialogue and found the meetings helpful in clearing up at least much of the misunderstanding. One very successful meeting with Illinois Mennonite Conference leaders was held at Goshen, September 18-19, 1979.[98] Not all the strain and misunderstanding has been strictly theological. An additional factor was the emergence in the U.S. in the 1960s of the long-haired and occasionally flag-burning and nihilistic "hippie" type of student. Mennonite college students with even the slightest hint of such characteristics upset Illinois Mennonites. It was even worse, of course, when some of their own number turned in that direction.

Such disaffected Mennonites tend to support religious causes other than their own. Even some (Old) Mennonites have preferred not to subscribe to the *Gospel Herald* because it is not sufficiently Fundamentalistic.[99] Some continue also to give their financial support, or at least a very substantial part of it, to non-Mennonite, Fundamentalistic institutions. One member at Calvary in Washington gave about $250,000 to Moody's while giving $1,000 to her own church. Recently in the Roanoke congregation two members gave land to Moody's worth close to $750,000.

Although the Illinois Mennonite Conference does a good job of meeting its financial quotas for Goshen College, the college clearly could do still better in attracting support from its constituents. Recent evidence comes from a report from the Waldo congregation at Flanagan, listing its students attending college in the fall of 1979. For whatever reasons, of eleven undergraduate students only one was at Goshen. Three were at Eastern Mennonite College, and two at Hesston College.[100]

The branch most affected in recent decades by Fundamentalistic influences has been the Evangelical Mennonite Church, as is brought out in various sources, especially *Anabaptists Four Centuries Later* by J. Howard Kauffman and Leland Harder. The authors, who included most of the Illinois Evangelical Mennonite congregations in their study, report that of five Mennonite branches studied, the "EMC is highest on the Fundamentalist Orthodoxy Scale and lowest on the Anabaptism Scale" (p. 341). However, one Evangelical Mennonite historian with close connections with Illinios sees some shortcomings in the Kauffman-Harder work. Stan Nussbaum thinks the authors were too negative on Fundamentalism, paying too much attention to the extreme "militant, heresy-hunting, exclusionist fundamentalism of the 1920s which admittedly lives on in some right-wing Protestant groups." Nussbaum wishes Kauffman and Harder had given more attention to the more moderate evangelicalism of the 1970s. He thinks also that some of the "conclusions" of the authors were really assumptions. He says that "if more attention had been given to the middle ground between John Howard Yoder and Carl MacIntyre ... perhaps the writers would not have had to conclude that Fundamentalism is an enigma for Anabaptists."[101]

The EMC has had a close relationship, including membership, with the National Association of Evangelicals since the founding of the latter in 1942. The church has felt that the task of promoting evangelical Christianity could best be done through such bodies as the N.A.E. The Evangelical Conference passed a resolution in 1966 urging local congregations to consider membership in the N.A.E. "so that they will have direct involvement in united evangelical activity." To quote Stan Nussbaum again: "EMC is more relaxed in its associations with evangelicals' than with Mennonites, and it has extensive NAE commitments.... The 'Evangelical' in the name 'Evangelical Mennonite' seems to be getting the lion's share of conference attention."[102]

At least two of the Evangelical Mennonite ministers in Illinois were formerly pastors of General Conference Mennonite congregations in other states. These men—L. R. Amstutz at Salem near Flanagan and

Emil Krahn at Groveland—apparently feel more at home in the more evangelical branch.

In conclusion, Fundamentalism among Illinois Mennonites has taken a course slightly different from that taken in other Midwestern states. During its main thrust in the 1920s, the Fundamentalist movement—together with the strains and stresses of cultural liberalism—did not result in congregational divisions in Illinois as it did in Indiana, Ohio, and Ontario. The loss of East White Oak to the Central Conference in the 1930s, however, was a Fundamentalist casualty. Yet since the 1920s and 1930s Fundamentalistic influences have continued perhaps more persistently in Illinois than elsewhere.

CHAPTER 13

Illinois Mennonites and War

Whether from Eastern United States or from Europe, the Amish and Mennonites came to Illinois with a heritage strongly emphasizing peace. As noted in chapters 2 and 3, one of their principal reasons for leaving Europe was their belief in and practice of nonresistance. After coming to Illinois in the 1830s and later, they faced no major military conflict that would test this faith until the Civil War. The Black Hawk War in 1832 was barely more than a skirmish, although a discouraging defeat for some Sac and Fox Indians in northern Illinois and Wisconsin. But even in this minor conflict John Engle, son of an Amish bishop, is reported to have served as a teamster.[1]

For Illinois Mennonites the Civil War did not involve serious, personal confrontation until the draft was introduced in 1863. Even then, thanks to the aid of Congressman Thaddeus Stevens from Lancaster County, Pennsylvania, who had many Mennonite constituents, the draft law provided that conscientious objectors who were members of a peace church could pay the government $300 in lieu of serving in the armed forces. The purpose of the act was to spur enlistments by threatening to invoke conscription. It "stimulated enlistments enormously," enabling some states and many districts to raise their quotas for the services without resort to the draft.[2]

The draft was invoked, however, in some Mennonite areas in Illinois. No available figures show how many Illinois Amish or Mennonites were drafted, how many of these entered the armed forces, and how many took the CO position. It is known, however, that there were some in each category. For example, Andrew Bachman, bishop of the Partridge congregation, accompanied several of his members to Springfield to arrange for their exemption on religious grounds. One of these was John Smith, who later became a leading Amish Mennonite bishop. He and others paid the commutation fee for exemption. According to the amended draft act of 1864, commutation fees were used for the benefit of sick and wounded soldiers.[3]

Christian Krehbiel of Summerfield has left us a brief account of his experiences with the draft. His brother Valentin, his brother-in-law David Ruth, and John Eicher were also drafted. The principle of nonresistance, the chief reason for the Krehbiels leaving Germany, had been firmly implanted in the family by their father. Christian advised members of his congregation, who had been persuaded to join an underground organization to defend the county, to remain faithful to nonresistance. At that time, said Krehbiel, the enemy was about to cross the Mississippi. But Krehbiel's stand was resented by some "undercover patriots" in the community. Calling him a rebel and traitor, a mob "apparently threatened" to hang him. He could not be intimidated. Later, he discovered that others of his American neighbors had testified to his loyalty to the Union. "In this I saw the protecting hand of God," he said. Krehbiel added, "Several of us had agreed to pool our money ($2,000) to secure substitutes...." His substitute, a young man from Germany, "was at once sent to the front into several hard battles, but was never wounded." At the close of the war the substitute contracted camp fever and returned home "looking like a skeleton. We were able to nurse him back to health." The young man returned to Germany where he married, but soon wrote that he was unable to support himself and family. "We sent him money to return with his family to America. They are now our good friends here in Halstead, Kansas," where Krehbiel moved in 1879. No doubt Krehbiel, like other conscientious objectors, wondered about the propriety of hiring someone else to do what he himself could not conscientiously do. But he at least continued a friendly interest in the welfare of the substitute and aided him generously.[4]

Christian Smith, whose parents, Christian and Magdalena Schrock Smith, died in the cholera epidemic in 1855 in what was later known as the Congerville area, is an example of one from an Amish family who went into the armed forces. He served in Company G, 108th Illinois infantry. He did not join the church, however, until after the war, in 1867. Born in 1846, according to one account, he joined church very little later, if any, than what Amish custom called for. How many Amish and Mennonite church members served in the armed forces it is impossible to state. With regard to the Civil War as a whole, Guy F. Hershberger has said that while many upheld their nonresistant position, others did not. It is clear, he added, that the American Mennonites did not teach their peace doctrine aggressively and were "not fully awake to the opportunities and obligations of the time."[5]

Some contemporary Mennonite leaders agreed with the assessment that the Mennonites were not teaching their peace doctrine aggressively enough. One of these was John F. Funk in Chicago. He became interested in the publishing needs of the Mennonite Church during the Civil War. The war stirred his interest, and he thought that Mennonites should have had more teaching on peace and nonresistance. This thinking resulted in his first published work, *Warfare. Its Evils, Our Duty. Addressed to the Mennonite Churches throughout the United States, and all others who sincerly [sic] seek and love the Truth.* This strong and eloquent diatribe against war was published in the prime war year of 1863. Christianity and warfare are mutually contradictory, said Funk. "The difference between the two is as wide as the distance between Heaven and Hell—the one has no dealings—no affinity, with the other" (p. 14).

When Funk's friend Bishop John M. Brenneman of Elida, Ohio, read the tract, he wrote to the author praising and thanking him for the timely work. He added that he too had thought of writing on the subject. But Brenneman seems to have had some questions about how frank one should be about publishing such sentiments in wartime. "I believe you have written the truth," he wrote Funk. "But it seemed to me that you ventured a little too far at this time, as you might get yourself into trouble for publishing your sentiments in such plain terms. I ... concluded that the people in Chicago must be more quiet and peaceible [sic] than they are here, or else you must be stronger in your faith than I am, as I would be almost certain, that if I would publish such a pamphlet here, that I would be arrested & imprisoned, if nothing worse would befall me." Brenneman thought Mennonites ought to be careful not to give offense to anyone if it could be avoided. But he thought God would use Funk as an instrument "whereby much good might be accomplished." Funk sent his booklet to a large number of Amish and Mennonite ministers, a list of whom Brenneman had helped supply. Incidentally, Funk's tract served as a prod to Brenneman to bring out his *Christianity and War,* which Funk published for him in Chicago also in 1863.[6]

Since the Spanish-American War was of such short duration and the draft system was not used, that war caused no serious confrontation of issues for conscientious objectors. The brief conflict did cause some concern, however, as is illustrated by the record of the Illinois Mennonite Conference which had its 1898 session during the course of the war. The conference appointed a committee composed of one Amish Mennonite (John Smith) and two Mennonites (John Nice and J. S. Shoemaker) to look up the United States and Illinois statutes "to ascertain whether there has been any provision made, by which our people may be exempt from military service."[7]

The war also stimulated further thought and expression on war and peace. M. S. Steiner, now back in Ohio but still remembered as the founder and the first superintendent of the Chicago Home Mission, strongly denounced war in a published sermon entitled "The Christian's Duty in Times of War and to Spain." After portraying the horrors of war he pointed out the duty of Christians "to do good, to love, to feed and to bring to Spain the gospel of peace and bread of life." He thought that if Christians had done their duty in evangelizing Spain and her colonies, the war probably could have been avoided.[8] An editorial in the *Herald of Truth*, June 1, 1899, was very critical of the methods used by the United States to bring "freedom" to the Philippines.

The Spanish-American War was so brief that it scarcely caused a ripple on the placid scene of peace, progress, and prosperity which existed at the turn of the century and after. It was the period of the Hague Peace Conferences, courts of arbitration, and strong and growing peace societies and movements. Many people thought optimistically that war as a means of settling international disputes was passing just as certainly as the old gladiatorial combats and dueling had passed. Illinois Mennonites, like others, were influenced and, one might add, deceived by the prevailing optimism. The emphasis of the times is illustrated by the title of J. S. Coffman's address at the dedication of the Elkhart Institute building in 1896, "The Spirit of Progress." Three years later, at the same institution, a commencement address by a student from Sterling, Illinois, illustrates even better the flowing rhetoric and excessive optimism of that day. Frank S. Ebersole, speaking on "Drum Beats and Heart Beats," stated—even in the midst of the Spanish-American War—that all old war practices were passing. Fainter "grows the drumbeat," he continued,

> the cannon shots are at longer intervals, the war horse smells no more the smoke of battle, the groans of the dying soldiers grow fainter and fainter until they are lost in a new and beautiful melody. It is the chorus by the celestial choir to the shepherds on the hills of Judea. How beautiful, how grand! "Peace on earth, good will toward men." It is the song destined to be ... the requiem of the drum-beat and the overture of the heart-beat.[9]

More mature scholars were also misled. C. Henry Smith wrote in the *Christian Monitor* of May 1910, as follows:

> The signs of the times indicate that war is on its last legs. Even the most casual survey of the history of the human race must convince the most skeptical of this truth.... There is no ground whatever for believing that the trend of history along this line shall be turned back. The same forces which have been responsible for making wars more and more scarce in the past ... are still at work today and will continue to be operative in the affairs of men until war shall be no more.[10]

Not all Mennonites nor all Americans were this optimistic on the eve of World War I, but the great majority were unprepared for the conflagration which came in 1914. And when it did come, few Americans foresaw that the United States would eventually be drawn into it. The Mennonites in Illinois as elsewhere were pleased with President Woodrow Wilson's proclamation of neutrality in the conflict. They were similarly pleased with Secretary of State William Jennings Bryan's efforts to maintain true neutrality between the opposing forces when it seemed that President Woodrow Wilson was veering a bit toward the Allies in his interpretation of neutrality. At first mere sideline spectators of a tremendously moving drama, Mennonites became increasingly concerned as the Wilson administration showed evidences of edging the country toward war. They were temporarily assured by the election of 1916 when the man who had been pictured as having "kept us out of war" won. They felt they had been "taken in" when the country found itself at war in April, 1917. Not a few of them believed that if William Jennings Bryan—who had resigned as Secretary of State in June of 1915 because of differences with Wilson over true neutrality—had been president, the United States would not have gotten into the conflict.

With the United States in a world war and with the enactment of conscription, the Illinois Mennonites found themselves in a new crisis for which neither they nor the government was prepared. Unlike in the Civil War, the president and the congress decided at the outset to use conscription. The act provided for exemption for conscientious objectors, but with the provision that "no person shall be exempted from service in any capacity that the President shall declare to be noncombatant." This law was passed on May 18, 1917, but the president did not define noncombatant service until March 20, 1918. When he did so, he defined it as a form of service within the military and required the wearing of the uniform. At first there was no segregation of conscientious objectors from soldiers, as there would be in World War II, and this caused additional strain and problems.[11]

The Illinois Mennonites tended to follow the lead of their co-religionists across the nation in this new crisis. For instance, the (Old) Mennonites meeting in their General Conference in August 1917, near Goshen, Indiana, drew up a statement of their position on war which also gave advice to members who had registered. The conference advised against military service, "either combatant or noncombatant." The work of this conference was influential not only in the (Old) Mennonite Church but at least to some extent in other branches as well.[12]

The Illinois Mennonite conscientious objectors shared the confusion which existed in all areas, since the government was inadequately prepared to take care of them when drafted. Apparently the higher government officials tried to be fair in their treatment of conscientious objectors (COs). It is difficult to determine President Wilson's attitude toward religious objectors. Of pacifists he said in November of 1917: "What I am opposed to is not the feeling of the pacifists, but their stupidity. My heart is with them, but my mind has a contempt for them. I want peace, but I know how to get it, and they do not."[13] Newton D. Baker, whose department of war administered the CO program, seems to have been more fair, even generous. He did not intend that any of his subordinates should mistreat COs, which did occur at times.[14] These cases of mistreatment no doubt were due not only to a lack of sympathy on the part of some subordinate officials but also to their lack of information and understanding of the law and the slowness of its implementation by Secretary Baker.

The experiences of the Illinois COs in the army camps were probably not the best, but they certainly were not the worst. For instance, in J. D. Mininger's list of religious COs at the Ft. Leavenworth federal prison, some 125 are indicated as being Mennonite, but only three were from Illinois: Joseph Eash of Shelbyville (listed as Mennonite, but probably Conservative Amish Mennonite); Edward R. Heiser [Hieser], Central Conference Mennonite from Tremont; and Daniel B. Teuscher, (Old) Mennonite from Fisher. Teuscher died at Ft. Leavenworth in November 1918 from influenza and pneumonia, but apparently not from mistreatment as did a few others.[15]

Those who did not go to prison at Ft. Leavenworth could and did have rough times too. Some have left accounts of their treatment, a number of whom report it as fair and decent. The treatment the COs received was a most strange mixture of brutish, devilish behavior on the one hand, and kindly, gentlemanly, considerate understanding on the other. So much depended therefore on the character of the individuals with whom the COs came in contact. Roy Buchanan of Metamora has given us a detailed account of his experiences. A recent but devout convert to the Mennonite faith, Roy interpreted "working for the military" pretty narrowly. But he left us an insightful view of the working of the military mind and the pressures used to get the COs to change their minds in favor of some kind of service in the army. Occasionally the best and the worst in man were demonstrated in the same individual, as was illustrated in his chef when Roy worked for five weeks in an army kitchen at Camp Dodge. For the first three weeks the chef did everything he could to make life for Roy as disagreeable as possible. Then the miracle happened! Calling Roy aside, the chef, under "great emotional stress and with tears and a new gentleness in his voice," apologized and added: "It's going to be different from now on." And it was. After "three weeks of drudgery plus a continued round of abusive language directed at me, then two weeks of the kindest consideration—I am convinced that nonresistance is worth while."

After being assigned to another part of the camp Roy would often go back to visit his new friend.[16]

Others from Illinois seem to have had an easier time than Buchanan had. But here too there was a variation in the treatment received. However, in few cases, if any, was life easy for the drafted COs. It took courage to stand out against the crowd. Quite often the harassment was limited to verbal abuse, but frequently enough it went beyond that to such tactics as turning water hoses on the COs, making them work hard under difficult circumstances, making them cook and eat their meals outside regardless of weather, ordering them to stand erect ("at attention") for hours, or threatening them physically if they failed to do as ordered.

After the first few months of floundering the handling of the COs in the camps improved, especially in June, 1918, when the War Department belatedly took two actions. The first was to include COs in the legal provision which authorized furloughs to men in the army "to engage in civil occupations and pursuits." The second was the establishment of a civilian Board of Inquiry to visit the camps and review all cases of COs. Those found to be sincere the Board recommended for furloughs, either to work on farms or to engage in relief work in France with the American Friends Service Committee. Both proved popular, positive steps, and many COs accepted one or the other option as recommended by the Board.[17]

One clear, typical example of better treatment of COs as a result of the above-mentioned action came at Camp Wheeler in Georgia. Here Mennonite boys, including a number from Illinois, had been forced to march around the camp very rapidly and pick up refuse, including horse manure, with their bare hands. The weather was hot and some collapsed. Another was arrested and put into solitary confinement. C. F. Derstine of Eureka, Aaron Augspurger of Saybrook, and Emanuel Troyer of Normal visited the camp early in July, 1918. Derstine reported that they "found a *sorry* bunch of abused boys. All forced into uniforms, nearly all were drilled. Worked till they fell down in a faint. One is so nervous that he could hardly stand or talk." These ministers discovered that the camp officials had not been informed of certain War Department rulings issued in June concerning the COs. At about the same time D. N. Claudon of Meadows wrote to Secretary Baker about the mistreatment of several Defenseless Mennonite boys in the same camp. When the camp officials found out about the new orders, they called the Mennonite boys to headquarters and allowed them to choose an alternate form of service. Nearly all selected farm furloughs.[18]

The commanding general at Camp Wheeler reported to his superiors regarding the COs quite differently from the report that Derstine sent to Loucks. He wrote that Rev. Derstine "expressed himself as being entirely satisfied with conditions at camp." Possibly General Lyon meant that Derstine would be satisfied with the anticipated changes.[19]

A study that the Mennonite Research Foundation carried out in 1948 and 1949 under the leadership of Melvin Gingerich has provided a great deal of information about Mennonite COs in World War I. The study included at least thirteen from Illinois. The pattern of experiences as revealed in the Illinois respondents' questionnaires is not greatly different from that indicated above: some physical abuse at first in a number of cases but later only the verbal type, if any. Most reported having had positive and helpful experiences. But one was very negative and bitter. His mistreatment was not physical violence, "*but* plenty hard on the nerves." He could not recall a few dates asked for in the questionnaire: "I have been wanting to forget the whole thing for the last 30 years." No minister visited him, he reported: "Nobody was interested in me, which was proved when I returned home by some of our own Mennonite brethren." That was why he left his home community for another, he said. In a note appended to the questionnaire he stated that under no circumstances did he want his name published with the report: "I have been double crossed by our own Clergy and members, which cut as deep as the ill treatment I received while in the service. I want to forget the whole thing. *(If Possible).*" This indeed was a minority opinion. His experience must have harmed him emotionally.[20]

The Schowalter Oral History Project carried out by Bethel College, North Newton, Kansas, also throws considerable light on Mennonite draftees in World War I. Only five of the interviews were with Illinois draftees, but they were important ones. The Mennonites interviewed included some who were in the army. Two were (Old) Mennonites and three were Central Conference. The two (Old) Mennonites—Levi Birkey from Hopedale and Daniel S. Deter from Morrison—did not take up service in the army. Of the three belonging to the Central Conference, one (Andrew C. Burky from Tiskilwa) went into the army as a noncombatant, one (John H. Miller from Hudson) took the more absolute CO position, and one (Lloyd Ramseyer from McLean County), who was drafted on the day of the armistice, had planned to go as a soldier and join the infantry.

These interviews, running from forty to fifty minutes each, are important because of the information they yielded not only about the men themselves but also about their churches and other factors in their environment. For example, Dr. Lloyd Ramseyer, president of Bluffton College, made perceptive comments not only about his own pilgrimage to a strong peace (CO) position but also about his East White Oak congregation and the Central Conference of Mennonites.

According to him the COs from East White Oak who refused to serve in the armed forces were not very popular even in their own congregation and received little support from it. John H. Miller, also from East White Oak, confirms the lack of support that Ramseyer mentioned. When asked why he thought so many in the congregation were not supportive of the CO position, Miller thought it was in part because a number were running for political office and feared the unpopularity of that stand.[21]

Roy Buchanan was among those who selected relief work as his alternate service. He no doubt was typical in feeling exhilaration in showing the positive and loving side of nonresistance by engaging in reconstruction rather than in the destruction of war. In the army he had to say "no," and he spent weeks in the guardhouse. "My conscience would not let me consent to military service. But wasn't there some way that a person could say 'yes'? I wanted to find some way of saying, 'I'm not a slacker; I *do* love my country; I'm saying 'no' to hate and war, but I want to say 'yes' to some kind of loving service to this poor mixed-up world." Relief work was Roy's way of saying "yes." It made a tremendous impression upon him—"wonderful memories, changing all my life at the mere mention of the word 'France.'" Much later—when almost eighty-one years of age—he wrote that the "most happy days" of his life "were in the devastated areas of France ... bringing comfort to a poor destitute people." Roy spoke for all Mennonite relief workers in France and elsewhere. Included in those from Illinois during and following World War I, in addition to Roy, were Edward R. Drange of Low Point; Albert J. Sommer, George O. Springer, Walter H. Smith of Metamora (all in France); Arthur W. Slagel of Flanagan; Mr. and Mrs. D. M. Hofer of Chicago in Constantinople and Russia; and A. M. Eash of Chicago in the Near East.[22] Most of this group volunteered for relief work and had not been furloughed from the army camps.[23]

During the war, Illinois Mennonites in the home communities also experienced some tension and disagreeable incidents. It is sometimes said, all too truly, that in time of war truth is the first casualty. The fact that the Mennonite churches followed the CO position officially and in practice, coupled with the fact that they were generally German in background and until recently in language, made them doubly suspect.

It was not only local hoodlums and rowdies who caused trouble for COs. New research, especially by Allan Teichroew, an archivist in the Manuscripts Division of the Library of Congress, has shown that because of the above-mentioned suspicion, military surveillance of Mennonites in World War I was widespread. An article he published in *The Mennonite Quarterly Review* (April 1979) includes a document,

"Note on the Mennonites," written and compiled by the Military Intelligence Division (MID) of the War Department. The list of security agencies which MID headed included the Bureau of Investigation,[24] the American Protective League, and state and local Councils of Defense. The MID document, known as the (R.J.) "Malone Report," is a mixture of truths, half-truths and untruths. "At the heart of the MID case," says Teichroew, "was the argument that Mennonites who rejected all military-related service, including noncombatant work, were less pacifistic than pro-German." Marlborough Churchill, new head of MID, stated there was "absolutely no question or doubt about the fact that the activities of the Mennonites and Amish . . . are doing as much harm with their pacifist and anti-war views as any similar organization in the country today, and that their actions ought to be silenced at once."[25] Fortunately, Secretary of War Baker, as pointed out above, was more tolerant than many of his subordinates.

The chief villain in the act in the minds of these subordinates was (Old) Mennonite Bishop Aaron Loucks of Scottdale, Pennsylvania, whose duties included visiting the camps to let the COs know and understand their rights under the laws. Of course most of the subordinate officials, who had been using virtually every means to get COs to take up at least noncombatant duty, did not like Loucks' forthright statements to the Mennonite boys that they neither had to work under the military nor wear the uniform. At times Loucks' advice was more restrictive than that coming from other Mennonite ministers, which, of course, was confusing to the COs, including those from Illinois.[26]

Government surveillance included the Illinois Mennonite communities, as well as the Mennonite men in camp. References in the "Malone Report" to specific Illinois Mennonite communities and their leaders are few. Bishop Andrew Schrock, mistakenly called "Old Order Amish," is reported as "very conservative, opposed to the war and to any support of war activities." The "Report" includes the following absurd statement about the Mennonites at Flanagan: "When asked to support the Red Cross, [they] replied that they preferred to give their money to the Germans, in their own way." C. R. Egle of the Salem Defenseless congregation, who was portrayed as "very influential in his church," "was made the subject of exhaustive investigation and interrogation." The "Report" spoke of Egle's "pronounced and excessive pacifism as well as the fact that he advised several Mennonite boys—his own son among them—not to wear the uniform." He also stated that boys who would put it on "would not be excommunicated," but their standing in the church would not be as good as that of those who refused to wear it. He added that President Wilson and Secretary Baker "approved the refusal of the Mennonite boys at Camp Wheeler to wear the uniform," and used Aaron Loucks as authority. Egle's church, continued the "Report," "had naturally been apathetic in the matter of supporting the Red Cross and purchasing Liberty Bonds. Feeling ran very high against him but was somewhat appeased by the discontinuance of German as the language of the services in his church and by indications of a more liberal spirit in supporting war activities." The "Report" concluded with a pretty dismal, bleak view of the Mennonites and COs: "The individual Mennonite draftee is in general narrow, bigoted, pig-headed, ignorant, slovenly, and selfish; he is unaccustomed to thinking for himself but follows stupidly along the lines of the traditions of his clan. Whether a sincere objector or just plain 'yellow' need not concern us here. He is at any rate, mighty poor material for the army."[27]

J. S. Shoemaker was also under surveillance during the war. Since Mennonites were considered "Germanic" in their national origins and thus suspect, and since they had missionaries in India, which was in the war as part of the British Empire, the Military Intelligence Board undertook to scrutinize the Mennonite Board of Missions and Charities and Shoemaker as its secretary. The Chief of the Freeport Division of the American Protective League, R. J. Stewart, investigated and reported to the Military Branch, War Department. Stewart explained the peace position of the Mennonites and how they could not support the war. He also explained that Shoemaker, whom he had known "for twenty-five years," was the leader of the Mennonites in that section. Stewart concluded that he "personally would consider it very dangerous at this time to permit the doctrine of this church to be spread in this County or in any other as the attitude of Mr. Shoemaker is no doubt the attitude of those high in authority of this church."[28]

One curious incident involving surveillance occurred in the Old Order Amish community at Arthur. On April 4, 1918, a former minister in the group, A. M. Kauffman, wrote a strange letter to President Wilson and Secretary Newton D. Baker about "shameful" acts going on in that Old Order community, suggesting that these people did not have "any just cause to demand exemption from military service." He added: "...you know their appeal to you is for exemption and this I claim is not loyal neither to God's command nor to our country or fellow man. God's command is love your neighbor as yourself. Now if we can't show a willing and a helping hand in winning this war, is it then possible that we love our neighbor as ourself and reap the fruits of his labor." On another occasion he wrote, "Now let us love our American soldier boys, give them a helping hand to whip the kaiser...." In a letter to his "Amish brethren" he wanted to show "by the help and grace of God" that "their dread and regret of going to war is uncalled for." Strange words indeed for a former Amish minister!

Government agents investigated the situation at Arthur and found that Kauffman was an "old man about 67 years of age" and a "former member of this church. He had some trouble with the leader of the church" and had been expelled four years earlier. "It would appear," reported one investigator, "that the charges made by Mr. Kauffman are occasioned by personal spite...."[29]

One form that local "super-patriots" at times used to "educate" their more backward neighbors was to daub Mennonites' automobiles and/or buildings, including churches, with yellow paint. The Metamora church, for example, was so "decorated" in 1918. On the one side was painted: "We Buy No Bonds." On the other: "We Are Slackers." The congregation left the paint on for a considerable length of time, thinking the mob might repaint it if removed immediately.[30] The Salem Defenseless church house at Flanagan, mentioned above, was also daubed with yellow paint. Elder Egle stated that the church's attitude in World War I "was firm on the doctrine of nonresistance, nearly all of our boys refusing to do non-combatant service in the camp.... The community was quite hostile for a time toward the Mennonites and our church was painted yellow and a demand was written on the side of the church building that no German should be preached any longer." At the East Bend church at Fisher, vandals splashed yellow paint only on the front door. They also put up a flagpole and flag. Some members wanted to remove it, but Bishop Peter Zehr instructed that it remain flying. It was left there until it became tattered. A similar flag incident occurred at the Hopedale church.[31]

Such paint and flag incidents may also have occurred elsewhere. At least there was further harassment in some communities. In some cases the draft boards were uncooperative. In Freeport, for example, the board was very unsympathetic with COs, which forced them to appeal to secure their CO status.[32]

One major cause of tension in Mennonite communities was the Mennonite attitude on buying war or "Liberty" bonds. Mennonites had little or no difficulty paying their taxes, since they believed they had scriptural support for that. But voluntarily buying war bonds was another matter. In 1918 after Russia was out of the war and Germany transferred troops to the Western Front to begin a terrific drive to end the war, Americans became tense and jittery with the advances of the Germans. The United States put tremendous pressure on its citizens to buy bonds and war stamps and make an all-out effort to win. The present writer recalls how a leading citizen of Eureka, chairman of the local Council of Defense, came out to the Roanoke congregation one Sunday morning in the summer of 1918 to plead the cause of buying bonds. He painted a bleak picture of the progress the German drives were making and what defeat of the Allies might mean. Such conflict, with more or less tension, was present in all Mennonite communities. At Freeport, for example, one member was buried in effigy on the courthouse lawn because he refused to buy bonds. Over the grave appeared this sign: "Here Lies A. J. Meck. He was born before the war and died at the time of the War Chest Drive."[33]

To make a long story short, community pressure became so great that after initial resistance to purchase, and after varied attempted compromises, many Mennonites bought bonds. At least some of them felt uneasy with war bonds on their hands and consciences, and many donated them to good causes such as their church colleges or other church institutions.[34] Even the conservative church at Morrison fell into line. Bishop John Nice and other leaders asked local government officials how to avoid having their homes or church painted yellow because of their CO position. "They were told nothing would happen if they bought war bonds and so that is what they did. The ministers and deacons bought them, too. Nothing was painted yellow."[35]

It is probably correct to say of the Illinois Mennonites in World War I, as Guy F. Hershberger has said of Mennonites nationally: "The various Mennonite groups demonstrated varying degrees of loyalty to the principle of nonresistance; but the majority of the conscripted Mennonites refused service of any kind under the military. A substantial minority accepted noncombatant service, while a few accepted combatant service." Hershberger also states that World War I made it clear both to the Mennonites and to the government that no form of service under the military was suitable for Mennonite COs. A second result was that "the farm furlough and the reconstruction program under the American Friends Service Committee pointed the way to the system of alternative service which was used during World War II." As to loyalty to nonresistance, a writer on the Kansas Mennonites in World War I concluded that "the degree of separation from the world was directly related to the rigidity of each sect's [branch's] stand on nonresistance."[36] The same statement, it appears, would be true of the Illinois Mennonites. Apparently no statistical breakdown of COs and the kind of work they accepted in World War I is available by Mennonite groups and conferences. But a statistical report of the Central Conference (largely Illinois) shows that twenty-six enlisted and forty-four were drafted. Of these, thirty-eight were in combatant service, twenty-seven in noncombatant work, and five accepted no service. Thus less than half of that group followed the teaching of the church on nonresistance.[37]

After World War I peace activity continued among Illinois Mennonites with varied intensity. In 1922 C. F. Derstine published an article with a significant title, "The World War Is Over—Not Yet." He sensibly argued that the immediate postwar period was a good time to press the cause of peace because people were fed up with war. He also stated realistically that Mennonites should plan as if there would be another war, in order that they might be better prepared than they were in the last one.[38] A little later Deacon David E. Plank of the Roanoke congregation feared that "we Mennonites are getting away a bit from the nonresistant doctrine.... We can talk about 'peace' without mentioning this unpopular doctrine, but the farther away we get from Christ's real and only remedy, the less effective our 'peace talk' will become." He felt that unless the Mennonites consistently and wholeheartedly followed the doctrine in time of peace they would find themselves in an "uncomfortable position" in another war.[39]

One matter that divided pacifists after World War I was the extent to which Christian pacifists should support all peace activities and movements, whether or not they were based on nonresistance. Mennonites, too, became divided on this question. There was a great deal of talk in this period about such matters as disarmament, peaceful settlement of disputes through the League of Nations and the World Court, and the outlawry of war. Some of the more Fundamentalistically inclined believed not only that the government must use the sword but that the church should not give advice to the government, and also should not work with peace advocates who were not biblically nonresistant. Some Mennonites even feared that disarmament might have led to "Red Revolution."[40]

Bishop J. S. Shoemaker of Freeport took a middle ground. He felt that all "movements that have a tendency to lead civil authorities, states, and nations to 'beat their swords into plow-shares, and their spears into pruninghooks,' are to be commended by all peace-loving people." But, he added, it was evident that "many of the present day peace advocates are simply legal, civil, and semi-Christian pacifists who are void of the true Christian pacifism as taught and exemplified by Christ and His apostles."[41]

A different Illinois Mennonite view of war shows the influence of dispensationalist millennialism with its postponement theory. Those Illinois Mennonites who accepted this theory of course claimed that the "sermon on the mount was given to Israel and not to the church," and that Paul, apostle to the Gentiles, "does not tell us to adhere to the sermon on the mount or to the ten commandments." Similarly, he "does not tell us that the Lord's Prayer is ours." Rather Israel is looking for that kingdom and not we."[42] While some Illinois Mennonites accepted the premillennial and dispensationalist view, the present writer has found no evidence that many accepted the postponement theory with reference to the Sermon on the Mount.

So the Illinois Mennonite peace witness in the inter-war period continued to take on various hues and colors. C. Henry Smith, still feel-

Illinois Mennonites and War 359

ing closely associated with Illinois, continued his passionate pleas for peace and peacemaking, arguing that if the Mennonites were to give up the principle they would lose the reason for their separate existence. The Ministerial Association of the Central Conference pledged support to its Peace Committee in its efforts to promote peace in line with the Mennonite peace heritage. The same group objected to affiliation with labor unions because in "spirit and often in practice" they were "at variance with the Christian principles of nonresistance an[d] nonviolence." In 1927 Pastor Ward S. Shelly and his Carlock congregation hosted a conference of peace churches—Friends, Church of the Brethren, and Mennonites. More activist than some, the conferees agreed among other things, to protest against compulsory military training, to try to work out "Christian solutions of some of the definite problems of foreign policy as they arise," and to mount an educational program in an effort to create the will to peace. Declaring that agencies such as the League of Nations and the World Court should be supported, they recognized a difference between warfare and the use of a police force. In March, 1939, a Mennonite peace conference was held at the Mennonite Home Mission in Chicago. This was said to be the "first time in American Mennonite history that representatives of seven Mennonite groups met to acquaint each other" with the peace attitudes, activities, and problems. Illinois was well represented. The Executive Committee of the Illinois Mennonite Conference, in cooperation with the Peace Committee of the (Old) Mennonite General Conference and with the Goshen College Peace Society, got together "for the purpose of working out a suitable program on the peace question." The group arranged for peace lectures and peace conferences in a number of the congregations. The attendance and interest in these meetings were good.[43]

A witness of a different tone was the following item reported by Pastor I. R. Calhoun of the Southwestern Gospel Tabernacle: "The Aaron Post of the American Legion, which is engaged exclusively in witnessing for Christ, had charge of the evening service Sunday, June 11. It was a time of inspiration and good fellowship." This was not the usual kind of report coming from Mennonite churches.[44]

Also different but less unusual was a report by the Northern Bible Society "To Our Mennonite and Amish Bishops, Ministers and Laymen," written by a Mennonite, probably a Mr. Bechler. He pointed out how "we as Mennonites" should be thankful for this land of freedom of worship and for a government which respects the rights of conscience. How can we as a "defenseless people" repay this great debt? He answered: by helping distribute Bibles in the United States to those who do not have them. We would not only be doing missionary work but also something to "help save America." Every "person or family or community that we win for Bible reading is added strength to our government in supporting the authority of the law of the land. We therefore reduce the possibilities for communism gaining a foothold in America." This was one way, thought the writer, in which we could demonstrate "real patriotism in our hearts."[45]

With the approach and outbreak of World War II in 1939, Mennonites again became very concerned. The passage of the Conscription Act of 1940 by Congress and the steps leading to the intervention of the United States in the war did not, of course, decrease the concern. But thanks to the experiences of World War I, the government officials and historic peace churches were now better prepared to handle the CO problem. This was due also to the fact that representatives from the peace churches had met on various occasions in the late 1930s and 1940 with government officials to keep them informed on COs.[46] When the Selective Training and Service Act of 1940 was passed, both sides agreed that men with conscientious scruples against both combatant and noncombatant military service should not be taken to the military camps as they had been in World War I. The law provided that all conscripted persons "who by reason of religious training and belief" could not conscientiously accept any service under the military should "be assigned to work of national importance under civilian direction." This was carried out through that part of the act that provided for the establishment of Civilian Public Service (CPS), which Don Smucker has called the "most far-reaching and comprehensive relationship to government in the history of the Mennonite Church."[47] Yet these relatively liberal, civilian provisions for conscripted COs did not come easily. It took a great deal of persuading of members of Congress. It would appear, Melvin Gingerich has said, "that the Brethren and Mennonites had taken the leadership in working out plans for action in case of conscription and war but that the Friends had taken the leadership in getting these concepts into the Selective Training and Service Act of 1940."[48]

Beginning in May of 1941, various Civilian Public Service camps were established to which COs were assigned to carry on such work as soil conservation, forestry work, assistance in hospitals (especially mental hospitals), and public health service. The administration of Civilian Public Service (CPS) was a cooperative arrangement in which the churches, chiefly the historic peace churches, assumed responsibility for the religious and other phases of camp life while the government was responsible for the work projects. The Mennonite Central Committee (MCC) was the inter-Mennonite agency responsible for the Mennonite CPS camps. In a few cases either the Brethren Service Committee or the Friends Service Committee cooperated with MCC in operating camps. In order to have a unified approach to the government the peace churches set up the National Service Board for Religious Objectors. Religious groups other than the historic peace churches had some COs—the Methodists, for instance, had 673—and these, too, had some representation on the above board.[49]

The Mennonites had by far the largest number of COs in these camps—4,665 out of a total of approximately 12,000. Of these, nationwide, the (Old) Mennonites had 59.5 percent of its drafted men in CPS, the Mennonite Brethren 36.4 percent, the General Conference Mennonites 26.6 percent, the Defenseless Mennonites 10.2 percent, and the Central Conference, with only eight of twenty-two churches reporting, 24 percent.[50] One authority has pointed to "considerable variation in the percentage of the different branches of the church as well as between the district conferences within a single branch of the church and also between congregations in the same district." The nationwide figures for all Mennonite draftees show that 39.6 percent chose regular military service, 14.5 percent accepted noncombatant service in the army, and only 45.9 percent chose alternative service. In other words only a minority of the most peace-minded of historic peace churches took the full-fledged CO position![51]

Unfortunately, it is difficult to get a breakdown of Mennonite draft figures by states, although there is one for (Old) Mennonites, the largest group in Illinois. The percentages were as follows: those taking regular army service, 38.6; those in noncombatant army service, 16.3; those in CPS camps, 45. All the other (Old) Mennonite district conferences, except one (Southwestern Pennsylvania, which had 41.8 percent in CPS), had higher percentages in CPS. But the Illinois (Old) Mennonite percentages were strikingly close to those of Mennonite draftees as a whole: 38.6 and 39.5 in regular army service; 16.3 and 14.2 in noncombatant service in the army; 45 and 46.2 in CPS.[52]

The Mennonite Encyclopedia (I, 607-09) lists the CPS camps and units operated either individually by the MCC or jointly with the Brethren or Friends Service Committee. About ninety percent were operated solely by MCC. Of the approximately ninety camps, units, and projects listed, only one was located in Illinois. This was at Henry, about thirty-five miles north of Peoria. It opened in November, 1941, and closed in November, 1942, when it was moved to Downey, Idaho. Leland Bachman of Morton served as the first director and Mrs. Bachman as matron. When the Bachmans transferred to a new camp at North Fork, California, in May of 1942, Mr. and Mrs. Ora Keiser of Kalona, Iowa, took their places. When a tornado struck the town of nearby Lacon the CPS boys offered their aid and contributed over 2,400 working days to its relief and construction. In addition to Camp Henry, operated in Illinois by MCC, however, there was a CPS unit under the administration of the Association of Catholic Conscientious

Objectors at the Alexian Brothers Hospital in Chicago, and at least twelve Mennonites served there. As to the number of men the various states had in Mennonite CPS camps, a survey showed that Illinois stood fifth in the list with 144. Kansas was first, Pennsylvania second, Ohio third, and Indiana fourth.[53]

The CPS system had both strengths and weaknesses. Since these have been ably discussed, especially by Melvin Gingerich and Guy F. Hershberger, they will not be repeated here. On balance it seems quite clear that the CO problem was handled much better than in World War I. Among both those drafted and the COs who remained at home, conditions and public relations were better. One reason for this was that the American public on the whole acted more maturely and less hysterically against all things German than in World War I. COs were not considered great heroes, of course. Far from it. They were resented, sometimes severely. For example, the Hopedale Mennonite Church was daubed with yellow paint, treatment that was much more common in the First World War than in the Second. The question of war bonds was still a problem for Mennonites. Church leaders and government officials made some progress toward a solution by providing special peace bond issues, the money supposedly to be used only for peaceful, constructive purposes.[54] This was hardly more than a Band-Aid, however, since the plan simply released more of other revenues for war purposes. But Mennonites could say that others were responsible for the war expenses, and they bought the civilian bonds in considerable amounts. As of July 31, 1944, Illinois was second highest in the purchase of these bonds ($648,612), surpassed only by Pennsylvania with the purchase of $1,179,042.50. The total bought as of that date was $4,769,673. The grand total purchased for the war period was $6,740,161.14.[55]

Though it is generally agreed that Mennonites were better prepared for the Second World War than they were for the first, and also that the government handled the CO problem much better in the second war, one problem continued to concern church leaders: the limited proportion of draftees taking the CO stand. As noted above, only 45 percent of draftees chose alternative service, although that was the official position of all the Mennonite groups. The Central Conference and Defenseless Mennonites (EMC) had the smallest percentages in the CPS camps. Their leaders were not indifferent. Harry E. Bertsche, for example, pastor at Salem and editor of *Zion's Tidings* (Defenseless), praised CPS and added that their conference had gone on record as "wholeheartedly supporting this work." His successor as editor, E. G. Steiner, said in 1944 that if another world war is to be averted, the Christian church must denounce war as sin. "Christ and war," he added, "cannot be harmonized. Either war must go or Christ must go. Love is stronger than force. Why not try love?"⁵⁶

Raymond L. Hartzler, editor of the Central Conference paper the *Christian Evangel*, and Alvin Beachy, editor of the section called "Our Peace Testimony" and a resident of Bloomington at the time, were both staunch advocates of nonresistance. Beachy wrote a strong editorial against war: "Watchman, What of the Night?" The occasion was the response that Mennonite pastors had given to a questionnaire which MCC had sent out to ascertain where the Mennonite boys were serving. Beachy noted that the General Conference Mennonite response was 100 percent, whereas that of the Central Conference was only about 30 percent. Only eight of the twenty-two churches in that conference had reported. He thought these facts were not "pleasant reading for some of us." He was alarmed and wondered whether the small response was due to lack of interest or lack of sympathy with the church's historic peace position. Of the eight churches reporting, out of a total of eighty-seven draftees (to Dec. 1, 1944) fifty-one had taken up regular army service (thus "repudiated the church's standing on war altogether"), thirteen had chosen noncombatant service in the military, and twenty-one had gone into CPS. Though not complete, the figures, thought Beachy, "should disturb us mightily. If ours is a heritage worth preserving, then it behooves us to remind ourselves that no generation can float into heaven on the reputation of the preceding one. Unless we make some investment in the heritage ourselves, it is extremely doubtful whether it will be anything but a dim, hazy memory in generations which will follow."⁵⁷

At least one minister, Ben Esch, pastor in one of the largest Central Conference churches in Illinois, was quite unhappy about Beachy's editorial, with the questionnaire, and with the way many Mennonite leaders were interpreting nonresistance. He felt strongly that the brethren should have manifested more tolerance with each other. He then pointed out what he thought were three examples of intolerance. One involved "a Mr. Harold Bender" who a few years earlier had been "sent to our church to speak on the M.C.C. program." Esch, who had entertained the speaker in his home, was "very much displeased when told that this man took the pains of telling others that Ben Esch had fallen so low in Mennonite doctrine that he has pictures of his sons [who had joined the navy] dressed in uniforms where they can be seen in his living room. I say that this parading the fact that a certain Mennonite preacher did not disown his sons because they decided to take regular service in the Navy is an example of intolerance." Another example, Esch thought, was when he was criticized by a Central Conference minister for telling a group of boys at a retreat about some of his son's experiences on board a cruiser. A third example Esch cited was a report that the new Mennonite Biblical

Seminary then opening up in Chicago refused to hire "one of the outstanding Bible teachers of our conference as a member of the faculty because one of his sons took noncombatant service instead of going CO. *If This Is True* it is a disgusting example of intolerance and a matter that must be explained before that institution can hope to meet any need in our conference." Esch wanted to be sure that his young men, most of whom were in "the regular service," would want to come back to the church after the war and not be lost to the church as a number had been after World War I. These young men, said Esch, wanted to share in the burdens as well as the blessings of democracy and therefore "have been led to stand along side of other young men in the unpleasant task of waging a war which they did not start or desire."[58]

It is not possible to say how many ministers felt as strongly on this side of the question as did Esch. Probably not many did. Moreover, while at one time Calvary was quite militaristic and was almost closed to the CO position some changes have been occurring there more recently, especially among the young people. Many are seriously considering and some accepting the CO option.[59]

But in the light of their own performance, many other Mennonite congregations could not consistently point a critical finger at Calvary because of its CO record. Calvary in Chicago (Defenseless) had twenty-two stars in its service flag.[60] One of these was gold representing a death in Normandy. In addition, two persons had received purple hearts and one had received the bronze star for exceptional merit. From Groveland (Defenseless) fifteen were drafted or enlisted, according to one record. At least fourteen of these were in the army.[61] A few statistics are also available from (Old) Mennonite congregations. Metamora had ten in the army and six in CPS; Hopedale, twenty in the army and eight in CPS; Freeport, one in the army and three in CPS; Fisher, fifteen in the army and eight in CPS; Arthur, four in the army and seven in CPS; Cullom, one in each.[62]

Apparently Illinois did its full share to support and operate the CPS program. Included in the CPS personnel from Illinois were, among others, Rev. and Mrs. Leland Bachman and Rev. and Mrs. Raymond L. Hartzler. Bachman, of course, served as director of several camps, including Camp Henry, and his wife served as matron. Hartzler, after serving as director of CPS camps at Bluffton and Medaryville, Indiana, helped expand and set up new dairy testing service units in Wisconsin and Michigan in 1943. Later that year he was appointed middle-states-area CPS supervisor and pastor. During the course of his labors with CPS, Hartzler became well acquainted with General Lewis B. Hershey, the Director of Selective Service. Hershey, who incidentally was from northern Indiana and of Amish Mennonite background, was sympathetic with the CPS program and helpful in setting it up and directing it in the right course. For example, when the Mennonites were considering whether they should ask for financial support from the government for the program, General Hershey advised against it. "If the government pays the cost," he said, "it will also operate the camps." If that happens, he added, "you and I will have lost a great advantage." Hartzler also reported that [about 1950 and 1951] the General helped remove the old barriers set up in 1943 against COs serving abroad in relief work.[63]

The draftees were not paid for work performed in the regular base camps and were given only maintenance wages of fifteen dollars per month in the special projects. MCC set up per capita quotas from time to time which it asked the constituency to contribute for the operation of the church's part of the program. Conferences varied considerably in their faithfulness in meeting these quotas. The different bodies also could and did make additional money contributions to their own members in the program, and such support also varied. For example, the (Old) Mennonites of Illinois apparently had 102 men in CPS. Of these a total of ninety-four, says the report, "received money from the CPS Committee at the rate of $2.34 per month plus a $10.00 payment made to those who were in camp in October 1944. A total of $8,792.69 was paid to our brethren, an average of $93.54. The largest sum paid to one man was $135 for four years, five months, and twelve days in camp. The smallest sum was $11.70 for five months. Altogther Illinois CPS men served a total of 310 years and four-and-one-half months, or an average of slightly more than three years each." Presumably eight men of the 102 total were not in camp long enough to receive payment.[64] With such meager payments, certainly no one was tempted to go into CPS for economic reasons!

Demobilization for Illinois Mennonite servicemen was something of a problem as it was for others, from several angles. One writer, probably Leland Bachman, wrote after the war that while the CPS system had terminated, "the spirit of service should never end within us." Unless this spirit continues to control us, "a large part of our testimony given through CPS will have been lost. I just now recall," he continued, "what a preacher of another denomination told the CPS men at Henry, Illinois, in the beginning of the CPS program. He said, 'You have now attracted our attention, but what we are going to watch is, what are you going to do after this is over to prove that you have something.' ... This opportunity is now ours to exhibit this spirit of service."[65] By and large these young men, along with many young ladies in the church, met this test in the years that followed.

Another problem that Mennonite boys faced when returning home was that of understanding the people who had remained there and had made more money than ever before because of high war prices, while those in service, especially in CPS, were laboring sacrificially. Another was differences in interpreting peace and nonresistance. And since so many draftees chose regular service, they and the COs faced the problem of fusing once again into one understanding brotherhood. Church leaders handled this last problem differently in different congregations, areas, and conferences. In some of the stricter bodies those who had chosen military service were automatically expelled and could not be taken in again until they confessed their sin. Other groups did nothing. Among the (Old) Mennonites practice was not uniform, some congregations requiring more of an adjustment than others. In 1945 delegates at the Illinois Mennonite Conference, after noting that statistics revealed a "laxity of teaching and example," bowed their "faces in shame and repentance," begged "forgiveness for our neglect and failure" in teaching, and pledged themselves "to more faithfully preach and teach" the principle of nonresistance. The conference also resolved that "in dealing with those who have erred" on this principle "we endeavor by love to effect a restoration to fellowship and to the joy of Christian service."

In practice the (Old) Mennonites took a sort of middle way. Hopedale is an example. This congregation, which had many more in the army than in CPS, was not clear what course to follow and postponed the holding of communion a time or two. Bishop Simon Litwiller, Minister Ben Springer, and Arthur W. Nafziger, an influential layman who had kept in close touch by correspondence with all the boys during the war, worked out a brief statement to which those who had served in the military felt they could agree. The main parts of the statement affirmed: "1. It is my sincere desire to fellowship with the church and I humbly beg the forgiveness of any I have offended. 2. It is my desire to live daily by the guidance of the Holy Spirit according to the Word of God. 3. I also want to exercise a Christlike forgiving spirit toward all the brethern [sic] and sisters." For several reasons, including the feeling that some in the congregation needed to affirm the statement as much as those who had served in the military, the bishop put the question to the entire membership. Thus all more or less reaffirmed the principle of nonresistance and could again experience the reality of unity and communion.[66]

What has been the attitude of the Illinois Mennonites on war since World War II? Has there been an erosion or an increase of nonresistance? Unfortunately, specific statistical studies are not available. Peace conferences, addresses, and writings have continued as much as ever. The official positions of the Mennonite bodies remained committed to the peace principles as strongly as before, with one or two exceptions. An exception is, for example, the Evangelical

Mennonite Church (formerly Defenseless Mennonites). It has diluted its position on nonresistance in recent years. Its *Manual* (1960, 31-32) states that the church's historic position is to "oppose the bearing of arms in warfare," but that the church "respects the right of individual conviction and recognizes that various positions will be taken on war and military service." In 1980 even that language was in process of change. A proposed revision stated that:

> ... we uphold our Christian youth who, because of faith and conscience, choose to express the law of love uniformly in personal, social and civil relationships and to seek exemption from or alternatives to combat service.... We also respect the right of individual conviction and recognize that various positions will be taken on military service and law enforcement. Therefore, we support those who choose to serve in agencies of civil government, such as the military or police force, because civil government is recognized as God's servant. Romans 13:4.[67]

This statement brings theory into line with the practice of this body. In the Kauffman-Harder study (*Anabaptists Four Centuries Later*, 1975), only 20 percent of EMC members surveyed (as compared to seventy-three per cent of all Mennonites) strongly agreed or agreed with this statement: "The Christian should take no part in war or any war-promoting activities."[68] Evangelical Mennonite historian Stan Nussbaum has said that the history of the EMC reveals a growing "indifference or indecision on a large number of peripheral issues" and "an increasing tendency to treat Anabaptist distinctives [including nonresistance] as peripheral rather than fundamental." He adds that during Henry Egly's time Menno Simons was the "pole star of EMC Doctrine." But "since the sunlight dawned on [Joseph] Ramseyer, it has become harder and harder for EMC to find that star."[69]

Of course, not all EMC members would agree with Nussbaum's assessment. On the other hand, some in other Mennonite bodies would agree that the same tendencies had appeared in their own Mennonite branches. The figures coming out of World War II indicated much practice in line with that judgment. The picture is a mixed one. While on the whole the peace witness continued strong, occasionally some voice was a bit muffled or even negative, or there were differences in interpretation and application. Illinois continued to have its share of good peace conferences and participated in others beyond its borders. Its speakers continued to produce valuable addresses and its writers good articles on peace. Heinz Janzen, pastor of Calvary at Washington, was one of these. A committed believer in nonresistance, Janzen thought Mennonites must "reinstate church discipline." "Will not permissiveness," he continued, "drag down what few ideals remain in the church? Already in some congregations the principle of nonresistance is a pulpit ideal completely rejected by the laymen."[70] It is probable he had his own congregation in mind, among others. The presence of the Mennonite Biblical Seminary in Chicago for a number of years added considerably to the state's Mennonite peace witness.

Fear of erosion of the peace principle existed among the Illinois (Old) Mennonites also. In 1952, as secretary of the Illinois Mennonite Conference, Richard J. Yordy told Harold S. Bender, "Some of us are faced with congregations in which a large minority no longer believe in non-resistance ... and we hardly know what to do to make our teaching effective." Yordy asked Bender to speak at the forthcoming Illinois Mennonite Conference to help the cause. To this same end the Illinois people welcomed closer cooperation with the (Old) Mennonite Church's denominational Peace Problems Committee, of which Guy Hershberger was chairman.[71]

Tensions that plagued most Americans as a result of the Korean War and the still more tragic and divisive Vietnam struggle also affected the Mennonites. In 1965 Warren R. Salzman of Heyworth, Illinois, was becoming increasingly concerned about trends in the General Conference paper, *The Mennonite*. He objected to a letter in an earlier issue which had suggested that Mennonites and others should refuse to pay war taxes. Salzman did not think the United States should have been hampered in carrying out its defense program. He felt that United States military power was not a threat of war or a threat against any country, but was to be used to defend the free world. "The threat of war today," Salzman continued, "is the result of the announced intention of leaders of other nations to dominate the entire earth by whatever means necessary. We must do what we can to stop communism, and it would not be to our credit if He should find us more on their side than His." Mennonites could not be neutral, Salzman concluded, and any action which hampered United States' efforts to stop communism would be aiding the enemy.

Similarly, Milt Sprunger from Washington defended Christian and Missionary Alliance missionaries in Vietnam whom some had criticized for close identification with American foreign policy in that country. Mrs. Wilton Ulrich from Flanagan thought that since the government recognized the right to alternative service, in lieu of military service, Mennonites did not have the right to object to the war in Vietnam. She thought the General Conference Church could not bring peace anyway, because Christ had said there would be no peace on earth. She added that pastors needed to be "standing in our pulpits shouting out some 'fire and brimstone' sermons to us."[72]

To what extent these opinions so typical of popular American attitudes were representative of Illinois Mennonites is difficult to say. Among Mennonite leaders in Illinois, it is quite clear that they were minority opinions. But the beliefs probably represented a much larger proportion of the laity. Many lay people, of course, held opposite opinions. Raymond Baer of Summerfield, for example, took strong exception to some statements made by a writer in *The Mennonite* (Jan. 20, 1970) to the effect that the war in Vietnam would open more of the area to Christian missionaries, and that we were fighting the war to let the Vietnamese determine their own future, democratically. Baer cited President Eisenhower's refusal to permit free elections in 1956, despite a previous agreement, because Ho Chi Minh and his followers would have won. Baer insisted that such a course could bring only dissent, polarization, and ruin in Vietnam and in the United States.[73]

Many other Illinois Mennonites also objected to our Vietnam policy. Keith Reimer of Chicago said President Nixon and his Vietnam policy were weighed in the balance and found wanting. The Woodlawn Mennonite and the Markham Community (Mennonite) Churches in Chicago publicly protested, organized peace caravans, handed out literature, and wrote local papers condemning U.S. Vietnam policies. This, said Stanley Bohn, Central District Conference Minister, was one of the boldest peace witnesses made.[74]

Beyond doubt, the Vietnam fiasco helped increase cynicism in the 1960s and early 1970s, especially among young people. And no doubt, Mennonites shared the trend. On the other hand, some reacted against this cynical, critical attitude. Mildred Brenneman of Pekin no doubt represented the feelings of a number when she wrote in *The Mennonite* (July 28, 1970): "... I want you to know that I love my country and will fly its flag on my car, at my door, and get others to do the same.... Ben Franklin, George Washington, Thomas Jefferson, Abe Lincoln, and many others built our U.S. of America and started it with prayer and with blood. Do the Mennonites," she continued, "want to help destroy it, now? I'm almost ashamed to say 'I'm a Mennonite.' Maybe I should have joined my mother's Baptist church." Catherine Huette of Morton was similarly critical of the *Gospel Herald* for its attitude toward the United States in its bicentennial year of 1976. (*GH*, March 2, 1976). She felt that Mennonites seemed so insecure that "we are not able to have any good feelings about our country and love God at the same time." She advised one writer who couldn't sing "God Bless America" to move to Russia and sing "God Bless Russia." She did praise some good articles on the subject. Asking for more "prayerful support" for the country, she concluded, "I am proud to be a Christian, happy to be an American, but have some anxious moments at being a Mennonite from the stand some of our 'leaders' are taking."

No doubt Robert S. Kreider's middle position was that of the majority. Born and reared in Illinois, in 1976 Kreider published in *The Mennonite* an article entitled "A Hymn of Affection for a Land and a People." Showing a love for his country, he condemned both extremes. He was critical, but in a loving, constructive way. He saw much to be liked and thankful for. This moved Elva May Roth of the Morton congregation to express similar convictions. She agreed there was much to criticize, but thought "there is still much that is good and inspiring." We could appreciate these things, she thought, without closing our eyes to the evils, which we should know about and work to eliminate.[75]

What effect if any did the growth of cynicism and disillusionment have on the CO position? Whether because of it or in spite of it, the proportion of drafted Mennonites taking that position became larger. In part, it could be because of the disillusionment. For part of the cynicism of young people had to do with their increased doubts about the supposed heroics and glamor of war. But there were also other fundamental reasons.

In 1956 Floyd Metz, Goshen College senior, made a valuable study for the (Old) Mennonites entitled "Analysis of the Draft Census of the Franconia, Illinois, Indiana-Michigan, Ohio, South Central and Pacific Conferences, January 1, 1952-April 1956." Metz thought that despite some weaknesses in the statistical analysis, the figures "probably" gave "reason for guarded optimism"; that is, a considerably higher percentage chose the CO position than in World War II. In these conferences the range of those selecting the CO position was from Illinois' low of 74 per cent to Franconia's high of 97.7. Put differently, in Illinois, 26 percent chose the military. The average for all the six conferences was 10.7 percent. In this study those in the armed forces included the minority who opted for noncombatant service.

In his summary Metz pointed out that the percentage of COs rose from about 50 percent in World War II[76] to 89.3 in this study. But he warned "one should not become over-optimistic because figures frequently do not tell the whole story." Metz attributed the significant increase in COs to the following:

> 1. An increased awareness on the part of the church to this problem as a result of the World War II survey. 2. An increased amount of education on the subject of Biblical nonresistance. 3. A greater number of young people attending our church colleges and high schools. 4. Less pressure and/or a lower emotional pitch on the part of secular society and hence less pressure on the young people of draft age. 5. With a few exceptions, more lenient draft boards.

Metz might have added another explanation: that I-W service did not require as much financial sacrifice as CPS had demanded.

In connection with the fifth point, it might be pointed out that the conference with the most lenient draft board (Franconia) had the highest percentage of COs. In connection with point three (to which seminaries should be added), it is significant that Metz's study shows that the college graduate group had the highest percentage of COs.[77]

Other evidence indicates that the higher percentage of COs continued in the 1960s and 1970s, due in part to the frustrations and disillusionment over Vietnam, and in part to more teaching, as noted above. Wrote Leland Harder in 1971: "The fact is that there has been a genuine renewal of commitment to the way of nonresistance among the young people of the General Conference [including the Central District], which began after the Selective Service Act of 1948 was enacted."[78]

Another study has indicated that the CO position has been rooted more strongly in rural than in urban life. Leland Harder made a study of this in the General Conference churches in 1960:

	Men in military service	Men in alternative service
141 country churches	43.4%	56.7%
124 town churches	60.5%	39.5%
85 city churches	71.8%	28.2%

"It would appear," said Harder, "that the more urban a Conference congregation, the less likely is a member to register as a war dissenter." Nevertheless, Harder insisted that General Conference's "post-war introspection has led to renewed commitment to the ethic of nonresistance."[79]

A growing trend and problem—which to some may seem a bit contradictory to this evidence that a higher percentage have taken the CO position recently—is the increasing involvement of peaceful Mennonites in politics and community affairs. One example of this is the Normal Mennonite congregation, until recently a part of the General Conference Mennonites only, but now affiliated with the Illinois (Old) Mennonite Conference as well. Recently for a number of years one of its members was the sheriff of McLean County. This fact, it seems, has not caused undue tension in the congregation or brotherhood. A humane, mild-mannered person, sensitive to the needs of offenders, John King used his powers of law enforcement constructively. He was reelected by a good margin for a second term. But however constructive and however successful a sheriff might be, in America the term "Mennonite sheriff" used to sound like a contradiction of terms, and probably still does to many Mennonites. But the point is, not to as many as formerly. Nor is this "new method of thinking" limited to the more "liberal" General Conference Mennonites in Illinois. One (Old)

Mennonite minister, who has the American Legion represented in his membership, recently stated that he thought he could accept a governor or United States senator as a member of his congregation.[80]

Another problem has been evangelistic outreach and inculcation. The veteran leader R. L. Hartzler expressed himself on this point in connection with the evangelistic crusade represented by Key 73—the renewal emphasis that Mennonites and others put on evangelism in the period around 1973. Hartzler raised the question that if too many are brought into the church too quickly without proper inculcation, especially from non-Mennonite backgrounds, what will happen to doctrines such as nonresistance? He thought we had not been very successful in this regard in the past. Apparently those who have succeeded most in outreach in the past, Hartzler continued, have not succeeded with nonresistance, and, vice versa. He concluded: "The prevailing pattern has been that where evangelism has been most stressed, the other has been weak or even challenged." Robert Harnish, who was pastor of the (Old) Mennonite congregation at Highway Village from 1951 to 1973, made a similar observation. Some in his congregation, almost totally non-Mennonite in background, had trouble with nonresistance. Belief in it was not made a test of membership. He accepted the people where they were, continued to teach the doctrine, of course, and believed that with time more and more, especially younger members, would accept it without difficulty.[81]

One issue current among the Illinois Mennonites as elsewhere is the payment of war taxes. Since such a large proportion of United States taxes now goes for the support of war, more people are protesting, even though the payment of taxes has biblical sanction. A few protest to the point of refusing to pay that portion which supports the military. This is illustrated by the case of Bruce Chrisman, thirty-year-old General Conference Mennonite of Ava in southern Illinois. In filing his federal tax returns Chrisman refused to pay the war tax and said in letters accompanying his returns that he had to decline on religious grounds, claiming exemption under the first amendment to the United States Constitution. Despite assistance from General Conference leaders James Dunn, Robert Hull, and Peter Ediger, Chrisman was convicted December 3, 1979, in United States District Court in Springfield, Illinois, for income tax evasion. He faced a sentence up to one year in prison and a fine of $10,000. On January 2, 1980, however, he received an unusual sentence: serving one year in Mennonite Voluntary Service. Delighted with the sentence, probably the first of its kind in a tax case, Chrisman was not happy that the court ruled the first amendment was not relevant in his case. He is appealing that part of the decision. Chrisman is married and has a two-year-old daughter.[82]

Another unusual case involving a conscientious objector was that of Abraham Warkentin, who lived in Chicago for some years in the 1930s and 1940s. Born in Russia, Warkentin came to the United States after World War I and sought to become a U.S. citizen in the 1930s. By this time the immigration and naturalization officials had begun to ask applicants for citizenship whether they would be willing, if necessary, to bear arms in defense of the country. Since as a CO Warkentin replied in the negative, the officials denied him citizenship. Other applicants in a similar situation were also denied citizenship during this period. This question of naturalization for CO immigrants was not resolved until some years later, when the U.S. Supreme Court reinterpreted the obligations of citizenship in such a way that defending the U.S. constitution was not equated with bearing arms.[83]

In concluding this chapter on the Illinois Mennonites on peace and war, it is probably in order to note C. Henry Smith's contribution to the furthering of the doctrine of nonresistance. Smith never forgot his Illinois connections. He maintained close contacts through visits, lectures, correspondence, and published writings. In particular his autobiography, "The Education of a Mennonite Country Boy" (changed later by his publisher to *Mennonite Country Boy, The Early Years of C. Henry Smith* [Faith and Life Press, Newton, Kansas, © 1962]), shows his continued attachment to his native state. This work and other writings also indicate the strong convictions he had on peace and war. For instance, in writing about his experiences as an undergraduate student at the University of Illinois, he stated:

> One other experience during the first weeks of that first semester I remember distinctly—my petition to the faculty to be excused from military training on the grounds of conscientious scruples. Then, as now, military drill was compulsory in all state universities [more precisely in all land grant colleges]. I was a Mennonite. Mennonites, like the Quakers, believe that love is a more potent solvent of social misunderstandings than hate, that force can never settle any problem affecting the relations of normal human beings, and that peace is always to be preferred to war among the nations of the world. Mennonites believe this so thoroughly that they have given this belief the sanction of a religious doctrine as essential and sacred as any other in their creed. Of all the religious principles which distinguish Mennonites from other Protestant groups I have always respected this as the most fundamental and one which it seemed to me was grounded on sound logic and correct social philosophy as well as on Scripture. It is the one bit of Mennonitism which remains longest with those Mennonites who, for some reason or other, have departed from their early faith for other associations and affiliations.
>
> Believing as I did that the war system was all wrong, I saw no consistency in drilling for war. I accordingly petitioned the faculty for release from this part of the university course, stating my reason for the request. It was, undoubtedly, an unusual and peculiar request. I was told afterward that only once before had a similar favor been requested, and

that by a Quaker student. It, evidently, was a question to be decided only by the highest university authorities, for I was sent to both the commanding officer in charge of the training, Major Fechet, and to President Draper. To my surprise, both the president and the major gave me a most courteous and sympathetic hearing. The major, especially, was most considerate and readily agreed that there should be the greatest freedom of conscience in this as in all other matters.[84]

Smith maintained these convictions throughout his life. A unique will that he wrote in the year of his passing (1948) is further evidence. Smith put the major portion of his estate into a trust, the income from which was to be used by his wife, Laura Ioder Smith. After her passing the income was to be divided into two equal parts. One part was to be used for scholarships at Bluffton and Goshen for descendants of Bishop John Smith (or for others at these two institutions as the Board of Directors of the Trust Fund might direct under certain circumstances). The other half of the income was to be used for the "promotion, and dissemination among the Mennonite colleges and churches, in such manner as the Board of Directors may see fit, of the traditional nonresistant peace doctrines as taught by the Mennonite church of America during the past two centuries." While teaching at Goshen College Smith and President N. E. Byers had taken initiative to organize an Intercollegiate Peace Association, to promote study of war and peace. This organization—with the word "Speech" later added to the name—has actively and uninterruptedly continued down to the present. Smith's will thus provides funds which, though not large, are enough to make an important impact on the Mennonite colleges and churches, and to carry forward effectively the concern for peace and nonresistance that the donor held throughout his life.

CHAPTER 14

Illinois Mennonites and Social Issues

This chapter will deal with the responses of the Illinois Mennonites to such social issues as race relations, civil rights, the temperance movement, labor-capital problems, women's rights, poverty, reform movements, and use of the political process. What should be the attitude of the Christian toward such problems? And if they are legitimate concerns of the church, how should Christians attack them? Few issues have produced more division of opinion and tension. No doubt part of the controversy has come from misunderstanding the meaning of terms. All no doubt agree that the gospel should be preached. But what gospel and how and to whom? Should the so-called "social gospel" be included? This is where much of the controversy has arisen. And the various viewpoints are represented among Illinois Mennonites as elsewhere.

There are those, usually the more conservative and fundamentalistic, who believe that preaching the gospel means proclaiming the story of Christ's crucifixion, resurrection, and ascension and man's regeneration through acceptance of him as personal Savior. That, plus guidance by the Holy Spirit and the reading of his Word, will take care of other problems. Others, however, believe the gospel, in addition to the story of human redemption wrought on Calvary, includes working on everyday problems which beset the Christian and applying the teachings of the Bible and especially of Jesus to their solution. As Ed Riddick, Mennonite lay minister of Chicago, put it: "There is the continuing necessity for prayer, spirituality, and the conversion of individual souls. But ministry takes on its full dimension only when we wrestle with war-spending, the problem of people living in squalor, labor relations, or unity and harmony within the shop and factory." Riddick added: "And we can attack these problems as an expression of faith...."[1]

The dichotomy between social action and evangelism has been

unfortunate and unnecessary. As George R. Brunk, well-known (Old) Mennonite evangelist, has said, "Let's bury this dichotomy between" the two. No doubt much of the misunderstanding and polarization of thought have come through the use, misuse, and abuse of the term "social gospel." This has meant different things to different people, but in orthodox circles it was often equated with salvation by good works in a social context instead of individual salvation through grace. This has given the terms "social action" or even "social conscience" bad connotations. However, such deductions are not necessary. The best definition or explanation of which the present writer is aware is that of William W. Sweet, a leading authority on American church history. He said the social gospel was an emphasis that developed in the post Civil War period and grew out of the labor disturbances of that period. Laborers accused the Christian churches of being more sympathetic with capital than with labor. This led some of the more progressive church leaders to study the implications of the biblical teachings, especially of Jesus, on social and economic questions. The teachings and writings of such men as Washington Gladden, Walter Rauschenbusch, Charles Sheldon, and others soon exerted wide influence and led to the development of a lively social consciousness and concern among Christians for the application of Christ's teachings to the social and economic problems facing them. Webster's definition of social gospel is even shorter and simpler: "The application of biblical principles and especially the teachings of Jesus to social problems."[2]

Evangelical Christians can thus be faulted on two grounds. They should not have put on the blinders which kept them from seeing the social implications of their faith and the obligation of the church to become involved in the everyday struggles of the working man. And they should not have permitted polarization to develop between them and the more liberal Christians over terms such as "social consciousness," "social concern," or even "social gospel," which in time were misused and abused by more extreme liberals. The dichotomy was not necessary. Even the theologically conservative Salvation Army with its "soap, soup, and salvation" slogan saw the need for social work in connection with evangelism. Fortunately, evangelical Christians have again begun to see the social implications of their faith, and in increasing numbers are broadening their concept of the Christian gospel.[3] In fact, a few evangelical Christians such as William Jennings Bryan had this broader view of the gospel at the very time the so-called social gospel arose. In this Bryan was in a minority. Had more evangelicals had the same foresight the polarization would not have occurred.[4]

Be that as it may, Illinois Mennonites like others struggled with the problem of applying their faith to the social and economic questions of the day. Some, of course, struggled more than others. In fact some groups experienced virtually no conflict at all. The very conservative, exclusive bodies, such as the Reformed Mennonites at Sterling, show virtually no social conscience or concern, for their intention has been to withdraw from the world. Amish groups show a bit more concern: for instance, their support of MCC. And among all groups there are differences of opinion.

According to Kauffman and Harder's study, which included a number of Illinois MC, GC, and EMC churches, the Evangelical Mennonite Church, which ranked highest on concerns having to do with faith, orthodoxy, and Fundamentalism or evangelicalism, ranked lowest or nearly so on such issues as race relations, welfare attitudes, and other ethical and social concerns. On the other hand, the Mennonite Church and the General Conference Mennonites, who in this study ranked high on the ethical and social concerns scales, ranked lower than the others on the Fundamentalist Orthodoxy questions.[5]

One should not assume, of course, that the EMC has been or is united in skepticism toward social concerns. Considerable evidence shows that quite a few members do have a growing social consciousness and think it ought to be still more evident in their church. William T. Pauley, education director and evangelist, thought every member ought to consider giving two years of Voluntary Service (VS) work for the church as "A Part of Their Education." He thought that through a sort of Christian "Peace Corps" the "physical needs of the people of the world" could "best be met by people who can offer spiritual help as well." Paul Jorg, at first skeptical about Mennonite Disaster Service (MDS), defended and promoted it when he found out that those in it were "interested primarily in sharing the love of Christ in word as well as deed." "Let's not pass by on the other side," he added.[6]

Already in 1949 the EMC author of an article, "Why Help the Negro," pointed out how Americans sinned against blacks and, though possibly individually innocent, were collectively responsible for righting the wrongs to "satisfy an angry God." In 1973 Evan Bertsche, who grew up at Gridley, wrote an excellent article on "Social Concerns and the Christian Layman," pointing out a number of areas where the Christian could profitably work out the social implications of his faith. These included: join VS through MCC; become a big brother to a needy boy; visit jails and prisons; visit Salem Children's Home; contact those in less fortunate circumstances such as in ghettos, in Appalachia, or on American Indian reservations, to see how one could help bear their burdens; volunteer services as a board member in local human service programs; "seek ways of reaching out to those alienated by our society—the drug addict, the alcoholic, the law violator"; establish a social concerns committee in each congregation through which "may be channeled outreach efforts to meet human needs as well as spiritual needs."[7]

EMC historian Stan Nussbaum has stated that "from the beginning the evangelistic concern [of the conference] was accompanied by a social concern, a concern to serve needy persons both inside and outside the church whether they responded to the gospel or not." The care of orphans, widows, and the elderly was one such concern. "Institutional work," said the Church's Annual Report of 1924, "does not give us salvation, but we do it because we have salvation. We should do all we can to help the poor and needy." Raising money for these ventures was just as important as raising money for home and foreign missions. Nussbaum mentions the denomination's Salem Gospel Mission in Chicago as the "project which most closely integrated social concern with evangelistic work." Founded in the stockyards district in 1908, the mission combined community service and a gospel witness. The workers served by "entering different homes, helping with the washing, mending clothes, caring for ... the sick, and cleaning up their homes.... It was felt by those in charge that it was only serving fallen humanity as Christ did when He was on earth."[8]

Additional evidence that the EMC has at least been struggling with the problem of social concern is that virtually the entire Winter, 1970, issue of its periodical *Build* was devoted to this matter. The contents indicate differences of opinion on the subject, some writers being more ready than others to acknowledge that preaching the full gospel should include the social and economic problems which the Christian faces in everyday life. One of those most strongly opposed to this approach was an Illinois pastor who was convinced that the ecumenical church or Council of Churches was a political or socialistic machine operating deceptively under a cloak of religion. He says that in Revelation 13 a beast comes out of the sea, representing a world government. Another beast comes out of the earth, representing a world church. The political beast has the second beast (religious forces) working with it to set up a world government and will then destroy it. The pastor then asks whether the socialists or one-worlders are not using the ecumenical churches as a tool to bring about their goal.[9]

The other writers were less extreme in their reaction to social action and saw some place for it in the life of the converted person. Two examples may typify their views. Charles Zimmerman, then president of the conference, said, "Our evangelism must insist that conversion is a beginning, not an end." No amount of social action and service, he continued, can be a substitute for the "explicit testimony to Jesus Christ. But equally, the proclamation of the Gospel will be empty if the one who makes it is not willing to deal honestly and realistically with the issues which his hearers have to face." Thomas Taylor wrote: "Many cry, 'Feed the hungry, help the sick and forget religion.' Others say 'Give them nothing but the gospel of Christ.' The Bible clearly tells us we must do *both*. Many will not listen to the gospel until love is shown them."[10]

In its Summer, 1974, issue *Build* published the document, "A Declaration of Evangelical Social Concern." This was a significant statement of the problem drawn up by some fifty evangelical churchmen who had met in Chicago in the fall of 1973 to discuss and to give expression to their conviction that "biblical faith and social concern are inseparable." It was a forthright acknowledgement that evangelical Christians were guilty of many sins of omission and commission in the fields of race relations, poverty and hunger, and international relations, among others. "So we call our fellow evangelical Christians to demonstrate repentance in a Christian discipleship that confronts the social and political injustice of our nation." *Build* published the statement "for our EMC constituency for consideration in our identifying with the spirit and content of the document and hopefully to motivate action consistent with the concern." As Ronald J. Sider has well said, the declaration indicates "that serious commitment to biblical social concern is growing rapidly among evangelicals." The editor of *Build* published also a slightly condensed version of Myron Augsburger's address at an MCC meeting in Chicago in January 1974. Entitling his address, "The Renewal of Social Concern Among Evangelicals," Augsburger expressed his oft-repeated conviction that "because of our emphasis on discipleship, I think we can hold the Gospel and social service together, instead of letting the two be divorced."[11] These examples show at least that EMC members, like other evangelicals, were exposed to an increasing concern for the social implications of their faith.

Even the still more conservative Krimmer Mennonite Brethren, in regard to their Lincoln Avenue Gospel Mission in Chicago, stated that the purpose of the mission was "to do welfare work, to edify believers and to win souls for Christ."[12]

The development of a social consciousness among the (Old) Mennonites in Illinois came slowly. Probably the rather strong fundamentalistic influences and the confusion over the so-called social gospel have had something to do with this. But early voices and signs also pointed in that direction. Already in the first issue of *Herald of Truth*, John F. Funk published an article by one "M. K." entitled "Man's Social Relations." The article emphasized that everyone should understand his relations to others and "the nature and demands of these obligations." Years later when Charles M. Sheldon published his *In His*

Steps—What Would Jesus Do? Funk promoted it, saying that it was "excellent" and that "everybody should read it."[13]

Social service was not ignored in the founding of missions. One early visitor to the recently established Home Mission in Chicago, having observed conditions in the city during the depression, wrote: "We believe that, according to the example of Christ, it is the duty of Christian people everywhere to aid in alleviating want and woe and helping this poor people out of their misery by clothing and feeding them, and above all, trying to save them from the pit of destruction and teaching them the principles of morality and Christianity."[14] With famine work as stimulant to the starting of foreign missions, social service was also a factor there.

In an article, "Joy in Saving Souls," a writer from Cullom, after speaking of the Christian's task of saving souls, includes this paragraph—a rather strange one for an (Old) Mennonite in 1905:

> The business of a true Christian is to conquer the world. This is a greater task than most of us realize, and invokes a wider view of life than we ordinarily take. We are not merely to kill sin in our own hearts, but we are to make the entire world better in its social, political, intellectual and religious life.[15]

This was a pretty advanced position for a Mennonite at that time.

As the twentieth century progressed more voices arose which indicated a growing social concern. The present writer remembers hearing Henry R. Schertz of Metamora speak on the two arms of the cross—one extending upward to God and reaching down to fallen man (regeneration), and the other reaching horizontally, a symbol of our obligation to serve our fellowman in his various needs. As someone has said, "the debt we owe to God we pay to our fellow man."[16] In a forthright article in 1924 A. E. Kreider represented the thinking of the more progressive element on this point. While we dare not minimize the value of doctrinal statements, it was quite impossible, he wrote, "to compress the living gospel of our Christ into a few statements or paragraphs. No formula or creedal statement can quite adequately express the gospel of God." Christ's gospel has proven itself a "power for social good," continued Kreider. Social conditions have been improved. "There is inherent in the gospel of Christ a moral and spiritual force which if properly released" will make this world more just. "God is a God of justice. His Gospel is a gospel of justice. Will God be worshipped acceptably unless those who receive His gospel strive to establish justice here among men? The message of the Church to be true to its founder must go beyond the preaching of harmless principles."[17]

By the 1940s Paul Erb was saying in the *Gospel Herald* that while the so-called Social Gospel as interpreted by some liberals was wrong, there was on the other side the following danger: "in orthodox theology, it is possible to put such an extreme emphasis on the individual nature of our salvation as to err seriously in the denial of the social implications of the Gospel. Our sense that we are responsible first to God may lead us to deny that we have responsibilities toward our fellow man." However the term "social gospel" might be misused, Erb continued, "the true Gospel is social." Jesus taught that we must contribute to the physical needs of people around us. John, James, and the Old Testament prophets preached justice for the poor and the helpless and condemned those who grew rich at their expense. Since there was great need in the world, and since America had an abundance, the time was near, wrote Erb during the war, for the churches to fulfill a great social obligation to the needy of the world. "There is danger," Erb concluded, "that ... we will forget that the true Gospel is social in all its implications. Sometimes our apparent orthodoxy may merely be an excuse behind which we protect ourselves so that we may continue to live in luxury and comfort while others starve and freeze."[18] Such words from a well-known leader were surely influential.

After mid-century the growth of a social conscience in the Illinois Mennonite Church was still more evident. An interesting example of the combining of the evangelistic and the social is the Ulrich Foundation, formed in 1949 by Ray Ulrich of Roanoke to serve in Puerto Rico and elsewhere. This organization worked alongside but was not organically connected to the Mennonite Mission Board program. Its purpose was to witness in a spiritual way and yet at the same time to challenge Puerto Ricans to make better use of their resources, especially agricultural, and to help them help themselves. Or, as Harold Zehr put it, it tried to get the people to "make a spiritual approach" to their "social and economic problems." With this in mind the Foundation carried on a program of agricultural experimentation, demonstration, education, and extension work. Dr. George Troyer, medical missionary, was interested in helping the Puerto Ricans economically as well as spiritually, and deserves credit for initiating the program which Ulrich carried out through his foundation.[19]

Pastors and other leaders at mid-century began to emphasize more clearly and more frequently the social implications of Christianity. A few examples must suffice. In a missionary sermon at Willow Springs, Tiskilwa, C. Warren Long outlined the congregational goals, which included providing a "Prophetic Voice" in the community and a "Christian service and relief program to give assistance to any person in need." LeRoy Kennel wrote that as a servant-people those in the Lombard congregation were "co-laboring with our Lord even as he goes before us in self-giving ministries wherever there are hurt and hunger." He continued: "Our mission means social action which is the good news that we can live together by the spirit rather than by the flesh.... Acting out the good news may appear ... to some as an overstressed emphasis, but these are unbalanced times." Kennel concluded that "our mission means identifying closely with the community, being there as a Christian source of concern for justice and love." A few months earlier Kennel had put it in these words: "These needs, viewed from the stance of evangelism and social concerns—right relations with God and with fellowman—are the front lines in which the congregation is called to serve." About the same time (1966) Kennel reported on a meeting of the Inter-Mennonite Ministers' Retreat at Camp Menno Haven, where they discussed the mission of the Mennonites in Illinois. The discussion included "the theological base, the geographical and sociological status ... population trends ... and special sphere for total mission, including business, poverty, prisons, politics, race, nationalism and militarism."[20]

In 1974 Paul O. King of Freeport addressed the Illinois Conference, of which he was president, on the topic, "What Are the Issues We Face as a Conference?" Among other emphases he said, "If your gospel is not touching the issues and problems of the community, it is not Biblical preaching." Aden Yoder of Hopedale said that one of the goals of the church must be service—giving a cup of cold water "to any and to all in the name of Christ." Mark Lehman of Rehoboth praised Church of the Brethren theologian Dale Brown for saying in 1971 that there "is hope in the area of evangelism in that the break between the personal and the social is mending.... The new thrust of the church seems to be from those with a conservative faith, but with a social conscience." Jim Harnish of Eureka, a layman from the Roanoke congregation, believed there was more to being the people of God than "proclaiming the gospel and administering the sacraments." He thought that while it was important to be "faithful in observance of temple worship," it was also important to "be an instrument of God in confronting the 'principalities and powers' which have made the temple (God's world) a den of thieves." He added that while we should be concerned about prayer we should also be concerned for being instruments "in building a more just society."[21]

In a powerful article, "Social Concerns and Christ's Call," Norman Derstine at Roanoke wrote that "it may surprise you when I say that I believe in the 'social gospel.'" Quoting Matthew 25:41-46, he said he had a right to believe in it "because this is the standard by which you and I will be judged.... We ought to find out [therefore] what this means for us.... Jesus did not teach that meeting social needs is the 'way of salvation,' or 'the way to bring in the kingdom.' But neither did He overlook the realistic fact that the person who is really a part of His kingdom has a sharp social conscience and concern." Pointing to the

Good Samaritan Derstine continued: "The Christian faith does not seal us off from world need. Rather, Jesus clearly taught and demonstrated that the person who has genuine faith cannot pass by 'on the other side' of social concerns." Bringing the application down to date, Derstine made a plea for those in our ghettos, especially the blacks. With complete approval he quoted a writer who said, "Any religion that professes to be concerned with the souls of men and is not concerned with the slums that damn them and the economic conditions that strangle them—is a dry-as-dust religion."[22]

Another Illinois Mennonite who saw and expressed the social implications of Christianity was a young man of the Waldo congregation, Rick May. As a student at Goshen College he actively participated in its various activities, including those of a small K *(koinonia)* fellowship group, and was well liked on the campus. But there was another Rick May—"the one who lived in constant struggle and search for something deeper in life." In the fall of 1970 this search led him to Koinonia Farms in Georgia. There Rick experienced social injustice in a new way "when he was asked to leave a Sunday morning service at a white Baptist church because he had come with a black brother. The tremendous impact of these experiences led Rick to a response of radical, deep commitment to Christian discipleship." With firm conviction he wrote to a friend: "I'm really getting hooked on this 'love' of Christ for fellowman." One of Rick's favorite hymns well illustrates the vertical and horizontal dimensions of the cross:

> I bind my heart this tide
> To the Galilean's side,
> To the wounds of Calvary,
> To the Christ who died for me.
>
> I bind my soul this day
> To the brother far away,
> And the brother near at hand,
> In this town, and in this land.
>
> —*Lauchlan MacLean Watt,* 1907

In September 1971 Rick arranged for his eyes to be used by others after his death. Little did he realize that a few days later, on September 21, 1971, he would be killed in an automobile accident. Though the human voice of this Christian activist is silent, the life he lived continued to speak loudly. As Norman Kauffmann aptly said at Rick's memorial service at Waldo on September 24, "Death does not interrupt what Rick has begun here at Waldo and continued at Goshen and Koinonia Farms."[23]

Such explicit expressions of the social conscience developed earlier among the General Conference Mennonites than among the (Old) Mennonites. But here, too, there were and are differences of opinion. Some felt that too many people were social activists and not enough were preaching the old gospel of Jesus Christ and his crucifixion, resurrection, and coming again. In 1966 one sister from Flanagan was bothered because she thought the pastors and conferences spent too much time and effort on government and race issues. She thought it was high time to get back to the Bible and begin thinking and preaching "about what the Christian must be watching and preparing for, Christ's coming to earth again." She thought, too, that ministers ought to be "standing in our pulpits shouting out some 'fire and brimstone' sermons to us." In 1966 a brother from Deer Creek thought the social activists were changing truth into lies. He thought too many of them, especially the demonstrators, were disobeying the law and thus, according to Romans 13, were disobeying God. Christ, he contended, was not a revolutionary, for he could not have been that and our Redeemer at the same time.[24]

But by the 1950s the Illinois General Conference Church seems definitely to have been on the side of combining social conscience with evangelicalism and evangelism. Ward Shelly of Washington, for example, agreed that social action could be overemphasized and that Mennonites needed more evangelical zeal, but he insisted that the gospel "must be backed by action." Church leaders, he added, should remind members of their social responsibilities. Heinz Janzen said the Great Commission still stood. Christ was still able to transform. The Mennonite combination of biblical truths with deeds of love was still potent. Christians must go where the people are. Giving a warm blanket or cup of cold water or hot coffee may lead to hearts being warmed by the Savior. "Christian demonstrations for human rights may show a disillusioned Negro that God cares for both body and soul."[25]

Marie J. Regier of the Woodlawn congregation in Chicago also made a strong case for the broader interpretation of preaching the gospel. She felt that some letters in *The Mennonite* objecting to social protest were so "out of focus" that she had to reply. When someone wrote that marches and demonstrations "inevitably" resulted in "riots and violence" she replied that such analysis was not true: "They very often prevent these." She also wanted more proof before believing that many of the demonstrations were "promoted and planned by the communistic forces." Regier pointed out that the author of "Oh Love That Will Not Let Me Go" was having wonderful fellowship with Christ on a ship, quite oblivious to the slaves chained down in the lower deck. "The Gospel of Jesus Christ cannot be divorced from social issues." As to critics of social action, she believed that if they would come to the city and get acquainted with conditions there, they would probably see the need "for social reform as well as handing out tracts." Larry Voth, pastor of the Markham Community Mennonite Church, also emphasized the community idea. He felt that whatever happened in the community was partly the responsibility of the church. "Like Christ, I try to touch people at their point of need.... This church finds its meaning in people's lives in society.... Its life does not depend on two hours on Sunday morning.... I draw no limits where church and community begin and end." Relations between the church and political figures should also be close, and they should work as a team.[26]

Perhaps the person who used the strongest language in showing the absurdity of trying to separate these two parts of the Christian gospel was Vincent Harding, a black who was associate and co-pastor of the Woodlawn Mennonite Church in Chicago in the late 1950s and early 1960s. Emphasizing the way of the cross, Harding called upon the Mennonite churches to face the injustices inflicted on Negro neighbors:

> For who can walk through Chicago's black ghetto and say: never mind about your miserable, frustrated crowded lives, and your burning houses, we'll just save your burning souls. Who can see the area of a few miles where over 600,000 Negroes are imprisoned, and say: never mind about the unscrupulous real estate dealers and the crooked policemen with their brutal ways, just accept the gospel? Who can say that without speaking blasphemy? For a salvation that does not deal with man's condition as he is, and a gospel that does not include concern for this freedom is surely a perversion of the Good News. It would be opium, not good news.[27]

For years to come, many Mennonites and others would squirm under the impact of Harding's trenchant speeches and writings.

Aside from words, what were some actual Mennonite responses, especially in Illinois, toward particular social issues? One set of issues was race relations and civil rights, including slavery. Apparently Mennonites never owned slaves, even in Virginia; or if there is slight evidence of one or two or three cases, it is inconclusive. Anabaptist theology made no room for slavery, and Mennonite confessions such as the Burkholder Confession of Faith produced in Virginia in 1837 prohibited owning or trafficking in slaves. A famous document, "The Earliest Protest Against Slavery Resolutions of Germantown [Pa.] Mennonites February 18, 1688," unfortunately is incorrectly labeled in two respects: it was not the first protest against slavery, and it was not a Mennonite paper. However, three of the four Quakers who signed the protest had a fairly recent Mennonite heritage, and "it is entirely probable that the main motivation for their protest to slavery came from their Mennonite background, not their more recent affiliation with Quakerism."[28]

Long before the Civil War Mennonites had become *Die Stillen im Lande* (the quiet in the land). There are few records available of their concern about slavery and race relations. Most Illinois Mennonites were no exception. To be sure, John F. Funk, who came to Chicago in 1857, was an exception and symbolized a new turn of events. Already in Pennsylvania he recorded in his diary his observations of "old Isaiah," an "old negro [who] was a subject of much curiosity to me. I looked him over and over . . . from head to foot as though I would discover something in him which I could not see or discover in anyone else." But Funk found nothing and marveled that this person, like himself, was God's creation, although he had been a slave. Mused Funk, in America all men are supposed to be free! Also shortly before he moved to Chicago Funk expressed indignation over "Border Ruffianism" and "Bleeding Kansas." In beautiful but searing, scorching prose he wrote with such a concern for freedom that he sounded quite the opposite from "the quiet in the land"! That was before Funk's conversion in 1858. But the young man continued the same concern afterward, though in less strident language.

Funk strongly favored Lincoln in 1860 and did what he could to get him elected. "Four evenings out of seven are taken up with church and prayer meetings," he wrote to his parents in 1860, and "two of the remaining ones are devoted to political affairs." Part of his activities on these nights was to participate in torchlight parades, one of which was two miles long: "and such a great, glorious, good old time was never known in this city." After what Funk called the "Glorious Republican victory" was accomplished, he wrote: "Free Republicanism has once more achieved a noble triumph over Pro-Slavery Democracy and Rowdyism. The first gun of 1860 has been fired and the voice of Liberty, in thunder tones, has gone forth to the greetings of the world."[29] Funk continued to condemn the miserable treatment and injustices blacks received from whites. In 1864 he read in *The Anglo African* an incident in which a black invalid was lynched. "How earnestly," Funk wrote, "we ought to beseech Him to remove all [our] wicked prejudices," and "how much and how humbly we ought to pray that God will forgive our people for all the wrongs inflicted upon the colored race."[30]

If only, in line with the Mennonite record regarding ownership of slaves, one could say also that they had no race prejudice! Unfortunately, this is not true. Surely they did not always recognize their prejudice. In this respect many of them were influenced too much by the prevailing culture of the post-Civil War era and went along too readily with the "accommodations" (i.e., segregation patterns) imposed on the blacks in the later nineteenth and twentieth centuries. There were occasional Mennonite voices of protest, but there were also Mennonite defenders of the "establishment." In 1899, for example, Illinois subscribers to the *Herald of Truth* read: "We find of all the races, the white has reached the greatest perfection—physically, intellectually, and, above all, morally."[31]

In 1900 H. P. Krehbiel, born and reared at Summerfield and later to become a prominent General Conference Mennonite leader, wrote a prophetic article on race relations. He was ahead of his time by a half century. Despite palaver about the blacks being satisfied with segregation, Krehbiel was much concerned about the discrimination against them. "In all directions," he remarked, "the citizen of darker hue is pushed back." No wonder "the black man chafes under these slights, insults, and outrages." Krehbiel predicted serious trouble someday: "The wronged will become desperate, then ... dangerous. God hears their cry—if man will not."[32] Even among Mennonites such voices of protest in that period were few.

Some Mennonites discussed the starting of mission work among Hispanics in the U.S., and at least a few were conscious of the "racial" implications. When Spanish Americans, especially Mexicans, began to move to Chicago in large numbers in World War I and later, many began to settle near the Home Mission. As the mission workers did visitation they began to contact some of these and to invite them, especially children, to attend services. A few responded, and later the number grew. Language was a problem, of course; the mission needed workers who could communicate in Spanish. Among those who could serve, at least temporarily, were missionaries on furlough from Argentina.

Spanish services attracted some adults as well as the children, and soon the question of baptism and church membership arose. The mission workers wrote to the Mennonite Mission Board at Elkhart for advice: "Shall the work be carried on here at the mission, or shall some hall be rented, where more segregation is possible? It is naturally to be expected that some difficulties will arise with reference to the mixing of the races." P. A. Friesen, missionary to India home on furlough and superintendent of the Home Mission in 1932, thought that from the financial angle it would have been better to have the Mexicans attend services at the Mission, but he said there was "so much race prejudice, I am afraid it would break up the congregation." He added that the existing race prejudice seemed "awful to us foreign missionaries."[33]

The Mission Board asked Friesen to seek a hall for the Spanish services. In the meantime the work grew, and a new Mexican congregation was organized in 1934 as a subdivision of the Home Mission. Edwin Weaver, who became the new Home Mission superintendent in

1933, hoped at first to combine the two congregations into one integrated church but soon saw that it would not work. The Mexican congregation then secured its own meetinghouse nearer the Spanish-speaking population. Although prejudice was not the only reason for this move, it was a factor. One prominent longtime member of the mission, who was also Sunday school superintendent, indicated his feelings in a letter to the Mission Board secretary: "The writer never was strong for mixing the Mex. into our church building with our whites (having contacts with Mexican living conditions in Okla. and new Mex.) however I understand that your Board and our District [Board] had no objection to baptizing into our congregation. Our attendance generally slumped from about then on."[34]

The Mexican work continued to prosper. When a new superintendent of the Mexican Mission, David Castillo, a native of Mexico, decided to marry Elsa Shank, daughter of Argentine missionaries, some raised a question because of the so-called mixed marriage. Sanford C. Yoder, secretary of the Mission Board, wondered what Elsa's marriage to "a man of another nationality" would mean for the mission, and whether it would not be "better for them to move to Argentina and work there where there is not the discrimination against mixed marriages that there is here in the United States.... As far as I am concerned, there would be no partiality or discrimination made, but I could not guarantee that that would be true of all." However, as a student of the subject has said, probably Yoder's reservations about the Shank-Castillo marriage was a case of a leader thinking prejudice was a greater problem in such a situation than it actually was. The couple worked in Chicago until 1940, when they moved to La Junta, Colorado, to take charge of a Spanish-speaking congregation there.[35]

As late as January 1943, the church paper which the Illinois (Old) Mennonites read most widely *(Gospel Herald)* referred to birth control as "race suicide." An editorial said it was contrary to the biblical admonition to: "Be fruitful and multiply, and replenish the earth." The longer Christian people used birth control and others did not, "the more completely the white race will become overwhelmed by the hordes of colored (and renegade white) races." But by 1946 (the editorship having changed in 1944 from the veteran Dan Kauffman to Paul Erb) the tone was different. The *Herald* noted that the Federal Council of Churches had recently made a statement to the effect that the existing pattern of racial segregation was unnecessary, undesirable, and a violation of Christian love and brotherhood. Then it continued: "The Mennonite Church dare not be behind the more liberal denominations in its recognition of the evils of segregation. There must be nothing in our attitudes or our method of work which suggests to other people that the white folks consider themselves superior."[36]

Among Mennonites as in the U.S. generally, the struggle over racial equality and the ending of racial discrimination became more intense in the 1950s and 1960s. Unfortunately, Mennonites as well as other Christians did not by and large increase their concern until after the United States government had taken the lead with the famous 1954 Supreme Court decision against school segregation. The Illinois Mennonites helped prepare and support new denominational statements on race relations, such as "The Way of Christian Love in Race Relations" (1955) and "Urban-Racial Concerns" (1969) by the Mennonite Church, and "The Christian and Race Relations" (1959) by the General Conference Mennonites. These were efforts to "tell it like it is," saying racial segregation and discrimination were sin and calling for repentance for failure to recognize it as such.[37]

Another example of conference action on this matter was a motion of the Illinois Mennonite Conference (MC) in 1964 "affirming our sympathy with the aspirations of American minority groups for equal human rights." It acknowledged with humility Mennonite failures in the past, pledged wholehearted support to the government's effort to effect "justice and equality for all men as evidenced in civil rights legislation," and reaffirmed the statement "The Way of Christian Love in Race Relations." Also, the year before, this conference had sent a letter to President Kennedy expressing appreciation for his civil rights concerns and for the leadership he was providing in protecting basic human rights for all persons.[38]

At Meadows and Metamora in 1964 the General Conference and (Old) Mennonites in Illinois held local joint conferences on race relations. These proved very valuable. Mark Lehman of Rehoboth was one of the speakers. Raymond L. Hartzler thought Lehman's presentation "... was the best thing in the matter of racial understanding that I have hear[d] yet. It stood out above any other attempt in giving a clear and moving picture of what the negro people have to confront in life. The citing of case after case to illustrate and press the point ... was most effective." Lotus Troyer concurred with Hartzler.[39]

Holding conferences and writing official statements of the ideal situation was one thing. Getting all the members to live up to the ideal in their thought and practice was another, even in supposedly enlightened times. In an article as late as 1978 Vic Reimer quoted John Burke, black Mennonite minister in Chicago, as saying: "I can name you a Mennonite church which is a hotbed of racial prejudice. And it always has been." Fortunately, however, there seems to have been a growing number who tried sincerely to live up to the ideal. Harold Zehr, editor of the *Missionary Guide*, also wrote that it takes more than statements and laws and their enforcement to bring about integration. We begin to integrate by understanding and respecting each other, "accepting each other and sharing personally regardless of race and color."[40]

Apparently such acceptance, understanding, and sharing still did not come easily. When farmers started growing tomatoes on a large-scale commercial basis in the Flanagan area, some Mennonites opposed the tendency because it would bring migrant workers and their problems into the community. But the workers came, and then the question of inviting them to church services. They were invited, but at first none came. Finally one large family that remained after the harvest started coming. The Christmas program that year, said the reporter, would have strange names on it—not only Ulrichs, Yordys, Forneys, and Roeschleys, but eight Chavezes![41]

Articles on the subject of race and civil rights in *The Mennonite* and the *Central District Reporter* brought mixed responses. Both papers took a strong position in favor of the minorities. Although most of the responses were favorable, quite a few were opposed. Some of the controversy centered on the activities of Martin Luther King, Jr. One typical anti-King letter came from Washington. Leonard W. Hesselein, expressing himself as "burned up," said, "I never did believe in King.... I wish you would show me one thing in writing where ... King ever said anything bad about communism. Why is it these writers criticize us for being in Vietnam and say nothing" about the evils of communism? "I could mention many other articles by other writers in *The Mennonite* that sound anything but American." Typical of the other side was O. W. Baer of Trenton near Summerfield. Baer viewed King as "one of the great social prophets of our day in the tradition of the prophet Amos."[42]

Favorable also was a response from Jim Harnish of Eureka. He said *The Mennonite* afforded the equivalent of a graduate course in American minority history. "All of us white people," he continued, "could use the experience of sitting in an interracial group, where the speaker reads excerpts from the accounts of how it was on the slave ships coming to America and the slave market after getting here, and feel the guttural moaning of black throats along with the shuffling of black feet as they identify with their hurting forbears [sic]." He added that white would be "the farthest thing from beautiful during such an experience." Harnish was disturbed that there was so little feeling of repentance on the part of whites because of these "institutionalized remnants of ... injustice" still with us, and so little feeling of responsibility to do something about them.[43]

One sister pleaded for segregation, saying that God would hold us personally responsible if we allowed desegregation to go on unchecked and adding there was "absolutely nothing the communists would love more than a mongrelized America that they could easily enslave." To such views Glen L. Boese of Chicago was quick to reply. He said segregation was never God's law. The Bible was clearly against it. "Love knows no segregation," he added, quoting social gospel writer Walter Rauschenbusch to support his position. Nor was Emma R. Jones of First Mennonite Church of Chicago afraid of desegregation and where it might lead. Jones, who was also a member of the Chicago Board of Education, thought that interracial marriage was no more wrong than marriage within the same race. Like colors in a garden, the "world will be one beautiful garden—interracial marriage and all."[44]

Renette Thiessen of Summerfield was enough of a social activist that she decided to go to Selma, Alabama, in 1965 and take part in a march for Negro rights. She was impressed by the speakers, all of whom characterized the movement as a powerful, nonviolent revolution. Said black leader Andrew Young: "We won't break a window, we won't fire a shot, we won't even curse; but we're gonna love the hell out of Alabama." Renette was also deeply moved by Martin Luther King's closing address and by 50,000 people joining hands and singing "We Shall Overcome."[45]

In one address Harry Spaeth, pastor of First Mennonite Church in Chicago, well illustrated the racial problem that many Mennonites faced in the city. Spaeth was apparently moderate in his views, no doubt too moderate for some. He spoke of the changing demographic patterns and the tendency of whites to move out of a community when blacks began to move in. Most whites moved, he said, "because they expect living standards to go down and crime to go up—an opinion not altogether without foundation." "Some feel," he continued, that rural Mennonites did not understand the situation "or they would not preach integration," and that those "who *talk* so much should try living with Negroes in a large city." Spaeth thought the only way integration would work would be if a large number of white families were to remain and thus "give a living witness to faith." Christians could prove their faith more effectively, he suggested, "by a willingness to put it into action in this way ... even though it may not be easy." He challenged those who were really concerned about this problem seriously to consider joining his church group in this effort.

Blacks seemed sometimes to concur with Spaeth's last point. One black advised the pastor to stress more the "importance of living together, rather than focusing only on getting Negroes into the church." A black sister in Chicago asked: Since Christ's mission on earth was to seek and save the lost, "how are you going to learn to know, help, and love others of different classes and races if you are continually running from them? ... I have the burning desire and zeal to learn, to work, and to serve our fellowman. So I admonish you, my brother, to stop running from me and learn to live with, work with, and love all men."[46]

The Illinois Mennonite congregation that became most involved in the civil rights movement and race relations was the GC Woodlawn Church in Chicago. This congregation developed around the Mennonite Biblical Seminary after it was located on South Woodlawn Avenue in 1946. Because of demographic changes the area soon changed more and more from white to black. In line with its ideals for the church of Christ, the seminary group saw the opportunity to operate a racially integrated congregation. It became, as S. F. Pannabecker put it, "a laboratory in interracial developments." In 1956 Delton Franz, a white, became its minister with Vincent Harding, PhD candidate in history at the University of Chicago, a black co-pastor. The work progressed quite well for some years. In addition to the chief goal of bringing people to Christ and into the church, the stated purpose at Woodlawn was to "break down the barriers of race and class through our identification as Christians with those of the community with whom we can share our lives." The local church board felt that in view of the racial hatred it was "especially important that Negroes experience the love of Christ also through white persons."

Probably no white Mennonite put the case for integration more strongly than did Elmer Neufeld, for some time associated with Woodlawn and shortly to become an outstanding General Conference leader. When the Mennonite Biblical Seminary Board decided in 1957 to move to Elkhart, Neufeld said the Woodlawn Church must continue and that its aim must be "integration" rather than "indigenization." The "separate but equal" doctrine, he held, had no place in the Christian church. Such separation was sin. His following comment no doubt was a summary of prevailing sentiment at Woodlawn:

> We must catch a great new vision of the church in which fellow Negro Christians sup with us at our 'faspas,' live in our communities, kneel with us at the communion table, share in our footwashing, attend our schools, participate in our retreats, enter our schools of nursing, sit on our Boards, preach from our pulpits—joining hands with us in extending the call of Christ. ". . . that they may become perfectly one, so that the world may know that thou hast sent me and hast loved them even as thou hast loved me."[47]

Delton Franz, the white pastor, supported this position strongly. When the seminary moved, Franz insisted the work at Woodlawn must continue. The gospel is not on trial, but the Mennonite brotherhood is, he said. The Christian church has done so much to drive the Negroes from the church; how much will the Mennonite church do to continue to meet the needs of this community? The Mennonite church would be derelict, Franz insisted, if it did not remain to carry on. In a strong article he forthrightly answered: "Why Is Woodlawn Church in the

Middle of Chicago's Civil Rights?" Chicago, he explained, was the first Northern city chosen for a full-scale civil rights campaign, and one of the two specific areas for focus was Woodlawn's neighborhood. He described terribly deteriorated ghetto conditions and said these will be overcome only when "Christians and all men of goodwill *act.* Our pitfall even as Christians is all too often ... to evade the cost of bearing the cross, which the taking of action may bring. Instead we stall by trying to think out pious religious answers to ugly and practical problems.... The biblical stance is that we are called upon to *act* ourselves into a new way of thinking rather than to try to *think* ourselves into a new way of acting."[48] Not all in the General Conference denomination agreed with Franz and others at Woodlawn. A good many thought Franz was too far out in front. Franz summed up their position as: "The Negro should have a better chance, but all that marching should stop! All the tension caused by these demonstrations is bad! This demonstrating is going too far!"[49]

Harding, the black co-pastor, was, if anything, even more blistering in attacking Mennonite passivity. In "An Open Letter to Mennonites" he asked how anyone could be "the quiet in the land" "in the face of today's American tragedy? Is it possible for any group which takes seriously its Christian faith to be silent at such a time as this?" When a military training bill was before Congress, said Harding, Mennonites very actively made their voices heard on Capitol Hill. But, "where are the letters protesting the inaction of Congress and the President on the segregation controversy in the schools? Where are our representatives to plead the cause of Negro boys and girls whose welfare is endangered and whose educational freedom is being stifled?" He thought it would be more Christian to "protest against wrong done to others, rather than waiting until we are hurt before we raise our voices."[50] Later Harding left Woodlawn and moved to the South, where he became still more militant. At the Mennonite World Conference in Amsterdam in 1967 he gave two addresses, "The Beggars Are Marching ... Where Are the Saints?" and "The Peace Witness and Modern Revolutionary Movements." His stinging, satirical remarks about complacent Mennonites being satisfied and silent about a status quo in which the poverty-stricken masses contributed to the wealth of others (including Mennonites) was too much for many. They criticized him vehemently. But a minority, including *The Mennonite* editor Maynard Shelly, defended him. If such prophets go unheeded, Shelly argued, the "horrors of the Ukrainian steppes of fifty years ago [the Russian Communist Revolution] may well appear on the prairies of North America." Marie Regier of Woodlawn thought the Holy Spirit had "sent a modern prophet in the form of Vincent Harding." "Isn't it perhaps high time," she added, "that a modern prophet awakes us?"[51]

In the meantime the Woodlawn congregation did constructive work. One worker there aptly pointed out how she saw God expressing his love toward man in the community: a job retraining program for middle-aged unemployed men and help in finding employment; a country "fresh air" program for children; money collected to rebuild bombed and ruined churches in Mississippi; and "a listening ear and understanding heart for many." Ed Riddick, a black Baptist minister who joined the Woodlawn church, also paid it a high tribute. Working with people with "strange teutonic names," he wrote: "I came, I saw, and it conquered me.... I came to know a dynamic and meaningful fellowship which defied all barriers of race or color."[52]

One service that the congregation operated was a bookstore and coffee shop (The Quiet Place). Located between a tavern and a five-story tenement building, this institution "touched the lives of scores of people who otherwise would never have entered a church building." The serving tables carried cards with a quotation from George McLeod: "Christ did not die on a cross between two candles in a cathedral, but on a cross between two thieves on the town garbage dump; and because that is where he died and what his life was about, that is where we should be and what we should be about." That indeed was what Woodlawn was about. Franz said the aim was to talk with people in a place less formal than a church and to take a Christian witness to the man on the street. We must learn, he added, how to help people to feel free to express their concerns, problems, hopes, fears, and how to share our faith more attractively.[53]

Franz and his supporters thought they should also do what they could to rehabilitate a slum area which was 99 percent black. In Franz's words, they wanted "to invest a portion of our strength, our love, and our talents in the welfare of those whose lives have been thwarted by the squalor and despair which come from slum living." This project, Franz reasoned, would acquaint our constituency with the dynamics of urban poverty."[54] The civil rights movement and race relations took on new meaning to those who saw the problem in terms of the Woodlawn area. As one rural Mennonite who came there to work asked: "Where is the Christian in these suffering trying times today?"[55]

The struggle for civil rights took a new turn at Woodlawn in the late 1960s. In January of 1966 Curtis Burrell, a black, accepted a call from the Woodlawn congregation to become associate pastor with Franz. Curtis had been born in St. Louis. According to his own story, he was the victim of a broken home who soon found himself in drug-related and other crimes and landed in the Missouri state penitentiary. Thanks to the work of Hubert Schwartzentruber, Burrell became converted to Christianity, attended Hesston College, and then graduated from Goshen College in 1959 and from Goshen Biblical Seminary in 1962. He then went back to Chicago ("which I knew when I was a drug addict"), where he began a promising career of Christian service. He was deeply moved when he pondered the difference in his work and situation—"when I think of the potential which God has in mind for people who are caught in the same hell I once knew."[56]

For some years Burrell worked with and retained the confidence of the congregation and the conference. Like Harding before him and Franz the pastor, he was strongly for civil rights and ready to act, including to march and to demonstrate. On one occasion, near the end of his sermon but before the close of the service, Burrell led a march "from the church to the world" to demonstrate at the store of a Greek grocer-landlord who for a long time, it was felt, had been exploiting the people.[57]

By the later 1960s Burrell was influenced by the Black Pride and Black Power Movement and soon began to emphasize it more than some thought he should. He praised Muhammed Ali for turning "his back on American wealth for the sake of conscience" and upheld him as a model for youth, especially black youth. Black power, said Burrell, may provide the "heretofore missing link between the freedom movement and the realization of freedom." At the same time Burrell seemed to share the anti-white feeling developing among some blacks in the community. White workers at Woodlawn more and more felt the increasing black militancy, and at least some complained about harassment, violence, and burglary. There had been some thought of supplying another white pastor after Franz left in 1967, but Burrell thought a white pastor would be working under a handicap. He also urged that a full-time secretary would be more necessary and helpful than another pastor. Meanwhile even the coffee shop began to have problems. Black militants came in and asked whites working there why they could not be replaced by blacks. Thus it became more and more difficult to continue Woodlawn as an interracial church. Yet the consensus seemed to be that the effort should continue.[58]

Also in the late 1960s Burrell became increasingly involved in urban renewal in his area. He was made president of the Kenwood-Oakland Community Organization (KOCO), a private organization founded by Jesse Jackson, an associate of Martin Luther King, Jr., and funded by the Community Renewal Society of the United Church of Christ. Burrell was also appointed to Mayor Richard Daley's Model Cities Planning Council. In an effort to help Chicago's most powerful southside youth organization (or gang) to use its energy constructively, Curtis joined what was then called the Blackstone Rangers. He even put some Rangers on KOCO's payroll. When they became too demanding, Burrell dismissed them. To make a long story short, "Gang harassment began," according to the story in *The Mennonite* (May 30, 1972). "Shots were fired at Mr. Burrell and others. On July 30, [1970,] the church was burned, a case of arson according to city fire officials." Some thought was given to rebuilding and a few preliminary efforts were made. In fact, on the Sunday after the fire (August 2, 1970) Burrell organized an elaborate service at the site of the burned-out church, a service which sounded like the kick-off of a drive for a new building. Delton Franz and other conference officials attended and spoke. Jesse Jackson gave the main address. Pastor Burrell spoke to the effect that out of these ashes "a new resurrection" would take place. "We have been dead, but like Lazarus, we are coming forth." The money, however, came in too slowly, and the building, to the disappointment of Burrell, was sold to a Baptist group in 1972.[59]

There were problems other than the building. Differences of opinion had arisen not only between Pastor Burrell and the conference leaders, but also in the congregation. The differences were both practical and theological. The controlling board and others felt that Burrell "had gotten too dictatorial and that his theological and moral views were far removed from fundamental Bible Christianity." On the other hand, Burrell felt that the General Conference Mennonite Church "deserted and left us. There was no attempt to understand the theology we express. They have not known how to deal with blacks. We need self-expression, and we don't need Mennonites to tell us that." Within a few months in 1971 the KOCO board dismissed Burrell as chairman, and the Central District missions committee cut off his salary. But in 1972 Jacob Friesen, conference minister, was still prepared to make some money available at Woodlawn that would "specifically help people" and was "trying to find ways to communicate" that were "more meaningful."[60]

The "noble experiment" in better racial understanding and relations came to an end with the differences and misunderstandings apparently not cleared up. But much good had been accomplished and many people helped, despite the pain and struggle. Franz, very close to the scene for eleven years, has said that the work terminated because of "a complexity of factors—leadership factors, aggressive neighborhood violence, the escalating deterioration of housing and services." But he believed that many lives were touched through a new discovery of the love of Christ in action and a more meaningful way of the cross in relation to the poor and oppressed.[61]

If the amount of literature available is a measure, the civil rights and race relations problem claimed more attention among Illinois Mennonites than did any other social issue. People have been awakened to the issue as never before. Despite the distance still to go, progress has been made—as is well illustrated at Calvary in Washington. One of the more fundamentalistic congregations, Calvary has been quite conservative on race relations as on many other social issues. Change may come slowly, but it comes. In 1979 Calvary had a black teacher in its daily vacation Bible school. The young people there as elsewhere are frequently the catalysts of change.[62]

Chicago area worker Laurence M. Horst represented thinking in advance of most white Mennonites on the subject of race relations. In the summer of the Watts riots in California (1965) he wrote prophetically: "The bills [from slavery and racism] are now due and payable. It may just be that if the church fails to suffer with the Negro now in this day when he is calling for ... help ... we shall suffer violence and death at the hand[s] of those we have refused to help." Horst concluded that the church must "be a leader in this ministry of healing." If she "finally take[s] seriously her assignment to be 'neighbour [sic] unto him that fell among the thieves,' then healing can take place and a community of desirable Christian brotherhood can be established."[63]

The problem of intoxicating or alcoholic drinks was another social issue claiming the attention and concern of the Mennonites. Schleitheim, the earliest Anabaptist confession, forbade patronage of drinking places. Many statements in the writings of Menno Simons also oppose use of alcoholic drinks. The early Anabaptists did not generally require total abstinence but they did have "a very sensitive conscience on the question of alcoholic drinks." In time this conscience may have become less sensitive, for Mennonite immigrants to America generally had no scruples against moderate drinking. The Mennonite names Leisy (some with that name lived at Summerfield) and Overholt became associated with brewing and distilling. When the temperance and abstinence movements developed in the nineteenth century among mainline Protestants and some Catholics, the Mennonites were not quick to join. But by the last decades of the century a few Mennonite voices began to speak. Two in Illinois were Peter and John Ropp, sons of Christian. Peter was a convert to the temperance cause as early as 1874, but not John. When Peter built a barn in that year and did not pass out the beer, John thought the idea of "raising a barn without a little beer" was ridiculous. Yet ten years later John and his wife, Mary, were "both outspoken enemies of the saloon or intoxicating liquor ... of any kind, in any manner, shape or form." For many years Mary was an active worker in the Women's Christian Temperance Union (WCTU). Joseph Stuckey was also said to have been a strong temperance man.[64]

How much influence Frances E. Willard of Evanston, Illinois, powerful WCTU leader and popular writer and speaker, had on Illinois and other Mennonites is impossible to say. No doubt the influence that came from her and especially from her Methodist Church and other Protestants was considerable. The influence operated in this case much as it did in the case of a number of the elements of the "Great Awakening" discussed earlier. The rise of Sunday schools among the Mennonites and the introduction and continuance for several generations of the quarterly temperance lessons surely had important influence.[65]

Mennonites were agreed that drunkenness was sin and as such could not be tolerated in the church. By the end of the nineteenth century there was a growing belief that he who sold liquor also sinned. But the belief was not unanimous. For example, the supposedly true story was told of a member of the Partridge church who was a bartender in Peoria and was excommunicated—not, however, because he tended bar but because he put a dashboard on his buggy, parted his hair, and wore a "boiled" shirt.[66]

Perhaps more to the point was the attitude of the emerging church leader John F. Funk. Funk's attitude toward total abstinence was at first a bit mixed. But he clearly saw the evils of drinking, condemned them, and in total context came out strongly against drinking. His conversion in Chicago in 1858, his association with Moody, and his Sunday school work with children were no doubt influential in determining his position. In 1881 he wrote in his paper that "the custom of keeping whiskey in the cupboard for the family and hired hands, although handed down to our fathers by the venerable practice of ancestors, has been weighed and found wanting."[67]

By the turn of the century the saloon—that "den of iniquity"—was under increasingly heavy attack. In 1895 Mennonite George H. Summer of Metamora, later minister and bishop, replied to an article in the *Herald of Truth* that seemed too defensive of the saloon: "there are only two ways ... if the saloon does not lead souls to heaven, it leads them to hell.... The power of darkness is the ruler of the saloon." And "for those that frequent those places [and] say *they can't* see any harm in it," Summer added, "... we as Christians should do all we can to help those and lead them to the One that opens the eyes to the blind." Summer was probably influenced by his uncle Bishop John Smith, one of the first Amish Mennonite leaders to take a stand against the saloon and liquor traffic.[68]

In 1890 the Western District A. M. Conference of which Smith was a part said that saloons should be shunned. The Illinois Mennonite Conference in 1900 stated that members who patronized saloons should "first be admonished as to the error of their way. After all Christian efforts have failed to persuade such to quit this evil habit, the church should deal with them according to their sin." In 1908 this conference took a still stronger position: "Since the liquor traffic, which is contrary to the word of God, is a destruction to the home, a menace to the nation, therefore we urge our people to suppress it by every possible means where they do not violate the principles of nonresistance." For by this time the Illinois Mennonites were thinking the liquor traffic was evil and saying that they should do something about it. John Ropp of Bloomington replied forcefully to a question in the *Herald of Truth.* The question was: "Is it right for a Christian to sign a remonstrance against granting a liquor license? In other words should we assist in resisting and regulating the deeds of the ungodly?" Ropp responded that the liquor traffic was the "greatest curse of Christendom" and therefore it was every Christian's duty to do all he possibly could to get rid of it, including praying, voting, signing remonstrances, and any other means that the Christian could consistently use. He cited James 4:17: "Whoever knows what is right to do and fails to do it, for him it is sin."[69]

The Central Illinois Conference of Mennonites was if anything even stronger in the stand it took against the liquor traffic. When the conference was organized in 1908 its constitution stated: "Conference also recognizes that the Bible teaches that no drunkard shall enter the kingdom of heaven, Gal. 5:21. Therefore, a congregation that tolerates among its members the drink evil, can not be regarded as Christian, and can therefore not be a congregation in this conference. Recognizing in the so-called saloon and all kinds of drink houses where strong drink is dispensed, one of the greatest and most common evils in human society, there [sic] should in no wise be countenanced by our congregations and members of our conference." In 1910 M. P. Lantz of Carlock pictured in vigorous language the evils of the liquor traffic which was penetrating political, economic, and social life and asked, "shall the saloon or the anti-saloon element control the state?" Only by "voting directly against the accursed business can I or you, dear brother, rest with a clear conscience." He thought that every pastor in the conference ought to preach on the "Duties of Christian Citizenship, with special reference to the liquor question."[70]

From its founding in 1910 *The Christian Evangel,* like other Mennonite periodicals, carried many articles on temperance and the liquor traffic, some of the periodicals having special "Temperance Sections." In such an article George Gundy, Central Conference leader from Meadows, wrote about the saloon as a "Modern Maloch." Like the old, the modern Maloch waits with outstretched hands to receive its uncounted thousands of victims and destroy them—men, women, and children. Gundy thought the minister who was not against the saloon was not worthy of his title. He thought too that the highway robber was "a better citizen than the saloon keeper." The robber took one's money, but the saloon keeper "takes your money and puts a bottle of liquor into your pocket which will destroy the body and many, many times sends the soul to a drunkard's hell."[71]

On the other hand, even some Mennonite ministers were not as opposed to liquor and saloons as strongly as many thought they ought to have been. There was some Mennonite preaching in the 1910s in Illinois against women voting, as provided in the proposed nineteenth amendment to the U.S. Constitution. One minister was said to have opposed the amendment not only because he thought women should not vote but because he feared that women would vote against liquor.[72]

Some even among those opposed to liquor were ambivalent about using the political process for Prohibition. But by the time the U.S. entered World War I (1917) little of this opposition remained.[73] One authority has stated that most Mennonites actively supported the prohibition movement and took part in local option and state elections, voting against the liquor traffic. In some areas "even the most conservative leaders urged their members to go to the polls to vote on the liquor issue."[74] The percentage of Illinois Mennonites voting on the issue is not known, but it was probably as high as in other states if not higher.

No doubt Illinois Mennonites shared the somewhat naive hope some put in Prohibition when the eighteenth amendment took effect in 1920. Billy Sunday, a famous non-Mennonite evangelist whom Illinois Mennonites read about and often heard, declared that: "The reign of tears is over. The slums will soon be only a memory. We will turn our prisons into factories and our jails into storehouses and corncribs. Men will walk upright now, women will smile, and the children will laugh. Hell will be forever for rent."[75]

Disillusionment soon came. As early as 1922 Illinois Mennonites were reading in one of their church periodicals that the millions who still had "depraved appetites" and the thousands who would do almost anything to make money were combining with the underworld in a "desperate effort to break down the prohibition laws."[76] This is not the place to discuss the pressures and propaganda that brought about the repeal of national Prohibition in 1933. Suffice it to say that the battle for temperance continued, and Illinois Mennonites did their part. David E. Plank, deacon in the Roanoke congregation, is a good example. Already in 1917 he had published a book entitled *The Temperate Life*, much of which sounds up-to-date for the 1980s. The Christian, he held, should lead a temperate life not only in drink but also in food, dress, and total deportment. Mary Grove from Cullom called attention to Plank's book in 1932 when it was clear that the eighteenth amendment would soon be repealed. In 1934 Plank wrote several articles in the *Gospel Herald*, in which he pleaded for total abstinence as the "only safe, God-approved course. Moderate drinking is a fool-hardy risk, and a sin. Drunkenness is a crime against God, against ourselves. Dear reader, will you go all the way and touch not another intoxicating drink?"[77]

Others also appealed against the liquor interests. At times it seemed like a hopeless cause, with liquor consumption, alcoholism and drink-related crimes on the increase. In the days of the New Deal, President Franklin D. Roosevelt, who had done much to bring about repeal, talked about the good, abundant life his New Deal had brought about. One Illinois Mennonite repeatedly rejoined that the only abundant life he saw Roosevelt bringing was abundance of liquor and the evils flowing from it.[78] A. N. Mitchell from Groveland published a strong attack against alcohol and cigarettes, characterizing them as two of the worst evils and leading to "moral degeneracy." These were not for Christians. Yet too many were being influenced by the propaganda of the liquor and tobacco interests. In 1953 Bishop A. C. Good of Sterling congratulated the *Gospel Herald* for asking people to pray for the new president (Eisenhower). Good broadened the appeal by asking readers to pray also for a "dry" White House. He thought that liquor was the "cause of much of the bungling in Washington in the last 20 years. Isn't it time for the voice of the church to be heard?"

With somewhat different emphasis, Marion Dechert and others at Woodlawn thought in 1966 that Mennonite teaching on alcoholism lacked depth. They suggested that not only the evils of alcoholism but also its causes should be studied. "We need to ask why men seek solace in drink and inquire what Christians must do about these things which 'drive men to drink.'"[79]

In 1969 Lulu Smith, an active worker in the Roanoke congregation, was another who wanted Mennonites to show more vigor against alcohol. In a letter to the "Readers Say" column (*GH*, June 10, 1969) she inveighed against its evils, cogently asking why we got so excited about poverty, hunger, malnutrition, death on the highways, murder, and other crimes, and yet remained quiet about one of the main causes—the "monster, alcoholism"? She regretted that the Mennonites were doing less on this than other churches. "I hope for the day," Smith added, "that every Mennonite church will go on record as having done something about this." "Let us as a church keep silent no longer."

Such appeals hardly had the success that many hoped for. Drinking and its consequent evils increased. Even Mennonites, it seemed, lost some ground. In the 1950s Harold S. Bender had written: "Meanwhile the pattern of total abstinence has become thoroughly established among American Mennonites of all branches, most of whom today would not knowingly tolerate among their membership the drinking of alcoholic beverages." If true for the 1950s, the statement would not be correct for the 1970s and 1980s. Unfortunately, Mennonites too have been influenced in recent decades by the liquor-pervading culture in which they live. One evidence of this is several strong articles in the May 18, 1976, issue of the *Gospel Herald* calling attention to this problem. Among them are "Whatever Is Happening to Abstinence" and "An Alarming Trend." Harder and Kauffman's study, referred to earlier, indicates that only fifty percent of the Mennonites surveyed believe that moderate drinking of alcoholic beverages is always wrong. There is no evidence to indicate that Illinois was particularly different in this respect.[80]

The use of tobacco was quite common among American Mennonites until the close of the nineteenth century. One authority says that "smoking and chewing were so common among all the Mennonite groups of Swiss-South German background as to be almost universal. There was also some use of snuff." Even some of the older women smoked pipes in the home. Chewing was so usual even during church services that "spittoons were found behind the pulpits in some of the meetinghouses." As for tobacco chewers not behind the pulpits, the reader will recall from an earlier chapter that in the 1870s one Mennonite conference called for more cleanliness because worshipers could not kneel for prayer without landing in tobacco spittle![81]

Mennonites who opposed both tobacco and liquor often bracketed the two together. But attacks on tobacco never rose to quite the same emotional pitch as did those on drinking. Nor did they produce as much literature. Yet with the coming of the Mennonite Awakening, opposition to tobacco increased. The coming of the Russian Mennonites, some of whom opposed tobacco, probably gave additional impetus. In 1890, for example, the Illinois Mennonite Conference stated that using tobacco was conformity to the world just as much as was dressing fashionably (although it did approve "necessary" use of tobacco). A few years later J. S. Shoemaker gave the conventional arguments against tobacco: While not specifically condemning its use, the Bible does condemn fleshly lusts and teaches cleanliness of flesh and spirit; tobacco use is a bad example; it is a waste of money that could serve better ends, such as missions; it is worldly conformity; it offends others. Deacon David E. Plank included a chapter against tobacco in *The Temperate Life*. Plank concluded that smoking cigarettes was the worst form of use.[82] It is perhaps ironic and a bit puzzling that the more liberal Mennonites in Illinois and the most conservative (Old Order Amish, for example) have been less strict against use of tobacco than have the groups in between. This pattern is not unique to this state, however.

Another social issue had to do with justice for laborers. So long as American Mennonites were a rural people they had little consciousness of labor-relations problems. When in the twentieth century more and more of them sought work in factories and when still later an increasing number became owners and operators of businesses and factories, they began to face the problem. Among those thus concerned was I. R. Detweiler, pastor in the 1930s at Normal. The church, he felt, must cry out against the great evils "that are threatening to destroy our civilization," including the exploitation of laborers through low wages, long hours, and poor working conditions. The workers, he added, have been deprived of their "just and equitable share."[83] But because of its commitment to nonresistance, the church faced the problem with some ambiguity. Church leaders were concerned with social justice on the one hand—although perhaps not always as much as they should have been. They had some reservations about labor unions, which were organized to secure higher wages and better working conditions for laborers. While generally agreeing with the goals of labor unions, Mennonites typically raised several objections. One, which was probably out of date in the twentieth century, was that they were secret societies that required members to take oaths to join. A strong emphasis was that joining violated the biblical injunction against being unequally yoked with unbelievers. More compelling reasons were the monopolistic nature of unions and their use of force and sometimes violence to attain their ends.

In 1904 the Illinois Mennonite Conference decided that candidates for membership who belonged to labor unions could not become members because "all who are oath-bound are contrary to God's Word," and also because unions "tend toward rioting, cause divisions and compel submission regardless of conscientious scruples." In 1910 the same (Old) Mennonite conference asked that since "labor unions are not founded upon Gospel principles and are destructive to personal liberty," church members give up their union membership. It reaffirmed this action in 1913.[84]

By the 1930s when unions were making considerable gains under New Deal legislation, many Mennonites had taken jobs in factories. So the brotherhood faced the problem again. In Illinois the matter was a problem chiefly for the (Old) Mennonites and a few of the smaller conservative groups. The (Old) Mennonites' general conference was trying to effect some sort of compromise whereby church members could pay the equivalent of union dues—in some cases as members, in other cases not—but not engage in any coercive activity that would violate their peace principles. In the 1940s the Illinois Mennonite Conference labored with the denomination's Committee on Industrial Relations and later its Committee on Economic and Social Relations to reach agreements with a number of unions operating in Illinois. Although these arrangements generally worked quite well,

(Old) Mennonites have since felt less need for them and now they are seldom used. Probably also the unions themselves have become more accommodating, due in part to an atmosphere created since the late 1940s by the passage of the Taft-Hartley Act and right-to-work laws in several states.

Though these special arrangements with the unions involved mainly the (Old) Mennonites and the Brethren in Christ, this does not mean that others were not concerned. In the Kauffman-Harder study (1975) referred to earlier, the question was asked whether respondents agreed with the following statement: "A church member should not join a labor union even if getting or holding a job depends on union membership." Twenty-five percent of (Old) Mennonite repondents agreed, 10 percent of General Conference Mennonites, and 8 percent of the EMC. With the statement, "A church member who owns or manages a shop should refuse to recognize or bargain with a labor union," the percent agreeing were 31, 12, and 11 respectively.[85]

On the status and role of women, Mennonite views have been far from uniform. But the trend among the Illinois Mennonites as elsewhere has been toward more equality. Among early Anabaptists, women had played important roles. Many had given vigorous, intelligent testimonies for their faith and suffered martyrdom. Later the congregations reverted more to the typical patriarchal attitude of their surrounding culture. This is illustrated by the comment of Christian Snavely, a Mennonite preacher at Shannon near Freeport. In 1890 he wrote: "There has Been quite a Revival in Shannon some fifty Souls have been Converted, a Woman preached." But despite the fifty souls, Snavely continued: "Dear Brother I have no faith in Women preaching its Contrary to Pauls teaching. Paul Wants women to be Silent in church Not alone to preach.... I would like to see what Kind of Fruit they Bear. The tree is known by the Fruit."[86] In America the very conservative Mennonite groups maintained "the patriarchal type of family life with a corresponding place for women." In the more progressive groups "(MC, EMC, GCM ...) since 1900, women have gradually moved into full participation in all aspects of church life and service, except in the ministry and in office-holding in general congregational life."[87]

However, for many years even after 1900 equality was slow in coming, even in the more progressive bodies, especially in those prescribing the prayer veiling. For a long time in Illinois as elsewhere the idea prevailed that women were to wear the veiling as a sign of submission to men. J. S. Shoemaker stated in 1904 that women were to keep silent in "church conferences, councils and other public religious assemblies, where the instruction and teaching was to be of an authoritative nature." Women were to be submissive to men and were not to assume the authority to preach, teach or give counsel to men. "Man is the head of the woman ... and it is the revealed will of God that public religious teachers should be men, not women. All authoritative teaching and church government has been divinely laid upon the shoulders of men." Shoemaker said women were not to be barred from helping in other capacities, such as praying and prophesying. But they were not to usurp the sphere allotted to men, and were to indicate their submission by wearing the devotional covering.[88] Shoemaker's words were in line with what the Western District A. M. Conference, for instance, had said in 1895: that women could serve as Sunday school teachers and "helpers in the church and ... be engaged in all good works," but not as Sunday school superintendents or ministers.[89]

With some variations from place to place and from individual to individual, this remained the prevailing sentiment in the (Old) Mennonite Church for many years.[90] Erosion of that traditional pattern did begin to occur in missions, both at home and on the foreign field. Women, of course, filled important places in the founding and operating of Mennonite and Brethren in Christ missions in Chicago. The same was true of foreign missions. Change came also through establishment of women's organizations such as the sewing circles. And in the Sunday school movement women were important almost from the beginning as promoters, teachers, and conference speakers. For example, at a one-day Western A. M. Sunday school conference at Roanoke in 1906 four of the speakers were women.[91]

In any case, by the 1950s and 1960s and especially the 1970s, Mennonites were discussing the role and status of women in the church and society as never before. Some Illinois Mennonites were in the forefront. No doubt the pioneer work, noted earlier, of Lydia H. Smith (1860-1941) in organizing and promoting women's sewing circles and other activities had helped enlarge Mennonite perceptions. Lydia Smith's granddaughter Lois Gunden Clemens, also born and reared in Illinois, was a pioneer in a later day. In 1970 she gave a series known as the Conrad Grebel Lectures, published the following year under the title *Woman Liberated.* In them she made a strong plea for true partnership between man and woman and the full release and use of the powers of both in the work of the church. She was the first woman to give the Conrad Grebel Lectures, after fourteen Mennonite men—asked by a committee of men—had preceded her.

In 1970 Mrs. Linda Beher of Villa Park saw the woman's liberation movement as one that gave her sex more options to follow: "Look, sisters, you have options; you can choose, as men have always chosen, what life role you wish to fill.... That's what the movement is all about." She added that women should be themselves, not pressed into a mold to be someone else. Louise Newswanger from Normal thanked the editor of *The Mennonite* for publishing an article by Dorothy Yoder Nyce on "Partners in Partnership." The author, an (Old) Mennonite, had pleaded for equality and a true partnership between husband and wife which would permit more flexibility in roles and work.[92]

Yet, despite some advanced views on women's roles, Illinois Mennonites were far from united in their thinking. In 1975 Percy Gerig, then pastor at Roanoke, held the traditional view that man was given authority over woman, but in love—just as Christ was in subjection to God, yet equal. God's order of roles has been: God the head of Christ, Christ the head of the church, and man the head of woman. "As Christ is the Head of the church the husband is the head of the wife. As the church is subject to Christ, let wives be subject to their own husbands in everything." Gerig also said: "My wife is my greatest co-worker, but not in leadership." He felt that this delineation of the different roles of the sexes did not make women inferior to men.[93]

In 1968 Don Roth, a pastor reared in the Salem congregation near Flanagan but now serving elsewhere, held similarly traditional views. In Genesis, he wrote, God held authority over man, and gave man authority over the wife. "The wife is to obey her husband and the husband is to obey God." Mankind's first sin, he added, was that of the woman's "disobeying her husband." Roth put his view in an article he entitled "What's Gone Wrong?" "The refusal of wives to obey their husbands," he declared, "is the one most frequent cause of decadence in our world today."[94]

In 1970 Peter Ropp, great-grandson of the pioneer bishop Christian Ropp, responded strongly in *The Mennonite* against what many thought was an extreme article on woman's liberation. The article had even characterized Paul as "that neurotic chauvinist" who wrote most of the guidelines for the church. Ropp asked why, suddenly, do so many want to be liberated from everything? "Why do so many clamor for recognition they do not deserve? ... Why do women want to be liberated from the most wonderful occupation God ever offered 'the rearing of a Christian family' so they can enter 'the great ulcer factory,' the business world of men?" He broadened his field of protest and asked further why young folk singers "have to holler at the top of their lungs? Are they trying to be heard above the din of battle and the noise of exploding bombs?" Ropp thought that we ought to follow the sign displayed in some implement stores: "When everything else fails, try reading the directions." He was referring to the way of Jesus Christ, and what Jesus had to say about love, peacemakers, the meek, the merciful and doing unto others.[95] No doubt many others in the state shared Ropp's sentiments but did not bother about writing articles or letters for their church papers.

As noted in chapter 9, in recent decades Illinois Mennonites have changed their views somewhat with regard to divorce and remarriage. These changed views probably had some connection with the changing attitudes regarding women. In any case, in 1974 one young sister from the Boynton congregation in Hopedale got the misinformation that the Associated Mennonite Seminaries at Elkhart, Indiana, were dodging the divorce issue. She protested that the seminaries are preparing pastors, and anybody knew "that in this age *future* pastors will come head on into divorce problems. The divorce rate is growing among Mennonite people." If our seminaries, she added, "can't give us answers as [to] how to cope with this issue who can we go to for help?" Jacob Friesen, Central District Conference minister, assured her that the seminaries were seriously studying the problem.[96]

The really big issue concerning the role of women which agitated Illinois Mennonites has become that of ordination to the ministry. That was of course the question raised in chapter 9 concerning Emma Richards at Lombard. Someone has said that Emma Richards was the "first licensed woman minister among North American Mennonites." This is not quite accurate. Vinora Weaver (later Mrs. Earl Salzman) was, in effect, licensed to preach in the 1920s in a small church near Danvers. She preached under the authority of Emanuel Troyer, who wanted to ordain her. Because of plans for marriage she actually preferred not to be ordained, but after her marriage she still preached on numerous occasions. Even before her, Ann Jemima Allebach was ordained in 1911 at First Mennonite Church in Philadelphia, Pennsylvania—not for a particular church, but to "go out and preach the

Source: Emma Sommers Richards, Lombard, Ill

Emma Sommers Richards, first woman ordained as Mennonite minister in Illinois; ordained June 17, 1973, at Lombard Mennonite Church, Lombard, Illinois.

gospel." Before an early death she preached in several churches, but more in a Reformed congregation on Long Island than elsewhere. She seems to have been the first Mennonite woman ordained in North America.[97]

No doubt on this point as on others Mennonites have been influenced by their cultural milieu. In this case influence has come from the contemporary women's rights movement. For some time Mennonites have been studying afresh the role of women in the church, emphasizing the teachings of Jesus on the subject, and reinterpreting Paul's statements about keeping silent in the churches. One such important study was authorized by the (Old) Mennonite Church's General Assembly in 1973 and published later as *Women in the Church*. Much of the initiative for this came from Illinois, especially from the Lombard congregation. The charter membership list of this young congregation included some from other branches in addition to (Old) Mennonites. In 1971 eleven members had sent a petition to the Lombard church council requesting that the council "take necessary steps to study (with a view to future action) the desirability, possibility, and timing of the ordination and licensing of Emma Richards to serve as part of a team ministry for our congregation." The congregation approved this recommendation.[98]

Richards was then licensed by the Executive Committee of the Illinois Mennonite Church Conference. At the same time the committee decided to have the conference study the question of women's ordination. At first (1972) the conference turned down Lombard's request to ordain Richards fully. In the meantime the study committee reported to conference. It took a strong position on recognizing all the gifts of all the members of the body of Christ, male and female, and said the separation of God's people into clergy and laity "is not a part of the Anabaptist-Mennonite heritage. We have always emphasized the priesthood of all believers." The report brought strong opposition and precipitated a vigorous debate among the conference delegates—so vigorous that one delegate who had only recently changed from Methodist to Mennonite wondered whether some Mennonites took their pacifism seriously. Those opposed to the report were only a small (albeit vocal) minority, and so the conference accepted the study committee's recommendation. Lombard was permitted to ordain Mrs. Richards. She was ordained in 1973, testifying that since early in life she had felt the call to preach.[99]

A few years after Mrs. Richards' ordination, Ed Springer of Markham Community Church said he was not excited over the discussion about the ordination of women or their being placed in a leadership role. "Why not?" he asked. He thought the obvious answer was that they should be. He thought it best to look to what Jesus had said about women rather than to Paul. But even Paul had said that all are one in Christ. He added that we are all equally blessed and equally called into his service; it "is sin when our gifts and callings are denied."[100] While Mrs. Richards' case was no doubt a milestone in Illinois Mennonite history, Springer's thinking was probably still ahead of that of the rank and file. Except in smaller conservative groups, Mrs. Richards' experience will undoubtedly make it easier for the great majority to come to Springer's position, if indeed they are not already there.

On an issue closely related to women's roles, the veteran Mennonite leader, R. L. Hartzler, has commented on abortion. In times past, he said in 1975, as the church allowed important issues to drift from declared standards, it "winced, hesitated, shrugged its shoulders, accommodated more and more, and finally tacitly condoned." Should we do the same on abortion? he asked. Quite certainly we shall if the present drift goes on, he insisted. Hartzler proposed having a conference of theologians, doctors, social workers, pastors, on either a conference or inter-conference level, to study and determine on what basis, if any, abortion might be justified. "Such bases," he thought, "might be rape, question of life or death ... of the mother, evidence of marked physical deformity or mental retardation to be the lot of the child when or if born, to mention a few." Churches or conferences could appoint review committees to study the matter in the light of the findings and guidelines of such a conference and thus help involved members resolve the matter. Some might not support such a procedure, he conceded, but drifting into a de facto position would probably bring more questionable attempts at solution.[101]

Hartzler was right in proposing that the abortion problem should be faced and studied. How widespread the issue has become among Illinois Mennonites by the 1980s is impossible to say. Clearly it is growing. In a recent case the pastor of the Roanoke congregation resigned partly because of this matter.[102]

Another social concern throughout church history has been how Christians should organize their social and economic life. One branch of the Anabaptists, the Hutterites, decided that no one should have private property, but all have their possessions in common. Most of the Anabaptists did not decide on this course. However, occasionally groups within the Mennonite body have felt that community of goods was the best Christian course, if not the only one. Even more often, individuals here and there have raised the question as to why Christians do not have all things in common as in the days of the apostles. In 1904 one brother asked this question in the *Herald of Truth*, and J. S. Shoemaker was asked to answer. The Illinois bishop replied that it was not practicable because of geographical scattering, different environments and circumstances, and the "peculiar personality of many Christians." He also said that community of goods was not a gospel requirement. The early Christians did not establish a formal community of goods, but out of love and fellowship the rich sold their possessions "that distribution might be made among those who had come from a distance and had not with them the means of support." Shoemaker concluded that they "abandoned this method after they were scattered abroad."[103]

This rationale has satisfied the Mennonites by and large. In recent years, however, a few in Illinois have felt that community of goods should be emphasized more than traditionally. While all agreed that, in the words of George Blaurock, "he who is a good Christian should share what he has, else he is none," those few have felt that the best way to carry this out is through the intentional community with all property held in common. Illinois has two Mennonite-related intentional communities. The older and larger is Reba Place Fellowship, in south Evanston just north of metropolitan Chicago. It had its origins in the minds of a group of seminary students and relief workers who had been in Europe and who were "deeply challenged by the rediscovery of Anabaptist thought" which was then going on at Goshen College and elsewhere. "What began as a discussion," says Virgil Vogt, chief leader, "turned into a deliberate seeking of fellowship by people who longed to live their lives in 'Christian community.'" They soon felt led to become a church congregation in a large city because the "twentieth century ... needed loving communities of people in the centers of mass population where loneliness and alienation seemed most severe." One family bought a house at 727 Reba Place in Evanston in 1957. Other young families as well as single men and women soon followed. Today (1980) Reba Place has a community of about three hundred adults and children. The group has come from several denominational backgrounds, and many have found Christ for the first time. The community has a common treasury "to which we bring our economic assets and earnings," and from which funds are allocated for each person's needs. Income in excess of these needs is distributed elsewhere. Though many members go outside the community for work, they all live in houses and apartments near each other in order to be able to congregate easily. The congregation is a member of the Illinois Mennonite Conference and of the Church of the Brethren. Reba Place represents a historic and significant movement and no doubt is causing many more Mennonites, whether in traditional or intentional communities, to reevaluate their ideals for caring and sharing.[104]

A younger intentional community is Plow Creek near Tiskilwa. Started in 1971, Plow Creek grew out of Reba Place and is much smaller. In that year several families set out to begin a new community on a newly purchased farm. As of 1981 it was supported by income from gardening, and various construction and other jobs outside the community. In 1978 the group numbered about sixty-five. Church membership in 1980 was twenty-nine. The group's thinking seems well illustrated by two of the members, Jim and Donna Harnish, who said that Christian commitment increases as one moves from the traditional church to the house church and then, "much more so," into the intentional community where everything is shared with everybody else. They thought that in "acquisitive, competitive, materialistic" society it was "all but impossible ... to affirm God's will and purpose for his creation." The Harnishes hoped the new form would be an instrument in the renewal of the church and in calling "it into a life of more radical discipleship." The minister at Plow Creek is Conrad Wetzel, a former leader at Reba Place.[105]

Illinois Mennonites have accepted Christian intentional communities as a way of life for those who have conviction on that point. At the same time, all are strongly opposed to Marxist communism. Yet not all have responded to Marxist communism the same way. Some have been ready to follow a "get-tough" policy and label others as "soft on communism." Others have thought that we needed more clarity in our statements to avoid misunderstanding, and especially more study of the causes of communism. In October of 1973, David Augsburger, then of Chicago, wrote an excellent article in *The Mennonite*, "Who Brings Communism?" Quoting at length from John Drescher, editor of the *Gospel Herald*, Augsburger pointed out that injustice brings communism; unjust laws favoring the rich bring it; preachers bring it when they ignore the social implications of the gospel; luxurious living brings it; businessmen who secure big profits and pay low wages bring it; professional people who charge exorbitant fees bring it; legislators who think more of the next election than of the next generation bring it; in fact, all who put personal gain before concern bring communism. "The Christian answer is not an answer to communism," Augsburger declared; it "is an answer to communists."[106]

At least a number of Illinois Mennonites have addressed themselves to questions of wealth, capitalism, materialism, conservation, poverty, hunger at home and abroad, and helping the poor and unfortunate. They have offered many articles, addresses, and sermons on how Christians should treat the poor, always buttressing their remarks with many Scriptures from the Old and New Testaments. Very early John F. Funk in his sojourn in Chicago discovered what poverty was like in a large city. When he visited homes of some Sunday school pupils in 1861 he was deeply moved by what he saw. In his *Herald of Truth* he continued to stress the poverty theme, and his descriptions were strikingly similar to what Home Mission workers would say forty and fifty years later.[107]

Pius Hostetler of Shelbyville and Roanoke was skeptical about the possibility of being a wealthy Christian. In 1915 he wrote that Christians who added farm after farm to their holdings were in danger. In line with the thinking of others, he said that poverty did not save anyone but that it "tends or leads to more humility and such conditions that are needful to our acceptance of the plan of salvation." On the other hand, he thought that riches tended to lead toward "pride and high-mindedness" and away from God. D. L. Christophel of Tiskilwa also thought that Christians could be faithful more easily if they were not encumbered with worldly goods. In similar vein C. F. Derstine of Eureka wrote in 1920 that there were two classes: "the full and the empty, the rich and the poor." Being rich was in itself no "certificate for hell," and poverty was no passport for heaven. "But to be rich, and allow at our doors, millions to starve for lack of food, is following the steps of him who opened his eyes in hell. I cannot see how any man in these days can add house to house, and dollar upon dollar in bank accounts and feel like a follower of Christ."[108]

Yet the rank and file of Illinois Mennonites have had no trouble living under the capitalist system. Most of them defend it; only occasionally does it come in for serious criticism. Yet it has had critics, even apart from those in the intentional communities. During the Great Depression C. W. Long of Peoria quoted favorably a local pastor who had blasted a capitalism that had "permitted or made possible 273 families to gather into their possession $409,500,000 in the short space of twelve months, while from five to ten million families are practically destitute." Long then added: "I have been wondering how and where our Mennonite rural and city industrialists have been placing their value."[109]

The problem of materialism among Mennonites is not new. Illinois has had its share. As noted early in this study, "Mennonites have a nose for good land." The rich Illinois soil on which they settled has probably helped produce a spirit of materialism on the part of too many. The sin of materialism has been compounded with a spirit of excessive individualism. The Mennonite farmer has often said, "This is *my* farm. I have worked hard for it, have saved my money, and now the land is mine and nobody is going to tell me what I should do with it." The wealthy farmer has enjoyed the social prestige attached to land ownership. Only a few Illinois Mennonites have thought materialism was such a problem as to require some radical solution such as intentional community. The majority have said it could be handled by proper teaching on priorities, values, and good stewardship.

One hopeful sign has been that the critics have been speaking out.

In 1974 Don Schrader of Freeport, for example, questioned the tendency to spend too much money on local building programs and on large operating budgets, and not enough on feeding the hungry and healing the sick. Are the "cushioned pews, stained glass windows, endless meetings, doctrinally exact sermons, tons of tracts, and soothing organ music pleasing to God," he asked, "when we give only our used clothing and our left-over crumbs to the poor & hungry? Faith is not carefully worded creeds. Faith is love for God and man in action."[110]

Increased emphasis on Christian stewardship came from various quarters, both in writing and preaching. For example, in 1964 Pastor Norman Derstine at Roanoke wrote in the *Gospel Herald* about how the Christian should look at wealth and possessions. In an article entitled "The Church Community and Covetousness," he stated that the church has become more worldly through the eagerness of its members to gain wealth and possessions for selfish reasons. He emphasized that the problem was "to recapture the true nature of the church and its full expression in the life of stewardship in the individual life of believers and in the brotherhood." He appealed for, among other changes, more vigorous approaches to discipleship and to teaching stewardship. In the 1960s and 1970s Milo Kauffman of Hesston, Kansas, also helped develop teaching on stewardship in Illinois. A noted authority on the subject, Kauffman gave his stewardship lectures in the state while serving as interim pastor at Tiskilwa and elsewhere, and on other occasions.[111]

Good stewardship involves also the proper use of the soil and other natural resources. Illinois Mennonites have done their share toward this reform also. By and large they have been good farmers. At Metamora on Soil Stewardship Sunday in 1957, Roy Bucher preached a sermon on "The Earth Is the Lord's." Stressing the Christian farmer's duty to conserve the soil, he hoped many in college would go back to the farm. The *Missionary Guide* editor thought the message important enough to publish in the paper's columns (Aug. 1957). Walter Bode of the North Danvers congregation, a member of the Board of Supervisors of the Soil Conservation District in McLean County, published in *The Mennonite* an excellent article entitled "Holy Ground." He said the church preaches much against sin, but how about preaching against "one of the greatest sins against the human race, which is the destruction of the soil"? Robert Yoder of Eureka wrote an equally good article entitled "The Good Earth." Concerned with the Christian's attitude toward land, he summed up with a quotation from C. W. Gees: "For truly the earth is the Lord's and the fullness thereof, but the responsibility for its stewardship is vested in man."[112]

Whatever may be said about too many Illinois Mennonites suffering from materialism, by and large and increasingly they have also been generous in contributing to worthy causes. Especially, they have shown strong social concern for hungry and destitute people at home and abroad, and have supported the Mennonite Central Committee (MCC) and their mission boards to meet these needs. Perhaps this growing support indicates that the teaching on Christian stewardship has been bearing fruit.

Support of MCC by Illinois Mennonites has been impressive. In recent years Mennonites in a number of states and provinces have organized relief auction sales, giving the proceeds to MCC for relief throughout the world. Illinois has one of the oldest and largest. In 1958 veteran lay church worker John Roth of Morton, having heard of a relief sale in Pennsylvania, talked with other Mennonites about having one in Illinois. The state's first Mennonite relief sale followed in 1959. Held annually for the first seven years at Congerville, the sales soon grew to such proportions that the controlling board had to move to larger facilities. These they found at Exposition Gardens in Peoria. Geographically, this has been conveniently near the center of the largest concentration of Mennonites in the state. Net proceeds of the annual sales have grown from $5000 received in 1959 to $148,178 in 1980. Considerably more than $1,000,000 has already been received and sent to MCC for service of compassion "in the name of Christ." "A volunteer labor force of more than 1,000 people contribute their time, talent, and financial gifts by helping in preparation weeks prior to the sale as well as on sale day." It is a tremendous community effort. Most of the items sold are donated. Included among them are the ever popular fine quilts—always good money raisers—which for many months before sale day women work to prepare. Because of distance the Amish and Mennonites at Arthur have their own separate relief sale. Hence the total contribution from Illinois is greater than indicated above.[113]

As Illinois Mennonites have responded to social issues, they have struggled with the challenge of the cities. Their response has been rather ambivalent. Nearly ninety years ago the more venturesome among the "rural" Mennonites were ready to accept the challenge and started city missions. But, as noted in chapter 11, there were doubters who thought that the Mennonite genius could be put to work more effectively and more efficiently in the rural environment. In the twentieth century some Mennonite scholars emphasized this rural motif. Many Mennonites questioned whether the more conservative groups could successfully promulgate the Mennonite distinctives in the cities. Nevertheless, city missions and churches continued and increased in numbers, although hardly with outstanding success.[114]

In recent decades the question has come up for new scrutiny. A good example is a General Conference Mennonite study headed by Leland Harder and published in the late 1950s and 1960s. The study covered, among other matters, a number of issues under the title "The Mennonite Church in the City." Some who contributed, including Harder, had served a number of years in Illinois. Harder pointed out that just "when home missions was due for new emphasis ... [the General Conference Board] of Home Missions was dissolved [in 1950] after 84 years of existence. It is precisely such a board as this which can devote its full time to grappling with the [urban] crisis of our generation that is needed for today's situation." Actually the Home Mission Board had been combined with that for foreign missions into one board. As a result of the new urban challenge to Mennonites the General Conference Board of Missions established a new Committee on City Churches (also called the City Church Committee).[115]

Others were also concerned about meeting the urban challenge more effectively. In the 1960s and 1970s Laurence M. Horst, an (Old) Mennonite worker in Chicago, conceded that Mennonites had not been very successful in the urban world. He thought possibly they had given too rigid a biblical interpretation on some of the distinctive doctrines. To be understood, Scriptures have to be interpreted in the light of their own day: "Who wrote them? To whom were they written? To what special problem were they written? ... What sociological need called them forth?" Horst added that when Paul wrote that women should keep silent in church and that if they want to know anything they should ask their husbands at home, "he was speaking to the Corinthian church and not to my church."

Another time, even more forcefully, Horst wrote: "Nothing seems clearer in the Scriptures than that the church belongs in the city. It seems that this has been a point of disobedience for the Mennonite Church." Horst thought Mennonites, despite their past record, were uniquely suited to work in cities; they were a caring people, they were "willing to work hard and sacrificially," and they had "an understanding of faith in the Gospel of Jesus Christ which affirms that men can be changed." Somewhere, continued Horst, "we became a bit confused about what separation from the world ... has meant [,] going into our rural ghettos and penning ourselves apart from the centers of real need." David M. Whitermore, appointed by the various Mennonite groups to be the coordinator of all the Chicago area Mennonite churches (eighteen in 1981), has been enthusiastic about the urban challenge. "Chicago needs us and ... we Mennonites need Chicago," Whitermore has said. He thought Chicago was a good place to carry out the "Anabaptist vision of the lordship of Christ as the basis for our discipleship."[116]

In 1978 another writer affirmed the Mennonites' need of the city, "just as they discovered they need overseas cultures, long regarded only as primitive arenas for missions outreach." "Ultimately," he added, "Mennonites need the city to keep a vital faith," even though, ironically, "this is just the opposite of what most of us have long believed." Mennonites had believed that if they could only stay away from the evil influences of the wicked city, they could keep their faith strong. But what the Illinois Mennonites now seemed to be saying, the writer noted, was that the gospel was universal and therefore adequate for all conditions of mankind. A faith to be kept with integrity must be able "to experience the pluralism of the city—all its different ideas and practices—without wilting." In 1965 Richard Yordy, president of the Illinois Mennonite Church Mission Board, asked: "Will new churches overcome [the] Mennonite urban pattern of the past 70 years and become large enough to be strong ministering congregations, or will a significantly different form of pastoral ministry, oversight and building pattern become necessary?" In any case, Yordy and the board, as well as the conference to which he reported, felt that they had to seek new, creative ways to serve more effectively in urban areas than they had in the past.[117]

Finally, in their responses to social issues, how have Illinois Mennonites looked on participation in community, state, and national politics? They have shown much ambivalence. In general, because of their isolation, their suspicion of the ruling authorities, and their view of nonresistance, early Mennonites outside and within Illinois tended to stay out of politics. There were exceptions, however, from Germantown onward. These exceptions became greater in the later nineteenth and twentieth centuries, especially among the more progressive groups. This was true of Illinois Mennonites. Of course voting was more common than office-holding, but even here the holding of lower offices was not unusual except among the small, very conservative groups. The doctrine of nonresistance continued to be a deterrent if the office-holding involved a use of force.

Although John F. Funk did not run for political office, perhaps few if any Illinois Mennonites have been more active in the political process than was Funk during his Chicago years. As noted earlier, Funk's close identification with the antislavery cause made him avidly pro-Lincoln and a "political enemy" of Stephen A. Douglas. Already in 1856 he worked ardently for the election of John C. Fremont, in 1858 for Lincoln over Douglas as senator, and in 1860 for Lincoln as president. He spent many hours in politics, as indicated in that letter to his parents in 1860: "Four evenings out of seven are taken up with church and prayer meetings, two of the remaining ones are devoted to political affairs. Last Tuesday evening Senator Seward came here and made a speech and everybody came to hear him." Funk was a member of the "Wide-Awakes," a club that campaigned for Lincoln by various means, including torchlight parades. After one parade he said that "such a great, glorious, good old time was never known in this city." After Lincoln and Hamlin's victory, Funk reported in fervid rhetoric the "glorious Republican" triumph: "On the wings of Electricity the news has gone abroad all over the land, and Ten thousand hearts, thrilled with enraptured delight, have made the very welkin ring with shouts of joy and congratulations over the victory we have achieved." After Funk's marriage in 1864 his wife "put her foot down on the torchlight marching, because he was burning holes in his one and only decent coat." Funk retained his interest in politics throughout life, although he became less enthusiastic about it.[118] In 1896 (Oct. 15) his *Herald* stated editorially that "it is unbecoming for a Christian to intermeddle with the political uproar" of a campaign. The *Herald's* statement was a far cry from Funk's own "uproarious" campaign in Chicago thirty-six years earlier, on the eve of the Civil War.

A different kind of political involvement was that represented by Christian Reeser, Sr. A little older than Funk but ordained as an Amish Mennonite minister in the same decade (1860s), Reeser participated more quietly and less actively. He, too, voted for Lincoln in 1860 and 1864. But it is said that otherwise he voted for every Democratic ticket from James K. Polk in 1844 to and including James M. Cox in 1920. He was more than 100 years of age when he voted in 1920—quite a record for an Amish Mennonite minister![119]

In 1867, the same year in which he moved his publishing business to Elkhart, Funk briefly reported in his *Herald* the meeting of an (Old) Mennonite Conference in Indiana. At that time the Illinois (Old) Mennonites, although not the Illinois Amish, were a part of the Indiana Conference. The conference cautiously decided that under certain conditions, apparently depending on the wording of the state law, church members could hold a public office such as road supervisor. In 1891 the Western District A. M. Conference, of which Illinois Amish were members, decided that church members could not accept the "worldly offices, except school director, road master and post master." At various times J. S. Shoemaker of Dakota held the offices of township supervisor, assessor, tax collector, and school director. Later, however, he seemed to take a more conservative position. In 1904, for example, he asked: "... how can we be truly nonresistant, if we hold office or help elect others to an office, by virtue of which he would be under obligation to violate the doctrine of Christ?" The Christian's citizenship is in heaven and "his standing before God is too high and noble to allow himself to stoop to that which is 'of the earth earthy,' and become entangled with that which belongs to 'Caesar.'" In 1905 he advised against using the ballot box to fight the evil of drinking, because he thought this would be a compromising way of dealing with the problem. Possibly Shoemaker changed his mind later when local option laws and prohibition became ballot issues. If he did not, many Illinois Mennonites disagreed with him.[120]

An increasing number of Illinois Mennonites began to feel they should take part in the public decision-making process, not only on moral issues such as liquor but also on others. To be sure, many still held the traditional view that nonresistant Mennonites, to be consistent, should stay out of politics and not hold office. Some even said that Mennonites should not vote. The Christian should obey the government (where he could do so conscientiously) and pray for it, but not get "entangled in politics . . . and in other forms of worldliness."[121]

But more and more Illinois Mennonites thought that there was a place for Christians in politics. In 1968 Norman Ringenberg of Flanagan wrote that while it was not necessary to preach partisan politics in the Sunday morning worship services, Christians should have discussion groups, and get help from other Christians on the various issues. He questioned, "How can we, as Christians, expect to have a Christian government and nation if we don't mix religion and politics?" In 1968 also, John C. Stutzman from Carlock said that ministers should not take partisan positions in the pulpit but that voters should act according to their Christian convictions. In the campaign the same year, Mary Rich Ball of Bartonville advocated support of candidates who were dedicated to acting on "the issues of Vietnam, civil disorders, poverty, space, foreign aid and taxation." In rendering "unto Caesar" what belongs to him, she wrote, our duty in economic, social and political affairs "is very evident." "God's power can redeem society by transforming human nature." Peter G. Schultz of Chicago warned that in maintaining law and order, which was emphasized much at the time, the Christian must do so in such a way that he does not identify with injustice.[122]

Illinois Mennonites like those of other states were more likely to be Republicans than Democrats. Occasionally this involved considerable soul-searching. In 1964 when it appeared that Barry Goldwater, the Republican candidate for president, was more likely to lead the country into war than was the Democrat Lyndon Johnson, apparently a number of Republican Mennonites voted Democratic. One Washington (Ill.) Mennonite asked: "Isn't he (Goldwater) the most dangerous candidate we have had in a long time?" This person hoped that Mennonites would not vote *only* for reducing federal expenditures "while wearing blinders for the really crushing needs of our times."[123] On the other hand, though precise figures are lacking, it seems that many Mennonites preferred the conservative Goldwater over the more liberal Johnson.

In September of 1968 *The Mennonite* polled every twenty-fifth subscriber as to political preference between Richard Nixon, the Republican candidate for president, and Hubert Humphrey, the Democratic. It also asked for comment on what the respondents thought were the most important issues. As of that time 59.3 percent had decided for Nixon and only 6 percent for Humphrey. But 28.7 percent were still undecided. Vietnam was the big issue. Many felt that Johnson had deceived them about Vietnam; as a result Humphrey, Johnson's vice-president, suffered. In an editorial in the October 22 issue Maynard Shelly, referring to the poll, found something more significant than the fact that Mennonites favored one candidate over another. This was the fact that when he asked what concerns the Christian should have for the political life "no one said that these things were outside the faith-life of a Christian." At the beginning of the century the protests against discussion of political issues would have been many and strong. But the "times have changed because we have changed." Shelly concluded, "Praise God, for he has opened our eyes. Having done that, He can and will use us."[124] Although this survey included more than Illinois, probably the preferences for that state alone would have been much the same.

Of course the above survey was among the more progressive General Conference Mennonites. Yet evidence suggests that the (Old) Mennonites and other groups have also been changing their views as to political participation. Recently, as noted earlier, the minister of one of the larger (Old) Mennonite congregations stated that he would be comfortable and happy to have the state governor be a member of his church. This presumably would apply also to other high governmental officials. In 1980 another person, Leroy Kennel, ordained but with no charge at the time, announced his candidacy on the Democratic ticket for the United States House of Representatives. He was nominated without opposition but being in a heavily Republican district in the suburbs west of Chicago he lost the November election. Kennel decided to run at the request of James Wall, Democratic State Committeeman and editor of *The Christian Century*. "When I was asked," Kennel stated, "I considered that an alternative voice—one which expresses what we have been researching in our studies of biblical and Anabaptist lifestyles—deserves to be shared by whatever means are available." Kennel is a member of the Lombard congregation and a teacher at Bethany Seminary. He has been pastor at Lombard and earlier at Metamora.[125]

All of the above indicates, as Maynard Shelly said, that the "times have changed because we have changed." But while a majority of the Illinois Mennonites were ready to accept the changes, not all of them could rejoice and praise God quite as loudly as Shelly did.

CHAPTER 15

Illinois Hispanic American and Afro-American Mennonites: The New Urban Challenge

Among the changes in recent Illinois Mennonite history is the development of Hispanic American and Afro-American Mennonite churches. This began at a time when Mennonites were a bit ambivalent as to whether in the future they should emphasize ministry in urban areas, or more in rural. Leaders such as Guy F. Hershberger and J. Winfield Fretz were emphasizing rural work, particularly because of the supposed Mennonite genius in tilling the soil. Fretz, of course, even questioned whether Mennonites should have been spending resources on city missions. In addition, many Mennonites still feared the city, because to them it typified "exaggerated evil, diverse people, fast living, complex organization, and an open community where anyone can be our neighbor."[1]

Soon after the Mennonites had started missions in Chicago around the turn of the century, population patterns began once more to change, as they had frequently before. Among the changes was the coming of many blacks from the South and the influx of Latin Americans, especially Mexicans from Texas and Mexico. Attracted by relatively high wages, especially during World War I, the newcomers fared reasonably well until the Great Depression of the 1930s. A large number of the Mexicans settled within a mile of the Home Mission, some quite close. Beginning about the 1920s, as mission workers visited in the community they began to encounter Spanish-speaking people and to invite the children, who could speak English, to attend Sunday school. At first a few responded, and then more. Soon the mission workers discovered that some parents, even though most were at least nominally Roman Catholic, desired to come also and did. But since the parents did not understand English, they wanted some services in Spanish.[2]

Thus Mennonites got into Spanish-language work inadvertently more than by design. To meet this new challenge they asked J. W. Shank, missionary on furlough from Argentina, to help. Shank was rooming at the Home Mission while attending Bethany Biblical Seminary. Of course he spoke Spanish fluently, and he gladly accepted the temporary assignment. Since the time was 1932, at the depth of the Great Depression and its unemployment, many people were in great need. Thanks to the generosity of rural Mennonites in Illinois and elsewhere, tons of food came to the mission for distribution to the community's unemployed, most of whom were Mexicans.[3]

The Spanish work grew and prospered—almost embarrassingly so. As noted in the previous chapter, when some wanted baptism and membership the question arose as to whether the work should continue as a part of the Home Mission or whether, because of some race prejudice, the work among the Mexicans should be separate and at a different location. This latter view prevailed. Apart from prejudice another reason—indeed the open, public explanation—was that the church should be nearer the center of Mexican settlement. There was, of course, truth in this contention. But the separation did not occur immediately. Shank held Spanish services at the mission on Sunday afternoons and twice or so during the week. According to reports, from thirty to forty and occasionally more attended the Sunday services. They "show great zeal and earnestness in their work, and a number are turning to Christ." Some twelve to fourteen of these joined the church during the time the group met at the Home Mission.[4]

Unfortunately for the new work, the Shanks had to return to Argentina in 1933. That left the group without a leader. After a short period Mission Board Secretary S. C. Yoder asked Nelson Litwiller, another Argentina missionary on furlough, to serve temporarily. Teaching part time 120 miles away at Goshen College during the year 1933-34, Litwiller consented to commute to Chicago to preach. While doing so he became acquainted with David Castillo, a recently converted Christian who had been born in Mexico. Litwiller invited him to the Mennonite Spanish services and soon became impressed with Castillo's devotion, ability, and interest in Protestant Christianity as interpreted by the Mennonites. Readily accepting Mennonite understandings as his own, Castillo soon began to make important contributions to the Spanish work. Litwiller arranged for him to take a short Bible course at Goshen College in January, 1934. Board secretary S. C. Yoder, who was also president of Goshen College, became impressed with Castillo and supported Litwiller's suggestion that the young man became pastor of the new Spanish group.[5]

Up to this time the Spanish ministry was carried on at the Home Mission. Now the mission sought a meeting place nearer the center of the Mexican community. Edwin Weaver, the new superintendent at the Home Mission, supported the move, as did Castillo. In September 1934 the congregation moved to a rented hall at 1128 South Halstead Street. The Illinois Mennonite Conference's mission board and the conference itself, along with the (Old) Mennonites' general mission board, agreed to assist financially. Lester Hershey, son of still other Mennonite missionaries to Argentina, succeeded Castillo as pastor in 1940 and served more than six years. One problem since has been a rapid turnover of ministers—at least fourteen from 1947 to the present (1980). All have been capable leaders, but nearly all were missionaries on furlough or retired. The list included Orley Swartzentruber, D. Parke Lantz, Elvin Snyder, Frank Ventura, J. W. Shank, William Lauver, John Litwiller, Mario Snyder, Don Brenneman, Albert Landis, J. Weldon Martin, Neftali Torres, William Hallman, and Ronald Collins. (Incidentally, Don Brenneman, who was ordained at this church, was the fifth successive generation of ministers in the Brenneman family.)

Despite turnover of ministers and a shifting population, the church's growth has been substantial, although like at most Mennonite missions, not phenomenal. It had fourteen members when it started in 1934, forty-nine in 1944, and according to the *Mennonite Yearbook*, eighty-nine in 1980. Attendance at Sunday school and church services, however, has been larger. At first considered an extension of the Home Mission, in 1942 the group organized as a separate congregation, with the name "Mennonite Mexican Church." Later, apparently about 1959, it changed the name to "Second Mennonite Church." Because of city renovation projects it has had to move its meeting place several times since 1934. In 1954, about two years after completing a new sanctuary, it moved to Blue Island Street and in 1964 to its present location at 2520 South Lawndale.[6]

This Mexican-American congregation has been active in its ministry, and the good work it has accomplished cannot be measured solely in terms of its membership. For instance, during his pastorate Lester Hershey founded *El Heraldo Mexicano*, which extended the voice and outreach of the church far beyond its local community. Begun as a monthly paper in March, 1941, the publication announced in its first issue that it was not only for people of Mexican descent in Chicago but for those elsewhere in the United States as well. In an article, "Do You Have a Spanish-speaking Friend?" published in the *Gospel Herald* (July 29, 1943), Hershey asked readers to send him names and addresses in order that he might send the paper free. At first the paper was mimeographed. But from November of 1942 on it was printed and the name changed to *El Heraldo Evangélico*, to appeal to all classes of Hispanics in the United States, not only Mexicans. With the help of other editors, Hershey, who with his wife moved to Puerto Rico in 1947, continued his connection with *El Heraldo* until December 1961. Printed at Scottdale, Pennsylvania, beginning in 1946, the paper was merged in 1962 with *La Voz Menonita* of Argentina to become *El Discípulo Christiano*, published for Latin-American Mennonites throughout the hemisphere.[7]

Source: Oyer, *What Hath God Wrought?*

David and Elsa Shank Castillo with daughter Anita. She was daughter of missionaries J. W. and Emma Shank; he was from Mexico and was the first Hispanic Mennonite (MC) minister for the work among Mexicans in Chicago that later became the Lawndale Mennonite Church, 1934-1940.

Members of the Mexican congregation were active in promoting the gospel. John Ramírez, for instance, preached among the Puerto Ricans employed by Mennonite farmers in Pennsylvania. Some of these accepted the invitation to move to Chicago. The Mario Bustos family of this congregation has also been active in outreach. Licensed in 1958 at Second Mennonite to preach, Bustos, in the same year and with the blessing of and some support from his congregation, opened a Spanish work in Milwaukee, Wisconsin. The Illinois Mennonite Conference's district board and the (Old) Mennonite's general mission board also assisted the work in Milwaukee. Bustos provided good leadership for a number of years until called to serve a Spanish-speaking church in New Paris, Indiana. Elvin Snyder, former missionary in Argentina, also served in Milwaukee capably for a few years. Aside from these men, however, the problem of securing adequate leadership has persisted. Largely for this reason the work closed for a short time, reopened under the leadership of William and Eleanore Shumaker, and again closed. The congregation, organized in 1959, was a member of the Illinois Mennonite Conference.[8]

The influence of Second Mennonite Church extended also to the western part of Illinois. In 1963 Mac Bustos, brother of Mario, moved from Chicago to the Davenport, Iowa-Rock Island, Illinois, area to shepherd a work among the Spanish begun in 1960 by Gladys Widmer of Wayland, Iowa, a missionary who had worked mainly in Puerto Rico. The missionaries served the Spanish migrants and held services at various places in the quint-cities cluster. In May 1964 they dedicated a building in Davenport. There is also a congregation in Moline. At the outset the Illinois Mennonite Conference helped support and supervise this work. Soon the Iowa-Nebraska Mennonite Conference (also MC) accepted the oversight. Thus the congregation is listed in the 1980 *Mennonite Yearbook* under the Iowa-Nebraska rather than the Illinois conference.[9]

Meanwhile in Chicago new phases of the Spanish work opened up. As noted earlier, when the Home Mission was forced to move in 1959, a nucleus continued to worship in the old area rather than go to Englewood. About that time a new movement of Spanish-speaking people into the Home Mission area began. Sadie Oswald and others in the Mennonite Community Chapel showed genuine interest in these people and invited them to services. A number accepted. Victor Ovando, a converted Catholic priest from Nicaragua preaching in Defiance, Ohio, accepted a call to work with the Spanish-speaking part of this congregation. The group prospered for a while and first moved to its separate quarters nearby, then a bit farther away to 2434 South Pulaski, and finally to 2628 South Komensky. Unfortunately, after initial progress the church, known as Iglesia Menonita Evangélica,

Source: *Lawndale Mennonite Church* (directory), 1975.

Lawndale Mennonite Church, a largely Hispanic congregation, with minister Ronald Collins, 1975.

came to a standstill. By the latter 1970s the Mennonites no longer supported this outpost. Ovando continued his work independently.[10]

Another Spanish-speaking Mennonite church grew out of the Mennonite Community Chapel in 1972. Guillermo Espinoza and his wife, natives of Bolivia, accepted an invitation to start such a work and in August Espinoza baptized six people in Lake Michigan. He characterized this event as an "inspiring experience for the young church," which became known officially as "Iglesia Evangélica Menonita." In a valuable account of this congregation, Espinoza has discussed its problems. One has been a large number of illegal immigrants or "wetbacks" who "come to church in search of all kinds of help, from food and clothing to work and security" but, according to Espinoza, seldom seemed to be "sincerely seeking God." This put the pastor "in a difficult situation regarding his conscience." Despite this and other problems the congregation, with some assistance from the Illinois Mennonite Conference and the (Old) Mennonite Board of Missions, made progress in various ways. In 1975 it purchased a building at 1021 West 19th Street suitable for worship. The membership numbered forty-five in 1980.[11]

Espinoza had strong feelings of sympathy and kinship for his fellow Hispanics, even though he was a Bolivian and most of the people he worked with were of Mexican background, and even though nearly half were illegal aliens. He was concerned about helping them educationally as well as spiritually, believing that education also helped them economically. In making plans for another church still farther south in Chicago he sought facilities which could be used for both purposes. In 1977 he found a suitable building at 1649 West 51st Street and started another Latin-American church, which included some educational work. By 1980 it had sixty members. Within a short time he was planning to found another congregation still farther south for the same purposes. In fact his strong missionary interest extended to other areas as well, including the reopening of the work in Milwaukee.[12]

Work among the Hispanics in Chicago has not been easy. Even so, new congregations were being formed as late as 1980. Edwin and Marcella Stalter bring this out in their booklet, *Illinois Mennonite Conference in Mission* (1980). Moreover, Espinoza and others, including the Illinois Mennonite Conference, have been deeply concerned about the high rate of unemployment among the Hispanics and other minorities. This, in Espinoza's poignant words, "leads us many times to unemployment offices, factories, schools, etc., etc., with the objective of orienting and helping the brethren who are 'foreigners' in all possible ways, for they are affected by this socio-economic problem, long lines and hours, with the bitter reality of what this involves, with direct and indirect impact on the church families," which has "made us conscious of the reality, though dramatic and under circumstances tinged with cruelty in which our people live."[13]

Just a few years after they began Spanish-language work, Mennonites in Illinois also began Christian ministries among blacks. Some new work came by deliberate, advance planning, for instance at Bethel in Chicago, and some by accident of population shifts, as in the case of First Mennonite in Chicago.[14] When the work at Bethel began in 1944, mission among blacks was not new for Mennonites. As early as 1898 some in Pennsylvania had broken ground in this field. In fact, the pioneer Mennonite black worker in Chicago, James H. Lark, came from that state.

To a considerable extent the Bethel work grew out of the Chicago Home Mission. Lester Hershey of the Mexican Mennonite Mission also favored and supported it. In the spring of 1944 a Goshen College voluntary service group made a thorough survey of the area around 14th Place and Laflin Street. As a result the church councils of the Home and the Mexican Missions recommended that the Illinois Mennonite Conference, through its district mission board, open work among blacks. The conference and the mission board accepted the report and in May 1944 decided to give support for one year under the Home Mission's local board (Walter Yordy, William Brenneman, and Theodore Wentland). The (Old) Mennonites' denominational mission

Source: Oyer, *What Hath God Wrought?*

James H. Lark (1888-1978), first black minister of Bethel Mennonite Church, 1946-1956, and of Rehoboth Mennonite Church, 1949-1952, and first (Old) Mennonite black bishop; with Sunday school children at Dearborn Street, Chicago, in 1947.

board had also sanctioned and supported the project. Under the leadership of Lester Hershey, Walter Yordy, and Mr. and Mrs. James Lark, who had been brought in from Quakertown, Pennsylvania, for the occasion, a successful summer Bible school for black children was held in the summer of 1944. In late August, shortly before the close of the summer Bible school, the workers held a meeting and organized the Bethel Mennonite Church.[15]

Lark had been asked to take charge, and he and his wife moved into a home near the mission. In 1946 he was ordained minister and in 1956 bishop. He was the first black minister and bishop in the Mennonite Church. For a meetinghouse, those in charge rented a building at 1434 South Laflin. The work grew. But growth, as well as the changing character of the area, posed continuing problems of securing adequate facilities and sufficient personnel. At times the congregation asked workers from Moody Bible Institute to assist. In November 1947 the enrollment at Bethel was given as ninety, with an average attendance of sixty and membership of twenty-four. The congregation had already started a mission outpost on Dearborn Street with an enrollment of forty and a membership of twelve. Lark's report to the Illinois District Mission Board in 1948 showed that the congregation was having a healthy, normal growth and activity. He reported on baptisms, communion services, his ordination, guest speakers, sewing circle work, summer camp, summer Bible school, fellowship dinners, Mothers' Study Club, Christmas activities, and the branch mission ministry on Dearborn Street. The summer camp mentioned was Camp Ebenezer in Holmes County, Ohio.[16]

In 1949 the various boards agreed that the denominational mission board should take over financial responsibility for Bethel. The Illinois district mission board hoped the transfer would mean better support and greater effectiveness. One problem the congregation faced was a parsonage for the Larks and adequate quarters for worship. Condemnation of the building in the area because of the city's renovation program compounded the problem. Also, a fire in the building where the group held services destroyed some of the Larks' property. Lark was released from responsibility at Bethel in order to solicit money for a new worship center. In the interim Paul and Lois King took over the Bethel leadership. The congregation was pleased to be able to dedicate a new building in September of 1954. Another source of delight and satisfaction was the summer Bible school attendance in July of that year. Three hundred and twenty attended the first day and 373 a few days later. The civil authorities also looked with favor on the Bethel program because it seemed to be improving the moral tone of the community.[17]

Lark conducted an energetic, aggressive mission outreach. Soon after establishing the Dearborn Street outpost he began another at St. Anne near Kankakee. There, with the help of a group from northern Indiana, he bought land and built a cabin in the summer of 1949 to serve as a summer camp for Chicago children and young people. He apparently thought a camp some sixty miles south of Chicago would be more convenient than the distant one in Ohio. He had ambitious plans to found other posts throughout Chicago. Perhaps this energetic spirit is what prompted one Illinois minister to write: "The relation between Lark and our [Illinois district] Board puzzles me. I[t] seems Lark is ten jumps ahead of someone, and it appears to be our Board."[18] This work at St. Anne, the center of a considerable black population, developed into a permanent church, Rehoboth, where Mark Lehman and others have served as pastors. Rehoboth's membership was thirty-eight in 1980. Like Bethel, it received support from the denominational board, until 1980 when the Illinois Mennonite Conference relieved Elkhart of this responsibility.

After a good beginning and good progress for a decade or so, the work at Bethel experienced difficulties. For a short time in the 1950s Lark was inactive as a minister because of a misstep he had taken. He acknowledged his mistake, made things right, and before long was again actively promoting his favorite cause—the extension of the Mennonite witness in urban areas. He moved to St. Louis where, in the words of Nelson Kauffman, the Mennonite Board of Missions' secretary for home missions, he served "very satisfactorily." He helped extend this ministry not only in Chicago and St. Louis, but also in Fresno and Los Angeles, California; Saginaw, Michigan; Wichita, Kansas; East St. Louis, Illinois; and elsewhere. At his funeral service on January 14, 1978, fittingly held in Chicago at the Bethel Mennonite Church which he had founded, LeRoy Bechler, pastor of Inglewood Mennonite Church in Los Angeles, said: "Before us lies history, for Rev. Lark was a man who was 50 years ahead of his time in vision and concern for the growth of the Mennonite Church in the urban areas of our nation." The high respect in which this man is held is also indicated by the recent establishment at Goshen College of the James H. Lark Scholarship and Leadership Program, designed to train Mennonite blacks for leadership roles in their churches, largely in urban areas.[19]

After Lark left, Bethel was faced with a leadership problem. A number of leaders served too briefly to carry out effective programs. Some, such as Paul and Lois King, did a good job of pushing forward. Others experienced turmoil and challenges to their leadership. Joe L. Holloway, installed as pastor in 1963, was discouraged at times. In 1964 membership was down, the faithful attendants being mostly women. "It is very discouraging to preach to only women most of the time," Holloway reported. More encouraging was the good work of the day care center, which the community appreciated and praised. Even this, however, brought problems. In 1969 a group of militant blacks attempted to get control of the center under conditions which the congregation as a Mennonite group could not meet. When negotiations were broken off, threats came. But the community rallied to the defense of the church and the crisis passed. Under the leadership of Leaman Sowell who, as of 1980 had been pastor for a considerable length of time, the work seemed again to be moving forward.[20]

Another church in Chicago that was not started for blacks but became predominantly black through population shifts is Englewood. This of course was a continuation of the Chicago Home Mission, which had to move in 1957 when the city authorities decided to build an expressway where the mission was located. The congregation moved to 832 West 68th Street in the Englewood area, establishing Englewood Mennonite Church. Mostly white at first, the congregation is now largely black. Upon the recent death of Ambers Wright, Louis Hagens assumed the leadership. The membership as of 1980 was fifty-three.[21]

A General Conference congregation, Markham Community Mennonite Church, began in 1955 as Mennonites from Chicago moved to the south suburban area. Under the leadership of Ronald Krehbiel eighteen charter members organized the congregation in 1957. Meeting at first in a community building symbolized what the congregation throughout its history has tried to be—a "helping-healing" influence in the community. During the next two years the congregation worked to construct a meetinghouse at 16200 South Kedzie, the dedication taking place in August, 1959. Lawrence Voth, who became pastor in 1961, said the church wanted to "give stability to a sea of restless souls who have little stability in any part of life. We want to make Christ relevant to the problems in Markham." Probably alluding among other things to the fact that many blacks were moving into the community, he also wanted the congregation to take seriously Saint Paul's teaching that "in Christ there is neither Jew nor Greek." This included the difficult task of resisting racial and cultural exclusiveness so typical of American church life. The membership of the congregation has had a steady growth. By 1964 Markham's membership of forty-seven included five blacks. In 1975 the membership of ninety was about half black.[22]

Since 1964 the Markham congregation has tried to be a "helping-healing" influence in the community through the operation of a day nursery. In 1967 it was reported that most of the children came from (sometimes broken) homes in which both parents worked. There has been much demand for such services, and the Markham facilities, both for the congregation and the day nursery, have been enlarged several times since the beginning. Pastor Larry Voth was convinced of the value of the nursery. "I would certainly encourage you to establish a Day Nursery in your church," he wrote to a friend. "We have found that it has been an extremely welcome facility in our town and certainly has given us unusual opportunity for service."[23]

In addition to helping the children directly, the workers hoped to reach the parents through the children. The staff has consisted of local volunteers and young people assigned by the denominational headquarters to Markham as voluntary service workers. In cooperation with the Markham Sheltered Care Workshop housed in the Trinity United Church of Christ nearby, this combined ministry has become a kind of "experience outpost," with workers, including students from Mennonite colleges, coming from other parts of the United States and from other countries. The period of their service has ranged from two weeks to two years, with a few deciding to cast their lot with the community and remain indefinitely. In any case, this "church community has provided a context in which many different young people have been able to experience urban society and the problems and possibilities of the Church as it seeks to minister in this society."[24]

Markham continued its progress under the leadership of Ed Springer, who succeeded Lawrence Voth as pastor in 1973. A significant development in this period was working out affiliation of the Mennonite congregation with the nearby Trinity United Church of Christ, an affiliation begun in 1971. The two groups worked together not only through a shared pastor but also through various cooperative activities such as Sunday evening meetings and joint summer worship services. The Markham "Brief History" states that just as the earlier experience of racial changes "brought a new sense of what it means to be the Body of Christ, so too this new sharing across denominational lines has brought a renewed challenge to manifest the life of the Spirit in both its oneness and its diversity." Springer, however, resigned at the United Church of Christ in July 1976 in order to devote full time to Markham. In 1977 he resigned at Markham also. After more than a year of lay leadership in the congregation, Menno and Margaretha Ediger became copastors.[25]

Another General Conference congregation, First Mennonite Church in Chicago, also underwent a transition from white to black in recent years as its neighborhood changed. As one of the more thoughtful white members wrote in 1966, the transition was interesting as well as challenging. "There have been much thought and heart searching as this is a new way of life." Henry Spaeth, the white pastor, resigned in 1968. He felt strongly that, in the "age of black power," the congregation needed Negro leadership. Later in the year Arthur L.

Jackson, a blind black, was installed as pastor. According to a report in the *Central District Reporter* (Sept. 17, 1968) he had been an (Old) Mennonite minister in the Spencer congregation in the suburbs of Toledo, Ohio, and before that had had pastoral experience in the Franconia Conference in eastern Pennsylvania. The same periodical (Sept. 21, 1971) states he was ordained at First Mennonite in July 1971. Apparently before that he was only licensed. Despite his handicap, and despite the fact that his wife was also blind, he was remarkably active in the congregation and community. John H. Burke is the present pastor.[26]

Illinois Mennonites have been exploring the possibility of working among other minorities, for example, Orientals. As one leader put it, "More New Things Need Doing." No doubt they will be done.[27]

Clearly, by the 1970s the Illinois Mennonites were feeling new challenges from the city. In a sense history was repeating itself. In the 1890s, as noted earlier, a small but growing minority was challenged to open mission work in Chicago. Those Mennonites were not well prepared. Mennonite ruralism and then the Hershberger-Fretz school of thought began to cast doubt as to whether Mennonite priorities were in the right place and whether the Mennonite genius did not continue to point to rural areas as more promising and fruitful for Mennonite outreach. Even in the 1950s, when young rural Mennonites came to Chicago to attend seminary or university and work in the churches they were disturbed and shocked to be confronted with squirming youngsters whose interests centered "mostly around Elvis Presley, murder mysteries and movies, comics, gangs, boyfriends, dancing, and bubble gum." How does one communicate the gospel to these children "from crowded tenements and broken homes?" they asked. Old techniques and lectures were hardly adequate! Where else, they added, could you find a seventh-grade girl who stayed out all night with a boy, a girl learning to steal clothes in a store, an eight-year-old boy who stole cupcakes by hiding them in his shirt, a sixth-grade girl carrying a knife and a flashlight for protection while coming to junior choir? Such situations, concluded the writer, forced a "startling realization of how far removed we [in rural areas] live from the frightening temptations and deep spiritual needs of these city children."[28]

The urban racial explosion in the 1960s and developments since have caused much heart-searching and review of priorities. Illinois Mennonites have begun to experience a sort of "second awakening" to the needs of the city. They have realized that despite some past failures and difficulties for the so-called Mennonite rural genius, the hard-core inner city is still a part of the world to which they are commanded to proclaim good news. More and more Illinois Mennonites have come to believe with David Whitermore, coordinator of inter-Mennonite ministries in Chicago, that: "We have put literally millions and millions of dollars overseas. I would like to see some of the fruits of that work and learning put to use for urban ministries. There needs to be preparation for mission in the city just as much as there is for mission overseas."[29]

Several perceptive articles published in 1978 have indicated awareness of this "new way of life"[30] for Mennonites. Ivan Kauffmann, a minister from Hopedale serving at Lombard as general secretary of the (Old) Mennonite General Board, has written five installments on "The Urban Mission and the Mennonite Church." He pointed out how the matter of the Mennonite witness in the cities, despite difficulties and some earlier failures, was a tremendous concern at the General Assembly of the Mennonite Church in 1977. Kauffmann thought this was the "Macedonian call" coming to the Mennonites. Especially germane was his third article, "Help! Help! Help!" He strongly appealed for help to enable the urban congregations to experience greater participation with the total church, for help to provide and prepare more urban leaders, and for help to make more resources available for urban needs. "The urban mission call for help is an urgent one. Too long a delay will be costly," concluded Kauffmann.[31]

Vic Reimer wrote about the same time (Nov. 21, 1978) in *The Mennonite* on "Mennonite Witness in Chicago." Among other considerations Reimer pointed out urban leaders' frequent concern that "rurally oriented Mennonites (even those who live in cities are still likely to think in terms of rural values) do not have a clear understanding of urban conditions and how the church functions in that setting." This problem is still greater where there are additional racial and cultural barriers to understanding, as in the case of minorities. George Classen, the pastor of a Chicago inner-city storefront church, said that churches of Mennonite background expected city congregations, even minority churches, "to be just like them." "Some of the easy rules and regulations that conferences pass," he added, "go well for long-established churches with a firm Christian heritage, but they are neither realistic nor practical for many city congregations." Since Mennonite teachings did not necessarily conform to the inner-city people's "culturally accepted norms of virtue and responsibility," added Classen, "there is a gap between the expectations of other Mennonites and the reality."[32]

Other tension points have had to do with the meanings of success and of being "Mennonite." Many inner-city churches, especially the minority groups, receive subsidies. Is such a church successful? Many Mennonites might say "no." But success in the inner city would likely be measured in terms of ability to hang on and survive. "That is the benchmark," said George Classen. As coordinator David Whitermore has stated, it is important for the entire church family "to realize that some city churches—particularly those in changing neighborhoods, in foreign culture and language settings, and in poverty areas—are mission outposts," and need support just as foreign missions do.[33]

Being "Mennonite" has not necessarily prevented painful and bitter problems of racial and cultural identity and integrity. At a Chicago workshop for Mennonite church leaders, the participants were asked to name four reasons for wishing death. In answering this strange request blacks and browns included their skin color. It was not always "cool" to be black or brown, they said. It could be a burden to be nonwhite and non-Mennonite, but it could also be "an oppressive burden to be nonwhite and Mennonite."

There has been a brighter side. Chicago area Mennonites have tried with some success to be creative in meeting these hurts. To the question, "Can Chicagoland form an accepting, supportive Mennonite fellowship across cultural and racial differences?" the answer has been "yes." One reason for Mennonite mutual support is the need for a vision which includes the goal of an "Anabaptist theology adapted to the needs of the city and creatively incorporating the diversities of the city." For this purpose Chicago Mennonites have organized various educational activities. For example, a "Retreat to Develop Urban Church Leadership," held at Camp Menno Haven in 1977, was attended largely by Latinos and blacks and only a few Anglos. Dale Suderman spoke on Anabaptist history in such a way that the group could easily identify with the historic movement. He stated that many of the earliest Anabaptists were educated city people. Chicago Mennonite youth "identified with their spiritual ancestors in ways they could not with many areas of 20th-century rural Mennonites." One camper was inspired by the thought that he was a real Mennonite even though he was "a Castro from Chicago and not a Yoder from Goshen." A similar type of seminar was held in Chicago in January of 1980. Lee Hochstetler, pastor at Grace Mennonite, told the group there: "For too long urban churches have been stuck with picking up the pieces from the destruction caused by social problems.... But this week, veteran urban church workers helped us to see that we must work to change the systems that cause the problems." Bennie Whiten of the Community Renewal Society told the group that we needed to help "people gain control of their own communities and of their own lives." If we do that then "we are also helping ourselves." "If my brother or sister is impoverished, then I am ... impoverished too." The participants had high praise for the week-long event.[34]

In concluding his discussion of the "Mennonite Witness in Chicago," Vic Reimer also saw the brighter side: "But I also sensed a creative movement of Christ-motivated persons seeking not only to survive, but to live warmly and openly across the barriers of race, culture, and ethnicity. There were good feelings because the problems were being faced. In diversity there will be joy and strength and peace." Probably no one has understood the recent issues surrounding Mennonite work in the city better than has David Whitermore, coordinator of Inter-Mennonite Affairs in Chicago. Neither has anyone worked harder nor done more to bring Chicago Mennonites together as a family, despite differences. Whitermore too stressed the fact that in a family of Christ-motivated persons there could be joy, strength and peace in diversity.[35]

Among the more significant Illinois Mennonite developments in recent decades has been not only a new outreach and meeting a new challenge from the cities; there has also been the challenge of making urban Anabaptist disciples of different hues and colors. As that happens, the term "ethnic Mennonite" means less and less.[36]

CHAPTER 16

Other Developments and Trends in Recent Decades

The impact of the city on Mennonites[1] has not been only in missions and in congregations of non-traditional ethnic background. Various studies have shown that the urban trend includes "rural" Mennonites. One study states that church membership growth in Illinois in recent decades "seems to have been largely Urban-Mission congregations; while at the same time the 'Rural-Original congregations' have shown a decrease in membership." In 1940 the Peace Problems Committee of the Mennonite Church conducted a survey of Mennonite men between eighteen and sixty-five to ascertain how many were employed as farmers and how many had non-farm jobs. For all (Old) Mennonites in North America, 60% of the men were engaged in farming and 40% had non-farm jobs. For Illinois the comparable figures were 63% and 37%. In 1965 the Mennonite Research Foundation conducted valuable family census surveys, headed by Melvin Gingerich, among (Old) and Conservative Mennonites. Gingerich and his colleagues found that in Illinois 43.5% of the employed men in the sample were farmers. The Illinois percentage of farmers was slightly higher than the North American (Old) and Conservative Mennonite average of 38.9%[2] Another measure of ruralism was of course residence. Two years earlier, in what he had called "The Mennonite Family Census of 1963," Gingerich had surveyed the residences of (Old) Mennonites in Illinois and found them to be: Urban 36.2%, Village 18%, Farm 45.8%. He used the guideline followed by the United States Census Bureau, classifying as urban any municipality of 2,500 population or more.[3]

As to the shifting of population from rural to urban, one authority has stated that Mennonites are moving *toward* the cities rather than *into* them. This statement applies particularly to the larger cities. To be sure, Mennonite congregations in a metropolis such as Chicago have been increasing in number. But even there, members of the older established churches have tended to move to the suburbs. So the "urban trend" among Mennonites is toward the towns and smaller cities. Lately even in rural Illinois only a minority of the general population is made up of farmers, for rural areas have experienced rapid increase in percentages of nonfarm population. The whole Bloomington-Peoria region is a splendid example of an area "clearly under urban influence." One conference report in 1965 indicated that the rural Mennonite churches in Illinois were growing, but at a declining rate. In fact eight churches had suffered actual decline in membership, and of the eight, six were rural. It also said that the greater the distance from the city, the greater the likelihood of slow growth or decline. Arthur, Cullom (now extinct), Waldo at Flanagan, and Willow Springs at Tiskilwa were examples. This same report indicated that "most rural churches have not related very effectively to rural nonfarm people," and added: "This is the most urgent evangelistic responsibility for many rural churches."[4] The General Conference congregation at Tiskilwa is another illustration. In 1972 the pastor reported a common complaint of churches in its situation: "The work at Tiskilwa is not progressing by leaps and bounds, but we are 'plugging on.' ... We have very few young people. After High School graduation they either leave for college or secure work elsewhere. That seems to be the small town problem."[5]

Thomas Yoder with Gerlof Homan and Lotus Hershberger, all of Normal, recently (1980) made a study of occupational changes among Illinois Mennonites. Dealing only with the MC, GC, and EMC groups, the study shows that the urban trend has continued and also indicates a proliferation of jobs which the Illinois Mennonites perform. While one should allow for a certain percentage of error, this study indicates a further proportionate decline in Mennonite farm population as compared with earlier figures, a trend confirmed by other authorities. But the decline in Illinois, according to Yoder, was not as great as it was churchwide.[6]

There are exceptions, of course, to the suggestion that congregations under urban influence grow most. Summerfield near East St. Louis and St. Louis has had a struggle to continue existence as a congregation. In 1974 one member reported that "the majority of our congregation is retired, and for quite a few of them the Social Security check is their only source of income." In addition, the group apparently experienced some disagreement on whether there was "any future for a separate Mennonite church in Summerfield." Some members had joined other churches, either through marriage or because of the local Mennonite church's uncertain future and a problem of retaining pastors. So the group is small, with a membership only of some twenty. Yet the remnant is composed of those most interested in retaining a Mennonite identity. George Dick, located in Bloomington

Glenn Ebersole farm near Sterling, Illinois, an example of a present-day Illinois Mennonite farm.

Eureka Hatchery, owned by Ralph Imhoff in Eureka, Ill., 1948; an example of modern Illinois Mennonite small business.

Other Developments and Trends in Recent Decades 439

150 miles away, travels to Summerfield and serves as minister.

As a whole, however, the Illinois Mennonite churches have continued to grow and prosper in recent decades.[7] Considerable evidence suggests that evangelism has increased. In 1976 Pastor Ward Shelly at Calvary in Washington, for example, led his congregation in an evangelistic thrust in various ways. In addition to having its own evangelistic services and stressing proclamation in its regular services, Calvary took the lead in various activities, including a Sunday school and a clothing distribution center in a high-crime area in Peoria. Earlier (1966) Shelly as chairman of the General Conference evangelism committee presented a resolution to the triennial session of the General Conference asking all congregations to emphasize evangelism more. The resolution passed. In 1973 the General Conference group called a meeting in Chicago to discuss new ways of church planting, such as house churches, intentional communities, and interdenominational congregations. As Ward Shelly said: "There is only one way of salvation, but there are many ways of evangelism."[8]

Other voices confirmed the evangelistic thrust, including (Old) Mennonite ones. Writing in 1973, Ivan Kauffmann emphasized evangelism as an important church goal. Carl Newswanger as editor of the *Missionary Guide* wrote that it was time for new church planting. In 1969 the Illinois Mennonite Mission Board accepted as a goal the establishment of fifteen new congregations in the following decade, and said that "we call congregations to prayer, spiritual renewal and personal response that this outreach goal may be achieved." The board significantly added that the call to evangelism must "encompass the whole need of man (social and spiritual)," and include a "commitment to peace and service" and to helping each other. Richard Yordy was asked to give full time to the church in mission in Illinois.[9]

A similar spirit activated the Conservative Mennonites in the Arthur area. Milton Otto was asked to visit the churches of his conference in the interest of missions. In 1972 some members from Arthur attended the so-called "Explo 72" at Dallas, Texas, an interdenominational evangelistic conference, and were affected by it. The young people became excited about evangelism, wrote delegate Danny Otto. "This is your invitation to come help change the world." But after witnessing the demonstrations and protest marches of the 1960s, Otto made it clear that we "can only change the world by changing individual people in the world. The only way to change people is through Jesus Christ." As did other groups, the Conservative Mennonites used radio to spread their message.[10]

Recent decades have also been times of anniversary celebrations, including centennials, which spring from a people's sense of maturity. In recent years such celebrations have become increasingly elaborate.

There have been anniversaries with historical addresses and the publishing of congregational histories. There have been historical skits and plays, some of them quite detailed. Some Illinois Mennonites have written histories of their congregations at the time of the centennial and then dramas later. In 1954, for instance, Hopedale members wrote *100 Years at Hopedale* and then in 1976 they had Carolyn Nafziger produce *The Hopedale Story: A Historical Drama About the Hopedale Mennonite Church.* With encouragement and help from Pastor Aden Yoder and from former Pastor Ivan Kauffmann, the congregation very ably presented the play during a Heritage Weekend in September of 1976, as a contribution to the United States Bicentennial. In 1979 the First Mennonite Church of Morton also presented a detailed drama presenting the highlights of its history. In this case the congregation—constituting a merger of Goodfield and Pleasant Grove—was celebrating the centennial of the first meetinghouse at Pleasant Grove. Both the Pleasant Grove and Goodfield congregations had been organized earlier.[11]

In 1978 the Groveland Evangelical Mennonite Church also held a weekend of rather elaborate centennial services. Here also the occasion was the anniversary of its first church building rather than the origin of the congregation, which had Amish beginnings in the 1830s.[12] Roanoke celebrated the seventy-fifth anniversary of its first meetinghouse in 1950, and then its centennial in 1975.[13] Its beginning as a separate congregation was a few years prior to erection of its first church building.

Some Illinois congregations have taken up the practice of having "Homecoming" celebrations. Metamora, for example, had its first one in 1940. The featured speaker was the native son and pioneer Mennonite historian, C. Henry Smith, who gave an informative and well-received talk entitled "One Hundred Years Ago—An address delivered at the first Home Coming celebration of the Old Partridge congregation near Metamora, Illinois...."[14]

Anniversary celebrations in and of themselves do not constitute growth. But emphasis on evangelism among Illinois Mennonites has resulted in gradual expansion. In 1922, in Illinois, the (Old) Mennonite Church for instance had 1,958 members in seventeen congregations. In 1966 there were 3,736 members in thirty-seven congregations, an average increase of about 1.5% per year. In 1978 the membership for the two largest bodies was 2,223 for the General Conference body and 4,239 for the (Old) Mennonites. In 1980 the respective figures were 2,297 and 4,297. Even this modest growth compounded the problem of supplying enough ministers, which with recent emphasis on training has become even greater.[15]

Along with growth in numbers Illinois Mennonites have shown

modest growth in financial giving to the church. Increased teaching on evangelism went hand in hand with a new emphasis on Christian stewardship. Lester Janzen, stewardship secretary of the General Conference, conducted stewardship seminars and conferences in several of the churches, to some of which other Mennonites were also invited. Participants have testified to the effectiveness of these meetings. To illustrate, Mrs. Roy Ehresman from Flanagan wrote that she was impressed with Janzen's idea that her money was herself—"my time, my ability and my energy converted into a medium of exchange. My money talks and I determine what it says: Do I really prefer hospitals to taverns; do I really prefer to send missionaries or missiles; do I prefer New Testaments to filthy magazines; do I prefer to bless or curse, to heal or kill?" As to other congregations, she pointedly added: "If you prefer not to have your individual members reevaluate their lives in terms of what really counts, do not invite Lester Janzen for stewardship day. It takes too long to forget!" Milo Kauffman, of course, also influenced Illinois Mennonites in favor of stewardship. In 1974 First Mennonite at Morton approved an annual budget that increased its

Source: Archives of the Mennonite Church

Noah E. Byers, J. Frederick Erb, Aaron C. Good, Harvey E. Nunemaker, Robert Keller, Harry F. Weber, and Amos E. Kreider at Centennial Celebration of Science Ridge Mennonite Church near Sterling, June 27-29, 1958.

designations to churchwide causes to 10 percent above askings. Kauffman, interim pastor, explained: "We felt it only fair to do this since we are blessed financially above many. We should help make up what some churches are unable to do." A few years earlier East Bend, influenced by a stewardship conference, had also increased its giving to mission causes.[16] Apparently other congregations had also caught the spirit of increased giving. The Illinois Mennonite Church Conference *Reports* (1975, 12 and 1979, 10) indicate that from 1971 to 1977 giving through the regular budget increased from $247,791 to $620,577, although a slight decrease followed in the next two years.

In the September 25, 1979, issue of the *Gospel Herald*, Mildred Schrock, administrative assistant for the Mennonite Church General Board, published an article, "Mennonite Church Giving—1978." Mennonite Church members in that year gave an average of $361.24 to the church program through the regular channels, an 11½ percent increase (roughly equivalent to inflation) over the previous year. In fact, there had been similar increases for several years. One should add that the amounts reported here did not include monies given directly to MCC such as that raised at relief sales and other direct gifts. Schrock gave a breakdown of per-member giving by (MC) conferences. The per-member giving in Illinois was $439.73 as compared with that average of $361.24. This was not the highest, but it was near the top.[17] Comparable MC figures for 1979 show an increase, but again hardly more than enough to offset inflation. In the Illinois Conference (MC) per-member giving was $486.59, exceeded only by the Franconia Conference in Pennsylvania with $529.14 per member reported. The MC average was $403.49, which was only about 5 percent of income.[18]

Another form of Illinois (Old) Mennonite giving was donations to Goshen College. In a ten-year comparison the per-member giving from Illinois was higher every year, usually much higher, than that from any other conference. Of all the conferences only Illinois, in 1976-1977, ever gave 100 percent of the amount asked, and in other years it was much the closest. Indiana-Michigan per-member giving was second, and that of Ohio a distant third.[19]

Part of the teaching on stewardship included emphasis on estate planning. Leaders encouraged members to manage and plan so as to leave some of their estates to the church upon decease. This included making annuity gifts to the church and its institutions, under which agreements the annuitant would receive interest during his lifetime and then at death leave the principal to the church. R. L. Hartzler was one of those most active in promoting this plan.[20]

Not all Illinois pastors were satisfied with the church's program of giving. When Mennonite Church officials reported in 1977 that contributions were not coming up to the levels hoped for, one pastor

Other Developments and Trends in Recent Decades   443

who claimed to speak for a large "silent majority" complained that if one disagreed with parts of the church's program and the methods used for promotion he was put down as disloyal and almost dechristianized. He thought that such people used nonsupport quite properly "to get the message across. Many of us," this pastor added, "believe too many boards and commissions are too concerned about their own commission and not the Great Commission." Let them design "a board or commission to exalt the Lord Jesus instead of genealogy or organization and see if this board or commission lacks funds."[21] No doubt many agreed with the pastor, although probably not the majority.

One very visible change in recent decades has been in the architecture Illinois Mennonites have used for church houses. In earlier centuries the Anabaptists and Mennonites had broken with the Catholic medieval idea that it was necessary or desirable to build huge, ornate cathedrals "for the glory of God." In fact in the early years of persecution they were not allowed to construct houses of worship—or, if they were, in some places the buildings had to be concealed from public view. In any case, for whatever the reasons, if and where meetinghouses were used they were simple structures in line with the simple lifestyle of the Mennonites. An additional influence in America probably was the plain meetinghouses of the Quakers. Therefore for many years after they began in the 1850s to use meetinghouses for worship in Illinois, Mennonites and Amish Mennonites erected severely plain buildings, rectangular, with saddle roofs, vestibules at

Source: Roanoke Mennonite Church Centennial Year, 1875-1975.

Roanoke Amish Mennonite Meetinghouse, built in 1875, showing traditional frame meetinghouse architecture.

the entrance end, and usually an annex in the rear. Usually they were frame structures. Despite the progressivism of the Stuckey and Egli groups, those branches also continued to reflect their Amish origins and to maintain such architecture.[22]

In more recent years, however, the Stuckey and Egli groups have changed more to forms used by other Protestants. Not far behind them, (Old) Mennonites also have considerably changed their meetinghouse style as they have built new buildings. In the process of replacing the earlier more simple structures, Mennonites have been in danger of imitating other churches without thinking enough of their own principles or traditions. That is not to say they had to keep traditional design rigidly unchanged, or that they could not consider aesthetics. An earlier departure from the traditional, for example, was a new meetinghouse that Roanoke erected in 1920. In the words of Harry F. Weber this new building was:

> a fine new brick structure ... very practical and useful ... for worship and Bible School ... erected with the idea that it was not consistent to build useful barns and fine homes, and a second-rate building for the service of God. The idea in construction was neatness, utility, and service, avoiding the elaborate and showy. The building has a high ceiling with good acoustics, containing a small side room which can be used to

Source: Roanoke Mennonite Church Centennial Year, 1875-1975.

Roanoke Mennonite Church, built in 1920, showing influences of mainline Protestant church architecture. The building still forms the main part of the church, although remodeled in 1956 with large wings added.

accommodate the overflow whenever necessary. It also contains a mothers' room with the necessary equipment for the convenience of the mothers and the comfort of the children. There is a spacious basement with one room which is used for Junior meetings, also rooms for the convenience of men and women, and a primary room for the youngsters.[23]

Since about 1920 the trend away from the traditional in church architecture has accelerated.[24] In an article entitled "Buildings, Buildings, Buildings," Richard J. Yordy, an Illinois (MC) leader, said that there was danger "of a church building idolatry." But, Yordy conceded, the Illinois (Old) Mennonites' mission board has tried to "upgrade the beauty and utility of buildings used by newer churches." There was a widespread feeling that some of the earlier mission church buildings "by their severe plainness and cheap construction [had] had a negative influence on the Christian witness in our society." Among the guidelines which Yordy suggested was that the "structure should appeal to the entire community in which it is located as a fitting headquarters for the Christian congregation."[25]

The Old Order Amish of course still do not build meetinghouses. A few other small, conservative groups have not departed widely from traditional architecture. A scan of pictures in Mennonite periodicals since World War I indicates that all other branches have changed their church architecture considerably. Yet in most cases the "idea in construction was [still] neatness, utility, and service, avoiding the elaborate and showy."

Along with growth in numbers and in church building came growth in Illinois Mennonite institutions—Salem Children's Home, Bloomington Mennonite Hospital, and the homes for the aged at Eureka and Meadows. The founding and earlier history of these institutions was noted in chapter 11. The institutions also have enthusiastically celebrated their various anniversaries. For the 75th anniversary of the Salem Children's Home in 1971, E. E. Zimmerman, EMC historian, wrote a short history of the institution, briefly chronicling the various stages of growth. Another writer has pointed out that the institution's annual budget grew from $75,000 in 1963 to $250,000 in 1973 and to $488,750 in 1979.[26]

The number of children the Salem Home serves has actually decreased in recent years because the state of Illinois has changed its philosophy on the use of such institutions. But services rendered have continued to grow. This can be seen in the following developments:

1964—Developed cottage concept for residential care
1966—Social work program begun
1968—Received child welfare agency license
1971—Completion of third cottage
1975—Developed Vocational Boys Program

1977—Hired fourth social worker
1977—Established Developmentally Disabled Program.[27]

The institutions at Eureka and Meadows for serving older people have grown substantially. Since their openings in the early 1920s both have increased their capacity and facilities some four or five times. About 1960 the Eureka Home began building cottages so that the elderly could live independently and yet have the services of the Home. In 1965, in order to meet state requirements, the administration completed and dedicated a 48-bed nursing center. This facility replaced an existing 14-bed infirmary. Since the Home had been serving not only Mennonites but people of many religious faiths, the community wanted to help in this endeavor. In fact the federal government, Mennonites of Illinois, and the Eureka community all provided funds.

Superintendents of the Eureka Home since J. D. Smith have been Clayton Sutter, Earl Greaser, and Frank Kandel. The most recent expansions of consequence at Eureka have been the building of a large apartment complex, finished in 1979, further enlargement of the nursing center in 1980, and some current renovations. The Home plans also to set up a "retirement community without walls" to be known as the "Illinois Elderly Service Program." This plan, worked out in cooperation with the Mennonite Board of Missions, calls for a voluntary service unit at the Home. Unit members will offer assistance to needy elderly people who would otherwise need institutional care, but who with some help can live in their homes. According to the plan this service will go into effect in 1981. As Tilman Smith, liaison person with the board, has said: "Our overall goal is to help older citizens live better and longer independently." Since such aid can be given more cheaply than institutional care, the government offers financial assistance.[28]

The Meadows Home, still under the auspices of both the General Conference and Evangelical Mennonite churches, underwent similar development, part of it due also to changing state and federal requirements. After a new wing was added in 1952 and nursing care facilities in 1966, the bed capacity stood at 66. Since then the institution has provided duplex cottages for independent living and in 1977 dedicated a 94-bed addition. The net increase in capacity was not quite 94 beds, however, since the new addition replaced an older part. Like the Eureka institution, the Meadows Home serves people of many religious faiths. Only about half the residents are Mennonite, and financial support comes from the local community, as well as from the Mennonite churches and the government. Significant support comes through bequests such as one in the will of the late Purley and Viola Bertsche, which provided some $250,000. David D. Schrag has been the administrator for some years. Lotus Troyer, pastor of the Flanagan Mennonite Church (GC), gave part of his time to the Home as chaplain and director of development. In 1980 George Classen of the North Danvers Church replaced Troyer at the Home.[29]

Thus in the twentieth century Illinois Mennonites have become increasingly conscious of the problems of the elderly. A growing literature attests to their concern—for instance, a 1959 article by Art Nafziger of Hopedale, "Golden Age Groups in Our Churches." The author pointed out how significantly old people have contributed and still contribute to the church. "The MYF," he said, "is not the church of tomorrow nor are the oldsters the church of yesterday." Rather, all members are the church of today. We must not neglect any of them.[30]

About 1961 Professor Carl F. Smucker of Bluffton College and Robert L. Steiner, a social worker who had been one of Smucker's students at Bluffton, published *A Research Study of the Aged—in a Central Illinois Mennonite Community*. They had carefully researched ten General Conference Mennonite congregations in the area, and they wanted to "present available data on aging so that local churches might be more aware of the needs in their respective congregations." They hoped the churches would "become more sensitive to each individual, older person and ... better plan to meet his needs." While the survey was to benefit the entire General Conference Church, those in charge thought that an in-depth study of a representative area would serve their purposes better than would a churchwide random sampling. They secured the names of all those General Conference church members 65 or over in central Illinois (354 persons), including those in retirement homes. All but a few who were away from home or were too ill or senile were interviewed.

Smucker and Steiner's conclusions emphasized that "no person living in a home for the aged was dissatisfied with these [living] arrangements—despite the prevailing apprehension about 'putting the older folks away.' ..." The least satisfactory arrangements had respondents living at home alone or with others in their homes. For those living alone, loneliness was a great problem. The researchers found considerable acceptance of the idea of separate cottages or apartments where some association and services could be provided but where the person could have some privacy and freedom. Some old folks were having a hard time financially and others feared they might have in the future. Many wanted part-time employment. The people usually had not prepared for retirement; they drifted into it. Men had more difficulty in adjusting to retirement than did women. Both men and women, because of the strong Mennonite emphasis on work, were not prepared to use leisure time very constructively. On this and other points, especially the idea of preparing for retirement, Smucker and

Steiner suggested that the church ought to make further studies.[31]

Probably the Illinois Mennonite institution which has grown most in recent years is the Bloomington Mennonite Hospital. Its earlier history has been noted in chapters 5 and 11. Coinciding largely with the administration of William E. Dunn (1959-) and his able assistants, some of the more significant recent accomplishments, according to historian Steven R. Estes, have been: improved heating and laundry facilities; piped oxygen to a new hospital wing; an improved communications system; a more active auxiliary, which started a program of annual equipment gifts to the hospital; installation of the Brewer system, which provides a time-saving plan for dispensing drugs; full-time chaplains—Ben W. Krahn, Samuel M. King, and others; and addition of a physical therapy department and an intensive care unit.

By mid-1960s the hospital faced a problem, near the surface for a long time, of whether the Bloomington-Normal area needed three hospitals. Many thought not. So the Mennonite Hospital Association considered various options. One was merger with or sale to another hospital. Another was large expansion, to allow Mennonite Hospital to provide new kinds of health care. In a special meeting on November 22, 1965, which Estes has described as "one of the most significant ever held by the Mennonite Hospital Association," the authorities voted by an overwhelming majority for expansion. A few months later they added plans for a 76-bed nursing care wing for older citizens—an extended care unit, as the government called it. A development office was organized, headed initially by Erwin C. Goering, to raise the funds for this and future expansion. By the fall of 1970 construction was completed. All of this permitted a remarkable range of health services to the community: acute care, intensive care, self-care, home care, rehabilitative care, long-term care, post-coronary care, adult day care, ambulatory care, and homemaker service. (Recently this homemaker service was incorporated into the home care program.) Also, in 1977 the hospital began offering 24-hour emergency service with full-time physicians. Outpatient services, started in 1949, have grown tremendously. In 1978 the hospital served more than 21,000 outpatients— more than three times as many as those admitted to hospital beds. In 1981 Mennonite Hospital began another expansion program; this time the cost was $11,400,000.[32]

A somewhat opposite change at Mennonite Hospital, but one not likely to impede growth, has been the closing of the obstetrical department in 1968. This was done partly as a gesture of cooperation with the other hospitals. Because of a strong reputation for excellence in this area (at "one time nearly half of the babies born in McLean County were delivered at Mennonite"), the decision did not come easily. But

Source: Mennonite Hospital Association, Bloomington, Ill.

Mennonite Hospital in Bloomington, Illinois, 1980.

the community wanted less duplication of effort, and the obstetrical facilities at the other two hospitals were new and adequate. Another form of cooperation was establishment of the Bloomington-Normal School of Radiologic Technology. The three hospitals and the local radiologists acting together opened the school in 1966.[33]

Among other significant developments was a decision in 1976 to construct a new health center. Its purpose was to supplement the physical treatment by paying attention to the mental, emotional, and spiritual needs of patients. Through this center, as well as through the chaplaincy, Mennonite ministers have become active members of the health care team. Named in honor of the veteran leader Raymond L. Hartzler, the center was completed and opened in 1977. In 1979 the Hospital Association erected a physicians' office building, which was located in the R. L. Hartzler Health Complex. In 1978 it extended services still further by purchasing and beginning to operate the local hospital at Eureka, Illinois.

Strong emphasis on eye care has continued at Mennonite Hospital, and addition of highly sophisticated equipment has encouraged eye specialists to come to the community. It is one of the most important eye care centers in the state.

The Mennonite Hospital School of Nursing also has experienced change and growth. In an effort to offer a better combination of nursing theory and clinical experience the administration expanded the curriculum and arranged for the freshman class to attend Illinois State University in Normal, securing twenty-seven credits in the basic sciences and humanities. In 1968 the school received accreditation from the National League of Nursing. Also in 1968 the Hospital Association revised its constitution, enlarging its board and including some non-Mennonites.[34] Through these and other developments the hospital's administration has remained committed to providing the highest levels of health care in a Christian setting.[35]

Another change among Illinois Mennonites in recent decades has to do with a less optimistic view of progress. As noted earlier, turn-of-the-century Mennonites were caught up in the "spirit of progress," as exemplified by John S. Coffman's noted address on that topic at Elkhart Institute in 1896. In September, 1910 the Central Conference's *Christian Evangel* editorialized, "Will the World Be Won?" "Why ask the question?" the editor queried. "Is God's power limited? Is His method of winning the world a partial failure? I think not," the editor answered optimistically. "Surely such thoughts have no place in our conception of the God we love, worship and obey." C. Henry Smith wrote, also in 1910, that war was "on its last legs." With many others, he thought Christian principles would sweep the world.[36]

But in his own lifetime and in his own thinking Smith saw a decline in optimism. Speaking at the Metamora Church in the early 1940s, during World War II, he said that by 1900 it had seemed that the worthy social goals of religious toleration, civil liberty, democracy, and peace were "in a fair way of being realized. The world was almost safe for democracy; peace conferences and arbitration treaties seemed on the verge of ushering in a new technique for the settlement of international quarrels." Then had come World War I, the Great Depression, and troubled times thereafter. These had "turned us back once more toward the dark ages from whence we came with political and social ideals more vicious by far than those we had discarded ages ago. At no time for centuries has religious toleration, and the very existence of religious faith itself, to say nothing of democracy and peace[,] been so challenged and threatened throughout a large part of the world as today."[37]

In this sober vein Smith spoke for a good many Illinois Mennonites. Since he spoke, events by and large have done little to restore the old optimism. Young people especially have often become more pessimistic and critical of our institutions. Yet times and moods change. Perhaps by the late 1970s and early 1980s the majority of Illinois Mennonites can be classed as "realistic optimists" or maybe "optimistic realists."

However, there is continued idealism and a critical attitude toward materialism among some younger Illinois Mennonites. This has resulted in the establishment of intentional communities. As noted in chapter 14, two Mennonite-related ones are Reba Place in Evanston and Plow Creek near Tiskilwa. Very few other such Mennonite communities exist in North America. The Hutterites, related historically to Mennonites, have property in common. Perhaps the number of such communities will increase. In 1975 the Mennonite Community Association sponsored a conference at Tiskilwa on the theme "In Search of Community." The Willow Springs and Tiskilwa Mennonite congregations assisted, and about seventy people attended. The conference used resource persons from the Fellowship of Hope, an intentional community at Elkhart, Indiana, as well as from Plow Creek and Reba Place. They discussed such topics as "Membership and Commitment," "Money and Property," "Leadership and Followership," "Decision-Making," and "Problem Solving." One speaker stated that the confession that "Jesus is Lord," was the basic commitment for membership. Another remarked that organizational leadership was not so important as the Spirit of Jesus. "What we are looking for is radical discipleship.... If you have found forms where you can be more faithful, we want to know about them."[38]

More than 500 people met at Reba Place in 1979 for a similar conference, with a few additional Mennonite and a number of non-

Mennonite intentional communities participating. Most of these apparently were a part of the Shalom Covenant, a network of Christian communities from the Midwest organized in 1974 "to provide mutual support, fellowship, and a more objective balance for churches which have incorporated a community lifestyle." Within Shalom Covenant each church community "continues to actively participate in its respective denomination." The conference dealt with such topics as "Enriching Personal Devotional Life," "Seeing God in Nature," "Affirming Each Other as Sisters," "Men's Sharing Groups," "Inner Healing," and "Cultivating a Vibrant Family Life."[39]

Another change has been more use of lay persons for the work of the church. A good example is the General Conference organization of Central Illinois Mennonite Men, begun in 1964. These laymen felt that they should become more active Christian witnesses and make the church a more powerful force in their communities. Desiring to enlist as many men as possible, they also wanted to "achieve a real feeling of unity among the churches resulting from working together." Sponsoring music programs, prayer breakfasts, study seminars, and other activities, they looked upon themselves as an arm of the church to be used where opportunity afforded.[40]

This emphasis on lay effort has come along with a renewed idea of the priesthood of believers and a decreasing emphasis on hierarchy. For the Illinois Mennonites this has meant less control by bishops and conferences and more congregational control, together with a growing appreciation of the role of women, youth, and all lay persons. A declining (Old) Mennonite emphasis on district conferences coincided, to some extent at least, with the promulgation in 1971 of a new "General Assembly" structure and regional organization. All factors point to a trend away from conference-wide legislation and toward congregations deciding particular issues and cases as they see fit or discern God's will. The divorce question illustrates the shift. Instead of having a rigid conference statement which attempted to cover all the various cases (as most groups had formerly), the major bodies now have statements which continue to emphasize the high view and permanency of the marriage relationship, but which no longer state inflexibly that no divorced and remarried person can under any circumstances be a member of the church. Since Illinois Mennonite congregations now have more leeway, there are a few more divorced and remarried members in them than formerly. Occasionally, however, a conference statement may not reflect the actual, up-to-date practice.[41]

Greater congregational control has been discussed earlier in connection with such matters as the clerical garb, the prayer veiling, musical instruments in worship, various expressions of nonconformity, and the changing role of women in the church. No doubt the

Lombard experience of "ordaining" or "commissioning" a woman for preaching will become more common in the near future. Lillia (Mrs. William) Espinoza in Chicago, for example, has been licensed to preach and will probably be ordained.[42]

Still another change involving more congregational control has been in the method of selecting ministers. At first nearly all Illinois Amish and Mennonites used the lot, although Summerfield and some of the Chicago mission groups probably did not. The Egly and Stuckey groups, after they broke from the Amish, soon discontinued it. But the more conservative groups, including the (Old) Mennonites, continued the practice well into the twentieth century. Some of them still use it. On the other hand, Hopedale, conservative as it was in some respects, was a pioneer among the Illinois Amish Mennonites in discarding it. In 1892 the congregation ordained Daniel Nafziger and Joseph Egly by majority vote. Minister Benjamin Springer, 1881-1968, stated that he could not remember that Hopedale ever used the lot. At present, virtually all except very conservative congregations have shifted from the lot to congregational vote.[43]

Another change, greater emphasis on education among the Illinois Mennonites, is simply a part of the American experience. When the present writer was graduated from the eighth grade in Illinois in 1915, it still was not common for Mennonite youth to go to high school. In his talk at the Metamora Mennonite Church in 1940, C. Henry Smith stated that in the 1890s he and three of his cousins—Ben Schertz, John Camp, and Christ Imhoff—"were the first boys from this congregation ever to attend the local high school." He added, "And as far as I know we were the first from any of the Amish communities throughout the whole of central Illinois. We had few successors in our own generation."[44] Mennonites followed the American trend, although not always closely, and during the latter 1910s and in the 1920s and 1930s, and especially in the 1940s and after, the number going to high school and then to college increased considerably. In the meantime compulsory school laws began requiring attendance until age 16. It is probably correct to say that after World War II a considerably larger percentage of Illinois Mennonite youth were going to college than went to high school in 1915. During World War II the story was different. Some were drafted and others who would have gone to college remained on the farm to avoid being drafted. Some feel that one result was that the church suffered a gap in trained leadership.[45] But by 1966, according to one study, about three fourths of the MC pastors "had at least some college level training."[46]

According to Thomas Yoder's survey, which included educational attainment, by 1980 Illinois Mennonites were faring comparatively well. Yoder states that among the three main groups (MC, GC, and

EMC) in 1972 "the percentage of persons . . . completing eighth grade, high school, and college and then earning a graduate degree . . . [was] higher than among the three groups churchwide."[47]

Part of the educational picture which involves some change as well as a problem and challenge is a growing tendency for Mennonite youth to attend non-Mennonite colleges. Attending non-Mennonite colleges is of course not new and some persons loyal to the denomination have had good reasons for doing so. But with more secularization and acculturation of Mennonites the problem has become greater. In 1973 Paul O. King, then moderator of the Illinois Mennonite Conference, expressed concern. He pointed out that in 1972-73 one hundred and two (Old) Mennonite students from Illinois attended Mennonite colleges, while 169 attended non-Mennonite ones. If the trend continued, he asked, what would it mean for preparing Mennonite youth for leadership, and how would it affect the communication of the Mennonite faith, heritage, and discipleship values to youth? Also how would it affect the support of church colleges, which serve Mennonite young people and provide leadership? King believed congregations should discover and call out potential leaders and assist them in securing training for pastoral ministry and mission service.[48] George Dick, General Conference pastor at North Danvers, had expressed a similar concern earlier, although he had emphasized financial support of the church schools as well as student attendance.[49]

In a study entitled "Mennonite Church Students—Fall 1979," Paul Bender has stated that the total of (Old) Mennonite Church members of college age in Illinois in 1979 was 446. Of them, 242 were actually in college and 109, or only 45 percent, were in Mennonite colleges—the lowest percentage in the Middle (U.S.) conferences. But seen another way, the Illinois record was good. About 16 percent of the total college-age Mennonite Church members attended their church's colleges, but 24 percent of Illinois' college-age (Old) Mennonites were attending. In other words, 54 percent of all (MC) college-age people in Illinois were in college in the fall of 1979, and 24 percent of all these college-age people were in their church's colleges.[50]

As noted earlier, one way in which a few congregations have been encouraging their young people to attend Mennonite colleges has been to pay part or all of the tuition. The idea is not new. Already in 1912 Aaron A. Augspurger, Central Conference minister at Saybrook, broached the subject. Conditions, he said, "are wonderfully changed." The simple life of the forefathers and the church were being challenged and threatened. The Central Conference had become "highly prosperous financially," a circumstance that leaders had "a hard struggle to keep pace with spiritually." "The rising tide of education and financial prosperity," he continued, "have paved the way for new difficulties in the future that we have not had in the past." Leaders had to be ready to meet the new conditions. But, Augspurger asked, where were the leaders? He suggested that each congregation set up a ministerial aid fund for the training of future ministers. He also urged his conference, which apparently had already started such a fund, to increase its contributions. The church had to do a better job of providing trained leaders and teaching because "very few of our younger members are able to tell what they are."[51]

Such a Mennonite voice in 1912 was a cry in the wilderness. But in time even the more conservative (Old) Mennonites heard it. In 1954, following the death of Henry R. Schertz, the Metamora congregation established the H. R. Schertz Memorial Scholarship Fund to aid and encourage needy students from that and other (MC) congregations in the state to attend church schools in preparation for Christian service. The Illinois Mennonite Conference has set up a loan fund from which Illinois students attending Mennonite seminaries can borrow money without interest.[52]

While several Illinois congregations are now aiding students in the late 1970s and early 1980s, the outstanding example dollar-wise has been the Mennonite Church of Normal (GC and MC). This 372-member congregation raised more than $40,000 in student aid for the 1978-79 school year. Sixteen students each had their tuition paid in full at Bethel College (GC institution in Kansas), at Bluffton College, or at Goshen College. According to Pastor James Waltner, the financial assistance "has definitely made a difference in the number of our high school students considering a Mennonite college." The figures for 1980-81 are still more impressive. Twenty-one students at Goshen, Bethel, Bluffton, and Mennonite Hospital had their tuition and fees paid, costing $65,000. Strictly and technically speaking, the fund is not made a part of the regular church budget but is raised by a volunteer group within the congregation. Perhaps that arrangement has helped the plan succeed. The aid is in the form of grants that do not have to be repaid. Students are encouraged, however, to "contribute back to the scholarship fund if and when they can."[53] No doubt this commendable practice will become more and more common.

One specific recent development has been the founding of Trinity Mennonite Church at Morton, which separated from First Mennonite. The circumstances of its organization were unfortunate, but the total membership of the two congregations is now considerably larger than it was at First Mennonite, and both groups are still in the same conference (MC). The story of the separation is hopelessly detailed. In short, as a result of differences and misunderstandings, the congregation asked conference leaders for help. In May, 1977 these leaders took soundings and found much polarization. One problem area was decision-making in the congregation. A substantial number felt they had no or very little voice. Quite a few felt also that their gifts were hardly being used.

Another divisive issue was forms of worship, or "the kind of piety in worship." The issue involved the charismatic experience, although to what extent that helped cause division is difficult to say. Trinity Mennonite Church, the group that left First Mennonite, has stated that they are "not a charismatic nor anti-charismatic church, but simply a New Testament believers church of the Mennonite Anabaptist tradition." Yet clearly they wanted freer forms of worship, with testimonies by the laity playing a larger part. One of their concerns "was a lack of openness to sharing in worship and a criticism of those who testified for Jesus."[54]

A third problem was leadership. Some were dissatisfied with the pastor. Others felt that the elders and some other individuals exercised too much power and refused "to share leadership responsibilities with the whole congregation." There seemed not to be a harmonious, smoothly working relationship between the pastor and the elders.[55]

Conference officials made some suggestions for improvement. They also pointed out the many strengths they had found in First Mennonite: "Its friendliness, hospitality, service interests, relief sale supporters, zeal for the Lord, etc.," plus the "very many good comments about the pastor" and his ability as a "good Biblical expositor."

Despite hopes and efforts of the conference officials and others, separation occurred in August of 1977. Meeting for some months in temporary quarters for services, the Trinity group began the erection of a new church building in Morton in August 1978 and dedicated it in September, 1979. According to Trinity's first *Annual Report* 1977-1978, one hundred and eight members transferred from First Mennonite. First Mennonite's membership had been 279, so those leaving were a large minority. Trinity's membership as of 1980 was 137. On October 1, 1977, Mahlon and Dorothy Miller "accepted the congregation's call to serve ... as Shepherding Elders." Quite a few of the new congregation were of non-Mennonite background, but the group seemed strongly determined to uphold the "basic tenets of [Christian] faith as held by the early Mennonite Anabaptists." They also wanted to stay with the Illinois Mennonite Conference. In the spring of 1979 the conference accepted Trinity's application for membership. Already in August of 1977 the new group stated to First Mennonite: "Our congregation has agreed that we are anxious to be a sister church to First Mennonite, and to work toward that goal in the spirit of love and brotherhood. We recognize that there are some differences between us, but we are hoping that the Mennonite Church will send us off with their blessing, and commission us to be God's people as we establish our witness and outreach in the community." Trinity is also on record as accepting "without reservation the authority of Jesus Christ as Lord of the Church, the Scriptures as God's Word, and the New Testament as our rule of faith and practice. We accept the 1963 Mennonite Confession of Faith and are affiliated with the Illinois Mennonite Conference." Their statement of belief indicates they are evangelical, evangelistic and nonresistant, and that membership is "only for those who have repented of their sin, received Christ as Lord, [been] transformed by [and filled with] the Holy Spirit, commit[ted] themselves to each other, and are seeking to live obedient Christian lives."[56]

Differences of opinion which lead to separation are always regrettable, as both sides freely conceded. Both groups also expressed a deep desire for Christian love, forgiveness, and reconciliation.[57] Though the Metamora congregation was reluctant to release him, James Detweiler, who went to First Mennonite as pastor, has been and no doubt will continue to be a healing, helpful influence. It is altogether possible, some think, that the combined Christian witness of the two congregations will be greater than the witness of the one congregation was before.

The charismatic movement, which has found homes in many Christian churches in recent years, has also influenced Illinois Mennonites. Especially in the congregation at West Sterling differences of opinion have arisen concerning it. The pastor, Harley Stauffer, has been very influential in the congregation during the past ten or eleven years. In 1979 he took a leave of absence to accept a radio ministry offered by a Sterling station. Jared Yoder, a member of Zion Chapel, a charismatically inclined fellowship at Goshen, Indiana, was secured as interim pastor.

In the fall of 1979 problems arose at West Sterling over interpreting the work of the Holy Spirit, over what some thought was a trend away from the Mennonite Church, and over the relation of the conference to the local congregation. Some wanted the help of the conference in settling their problems, and others did not—or at least they objected to the way in which the matter was handled. Stauffer felt that the charismatic movement was not the main problem. He said that the movement had been influential in the congregation ever since the time of Holy Spirit Festivals at Goshen College in 1972 and 1973, which he and others of the congregation attended.

In any case, in the winter and spring of 1979 some members, including the Stauffers, withdrew from active participation in the congregation. Yoder, whose theology and methods seemed out of line with the Illinois Mennonites including many at West Sterling, terminated his ministry at the end of the interim period. The congregation, most of whom wanted to continue as a part of the Illinois Mennonite Conference, have been searching for another pastor. John Troyer of the Dillon church has been assisting on a temporary basis.[58]

A recent development in southern Illinois appears in the 1980 *Mennonite Yearbook.* That directory lists three new Mennonite congregations: Ewing (21 members), Mt. Pleasant at Anna (43), and Orchardville at Keenes (35). These are a part of the Eastern Pennsylvania Mennonite Church Conference district, a group which separated from Lancaster Mennonite Conference in 1969 when its members thought the Lancaster Conference was giving up too many Mennonite positions and practices. In addition to being quite conservative, the breakaway group is also premillennialist. The name of their mission board is "Mennonite Messianic Mission Board." They take a strong position against participating in the armed services. Any member who enters the armed forces, either as a combatant or noncombatant, automatically forfeits church membership. However, thankful for the alternative service provision for conscientious objectors, the group does not believe in protesting against the draft or against so-called war taxes. They believe that Christians are "required to pay our taxes," that "tax monies belong to the government," and that government is "solely responsible for the use of its monies." Members "are not permitted to take part in protest demonstrations or in the so-called peace movement."[59]

As of 1980 the conference had forty-six congregations with 2,381 members. Although located largely in Pennsylvania, it has a few congregations in other states and also in British Columbia and Guatemala. The group's church periodical is *The Eastern Mennonite Testimony.* Two conference leaders, who also carry important leadership responsibilities in Illinois, are bishops Isaac K. Sensenig and Jesse Neuenschwander.[60] The lines of communication and fellowship for the new congregations in Illinois are east-west, largely into Pennsylvania, and not north-south with the other Illinois Mennonites.

CHAPTER 17

Toward Mennonite Cooperation and Unity

Denominations which emphasize congregational life and control as much as do many Mennonites are likely to have problems maintaining unity. From their origin Anabaptists held many different points of view. At first in America, however, Mennonites, except for the Amish division, were quite united. Most of the schisms for which Mennonites and Amish have become notorious did not occur until the nineteenth and twentieth centuries. Since Mennonites have been quite individualistic and schismatic, the number of groups in North America constantly changes. So to give a precise number is difficult. Some seventeen or eighteen groups can be identified in the twentieth century. According to the 1980 *Mennonite Yearbook* (p. 146), there are twenty-one branches in the United States and Canada. That number includes the Hutterian Brethren, the Old Order River Brethren, and the Brethren in Christ, all of whom are related but not Mennonite; it does not include nearly all local variations.

Illinois has only some nine Mennonite branches, and some of those have only one, two, or three congregations: three connected with the Eastern Pennsylvania Mennonite Church, and one or two each with Reformed Mennonites, Mennonite Brethren, Beachy Amish Mennonites, and Conservative Mennonites. It has a few independent Mennonite congregations. For thirty-five or forty years after Mennonite beginnings in Illinois (about 1830) there were essentially only the two bodies—the Amish and the Mennonite, with some differences among the latter, as represented by the Summerfield group and the Reformed congregation at Sterling. The number increased with the coming in 1865 of Amish who remained Old Order, in the Defenseless Mennonite division in 1866, and the Stuckey Amish separation in the 1870s. The number of Mennonite branches in the state further increased around 1900 with several bodies establishing mission churches in Chicago.

Thus Illinois presents a Mennonite mosaic almost as complicated as anywhere. Growth toward cooperation and unity in Illinois is a mixed story. But at least so far as the two major groups are concerned—the MC and the GC—the state is probably among the leaders. The more capable church leaders and laity have never forgotten Christ's prayer for unity—"that they may be one." Illinois has had a number of such concerned people.

Illinois Mennonites have shared a common heritage which many have found very meaningful. In addition to close physical contact as neighbors, many have had connections with more than one body through intermarriage and birthright. A good example of this is Edwin J. Stalter, a current Mennonite Church leader whose mother was from the Central Conference and whose wife had been Evangelical Mennonite. A number of twentieth-century leaders and laity in the Central and then General Conference came from the (Old) Mennonites. Such changes at times may cause people to react against and to dislike the old church; but it need not always turn out that way. Some eight or ten ministers in the Old church who joined the Central Conference in the 1910s and 1920s and labored a number of years in Illinois retained a respect for their earlier church home and served as bridges of understanding between the two groups. For example, Raymond L. Hartzler, who graduated from Goshen College in 1918, wrote: "I shall always cherish [my] (Old) Mennonite background and training and particularly the spirit of my Alma Mater as expressed in her motto, 'Culture for Service.' What better motto could any church college espouse?"[1]

Already in the nineteenth century there were Mennonite voices calling for unity. They were voices in the wilderness, but made themselves heard almost as soon as divisions occurred. Ironically, John H. Oberholtzer, the center of an important division in Pennsylvania in 1847, raised such a call. At least as early as 1856 in *Das Christliche Volksblatt* he first publicly proposed a union of all Mennonites. The General Conference Mennonites which Oberholtzer helped organize in 1860 included his proposal for union as one of its goals. At first this affected Illinois directly only at Summerfield, but later it involved large numbers when the Central Conference people became a part of the General Conference body in the 1950s.[2]

More to the point in Illinois was the case of Joseph Stuckey. In 1871, when differences with his Amish brethren were beginning to surface, Stuckey published four letters from the Amish division in Switzerland and Alsace in the 1690s. In a preface, Stuckey said he wanted to see what the points of misunderstanding were and, for unity's sake, try to avoid such mistakes in the future. He continued:

> We are people surrounded by weakness, but if we can see where others have erred then we can guard ourselves against such errors.

Therefore it has been considered worthwhile to collect these old letters again in order to examine them since so many errors arose from the Jacob Amman [sic] division in 1693 and have been preserved to this very day. Also it may contribute something to closer connections with each other and perhaps to heal the division which would of course be desirable.[3]

One of the earliest Illinois voices in the wilderness was that of Christian Erismann, the Amish schoolteacher in the post-Civil War period. Erismann frequently confided to his diary a concern and prayer for Mennonite unity. As a layman he attended a number of Amish and Mennonite conferences and worshiped with various groups. He could not understand that God would insist on the use of hooks and eyes and why there should have been so much emphasis on this point. "O, gebe Got [sic] seinen Segen, dass die Mennonitten sich wieder vereinigen würde, dies wäre mein sehlichster Wunsch." ("O, for God to give his blessing that the Mennonites might again become united would be my most ardent wish.")[4] On Christmas Day apparently in 1865 he reported attending a Mennonite (probably Amish) church. After the service the members debated about hooks and buttons. Erismann wrote: "... if only this would stop and were different and that once we Mennonites would have peace. How nice it would be, how much better, if the Mennonites would become unified to work together in a unified effort to strive" toward a goal.[5]

According to H. S. Bender the "first all-Mennonite organization" was the Mennonite Aid Plan organized in Indiana in 1882. Soon after its founding Mennonites in Illinois and elsewhere became a part of it. In 1912 its headquarters were moved to Freeman, South Dakota.[6]

John S. Coffman's work as evangelist in Illinois also pointed toward closer cooperation, if not unity. Although a Mennonite Coffman also served Amish Mennonites, including groups who had separated from the old church. In March of 1889, for example, he included the Stuckey churches at Washington and North Danvers in a preaching tour. Jonathan Kurtz of Topeka, Indiana, served with Coffman on this mission. That the old contacts with the Stuckey followers were not wholly discontinued is evident also from a report of the travels of Joseph Buerckey, Amish Mennonite leader of Tiskilwa. On January 17, 1891, he went to Danvers "where we met at Pre. Jos. Stuckey's ... with several other brethren" and on March 18 "attended a large meeting at North Danvers Mennonite church." From there he went to Flanagan, where he "attended four meetings in the old and new churches." The report does not indicate which these were, but obviously they included some that had separated from the old church.[7]

Jonathan Kurtz visited Illinois again in the fall of 1891. He was accompanied by Jonathan P. Smucker of Nappanee, Indiana. A Metamora correspondent saw the trip as contributing to unity, saying: "I believe it is good for ministers to visit one another more that brotherly love may be more cultivated among us, and that we may show that we are of one mind, and working together in the vineyard of the Lord.... There is but one way open for us, and that is to be united and harmonious in our work, if we would reach the desired land."[8]

Other early sentiments for unity came from John Smith of Metamora, the Amish Mennonite bishop. In 1893 he made a plea to the Illinois Mennonite Conference that bears repeating: "It matters not what we are called, Amish or Mennonites or any other name. Let the heart be right so that we may work to the upbuilding of the church in a way that will stand before God."[9]

The Congo Inland Mission was of course inter-Mennonite and its successor, the Africa Inter-Mennonite Mission still more so. Even the beginning of missions in India—at least the relief work which led to missions—for a time "assumed a quasi interMennonite character." While the Old church contributed most financially, "practically all Mennonite groups shared in the contributions." Some leaders from the other groups also served in the administration, including D. F. Jantzen, David Goerz, and H. H. Regier.[10]

After the turn of the century pleas for cooperation and unity increased. Mennonites easily agreed with Fannie E. Ebersole from Freeport that in "heaven all is love, peace and union, and as it is in heaven, so should it be on earth among God's people." So had Christ prayed in the Lord's Prayer and in John 17. Mennonites found it hard to put these noble, professed principles into effect in church organization, life, and work. But there were those who made the attempt, some prematurely and others with some success as the twentieth century moved on.[11]

The 1910s showed considerable activity and some progress in this effort. The organizing of the Central Illinois Mennonite Conference in 1908 and the founding of its publication, the *Christian Evangel,* in 1910 furthered the discussion. Incidentally, most of the paper's editors during its lifetime (1910-57) were former members of the (Old) Mennonite church. Aaron Augspurger, associate editor and a conference leader, stated that the separation from the old group and the "dissipation of our Christian forces" was deeply deplored. He firmly believed that the church should be composed "of one great army," divided, of course, into regiments, but "all in perfect harmony and cooperation, with the spirit of Christ prevailing everywhere." He thought that his conference, though born of the spirit of the age—"the spirit of disintegration [rather] than of unity"—would in time, after its mission was fulfilled, be "reabsorbed into the great body of Jesus Christ and lose its identity."[12]

On August 19 and 20, 1913, a first All-Mennonite Convention in America was held at Berne, Indiana. Illinois was well represented. Such a meeting had been advocated for several years. In 1910 the editor of *The Mennonite*, I. A. Sommer, had suggested a conference of representatives from the various Mennonite bodies to discuss similarities and differences and to see whether the former were not greater than the latter. Aaron Augspurger of Saybrook was the first to endorse the idea; many others approved. Then opposition from the outspoken (Old) Mennonite scholar John Horsch derailed the movement.[13] When that happened, President Noah E. Byers of Goshen College, formerly from Illinois, wrote an article in *The Mennonite* (Aug. 18, 1910) which revived interest. He warned that Mennonites could unite only "on the basis of a distinctively Mennonite interpretation of New Testament teachings and some agreement as to the application of these principles to the conditions of our modern life." And he emphasized the necessity of getting to know each other better and to ascertain others' actual beliefs, and also proposed a plan of procedure.

All of these efforts finally led to the Berne meeting in 1913. Although there is no record of the number from Illinois who attended, the *Report* indicates that in addition to Byers, who deserves much credit for calling the meeting, six Illinois men took prominent parts: Valentine Strubhar of Washington, Albert B. Rutt of Chicago, C. R. Egle of Gridley, Aaron Augspurger of Saybrook, Emanuel Troyer of Normal and D. N. Claudon of Meadows. C. Henry Smith, of course a native of Illinois, addressed the conference on the history of the American Mennonites. Among other points he emphasized the Mennonite tendency toward division. But he thought the tendency was now in the other direction; and he and others made a strong plea for cooperation.[14]

At irregular intervals until the 1930s a number of other All-Mennonite Conventions occurred. The second met at the Carlock (Ill.) Mennonite Church in 1916. Five hundred and nineteen registered at that convention compared with 143 at Berne. In all subsequent conventions Illinois played an important role. It appears, however, that Central Conference people were more active in them than were (Old) Mennonites, the largest group. Clearly, the more progressive groups were more ready for closer cooperation and unity than were the more conservative ones, including the Mennonite Church.[15] In fact the progressives seemed often to be calling for a unity based on their own positions.

In the same year in which occurred the first All-Mennonite Convention, C. Henry Smith along with N. E. Byers and one or two others moved from Goshen College to the newly reorganized Bluffton College in Ohio. This, too, represented a part of the movement toward closer Mennonite cooperation and unity. The Bluffton group hoped their new institution—known before 1913 as Central Mennonite College—would serve and represent a number of Mennonite bodies. The same forces and influences brought into being the all-Mennonite seminary at Bluffton a few years later. Byers and Smith had hoped that the board that controlled Goshen College would have been more sympathetic to the unity movement. Had it been, according to Smith, "undoubtedly Goshen, as the largest of the colleges at that time and as the most centrally located, would have been the beneficiary of the seminary and the enlarged constituency from the unaffiliated branches."[16]

In 1926 Harvey E. Nunemaker, editor of the *Christian Evangel*, wrote that the Central Conference had always favored closer Mennonite cooperation and unity. Already in 1924 it had passed a resolution stating the Conference was a body of Mennonites who wanted closer ties with Mennonite groups who were of "kindred faith." Nunemaker heartily invited all such "to effect with us a closer cooperation." Yet he was realistic and realized that "some of our congregations would not be ready for the actual step [of union] without considerable education on the matter." At the same time Ben Esch of Calvary wrote a prophetic article on "A Union of Mennonites." Stating that Mennonites were becoming better acquainted with each other, he thought the time was approaching when "greater cooperation and unity would take place." Some leaders, he added, might delay the movement, but they could not stop it. "Language, customs, personalities, etc., are no longer ... determining factors," but rather the "basic principles of the Mennonite church."[17]

The chief problem the unifiers faced and failed to comprehend was the strong beliefs that the (Old) Mennonites still had in certain marks of nonconformity, the head covering, foot washing, and other doctrines and ordinances that the more liberal group called "nonessentials." Although J. S. Shoemaker was relatively moderate within the old church, in a *Gospel Herald* article in 1920 (May 6) he lashed out against decline in standards of separation from the world. People are telling us, he said, "that it is not necessary for the Church to be so distinct from the world in conduct, conversation, and manner of dress. They say, 'We will have more influence for good if we follow more closely the world's standard in dress.' This is a deception of him who transforms himself into an angel of light in order to deceive, if possible, the very elect."

Despite the progressives' and the (Old) Mennonites' failure to agree, and despite the fact that the seminary at Bluffton eventually had to close, the unity movement proceeded in other quarters. Defenseless and Central Conference Mennonite people in Illinois worked together to found the Congo Inland Mission, the hospital in Bloomington, and the old people's home at Meadows. In Chicago also various Mennonite mission groups early learned the advantages of frequently working together. For example, the first quarterly meeting of Chicago Mennonite missions and churches occurred on November 28, 1907, at the Home Mission. This was one of the earliest attempts to have the various Mennonite bodies work together.[18]

World War I gave the unity movement an important boost. One writer has said that this war shook up the Mennonites "from top to bottom as it did the rest of the world, to reveal the basic need for fellowship and unity among them both nationally and internationally, and thus to bring about the functional unity of American Mennonites through which the stream of culture was to flow again."[19] Both during and after the war Mennonites learned to cooperate as they had not done for centuries. Relief work, especially with the founding of the inter-Mennonite Central Committee in 1920, "acquainted the different bodies ... in America with one another, so that they discovered the many things that we do have in common, over and above the several differences...." So wrote P. C. Hiebert, for many years MCC chairman. He continued: "We have realized that we can work side by side in a great common cause, without in the least infringing upon the individualistic characteristics of any one group."[20] Undoubtedly MCC has been one of the most (if not the most) important factors in bringing about better understanding and closer relations between the various Mennonite branches. Illinois has done its full share in supporting the organization with finances and personnel. Through their many inter-Mennonite contacts they have broadened their horizons, have "rediscovered Mennonites and Mennonitism,"[21] and in many cases have found that their similarities were surprisingly great.

In the 1930s the potential for unity continued to appear. Even though it was premature, the temporary union between *The Mennonite* (GC) and the Central Conference *Christian Evangel* published in Illinois was one of these. Said the editor of the combined organ: "With this issue we are beginning a new day in Mennonitism.... We are entering a new era.... The church needs to sense the change which is being brought about.... May this union project of the *Christian Evangel* and *The Mennonite* point the way to other union projects, especially within our own Mennonite household."[22] The editor's wish came true. Even though this union project continued only two years at that time and the permanent merger waited until later, the venture did point and lead to other and greater union projects. When separate publication resumed, Editor William B. Weaver of the *Evangel* wrote that its purpose would remain the same as from the beginning: "to promulgate and encourage the activities of our Conference and to support all worthy efforts for a closer cooperation among the various Mennonite groups."[23] I. R. Detweiler, pastor at Normal, insisted that Mennonites needed to work together in order to conquer great evils "that are threatening to destroy our civilization," such as war, the race problem, illiteracy, economic injustice—low wages, long hours, and other bad labor conditions—and lack of religious education.[24]

The 1940s brought a big step toward Mennonite unity. World War II "gave the greatest impetus to inter-Mennonite cooperation through the joint effort of all major Mennonite bodies to define a common peace position in the United States and to administer Civilian Public Service." MCC took on additional activities and responsibilities and "became the one truly all Mennonite inter-Mennonite organization," enjoying "immense prestige and good will."[25] Even aside from war concerns, farsighted leaders were emphasizing the need for more cooperation among the Mennonite bodies. Raymond L. Hartzler of Bloomington is a good example. In an editorial in the *Christian Evangel* in 1945 he forcefully and prophetically spoke out for greater cooperation in seminary and Bible training, publication of Sunday school and other Christian literature, summer camps and conferences, mutual aid, and retirement benefits for ministers and missionaries. He stressed especially the importance of properly training future leaders if the Mennonites are to retain their historic faith. These and other tasks could not be done alone. "Joining our concerns, resources and efforts with those of some other like-minded group seems to be the solution in these, as in some other areas in which we are now active. More cooperative outlets or channels must thus be found." As Hartzler faced the expanded work of the church in the 1950s he wrote: "Let us set ourselves with resolution and humility; but, above all, let us do it *together.*"[26] In fact, Hartzler has lived to see virtually all of this cooperation become reality.

As the Illinois Mennonites approached and passed mid-century, more and more of them were coming to the position of R. J. Hartzler of East Peoria. In 1954 the *Gospel Herald* editor wrote about the progress that had been made in healing the Amish schism, and expressed the hope that someday the rift would be healed entirely. In response Hartzler wrote: "God speed the day when this can be said of all Mennonite churches! We can cooperate in times of war, and in projects of relief to the needy—why can we not live and love as we should in our daily walk together?"[27]

Inter-Mennonite organizations, meetings, and activities have increased remarkably in recent decades. The Illinois Mennonite nurses formed such an organization in 1948 to serve the needs of nurses as Christians, to expand the role of the missionary nurse, and

Adelphian Male Chorus organized in 1926 with members from Metamora, Roanoke, Union, and Calvary Mennonite churches. Arthur Schertz (sitting third from left) was assistant director, and Walter E. Yoder (sitting fourth from left), director; ca. 1930.

Source: Tilman Smith, Goshen, Ind.

to give aid to needy student nurses in training. Inter-Mennonite ministers' fellowship meetings began in Illinois about the mid-1950s. Pastors, especially from the major groups—GC, EMC and MC—"met in this unofficial way to spend time in Bible Study and to discuss matters of common interest." At an early meeting they talked of forming a Mennonite Disaster Service, which was later organized and affiliated with the national organization. Illinois soon had occasion to use this service following a tornado south of Summerfield in 1957.[28]

Because of the large number of Illinois congregations involved, the merger of the Central District Conference (formerly the Central Conference of Mennonites) and the Middle District of the General Conference was an important step for Mennonites in the state. One leader speaking on "How We Came to Where We Are" stated that "we are where we are because the reasoned judgment of the conference chose to take that way, each successive step being taken with the feeling that a movement for unity is in keeping with the spirit and purpose of our Lord, and in answer to His prayer, 'That they all may be one.'" A strengthened Young People's Union was one result of the merger. Lotus Troyer, pastor of the Meadows congregation and president of the newly merged Central District Conference, spoke in 1958 on "A United Church At Work." Pointing out that history had shown too many divisions in the church, he said it had also shown many points of common interest. He pointed to MCC as the classic example. "A United Church at Work," he continued, was "united in our efforts to make Christ known through evangelism, education, publication, peace and service, hospitals, homes for the aged, retreats, auxiliary organizations, embracing the youngest to the oldest, the cause of missions at our own doorstep and in the farthest recesses of the earth."[29]

The trend in the state in recent decades has been similar to that in North America. The story of greater inter-Mennonite activity is well summarized by H. S. Bender in *The Mennonite Encyclopedia* ("Inter-Mennonite Relations," III, 44-48) and by Paul N. Kraybill in *North American Inter-Mennonite Relationships* (Rosemont, Ill., 1974). Kraybill listed the numbers of inter-Mennonite projects organized in various decades (p. 1):

Decade	Number
1911-20	2
1921-30	1
1931-40	0
1941-50	8
1951-60	18
1961-70	23
1971-74	20

Actually the decade 1911-1920 ought to include the Mennonite Hospital at Bloomington, which was inter-Mennonite from its beginning in 1919. The above list also overlooked a number of local inter-Mennonite projects. In any case, such activities grew phenomenally after mid-century. Illinois is not only keeping up with the procession but is moving more rapidly than some other areas.

One development in 1958 which involved Illinois both directly and indirectly was the moving of the Mennonite Biblical Seminary from Chicago to Elkhart, Indiana. For various reasons the seminary arrangements in Chicago became less satisfactory after some ten years. The long daily trips required for commuting to Bethany, together with increasingly overcrowded conditions in the Woodlawn community, due largely to urban renewal in adjacent areas, caused seminary officials to seek a new location. The old ideal of an inter-Mennonite seminary program also loomed large again. The move to Elkhart came when Mennonite Biblical Seminary struck an agreement with Goshen College Biblical Seminary to form the Associated Mennonite Biblical Seminaries. The Goshen seminary eventually moved to the Elkhart campus, where the two institutions have since carried on a unified program under a single dean, while maintaining separate presidents and legal and institutional identities.[30]

For MC and GC unity, the seminary arrangement at Elkhart has been immeasurable. Other Mennonite bodies have been invited to join, but so far only the GC and the MC groups have chosen to participate. One (Old) Mennonite institution—Eastern Mennonite Seminary at Harrisonburg, Virginia—has not joined. Yet the Elkhart venture seems to be very successful. Enrollment has grown substantially, with Illinois sending its full share of students and money. If the joint seminaries can provide the future leaders of the two largest Mennonite bodies in Illinois, they will contribute greatly to future unity. Heinz Janzen, former pastor at Washington, has said: "Here the students study together for three years. When they go out into the churches they say: 'We worked, studied, and prayed together for three years, why can't we continue to do this out on the local level?' " To be sure, a significant amount of inter-Mennonite educational activity had already occurred on the college level. One additional matter in connection with the various Mennonite colleges and seminaries, which made it easier for some groups to work together, was that those institutions did a good job of promoting such Mennonite distinctives as peace and nonresistance.[31]

In any case, by the 1960s and 1970s one finds in the Illinois records more and more Mennonite "togetherness." According to one report, the "first all-Mennonite youth fellowship get-together, including Meadows, Salem, Flanagan, and Waldo congregations . . . was held at East Bay Camp near Bloomington" in 1959. By then the (Old) Mennonites with their nurses' training school at La Junta, Colorado, closed were associating more with the other groups in operating and supporting the Mennonite Hospital at Bloomington. Harold Zehr consented to serve on the Board and, as editor of the *Missionary Guide*, promoted it vigorously. Other (Old) Mennonites became increasingly involved in the administration of the hospital.[32]

The growth toward unity, particularly between the GCs and MCs, became evident in various ways, including more pulpit exchanges, more inter-Mennonite ministers' fellowship meetings, more inter-Mennonite student fellowships, and closer cooperation between conferences. In 1960, for example, Roy Bucher of Metamora gave a series of "Spiritual Life Messages" at First Mennonite in Normal. In 1961 C. Warren Long of Tiskilwa gave a series of "much appreciated" pre-Easter messages at Summerfield.[33]

The inter-Mennonite student fellowship at Champaign-Urbana illustrates what has been happening in university cities in recent years. In 1961, after meeting for some time informally and irregularly, Mennonite students at the University of Illinois organized an Inter-Mennonite Student Fellowship. With the help of Virgil Brenneman of the Mennonite Student Services Committee and Pastor J. Alton Horst of East Bend the students organized and elected Keith Sprunger (GC) as president. Already in 1960 Horst and R. L. Hartzler had been asked by the Illinois Inter-Mennonite Ministers' Fellowship to encourage and promote such fellowships on the various college campuses in the state. Church leaders were "interested primarily in maintaining contact with [Mennonite] students" and in assisting them "in gathering for fellowship and organizing for witness."[34] In 1964 the Champaign-Urbana group organized itself as the First Mennonite Church with dual membership in the Central District Conference (GC) and Illinois Mennonite Conference (MC). The congregation celebrated its first communion service April 19, 1964, with a membership of fifty, including some Mennonite Brethren. It also included local residents in addition to students. Richard J. Yordy and James Dunn have been two of the pastors.[35]

Yordy, an (Old) Mennonite leader who believed in closer cooperation between the various bodies, also believed in proceeding cautiously. In an article in 1963 he pointed out the advantages of the growing inter-Mennonite unity which he had observed in Illinois and elsewhere. But he also suggested concerns and dangers. He stated that as "members of the Illinois Conference [MC], we are sometimes the cause of concern among Mennonite churches seeking to hold a more conservative emphasis." The conference study that led to a fully supported ministry (1947), "relaxing the requirement of the 'plain suit'

Source: Mennonite Biblical Seminary, Elkhart, Ind.

Mennonite Biblical Seminary on Woodlawn Avenue, Chicago, showing (from left to right) Woodlawn Mennonite Church, the offices (in the tower), and the library and study rooms; 1946-1957.

[for ministers] (1949), statement regarding redemption and church membership for those involved in divorce and remarriage (1956), giving administrative responsibility to pastors (1956), [and] study of church music usage which left an option for instruments in worship ... (1958), [has] brought some degree of uneasiness in the brotherhood at large." Yordy concluded: "Unless we undertake to maintain openness with our brethren and a willingness to accept their brotherly address, we may be contributing to the breakdown of our church-wide unity."[36] This was wise counsel. The saving feature in the situation was that changes were occurring in other parts of the brotherhood also, including a growing cooperation and unity.

In editorials and other articles the leading periodicals of the two major groups in the state—the *Gospel Herald* of the (Old) Mennonites and *The Mennonite* of the General Conference body—encouraged the trend toward cooperation. Upon retiring as editor of the *Gospel Herald* in June, 1962, Paul Erb wrote about changes in the Mennonite Church during his editorship. He saw some as good and some as not. People had reacted differently to the changes and the tensions they frequently produced. There was much emphasis during this period on the "Scriptural doctrine of unity" and, the editor added, "however much we may regret certain changes, we have considered division the greater sin." He also pointed out how inter-Mennonite cooperation had grown through such activities as Mennonite Disaster Service, publication of curriculum materials, seminary education, mental hospitals, *The Mennonite Encyclopedia*, Mennonite Mutual Aid, and Mennonite World Conference. *The Mennonite* published Erb's statement. In fact, increasingly in recent years, *The Mennonite* and *Gospel Herald* have planned issues jointly and published many of the same editorials and articles.[37]

In 1965 the Illinois Mennonites, particularly the General Conference and the (Old) Mennonites, were reading a remarkably forthright "Call to Unity." It was an editorial written by Paul Erb's successor as editor of the *Gospel Herald*, John Drescher, and republished in *The Mennonite*. Probably it was the strongest plea for unity ever written even until today by an editor of the *Herald*. Drescher said that Mennonites "are overdue for a call to unity.... Too often we have presented a picture of spiritual impotence, division, and contention rather than love, concern, and unity in Christ." Noting the move of the General Conference Mennonites in their triennial convention a few weeks before to "end the existing divisions in the Mennonite family," he asked: "What will our response be? ... Should there be an hesitancy on our part to honestly evaluate our position toward fellow Mennonites? Have we ever looked carefully to really see what our differences are? What is our vision of Christian unity? If our vision is a bit foggy, are we willing to seek to clear it? Certainly we believe in Christian unity. We could not believe the Scripture and believe otherwise." But we as Mennonites, the editor continued, "have hardly begun to grapple with the problems of Christian unity. Too often we have been busy bolstering our divisions and differences until some things have become magnified out of proportion."

Drescher conceded that before union could occur many problems and misunderstandings needed to be addressed. One of these "will be to frankly face old prejudices, petty differences and fleshly feelings. We must rid ourselves of sneaking suspicions and pre-conceived notions. This will test our openness to the Holy Spirit and His leading." In this search for unity we will have to learn how to handle differences, he said. There will always be various interpretations. "We find this true even within congregations and conferences." But it "is a condemnation on our heads when we stand condemning those we call liberal and unorthodox while they unite in statements recognizing the deity and lordship of Christ and the authority of the Scripture and we create new divisions and take a separatist attitude." Drescher felt that we needed to "trust others just as much as we want others to trust us"; that we must be as ready to listen to them as "we are to have others listen to us"; and that in humility and under the guidance of the Holy Spirit as the unifying factor we must be "willing to search together as true disciples of Christ and allow His Word and Spirit to search us."[38] Such an editorial, from a rather conservative source, could not help but have a significant effect on *Gospel Herald* readers in Illinois and elsewhere.

About the same time and in response to the same General Conference effort to give Mennonite unity a nudge, Arnold W. Cressman, (Old) Mennonite pastor and leader in Christian education, wrote an article in the *Gospel Herald* entitled "Oberholtzer, We're Sorry." This is a very forthright, candid statement to the effect that Oberholtzer had been right in 1847 and that the (Old) Mennonite Franconia Conference had been wrong. Cressman said the least the (Old) Mennonites could do now was to listen to the General Conference people who were making overtures toward cooperation and unity. They were "right," he wrote. "They have asked that the quarrel be forgotten, that we explore together the possibility of union. They are to be commended for acting redemptively. We would be most unchristian and unkind to refuse to explore." This was not the time to lay blame, Cressman continued. "It is time rather to confess our sin. The old wounds have in fact healed.... If Oberholtzer was ahead of his time in advocating Sunday schools, leadership training, missions, conference constitutions, and minute keeping, let us admit it. And let us note that all of these things we now endorse. Perhaps it was not the church's fault that somebody was ahead of it. But it is the church's fault when it catches up with its dead prophets and still ignores them." One Illinois writer no doubt represented widespread sentiment in the state when she wrote that she was in "hearty agreement" with Cressman's views. As a former GC member she was "very hopeful" that we could "sometime soon give a more united witness." She realized that uniting churches was not "as easy as talking about it" and that there would be problems, but she was "certainly in favor of exploring the possibilities."[39]

General Conference voices, including *The Mennonite*, supported these efforts vigorously. This could be expected because of the church's goals laid out when the conference started in 1860. In 1964 Stanley Bohn, General Conference leader who had studied at Mennonite Biblical in Chicago and had served as pastor for a short period at Normal, wrote a letter to *The Mennonite* on the "Stewardship of Separated Mennonites." In clever, gentle satire he asked whether it was good stewardship for the General Conference and (Old) Mennonites to maintain separate, duplicate establishments in publication, educational and mission activity. "It gets expensive." He thought it demoralizing and for peace churches, embarrassing, to support separate but identical programs. Bohn continued:

> In my bad moments I wonder if the comparatively high rating we smaller denominations have in per capita giving isn't nullified by the extra "fee" we are paying for smaller private family-club churches that cannot cooperate with other groups. In my irreverent moments I wish Oberholtzer would have spent some extra cash one hundred years ago to buy a collarless coat to wear to ministers' meetings and pencils and paper to take his minutes instead of starting a new denomination over these issues. I would buy him a lifetime supply to get out of having us support two identical programs. I just can't afford to support two clubs when there is malnutrition, people sleeping in cars, churches fleeing to suburbs outside my study windows.
>
> But we have one consolation. We peace-church denominations do make a powerful witness. We show how expensive it is not to be peaceful Christian brothers. That should be a lesson for these non-peace denominations that are always cooperating and sometimes merging and don't have the peace witness we do.

One GC leader and pastor responded that Bohn's letter ought to be required reading from *every* Mennonite pulpit.[40]

The editor of *The Mennonite*, Maynard Shelly, also made strong pleas for unity. In 1964 (July 28), after telling the story of a jilted suitor, he wrote that the GC Mennonite Church "has been trying to marry itself off with some other Mennonite group for a long time" but the "response has been discouraging. Could it be," he humorously continued, "that the deodorant ads are really talking about us? Or are we the awkward suitor?" In this and in a second editorial (April 20, 1965) the editor had in mind the GC triennial conference to be held in July of 1965, in which the subject of unity was again to be discussed. He wisely pointed out that "perhaps we've seen things too much from our point of view. It has been easy to brush off the fears of those other Mennonite groups as silly and petty." In order to seriously discuss the problem of unity "it might be well to tackle the problem from this side." In a 1965 editorial entitled "I've Been Thinking About Joining Another Church," he said here we are "with a sackful of organizations and a lot of knotty questions about our relatives." Why not "de-organize" and go in the opposite direction? As we face the question of unity for the "umpteenth" time "why don't we just apply for membership in the (Old) Mennonite Church and/or the Mennonite Brethren Church?" Some say it isn't that simple. "Well, it isn't that complicated either. Don't we often wake up on a frosty morning to find a long lost relative on our doorstep? It's just an old custom among Mennonites. Why don't we just pick up our buildings, boards, and noisy editors and say to one of our sister groups, 'Here we are. Where shall we put the stuff?' They might be a bit surprised, but I'm sure they're hospitable." The editor then concluded: "The General Conference is on record to go part of the way.... We can't wait until everything comes our way. If we want a family reunion, and if we want it in our lifetime, we'll have to be willing to sacrifice a lot."

Of course some thought the above statements were too simplistic, not sufficiently taking into account the differences between the groups which still existed in the 1960s.[41] Nevertheless, such articles and editorials in their leading church periodicals could not help but influence the thinking of many Illinois readers in the direction of cooperation.

So the trend toward cooperation and unity continued. Many agreed with a farmer at Summerfield who pointedly asked how Mennonites could be effective witnesses "in solving the world's problems unless we first demonstrate our ability to cooperate and resolve our differences with other believers." The Chicago metropolitan area churches continued to point the direction. Adding to the history of inter-Mennonite cooperation in Chicago, Evanston also was founded as a varied group containing, among others, MBs, GCs, MCs, and EMCs. Pastor Laurence Horst reported that the way the groups worked together was "a unique feature." When Mr. and Mrs. James Bertsche (EMCs), who had helped organize the church, left for mission work in the Congo the congregation gave them a love offering for the purchase of a washing machine.[42]

Mennonite cooperation in Chicago went forward still another step in the mid-1960s. In order to work together more effectively in forwarding a united witness the thirteen or fourteen metropolitan congregations set up a Chicago Area Mennonite Council and appointed a coordinator and eventually a Steering Committee. Conference and other church leaders in Chicago agreed that united planning would help Mennonites advance "into new geographical areas as well as into new kinds of ministries." There might be cases also where they could "share in counsel, personnel, and finances." In fact these leaders were asking "whether our entire home missions expansion should be considered on an inter-Mennonite basis." LeRoy Kennel was the first coordinator. Mission boards and conferences were to pay whatever part of the costs the area congregations could not carry. But instead of the Chicago mission churches being directed mostly by distant mission boards as in the past, more planning was to come now from the new council and the churches themselves.[43]

In the 1960s and since, the practice of having various inter-Mennonite meetings has gained momentum in Illinois. Since 1950 there have been annual Inter-Mennonite Ministers Retreats, generally at Camp Menno Haven, to discuss matters of common concern and to help church leaders along with their wives become better acquainted. One pastor stated that since 1955 this retreat "has been his most significant experience in inter-Mennonite relationships." But inter-Mennonite meetings have involved young people and quite ordinary folks as well as church leaders.[44]

A practice of exchanging pulpits and conference speakers has likewise accelerated, moving considerably beyond the older custom of conferences exchanging greetings. In 1958, for example, Roy Bucher invited H. N. Harder, General Conference minister at Normal, to address the (MC) Illinois Mennonite Conference. Bucher wrote: "We would like to continue the good relations and fellowship we have had with your conference and we would therefore like to invite you to serve on the program." In an equally warm letter Harder replied that he was glad for the opportunity to speak. He added: "... the fellowship with you and other brethren of your conference has been a real happy experience for me since coming to ... Illinois. There are ever so many things, I feel, I have in common with you that I find it always refreshing to fellowship with you brethren. This exchange in pulpits has been a wholesome practice and we should continue in this."[45] Although not all Illinois General Conference and (Old) Mennonites felt as warm about such new inter-Mennonite relations, this exchange of letters suggests a new direction.

Part of the growing cooperation was a 1966 meeting of the executive committees of the Illinois Mennonite and the Central District (GC) Mennonite Conferences, at the home of Richard D. Miller in Meadows. The Central District included a number of other states, but the discussion focused on Illinois. Agenda items were:

1. A period of Bible study and learning to know each other in Christian faith and fellowship.
2. A study of our conference organizations.
3. A geographical study of the congregations.
4. An analysis of the areas of our church life.
5. Dual-conference membership functions.
6. Planning and sharing information together to avoid duplication of efforts.

At that time the Illinois Conference had thirty-seven congregations with approximately 3,700 members. The Central District had sixteen Illinois congregations with about 2,400 members. The group noted with favor the growing cooperation among the Chicago-area Mennonites and hoped for similar developments in and around Peoria. Actually, both conferences' old mission congregations in Peoria had already united' in 1971. The committees also felt that in the formation of churches in the future there should be "strong inter-Mennonite cooperation." The group also encouraged dual conference membership for the new congregation in Champaign, as well as elsewhere under certain conditions. Another matter discussed in this meeting, and elsewhere in Illinois, was the sharing of church periodicals among the ministry. The groups suggested that *The Mennonite* and the *Gospel Herald* might be supplied at half price and the *Central District Reporter* (GC) and the *Missionary Guide* might be provided free. Harold Zehr, editor of the *Guide*, favored making *The Mennonite* and the *Herald* available to ministers in each other's church, on grounds that "the sharing of information is one of the most important ways of extending our fellowship at this juncture." The group appointed Gordon Dyck (GC) and Richard Yordy (MC) to add a third member and then to act as a committee to study further "the Mennonite Mission in Illinois."[46] About the same time the Illinois Mennonite Conference Mission Board and the Central District Mission Committee began to meet and discuss how better to work together.[47]

Momentum toward cooperation and unity increased in the 1970s. With the reorganization of the Mennonite Church into regions (it was thought the regional divisions would become more significant than they actually have) Region IV (MC) and the Central District covered roughly the same Midwest territory, including Illinois. Officials of these two groups also met to explore cooperation in new fields as well as in old ones such as pastoral training, relief sales, workshops, seminary support, use of the same Sunday school materials and church hymnals.[48]

No doubt the organizing of an Illinois Mennonite Historical and Genealogical Society on an inter-Mennonite basis gave impetus to further unity. In the hands of capable leaders from the beginning, the organization has enjoyed a substantial growth, achieving a membership of about 500 in 1980. It actively promotes the history of the Mennonites and the collection and preservation of their historical materials. In 1974 it began publishing a quarterly magazine, which W. Richard Hassan of Rockford has edited from the beginning. It maintains a library in the Mennonite Church of Normal and a museum in the old meetinghouse of the Congerville Mennonites. A recent, ambitious project has been the purchase of a six-acre site about two and a half miles west of Metamora. The site committee recommended this location only after a careful consideration of several others. The location is fairly central for Mennonites and, being near the site of the old Partridge Creek meetinghouse built in 1854, is in a historic community. There the Society will have its headquarters, library, archives, and museum. In 1981 the Society constructed a building for this purpose and dedicated it on November 15. As mentioned earlier, the historic Sutter barn at Hopedale, built in 1868, and in which the 1875 session of the *Diener Versammlungen* was held, was recently given to the Society. It has been dismantled and will be reerected on the new site. The Society is thinking of erecting a few additional buildings, possibly including a pioneer schoolhouse and a replica of the old Partridge meetinghouse. The *Journal-Star* of Peoria has offered an interesting local non-Mennonite reaction. Many people who know about the Mennonites only through the Mennonite relief sale, the paper has said, "will be able to add to their knowledge by visiting a museum three miles west of Metamora." And:

Source: Clarence Imhoff, Roanoke, Ill.

Illinois Mennonite Historical and Genealogical Society building containing the Society's headquarters, library, archives, and museum; near Metamora, dedicated November 15, 1981.

Toward Mennonite Cooperation and Unity 479

> We are enthused about the news of the Mennonite historical development, complete with church, school, barn, woodshop, and museum, which will be raised on a six-acre site near Metamora. They say it will take about five years to put the whole attraction together.... We don't know exactly how it will turn out—we have a vision of a small-scale New Salem without Lincoln logs—but we do know the Mennonites never do anything half way. We can hardly wait for the opening.[49]

Since much material on Mennonite history has been produced since the 1920s, when Harry F. Weber did his research for the *Centennial History of the Mennonites of Illinois*, the Society has assumed responsibility for publishing the present new history, to bring the account down to the present.[50]

A few Illinois churches from different conferences merged in the 1960s and 1970s, no doubt setting precedent for the future. Apart from Chicago, Champaign, and Peoria, perhaps the most notable merger to date was at Normal, where the older First Mennonite Church in Normal (GC) and the younger and smaller Mennonite Church (MC) in Bloomington have come together. The two began working together some eight years before they actually merged. In 1968 they jointly sponsored a get-together for about forty Mennonite students attending Illinois State University in Normal and Wesleyan University and Mennonite School of Nursing in Bloomington. This they repeated for a larger turnout in 1970. In 1971 they successfully ran a joint daily vacation Bible school. An "Inter-Church Task Force Report" of 1975 summarized what happened thereafter:

> The official church boards have met quarterly. A variety of cooperative endeavors and programs have resulted. A joint Summer Bible School has been held for the past four years. A variety of Sunday evening activities have been jointly sponsored, including Homebuilders, hymn sings, picnics, communion, as well as quite a number of services with local or visiting speakers. Special choir programs have been planned and given both at Christmas and Easter. Pulpit exchanges have occurred. The youth groups have met together and presented services in both churches. The two churches have jointly sponsored outside groups to this area. The presentation of plays and choir programs are examples. The Men's Breakfast groups are presently meeting together and there is some sharing in small groups among the women.

After such activities the next step was no surprise. The two groups recognized there would be practical problems such as supporting two duplicating sets of denominational institutions, but they thought the advantages were greater. So they merged, keeping membership both in the Central District Conference (GC) and in the Illinois Mennonite Conference (MC). The merger was completed officially September 26, 1976. "If it can happen anywhere, it can happen here as we continue to work with patience and love," reported James Waltner, pastor at Normal. Carl Newswanger, pastor at Bloomington, became copastor. The united group used the larger facilities of the Normal congregation. In 1980 they constructed a new meetinghouse on the west side of Normal.[51]

What happened at Normal is probably an omen of the future. For instance, Boynton and Hopedale have been considering merger or some degree of it. In 1975 Edwin Stalter, (Old) Mennonite conference minister in Illinois, reported that the previous year had been one of closer fellowship with General Conference congregations. In most of the areas where churches of both groups existed they "met in fellowship and cooperated in a number of projects." Stalter hoped that a full-time youth worker might serve both groups.[52]

Inter-Mennonite cooperation in Illinois probably has developed most fully in the case of the annual MCC relief sale. Donald F. Roth of Morton (MC) and Delton Litwiller of Emden (MC) have been cochairmen, assisted by a number of other officials and board members from various Mennonite groups in different parts of the state.[53] In fact, the sale enjoys wide support not only among Mennonites but also among others. For example, for a number of years about 125 men from the Morton Apostolic Christian Church have been directing the traffic and helping with parking.

Elva May Roth of Morton has testified that in addition to raising significant sums for relief, the sales "are one of the finest expressions of working together for a cause, and the fellowship that results, that I have ever experienced." All ages and all kinds of people work together. "The sales," she continued, "are the one effort in which all the Mennonite groups of Illinois, from the Conservative and Amish to the General Conference and Evangelical Mennonite, ... including the [non-Mennonite,] isolationist Apostolic Christian, join efforts for the one cause." Many others also, she added, have been drawn in since the cause appealed to them and they wanted to help. The sales have provided a positive witness in the community.[54]

As one looks over the history of the Illinois Mennonites in the 1970s and the advance into the 1980s, the trend toward cooperation and unity is clear. Of course the logical next step would be joint meetings of the church conferences. And indeed the Central District Conference (GC) and the Illinois Mennonite Conference (MC) held such a joint meeting, very successfully, at Normal in April of 1981.[55] Nor was that the first case of GC and MC Mennonites holding a conference jointly. Already in 1972 the South Central Conference (MC) and the Western District Conference (GC) had met together. Even more significantly, in 1975 the Eastern District Conference (GC) and the Franconia Conference of the (Old) Mennonites met jointly for the last

Source: Archives of the Mennonite Church.

Illinois Mennonite Relief Sale Committee in 1960 at Congerville, Illinois, with (left to right): Ralph Vercler, John Roth, Charles Hoffman, Clarence Yordy, Kenneth Burkey, Homer Springer. Presumably the men themselves did not make the quilts.

session of each group's conference—for the first time since 1847 when the "Oberholtzer" affair had divided those groups! Any joint meeting of those two bodies must bode well for the future.[56]

However, the trend toward unity has not touched all branches equally. With some significant exceptions Evangelical Mennonites have, as reported earlier in this book, felt generally more comfortable with the National Association of Evangelicals than with fellow Mennonites. According to one study EMC members, when asked "would you like to see your denomination unite with some other Mennonite groups?" replied "yes 9%, no 48%, uncertain 43%." Stan Nussbaum, EMC missionary and historian, has said: "EMC has taken note of the Anabaptist bandwagon, but has not climbed aboard." Pastor Milo Nussbaum at Grace in Morton thought EMC might rate a C+ in cooperation and F in unity. Perhaps he was too modest at least in rating their cooperation.[57]

For the General Conference Mennonites and the Mennonite Church in Illinois, the growth toward cooperation and unity seems irreversible. The two North American bodies plan to have the General Conference (GC) and the Assembly (MC) meet at the same time and in the same area in 1983, with some joint meetings. The location will be in eastern Pennsylvania, where the Mennonite story in this land began 300 years earlier, and celebrating the tricentennial jointly will add to the "togetherness." All this does not mean that full organizational union will come soon, for unity and organizational union are not necessarily the same. During an interim period the emphasis may well be on regional cooperation and planning of the kind often done in Illinois. One General Conference leader has asked, "Might it not be more meaningful to have the [GC] churches seek to work together with other nearby Mennonite churches than to unite General Conference congregations from a distance?"[58] Donald Nester, coordinator of Central Illinois Regional Youth Work, reported to the Central District Conference in 1972: "It is my conviction that regional and inter-Mennonite planning for Central Illinois General Conference youth can be very fruitful." Though much has happened in the decade since his statement, very likely regional cooperation between the groups will become still more meaningful, especially since the Central District of the General Conference is a much larger area than just Illinois.[59]

Another example of the unity tendency in Illinois was peace workshops that the GC and MC groups promoted in 1975. These were held in Chicago, Sterling, Washington, and Normal on the same day, September 6. An able peace leader from outside the state served at each workshop as resource leader. As one participant reported, it was a good experience for members of the two groups to meet together at the various places and gain insights from each other. Another straw in the wind is a practice wherein the Flanagan (GC) and the Waldo (MC) congregations have a joint young people's Sunday school class. They also have other activities together, including some Sunday evening young people's meetings.[60]

Recent decades have seen remarkable growth toward inter-Mennonite cooperation and unity—a trend that will, no doubt, continue in the future. Very likely the process will be selective, as it is at present. Some groups and conferences will continue to be warmer to the idea than will others, and some congregations within the same conference will move more rapidly toward the goal than others. A few apparently will not go along, as some have not in the past. In any case the process could and would be helped if the wise counsel left by GC scholar S. F. Pannabecker were followed by all groups. What is needed, he wrote, is not compromise but understanding. "We of the General Conference have too often expected others to agree with us without trying to understand their reasons for hesitancy." Perhaps in rejecting so-called nonessentials, a term never defined, "we have sometimes lost an element of truth." Perhaps the (Old) Mennonites have "preserved a sense of modesty that we have discarded as nonessential. Perhaps the Mennonite Brethren[61] have preserved an emphasis on rebirth and heartfelt religion that we have lost in discarding pietistic ways of evangelism. Have we sometimes thrown out the baby with the bath? We want to retain our emphasis on cooperation based on essentials, but we want to retain the values symbolized in nonessentials." Truth, Pannabecker concluded, is "attained not by pressing a particular viewpoint but by allowing the Holy Spirit to direct growth and humbly seeking enlightenment."[62]

CHAPTER 18

American Acculturation and Keeping the Faith

The foregoing chapters have traced the story of the Mennonites in Illinois, including changes and trends in recent decades. This concluding chapter will attempt to summarize the problem of keeping the faith in an American setting that pulls strongly toward acculturation.

Such summarizing is not an easy task. So much depends on the individual's view: What is the faith that is to be kept? The Old Order Amish view at Arthur is quite different from that of the EMC or the GC or the MC. The Old Order group is the least acculturated (or assimilated or Americanized). In his *Story of the Mennonites* (1941), C. Henry Smith entitled his last chapter "Keeping the Faith," and discussed only the oath, briefly, and war and nonresistance more fully. He felt that nonresistance was the most characteristic belief of the Mennonites.[1] In this present discussion the concept of the faith to be kept will be defined in broader terms.

The EMC view of keeping the faith is quite different from that of other Mennonite groups. Furthermore, it is quite different today from what it was fifty years ago. Henry Egly, the founder, would affirm the continued emphasis on the new birth, but would probably turn over in his grave if he knew how his church has given up the Amish and Mennonite "distinctives." Stan Nussbaum has pointed out "an increasing tendency to treat Anabaptist distinctives as peripheral rather than fundamental."[2] In the Spring, 1979, issue of the EMC periodical *Build*, Editor Andrew W. Rupp asked, "Is EMC Mennonite?" He explained that EMC has done some grafting which has produced a better fruit—new life "that has given EMC some different fruits and some different hues to other fruits." After mentioning some affirmative and some negative answers to the above question, the editor concluded: "No, EMC is not 'Mennonite'; it is 'Evangelical Mennonite,' and that is different!"

The foregoing suggests the matter of boundary maintenance and barriers to acculturation. Amish and Mennonites have used various barriers to prevent assimilation and maintain separation from the world. A few of the more conservative groups such as the Old Colony Mennonites in Mexico have used geographical isolation. Of course in Illinois geographical isolation has long been impossible. So groups have used other types of separation and other barriers, such as language, dress, and nonparticipation with outside groups in entertainment and other relationships. Studies "support the hypothesis that boundary maintenance is positively associated with adherence to Mennonite norms." Systemic linkage to the outside world is the other side of the coin of boundary maintenance. The more of these linkages there are, the greater the amount of acculturation likely to take place. Sociologist J. Howard Kauffman has said, "The empirical evidence supports the theory quite consistently: If boundary mechanisms are weakened and systemic linkages are increased, adherence to Mennonite norms will greatly diminish and substantial assimilation will take place."[3]

Regarding dress and the German language as cultural barriers, it is difficult to say which disappeared first in Illinois. While the pace of change was different with different groups, the major Amish and Mennonite bodies changed both language and dress quite markedly in the latter part of the nineteenth and the first part of the twentieth centuries. To be sure, Defenseless and Central Conference Mennonites changed earlier in dress than did (Old) Mennonites. One person born shortly before 1900 and reared as an Amish Mennonite has said that when he was a youth at home it was "normal to be abnormal" in not conforming to all the ideas of the surrounding culture—in dress, cosmetics, school dances, entertainment, and even in language.[4]

Mennonites' long battle over language pretty well ended by World War I. By the latter nineteenth century, with the establishment and growth of public schools in Illinois—taught in English, of course—the battle had already been tilted in favor of English. Amish and Mennonite efforts to have their own German schools could not match the public schools' influence. Nor were efforts to teach the language in Sunday school sufficient to retain German. Of course, with the passing of German services and Sunday schools there was less reason to teach the language. Except for the Old Order Amish and a few other small conservative groups, the congregation at Hopedale and Salem at Flanagan were among the last Illinois Amish and Mennonites to use German for worship. They did so until about World War I.[5]

Well before World War I, most Illinois Amish and Mennonites had given up German. Occasionally there might still be a German hymn or Sunday school class or sermon, but those were only remnants. Then about 1917 and 1918, with the war, anti-German hysteria so overran the country that Americans considered it unpatriotic and in some areas made it almost dangerous to use German. Amid such emotionalism Illinois Mennonites' pacifism was a big enough cross to bear, without coupling it with an unpopular language. Mennonites in Illinois did not want to be considered unpatriotic over an issue which the great majority no longer considered vital. Having immigrated earlier, they were not as devoted to German language and culture as were the Russian Mennonites farther west.[6]

In any case the transition to the language of the country was tremendously significant for the American acculturation of Illinois Mennonites. By opening doors and windows to higher education, periodicals, and literature the change gave Mennonites access to a vast and rich cultural heritage that in the end tended to make the Mennonites Anglo-Saxon in their thinking rather than Germanic.

Another matter closely related to the weakening of nonconformity and the increase of acculturation had to do with *"Die Stillen im Lande"* (the quiet in the land) becoming more aggressive in Christian work. As Donovan Smucker pointed out while living in Chicago, Mennonites believed in the "Go ye!" of the Great Commission and the "Separate ye!" of the nonconformity principle—but not all Mennonites and not always. For many years "Separate ye!" had won over "Go ye!" It still wins among the Old Colony Mennonites of Mexico and among most Old Order Amish. But among most Mennonites of the Great Awakening period and since, "Go ye!" has won. Yet the two imperatives have continued in tension. As Smucker stated, some Mennonites have abandoned witnessing to stay pure and clean, while others have abandoned separation in hopes of witnessing more effectively. Both commands are "deeply imbedded in Scripture and in the experience of genuine church life."[7]

Others have also pointed out this seeming dilemma. In writing about the general Protestant evangelization thrust in 1973 ("Key 73"), R. L. Hartzler thought the emphasis was proper and necessary. But, he added, it raised the problem of proper teaching in that if too many are brought into the church too quickly without proper inculcation, what will happen to doctrines such as nonresistance? Hartzler thought Mennonites had not been very successful in this regard in the past, since those who have succeeded most in outreach in the past have not succeeded with nonresistance. Likewise, those who have stressed inculcation have succeeded better with nonresistance. Looking at the experience of World War II, he continued: "The prevailing pattern has been that where evangelism has been most stressed, the other has been weak or even challenged. What now if Key 73 produces the anticipated results?" Hartzler thought the Old Order Amish were a good example of those emphasizing inculcation and EMC a good example of those emphasizing evangelism.[8]

Using the Hutterites as his example, one prominent non-Mennonite authority has also observed this tension between "Separate Ye" and "Go ye." Roland H. Bainton has stated that the Hutterites have achieved success in Canada and the United States "by abandoning the missionary command, and they have been able to preserve the ancient pattern because of the isolation." But Mennonites, he continued, "have been more concerned to maintain the missionary emphasis, and have a greater concern to reach out to the society round about, and thereby they have been modified." He pointed out that this was a problem not only for Mennonites and Hutterites but for all mission-minded Christians "because there is no possibility of carrying the gospel to other people without some kind of accommodation." Even the change of language is an accommodation. "Likewise there has to be a certain accommodation to culture. This raises the question of how far can you go." Bainton concluded: "There is a point beyond which we cannot go. But if there is no accommodation, Christianity is unintelligible and cannot spread. If there is too much accommodation it will spread, but will no longer be Christianity. How shall we determine what is the true core?... We must go back to the Biblical norm."[9]

In 1959 Roy Ingold, while in charge of mission work in Gibson City, wrote to Vern Miller, the leader of a mission church in Cleveland, Ohio, asking to what extent his congregation insisted on adherence to the Mennonite distinctives. Miller's reply is informative: "Our church ... is in no sense antiMennonite.... [Yet] we do not insist on a convert accepting all our doctrine immediately. We baptize and give communion to all who are saved. Since we don't insist on Mennonite practices our people are much more favorable to them. About half of our people wear coverings. We have not insisted on nonresistance but are teaching it." Miller concluded: "We don't insist on them being Mennonites to be members of the church but they know that we are sponsored by the Mennonites and" in "some way affiliated with the local conference."[10]

At Highway Village, where the group was almost totally non-Mennonite in background, Robert Harnish pursued a course quite similar to that of the Cleveland congregation. He accepted people where they were and he and the members decided on policies which were quite flexible regarding dress, the use of musical instruments, and nonresistance. The congregation taught nonresistance but did not make it a test of membership. Harnish thought the young people were accepting the principle more readily than the older ones.[11] Already in 1947 a city missions conference reported that missionaries were called to preach Christ rather than Mennonite culture, which do at times conflict. The church, continued the report, needs to "have forbearance with the city mission problem in considering application of her standards to the non-Mennonite believer" and must consider "the problem of psychological adjustment required on the part of a non-Mennonite convert" in accepting Mennonite doctrines.[12] Whatever the connection between inculcation and evangelism, in a survey of (Old) Mennonite outreach, the Illinois Conference and the South Central were listed as the most effective in winning non-Mennonites. As noted earlier, other (Old) Mennonites often looked upon their Illinois counterparts as being more liberal in interpreting nonconformity.[13]

When Illinois Mennonites began to see the tension between a too rigid interpretation of separation from the world on the one hand and involvement in mission in the world on the other, they were merely moving along with the main stream. Edward Stoltzfus, moderator of the Mennonite Church, said at the 1977 General Assembly: "Brothers and sisters, the model of cultural separation from the world is dead. It is no more. This model, separation from the world, cannot serve us well any longer. We need a new model for our life in this world." Later in the address he added: "The Mennonite Church is changing—it is changing from an emphasis on separation to an emphasis on incarnation, from preservation to involvement." Coming from the elected head of the (Old) Mennonites, these were strange, not to say shocking, words. Not everyone agreed. But Stoltzfus had explained that the new "incarnational model" called for was a new messianic community and still required separation in that its "life of faith, its values, its ethics, its hope for the future are separated from the world's values, ethics and hopes." The church's "presence in this world is for the world. *To be separated to Christ means to be turned toward the world,* to love it as God loves it, to work for its redemption, and fulfillment as God works in Christ. The church exists in and for the world."[14] This address, published in a slightly condensed form, was no doubt influential among Illinois readers. At the least, it indicated that changes occurring in Illinois (Old) Mennonite congregations were quite representative of those across North America.

Even Mennonite benevolence, according to one writer, has been an expression of acculturation. In an article entitled "Mennonite Benevolence and Civic Identity: The Post-War Compromise," James C. Juhnke put forward a thesis about American Mennonites in general that may well apply to those in Illinois. He pointed out that the peaks "of benevolent enterprise have coincided with the peaks of American nationalist-militarist enthusiasm" and asked, "Is American nationalism one of the sources of American Mennonite benevolence?" Juhnke's thesis was that Mennonite relief and service programs have to quite an extent been products of acculturation. Mennonites could not fight and kill, he explained, so in order to be good citizens they looked for a substitute that also called for similar sacrifice and service. The older, traditional explanation has been that Mennonite benevolence was "an internally generated phenomenon which arises from the peculiar history, traditions, and characteristics of the Mennonite churches." In other words, "the spiritual motivational basis for that response came from within the Mennonite community."[15]

Juhnke has said that in other areas of Mennonite life also, "it is obvious that acculturation to American models has had deep and permanent effects. Mennonites began speaking the English language, using advanced farm machinery, playing organs in their churches," some of them abandoning foot washing and prayer coverings, "naming their children Harry and Nancy, attending football games and crowning homecoming queens, shaving their beards and sometimes growing them again—all in imitation of American culture."

Juhnke conceded that to suggest Mennonite benevolence is a product of American acculturation "may be deceptively simple." He admitted that human motivations are complex—multicausational rather than single. But he argued convincingly that Mennonite benevolence has had some relation to militant American nationalism. "The Mennonite Central Committee, long understood as a chapter in the recovery of the Anabaptist vision, is also a footnote to American nationalism."[16] Church officials' experience in Vietnam War times has tended to confirm Juhnke's argument. The officials found that the number offering themselves for the Voluntary Service Program decreased with the end of the draft in 1973.

On another subject dear to Mennonites, Juhnke has also strongly suggested that arrangements which the peace churches have worked out with the government to accommodate conscientious objectors have been too much of a compromise—the "Great Compromise" he has called them. In his view concessions by the government have made the Mennonites too complacent, too self-satisfied, and too inclined to lose or at least mute their prophetic voice. They already have what they want. "Why speak out against universal military training, when we are already exempted? Why witness against the military-industrial complex, if our churches are tax free?" Juhnke proposed that Mennonites may have to move beyond that Great Compromise.[17] Not all in Illinois would agree, but some, particularly some younger ones, would.

Surely, as Illinois Mennonites have experienced acculturation they have held differing views of keeping the faith. Yet, without question, in the ways the major Mennonite bodies have dealt with a number of the traditional Mennonite distinctives, considerable shifting has occurred. As noted in previous chapters—especially in IX, XII and XV—there have been changes in the interpretations of Scripture regarding amusements, use of musical instruments, business and labor relations, the prayer veiling, divorce and remarriage, lodge membership, and dress and other expressions of nonconformity.

According to one brother, the ordinance of the holy kiss, even among the (Old) Mennonites, was losing favor already in the early 1930s. This person, a deacon, believed in the practice and rejected the two chief arguments against it—that it was unsanitary and embarrassing. He conceded, however, that whether to kiss or not to kiss was at times a problem. "It is quite embarrassing to know how to approach even some Mennonite ministers," he wrote, "for while we appreciate the kiss ourselves, there are those who do not seem to appreciate it." As to dress, things have changed much since 1921 when a C. F. Derstine article offered "A Glimpse at the Bonnet Question"—with twenty-one reasons why the bonnet was the scriptural and proper headgear for women. Lodge membership was already a problem in some Mennonite churches as early as 1923. The pastor of one church wrote that they had "quite a mess" on their hands. "We've had three men in church here who belong to lodges. Of late a number of our young men joined [the] Klan." On the previous Sunday the congregation had voted on the question of expelling them. "Twenty voted in favor of expelling and forty-nine against. The preachers are up in the air and its [sic] a question as to what will happen. They may vote my congregation out of conference." Conference did not reject the congregation, and the pastor continued to serve there for many years.[18] It should be pointed out, however, that lodge membership among Mennonites in the 1920s was probably pretty rare.

These and other instances of the erosion of Mennonite distinctives mentioned in earlier chapters clearly indicate that by the 1980s the question whether the Illinois Mennonites were keeping the faith was a relevant one. Or Illinois Mennonites were measuring by changing criteria. Not all would give the same answer. Quite a few would agree with some of the changes but not all of them. One older minister, for example, agreed that dropping the plain coat requirement for ministers was not "departing from the faith in any way." But while he also agreed that divorce and remarriage cases had to be considered individually, he felt there was "too much liberality along that line in most cases." He also saw disappearance of women's prayer veiling as departure from the faith. But even he concluded that many had grown in spirituality and that for most members "probably you could say they are keeping the faith."[19]

The majority in the major bodies would no doubt insist that they have been keeping the faith. Otherwise, logic would compel the majority to change its course. They would say that they still stick to basic principles but that application of the principles has changed. Nonconformity, for example, is still good Mennonite belief in Illinois in the 1980s, but most people put the emphasis at a different place from where it was earlier in the century. Many feel that former emphases and interpretations were superficial. So they put less stress on nonconformity in particular styles or forms of clothing but still believe in it with regard to practices they regard as wrong, including going to war. Concepts of simplicity are still present among Illinois Mennonites who do not wear a distinctive garb. As one authority has well said: "If Mennonites remain true to their heritage they will continue to stress the principle that all of life, including its expression in the kind of clothing worn, must be brought under the scrutiny of New Testament standards relating to humility, stewardship, modesty, and simplicity."[20]

Beyond question, the pressure to conform to secular American society has been and remains tremendous. Modern transportation and communication, especially radio and television, have vastly increased this pressure to conform. The pressure has become so great that one can understand why some—especially those with little or no sense of mission to others—should seek isolation or very strong cultural boundaries as solutions.

But geographic isolation also has its limitations, as anyone knows who is conversant with the history and spiritual condition of the Old Colony Mennonites in Mexico. Illinois Mennonites as a whole have chosen to emphasize the strengthening of the inner defenses to enable the believer, in a world in which there is much antagonism to his principles and way of life, to experience the truth that "he who is in you is greater than he who is in the world" (1 John 4:4). It was in this spirit that the veteran church leader A. C. Good (1881-1978) worked throughout a long active career. As he was growing old, he wrote: "I love to think of the church in victory. We are not playing the role of the defeatist—praise the Lord." The church is built on a rock, "and the gates of hell shall not prevail against it." "Whatever happens to the nations of the world, the church marches on to victory. She knows no defeat."[21] Good's ninety-seven years spanned many changes among the Mennonites, including less rigid application of the Mennonite distinctives. But the great majority would no doubt agree that he "kept the faith."

Like Good, many others also kept the rock Christ Jesus as the foundation of faith. One leading periodical, *The Mennonite*, has had from its beginning in 1885 Menno Simons' favorite motto: "For other foundation can no man lay than that is laid, which is Jesus Christ" (1 Cor. 3:11). Among others Joseph D. Hartzler at Waldo also epitomized "keeping the faith" by keeping Christ foundational. At Hartzler's funeral service Edwin J. Stalter, who had worked closely with him for years and knew him well, pointed out that while J. D.'s life span (1884-1970) covered a host of theological ideas, "Orthodoxy, Fundamentalism, Liberalism or Modernism, Neo-orthodoxy, demythologization, New theology, etc. . . . [his] faith in Christ was kept." He kept his vision on Christ who changes not. "Each generation," said Stalter, "must focus its Christian vision according to the environmental factors that relate to Jesus Christ. He is the unchanging and consistent factor of our faith, . . ." among the generations, the same yesterday, today, and forever. "Men of other days could have lived in our day, and we could have lived in theirs. But the common denominator for faith in all ages is Christ Jesus." Stalter concluded: "An unspoken voice is here today. A silent testimony is given for our comfort and edification. It is the testimony of Brother J. D. 'I have kept the faith.' "[22]

The Illinois Mennonites, like many Christians in the Western world, face serious problems of materialism and affluence, complacency, individualism as over against community, secularism, too much acculturation, a too restricted view of the gospel, and "not enough willingness for adults to become mature disciples through dialogue and study of the Word and our times." Yet while in some ways they were doing better and in others perhaps not so well, it could well be that on balance Illinois Mennonites were doing a better job of keeping the Christian faith in the 1980s than did their forefathers a century earlier.[23]

In any case Illinois Mennonites face the future with much confidence. Ivan Kauffmann of Lombard has said that "the coming years will be exciting times for the church. They will be times of testing, but they will also be times of victory and growth. It is my opinion that God is at work in the midst of our church, and that in the coming decade there will be growth and expansion [and inter-Mennonite cooperation] such as we have not seen in our 300-year history in North America. . . . It will be an exciting future."[24] That future, of course, is in the hands of God. Yet it is clear that as of 1981 the Illinois Mennonites were searching, praying, and working hard not only to keep the faith but to make it still more relevant and effective in a needy world.

Notes

Key to Abbreviations

AMC—Archives of the Mennonite Church, 1700 S. Main, Goshen, Ind.
AMBS—Associated Mennonite Biblical Seminaries, 3003 Benham, Elkhart, Ind.
CC Yrbk—*Central Conference Mennonite Church Yearbook* (with year)
Cen Dist Rep—*Central District Reporter*
Chr Evan—*The Christian Evangel*
EM—*The Evangelical Mennonite*
EMC—Evangelical Mennonite Church
GH—*Gospel Herald*
GW—*Gospel Witness*
HT—*Herald of Truth*
IMC—Illinois Mennonite Conference
IMCR—*Illinois Mennonite Conference Reports*
IMHGS—Illinois Mennonite Historical and Genealogical Society
Menn—*The Mennonite*
MCD—*Mennonite Cyclopedic Dictionary*
ME—*The Mennonite Encyclopedia*
MH—*Mennonite Heritage*
MHB—*Mennonite Historical Bulletin*
MHLB—Mennonite Historical Library at Bluffton College, Bluffton, Ohio
MHLG—Mennonite Historical Library at Goshen College, Goshen, Ind.
ML—*Mennonite Life*
MLA—Mennonite Library and Archives, Bethel College, N. Newton, Kan.
MQR—*The Mennonite Quarterly Review*
M Yrbk—*Mennonite Yearbook and Directory*
MG—*Missionary Guide*
NARS—National Archives
ZT—*Zion's Tidings*

CHAPTER 1. Illinois When the Mennonites Came

1. The full title of the Act is "An Ordinance for the government of the Territory of the United States northwest of the River Ohio."
2. These two ordinances appear in many books of United States history readings, e.g., Henry Steele Commager, *Documents of American History*, various editions.
3. Quoted in A. C. Boggess, *Settlement of Illinois* (1908), 97.
4. *The Encyclopedia Americana* (1974), s.v. "Illinois."
5. Boggess, 134 ff.
6. J. M. Peck, *A Gazetteer of Illinois* (1837), as quoted in Willard H. Smith (see note 8).
7. Official United States census as quoted in *The World Almanac 1966*, 324.
8. Willard H. Smith, "The Westward Movement into Illinois" (graduate research paper, University of Michigan, 1929), 24, copy in author's possession.
9. *Dictionary of American History* (1946), s.v. "The Illinois and Michigan Canal," by Paul M. Angle.
10. *Ibid.*, s.v. "The Illinois Central Railroad," by Paul W. Gates.
11. See, e.g., Emerson D. Fite, *Social and Industrial Conditions in the North During the Civil War* (1930), 14ff.
12. Arthur C. Cole, *The Era of the Civil War 1848-1870* (1919), 75-76.
13. *Ibid.*, 83-85.
14. *HT*, Mar. 15, 1892.
15. Madge Pickard and R. Carlyle Buley (1946), 36; see also dedication page.
16. *HT*, Nov., 1871, 174-75.
17. Milo Custer, "Asiatic Cholera in Central Illinois 1834-1873," *Journal of the Illinois State Historical Society* 23 (April 1930), 113ff.
18. Homer C. Hockett, *Political and Social Growth of the American People, 1492-1865* (3rd ed., 1940), 688.
19. Theodore C. Pease, *The Story of Illinois*, (3rd ed., 1965), 128-131; Theodore C. Pease, *The Frontier State 1818-1848* (1918), chapter 19.
20. *Dictionary of American Biography*, XI, 434-35.
21. *ME*, s.v. "John Fretz Funk," by Harold S. Bender.

CHAPTER 2. Origins and Growth of the Mennonite Settlements in Illinois to the 1870s

1. J. C. Wenger, *The Mennonite Church in America* (1966), 27.
2. *Ibid.*, 29; Harold S. Bender, *Conrad Grebel, c. 1498-1526: The Founder of the Swiss Brethren Sometimes Called Anabaptists* (1950), 137ff.; *ME*, II, 572; Cornelius J. Dyck, ed., *An Introduction to Mennonite History* (1967), 33-35.
3. Wenger, 29-30; conf. with John Oyer, March 16, 1981, at Goshen, Ind.
4. Delbert Gratz, *Bernese Anabaptists* (1953), 5-7.
5. For those wishing to read more on recent scholarly research on the complicated story of the origins and character of Anabaptism, see, for example, the following: James M. Stayer, Werner O. Packull, and Klaus Depperman, "From Monogenesis to Polygenesis: The Historical Discussion of Anabaptist Origins," *MQR* 49 (April 1975), 83-121; James M. Stayer, "Reflections and Retractions on *Anabaptists and the Sword*," *MQR* 51 (July 1977), 197-212; James M. Stayer, "The Swiss Brethren: An Exercise in Historical Definition," *Church History*47 (June 1978), 174-95; Carl S. Meyer, ed., *Sixteenth Century Essays and Studies* (1970), I, especially the chapters by Paul Peachey and Abraham Friesen on Marxism and Anabaptism.
6. *ME*, III, 522-25.
7. Dyck (see note 2), 40; *ME*, III, 525.
8. J. C. Wenger, *The Doctrines of the Mennonites* (1950), 71-75.
9. Readers who desire to read more on the European background of the Mennonites can find many good works, including: John Horsch, *Mennonites in Europe* (1950); C. Henry Smith, *The Story of the Mennonites* (5th ed., revised and enlarged by Cornelius Krahn, 1981); Wenger (see note 1), chapters 1-4; Cornelius J. Dyck, ed., *An Introduction to Mennonite History* (2nd ed., 1981), chapters 1-10; and the monumental *Mennonite Encyclopedia* (4 vols., 1955-59), an excellent, scholarly source on thousands of topics on the Anabaptists and Mennonites in Europe and America.
10. *ME*, IV, 136-138. For further reading on this wave of Mennonite migration see C. Henry Smith, *The Mennonite Immigration to Pennsylvania in the Eighteenth Century* (1929).
11. By 1820 religious persecution in Europe had declined, but something new, namely conscription into the armed forces, put Mennonites in a difficult position.

12. Quoted by Harold S. Bender, "Causes for Emigration to America," in Wenger (see note 1), 51.
13. Jacob Krehbiel, *Krehbiel History and Family Records* (compiled and mimeographed by Howard Raid, 1963), 12ff.; copy in MHLG.
14. John S. Oyer, "Life Among the Early 19th Century Amish-Mennonite Immigrants to Illinois" (summary), *MH*, Dec. 1976. Complete address given at Metamora, Oct. 30, 1976, to the Illinois Mennonite Historical and Genealogical Society, is on cassette in the possession of writer.
15. C. Henry Smith, *The Story of the Mennonites* (4th ed., 1957), 570; Arman Habegger, *Menn*, June 17, 1975, A-12.
16. C. Henry Smith, *The Mennonites of America* (1909), 496-97. For a discussion of the Indians of the area just before the Mennonites came, see C. Henry Smith, *Metamora* (1947), especially chapter 11.
17. Smith, *Mennonites of America*, 284-85, 489; *HT*, Nov. 22, 1863, Sept. 1864, Jan. 1867, Mar. 1878; Harry F. Weber, *Centennial History of the Mennonites of Illinois 1829-1929* (1931), 134-36, 600; *ME*, IV, 658.
18. *MG*, Oct. 1948; *HT*, Oct. 1870, July 1871, Dec. 1877, Dec. 1, 1891, May 15, 1897; Mary Kauffman, "Bishop Joseph S. Shoemaker—A Short Biography," *Christian Monitor*, July 1936; Eldon Kortemeier, *The Life and Growth of the Freeport Mennonite Church* (1959), 7-10, 14 ff; Weber, 142-43; J. S. Shoemaker, "[Auto] Biographical Notes," box 1, J. S. Shoemaker mss., AMC.
19. For a good discussion of this see Kortemeier, 14.
20. *Ibid.*, 16; conference with Paul King, Oct. 14, 1978, at Goshen, Ind.
21. For this difference of opinion see Kortemeier, 15, including footnote 11; J. S. Shoemaker, et al., "History of the Freeport Church," J. S. Shoemaker mss., III-13-18.1, AMC.
22. *MG*, Apr. 1950, Aug. 1958; Salinda D. Hershey and Mary S. Denlinger, "A Trip West," *HT*, Nov. 15, 1891, March 1, 1899; Weber (see note 17), 152-53.
23. *MG*, Apr. 1950, Aug. 1958; *Christian Monitor*, Sept. 1948; *Sterling Daily Gazette*, Apr. 1, 1898, reprinted in *Christian Monitor*, Sept. 1948; *ME*, IV, 489.
24. Hazel Nice [Hassan], "History of the Morrison Red Brick Church," 1-3; Weber (see note 17), 162-63; Eunice Deter, *Descendants of Ulrich Steiner* (1947), 49ff.; *HT*, June 1867, 90.
25. *HT*, Sept., Dec. 1866, Jan. 1867, March 1872; Hazel Nice Hassan, *The Nice Family History—Descendants of Henry Clemmer Nice* (1965), 35-37.
26. Thomas Yoder, *The Cullom Mennonite Church* (1975), 3-6; Weber (see note 17), 167ff.
27. Yoder, 21. *HT*: Sept. 1864, 56; July 1873, 121-22.
28. Solomon Lehman to Christian Lehman and family, May 2, 1869, published in *MHB*, July 1977. Letter supplied by Wilmer D. Swope, Leetonia, Ohio.
29. Quoted in Hazel Hassan, "The Early Mennonites of Jo Daviess County," *MH*, March 1977.
30. The best sources of information about Scales Mound are two articles by Hazel N. Hassan, both in *MH*, March 1977. In addition to the article mentioned in note 29, see also her "The Hammer Cemetery," listing names and dates of many Mennonites and others buried there. See also *History of Jo Daviess County, Illinois* (1878), 372, 790, 793; *HT*, Dec. 1878, 211.
31. Funk diary, May 28, 1865, AMC; Funk, autobiography (two bound volumes written in first person and in Funk's handwriting), pp. 94B-95B, box 48; document about his first sermon, box 49; John F. Funk mss., AMC. John A. Hostetler, *God Uses Ink: The Heritage and Mission of the Mennonite Publishing House after Fifty Years* (1958), 38. *HT*: Dec. 1864, 84; Jan. 1865, 3; March 1872, 41, 42; Oct. 1885, 319; Feb. 1, 1901, 47. *ME*, s.v. "John Fretz Funk" and "Gardner," 421-23, 439; Edwin J. Stalter, "Gardner Mennonite Church," *MH*, Sept. 1976.
32. J. Winfield Fretz, "First Mennonites in Chicago," *ML*, April 1953, 56-57.
33. Ivan W. Brunk to author, Dec. 21, 1976; Ivan W. Brunk, "Brunk Ancestors," *MHB*, July 1976; Ivan W. Brunk, "Noah Brunk," unpublished mss. in my possession, courtesy of Brunk; Coffman diary, Nov. 23, 24, 25, 1895, J. S. Coffman mss., AMC; *HT*, Feb. 1878, 30-31.
34. Ivan Brunk, "Mennonites in Henry County Illinois," *MH*, March 1976; Ethel Estella (Cooprider) Erb, *Story of Grandmother Heatwole-Brunk-Cooprider* (n.d.), 21-30; Reuben J. Heatwole to John S. Coffman, April 11, 1865, published in *MHB*, Jan. 1974; Paul Erb, *South Central Frontiers: A History of the South Central Mennonite Conference* (1974), 163-67; Daniel F. Driver to John F. Funk, March 20, 1867, John F. Funk mss., AMC; J. C. Wenger, *Faithfully, Geo. R.: The Life and Thought of George R. Brunk I (1871-1938)* (1978), 23-25.
35. *HT*: April 1878, 67; March 1879.
36. *HT*: June 1871, 94; March 1872, 44; Feb. 1877, 31; May 1877, 74-75; Nov. 1878, 190; Dec. 1879, 230; Jan. 1880, 11; March 1880, 51; June 1881, 113-114; May 1881, 84-85; July 1881, 110-111; March 1, 1883, 73; April 1, 1883, 106. Edward Yoder, "Henry Yother (1810-1900)," *MHB*, June 1944; G. R. Risser to J. S. Coffman, Jan. 18, 1884, box 7, J. S. Coffman mss., AMC. Another example of early Illinois settlers who were descendants of Mennonites is the Ebys (or Abys) of Peoria and surrounding counties. See Malvin Stanton Aby, and Franklin Stanton Aby, MD, *The Aby Family of Peoria County Illinois* (1924), 8ff.

CHAPTER 3. Origins and Growth of the Amish Mennonite Settlements in Illinois to About 1878

1. Milton Gascho, "The Amish Division of 1693-1697 in Switzerland and Alsace," *MQR*, 11 (Oct. 1937), 235ff. *ME*, I, 90-99: "Amish Division," "Amish Mennonites," and "Ammann, Jakob;" John A. Hostetler, *Amish Society* (3rd d., Baltimore and London, 1980), 31-47.
2. C. Henry Smith, *One Hundred Years* (address at Metamora, Ill., 1940), 11; copy in MHLG.
3. Delbert Gratz to author, Feb. 1, 1981; on this point, as well as others, Thomas Yoder and Steven R. Estes of Graymont, Ill., who have been and are doing research on the Illinois Mennonites, have generously shared their material with this writer. Mrs. Myrna Park of Normal has likewise put at the writer's disposal a rich collection of family and other historical records.
4. Walter Ropp, in Pete Ropp, compiler, *Christian Ropp 1812-1896* (1977), 12-13. This account contains a translation of a brief autobiography of Christian Ropp, which differs slightly from a version in C. Henry Smith's *The Mennonites of America* (1909), 479ff., and in Harry F. Weber's *Centennial History of the Mennonites of Illinois* (1931), 83ff. But in essentials the two translations are the same.
5. Pete Ropp, compiler, 4-8, 15.
6. See "Apostolic Mennonite Church" and "Butler County, Ohio," in *ME*, I, 137-38, 486.
7. Newton Bateman *et al.*, eds., *History of McLean County*, (1879), 658, 659.
8. Leo Driedger, "Native Rebellion and Mennonite Invasion: An Examination of Two Canadian River Valleys," *MQR* 46 (July 1972), 290-300.
9. *Ibid.*, 361; *MHB*, Oct. 1974, 3.
10. *The Portrait and Biographical Album of McLean County;* (1887); conference with Steven R. Estes, Oct. 17, 1978, at Goshen, Ind.; see also Hazel N. Hassan, "Peter Maurer, Pioneer," *MH*, Sept. 1979.
11. See Weber (see note 4), 78, and his Appendix I. But see also ms. by Samuel E. Maurer, "Life of S. E. Maurer," 1-2; and Valentine Strubhar, "A Short Hist. of the Peter Strubhar Sr. Family . . .", 1; copies of both in the possession of Steven R. Estes, Graymont, Ill.
12. Smith, *One Hundred Years* (see note 2), 4; *HT*, May 1, 1888, 141.
13. *History of Kankakee County, Illinois* (1906), 793-794; *Chenoa Times*, Sept. 28, 1911, as reported by Steven R. Estes.
14. Information from Charles Claudon, Park Forest, Ill., who is writing a Claudon family history, and from *Bloomington Pantagraph*, Jan. 1, 1894, through courtesy of Steven R. Estes, Graymont, Ill.
15. *HT*, Apr. 1872; see Steven R. Estes to author, June 8, 1977, for citation for John and Mary Rupp trip to Europe.
16. Conferences with Ernest J. Bohn, Oct. 10, 1977, Apr. 18, 1978, at Goshen, Ind. Ernest thought his parents joined the Roanoke congregation.
17. Arthur Nafziger and Richard Hassan, "Interview with Christian E. Martin," *MH*. Dec. 1974; W. H. Grubb, *History of the Mennonites of Butler County, Ohio* (1916), 27; *MHB*, July 1954.
18. Paul M. Schrock, *Four Score and Ten: The Story of Joseph Schrock 1852-1943* (mimeographed, 1972), 2-5; copy available MHLG.
19. Melvin Gingerich, *The Mennonites in Iowa* (1939), 329.
20. Kathryn Schertz to C. Henry Smith, Sept. 16, 1935; George I. Sommer to C. Henry Smith, March 15, 1938; C. Henry Smith mss., MHLB. *HT*, March 1905, 79; *GH*, March 14, 1940, 1070.
21. *ME*, II, 810; J. C. Wenger, *The Mennonites in Indiana and Michigan* (1961), 240.
22. Weber, (see note 4), 79.
23. *ME*, III, 560.
24. Smith, *Mennonites* (see note 4), 228-31; Weber (see note 4), 79-82.
25. Locations cited in note 24; conference with Nelson Springer and Lena Lehman, May 17, 1978, at Goshen, Ind.
26. M. P. Lantz to C. Henry Smith, Apr. 3, 1923, C. Henry Smith mss., MHLB; Smith, *Mennonites* (see note 4), 231; for a good historical summary of the Amish settlements in Illinois and the organization of congregations among them see Steven R. Estes, "History of Partridge Creek Meeting Traced," *MH*, June 1980.
27. Smith, *One Hundred Years* (see note 2), 5.
28. *Ibid.*, 4-5.
29. C. Henry Smith, "The Amish of Illinois," *M Yrbk*, 1907, 20.
30. Conference with Lena Gerber Lehman, May 26, 1978, at Goshen, Ind.; conference with Mrs. Ruth King, Sept. 27, 1979, at Morton, Ill.; Elva Mae Roth, "The Pleasant Grove Church," *MH*, June 1977; Weber (see note 4), 220.
31. Published in Smith, *Mennonites* (see note 4), 479-84; also in Ropp (see note 4), 4-10. Compiler Ropp says that much of this information was obtained by Edwin O. Ropp and Walter A. Ropp.
32. Ropp miscellaneous papers, on Christian Ropp and wife and children; unpaginated; photocopies in my possession, courtesy of Steven R. Estes, Graymont, Ill.

Notes for Pages 67-85

33. Ropp (see note 4), 21.
34. Christian Erismann diary, Feb. 7, 1869, 50, AMC.
35. Edwin O. Ropp papers, AMC; conference with Steven R. Estes, Oct. 17, 1978, at Goshen, Ind.
36. Alma Kaufmann, "History of the Willow Springs Mennonite Church Near Tiskilwa" (unpublished ms., 1973), 1-2 (sent to writer through courtesy of author); Amanda Sears et al., *The Albrechts 1836-1969* (1969), 3-4.
37. Locations cited in note 36; Mrs. Henry (Harriet) Albrecht, "The Albrecht Family of Bureau County," *MH*, June 1977.
38. Locations cited in note 37; Weber (see note 4), 226-30.
39. *A Brief History and the Constitution* (1957), North Danvers Church Archives; Weber (see note 4), 634.
40. William B. Weaver, *History of the Central Conference Mennonite Church* (1926), 67-73; new information about Stuckey's birth year (1826 instead of 1825) comes from Mrs. Grace Croft, Provo, Utah, to Steven R. Estes, Graymont, Ill. She has a prayer book of Joseph's father in which the names and birth dates of the children are listed.
41. Weaver, 78-79; Minnie Brenneman to C. Henry Smith, Nov. 26, 1923, C. Henry Smith mss., MHLB.
42. Arthur W. Nafziger, Hopedale, Ill., great grandson of Christian Nafziger, has shown the writer this "Certificate of Domicile" and the "Testimonial"; Arthur W. Nafziger mss., AMC. See also Arthur W. Nafziger et al., *100 Years at Hopedale* (1954), 7-9.
43. Nafziger et al., 10, 16-17.
44. Edwin J. Stalter, *The Mennonites of Waldo 1860-1960* (1960), 2-4; Stalter, *Notes on Some Early American Stalters: Joseph, John, Jacobina* (private, n. p., 1969), 3-4.
45. Historical Committee, *Roanoke Mennonite Church Centennial Year 1875-1975* [1-2]. See also Schrock (see note 18), 2-4.
46. For an excellent biography of Christian Reeser, Sr., we are indebted to one of his great-granddaughters. See Ethel Reeser Cosco, *Christian Reeser: The Story of a Centenarian* (n. d.), passim.
47. Verle and Margaret Oyer, *Jacob Zehr, 1825-1898, "Mackinaw Meeting" Preacher* (1964), 1-4, 7-9; Jacob Zehr obituary, *HT*, March 15, 1898.
48. Edwin O. Ropp papers (under title "C Ropp—Probation), AMC.
49. Nafziger et al. (see note 42), 9ff.; J. J. Sommer, "Sommer History 1934," unpublished, in C. Henry Smith mss., MHLB.
50. Letter from Bureau County, in C. Henry Smith mss., MHLB.
51. Franklin L. Kenyon, ed., *Roanoke Centennial History . . . bridging the years, 1874-1974* (1974), 8; Oyer and Oyer, 4; A. J. Fretz, *A Brief History of Bishop Henry Funck and Other Funk Pioneers* (1968), 729ff.; conference with Nelson Springer, who checked Funk genealogies, March 18, 1978 at Goshen, Ind.; *Past and Present of Woodford County, Illinois* (1878), 573.
52. See note 17 in chapter 1. The story of Peter's loneliness and experience with the cup of water has been handed down in the Smith family.
53. Albert and Bertha Reedy Zehr, "The Life and Family of Samuel S. Zehr" (unpublished, 1976), 1.
54. This important Erismann manuscript is in the AMC. Nelson Springer deserves much credit for transcribing the important parts from the handwritten Gothic German into modern script. See also Springer's paper, "Schoolteacher by Accident, Churchman Without Office," read before the Illinois Mennonite Historical and Genealogical Society at Hopedale, Oct. 28, 1978.
55. E. E. Zimmerman, compiler, *Rinkenberger Family Record* (1949), 11-12.
56. Christian Erismann diary, March 23, 1868, AMC.
57. C. Henry Smith, *Mennonite Country Boy: The Early Years of C. Henry Smith* (1962), 127-28.
58. John A. Hostetler, "Amish Problems at the Diener-Versammlungen," *ML*, Oct. 1949.
59. These proceedings were printed annually, first by John Baer and Son of Lancaster, Pa., and then by John F. Funk of Chicago, Ill., and Elkhart, Ind. The general title of these reports (with a few minor variations) is *Verhandlungen der Diener-Versammlung der Deutschen Täufer oder Amischen Mennoniten* (1862, etc.). I shall use the abbreviation VDV1 for the first year, VDV2 for the second meeting, etc., to VDV16, the last meeting. See VDV1, 1ff.
60. There is a good article on them in *ME*, II, 56-57. The best treatment of the conferences is the article by John A. Hostetler. See also Pannabecker, *Faith in Ferment: A History of the Central District Conference* (1968), 14-19; Weber (see note 4), 179-86; and James O. Lehman, *Creative Congregationalism . . .* (1978), 79-91.
61. VDV1, 1-18.
62. VDV2, 3-15.
63. VDV3, 3-15.
64. VDV4, 5, 8.

65. VDV5, 1ff; 10-13; Christian Erismann diary, May 24, 1866, AMC.
66. VDV6, 8 and VDV7, 7.
67. VDV9, 9-14, 36.
68. VDV14, 1875, 19, 20.
69. *ME,* I, 97.
70. *Family Life,* Jan. 1973; James N. Gingerich, "*Ordnung* and Amish Ministers Meetings of the 1860s" (unpublished, 1980, copy in MHLG), 15.

CHAPTER 4. The Central Conference Mennonites in Illinois to 1957

1. Samuel Floyd Pannabecker, *Faith in Ferment: A History of the Central District Conference* (1968), 32.
2. Olynthus Clark, "Joseph Joder, Schoolmaster-Farmer and Poet 1797-1887," *Transactions of the Illinois State Historical Society* (1929), 135-65.
3. VDV12 (see chapter 3, note 59), 1873, 25-26; Pannabecker, 35; Clark, 97; conference with S. F. Pannabecker, Aug. 31, 1977, at Goshen, Ind.; *ME,* II, 56. The writer wishes to recognize the help of others, especially Elizabeth Horsch Bender and James Gingerich, in arriving at a proper understanding of this translation.
4. VDV11, 1872, 9, 14, 21-22; VDV12, 1873, 25-26.
5. Steven R. Estes, "Heaven's Temple," ms. in MHLG. Mr. Estes is studying both Christian Ropp and Joseph Stuckey.
6. William B. Weaver, *History of the Central Conference Mennonite Church* (1926), 95-96.
7. C. Henry Smith, *The Mennonites of America* (1909), 251.
8. This number has been misstated in some writings. One account states that the "Amish congregations of Central Illinois, with the exception of the Mackinaw Church [,] stood by their leader. . . ." The *ME* also states that "most of the Central Amish congregations stood with Stuckey. . . ."; Weaver, 97; *ME,* IV, 647.
9. Weaver, 72.
10. *A Brief History and the Constitution* (brochure, 1957, in North Danvers Church Archives), used through the courtesy of the present pastor, Elmer A. Wall.
11. *Ibid.*
12. *Ibid.;* Elsie I. Sloneker, *A Brief History of the North Danvers Mennonite Church* (1972), 8.
13. Sloneker, *Centennial Anniversary of the North Danvers House of Worship 1872-1972* (1972), 3, 16-17, in my possession; conference with R. L. Hartzler, April 21, 1977, at Bloomington, Ill.; "Minutes of the Board Meetings of the North Danvers Mennonite Church," in that church's archives.
14. "South Danvers Mennonite Church," *CC Yrbk,* 1922, 22-23; Weaver (see note 6), 79-81; *ME,* IV, 1127; Steven R. Estes, "Bishop Peter Nafziger (1789-1885), an Amish Apostle" (unpublished, 1977), 5-9, in MHLG.
15. Valentine Strubhar, "A Condensed History of the East [Washington] Mennonite Church Now Known as the Calvary Mennonite Church" (unpublished, 1940), in MHLG, courtesy Steven R. Estes; W. Richard Hassan, "Valentine Strubhar and the East Washington (Calvary) Church," *MH,* Sept. 1975, 27-28, 35; *ME,* I, 494 and IV, 1127; *Cen Dist Rep,* Sept. 20, 1966; conference with Steven R. Estes, Oct. 17, 1978, at Goshen, Ind.
16. Steven R. Estes, "The Nebraska Brethren: The Origin and Early Development of the Flanagan Mennonite Church" (1978 copy in MHLG), 1-24; *Menn.* Oct. 19, 1976, A-4; Steven R. Estes to author, Feb. 17, 1981.
17. *CC Yrbk,* 1924, 19-20; *Cen Dist Rep,* July 1966, A-1; *ME,* III, 547; Harry F. Weber, *Centennial History of the Mennonites of Illinois, 1829-1929* (1931), 467-69; Steven R. Estes to author, Feb. 17, 1981.
18. *CC Yrbk,* 1943, 6, 5-8; *ME,* IV, 750-51.
19. *ME,* I, 119; Pannabecker (see note 1), 203; Weaver (see note 6), 87-89; Joseph Stuckey, "Memorandum Book," 15, in MHLG.
20. *CC Yrbk,* 1924, 18-19; Raymond M. Yoder, "A Rural Harvest," *MG,* June 1950; conference with Raymond M. Yoder, July 17, 1978, at Goshen, Ind.
21. The two Yoder sources cited in note 20.
22. Weaver (see note 6), 92-93; *Menn,* Sept. 20, 1960; *Bethel Church News* (Bulletin), Nov. 14, 1977, May 4, Aug. 30, 1978, copies at the Bethel Church.
23. Ruth Schilpp, "Boynton Mennonite Church," *WHAM,* Aug. 3, 1976, courtesy of (Mrs.) Anna Nafziger, Goshen, Ind., granddaughter of Mrs. Wittrig; Mrs. Albert Habecker, "The Boynton Mennonite Church," *MH,* Dec. 1976. Conference with Anna Nafziger, July 15, 1978, at Goshen, Ind.; she was reared in

Notes for Pages 100-120

this church and her parents were charter members.
24. Sources cited in note 23; Mildred May Brenneman to editor, Nov. 6, 1970, *Menn*, Jan. 5, 1971; Bloomington *Pantagraph* (clipping), about Nov. 9 or 10, 1923, available in C. Henry Smith mss., MHLB.
25. *CC Yrbk*, 1924, 18-19; see the yearbooks for the following years for ministers and statistics, including membership.
26. Weber (see note 17) says "forty" on p. 230, and "twenty-three" on p. 480.
27. *ME*, IV, 728; Weber (see note 17), 226-30, 480; conference with Ernest Bohn, July 18, 1978, at Goshen, Ind., *Cen Dist Rep*, Nov. 16, 1971.
28. *ME*, I, 540.
29. Ben Esch, "The Work of Father Stuckey," *CC Yrbk*, 4-6, 37; "Joseph Stuckey's Record of Marriages, Baptisms, Deaths, Communions, and Addresses," in North Danvers Mennonite Church Archives; Pannabecker (see note 1), 146; Weaver (see note 6), 73. J. C. Mehl to William B. Weaver, Jan. 29, 1926; D. J. Johns to Weaver, Jan. 25, 1926; both in William B. Weaver mss., AMBS. For Stuckey's writing, wide traveling and many spiritual ministrations see the files of *HT*, especially in the 1860s and 1870s, and of the *Christlicher Bundesbote*, especially for the 1880s and the 1890s.
30. Conference with Raymond L. Hartzler, Apr. 21, 1977, at Bloomington, Ill.
31. A. [Aaron] Augspurger, "A Brief History of the Origin of the Central Conference of Mennonites," *CC Yrbk*, 1922, 26-27; Augspurger, *Chr Evan*, Dec. 1929.
32. "The Future of the Central Illinois Conference of Mennonites," *Chr Evan*, Aug. 1912, 378.
33. *CC Yrbk*, 1935, 30-33.
34. Pannabecker (see note 1), 38-42, and chapter 12;
35. *Chr Evan*, Sept.-Oct. 1953.
36. *Ibid.*, Sept. 1949.
37. *Cen Dist Rep*, Dec. 1964, Jan. 1965, Nov. 16, 1976 (insert in *Menn*); *Menn*, Apr. 23, May 14, 1957.
38. [Raymond L. Hartzler], "Significant Eras in Our Conference History and Our Present Status," *Chr Evan*, Oct. 1953.
39. Oscar Julius Sommer, *History of Sommer Brothers Seed Company, 1905-1955* (1955), 13ff. and *passim*. The writer is indebted to Thomas Yoder, Normal, Ill., for the use of his notes from county histories on this and other points.
40. Augspurger, *Chr Evan*, Aug. 1912; conf. with Raymond L. Hartzler, April 21, 1977, at Bloomington, Ill.; conference with Heinz Janzen, April 1977, at Bluffton, Ohio.

CHAPTER 5. The Evangelical Mennonite Church (Defenseless Mennonites) in Illinois

1. Stan Nussbaum, *You Must Be Born Again* (1980), 22-23.
2. *Ibid.*, 2-3, 9; David N. Claudon and Kathryn E. Claudon, *Life of Bishop Henry Egly 1824-1890* [1947], 7-12; Henry Egly, "Autobiography" (unpublished, 1887), EMC Archives.
3. Egly, "Autobiography," 2.
4. Christian R. Egle, *Brief History of Salem Mennonite Church near Flanagan, Illinois* ... (1925), 3.
5. *Ibid.*, 4; E. E. Zimmerman to Thomas Yoder, Oct. 9, 1970, and Jan. 21, 1972, in the possession of Yoder, Normal, Ill., *EM*; Nov. 15, 1956, 7; June 15, 1965, 12. Albert Frey to Reuben Short, Dec. 3, 1949, Salem file, EMC Archives.
6. *EM*, Oct. 15, 1965; *Build*, Summer, 1971.
7. Egle, 7.
8. *Ibid.*
9. *Ibid.*, 10.
10. *Ibid.*, 5; Viola Zurlinder, *ZT*, Sept. 15, 1940.
11. Egle (see note 4), 6-7.
12. Quoted in Peter G. Schultz, "The Evangelical Mennonite Church in Illinois," *MH*, Sept. 1975.
13. Egle (see note 4), 8.
14. *Ibid.*; E. E. Zimmerman, "A Brief History of the Evangelical Mennonite Church Publications," *EM*, July 15, 1968; *ME*, II, 693.
15. Egle (see note 4), 8-9; *Goshen College Record*, Nov. 1905, 37-38.
16. Egle (see note 4), 9; William B. Weaver, *History of the Central Conference Mennonite Church* (1926), 163ff.; Harry F. Weber, *Centennial History of the Mennonites of Illinois, 1829-1929* (1931), 377ff.; Nussbaum (see note 1), 24 ff.
17. Egle (see note 4), 11.
18. *ZT*, Aug. 15, 1939; *EM*, Oct. 1953, March 15, 1956; E. E. Zimmerman, "Biography of Peter

Hochstettler 1834-1924," *EM*, Oct. 15, 1965; J. S. Coffman diary, Feb. 25, 1893, AMC.

19. Nussbaum (see note 1), 14. The following sentence was a part of Nussbaum's original manuscript but not included in the book: "To some EMC [Evangelical Mennonite Church] leaders, Ramseyer seemed to be adding new doctrines to the faith, amending the creed to say, 'You must have the new birth and later you must have the baptism of the Holy Spirit too,' or, 'You must be born again, and again.' "

20. Nussbaum (see note 1), 13; correspondence among E. G. Steiner, Reuben Short, and Walter McDowell (pastor at Groveland), April to May, 1961, *passim*, in McDowell file, Groveland congregation, materials, EMC Archives.

21. E. E. Zimmerman to Thomas Yoder (undated but received by Yoder, Oct. 12, 1971), in the possession of Yoder, Normal, Ill.; *ZT*, Oct. 15, 1938.

22. *EM*, Apr. 15, 1964.

23. See note 21; also *ZT*, Dec. 15, 1931.

24. *ZT*, Jan. 15, 1939; conference with Reuben Short, Nov. 6, 1979, at Ft. Wayne, Ind.

25. E. E. Zimmerman, *ZT*, Oct. 15, Nov. 15, 1938; *Build*, Fall, 1976.

26. See: the Nov. 15, 1966 issue of *EM* for an article by Schultz himself on "Calvary Mennonite Church"; *MH*, Sept. 1975; brief, unpublished manuscript by Schultz, "Calvary Memorial Church—1976," in Calvary file, EMC Archives.

27. Peter G. Schultz, "The Evangelical Mennonite Church in Illinois," *MH*, Sept. 1975; Zimmerman to Yoder (see note 21); Paul Rupp, "Oak Grove, Illinois, Evangelical Bible Church," *EM*, Sept. 15, 1958; EMC *Annual Report and Directory* for 1977 and other years, for church and Sunday school statistics. *EM*, Aug. 15, Oct. 15, 1955, Apr. 15, 1956.

28. *Conference Report of the Defenseless Mennonite Church of North America* ... Aug. 13-17, 1947; *EM*, Apr. 15, 1961; *Build*, Autumn, 1972, Summer, 1976. Milo Nussbaum to Reuben Short, Feb. 4, 1958, May 5, 1961; Short to Nussbaum, June 11, July 16, 1958, Dec. 9, 1960, EMC Archives (Groveland, Grace files). Conference with Milo Nussbaum, Sept. 25, 1979, at Morton, Ill.

29. *EM*, Sept. 1964, Aug. 1966.

30. *Build*, Spring, Summer, 1969.

31. *Ibid.*, Summer, 1979, 18.

32. Marie Diller Brown, "An Historical Study of the Development and Growth of the Evangelical Mennonite Church ..." (M. R. E. Thesis, Biblical Seminary in New York, 1951), 106-07; Brown, *EM*, May 15, 1965; *ZT*, Sept. 15, 1947; Driver, "This Is Our Church" [1967], 1 p., EMC Archives.

33. EMC *Annual Report*, 1948, 31; Nussbaum (see note 1), 51.

34. *ZT*, June 15, 1950.

35. *Ibid.*, July 15, 1951, Sept. 15, 1952; *Report of Inaugural Conference of The Conference of Evangelical Mennonites, 1953*, EMC Archives, 2-4.

36. For examples of comments stressing unity and harmony, see *EM*, July 15, 1953, Aug. 1953, July 15, 1955; for some indicating questions and doubt, see June 15, 1954, June 15, 1955, May 15, 1955, and Nov. 15, 1957.

37. *EM*, Sept. 15, 1962; document, "E. M. B. Conference," June 6-10, 1962, in EMC Archives.

38. Conference with Ancil Whittle, one of the United Missionary delegates, Sept. 4, 1978, at Goshen, Ind.

39. John R. Dick, "Too Old to Marry?" *EM*, Nov. 15, 1957; Nussbaum (see note 1), 51-52.

40. *Missionary Church, Inc., 1980 Directory*, 12-13.

41. J. Howard Kauffman and Leland Harder, *Anabaptist Four Centuries Later: A Profile of Five Mennonite and Brethren in Christ Denominations* (1975), 45-46.

42. Nussbaum (see note 1), 50.

43. *Ibid.*, 42, 46, 55, 57; conference with Harvey Driver, March 8, 1978, at Goshen, Ind.; "Is EMC 'Mennonite' "? *Build*, Spring, 1979, 2. E. E. Zimmerman to Reuben Short, Sept. 8, 1958; E. M. Roche to "Dear Bro. Short," Dec. 5, 1958; Groveland file, EMC Archives. Conference with Reuben Short and Harvey Driver, Nov. 6, 1979, at Ft. Wayne, Ind.

CHAPTER 6. The Old Order Amish in Illinois

1. Dan A. Miller, *History of Arthur, Illinois* ... (mimeographed, 1975), 9, 31; L. A. Miller, "Historical Sketch of Early Amish Settlers," Arcola *Record Herald* (clipping), internal evidence suggests 1920s, in the possession of Thomas Yoder, Normal, Ill.

2. Orva Helmuth, "The Amish of Arthur," *MH*, June 1975.

3. *Ibid.*; Dan A. Miller, 31; Arthur V. Houghton, "Community Organization in a Rural Amish Community at Arthur, Illinois" (BS thesis, University of Illinois, 1926), 35.

Notes for Pages 133-147

4. D. Paul Miller to author, Aug. 13, 1979; see also D. Paul Miller, *The Illinois Amish* (1980), 14, 18.

5. *ME*, IV, 512-13, II, 318; see also articles on the two settlements by David Luthy, *Family Life*, Nov. 1976, Aug.-Sept. 1977.

6. Judith A. Nagata, "Continuity and Change Among the Old Order Amish of Illinois" (PhD dissertation, University of Illinois, 1968), 255, 359; Orva Helmuth and W. Richard Hassan, "Menno Diener Talks of His Family and Church," *MH*, June 1975; Lois Fleming, "The Old Order Amish Community of Arthur, Ill." (MS Ed thesis, Eastern Illinois University, 1962), 83-87.

7. Fleming, 104ff., 120; Helmuth and Hassan; Nagata, 349-50.

8. John A. Hostetler, "Old Order Amish Survival," *MQR* 51 (Oct. 1977), 358-59; Levi A. Esh, "The Amish Parochial School Movement," *MQR* 51 (Jan. 1977), 69-75; "1977 School Directory 1978: Old Order Amish," in *Blackboard Bulletin*, Dec. 1977; Silas Hertzler, "Mennonite Elementary Schools, 1947-48," *MQR* 23 (April 1949), 108-112; A. V. Houghton, (see note 3), 67ff. Conference with Daniel Otto, Feb. 9, 1979, at Goshen, Ind.; Otto is a well-educated Conservative Mennonite from Arthur who was reared Amish. See also D. Paul Miller, *Illinois Amish* (see note 4), 40-42, 47.

9. Nagata, 81; Otto thinks the Amish had these amenities earlier than Nagata states. Conference with Otto (see note 8); conference with Samuel Petersheim, Sept. 20, 1979, at Arthur, Ill.

10. Fleming, 88.

11. *Ibid.*, 56ff., 67ff.; Nagata (see note 6), 101.

12. Victor Stoltzfus, "Amish Agriculture: Adaptive Strategies for Economic Survival of Community Life," *Rural Sociology*, 38 (Summer, 1973), 200, 202. This is an excellent study of the Arthur Amish. See also Fleming (see note 6), 65.

13. Fleming (see note 6), 63, 65.

14. Stoltzfus, 200-201.

15. *Ibid.*; Nagata (see note 6), 119.

16. Fleming (see note 6), 90ff.; Nagata (see note 6), 107ff., 117, 122, 334ff.; conference with Otto (see note 8); conferences with Menno Diener and Edward Nissley, Sept. 20, 1979, at Arthur, Ill.; conference with Victor Stoltzfus, Aug. 5, 1981; D. Paul Miller, *Illinois Amish* (see note 4), 30, 35-38. See Miller also for a listing of the occupations of heads of Arthur Amish households (pp. 57-148); close to half were non-farmers. This same pattern is occurring elsewhere. Thomas J. Meyers, a graduate student at Boston University, is (in 1981) doing a study of Amish of northern Indiana, for a PhD dissertation entitled "Stress and the Amish Community in Transition." He has generously shared with me the information that as of 1980 fewer than half of the Amish heads of households in northern Indiana were farmers.

17. Fleming (see note 6), 67ff.

18. Conference with Victor Stoltzfus, June 17, 1977, at Goshen, Ind.

19. Nagata (see note 6), 85-87.

20. *Ibid.*, 90-92; Fleming (see note 6), 101-02.

21. Nagata (see note 6), 317; *ME*, I, 172.

22. Nagata (see note 6), 155, 233, 345-47; conference with Stoltzfus (see note 18).

23. Nagata (see note 6), 92, 141-42, 374-76; conference with Stoltzfus (see note 18).

24. This was probably more true a few years ago when gasoline was less expensive.

25. Hostetler (see note 8), 360-61; Fleming (see note 6), 64; Stoltzfus (see note 12), 202; "Wisconsin v. Yoder," *Supreme Court Reporter*, Vol. 92A, 1531-1535; conference with Ernest Bennett, Jan. 19, 1979, at Goshen, Ind. C. L. Graber and H. J. King were also on the committee with Bennett, along with Russell Massanari and Ivan Kauffmann appointed by the IMC's mission board. See also Dick Williams and Elvan Yoder, *The Illinois Amish and Rockome Gardens* (n.d.), 18ff. The writer and his wife were guests of Mr. and Mrs. Elvan Yoder at Rockome, Sept. 22, 1979; the hospitality included a bountiful, delicious Amish meal in the Rockome Restaurant.

26. Levi A. Esh (see note 8), 75.

27. Menno A. Diener, *History of the Diener Family* (1964), 56.

28. John A. Hostetler, *Amish Society* (3rd rev. ed., 1980), 66-67, 77-78; D. Paul Miller (see note 4), 30-31.

CHAPTER 7. Smaller Mennonite and Related Groups in Illinois

1. Daniel Musser, *The Reformed Mennonite Church, Its Rise and Progress, With Its Principles and Doctrines* (1878), 237-42, 295ff. *ME*: II, 712-13; IV, 267-69.

2. John F. Funk, *The Mennonite Church and Her Accusers* (1878), 25,28; see also chapters 1,2,12,13.

3. *Good Tidings* (Reformed Mennonite publication, not to be confused with another of the same title), Jan. 1932.

4. A. M., "The Reformed Mennonites," in *ibid.*, July 1922, 2ff.

5. *ME*, IV, 268-69.

6. *Ibid.;* "The Sunday School Problem," *Good Tidings* (see note 3), April 1923.

7. *Sterling Daily Gazette,* April 1, 1898, quoted by Ira D. Landis in *Christian Monitor,* Sept. 1948; Harry F. Weber, *Centennial History of Mennonites in Illinois 1829-1929* (1931), 564.

8. Charles Bent, ed., *History of Whiteside County, Illinois* ... (1877), 438; Weber, 564; *ME,* IV, 268-69.

9. W. Richard Hassan, "The Sterling Reformed Mennonite Church," *MH.* March 1979.

10. Jacob Ernest Ruth, "A Journey in the Mid-Nineteenth Century," *MQR* 42 (July 1968), 203-10; "History of the Summerfield Mennonite Church," *Year Book of the General Conference of the Mennonite Church of North America, 1937,* 24-37; Melvin Gingerich, *The Mennonites in Iowa* (1939), 88.

11. C. Henry Smith, *The Story of the Mennonites,* (4th ed., 1957), 576.

12. Ruth, 203-10.

13. Christian Krehbiel, *Prairie Pioneer: The Christian Krehbiel Story* (1961), 42.

14. *ME,* IV, 13.

15. "History" (see note 10); *Verhandlungen der Allgemeinen Konferenz der Mennoniten von Nord-Amerika, Erste bis Elfte Sitzung* (1860-1887), 11, quoted in S. F. Pannabecker, *Open Doors: The History of the General Conference Mennonite Church* (1975), 52.

16. Quoted from *Verhandlungen* in Pannabecker, 55.

17. *Das Christliche Volksblatt,* Dec. 24, 1862, 42, quoted in Pannabecker, 54.

18. Krehbiel, 42-43; Pannabecker, 59.

19. Krehbiel, 43-44; W. Richard Hassan, "History of the Summerfield Church," *MH,* March 1978.

20. Krehbiel (see note 13), 71ff.; Pannabecker (see note 15), 91ff. *ME,* III, 236; "The Mennonite Board of Guardians," *HT,* Feb. 1874, 19-21. An excellent article on the important part John F. Funk played in the Russian immigration in the 1870s is Kempes Schnell, "John F. Funk, 1835-1930, and the Russian Mennonite Migration of 1873-1875," *MQR,* 24 (July 1950), 199-229. The best book on the Russian immigration in that period is C. Henry Smith, *The Coming of the Russian Mennonites; an Episode in the Settling of the Last Frontier, 1874-1884* (1927).

21. Pannabecker (see note 15), 99; Krehbiel (see note 13), 78ff.; *ME,* IV, 888.

22. Pannabecker (see note 15), 187; Hassan.

23. See Leland Harder, *Seventy-third and Laflin* (1952), 2ff.; J. Winfield Fretz, "A Study of Mennonite Religious Institutions in Chicago" (BD thesis, Chicago Theological Seminary, 1940), 49ff.

24. Copy of the paper is in MHLG; Pannabecker, *Faith in Ferment: A History of the Central District Conference* (1968), 275-76.

25. Pannabecker, *Faith,* 276-77; John T. Neufeld, "The Grace Mennonite Church," *ML,* April 1953.

26. *ME:* III, 589-90; IV, 977. [Frieda Claassen], *The Woodlawn Story* (1958), 1-5.

27. For a good, brief discussion of the history of this conference see Richard A. Showalter, *The Conservative Mennonite Conference* ... (1971), 1-16; also Merlin L. Swartz, "The Historical Background of the Conservative Conference" (1960), ms. in MHLG; *ME,* I, 700-02.

28. Conference with George P. Plank et al., Sept. 22, 1979, at Arthur, Ill.

29. Nagata (see chapter 6, note 8), 317.

30. *ME,* I, 172; *M Yrbk,* 1978. Strangely, the *Yearbook* for 1977 lists a third congregation, Prairie Chapel, with a membership of twenty-eight, which does not appear in the later editions.

31. *Life Preaching and Labors of John D. Kauffman* [1916], 1-5.

32. *Ibid.,* 30ff.

33. Part of Funk's report discussed above is printed in Weber (see note 7), chapter 56. Weber put the quoted parts in quotation marks and correctly cites *HT,* March 15, 1882, as the source. But for some reason the lengthy quotation is far from exact, although the sense is quite accurate.

34. *Mennonite Reporter,* March 5, 1979.

35. *HT,* Oct. 1880, 180-81.

36. See two articles by W. Richard Hassan—"John D. Kauffman, Sleeping Preacher," and "The Fairfield Amish Mennonite Church"—both in *MH.* Sept. 1977. For additional information on sleeping preachers note also the footnotes, especially to the first article, in *MHB,* Jan. 1971, which include Melvin Gingerich's "Sleeping Preachers."

37. Hassan, "Fairfield"; *M Yrbk,* 1978, 73.

38. Hassan articles cited in note 36. *ME:* III, 351; IV, 544. Conferences at Goshen, Ind., with Debra Hostetler, Oct. 28, 1978, and with Ray Hostetler, Nov. 4, 1978; both former members at Linn. Conference with Katie Kennell Reeb, May 8, 1981, at Eureka, Ill. Telephone conference with Linn's bishop, D. M. Hostetler, May 14, 1981. Agnes Albrecht [Gunden], diary AMC: Oct. 18, Nov. 1, Dec. 23, 1908; Nov. 7, 14, 30, Dec. 1, 1909.

39. J. W. Fretz (see note 23), 106 ff., 111-114; *ML* April 1953, 61. John T. and Catherine Neufeld, compilers, *Mennonite Work in Chicago up to 1961* (1961); unfortunately not paginated.
40. *ME,* I, 430.
41. Peter G. Schultz, "Brighton Mennonite Church" (ms. in Schultz's possession at Justice, Ill., 1969); conference with Peter G. Schultz, Nov. 3, 1978, at Goshen, Ind.
42. *ME,* I, 254; Alvin J. Beachy, "The Rise and Development of the Beachy Amish Mennonite Churches," *MQR,* 29 (April 1955), 118-40; conference with J. C. Wenger, Nov. 7, 1978, at Goshen, Ind.
43. Fleming (see chapter 6, note 6), 44-46; conference with Victor Stoltzfus, June 17, 1977, at Goshen, Ind.; conference with Sam Petersheim, Sept. 22, 1979, at Arthur, Ill.
44. Neufeld (see note 39), section on The Brethren in Christ Mission; Harvey Sider, *The Church in Mission* (1975), 68-69.
45. I am indebted to Rev. Dorance D. Calhoun, pastor of the Morrison church, for the information. See also Carlton O. Wittlinger, *Quest for Piety and Obedience: The Story of the Brethren in Christ* (1978), 132, 270-71, 174-77.
46. Walter H. Lugibihl and Jared F. Gerig, *The Missionary Church Association* (1950), 16; *ME,* III, 710-11. Lugibihl and Gerig's work is a good source for those who wish more information about this denomination.
47. *ME,* III, 710-11; conference with Rev. G. G. Waun, Nov. 9, 1978, at Goshen, Ind.
48. *GH,* Nov. 1912; *ME,* I, 138-39.
49. According to Frank S. Mead, *Handbook of Denominations in the United States* (1975), 29-30, there are over 10,000 members and 78 congregations in the United States, four congregations in Japan, one in Canada; *ME,* I, 138-39; Ruth C. Roth, "Church History: History and Practices of the Apostolic Christian Church," *GH,* Feb. 24, 1918; Orel O. Steiner, compiler, *Apostolic Christian Churches and Ministers in America and Japan* (1971), *The Silver Lining,* Oct. and Nov. 1976; Marilyn Klaus, "*Es Giebt Ein Wunderschönes Land:* A Story of the . . . Apostolic Christian Church of America" (term paper, AMBS, 1974, copy at AMBS), 19, 22, 25-26; [John H. Baumgartner], *The First One Hundred Years Dec. 24, 1870-Dec. 24, 1970, Apostolic Christian Church, Bluffton, Indiana* (1970), 29; *Menn.* Dec. 9, 1958, 768; conference with S. M. King (formerly chaplain at Mennonite Hospital in Bloomington), Nov. 15, 1978, at Goshen, Ind.; *Cen Dist Rep.* Sept. 1965, 1; Arthur Haab, *The Apostolic Church of America* (n.d.), 2 (in Willard H. Smith's possession, courtesy Mr. Haab); Carol Plummer, "The Apostolic Christian Church as a Believers Church" (term paper, Goshen College, 1975 copy in MHLG), 11.

CHAPTER 8. The Illinois Amish Mennonite Congregations and the Western District Amish Mennonite Conference

1. *ME,* II, 57, 118, IV, 932; Verle C. Oyer, "A Short History of East Bend Church," *MH,* Dec. 1977; Albert and Bertha Zehr, "The Life and Family of Samuel S. Zehr," unpublished paper loaned to me through the courtesy of the Zehrs, son and daughter-in-law of Samuel S. Zehr.
2. In his own record book, or "Church Book," as he calls it, Peter Zehr states the date was 1889. Other accounts give 1890 as the date. I am indebted and grateful to Mrs. Alva Cender of Fisher for lending me this "Church Book" in her possession.
3. Oyer; Albert and Bertha Zehr; Amelia Zehr Birkey, "Memories of My Father," 3, unpublished ms. in my possession through courtesy of Mrs. Birkey. See also Verle and Margaret Oyer, "East Bend Mennonite Church," unpublished ms. in my possession through courtesy of the Oyers.
4. *ME,* II, 118; *M Yrbk,* 1950, 65; Oyer, unpublished ms. (see note 3); Peter Zehr (see note 2), 5.
5. *ME,* II, 118; Oyer, unpublished ms. (see note 3); *M Yrbk,* 1978, 46; C. William Heiser, *History of East Bend Mennonite Church from 1889 to 1949* (1949), 6-13.
6. *ME,* I, 172; Agnes Albrecht [Gunden] diary, May 19, 1906, AMC; Orva Helmuth, "History of Arthur Mennonite Church," *MHB,* Oct. 1961.
7. This valuable record book is in the possession of Clarence Imhoff, Roanoke, Ill.; he kindly loaned it to me. Like all good historical documents this record reflects the lifestyle of the times: at a business meeting in 1912 proposition 3 (spelled "propersition") "carried that the out house on the north side of the church house is to be rebuilt to the plan of the trustees." The 4th "propersition" carried "that a side walk from the west door to the out house is to be made of Concread [sic] . . . ."
8. Agnes Albrecht [Gunden] diary, March 4, 1906, AMC.
9. Harmony Church "Record Book," 25; in the possession of Clarence Imhoff, Roanoke, Ill. Conferences with Mathilda Schertz Yoder and Tilman R. Smith, Dec. 1, 1978, at Goshen, Ind.
10. The terms Western District Amish Mennonite Conference and Western Amish Mennonite Conference were used interchangeably. I shall use the shorter one, and the abbreviation "A. M." for Amish Mennonite.

11. From records in archives of First Mennonite Church, Morton, Ill. Mrs. Elva Mae Roth, church historian, loaned the records to Ruth C. Roth, librarian at Eureka Public Library, who photocopied them and sent copies to me. I thank both. See also Elva Mae Roth, "The Pleasant Grove Church," *MH*, June 1977, 16.

12. This must have been a temporary arrangement, since it would have been unusual for an Amish Mennonite church in that day to have a kitchen included in its facilities.

13. Reprinted in Sugar Creek (Ohio) *Budget*, Sept. 29, 1904.

14. Wayne Gerber, "Biography of Bishop Samuel Gerber" (term paper, Goshen College, 1959, copy in MHLG), 4, 5, 13; see also *Conference Proceedings of the Western District A. M. Conference, 1890 to 1912*, and the *Reports of the Western District A. M. Conferences from 1913 to 1920*; *GH*, Nov. 23, 1954.

15. Melvin Gingerich, "Ten Leaders," *MHB*, Oct. 1940; Harry F. Weber, *Centennial History of the Mennonites of Illinois 1829-1929* (1931), 208-210.

16. Locations cited in note 15; *GH*, Nov. 4, 1947. Both Gingerich and Weber (p. 610) are wrong about the date of his ordination to the ministry.

17. Gingerich.

18. *ME*, III, 932-33.

19. These reports were later brought together and published in convenient form as *Conference Proceedings of the Western District A. M. Conference, 1890 to 1912*, and *Report of the Western District A. M. Conferences for the Years 1912-1920*. Since they are brief they will be referred to by year only, not by page number.

20. As *ME*, III, 932-33, refers to them.

21. Underscoring added by present writer.

22. "Report of Ninth Annual Meeting of the A. M. Ministers of Illinois" (near Goodfield), Apr. 30, 1918, (p. 1), in MHLG. Said Birky to S. C. Yoder: "When I have a problem I cannot settle, I take it to the congregation." Conference with Nelson Springer, Jan. 10, 1981, at Goshen, Ind.

23. I shall put the year or years in parentheses, if not used in the text, in order that the reader may refer to the conference reports for those years.

24. Thomas Yoder, "Ezra Yordy: A Man of Many Facets," *MH*, Dec. 1976.

25. I have not taken the time or the space to quote the numerous scriptural references the delegates used to support their conference resolutions. No doubt the relevance and appropriateness of some of these would be questioned more today than then.

26. See also *HT*, Jan. 1, 1897.

27. Agnes Albrecht [Gunden] diary, Sept. 27, 1906, AMC.

28. Martha Smith to C. Henry Smith, Sept. 11, 1899. C. Henry Smith. mss., MHLB. But the conference report for 1899 does not indicate that the matter was discussed.

29. *GH*: March 16, May 18, 1911; Sept. 1912; Sept. 1913.

30. *GH*, Feb. 17, 1921.

31. *GH*, July 20, 1916.

32. *HT*, Feb. 15, 1893, Feb. 15, 1894, Sept. 1, 1895.

33. J. S. Coffman, "Illinois Conference," *HT*, July 1, 1893.

34. Some *Proceedings* and programs of these conferences are available in MHLG, in the Dennis Summer Collection, AMC, or in the private possession of Mrs. Alva Cender, Fisher, Ill.

35. Weber (see note 15), 329; Harold Zehr, "A Brief History of Illinois Mennonite Conference," *Constitution and Brief History of Illinois Mennonite Conference and Subsidiary Organizations* (1962), 7.

CHAPTER 9. The Mennonites and the Development of the Mennonite Conference

1. June 15, 1886.

2. *HT*, March 1878, 53; Hazel Nice Hassan, *The Nice Family History: Descendants of Henry Clemmer Nice (1822-1892)* (1965), 38-40.

3. *HT*, Jan. 1877, March 1878.

4. *Ibid.*, Jan. 28, 1904; Harry F. Weber, *Centennial History of the Mennonites of Illinois 1829-1929* (1931), 601.

5. *HT*, March 1, 1899, Dec. 1, 1891; *GH*, Jan. 25, 1949; Eldon Kortemeier, "The Life and Growth of the Freeport Mennonite Church" (Mennonite History paper, Goshen College, 1959, copy in MHLG), 28-34; *MCD*, see under Matthias Eby, Martin Lapp, Joseph S. Lehman, Ephraim M. Shellenberger, Christian Snavely, and Christian Snyder; J. S. Shoemaker *et al.*, "History of the Freeport Church," ms., III-13-18.1, AMC.

6. *HT*: Jan. 1, 1903; June 30, July 14, 21, 28, Oct. 27, Dec. 1, 1904; Kortemeier, 38.

7. *HT*, Oct. 8, 1903.

8. Sara A. Reitzel to Coffman, Feb. 23, 1890, Box 7, J. S. Coffman mss., AMC.

Notes for Pages 192-208

9. *HT:* Sept. 15, 1890; Oct. 1, 1891; Feb. 1, May 15, 1892.
10. In addition to Coffman's diary, J. S. Coffman mss., AMC, see: *HT,* May 19, June 23, July 21, 1904; Lewis C. Good, *A Good Tree Grew in the Valley: The Family Record of Christian Good, 1842-1916* (1974), 205-07; A. C. Good, *A Life Sketch* (1980), 9.
11. A. C. Good, 10, 19; *MG,* June 1968, Apr. 1977.
12. Hazel Nice [Hassan], "History of the Morrison 'Red Brick Church' " (term paper, Goshen College, 1952, copy in MHLG), 4-5.
13. *Ibid.,* 2-5.
14. Henry Peter Krehbiel, *The History of the General Conference Mennonite Church in North America* (1938), I, 84-85; Hassan (see note 2), 32-40; J. S. Shoemaker, *GH,* Aug. 22, 1929.
15. Thomas Yoder, *The Cullom Mennonite Church* (1975). See especially pp. 8-13.
16. *HT.* Feb. 1874, Aug. 1877. Coffman diary: Dec. 19, 1877; Sept. 17, Oct. 5, 1878; Jan. 30, March 13, Apr. 6, 1879; J. S. Coffman mss., AMC. Yoder, 21.
17. J. S. Coffman diary, Sept. 24, 1882, J. S. Coffman mss., AMC; *HT,* May 1, Oct. 15, 1882.
18. *HT.* Nov. 15, 1882, Jan. 1, 1886, Nov. 1, 1889, June 15, 1891; *GH,* July 13, 1948; Coffman diary, Dec. 21, 1890, J. S. Coffman mss., AMC; conference with Susie S. Hoover, Jan. 10, 1979, at Goshen, Ind.; Vernon Snyder to author, Jan. 19, 1979.
19. Coffman diary, May 28, 29, 30, 1893, J. S. Coffman mss., AMC; *HT.* Sept. 15, Dec. 15, 1892; P. B. S. to Coffman, July 12, 1892, J. S. Coffman mss., AMC.
20. Conference with Clinton Reedy, Dec. 26, 1978, Goshen, Ind.
21. *HT:* June 1, 15, 1896; July 1, 15, 1896; July 15, 1897; Jan. 7, 1904; Aug. 10, 1905; Jan. 8, 1906.
22. Henry Koerner, quoted in Yoder (see note 15), 12.
23. Yoder (see note 15), 14, 25, 26, 67, 68.
24. Yoder (see note 15), 26-27; Weber (see note 4), 168-69.
25. *HT.* Apr. 1862; conference with J. C. Wenger, Jan. 11, 1979, at Goshen, Ind.
26. *HT.* June 1872; scrapbook of clippings in IMC Records, AMC. Nearly all these clippings are from *HT,* but the report of the first conference (1872) apparently is not.
27. *HT.* Aug. 1873.
28. *Ibid.*
29. HT, July 1875, July 1877, June 1878.
30. *HT,* July 1, 1882, July 15, 1883, June 15, 1887, July 1, 1889, June 15, 1890.
31. *HT.* July 1, 1892, July 1, 1893, June 15, 1894, June 15, 1895.
32. *HT.* July 15, 1897, July 1, 1898, June 15, 1900.
33. *HT.* July 1, 1899.
34. *HT.* June 23, 1904; *GH.* June 29, 1911, July 4, 1918.
35. *IMCR,* 1921, 4ff.; *GH,* June 30, 1921, Oct. 25, 1923, Oct. 23, 1924.
36. *GH.* Oct. 15, 1925, Oct. 21, 1926. *IMCR:* 1926, p. 4; 1933, p. 9.
37. *GH.* Sept. 1, 1927.
38. *GH.* Oct. 23, 1921, Sept. 1, 1927. *IMCR:* 1927, p. 6; 1931, 16-18. Paul Mininger to Roy Bucher, Sept. 17, 1948, IMC mss., AMC.
39. *IMCR.* 1938, 11. IMC *Proceedings:* 1959, 18-19; 1960, 23. *GH,* Oct. 20, 1944; *MG,* Oct. 1960.
40. *GH.* Oct. 22, 1946, Nov. 4, 1947. *IMCR:* 1947, 18-19; 1954, 14ff.; report of the Ministerial Study Committee of IMC (1954), IMC mss., AMC; *MG,* Oct., Dec. 1954.
41. *IMCR,* 1973, 9. For further facts about Illinois ministers see *MG,* Feb. 1959, p. 7. Of the forty-two men assigned from 1945 through 1958 nineteen were from Illinois and twenty-three from outside.
42. *GH.* Oct. 11, 1949; *IMCR.* 1950, 22, and conference program for 1953; Minutes of Special Business Meeting of IMC in connection with the meeting of Ministers' Fellowship on Nov. 30, 1953, IMC mss., AMC.
43. These examples are from the conference programs of 1932 and 1937.
44. IMC mss., AMC.
45. *IMCR.* 1943, 16-17.
46. Indiana-Michigan Mennonite Conference to the Mennonite General Conference [1939]; IMC to Executive Committee of Mennonite General Conference, Aug. 14, 1939; Executive Committee correspondence and minutes, IMC mss., AMC.
47. Executive Committee of Mennonite General Conference to IMC [1939], located as in note 46.
48. *GH.* Nov. 2, 1948.
49. *IMCR.* 1949, 24; Richard Yordy to G. G. Yoder, IMC mss. [1954], AMC.
50. Roy Bucher, IMC secretary, to Oscar Roth et al., Sept. 2, 1958, IMC mss., AMC. Conferences at Goshen, Ind.: with J. J. Hostetler, Jan. 31; with Vernon Schertz, Jan. 31; with Norman Kauffmann, Feb. 1, 1979.

51. "Recommendation Regarding the Ministry in the Illinois Mennonite Conference," Jan. 16, 1961; Rob't Harnish, IMC secretary to Walter Brubaker, Feb. 3, 1964; IMC mss., AMC.
52. *IMCR.* 1957, 4-5; conference with Laurence Horst (then conference moderator), Dec. 14, 1978, at Goshen, Ind.
53. *IMCR.* 1965, 6, 7, 24, 25; see also Clayton V. Beyler, "Meaning and Relevance of the Devotional Covering: A Study in the Interpretation of 1 Corinthians 11:2-16" (ThM thesis, Southern Baptist Theological Seminary, 1954).
54. "A Possible Redemptive Program for Those Involved in Divorce." 1952, IMC mss., AMC; "A Statement Regarding Redemption and Church Membership for Those Involved in Divorce and Remarriage," *IMCR.* 1956, 25-26; H. J. Zehr to Richard Yordy, Jan. 23, 1952, IMC mss., AMC; "Conference Notes, Thirty-sixth Annual Illinois Mennonite Conference, 1956," *MG.* Oct. 1956.
55. *MG.* Dec. 1949. *GH:* Feb. 15, 1940; Apr. 26, May 3, 1949; Feb. 13, 1951; Oct. 7, Nov. 4, 1952; Nov. 17, 1959; June 7, Aug. 23, 1960. *IMCR:* 1936, 18; 1939, 9-10; 1940, 9; 1941, 16-18.
56. *GH:* Aug. 23, Oct. 18, 1960; Oct. 10, 1961; July 22, 1975. *MG.* Aug. 1959, June 1961, Dec. 1951.
57. *ME.* IV, 145-46.
58. *MG.* Aug. 1951, Aug. 1965.
59. *MG.* Apr. 1946, Feb. 1952; *GH.* May 16, 1978; *MG.* Apr. 1978, 5-6.
60. Orva S. Helmuth, *History of the Arthur Mennonite Church* (1958), 1ff.; Nagata (see chapter 6, note 6), 324; *ME.* I, 172; statement of IMC Executive Committee, May 24, 1955, IMC mss., AMC.
61. *GH.* July 1, 1952, Oct. 26, 1954; conference with Mary Good, Apr. 20, 1978, at Goshen, Ind. See chapter 6 for the actual use of Rockome.
62. *MG.* June 1952, Dec. 1964.
63. *GH,* Jan. 25, 1940, Nov. 18, 1958.
64. *IMCR.* 1965, 54-55; *MG.* Feb. 12, 1957, Apr. 1959, Aug. 1962.
65. *MG.* July 1945.
66. *GH,* March 23, 1948; *MG.* July 1945, Feb. 1956.
67. *MG.* Apr. and Sept. 1946, Aug. 1950; W. Richard Hassan, *MH.* March and June 1980.
68. Locations cited in note 67.
69. *GH.* June 14, 1960, Jan. 31, 1961; *MH.* June 1977; *MG.* Apr. 1957, June 1960, Feb. 1977.
70. *MG.* Dec. 1950, Oct. 1960: conference with Norman Kauffmann, Feb. 17, 1979, at Goshen, Ind.
71. *GH:* May 20, 1952; July 5, Nov. 8, 1955; Aug. 14, 1956. *MG.* Dec. 1958.
72. Mrs. Richards' ordination is discussed further in chapter 14.
73. Ivan and Ann Brunk, *Lombard Mennonite Church History 1954-1974* (1974), 1-8; *GH,* Nov. 16, 1954, March 29, 1955; *IMCR.* 1973, 1; conference with Nancy (Mrs. David) Augsburger, Feb. 17, 1979, at Goshen, Ind.
74. *MG.* December 1956; conference with James Waltner, May 5, 1978, at Normal, Ill.; conference with Dawn Yoder, Feb. 19, 1979, at Goshen, Ind.
75. *Reba Place Fellowship* (n.d.), 1-5. This is a recent pamphlet probably written by Virgil Vogt. I am indebted to Vogt for sending me this and other good material on Reba Place.
76. *MG.* Dec. 1958. Conferences at Goshen, Ind: with Esther Meck Smucker, Jan. 18, 1979, and Aug. 25, 1981; with Donald Blosser, Aug. 25, 1981.
77. *MG.* Oct. 1961; conference with J. J. Hostetler, Feb. 13, 1979, at Goshen, Ind.
78. *IMCR.* 1964, 38; *GH.* Apr. 4, 1961; conference with Mary Smucker, Feb. 22, 1979, at Goshen, Ind.
79. Nafziger's chart, giving selected years from 1905 to 1964, is in *IMCR.* 1964, p. 9.
80. See, e.g., Sunday school attendance figures in *MG,* Dec. 1958.
81. *MG.* Dec. 1961.
82. Conference with Vernon Schertz, Feb. 23, 1979, at Goshen, Ind.; *MG,* June 1966, Aug. 1968, Apr. 1976; Orie A. Miller to C. Warren Long, May 25, 1968, Illinois Mennonite Historical and Genealogical Society Archives, Normal, Ill.
83. *MG.* Feb. 1949, 1952; Susie V. Koerner to L. A. Bachman, Feb. 18, 1947, IMC mss., AMC; conference with Clinton Reedy, Apr. 12, 1980, at Goshen, Ind.
84. The most convenient source for information on this point is the *Mennonite Yearbook.*
85. Zehr to Richard Yordy, Oct. 3, 1957, IMC mss., AMC.

CHAPTER 10. The "Awakening" Among the Illinois Mennonites: Publication and New Religious Agencies and Organizations

1. See H. S. Bender's article on "Evangelism," *ME.* II, 269.
2. See Theron Schlabach's writings, especially, "Reveille for *Die Stillen Im Lande:* A Stir Among Mennonites in the Late Nineteenth Century...," *MQR.* 51 (July 1977), 213-26; and *Gospel Versus Gospel:*

Mission and the Mennonite Church, 1863-1944 (1980), 31ff., 42-52 and passim.

3. *HT*, July 1, 1899.

4. *HT*, Feb. 15, 1900, 52-54, Aug. 1, 1892, 225-26.

5. See his article, "A Few Points on American Mennonite History," *HT*, Apr. 1, 1902.

6. Theron Schlabach to author, Jan. 10, 1981.

7. John A. Hostetler, *God Uses Ink: The Heritage and Mission of the Mennonite Publishing House After Fifty Years* (1958), 33-35.

8. See, among others, C. Henry Smith, *The Coming of the Russian Mennonites: An Episode in the Settling of the Last Frontier, 1874-1884* (1927).

9. *HT*, July 1874.

10. Besides *HT* for 1873ff., especially 1874, see *ME* under "Funk, John Fretz," and "Krehbiel, Christian," "Goerz, David," "Zur Heimath"; also Christian Krehbiel, *Prairie Pioneer: The Christian Krehbiel Story* (1961), 70ff. But Krehbiel was in error when he said (p. 71) that Oberholtzer "at that time was the publisher of the only Mennonite periodical in America."

11. William W. Dean, "John F. Funk and the Mennonite Awakening" (Ph.D. dissertation, University of Iowa, 1965), pp. 213-15. See also Edmund G. Kaufman, *The Development Of The Missionary and Philanthropic Interest Among the Mennonites of North America* (1931), 189.

12. Erismann diary, AMC: Nov. 24, 1867, Oct. 25, Nov. 7, 1868, Apr. 10 to June 24, 1869, especially pp. 88ff. Unfortunately Erismann's chronology is confusing at times. Parts at least were written after the events.

13. *HT*, July 15, 1889.

14. Reprinted in *GH*, Dec. 11, 1956.

15. For examples of citations to the language problem see *HT*, Jan. 1864, Sept. 1866, Dec. 1869, Dec. 1881, Sept. 1, 1891, Sept. 15, 1895, Jan. 5, 1905; *GH*, Nov. 18, 1909.

16. Henry Peter Krehbiel, *The History of the General Conference of the Mennonite Church in North America* (1938), 14-18.

17. Funk, autobiography (bound volumes in Funk's handwriting, written in first-person, in box 48, John F. Funk mss., AMC), 124B-129B.

18. Helen Kolb Gates to J. Clemens Kolb, March 25, 1931, Box 1, John F. Funk mss., AMC; *ME*, II, 421-22; *HT*, March 15, 1893.

19. Funk, autobiography, 90B-91B.

20. *ME*, II, 421-23. Funk diary, May 8, 1853, Feb. 13, 1859, John F. Funk mss., AMC Hostetler (see note 7), 27-30, deals perceptibly with Funk's Chicago years. Dean's study (see note 11) is also valuable.

21. Hostetler (see note 7), 31; Peter G. Schultz, "John F. Funk," *MH*, Sept. 1977.

22. Funk to Oberholtzer, Aug. 19, 1861, cited in Funk's diary, box 1, John F. Funk mss., AMC, and printed in *Christliche Volksblatt*, Sept. 4, 1871; Funk, autobiography (see note 17), 95B to 96B.

23. Funk, autobiography (see note 17), 104B to 114B. J. M. Brenneman to Funk, Oct. 17, 1863; Daniel Brenneman to Funk, Aug. 6, 1863; box 6, John F. Funk mss., AMC. Hostetler (see note 7), 35ff.

24. Funk, autobiography (see note 17), 129B; Hostetler (see note 7) 38ff.

25. Funk, autobiography (see note 17), 124B to 129B; Abraham Blosser to Jacob Mensch, May 16, 1885, published in *MHB*, July 1970.

26. Joseph Liechty, "From Yankee to Nonresistant, John F. Funk's Chicago Years, 1857-1865" (term paper at AMBS, 1979, copy in MHLG), 32-34.

27. Funk, autobiography (see note 17), 92B to 94B, 130B; A. S. Overholt to Funk, Apr. 12, 1866, Box 6, John F. Funk mss., AMC.

28. *HT*, Feb. 1865; Peter Stuckey to Funk, March 25, 1867, box 6, John F. Funk mss., AMC; *GH*, May 24, 1955.

29. *HT*, Dec. 1878.

30. *HT*, July 1, 1899; *GW*, June 19, 1907; *GH*, Apr. 11, 1908.

31. *CC Yrbk*, 1926, 15ff.

32. *Menn*, Oct. 18, 1960.

33. *Ibid*. *ME*: II, 693; IV, 1033. E. E. Zimmerman, "A Brief History of the Evangelical Mennonite Church Publications," *EM*, July 15, 1968.

34. *CC Yrbk*, 1936, 50-51; for the merger in the 1930s, see *Chr Evan*, Dec. 1933, Dec. 17, 1935.

35. See *Brotherhood Beacon*, Jan. 1971; and *Herold der Wahrheit*, Jan. 1912, Jan. 1955.

36. For a good summary of the coming of the Sunday school into America and into the Mennonite churches see: Harold S. Bender, *Mennonite Sunday School Centennial 1840-1940* (1940)—reprinted, somewhat revised, in J. C. Wenger, *The Mennonite Church in America* (1966), 144-181. *ME*, s.v. "Sunday school"; Funk diary, May 8, 1853, John F. Funk mss., AMC.

37. Bender, 47-56.

38. William B. Weaver, *History of the Central Conference Mennonite Church* (1926), 148; Samuel Floyd Pannabecker, *Faith in Ferment: A History of the Central District Conference* (1968), 155; *ZT*, Feb. 15, 1950; Hirstein, "A Reply," *HT*, March 1868.
39. *HT*, Dec. 1, 1890.
40. Bender, 28-31.
41. Report of Western District A. M. Conf., 1897, *HT*, Dec. 1, 1897; "Report of Illinois Conference," *GW*, June 19, 1907; *MHB*, July 1970, Apr. 1976.
42. *ME*, IV, 658-60; Pannabecker, 108; *CC Yrbk*. 1924, 17.
43. *MG*, Aug. 1958; *HT*, March 1891, May 1896, May 1897; "Notes of Geo. I. Sommer," of Metamora, loaned to me by Emma and Mary Sommer, Metamora, Ill.; Weaver (see note 38), 62; Christian Erismann diary, Aug. 12, 1866, AMC.
44. *HT*, Jan. 1867.
45. *ME*, IV, 661-62.
46. Bender (see note 36), 55.
47. *ME*, III, 622; *HT*, Feb. 1, 1886; Hostetler (see note 7), 39-40; Minutes of the Board, *GH*, March 4, 11, 18, 1952.
48. *ME*: I, 417; IV, 309.
49. John Schertz (from Roanoke), "Modern Evangelism," *GW*, Nov. 21, 1906; *ME*, IV, 309; John S. Umble, "John S. Coffman as an Evangelist," *MQR*, 23 (July 1949), 123-146; Strubhar, "A Condensed History of the East [Washington] Mennonite Church Now Known as the Calvary Mennonite Church" (unpublished, 1940, copy in MHLG).
50. See also Coffman diary, Feb. 9 and 15, 1890, J. S. Coffman mss, AMC.
51. *Ibid.*, Feb. 15, 1888; Barbara Coffman, *His Name Was John* (1964), 204-08.
52. *HT*, Aug. 1, 1899. For his work as evangelist, plus these broader interests, see Umble.
53. *HT*, Jan. 22, 1903, March 1, 1906; *GW*, Jan. 30, 1907; *GH*, Oct. 21, 1909; printed programs loaned to me by Mrs. Oliver Yoder, Eureka, Ill.
54. See secretary's "Yearly Report of the Society" *(Alles Mit Gott)*, March 11, 1891, in archives of Flanagan church; *HT*, March 15, 1891; A. J. Beachy, *Menn*. May 15, 1962; *ME*, I, 581.
55. Letta Schwartz, "Christian Endeavor," *CC Yrbk*, 1933, 47-50; Pannabecker (see note 38), 241; Horst, *GH*. Feb. 8, 1940.
56. J. L. Horst, "The Rise of the Young People's Bible Meeting," *GH*, Feb. 8, 1940; *HT*, June 15, Oct. 15, 1894; Paul Lederach, "History of Religious Education in the Mennonite Church" (ThD dissertation, Southwestern Baptist Theological Seminary, 1949), 195ff.
57. Conference with James Bertsche, Apr. 2, 1979, at Goshen, Ind.; Pannabecker (see note 38), 261.
58. *Chr Evan*, Nov. 1911.
59. "Report of the Young People's Conference," *Christian Monitor*, Nov. 1920; J. L. Horst, *GH*, Feb. 8, 1940.
60. *ZT*, Oct. 15, 1933.
61. Pannabecker (see note 38), 262.
62. *ME*, IV, 654-55.
63. *ME*, IV, 654-56; C. F. Yake, *GH*, Apr. 16, 1946; conferences with Mary and Katherine Royer, Apr. 4, 1979, at Goshen, Ind.

CHAPTER 11. The "Awakening" Among Illinois Mennonites; Education, Missions, Service

1. N. S. Gingerich, "The Mennonites and Education," *HT*, Feb. 15, 1900; John E. Hartzler, *Education among the Mennonites of America* (1925), 20-21; conferences with John Oyer and J. C. Wenger, Apr. 10, 1979, at Goshen, Ind.
2. For excerpts from Krehbiel's dedicatory address see *Menn*, Oct. 11, 1966.
3. Samuel Floyd Pannabecker, *Faith in Ferment: A History of the Central District Conference* (1968), 83. Perhaps it would be more correct to say that it marked the beginning of the end of the untrained ministry in that body.
4. See Samuel F. Pannabecker, "Its Spirit Lives On," *Menn*, Oct. 11, 1966.
5. Abraham Blosser to Jacob B. Mensch, May 16, 1885, printed in *MHB*, July 1970; Brenneman to Funk, March 18, 1867, John F. Funk mss., AMC.
6. H. B. Burkholder, "What Do You Read," *HT*, Feb. 1873.
7. Quoted in Barbara Coffman, *His Name Was John* (1964), 286.
8. Quoted without name and date—in 1890s—in *ibid.*, 286.
9. Coffman to Steiner, June 14, 1894, M. S. Steiner mss., AMC; I. Wilmer Hollinger, "M. S. Steiner: A

Biography of His First Thirty Years" (unpublished, 1965, copy in MHLG), 64-65, quotation on p. 65. These plans of Steiner apparently were similar to those which resulted in the founding of Elkhart Institute.

10. *HT,* July 1, 1892; West. Dist. A. M. Conf. *Proceedings* for 1895 and 1899.

11. Christian Erismann diary, Oct. 10, 1866, May 28, 1871, AMC.

12. Steven R. Estes to author, June 19, 1980; from Edwin O. Ropp mss., copies in AMC; H. C. Bradsby, *History of Bureau County Illinois* (1885), 439. No doubt there were others who sought more education, of whom we have no record.

13. *HT,* July 1, 1899, Jan. 1, 1904.

14. C. Henry Smith, *Mennonite Country Boy: The Early Years of C. Henry Smith* (1962), 48, 91.

15. *Ibid.,* 105.

16. Story told by Whitmer to Dr. Delbert Gratz of MHLB, who reported it to the writer, March 29, 1977.

17. Willard H. Smith, "C. Henry Smith, 1875-1948: A Brief Biography," *MQR* 23 (Jan. 1949), 7-15; C. H. Smith (see note 14), 199-200.

18. *Christian Monitor,* Sept. 1922, 658.

19. W. H. Smith (see note 17); see also *Menn,* July 12, 1906, and *GW,* Nov. 21, 28, 1906.

20. C. H. Smith (see note 14), 109-10, 181.

21. Noah E. Byers, "The Times in Which I Lived," *ML,* Jan., Apr., July, 1952.

22. "Relation Between the Day School and Sabbath School," *HT,* June 15, 1896.

23. Noah E. Byers, "C. Henry Smith as I Knew Him," *ML,* Apr. 1950; C. Henry Smith, "A Pioneer Educator—N. E. Byers," *ML,* Jan. 1948.

24. Obituary, *GH,* March 12, 1931.

25. Pannabecker (see note 3), 310, 312; *Who's Who Among the Mennonites* (1943), 195-96.

26. See Elkhart Institute and Goshen College annual catalogs for years from 1902 to 1908; *HT,* March 1, 1900, March 26, 1903, July 1905.

27. Hartzler to John Ropp, Nov. 1, 1914; Ropp to Hartzler, Feb. 7, 1916, March 1, 1916; box 2, J. E. Hartzler mss., AMC.

28. C. Henry Smith and J. Hirschler, *The Story of Bluffton College* (1925), 199ff.; for the founding of Bluffton College as an experiment in inter-Mennonite cooperation, see chapters 5-9.

29. Pannabecker (see note 3), 160, 171; *Chr Evan,* Oct. 1913.

30. Augspurger to Hartzler, June 13, 1913, box 2, J. E. Hartzler mss., AMC.

31. *Chr Evan,* March 1916; *Menn,* Sept. 30, 1920.

32. Weaver to Hartzler, July 22, 1923, Box 8, Hartzler mss., AMC; H. A. Alderfer to Lester Hostetler, Feb. 25, 1930, in Hostetler's possession, Goshen, Ind.

33. Smith and Hirschler (see note 28), 136.

34. *CC Yrbk,* 1937, 51-53.

35. *ME,* III, 714; Edmund G. Kaufman, *The Development of The Missionary and Philanthropic Interest Among the Mennonites of North America* (1931), 104-09, 123-24; James C. Juhnke, "General Conference Mennonite Missions to the American Indians in the Late Nineteenth Century," *MQR* 54 (Apr. 1980), 117-34, and *A People of Mission: A History of General Conference Mennonite Overseas Missions* (1979), 4-5.

36. *ME,* II, 352; Kaufman, Juhnke items cited, note 35.

37. *HT,* Apr. 1, June 1, 1892, Apr. 15, 1893; *GW,* Jan. 22, 1908.

38. *HT,* Dec. 15, 1892, July 1, 1886.

39. *ME,* III, 592, 715.

40. *GH,* May 4, 1916, July 4, 1918, May 12, 1921; J. S. Shoemaker, *GW,* Apr. 18, 1906, Roy Umble, "Mennonite Preaching, 1864-1944" (PhD dissertation, Northwestern University, 1949), 337; chapter 8 is on J. S. Shoemaker.

41. See, e.g., A. B. Rutt, in *GW,* Aug. 9, 1905.

42. Steven R. Estes, *Christian Concern for Health: The Sixtieth Anniversary of the Mennonite Hospital Association* (1979), 3-5.

43. *HT,* Dec. 15, 1892.

44. *HT,* Dec. 1, 1893; Theron Schlabach, *Gospel Versus Gospel: Mission and the Mennonite Church, 1863-1944* (1980), 58-59; Hollinger (see note 9), 48ff. These writings by Schlabach and Hollinger are the best works on the founding of the Chicago Home Mission.

45. Schlabach, 60-62.

46. *HT,* June 15, 1894, 1895, 1896.

47. Emma Oyer, *What God Hath Wrought in a Half Century at the Mennonite Home Mission* (1949), 1; Hollinger (see note 9), 53ff.; *ME,* III, 594.

48. Coffman to Steiner, March 3, 16, 1894, box 2, M. S. Steiner mss., AMC.
49. Steiner to Clara Eby, Jan. 10, Feb. 2, 1894, M. S. Steiner mss. in the possession of Mrs. J. C. Meyer, Goshen, Ind. Mrs. Meyer, a daughter of the late M. S. Steiner, graciously permitted me to read these letters written by him to Clara Eby, some before and some after their marriage. I thank her sincerely.
50. *Ibid.*, Sept. 17, 19, 22, 24, 1894.
51. "Superintendent's Report," Oct. 1, 1894, pamphlet of 16 pp. in MHLG; *GW*, Oct. 10, 1906.
52. *HT*, Feb. 1, 1894; "Special Conference," Aug. 15, 1895; "A Statement," Apr. 1, 1896.
53. John T. and Catherine Neufeld, compilers, *Mennonite Work in Chicago up to 1961* (1961); *HT*, May 1, 1896, 138, Nov. 1, 1897, 329-30.
54. *HT*, Feb. 15, June 15, Aug. 1, 1897; see Oyer, (see note 47), 5-15, for interesting accounts of the medical services and other features of the early mission.
55. Arnold C. Schultz, "A. Hershey Leaman: Pioneer Missionary," *MH*, Dec. 1975. See also diaries of Emma Oyer, in the possession of Mrs. Edna Oyer Bachman, Goshen, Ind. Mrs. Bachman kindly placed these at my disposal. *GW*: Apr. 24, 1907, 58; May 8, 1907, 89.
56. The bishop must have been either John Nice or J. S. Shoemaker, both of whom "shared in the care of the Home Mission congregation," according to Oyer (see note 47), 73-74. I am indebted to A. Miriam Leaman, one of Leaman's daughters living in Chicago, for this information, but she does not know why the bishop objected; letters to me, Jan. 6 and Feb. 5, 1979. See also Schultz.
57. *MG*, June 1958; *IMCR*, 1935, 6; *HT*, Jan. 15, 1900, 23; Oyer (see note 47), 101ff.; *GH*, July 24, 1951, 713; conference with Laurence Horst, Apr. 5, 1980, at Goshen, Ind.
59. *HT*, Jan. 15, 1900, 23; conference with Hartzler; Oyer (see note 47), 113-18; Walter Yordy, *GH*, Feb. 20, 1951. For an interesting and somewhat idealized account of an early Christmas dinner by Leaman see *HT*, Jan. 1, 1902.
60. Oyer (see note 47), 113; Schultz (see note 55); Emma Oyer, "The Chicago Home Mission," *GH*, Nov. 6, Dec. 4, 1919.
61. *HT*, Nov. 17, 1904.
62. Oyer (see note 47), 18-22, 33; *ME*, III, 628; *HT*, Oct. 22, 1903, 337; conference with Raymond Yoder, May 6, 1979, at Goshen, Ind.
63. *GH*, July 4, 1950; *MG*, Dec. 1957.
64. Mennonite Board of Missions and Charities, Executive Committee Minutes, May 1918-Apr. 1922, pp. 51, 54, 64, 93-94, 98, 101-103, 108, 109-10, 116, 117-19, IV-6-2, MBMC mss.; J. S. Shoemaker to Daniel Kauffman, Feb. 17, 1920, box 2, Daniel Kauffman mss., 1-20, AMC; conference with Ethel Good Yoder, May 28, 1979, at Goshen, Ind.
65. A. Miriam Leaman, "Biography of A. Hershey Leaman," *MG*, Aug. 1950; Schultz (see note 55).
66. Yoder's comment is appended to: A. L. Neff, "Boys Will Be Men," *MG*, Jan. 1947. Earl Lehman, "Fifty Years' Witness in the City," *GH*, Dec. 31, 1946; A. Miriam Leaman to author Feb. 5, 1979. For the view of a few Illinois Mennonites who felt that Leaman was a bit too "liberal" for the Mennonite Church of the 1920s on such questions as dress, life insurance, etc., see H. R. Schertz to J. D. Smith, July 24, 1924, in the possession of Thomas Yoder, Normal, Ill.
67. See Schertz's testimony in Oyer (see note 47), 55-60.
68. Oyer (see note 47), 22, 62.
69. *GH*: Aug. 23, 1955, 805; July 16, 1957, 657. Conferences with Areta Lehman and Lela Mann, May 2, 1979, at Goshen, Ind.
70. Conferences at Goshen, Ind., with: Raymond Yoder, May 6, 1979; Levi C. Hartzler, May 29, 1979; Areta Lehman, June 1, 1979.
71. *GH*, Oct. 8, 1957, 856; *IMCR*, 1964, 45; conference with Laurence Horst, Dec. 14, 1978, at Goshen, Ind.
72. *HT*, Nov. 1905, 360; *GW*: Oct. 1906, 443; Nov. 7, 1906, 508; A. M. Eash, *After Ten Years: A Brief Report of the First Ten Years of Work of the Twenty-Sixth Street Mission, 1900-1916* (1916), 7ff.
73. Eash, 38-41; *GH*, July 18, 1912, 244-45.
74. See reports by A. M. Eash, *GH*, Dec. 20, 1906, Nov. 28, 1908, March 24, 1910, July 24, 1913, April 6, 1916; Also *GH*, May 19, 1910, Feb. 8, 1912; Eash (see note 72), 77-78; J. Winfield Fretz, "A Study of Mennonite Religious Institutions in Chicago" (BD thesis, Chicago Theological Seminary, 1940), 71ff.
75. A. M. Eash to George H. Sommer, Sept. 18, 1923; A. M. Eash, "The Case of the Twenty-Sixth Street Mission ..." [1923]; Dennis Summer mss., AMC; Eash (see note 72), 102; *CC Yrbk*, 1924, 24.
76. Eash, "The Case," 2; "The 26th Street Mission," in Neufeld (see note 53); Pannabecker (see note 3), 181, 199, 268. A. M. Eash to I. R. Detweiler, Oct. 14, 1936; Detweiler to Eash, Oct. 20, 1936; Minutes, Central Mennonite Board of Home & Foreign Missions, Cen. Dist. Conf. Archives, MHLB. Amos Eash to W. B. Weaver, Feb. 2, 11, 1949, in W. B. Weaver file, AMBS.
77. Pannabecker (see note 3), 164ff., 180, 199, 266ff.

Notes for Pages 278-296   511

78. Mary Wiens Toews, *The True Life Story of the Wiens Family* . . . (n. d.); Fretz (see note 74), 84ff.; *ME*, I, 430; "Mission Work of the Defenseless Mennonite Brethren," and "Mennonite Bible Mission," in Neufeld (see note 53).
79. *Ibid., ME*, II, 560; *ML*, Apr. 1953.
80. See chapters 5 and 7.
81. *CC Yrbk.* 1931, 23; Pannabecker (see note 3), 165-66, 268; *GH:* March 1924, 995-98; Sept. 23, 1942, 941. Conference with J. J. Hostetler, June 8, 1979, at Goshen, Ind.
82. H. S. Bender, *ME*, I, 604; Fretz (see note 74), v-vi. See also Pannabecker (see note 3), 268-69.
83. *GH.* May 23, 1908.
84. *HT:* Apr. 15, 1897, 114; May 1, 1897, 129-30; July 15, 1898, 217; June 1, 1902, 161; Dec. 1, 1904, 385. *ME:* II, 300, 796-97; III, 714-16; IV, 1101.
85. G. L. Bender to George H. Summer, March 16, 1918, Dennis Summer mss., AMC; *GH,* Nov. 16, 1945, 632.
86. See especially L. B. Haigh, "A Present Need," *Chr Evan,* Jan. 1911; see Minutes of the Central Mennonite Board of Home and Foreign Missions, 1905-1945, 1 (Sept. 14, 1905), Cen. Dist. Conf. Archives, MHLB.
87. *ME,* I, 690; William B. Weaver, *Thirty-five Years in the Congo* (1945), 63ff.; Melvin J. Loewen, *Three Score—The Story of an Emerging Mennonite Church in Central Africa* (1972), 31ff.; H. A. Driver, "50 Years Ago," *EM,* Feb. 15, 1961.
88. M. L. Klopfenstein, *ZT,* Apr. 15, 1950; *EM,* Sept. 1957; Lotus Troyer, *Menn,* Dec. 6, 1960; James Bertsche, *Menn,* Apr. 9, 1974, 240; conference with James Bertsche, June 22, 1979, at Goshen, Ind., 115ff., 134-35.
89. *ME,* III, 31, IV, 86, 87. *HT:* June 1, 1896, 167; Dec. 1, 1896, 356. Schlabach (see note 44), 87-88.
90. C. C. Moser, *ZT.* Aug. 15, 1939, Jan. 15, 1940; Clara Roth, *ZT,* Jan. 15, 1941; E. E. Zimmerman, *75th Anniversary Salem Children's Home,* (1971) [1-3]; Ronald L. Kestner, "Reflections," *Build,* Summer, 1971; Steven R. Estes, "Daniel R. and Mary Claudon King: Founders of Salem Orphanage" [1979], in my possession, courtesy of Mr. Estes.
91. *ME,* II, 798-99.
92. Augspurger to Horsch, May 17, 1920, Jan. 3, 1921, Box 2, John Horsch mss., AMC.
93. *ME,* III, 628; *HT:* July 1, 1898, 202; July 15, 1901, 219. J. S. Shoemaker to Geo. H. Summer, Nov. 18, 1919, Dennis Summer mss., AMC; V. E. Reiff, *GH,* Aug. 31, 1922, 421. J. D. Smith, *GH:* Jan. 4, 1923, 791-93; Apr. 7, 1932, 24-25.
94. "Meadows Mennonite Home: for 50 Years a Caring Community, Fiftieth Anniversary Celebration, May 20, 1973," brochure in writer's possession; *ME,* III, 547; G. I. Gundy, *CC Yrbk.* 1931, 19-21; E. E. Zimmerman, "History of the Mennonite Old People's Home," *ZT,* Aug. 15, 1938; *ZT,* May 15, 1952; *EM.* Nov. 15, 1954, Apr. 15, 1966.
95. *Chr Evan,* Oct. 1922, 223; "General Conference Minutes," *GH,* Sept. 22, 1921.
96. Estes (see note 42), 9; conference with Raymond L. Hartzler, Apr. 21, 1977, at Bloomington, Ill.; *ME,* II, 817.
97. *ME,* III, 628-29; Raymond L. Hartzler, "A History of Mennonite Hospital" (unpublished, 1977, in my possession, courtesy of Hartzler), 1-2; see also Estes, (see note 42), chapters 1 and 2.
98. *The Menno-light,* June 1976, 10.
99. See Hartzler (see note 97), 3-6; for samples of his secretarial reports, see *Chr Evan,* March 19, 1935, Feb. 1937, Feb. 1940.
100. Letter, Raymond L. Hartzler to author, June 2, 1977; Maude Swartzendruber, *The Lamp in the West* (1975), VI, 272ff.; Hartzler (see note 97), 6-7; see Hartzler's reports in *Chr Evan.* Feb. 1945, March, Apr. 1946, Feb. 1947, Feb. 1957; *Menn.* Sept. 2, 1969, 519-20; Estes (see note 42), chapters 4, 5.
101. *ME,* IV, 974-75; Lydia Smith, "A Brief History of Illinois Sewing Circles," clipping in Science Ridge congregation papers, III-13-13, AMC; Abram Burkhart, *GW,* Oct. 16, 1907, 457-58. *GH:* Sept. 13, 1949, 914-15; Oct. 18, 1949, 1034.
102. "Minutes of Society," ms. in the possession of Steven R. Estes, Graymont, Ill.
103. *CC Yrbk.* 1931, 31-33; *The Congo Missionary Messenger,* Nov. 1929, 51-52; Estes (see note 42), 25-26.
104. "West. Dist. A. M. Conf. Report[s]": *GW,* Oct. 17, 1906, 452, 461; *HT,* Dec. 1, 1898, p. 357-58, July 15, 1892, p. 218, Oct. 15, 1892, p. 314.
105. *HT:* July 15, 1883, 216; March 15, 1886, 89; March 1, 1900, 76. *IMCR:* 1934, 9; 1956, 24-25. *GH,* Oct. 20, 1944, 580-81; *ME,* III, 588.
106. "50 Years of Helping One Another," pamphlet stapled into *EM,* Oct. 15, 1967; conferences with Eugene Lang, Aug. 22, 1978, and John Jennings, July 12, 1978, at Goshen, Ind. *ME.* I, 439.
107. III, 796-801.

108. Most of the *HT* issues for 1874 and 1875 list contributions.
109. See bibliography; see also *ME*, III, 605-09, IV, 284-91.
110. Conference with Vinora Weaver Salzman, July 17, 1979, at Goshen, Ind.; *GH*, Jan. 15, 1920, 797; P. C. Hiebert and Orie O. Miller, *Feeding the Hungry: Russia Famine, 1919-1925; American Mennonite Relief Operations Under the Auspices of Mennonite Central Committee* (1929), 343ff., 363, 365; J. D. Unruh, *In the Name of Christ: The Story of the Mennonite Central Committee and Its Service, 1921-1951* (1952), 12ff.; *ME*, 285-87.
111. David M. Hofer, *Die Hungersnot in Russland und Unsere Reise um die Welt* (1924). See also Hiebert and Miller, 340-42.
112. *MQR*, 44 (July 1970), 213; *GH*, Feb. 1, 1946. The beautiful tribute to Kratz by A. J. Miller, director of Mennonite Relief in Soviet Russia, 1921-26, was first published in Hiebert and Miller, 169-70.
113. Elva Mae (Schrock) Roth, "Mennonite Work Camp: Chicago, 1938," *MH*, Sept. 1979; *ME*, IV, 848-50.
114. *ME*, III, 614; *GH*, Aug. 8, 1912, March 1932.
115. See especially Schlabach's "Reveille for *Die Stillen Im Lande*...," *MQR*, 51 (July 1977), 213-26; his book cited note 44, 23-28, 42-53, and chapter VI; and his "The Humble Become 'Aggressive Workers': Mennonites Organize for Mission, 1880-1910," *MQR* 52 (April 1978), 113-126.

CHAPTER 12. Strain, Stress, Liberalism, Fundamentalism

1. *God Hath Spoken: Twenty-Five Addresses Delivered at the World Conference on Christian Fundamentals, May 25-June 1, 1919* [1919], 11-12.
2. Harold S. Bender, "Outside Influences on Mennonite Thought," *ML*, Jan. 1955, 48; quotations from text and footnote. The present writer recalls Bender's discussion in a faculty meeting at Goshen College in which he stated that Mennonites were fundamentalists with a small "f." This was in the 1940s or 1950s. Conference with J. C. Wenger, Aug. 7, 1979, at Goshen, Ind.
3. *Christlicher Bundesbote*, Aug. 9, 1900, 5.
4. Conference with J. C. Wenger, Jan. 30, 1979, at Goshen, Ind.
5. Conference of Steven R. Estes with Maurice Troyer, Apr. 29, 1979, as reported by Estes to author, July 23, 1979.
6. *GW*, Oct. 10, 1906, 440.
7. Steiner to Coffman, 4-20-94, box 9, M. S. Steiner mss., AMC.
8. Coffman "Diary Excerpts" in box 2, J. S. Coffman mss., AMC; *Elkhart Institute Monthly*, Apr. 15, 1899, 54.
9. *Sixty Years With East Bend* [1949], 7; "Illinois Conference," *HT*, July 1, 1898. J. S. Shoemaker, *GH*: Oct. 21, 1909, 467-68; Dec. 1922, 723, 734; Jan. 1944, 898-99. *IMCR*, 1929, 7-8; *GH*, Oct. 16, 1941, 611-12; *GH* editorials: Jan. 7, 1943, 865-66; June 10, 1943, 202; E. J. Stalter to H. J. Zehr, March 21, 1961, IMC Ex. Com. Sec. corr., AMC; conference with J. J. Hostetler, July 30, 1979, at Goshen, Ind.
10. William R. Moody, *The Life of Dwight L. Moody* (1930), 82.
11. See Emma Oyer diary in the possession of Edna Oyer Bachman, Goshen, Ind., e.g., Feb. 1, 1944, Feb. 4 and 7, 1947, Feb. 4, 1948. During her long period of service at the Mission Emma Oyer was known as a faithful attendant at these Moody meetings. In June 1920 while I was visiting her at the Mission, she insisted I accompany her to the Moody Church Tabernacle, for some meetings which turned out to be the Second World Conference on Christian Fundamentals. The first one had been held the year before at Philadelphia when the famous World's Christian Fundamentals Association was formed. Although too young at the time to realize fully the importance of these meetings, I later became very grateful for having had the privilege of attending this historic conference. I still have a copy of the printed program. Included in the list of books for sale at the conference was *God Hath Spoken* (see note 1), which I fortunately purchased.
12. S. F. Coffman to Hartzler, March 21, 1921, J. E. Hartzler mss., AMC.
13. Gerald C. Studer, rough draft of paper on Fundamentalist influences on the Mennonite Church, box 2, Studer mss., AMC; *ME*, I, 558-59; J. S. Coffman, *Outline and Notes Used at the Bible Conference Held at Johnstown, Pennsylvania, from Dec. 27, 1897, to Jan. 7, 1898* (1898), 4-5.
14. Quoted in Studer, 44.
15. For further reading on dispensationalism see C. Norman Kraus, *Dispensationalism in America: Its Rise and Development* (1958), esp. chapter 7.
16. M. S. Steiner to Clara Eby Steiner, July 10, 1894, in the possession of a daughter, Mrs. J. C. Meyer, Goshen, Ind. Steiner, like others, seemed favorably impressed with Moody's. In another letter (July 5, 1894, same location) to his wife he wrote: "Fred [S. F. Coffman] is missing some good lectures at the Institute." Studer, 40. E. E. Zimmerman, "History of Mennonite Hospital," *ZT*, Feb. 15, 1939.

Notes for Pages 310-325 513

17. Section on Clayton F. Derstine in Urie Bender, *Four Earthen Vessels.*
18. *GH:* Sept. 1920, 506-07; Oct. 7, 1920, 530-31.
19. *GH.* Oct. 19, 1922, 573.
20. *GH.* Oct. 4, 1923.
21. Whitmer to Derstine, Apr. 21, 1920, box 2, Daniel Kauffman mss., AMC.
22. Derstine to "Dear Brethren," n.d. (probably soon after Apr. 21, 1920), box 2, Daniel Kauffman mss., AMC. *GH:* Apr. 15, 1920; Jan. 8, 1952; Feb. 9, 1954.
23. I am indebted to Professor Jacob J. Enz of the AMBS for pointing out to me that in the original edition of Scofield's *Rightly Dividing the Word of Truth* there is a paragraph which is difficult to reconcile with the theory—a paragraph which some publishers later omitted without the author's knowledge. The paragraph is as follows:

> It may safely be said that the Judaizing of the Church has done more to hinder her progress, pervert her mission, and destroy her spirituality, than all other causes combined. Instead of pursuing her appointed path of separation, persecution, world-hatred, poverty, and non-resistance, she has used Jewish Scripture to justify her in lowering her purpose to the civilization of the world, the acquisition of wealth, the use of imposing ritual, the erection of magnificent churches, the invocation of God's blessing upon the conflicts of armies, and the division of an equal brotherhood into "clergy" and "laity."

See page 13 in 1951 edition; see also publisher's note.
24. E. L. Smith to Horsch, Nov. 29, 1933, box 5, John Horsch mss., AMC.
25. *GH.* Dec. 1919, 717-18; *Mennonite Church Polity* (1944), 67ff.; *GH:* Oct. 19, 1922, 572-73; Oct. 23, 1924, 589. Program of the Missionary Conference at Peoria, Dec. 29-30, 1924, IMC mss. AMC; program of the Mennonite General Conference held near Elkhart and Goshen, Ind., Aug. 1929.
26. *GH.* Sept. 20, 1923, 523.
27. *GH.* Sept. 3, 1925, 449; "Minutes of Local Committee Making Arrangements for General Conference at Eureka," in the possession of Thomas Yoder, Normal, Ill.
28. *GH.* Jan. 20, 1927, 898-99; Shoemaker to Hartzler, Feb. 15, 1918, folder 11, box 3, J. E. Hartzler mss., AMC; see also *GH:* Feb. 27, 1919, 850-52; Feb. 24, 1921, 938-39; and March 19, 1925, 995.
29. *GH:* Dec. 15, 1927, 802-03; Feb. 6, 1930, 914-15; Oct. 30, 1930, 658.
30. *Chr Evan.* July 1910, 6.
31. *Chr Evan.* Jan. 1933, 9-11, 19; *CC Yrbk.* 1935, 44-48.
32. Noah Oyer to Daniel Kauffman, Jan. 31, 1925, box 1, Noah Oyer mss., AMC; Oyer to author, May 11, 1921; Machen to Oyer, Nov. 15, 1928, box 2, Noah Oyer mss., AMC; Goshen College *Record* (Review Supplement), May-June 1926.
33. *In Memoriam: Dean Noah Oyer, 1891-1931* (1931), 36-37, copy in MHLG.
34. *Ibid.,* 88-89.
35. *GH.* Apr. 11, 1912.
36. *GH,* March 18, 1920, Jan. 28, 1926.
37. "Modernism vs. Fundamentalism," *GH.* May 22, 1924.
38. *GH.* Mar. 4, 1926, 993.
39. *GH:* June 25, 1925, 257-58; July 30, 1925, 353; March 4, 1926, 993. For examples of articles on Fundamentalism in *GH* by leading non-Mennonite Fundamentalists see issues of: Aug. 30, Oct. 4, 1923; Aug. 20, 1925. Daniel K. Kauffman. *Fifty Years in the Mennonite Church, 1890-1940* (1941), passim, especially chapters 9-11.
40. *GH,* Jan. 21, 1926.
41. *Ibid.;* Bender, "Outside" (see note 2); *ME,* II, 418-19.
42. *HT:* Apr. 1, 1895, 101-02; Feb. 1, 1899, 39. John Horsch to Coffman, March 3, 1896, box 3, J. S. Coffman mss., AMC.
43. *GH.* Dec. 1941, 810-11; James M. Gray, "Introduction," *Modern Religious Liberalism* (1968).
44. *Menn,* Sept. 30, 1920, 2; Augspurger to Horsch, May 17, 1920, July 12, 1921, box 2, John Horsch mss., AMC.
45. Augspurger to Horsch, Sept. 23, 1924, box 2, John Horsch mss., AMC.
46. *Ibid.,* Oct. 14, 1924.
47. *Ibid.,* Feb. 1, 1931.
48. C. Henry Smith to John Horsch, June 8, 21, 1924, Dec. 12, 1925; Horsch to Smith, June 16, 1924; boxes 2 and 3, John Horsch mss., AMC.
49. Bechtel to Horsch, June 29, 1925, box 3, John Horsch mss., AMC.
50. *Ibid.,* Mar. 8, Apr. 22, 24, 1926.

51. Burkhart to Horsch, June 7, 1925, John Horsch mss., AMC.
52. Shoemaker to Horsch, June 2, 1924, box 2, John Horsch mss., AMC.
53. *Christian Exponent:* July 1924, 239-40; May 21, 1926, 174-75.
54. Conference with Lester Hostetler (formerly *Exponent* editor), Jan. 27, 1981, at Goshen, Ind.; E. I. Culp, "Just a Word," *Christian Exponent*, July 18, 1924, 239; Walter E. Yoder to Lester Hostetler, Jan. 27, 1927, in Hostetler's possession, Goshen, Ind. Hostetler has kindly permitted me to use his valuable collection of letters.
55. Letter, Sept. 28, 1925, box 3, Hostetler collection cited note 54.
56. John Horsch, *Communism* (1937), 26-28; Lantz to Horsch, Apr. 23, 1937, box 6, John Horsch mss., AMC. The article on communism was also a chapter in Horsch's 1937 ed. of *Modern Religious Liberalism*.
57. Schrock to Hartzler, July 3 and 28, 1916; Hartzler to Schrock, July 5, 1916; box 22, J. E. Hartzler mss., AMC.
58. Albrecht to Hartzler, Nov. 1, 1916, box 22, J. E. Hartzler mss., AMC.
59. Shoemaker to Hartzler, Feb. 15, 1918, box 3, J. E. Hartzler mss., AMC.
60. Good to Hartzler: Feb. 9 and 14, 1918, box 3; Jan. 30, 1921, box 6; J. E. Hartzler mss., AMC.
61. Kreider to Hartzler, Feb. 14, 1920, box 5, J. E. Hartzler mss., AMC.
62. John S. Umble, *Goshen College, 1894-1954* (1955), 73.
63. *Ibid.*, 104-113; conference with Jesse N. Smucker, Aug. 30, 1979, at Goshen, Ind.
64. Hartzler to Egle, Aug. 15, 1921, box 6; Augspurger to Hartzler, Sept. 29, 1923, box 22; J. E. Hartzler mss., AMC.
65. Augspurger to Hartzler, Sept. 29, 1923, box 22, J. E. Hartzler mss., AMC.
66. Weaver came to North Danvers in 1922.
67. Weaver to Hartzler, May 23, 1923, box 8, J. E. Hartzler mss., AMC.
68. Eash to Hartzler, Aug. 16, 1923, box 7, J. E. Hartzler mss., AMC.
69. J. E. Hartzler, *Menn.* Aug. 28, Sept. 4, 1924.
70. Samuel Floyd Pannabecker, *Faith in Ferment: A History of the Central District Conference* (1968), 223-26. *Evidence of Modernism at Bluffton College* (1929), 1ff.; for W. S. Gottshall's letter to A. H. Miller, Pekin, Ill., see pp. 27-33. S. K. Mosiman to W. B. Weaver, July 6, 1934, Weaver file, AMBS.
71. *Chr Evan.* 1933, 42, 92, 213; *Menn* and *Chr Evan*, Apr. 17, 1934, 20; Pannabecker, 200-202; *CC Yrbk.* 1935, 26; these committee reports, together with the Minutes of Special Session of Central Conference of Mennonites at Normal Mennonite Church, Nov. 22, 1934, are in the Central Conference Archives, MHLB.
72. Walter Guth to W. B. Weaver, June 26, 1934; Ordination Committee Report, July 2, 1934; Board's Official Reply to Guth, July 18, 1934; James M. Gray to J. H. King, July 19, 1934; W. B. Weaver file, AMBS.
73. Herbert W. Schneider, *Religion in Twentieth-Century America* (1952), 107.
74. *GH:* Oct. 21, 1937; Dec. 5, 1940, 764; Nov. 13, 1941, 708-09; July 4, 1940, 282-83; June 18, 1942, 263-64; Sept. 19, 26, 1940, 529-30, 545-46.
75. *ZT.* July 15, 1944, Jan. 15, 1952; *EM.* June 15, 1957, 6; Charles Rupp, "Christian Higher Education and the E. M. C. Conference," *EM.* Apr. 1965.
76. "That Sunday School Lesson Question" (editorial), *ZT.* Feb. 15, 1949.
77. *EM.* July 1953.
78. *ZT.* July 15, 1932, Sept. 1937, July 15, 1938, March 15, 1939; J. Winfield Fretz, "A Study of Mennonite Religious Institutions in Chicago" (BD thesis, Chicago Theological Seminary, 1940), 84ff., 94ff.; *IMCR.* 1947, 30.
79. See Yoder's editorial, "When I," in *MG.* Aug. 1947.
80. Conference with Raymond Yoder, May 6, 1979, at Goshen, Ind. *IMCR:* 1947, 20; 1949, 22. *GH.* Oct. 11, 1949, 998-99. Howard J. Zehr to Raymond Yoder, Sept. 16, 1947; Zehr to A. C. Good *et al.,* Sept. 19, 1947; Good *et al.* to Zehr, Sept. 30, 1947; Howard J. Zehr mss., AMC.
81. Orie A. Miller to IMC Exec. Com., May 6, 1948, in IMC Exec. Com. mss., AMC. There is a large amount of material here covering this stressful period. In same collection, see also, e.g.: Harold R. Oyer to Exec. Com., no date (but 1948); Noah Roeschley's filled-in questionnaire to conference (1948); Ezra B. Yordy to Howard Zehr, Sept. 22, Dec. 5, 1949; H. R. Schertz to A. C. Good *et al.,* July 18, 1947; Schertz to "Brother Zehr," Jan. 31, 1949. Conference with Lena Lehman, Feb. 20, 1978, at Goshen, Ind.
82. *GH.* Nov. 4, 1946, 683-84. *IMCR:* 1947, 20; 1949, 23; 1951, 19-20; 1952, 24; 1953, 3. Exec. Com. Meeting Minutes for Nov. 1 and 2, 1948 and March 5, 1949, box 3; Harold R. Oyer to IMC Exec. Com., Dec. 4, 1951, box 2; Richard Yordy to Oyer, Dec. 12, 1951, box 2; IMC Exec. Com. mss., AMC.
83. Howard J. Zehr to Robert E. Zehr, Jan. 13, Oct. 1, Oct. 22, 1952; Robert E. Zehr to Howard J. Zehr, Oct. 21, 1952; Illinois Conference folder, Howard J. Zehr mss., AMC. Conference with Robert E. Zehr, Aug. 14, 1979, at Syracuse, Ind.

Notes for Pages 337-346

84. Harold Zehr to IMC Exec. Com., Apr. 26, 1951, box 3; report of the Exec. Com. to the East Bend congregation [1951]; Harold Zehr to J. A. Heiser, 6-29-51; Harold Zehr to Howard J. Zehr, Apr. 27, May 9, May 20, 1951; IMC mss., AMC. Alta Detweiler to Howard Zehr, May 23, 1951; Elmer R. Schrock to "Dear Brother," May 20, 1952; Ernest E. Smucker to Howard Zehr, May 23, 1951; Elsie and Dorothy [Birkey] to Howard Zehr, June 12, 1951; John R. Bruehl to Howard Zehr, Sept. 17, 1951; Howard Zehr mss., AMC. Ernest E. Smucker to H. S. Bender [June 7, 1954], in Smucker's possession, Goshen, Ind. Conferences with the following persons in the Fisher, Ill., area on Sept. 18, 19 or 20, 1979, have been very helpful: Verle and Margaret Oyer, Ivan Birkey, Mr. and Mrs. Bert Zehr, Mr. and Mrs. Alva Cender, Mrs. Alta Detweiler, Mr. and Mrs. Vernon Heiser, Mr. and Mrs. Emery Cender, Dan Teuscher, and Mr. and Mrs. Russell Massanari. Likewise at Goshen, Ind.: S. J. Hostetler, June 22, 1979; Ernest and Mary Smucker, July 9, 1978; Jay Zehr, July 16, 1978; Edna (Mrs. Howard) Zehr, July 7, 1979. See also "Report of the Executive Committee to the East Bend congregation, n. d. [Spring 1952]; Harold Zehr to "Dear Brethern" [sic], the East Bend Church Council [May 1951]; Howard J. Zehr to "Dear Christian Friends," June 20, 1952; all in the possession of Verle and Margaret Oyer and sent to me through their courtesy. Verle Oyer to author, July 14, 1980.
85. *IMCR*: 1952, 22-23; 1953, 3.
86. Richard [Yordy] to Ira Eigsti, Oct. 20, 1952, IMC mss., AMC; in same location, see also two documents, entitled "To Whom This May Concern," and "Consider the Following Facts in Their Relationship to the Present Condition of the East Bend Mennonite Congregation," which "The Committee" of the departing group sent to the East Bend members. See also reports of conferences mentioned in note 85.
87. Paper in my possession, courtesy Verle Oyer.
88. Kauffmann to Howard [Zehr], Jan. 14, 1965, Howard Zehr mss., AMC.
89. *MG*, Oct. 1959, 8; *GH*, Dec. 19, 1961, 1085.
90. *Menn.* May 22, Sept. 1962, 599.
91. *Menn*, Oct. 30, Nov. 6, 1962.
92. *MG*, Oct. 1976, 12. Stauffer to Zehr, Oct. 15, 1971; Zehr to Stauffer, Oct. 19, 1971; Howard J. Zehr mss., AMC.
93. Gordon Dyck to Pulpit Committee, Apr. 13, 1967; James Dunn to Gordon Dyck, June 21, 1967; Congerville file, Cen. Dist. Archives, MHLB. Conference with Paul Sieber, Sept. 25, 1979, at Peoria, Ill.; conference with Norman Kauffmann, Feb. 17, 1979, at Goshen, Ind.
94. J. C. Atherton to Stan Bohn, April (day not given), 1976; Elaine B. Bowers to "Gentlepeople of the Menn. Conf.," Apr. 10, 1976; Tiskilwa file, Cen. Dist. Conference Archives, MHLB; E. J. Stalter to Vernon MacNeill, Mar. 21, 1961, IMC Exec. Com. Sec. corr., AMC.
95. *MG*, Apr. 1974, 16, Oct. 1976, 12; on Gothard see also Ina Troyer, Delavan, *GH*, Dec. 10, 1974, 943; Neufeld, "Billy Graham and a Mennonite Church," *Menn*, June 19, 1962.
96. Richard Yordy to Jesse B. Martin, Oct. 3, 1961, box 2, IMC mss., AMC.
97. Roy Bucher, Sec., to Paul Mininger, Pres., and Harold Bender, Dean, Goshen Biblical Seminary, Sept. 11, 1958, Sec. corr., IMC Exec. Com. mss., AMC.
98. Conferences in Illinois with the following, in Sept. 1979: Russell Massanari, at Fisher; Aden Yoder, at Hopedale; Paul Sieber, at Peoria; Norman Yutzy, at Eureka, Ill.
99. Conference with John Harnish, June 14, 1979, at Eureka, Ill.
100. *MG*, Oct. 1976, 12. Conferences: with Ward Shelly, June 14, 1979, at Washington, Ill.; with Norman Yutzy, June 14, Sept. 28, 1979, at Eureka, Ill.; with James Detweiler, Sept. 25, 1979, at Morton, Ill.; with Mary Sutter, Nov. 29, 1979, at Goshen, Ind.
101. *Build*, Summer 1975, 12.
102. *EM*: Apr. 1957, 2; Sept. 15, Oct. 15, Nov. 15, Dec. 15, 1957. *1966 Annual Report and Directory* of EMC, 4; Stan Nussbaum, *You Must Be Born Again* (1980), 57; conference with Nussbaum, Aug. 13, 1979, at Goshen, Ind.

CHAPTER 13. The Illinois Mennonites and War

1. *Past and Present of Woodford County, Illinois* (1878), 269.
2. C. Henry Smith, *The Mennonites of America* (1909), 376-82; T. Harry Williams, *et al.*, *A History of the United States to 1877* (1969), 631-32.
3. Harry F. Weber, *Centennial History of the Mennonites of Illinois* (1931), 110, footnote; *ME*, I, 694-95; Edwin O. Ropp mss., copies in AMC.
4. Christian Krehbiel, *Prairie Pioneer: The Christian Krehbiel Story* (1961), 43-44. Is Krehbiel correct about securing a substitute? By 1864, when he said this happened, he could have paid the $300 commutation fee. *ME*, I, 695.
5. *History of Tazewell County, Illinois* (1879), 542; *ME*, I, 695.

6. John M. Brenneman to Funk, July 28, 1863, box 6; see also Funk's diary, Oct. 20, 1863, box 1; John F. Funk mss., AMC. Brenneman published his *Christianity and War* without his name attached. Funk states in his diary that he wanted it known that Brenneman was the author.
7. *HT*, July 1, 1898, 194-96. There is evidence that a member of the Rock Creek congregation enlisted in the Spanish-American War. Steven R. Estes to author, June 18, 1980.
8. *HT*, Aug. 1, 1898.
9. *Elkhart Institute Monthly*, Nov. 1898.
10. *Christian Monitor*, May 1910, 532.
11. G. F. Hershberger, *War, Peace and Nonresistance* (1944), 113-117.
12. *GH*, Sept. 6, 1917, 420.
13. Quoted from his address to the American Federation of Labor, Buffalo, N.Y., Nov. 12, 1917, *The Commoner*, Dec. 1917. Had Wilson lived long enough to see the numerous wars which followed his "war to end wars," he might have become less arrogant.
14. Possibly Baker was influenced in part by his wife, who was Quaker.
15. This list published by Mininger is in MHLG. According to his family, Teuscher died in the arms of a fellow prisoner who, as Teuscher found out shortly before he died, was also named Teuscher. But the family never found who he was or from where he came. Margaret and Verle Oyer to author, Jan. (n.d.), 1980.
16. Roy Buchanan, as told to Miriam Sieber Lind, "A Time to Say 'No,'" *Christian Living*, Sept. 1960, 34. This series ran in six successive installments in *Christian Living* from Sept. 1960 to Feb. 1961.
17. *ME*, I, 695-96; *GH*, June 13, 1918.
18. Aaron Augspurger to Newton D. Baker, July 9, 1918, Adjutant General's Records, reel 2, hist. mss., 8-29, AMC; C[layton] F. D[erstine] to Aaron Loucks, n. d. [ca. July 5, 1918], Peace Problems Com. folder, box 1, Loucks-Hartzler mss., AMC; Claudon to Baker, July 4, 1918, same as Augspurger to Baker; conference Mrs. Esther Nice with Hazel Hassan, Dec. 9, 1979, at Morrison, Ill., reported to present writer courtesy Mrs. Hassan; Margaret and Verle Oyer to author, undated [Jan. 1980].
19. Major General LeRoy S. Lyon to Adjutant General, July 17, July 29, 1918; Robert S. Henry Intelligence Office, Camp Wheeler, to Commanding General, July 30, 1918; file 383.2, Adjutant General's Office, War Dept., RG 407 NARS. This material was sent to me courtesy of Allan Teichroew, Washington, D.C.
20. Menn. Research Foundation Project #24-Questionnaires V-7-19, box 7-25, AMC.
21. Transcriptions of four of these interviews and a cassette of Ramseyer's are in MLA and in AMC.
22. *GH*, March 6, 1919, 877. Buchanan (see note 16); Jan. 1961, 24; Feb. 1961, 35. *GH*, July 1, 1969, 594.
23. For fuller accounts of CO experiences in the army camps in World War I, see C. Henry Smith, *The Story of the Mennonites* (4th. ed., 1957), 794ff.; G. F. Hershberger (see note 11), 119-22; Jonas S. Hartzler, *Mennonites in the World War* (1922), chapters 7-11.
24. Later called the Federal Bureau of Investigation.
25. Allan Teichroew, "Military Surveillance of Mennonites in World War I," *MQR* 53 (Apr. 1979), 98.
26. For a good example of this see "Malone Report," *ibid.* 110-14, 123-24, including footnotes. See also Roy Buchanan's reaction to this advice from the Iowa Mennonite ministers: (see note 16): Nov. 1960, 14-15.
27. Teichroew, 125-27.
28. R. J. Stewart to Military Intelligence Branch, July 30, 1918, MID RG 165 War Dept., NARS (see note 19).
29. File ILL., 17-76, SS records, RG 163, Suitland, War Dept.; Report by T. W. Quinlan, B of I Agent, Apr. 29, 1918, and Report May 15, 1918, by A. B. Bielaski; NARS (see note 19). Orrville, Ohio, *Courier-Crescent*, June 11, 1918, quoted in James O. Lehman, *Sonnenberg: A Haven and a Heritage* (1969), 168; *Herold der Wahrheit*, June 1, 1918, 264.
30. Arthur L. Smith to author, n. d. [Dec. 1979]; Smith stated that this information had been confirmed by Laura (Mrs. Joel) Schrock to Arthur L. Smith. Conference with Tilman R. Smith, Nov. 22, 1979, at Goshen, Ind.
31. Christian R. Egle, "Brief History of Salem Mennonite Church . . ." (unpublished, n. d.), 10, in my possession, courtesy of Edwin (Jack) Stalter; Margaret and Verle Oyer to author, n. d. [Jan. 23, 1980]; Arthur W. Nafziger to author, Jan. 23, 1980.
32. Conference with Esther Meck Smucker, Dec. 5, 1979, at Goshen, Ind.
33. Hazel Hassan to author, Jan. 15, 1980.
34. The present writer recalls how his father, John J. Smith, took Goshen College President I. R. Detweiler around in the Eureka-Roanoke community to solicit for the college. Detweiler received quite a few of these bonds.
35. Courtesy Hazel Nice Hassan who got the information from her mother, Mrs. Esther Nice, Morrison, Ill., Dec. 9, 1979.

36. *ME*, I, 696; Arlyn J. Parish, *Kansas Mennonites During World War I* (1968), 56.
37. *Menn.* Oct. 24, 1918, 1; consult also tape of interview with Dr. Lloyd Ramseyer, Schowalter Oral History Project II, interview 185, MLA and at AMC.
38. *GH*, Oct. 19, 1922.
39. *GH*, March 12, 1931.
40. Rodney J. Sawatsky, "The Influence of Fundamentalism on Mennonite Nonresistance 1908-1944" (MA thesis, University of Minnesota, 1973), 175-79.
41. *GH*, July 31, 1924, 355, 364.
42. E. L. Smith to Horsch, Nov. 29, 1933, box 5, John Horsch mss., AMC.
43. C. Henry Smith, "Mennonites and War," *CC Yrbk*, 1935, 48-51; Minutes of Ministerial Association of the Central Conference of Mennonites meeting, Dec. 3, 1937, Cen. Dist. Conf. Archives, MHLB; *CC Yrbk*, 1927, 20-23; Harold S. Bender, Sec., "Report of a Conference of Mennonite Peace Groups, March 10, 1939 . . .," *ZT*, June 15, 1939; *IMCR*, 1936, 11.
44. *ZT*, June 15, 1939.
45. *ZT*, July 15, 1939.
46. See, e.g., *ZT*, Feb. 15, 1940; *GH*, Feb. 22, 1940, 1004-1005.
47. *GH*, March 21, 1950.
48. Melvin Gingerich, *Service for Peace: A History of Mennonite Civilian Public Service* (1949), 50. This is an excellent, detailed work on CPS. See also *ME*, I, 696; Albert N. Keim, "Service or Resistance? The Mennonite Response to Conscription in World War II," *MQR* 52 (April 1978), 141-53.
49. Gingerich, chapters V to XVII give the details regarding setting up the program and the types of work carried on. See also excellent summaries in *ME*, s. v., "Civilian Public Service" by Melvin Gingerich, and "Conscientious Objector" by Guy F. Hershberger.
50. *ME*, I, 696-97; Pannabecker, *Faith in Ferment: A History of the Central District Conference* (1968), 234.
51. Gingerich (see note 48), 90; Howard Charles, "A Presentation and Evaluation of MCC Draft Status Census," in *Proceedings of the Fourth Annual Conference on Mennonite Cultural Problems* (1945), 87.
52. Guy F. Hershberger, *The Mennonite Church in the Second World War* (1951), 39-40.
53. *GH*, Jan. 8, 1942, 864; June 4, 1942, 204. Gingerich (see note 48), 124; *GH*, Aug. 11, 1944, 382.
54. *GH*, July 2, 1942, 299-300.
55. Conferences, at Goshen, Ind.: with J. Marvin Nafziger, Dec. 5, 1979; with Frederick Swartzendruber, Dec. 20, 1979; with Anna Nafziger, Dec. 21, 1979. Hershberger (see note 52), chapter XI; *GH*, Oct. 6, 1944, 534.
56. *ZT*, Apr. 15, May 15, 1942; June 15, 1944; March 15, 1946.
57. *Chr Evan*, Sept. 15, 1945.
58. Ben Esch to Alvin Beechy, Raymond Hartzler, and Harry Yoder, Sept. 15, 1945, W. B. Weaver mss., AMBS.
59. Conference with Pastor Ward Shelly, June 14, 1979, at Washington, Ill.
60. It is not clear how many of these, if any, were in CPS camps.
61. *ZT*, May 15, 1944, Apr. 15, 1946; E. E. Zimmerman and E. J. Krahn, compilers, *Groveland Evangelical Mennonite Church 1878-1978*, (1978), 20-21.
62. IMC, CPS Committee corr., box 1: Susie V. Koerner to Leland Bachman, Feb. 1947; IMC mss., AMC.
63. Gingerich (see note 48), 126, 128, 193ff.; *GH*, Nov. 20, 1941, 722; R. L. Hartzler to editor, May 31, 1977, *Menn*, July 12, 1977.
64. *IMCR*, 1948, 14.
65. *CPS Bulletin*, March 25, 1947.
66. *GH*, Oct. 26, 1945, 579-81; conference with A. W. Nafziger, Feb. 28, 1978, at Goshen, Ind. The statement is on loan in the A. W. Nafziger mss., AMC. Leland Bachman, "As Our Men Come Home," *GH*, March 15, 1946, 969-70.
67. These EMC Manual Revision Sheets were supplied to me through courtesy of Reuben Short at the Ft. Wayne headquarters; see also Andrew Rupp's editorial, "Is EMC Mennonite?" *Build*, Spring 1979, and letters about it in *Build*, Summer 1979; telephone conference with Rupp, Nov. 28, 1979.
68. J. Howard Kauffman and Leland Harder, *Anabaptists Four Centuries Later: A Profile of Five Mennonite and Brethren in Christ Denominations* (1975), 133.
69. Stan Nussbaum, *You Must Be Born Again* (1980), 35-36.
70. "Are Your Standards *Low* Enough?" *Menn*, Feb. 28, 1958.
71. Richard J. Yordy to H. S. Bender, Sept. 19, 1952; G. F. Hershberger to Roy Bucher and J. J. Hostetler, Nov. 24, 1959; IMC Exec. Com. Sec. corr., AMC.

72. *Menn:* Jan. 19, 1965, 44; Feb. 9, 1965; June 24, 1975, 405-06; Nov. 22, 1966, 715-16.
73. R. J. Yordy to H. S. Bender, IMC Exec. Com. Sec. corr., AMC.
74. *Menn* editorial, Oct. 3, 1967; *Cen Dist Rep,* Nov. 16, 1965, May 17, 1966; *Menn,* June 9, 1970, 403.
75. *Menn:* Jan. 13, 1976, 18ff.; March 2, 1976, 156.
76. Floyd Metz, "Analysis of the Draft Census of the Franconia, Illinois, Indiana-Michigan, Ohio, South Central and Pacific Conferences, Jan. 1, 1952-April, 1956" (Goshen College term paper, 1956, MHLG). Actually the figure for (Old) Mennonites choosing alternative service was 59.5 percent.
77. Metz, 5-6, 9-10, 21-23.
78. Delton Franz, "The Washington Office: Reflections After Ten Years," MCC Peace Section *Washington Memo,* July-Aug. 1978; conference with John A. Lapp, Jan. 2, 1980, at Goshen, Ind.; conference with James Waltner, May 5, 1978, at Normal, Ill.; Leland Harder, *General Conference Mennonite Church Fact Book of Congregational Membership* (1971), 30-32.
79. *Menn,* March 5, 1963, 151.
80. Conferences with James Waltner, May 5, 1978, at Normal, Ill.; and with Norman Yutzy, Sept. 28, 1979, at Eureka, Ill.
81. *Menn,* Dec. 12, 1972, 736-37; conference with Robert Harnish, May 3, 1978, at Tiskilwa, Ill.
82. *GH:* Jan. 8, 1980, 24; Feb. 12, 1980, 136.
83. For Warkentin's case in court, see Charles P. Schwartz, *Brief for Appellant in the United States Court of Appeals for the Seventh Court No. 6229 Abraham Warkentin, Appellant . . .* [1937], 1-44.
84. C. Henry Smith, *Mennonite Country Boy: The Early Years of C. Henry Smith* (1962), 194-95.

CHAPTER 14. Illinois Mennonites and Social Issues

1. *Menn,* Dec. 19, 1972, 749.
2. *MG,* Dec. 1971, 12; *Dictionary of American History* (1946), V, 107.
3. See, e.g., Carl F. H. Henry, *The Uneasy Conscience of Modern Fundamentalism* (1947), and Ronald J. Sider, *Rich Christians in an Age of Hunger* (1977).
4. See Willard H. Smith, *The Social and Religious Thought of William Jennings Bryan* (1975), esp. chapter 2.
5. J. Howard Kauffman and Leland Harder, *Anabaptists Four Centuries Later: A Profile of Five Mennonite and Brethren in Christ Denominations* (1975), 302-04; *GH,* May 1, 1973, 382.
6. *EM,* Sept. 15, 1967; *Build,* Spring, 1974.
7. *ZT,* Oct. 15, 1949; *Build,* Spring, 1973.
8. Nussbaum, *You Must Be Born Again* (1980), 19-22; E. E. Zimmerman, *ZT,* Oct. 15, 1938, 3.
9. *Build,* Winter, 1970, 23.
10. *Ibid.,* 3, 24, 21.
11. *Build,* Summer, 1974, Autumn, 1970; *Menn,* Jan. 1, 1974.
12. *ML,* Apr. 1953, 64.
13. *HT:* Jan. 1864; Aug. 1, 1899, 232.
14. *HT,* Jan. 15, 1894, 18-19.
15. Lewis D. Appel, *HT.* Feb. 23, 1905, 58-59.
16. Author heard H. R. Schertz say this in a Sunday School Quarterly Meeting in the Union Church in the later 1910s.
17. "The Gospel of God," *Christian Exponent,* Jan. 4, 1924, 9-10.
18. *GH,* Christian Doctrine Supplement (editorial), Feb. 1943, 1011.
19. Harold Zehr, *GH,* May 8, 1956, 448; conference with Lawrence Greaser, Jan. 18, 1980, at Goshen, Ind.; *The Foundation Echo,* May, Sept. 1954, Jan., Apr., Sept. 1955.
20. *MG:* June 1960; Apr. 1966, 16; Oct. 1966, 3.
21. *MG:* June 1974, 5; Oct. 1975, 14; Dec. 1971, 6. *Menn.,* June 10, 1969, 397.
22. *GH,* Aug. 10, 1965, 690-93.
23. "In loving Memory of Rick May," addresses given by David Eshleman, pastor at Waldo, and Norman Kauffmann of Goshen College, at Memorial Service, Sept. 24, 1971, Waldo Mennonite Church (in my possession courtesy Norman Kauffmann); Marilyn Houser, "As He Was Known," *Goshen College Record,* Oct. 1, 1971, republished in *MG,* Dec. 1971.
24. Mrs. Milton Ulrich, *Menn,* Nov. 22, 1966, 715-16; Donald D. Kamp. *Menn.* March 11, 1969, 179-80.
25. *Menn:* Sept. 23, 1969, 572; Jan. 4, 1966 (guest editorial).
26. *Menn:* Oct. 5, 1965, 624; Apr. 30, 1968, 319. *Cen Dist Rep,* June 17, 1969.
27. *Menn,* May 12, 1959, 294.
28. John Denny Weaver, "Some Background to the Position of American Mennonites on Slavery"

(seminar paper, Goshen Biblical Seminary, 1970, copy in MHLG), 1, 26-27; J. Herbert Fretz, "The Germantown Anti-Slavery Petition of 1688," *MQR*, 33 (Jan. 1959), 42ff., 54; H. S. Commager, *Documents of American History* (1963), I, 37-38.

29. Funk diary, Sept. 23, 1855; Funk to "Mr. Editor," March 8, 1860; John F. Funk mss., AMC. (At that time not all the states had their elections in November.) Helen K. Gates *et al., Bless the Lord, O My Soul: A Biography of John Fretz Funk, 1835-1930* (1964), 47-48; for the article on "Border Ruffianism" see *MHB*, Apr. 1973.

30. *HT*, Feb. 1864, 7.

31. Apr. 15, 1899, 119. This was written not by Funk, but by another Pennsylvania Mennonite.

32. Editorial in the *Review* (Oct. 1900), published by Krehbiel; discovered by Jim Juhnke and published in *Menn*, Apr. 15, 1969.

33. Chicago Home Mission workers to Executive Committee of Mennonite Board of Missions and Charities, Nov. 29, 1932; P. A. Friesen to S. C. Yoder, Nov. 20, 1932; IV-7-1, AMC.

34. F. D. King to S. C. Yoder, Sept. 16, 1935, Chicago Home Mission material, IV-7-1, AMC.

35. S. C. Yoder to Levi C. Hartzler, Feb. 10, 1937, Exec. Off. corr., box 3, IV-7-1, AMC.; J. Nelson Kraybill, "The Birth of the Chicago Mennonite Mexican Mission" (history seminar paper, Goshen College, 1978, copy in MHLG), 29.

36. *GH*: Jan. 7, 1943, 865; Apr. 2, 1946, 15.

37. For GC statement, see *Menn*, Sept. 1, 1959, 540. Copies of the MC statements are in MHLG.

38. IMC *Annual Report*, 1964, 6, 7; Roy Bucher to Pres. Kennedy, Aug. 12, 1963, box 3, IMC Exec. Com. Sec. corr., AMC.

39. Ivan Kauffmann to Roy Bucher, May 26, 1964; L. E. Troyer to Vern Preheim, July 6, 1964; location cited in note 38.

40. *MG*, Aug. 1963; *Menn*, Nov. 21, 1978.

41. *Cen Dist Rep*, Jan. 18, 1966, 4.

42. *Menn*: Dec. 31, 1968, 818; Jan. 14, 1969, 30.

43. *Cen Dist Rep*, Sept. 15, 1970, A5.

44. *Menn*, Feb. 19, 1957; *Cen Dist Rep*, Feb. 20, 1968, A6.

45. *Cen Dist Rep*, June 1965, Dec. 1964.

46. *Menn*, March 2, 1965, 139; *GH*, Sept. 21, 1965, 843.

47. *Menn*: Dec. 11, 1962, 789; Dec. 16, 1958; Nov. 12, 1957, 710-16. Samuel Floyd Pannabecker, *Open Doors: The History of the General Conference Mennonite Church* (1975), 271.

48. *Menn*, May 21, 1957; *Cen Dist Rep*, Feb. 15, 1966. See also his report of a trip to the segregated South—"Islands of Hope in a Sea of Despair," *Menn*, Feb. 24, 1959.

49. *Menn*, Sept. 28, 1965, 607.

50. *Menn*, Sept. 30, 1958.

51. C. J. Dyck, ed., *The Witness of the Holy Spirit, Proceedings of the Eighth Mennonite World Conference, Amsterdam* (1967), 128-29, 337-44. *Menn*: Oct. 3, 24, 1967, 648; Nov. 7, 1967, 679-80 (also editorial, same issue); Nov. 14, 1967; Sept. 12, 1967, 552; see Feb. 7, 1967, 82-83, for his bitter satire against the Mennonites.

52. *Menn*: Feb. 9, 1965, 9; Aug. 26, 1958.

53. Delton Franz to author, Jan. 31, 1980; *Menn*, Jan. 8, 1963, 25.

54. *Menn*, May 10, 1966, 320.

55. *Cen Dist Rep*, Feb. 21, 1967, A5-6.

56. *Cen Dist Rep*, Feb. 16, 1966.

57. *Ibid.*, Nov. 21, 1967; *Menn*, July 20, 1965, 467.

58. *Menn*: Oct. 11, 1966, 620-21; June 13, 1967, 397; Dec. 5, 1967, 739. Leonard Wiebe to Mrs. June Kirk, Aug. 14, 1968; Steve L. Goering to "Fred," Oct. 28, 1968; Cen. Dist. Conf. Archives, MHLB.

59. See also *Menn*, Jan. 14, 1969, 27; Mrs. Melvin Rensberger, *Cen Dist Rep*, Feb. 18, 1969; *Cen Dist Rep*, Sept. 15, 1970.

60. *Menn*: May 30, 1972, 362-63; Aug. 25, 1970, 507-08.

61. Franz to author, Jan. 31, 1980; conference with Stanley Bohn, Oct. 7, 1977, at Goshen, Ind. See also Curtis E. Burrell, Jr., "A Primer on the Urban Rebellion," *Menn*, June 18, 1968. L. L. Ramseyer to Gordon Dyck, Mar. 2, 1969; Don Schierling to Gordon Dyck, Mar. 20, 1969; Esko Loewen to Fred Unruh (Memo), May 8, 1969; C. E. Burrell, article on U.S. being a police state, n. d.; Woodlawn file, Cen. Dist. Conf. Archives, MHLB. *Chicago Tribune* and *Chicago Sun Times*, July 30, 1970; Jacob T. Friesen, "Debate Woodlawn Strategy," *Menn*, Sept. 7, 1971. Curtis Burrell, Jr., to Jake Friesen and Stanley Bohn, communication on tape, undated but some time after 1972—in the possession of Stanley Bohn, Newton, Kan.

62. Conferences with Ward Shelley, June 14, 1979, at Washington, Ill., and with Harry Yoder, Nov. 9, 1979, at Bluffton, Ohio.

63. *GH*. July 6, 1965, 586.
64. Information on the Ropps from the Walter Ropp mss. in the possession of Peter Ropp, Normal, Ill., courtesy Steven R. Estes; on Stuckey see *The Portrait and Biographical Album of McLean Co., Ill.* (1887), 835.
65. *ME*. I, 36-39.
66. I heard C. Henry Smith mention this several times; see also Smith's *One Hundred Years Ago*, (address at Metamora, Ill., 1940), 23; *HT*. Nov. 17, 1904, 374.
67. John F. Funk, *The Mennonite Church and Her Accusers* (1878), 175; Funk, "The Little Beer Drinker," "Journal," 1857, 58ff., 143 (trip to Illinois), box 1, John F. Funk mss., AMC; *HT*. Jan. 1881, quoted in *GH*. Jan. 17, 1956, 52.
68. *HT*. March 1, 1895; *GH*. Nov. 28, 1929, 715-16.
69. West. Dist. A. M. Conf. *Proceedings*. 1890, 10; *HT*. June 15, 1900, 188; *GH*. July 4, 1908, 221; *HT*. May 19, 1904, 165.
70. *Chr Evan*. Sept. 1910, 22-23.
71. *Ibid.*, Dec. 1910, 26-27.
72. I heard such preaching in the 1910s.
73. For an example of an article in *GH* which strongly favored temperance but did not advocate voting for prohibition see issue of Oct. 16, 1913, 454.
74. *ME*. I, 39.
75. Herbert Asbury, *The Great Illusion* (1950), 144-45.
76. *GH* editorial, Aug. 17, 1922, 385.
77. *GH*: July 28, 1932, 363; March 15, 1934, 1058-59; March 22, 1934, 1074-75.
78. F. D. King of Chicago to author on several occasions in the 1930s.
79. *ZT*. March 15, 1941; *GH*. Feb. 3, 1953, 98; *Menn*. Oct. 11, 1966, 621.
80. Kauffman and Harder (see note 5), 123; John Drescher to author, June 15, 1973; J. C. Wenger, in *The Gospel Evangel*. May-June, 1976, 8.
81. See chapter 9; *ME*, IV, 733.
82. David E. Plank, *The Temperate Life* (1917), 60. *HT*: June 15, 1890, 190; Apr. 15, 1897, 117-18.
83. *CC Yrbk*. 1937, 32-35; for Menno Simons' view on this see Menno Simons, *Complete Writings* (1956), 365-66.
84. *HT*. June 23, 1904, 205. *GH*: June 9, 1910, 157; July 10, 1913, 237.
85. Kauffman and Harder (see note 5), 147.
86. Snavely to Mensch, March 5, 1890, Jacob Mensch mss., Eastern Pa. Menn. Hist. Lib., Christopher Dock H.S., Lansdale, Pa.; microfilm copy in MHLG.
87. *ME*, IV, 972, 974.
88. *HT*: Sept. 22, 1904, 308. See also, 1904: Nov. 17, 370-71; Oct. 13, 330-31; Nov. 24, 381.
89. *HT*. Oct. 1, 1895, 298-99.
90. See, e.g., S. G. S. (possibly S. G. Shetler) in *GH*, May 2, 1940, 99, 108-09. But many by 1940 were taking a less rigid position on the role of women than was S. G. S.
91. Program in my possession.
92. *Menn*: Nov. 24, 1970, 726; March 19, 1974, 198.
93. *GH*. Apr. 22, 1975, 306-07.
94. *EM*. June 15, 1968.
95. *Menn*: June 3, 1970, 448; Aug. 11, 1970, 500.
96. Fanny Sutter to Jacob Friesen, May 6, 1974; Friesen to Sutter, May 10, 1974; Cen. Dist. Conf. Archives, MHLB.
97. Lois Barrett, *Menn*. May 25, 1976; conference with Vinora Weaver Salzman, Oct. 5, 1977, at Goshen, Ind. *Menn*: Jan. 18, 1977, 34-37; Dec. 12, 1972.
98. Ivan and Ann Brunk, letter to editor, *GH*, July 16, 1974, 556-57.
99. *Ibid; IMCR*. 1973, 1, 9-12; *Menn*, June 5, 1973. Dec. 12, 1972; *MG*, Dec. 1974, 4; Aug. 1973, 4; conference with W. Richard Hassan, Feb. 10, 1981, at Goshen, Ind.
100. *Menn*, June 15, 1976, A-11.
101. Hartzler, letter to editor, Oct. 3, 1975, in *Menn*. Nov. 11, 1975, 644.
102. Conference with Clarence Sutter, Feb. 4, 1981, at Goshen, Ind.
103. *HT*, Nov. 10, 1904, 364-65.
104. "Reba Place Fellowship" (11-page document published by Reba Place, Evanston, Ill., n.d.); "An Interview with Reba Place Fellowship," *Post American*, Sept./Oct. 1973, 8-11; J. Winfield Fretz, "Mennonite Community: Traditional or Intentional," *ML*. Dec. 1975, 5-7; Dave Jackson, *Coming Together* (1978), 173; conference with Jerry Lind, Feb. 19, 1980, at Goshen, Ind.
105. Jackson, 173; Jim and Donna Harnish, *Menn*, June 17, 1975, A-11.

106. *EM*, March 15, 1964; R. L. Hartzler, *Menn*, Nov. 28, 1961, 764; Drescher, editorial, *GH*, Feb. 18, 1970.
107. Funk diary, Jan. 27, 1861, John F. Funk mss., AMC; *HT*, Jan. 1881, 4. Ruth E. Buckwalter, *GH*: July 6, 1916, 274; Oct. 4, 1917, 507-08.
108. *GH*: March 11, 1915, 805; Oct. 20, 1932, 618-19; Apr. 24, 1930, 90-91; Feb. 26, 1920, 900-01.
109. *GH*. Sept. 24, 1931, 564.
110. *GH*. Dec. 24, 1974, 975; conference with R. L. Hartzler, Apr. 21, 1977, at Bloomington, Ill.; conference with Heinz Janzen, Apr. 20, 1977, at Bluffton, Ohio.
111. *GH*. May 12, 1964, 402-03; see Kauffman's books: *The Challenge of Christian Stewardship* (1955) and *Stewards of God* (1975).
112. *Menn*, May 6, 1958; *GH*, June 6, 1978, 453.
113. *Tazewell Publications*, March 8, 1979, 4. This is a section of *Tazewell News* and other Tazewell Co. papers; see same for March 12, 1977, March 9, 1978, March 13, 1976, all in writer's possession through courtesy of Don Roth, Morton, Ill.; *MG*. Apr. 1976, 12; Menn. Relief Sale Financial Report for 1980 sent to me by Dorothy Unger, Morton, Ill.
114. J. Winfield Fretz, "A Study of Mennonite Religious Institutions in Chicago" (BD thesis, Chicago Theological Seminary, 1940), v-vi.
115. Delton Franz, in *The Mennonite Church in the City*, 14th Issue, Oct. 20, 1959, 1-3.
116. Laurence M. Horst, *MG*, Feb. 1961, 4; Horst, *GH*. Oct. 19, 1965, 920-21; *Menn*, Sept. 21, 1976, Al-2; conference with Whitermore, Jan. 25, 1981, at Goshen, Ind.
117. Bruce Leichty, "Why Mennonites Need the City," *GH*, June 13, 1978, 474 (from *Mennonite Weekly Review)*; *IMCR*, 1965, 37-38.
118. Funk diary, Nov. 1, 1858; Funk to Mr. Editor, Mar. 8, 1860; box 1, John F. Funk mss., AMC. Gates (see note 29), 47-48.
119. Ethel Reeser Cosco, *Christian Reeser: The Story of a Centenarian* [1940s], 73.
120. *HT*. Nov. 1867, 168-69; West. Dist. A. M. Conf. *Proceedings*, 1891, 11; Roy Umble, "Mennonite Preaching, 1864-1944" (PhD dissertation, Northwestern University, 1949), 332. *HT*: Dec. 15, 1904, 405; Feb. 9, 1905, 42-43.
121. Louella Sanders, Dakota, Ill., *GH*, July 1931, 362.
122. *Cen Dist Rep*, June 18, 1968, A-5; *Menn*, July 9, 1968, 471; *Build*, Autumn 1968.
123. *Menn*, June, 30, 1964, 432.
124. *Menn*: Oct. 8, 1968, 620; Oct. 22, 1968 (editorial).
125. Conference with Norman Yutzy, Sept. 28, 1979, at Eureka, Ill.; *Mennonite Weekly Review*, Feb. 21, 1980.

CHAPTER 15. Illinois Hispanic American and Afro-American Mennonites: The New Urban Challenge

1. "Challenge of the City," *Menn*, Apr. 15, 1958.
2. Emma Oyer, *What God Hath Wrought in a Half Century at the Mennonite Home Mission* (1949), 130; J. W. Shank, *GH*, Dec. 1, 1932, 764.
3. Anna Yordy, *GH*, May 26, 1944, 146.
4. Oyer, 130-34; J. Nelson Kraybill, "The Birth of the Chicago Mexican Mission" (history seminar paper, Goshen College, 1978, copy in MHLG), 7-23.
5. *Ibid.*, 7-23.
6. *Ibid.*, 22-34; Ronald Collins to Steven R. Estes, Dec. 18, 1979, in the possession of Estes, Graymont, Ill. Anna Yordy, *GH*: May 26, 1944, 146; Aug. 4, 1944, 344; Dorothy Bean, Apr. 8, 1947, 43-44. *MG*: Oct. 1960; Aug. 1951, 15. *M Yrbk*. 1958, 1959. *IMCR*: 1935, 4; 1942, 3.
7. *El Heraldo Mexicano*, March 1941; *El Heraldo Evangélico*, Dec. 1961, 2; *GH*, Feb. 1, 1946, 840.
8. *GH*: Nov. 12, 1946, 712; Aug. 19, 1958, 785; Oct. 14, 1958, 977; Nov. 10, 1959, 972; May 10, 1960, 433. *MG*, Aug. 1958; Edwin and Marcella Stalter, *Illinois Mennonite Conference in Mission* (1980), 6.
9. *GH*: May 7, 1963, 392; June 4, 1963, 477; Apr. 28, 1964, 362; May 12, 1964, 408-409; Sept. 20, 1977, 709. *IMCR*: 1963, 10-11; 1964, 44-45; 1974, 15.
10. *GH*. March 20, 1962, 279; conferences with José Ortiz and Lupe de Leon, March 17, 1980, at Goshen, Ind.; Guillermo Espinoza, "A Presentation of the History of the Evangelical Mennonite Church, 1021 W. 19th St., Chicago" (unpublished, 1976, copy in MHLG).
11. Espinoza; see *M Yrbk* for membership figures.
12. Espinoza; Richard Hassan, Sec., "Minutes of the Church [IMC], Finance and Extension commission," May 21, 1979, copy in my possession.
13. Espinoza.

14. For a brief period in the late 1940s Mennonite conducted summer Bible school among blacks in Pulaski County in southern Illinois, and about the same time held services for a few years for the blacks in Gibson City. See *GH:* March 8, 1946, 953, 957; Aug. 23, 1949, 836.

15. *GH:* June 2, 1944, 160; Oct. 20, 1944, 578. Ill. Dist. Menn. Miss. Bd. *Report.* 1945, 8-9; Rosemary Freeney, "City Planning in the Chicago Near West Side Area . . ." (seminar paper, Goshen College, 1955, copy in MHLG), 48-49.

16. [Menn. Bd. of Missions & Charities], *Chicago Bethel Church Development* [1940s], 9-10. *GH:* Oct. 15, 1946, 616; Mar. 9, 1948, 230-34; May 4, 1948, 222-26.

17. Ivan Brunk, *MG,* Oct. 1948. *IMCR:* 1949, 12; 1950, 13; 1952, 19-20. *GH:* Feb. 7, 1950, 136; Nov. 4, 1952, 1086-87; July 20, 1954, 685; Oct. 5, 1954, 949.

18. Wilfred Ulrich to Raymond Yoder, July 12, 1949, in Thomas Yoder's possession, Normal, Ill. *GH:* July 19, 1949, 705; Nov. 24, 1953, 1126; May 20, 1956, 541. Conference with J. D. Graber, sometime in 1977, at Goshen, Ind.

19. Nelson Kauffman to Richard Yordy, Aug. 3, 1957, Incoming Letters, IMC mss., AMC; *GH,* Feb. 1978, 118; *IMCR,* 1962, 5; conference with Daniel Kauffman, Mar. 21, 1980, at Goshen, Ind.; conference with David Whitermore, Jan. 26, 1981, at Goshen, Ind.

20. Joe L. Holloway to "Dear Brother Bob," July 3, 1964, IMC mss., AMC. *GH:* Apr. 8, 1958, 331; Sept. 19, 1961, 822. *MG,* Dec. 1969; conf. with Dwight McFadden, Mar. 20, 1980, at Goshen, Ind.

21. *Menn Weekly Review,* Oct. 31, 1957; *GH,* June 25, 1957, 609; *M Yrbk,* 1980, 50.

22. *Menn:* Sept. 8, 1959, 558; Dec. 11, 1962, 789. "Markham Community Mennonite Church (A Brief History)" (1975, unsigned but apparently put out by the congregation), p. 1, courtesy Marlene Suter and Steven R. Estes, Graymont, Ill.

23. Voth to Mrs. Bechtel, March 29, 1966, Markham file, Cen. Dist. Conference Archives, MHLB; *Menn,* Sept. 22, 1970.

24. "Markham Community" (see note 22). *Cen Dist Rep:* Apr. 18, 1967, A8-9; Oct. 17, 1967, A2; June 15, 1971, A2.

25. *Menn,* July 20, 1976, A-4; Marlene Suter to Steven R. Estes, Jan. 18, 1980, in the possession of Estes, Graymont, Ill.

26. *Cen Dist Rep:* Jan. 18, 1966, A5; March 19, 1968; June 17, 1969. *Menn,* March 9, 1971, 163.

27. *Menn.* Aug. 31, 1976, 502; *MG,* Oct. 1970, 40.

28. Norma Voth, *Menn.* July 22, 1958, 436.

29. *Menn,* Nov. 21, 1978, 676; *Cen Dist Rep,* Jan. 18, 1966, A5.

30. *Cen Dist Rep,* Jan. 18, 1966, A5.

31. *GH:* Jan. 31, 86; Feb. 14, 133; the other installments are in Feb. 7, 21, and 28 issues.

32. *Menn.* Nov. 21, 1978, 676-77; reprinted in *GH,* Apr. 4, 1978, 269-71.

33. *Ibid.*

34. *GH,* Feb. 12, 1980, 137.

35. *Ibid.; GH.* Sept. 13, 1977, 688; tel. conference with David Whitermore, Chicago, Mar. 27, 1980.

36. See Edwin and Marcella Stalter, *Illinois Mennonite Conference in Mission* (1980), 1-14. These authors speak of "approximately 16 groups" in the Chicago area. One of the new groups is in Oak Park where David Whitermore serves as leader. They recently started Sunday morning services. *Forum,* Nov. 1979, 12.

CHAPTER 16. Other Developments and Trends in Recent Decades

1. See, e.g., *GH.* Nov. 25, 1947, 746; Kenneth L. Weaver, "When He Saw the City," *MG,* June 1965.

2. Weaver. *GH:* Nov. 15, 1949, 1119; Mar. 9, 1965, 202.

3. Melvin Gingerich, "The Mennonite Family Census of 1963," p. 11, box 7, I-3-3, AMC.

4. Conference with J. Howard Kauffman, June 6, 1979, at Goshen, Ind.; *IMCR* 1965, 37-38.

5. Alvin E. Applequist to Jake Friesen, May 1, 1972, Tiskilwa file, Cen. Dist. Conf. Archives, MHLB.

6. See Yoder's 1980 survey of occupations of Illinois Mennonites in Appendix I (Table I); conference with D. Paul Miller, July 26, 1981; tel. conference with Thomas Yoder, July 28, 1981.

7. Gordon R. Dyck, report on visit to Summerfield, Ill., Feb. 7, 8, 1969, Cen. Dist. Conf. Minutes, Cen. Dist. Conf. Archives, MHLB. In same archives, Summerfield file, see also: Gordon R. Dyck to Bruno Penner, Nov. 28, 1967; Carl Basinger to Ellen Koontz, July 5, 1969; Jacob T. Friesen to George and Helene Dick, Dec. 4, 1970; Marion Ruth to Jacob Friesen, Jan. 28, 1974. For a good recent history see W. Richard Hassan, "History of the Summerfield Church," *MH,* March 1978.

8. *Menn:* Mar. 16, 1976, A6; Feb. 15, 1966, A9; Oct. 16, 1973.

9. *MG:* Feb. 1974, 5; Dec. 1976, 16; June 1969; Dec. 1970, 5; Dec. 1973, 11ff.

Notes for Pages 439-453

10. *Brotherhood Beacon:* Apr. 1975, 40; Sept. 1972, 106. Henry Plank, "The Now Generation," Apr. 1971, 39.

11. The title of this play is *The First Mennonite Church Presents Its Centennial Pageant, "Cherish Our Past—Share Our Future": A Historical Drama in Ten Scenes.* At the same time the congregation published a brief history entitled *Centennial Celebration of First Mennonite Church Morton, Illinois.* Mrs. Ruth Gerber King and Elva Roth were largely responsible for the historical data which appeared in the above publications. See also *Pekin Times*, Sept. 1, 1976.

12. E. E. Zimmerman and Emil J. Krahn, compilers, *Groveland Evangelical Church 1878-1978* (1978).

13. The present writer participated in the 1950 celebration. See *Roanoke Mennonite Church Centennial Year 1875-1975* (1975).

14. This has been published in pamphlet form.

15. *MG*, June 1966, 4; *IMCR*, 1973, 9; GC and MC *Yearbooks*.

16. *Cen Dist Rep*: Nov. 19, 1968, A5; Jan. 16, 1968; Mar. 18, 1969, A4. *GH*: Jan. 22, 1974, 84; Nov. 20, 1962, 1029.

17. Conference with Ernest Bennett, May 6, 1980, at Elkhart, Ind.

18. *GH*, Aug. 19, 1980, 660-61.

19. "Church Giving by Year and Conference 10-Year Comparision," Goshen College Public Relations Office Release (1979).

20. *Cen Dist Rep*: June 18, 1968, A5; June 15, 1971, A7.

21. Percy Gerig, pastor at Roanoke, letter to editor, *GH*, Feb. 15, 1977, 142.

22. Levi Miller, ed., *The Meeting House of God's People* (1977), 12, 14ff.

23. *Ibid.*, 20, 47; Harry F. Weber, *Centennial History of the Mennonites of Illinois 1829-1929* (1931), 204-05.

24. Miller, 21-25.

25. *MG*, June 1965.

26. E. E. Zimmerman, *75th Anniversary Salem Children's Home 1896-1971* (1971); Vernon Zimmerman, "It's a New Ball Game," *Build*, Winter 1973; *Salem Children's Home—The Facts Are ...* (brochure, 1971, in my possession).

27. *Salem Children's Home—The Facts Are ...*; tel. conf. with Michael Kauffman, Flanagan, Ill., May 13, 1980; see also *Salem Children's Home* (pamphlet recently published, n. d.).

28. *MG*, Apr. 1950, Feb. 1963, Apr. 1964; copy of dedication service program, Aug. 29, 1965. *GH*: Nov. 15, 1960, 1012; Sept. 9, 1980, 720. Conference with Tilman Smith, May 29, 1980, at Goshen, Ind.

29. *Cen Dist Rep*. July 17, 1966, Sept. 19, 1972; *Menn. Weekly Review*, Nov. 24, 1977; *Build*, Winter 1978, 21, *Menn*: Sept. 17, 1974, A3; Apr. 20, 1976, A5; Oct. 19, 1976, A5; Apr. 19, 1977 (Cen. Dist. Edition), A5; Steven R. Estes to author, Feb. 17, 1981.

30. *MG*. Apr. 1959, 3.

31. Carl F. Smucker and Robert L. Steiner, *A Research Study of the Aged in a Central Illinois Community* (1961), preface, 1-3, 37-39.

32. Steven R. Estes, *Christian Concern for Health: The Sixtieth Anniversary History of the Mennonite Hospital Association* [1979], 87-99 (see pp. 96-98 for Estes' explanation of the above-mentioned kinds of care); Menn. Hospital *News Release*, Jan. 16, 1981.

33. *Ibid.*, 94-95.

34. *Ibid.*, 93-102.

35. *Cen Dist Rep*. Apr. 16, 1974, A4ff.; in addition to Estes, see recent issues of *The Menno-light*, especially Feb. 1975, Dec. 1975, June 1976, Dec. 1976, Feb. 1977, Aug. 1977, and Apr. 1979 "Special Anniversary Issue, 1919-1979." See also "Mennonite Hospital Today," 4-page brochure revised as of 1978. According to this, the hospital had at that time 250 beds, 579 employees, and 115 physicians, representing 18 specialities, on the medical staff. *Menn*: Sept. 16, 1975, A5; Apr. 19, 1977, A5. *GH*. June 21, 1977, 500; *Menn. Weekly Rev.*, July 6, 1978.

36. *Christian Monitor*, May 1910; *Chr Evan*. Sept. 1911.

37. C. Henry Smith, *One Hundred Years Ago* (address at Metamora, Ill., 1940), 32.

38. *GH*. July 15, 1975, 501-02.

39. *GH*. June 12, 1979, 490.

40. *Cen Dist Rep*: Dec. 1964, A9-10; Oct. 17, 1972, Al. *Menn*, June 27, 1961, 424; *MG*. Feb. 1969.

41. See, e.g., EMC *Manual Revision* (mimeographed copy, 1979), Part III, 3-4; conferences with various Illinois ministers, 1979; Leland Harder, *General Conference Fact Book of Congregational Membership* (1971), 34-35.

42. *Illinois Mennonite Conference Yearbook*, 1979, 32; conference with Paul King, Oct. 23, 1979, at Goshen, Ind.

43. *ME*, III, 399-400; *HT*, Apr. 1, 1892, 107; conference with Nelson Springer, June 12, 1980, at Goshen, Ind.
44. Smith (see note 37), 29.
45. Conference with Tilman R. Smith, April 26, 1979, at Goshen, Ind.
46. James E. Horsch, "A Comparison of Past and Projected Changes . . . in the Illinois Mennonite Conference" (seminar paper, Goshen College Biblical Seminary, 1966, copy in MHLG), 9.
47. See Yoder's "Educational Attainment Among Illinois Mennonites, 1980," in Appendix I (Table III).
48. "To Think About," *MG*, Aug. 1973, 3.
49. George Dick, "Pastor's Report for June to January of 1966," in North Danvers Mennonite Church Archives.
50. Paul Bender, compiler, "Mennonite Church Students—Fall 1979," compiled for Mennonite Board of Education, copy in my possession; conference with Paul Bender, June 9, 1980, at Goshen, Ind.
51. *Chr Evan*, Aug. 1912, 379-80.
52. *GH*, July 13, 1954, 660; *IMCR*, 1975, 26.
53. *Menn. Weekly Rev.*, July 13, 1978; conf. with Dawn Yoder, Feb. 19, 1979, at Goshen, Ind.; Thomas Yoder to author, Sept. 26, 1980.
54. "Morton Evaluation, May 15, 1977," IMC document supplied to me through courtesy of Edwin J. Stalter, Conference Minister; "To the Elders and Membership of First Mennonite Church," Aug. 28, 1977, by the elders of the Trinity group, copy in my possession.
55. Sources cited in note 54.
56. *Ibid.*; *Trinity Mennonite Service of Dedication* (Sept. 30, 1979), copy in my possession; Edwin J. Stalter to author, Nov. 3, 1979. Conferences with the pastors and leading members of both congregations in Sept. 1979, and with Pastor Mahlon Miller at Elkhart, Ind., in Oct., have been very helpful.
57. Herbert Roth, "Chairman, Elders Report to First Mennonite," Sun., Aug. 21, 1977; Clayton Eigsti, "A Witness to a Church Division," Jan. 1, 1978; *Trinity Annual Reports*, 1977-78, 4, 6; all in my possession.
58. Edwin J. Stalter to author, Nov. 3, 1979. Conferences, at Goshen, Ind., with: Victor Hildebrand, April 21, 1980, and June 17, 1980; Phil Helmuth, May 26, 1980; Harley Stauffer, June 6, 1980; Norman Yutzy to author, Sept. 13, 1980.
59. *M Yrbk* 1980, 97-98. *The Eastern Mennonite Testimony:* Jan. 1970, 7; June 1980, 67-68. Conf. with J. C. Wenger, June 18, 1980, at Goshen, Ind.
60. Sources cited in note 59.

CHAPTER 17. Toward Mennonite Cooperation and Unity

1. J. C. Wenger, *The Mennonites in Indiana and Michigan* (1961), 285.
2. *Menn*, Oct. 18, 1968, 668; A. J. Beachy, May 15, 1962, 326; *ME*, III, 470.
3. Joseph Stuckey, *Eine Begebenheit, die sich in der Mennoniten-Gemeinde, in Deutschland und in der Schweiz, von 1693 bis 1700 zugetragen hat* (1871), preface. (Unpublished English version of preface was used, trans. by Nelson Springer. Both the published work and the translated preface are in MHLG.)
4. Erismann diary, 1867, p. 30, summer 1868.
5. *Ibid.*, apparently 1865. It is interesting that Erismann would use "Mennonite" instead of "Amish," almost as if he did not want to recognize the Amish division.
6. *ME*, III, 588.
7. Coffman diary, Mar. 12, 13, 14, 16, 18, 1889, J. S. Coffman mss., AMC; *HT*, Mar. 1, 1891, 73.
8. *HT*, Nov. 15, 1891, 347.
9. "Illinois Conference," *HT*, July 1, 1893.
10. *ME*, II, 797.
11. "Christian Unity," *HT*, Oct. 1, 1903, 315, 317.
12. *Chr Evan*, Aug. 1912, 378.
13. *GH*, May 26, 1910, 114-15.
14. *Echoes: A Book Containing the Report of . . . The First All-Mennonite Convention in America . . .* (1913), 11, 38-50, *passim*; P. G. Schultz, *MH*, Dec. 1975; *CC Yrbk*, 1926, 19-21; Noah E. Byers, "The All-Mennonite Convention," *ML*, July 1948, 7, 8, 10; C. J. Dyck, "The Mennonite World Conference: A Brief Introduction," *MQR* 41 (July 1967), 278-80.
15. Lester Hostetler, "The Ninth All-Mennonite Convention" (1936), *CC Yrbk*, 1937, 29; Dyck.
16. *ML*, Jan. 1948, 44-46.
17. *Chr Evan*, Apr. 1926, 76-77; Weber, *Centennial History*, 527; Harvey E. Nunemaker to Lester Hostetler, March 26, 1926, Lester Hostetler mss., in Hostetler's possession, Goshen, Ind.

18. John T. and Catherine Neufeld, compilers, *Mennonite Work in Chicago up to 1961,* 47; Stan Nussbaum, *You Must Be Born Again* (1980), 19, 21, 24.
19. Harley J. Stuckey, "Cultural Interaction Among the Mennonites Since 1870" (M. A. Thesis, Northwestern University, 1947), 79-80.
20. Peter C. Hiebert and Orie O. Miller, *Feeding the Hungry: Russia Famine, 1919-1925; American Mennonite Relief Operations Under the Auspices of the Mennonite Central Committee* (1929), 414-15.
21. Words taken from the title of a sermon which the present writer preached in the Woodlawn Mennonite Church in Chicago in the spring of 1946.
22. *The Mennonite and The Christian Evangel.* Jan. 2, 1934, 13.
23. *Chr Evan,* Jan. 1936, 3.
24. "Church Union," *CC Yrbk.* 1937, 32-35.
25. H. S. Bender, *ME,* III, 46-47.
26. *Chr Evan:* Aug. 1945, 171, 73; Oct. 1953, 163-64.
27. Letter to editor, *GH.* March 2, 1954.
28. *MG,* Oct. 1948; *GH.* Feb. 10, 1953, 132; *MG,* June 1956; *Menn,* Feb. 4, 1958; "Program for Ill. Inter-Menn. Ministers Fellowship ... Metamora ... May 14, 1956," MC Conf. Ill. material, vertical file, MHLG; *Menn,* May 7, 1957, 292.
29. R. L. Hartzler, *Chr Evan,* Feb. 1957, 23-24. *Menn:* Nov. 11, 1958, 702; Apr. 29, 1958, 259.
30. Samuel Floyd Pannabecker, *Ventures of Faith: The Story of Mennonite Biblical Seminary* (1975), 55-57, 99-102, and *passim;* see also "Memorandum of Agreement Between the Associated Mennonite Biblical Seminaries," 1957, in MHLG.
31. Conferences with Robert Yoder, March 2, 1979, at Goshen, Ind., and with James Waltner, May 5, 1978, at Normal, Ill.; *Menn,* Nov. 21, 1972, 679.
32. *GH.* June 30, 1959, 612; R. L. Hartzler to author, June 2, 1977; *MG,* Feb. 1964.
33. *Menn:* March 29, 1960, 206; May 16, 1961, 334.
34. The committee of Horst and Hartzler was later enlarged to six, adding H. N. Harder, Paul Roth, Harold Zehr and Roy Bucher.
35. *MG:* Dec. 1960, 5; Oct. 1961, 4; June 1964, 5. *GH.* May 16, 1960, 457. *IMCR* 1961, 31; 1964, 43. *Menn,* June 2, 1964, 366.
36. *MG.* Feb. 1963, 8.
37. *GH.* June 26, 1962, 579; *Menn,* Aug. 14, 1962, 528.
38. *GH.* Aug. 24, 1965, 737; *Menn,* Sept. 7, 1965, 564.
39. *GH.* Aug. 3, 1965, 664 (republished in *Menn.* Sept. 21, 1965, 592); Elva Mae Roth, *GH.* Aug. 31, 1965, 770.
40. *Menn:* Jan. 14, 1964, 28; and (for William H. Stauffer's response) Feb. 11, 1964, 92.
41. See, e.g.: James A. Goering, *Menn.* Nov. 16, 1965, 719; John H. Yoder, *Cen Dist Rep.* Dec. 21, 1965, 1.
42. *IMCR* 1964, 38; *GH.* July 30, 1963, 659; telephone conference with Mrs. Bertsche, June 21, 1980; Henry J. Ruth, *Cen Dist Rep.* Nov. 21, 1967.
43. Report *On Chicago Area Mennonite Council Coordinator* (n. d.), box 3, IMC corr., (1964-66), AMC; *IMCR.* 1966, 15, 34-35, 46; "First Inter-Mennonite Ministers Meeting," *Menn.* March 5, 1963, 152ff.; *Cen Dist Rep.* June 18, 1974, A8; *GH.* May 7, 1974, 364.
44. *MG.* Oct. 1966, 3.
45. Roy Bucher to H. N. Harder, May 2, 1958; Harder to Bucher, May 5, 1958; IMC Sec. corr. (1956-59), AMC.
46. Minutes Inter-Mennonite Exec. Com. Meeting, Feb. 10, 1966, Ex. Com. corr.; Harold Zehr to Rob't Harnish, Mar. 18, 1966, box 3, IMC mss., AMC; *Cen Dist Rep.* Mar. 15, 1966, June 15, 1971; *MG:* Apr. 1966, 7; Aug. 1973, 3.
47. IMC Mission Board 1967 materials, box 1, IMC mss., AMC.
48. Howard Raid, "Cooperation Explored," *Menn.* Dec. 16, 1975, A5; *MG,* Feb. 1976, 11.
49. *Journal-Star.* Apr. 9, 14, 1980.
50. *MG.* Oct. 1969, Feb. 1970; *MH.* June 1974, Dec. 1976, June 1980; *GH.* July 23, 1974, 571.
51. *MG.* Oct. 1968, Dec. 1970, Oct. 1975, Dec. 1976; *Menn,* Oct. 21, 1975, A5. "Inter-Church Task Force Report," April 25, 1975; James Waltner and Carl Newswanger, Pastors' *Annual Reports* 1975, dated Jan. 18, 1976; Normal Church file, Cen. Dist. Conf. Archives, MHLB. *GH:* Sept. 30, 1975, 699; Oct. 12, 1976, 789.
52. *IMCR* 1975, 15; Gordon Dyck to Ivan Kauffmann, Jan. 1, 1969; Jacob Friesen to O. H. Augsburger, Apr. 18, 1974; Cen. Dist. Conf. Archives, MHLB.
53. *Tazewell Publications* (Supplement), March 9, 1978, March 8, 1979; conference with Mr. and Mrs. Donald Roth, Sept. 27, 1980, at Morton, Ill.

54. *Menn.* May 14, 1968, 348.
55. Tel. conf. with Norman Yutzy, Eureka, Ill., Aug. 7, 1980; conference with Thomas Yoder, April 11, 1981, at Goshen, Ind.
56. *Menn;* Nov. 21, 1972, 686; May 20, 1975, 320.
57. *1966 Annual Report and Directory of E. M. C.*, 4; *Build.* Winter 1973; Stan Nussbaum (see note 18), 58; conference with Milo Nussbaum, Sept. 24, 1979, at Morton, Ill. For a different EMC view see E. E. Zimmerman, *ZT,* Nov. 15, 1948: "The principles of our conference are similar to those held by the Mennonite denominations in general." See also Lester Rich, *Build,* Summer 1979, 213.
58. David Habegger, *Cen Dist Rep,* Apr. 18, 1972, A2.
59. *CC Yrbk,* 1972, 34.
60. Laura S. Oyer, *Menn.* Nov. 18, 1975, A5; conference with Steven R. Estes, July 29, 1980, at Goshen, Ind.
61. Or EMC.
62. *Cen Dist Rep,* July 23, 1974, A7.

CHAPTER 18. American Acculturation and Keeping the Faith

1. C. Henry Smith, *Mennonite Country Boy: The Early Years of C. Henry Smith* (1962), 194-95.
2. Stan Nussbaum, *You Must Be Born Again* (1980), 45ff.
3. "Boundary Maintenance and Cultural Assimilation of Contemporary Mennonites," *MQR,* July 1977, 229, 232, 237-39.
4. Stanley Bohn, "E. J. and Nora Bohn....," *Menn.* Sept. 16, 1975; conference with Ernest J. Bohn, Oct. 10, 1977, at Goshen, Ind.
5. Conference with Silas Nafziger, Sept. 26, 1979, at Hopedale, Ill.; Christian R. Egle, *Brief History of the Salem Mennonite Church near Flanagan, Illinois . . .* (1925), 10.
6. James C. Juhnke, *A People of Two Kingdoms: The Political Acculturation of the Kansas Mennonites* (1975), 155-57.
7. Smucker, *GH,* March 21, 1950.
8. *Menn.* Dec. 12, 1972, 736-37; conference with Hartzler, Apr. 21, 1977, at Bloomington, Ill.
9. *ML,* Apr. 1954, 98.
10. Vern Miller to Roy Ingold, June 8, 1959, IMC Ex. Com. Sec. corr., AMC.
11. Conference with Harnish, May 3, 1978, at Tiskilwa, Ill.
12. *GH,* Jan. 20, 1948, 65.
13. Royal Bauer, *GH,* March 29, 1949, 302-03. Not all authorities agree that this so-called tension between "Separate ye" and "Go ye" was a hindrance to missionary work. See, e.g., Theron Schlabach, *Gospel Versus Gospel: Mission and the Mennonite Church, 1863-1944* (1980), 155ff., and Schlabach to author, Feb. 13, 1981.
14. "Where 'on the way' is the Mennonite Church?" *GH,* July 12, 1977.
15. *ML,* Jan. 1970, 34-37. Despite Juhnke's statement, many would insist that the Anabaptist-Mennonite motivation did come, in large part at least, from within the community.
16. *Ibid.*
17. *Menn.* Sept. 23, 1969, 562-64.
18. David E. Plank, "The Holy Kiss," *GH,* Dec. 15, 1932, 786-87; Derstine, *GH,* Feb. 17, 1921, 130-32; W. B. Weaver to J. E. Hartzler, Nov. 15, 1923, folder 2, box 8, J. E. Hartzler mss., AMC.
19. John L. Harnish to author, Sept. 30, 1980.
20. Conf. with James Dunn, July 20, 1979, at Champaign, Ill.; Melvin Gingerich, *Mennonite Attire Through Four Centuries* (1970), 158.
21. *MG,* Feb. 1963, 3.
22. *MG,* Oct. 1970, 7, 9.
23. Conferences at Goshen, Ind.: with Paul Mininger, Sept. 13, 1980, with J. C. Wenger, Sept. 17, 1980, with Nelson Springer, Sept. 17, 1980. Norman Yutzy to author, Sept. 13, 1980; for a slightly different approach and interpretation see Calvin Redekop, "Patterns of Cultural Assimilation Among Mennonites," *Proceedings of the Eleventh Conference on Mennonite Educational and Cultural Problems* (1957), 99-112.
24. *GH,* Jan. 6, 1981, 7.

APPENDIX A

Survey of Occupations, Income, and Education Among Mennonites of Illinois

by Thomas Yoder

The survey conducted included the three major groups of Mennonites in the state of Illinois—Illinois Mennonite Conference (MC), Central District Conference (GC), and the Evangelical Mennonite Church. Survey forms were mailed directly to the pastor of each congregation, and for congregations not having a pastor listed, forms were mailed to the church addresses. Pastors were asked to distribute them to persons 19 and older through adult Sunday school classes or church mailboxes. The person receiving the form was instructed to indicate sex, marital status, level of education achieved, annual income category, and full-time occupation. The number sent to each congregation was based on approximately 18% of the total membership. Of the sixty-one congregations receiving forms, thirty-six (59%) returned them. The rate of return from these thirty-six congregations was 62%. Forty percent of the 1,225 individual forms were returned. The male/female ratio of the returns was 59% for the males and 41% for the females. More persons checked the occupational part of the survey than the parts dealing with education and income. The age breakdown of those completing the occupational checklist was as follows:

Age	Percent	Age	Percent
19—25	9	46—55	21
26—35	25	56—65	15
36—45	14	66 & Over	16

The breakdown for education and income was not tabulated.

The occupational results were categorized into basically the same classes as those used by Howard Kauffman and Leland Harder in their 1975 book.* The number and percent in each category were as shown in Table I.

TABLE I

Occupational Distribution of Illinois Mennonites by Sex

Occupational Class	Male No.	%	Female No.	%	% of Male & Female
Professional and Technical Workers	78	26	63	29.7	27
Business Owners and Managers	21	7	3	1.4	5
Sales and Clerical Workers	19	6	25	11.8	8.6
Craftsmen and Foremen	39	13	0	.0	7.6
Machine Operators	7	2	0	.0	1.3
Laborers (Farm and Non-farm)	21	7	0	.0	4
Farm Owners and Managers	76	25	5	2.4	16
Service Workers	18	6	24	11.3	8.2
Housewives	0	0	64	30.2	12.4
Students	3	1	0	.0	.6
Retired	20	7	28	13.2	9.3
Totals	302	100.	212	100.0	100.0
N=514					

Comparison of the 1980 occupational distribution of Illinois Mennonites with Kauffman and Harder's early-1970s study of Mennonites across North America suggests considerable movement of Illinois Mennonites into the professional and technical job category, especially among women in the areas of nursing and education. Percentages owning and managing businesses are about the same, but in the 1980 Illinois study higher percentages were working in sales, in clerical work, as craftsmen, as foremen, and as laborers. Additionally, among Illinois Mennonites in 1980 a greater percent of both men and women were farm owners or managers than among Mennonites churchwide in the early 1970s.

*J. Howard Kauffman and Leland Harder, *Anabaptists Four Centuries Later* (1975), p. 60.

Regarding income, very few Illinois persons in the retired category reported an income above the $9,999 level. Second, those with incomes of $20,000 and above were mostly business persons, farmers, accountants, physicians, and dentists. Persons checking the $60,000 category were from the medical profession and from farming. Table II indicates income distribution.

TABLE II

Income Distribution of Illinois Mennonites, 1979

Income Level	No.	Percent
$ 5—9,999	78	18.2
$10—14,999	109	25.5
$15—19,999	84	19.6
$20—29,999	99	23.1
$30—39,999	27	6.3
$40—49,999	14	3.2
$50—59,999	9	2.1
$60 and over	8	2.1
Median income $15,928		N=428
Mean income $19,725		

Compared to Kauffman and Harder's study, the percentage of persons among the Illinois Mennonites completing eighth grade, high school, and college, and earning a graduate degree was considerably higher than among the three groups churchwide a decade earlier. Table III offers the 1980 Illinois data.

TABLE III

Educational Attainment Among Illinois Mennonites, 1980

Level Completed	No	Percent
Eighth Grade	58	12.8
High School	171	37.6
Two Years of College or Training	84	18.5
Four Years of College	100	21.9
Master's Degree	31	6.8
Doctorate	11	2.4
Totals	455	100.0
Median number of years completed	12.0	
Mean educational level attained	13.36	

Among the Illinois Mennonites, those completing at least an eighth-grade level of education is at 12.2 percent, while churchwide among the three groups of Mennonites in 1972 it was 9.7 percent. Those completing only high school is 37.6 percent versus 26.4; those earning at least a college degree is at 21.9 percent compared to 9.9. The number earning a graduate degree is about the same, 9.2 percent compared to 8.2. The median number of years attained in school is also about the same, 12.0 versus 12.2. The mean educational level attained by Illinois Mennonites is 13.36. Of course, one might expect a bit higher educational level in 1980 than in the early 1970s.

APPENDIX B

Illinois Mennonite Congregations and Leaders

Compiled by Steven R. Estes

Key
Dates in parentheses indicate years of person's life; b. indicates "born," d. indicates "died."
bp, followed by dates: years as a resident bishop.
d, followed by dates: years as a deacon.
e, followed by dates: years as an elder.
f.s., followed by dates: conference field secretary acting as overseer in absence of a bishop.
l, followed by dates: years as lay minister or lay leader.
Dates with no further designation indicate years of service as a minister.
Asterisk (*) indicates non-residence in the congregation.

Explanatory Note
This appendix was compiled from a variety of sources including correspondence, interviews, *The Mennonite Yearbook* (1905ff.), *The Central Conference Yearbook* (1922-1957), *Year Book of the Central District Conference* (1957ff.), *Annual Report and Directory* (EMC, 1926ff.), and *The Meadows Home Round Robin and Family Bulletin* (1977ff.). Books consulted include C. Henry Smith's *Mennonites of America* (1909), William B. Weaver's *History of the Central Conference Mennonite Church* (1926), Harry F. Weber's *Centennial History of the Mennonites of Illinois, 1829-1929* (1931), and various congregational histories.

Full information is not available on every ordained person, but the researcher has tried to work as thoroughly as possible. Approximate dates are marked with "ca." (circa: about).

Usually, addresses of congregations are original ones, from the time the congregations were established. In some cases the modern address was not available.

Thanks are due the gracious persons who responded to the researcher's various requests for information, especially a letter of inquiry sent in 1979 to each Mennonite congregation in Illinois. Those good people and both Willard and Verna Smith helped make this compilation as complete as it is.

531

BEACHY AMISH MENNONITE

Pleasant View Church
Arthur, Illinois
Org. 1957

Simon G. Gingerich (1912-): 1957-1960s
Samuel E. Petersheim (1913-): 1957-1959; bp, 1959-
Menno B. Kuhns (1927-): d, 1957-
Dannie Diener

CENTRAL CONFERENCE MENNONITE CHURCH

(Note: Listed here are only those Central Conference Mennonite congregations which discontinued before the merger, in 1957, of the Central Conference Mennonite Church with the Middle District Conference (GC) to form the present Central District Conference (GC). Other congregations that began as Central Conference congregations are listed under Central District Conference, immediately below.)

Anchor Mennonite Church
near Anchor, Illinois
Org. June 10, 1894; discont. June 12, 1953

Aaron Augspurger (1865-1953): Jan. 10, 1894-1900; bp, 1900-1929
Samuel Ummel (1892-1969): 1, 1929-1933; 1933-1934
Roy Unzicker (1905-): 1, 1929-1933; 1933-1942; e, May 3, 1942-June 12, 1953.
Benjamin Esch (1887-1971): bp*, 1951-1952

Danvers Mennonite Church
(formerly Hessian Amish congregation and South Danvers
Mennonite Church (1841-1915)
Danvers, Illinois
Org. 1841; discont. 1943, when merged with North Danvers Mennonite Church

John Michael Kistler (1808-1876): 1841-1862; bp, 1862-1863
Peter Naffziger (1789-1885): bp, ca. 1850-ca. 1860
Christian Naffziger (1803-1893): 1853-1893
Christian Gingerich (1820-1908): 1862-1963; bp, 1863-1908
Michael Kinsinger (1814-1895): 1862-1895
Kilian Kennel (1832-1923): d, ca. 1866-1871
John Gingerich (1856-1931): Sept., 1885-1893; bp, 1893-1922
John Kinsinger (1854-1930): Sept., 1885-1893; bp, 1893-1922
Lawrence B. Haigh (1881-1963): 1921-Jan., 1922; July, 1922-Sept. 1, 1923
Harvey E. Nunemaker (1893-1972): 1, Mar., 1924-Mar. 29, 1925; bp, Mar. 29, 1925-Jan. 16, 1927
Vinora Weaver (1895-): 1, Jan. 1927-Apr., 1927
Peter D. Naffziter (1884-1954): September 1, 1927-June 29, 1930; e, June 29, 1930-1933
Roy F. Scott: 1933-Apr. 14, 1936
Frank McNutt: Sept. 12, 1937-June 1, 1938
Emanuel Troyer (1871-1941): f.s.*, 1937-June 30, 1941
Robert David Sommer (1920-): Summer, 1941
Melvin Hendricks (1911-): 1, Fall, 1941-Mar. 1, 1942; Mar. 1, 1942-Jan. 17, 1943
Allen Yoder (1874-1969)[1]:f.s.*, 1943

East White Oak Mennonite Church
Route 1, Carlock, Illinois; Org.
Fall, 1892; discont.[2] Nov. 11, 1934

---

1. Although not an Illinois resident, Allen Yoder, as Central Conference field secretary, took pastoral responsibility for the Danvers Mennonite Church in 1943.
2. Date of termination of conference affiliation.

Peter Schantz (1853-1925): 1892-
1900; bp, 1900-1910
Emanuel Troyer (1871-1942): April
21, 1899-1911; bp, 1911-1928
Earl Salzman (1895-1961): Nov. 24,
1920-1927
Reuben J. Zehr (1899-1972):
July 15, 1928-1930; e, 1930-
Nov. 11, 1934

*Chicago Mennonite Gospel Mission
formerly Mennonite Home Chapel
6201 Carpenter Street, Chicago,
Illinois
Founded June 20, 1909; discont.
1948*

Albert B. Rutt (1879-1962): Jan. 20,
1909-Apr. 9, 1912; bp, Apr. 9, 1912-
Jan. 2, 1917
Jacob Sommers (1878-1953): 1911-
1914
David D. Augspurger (1853-1935):
Jan. 2, 1917-June 25, 1918
Jacob Sommers (1878-1953): Jan. 2,
1917-June 25, 1918
LeRoy D. Hartzler (1881-1925): Jan. 2,
1917-June 25, 1918
Edmund T. Rowe (b. 1885): June 25,
1918-Oct. 1, 1929
Albert B. Michaelson: Oct., 1929-Apr.,
1933
Walter Guth: May 28, 1933-July 18,
1934
Lee J. Lantz (1873-1970): Aug. 5,
1934-Sept. 3, 1944
Robert David Sommer (1920-): Oct. 1,
1944-Aug. 11, 1946
Harold Thiessen (1922-): Sept., 1946-
Dec. 21, 1947

*Oak Grove Sunday School
near Hopedale, Illinois
Org. 1909; discont. 1916*

Aaron D. Egli (b. 1890): lay sup't,
1909-1916

*Spring Bay Sunday School
near Spring Bay, Illinois*

Org. ca. 1912; discont. between
1914-1928

Valentine Strubhar (1859-1941): ca.
1912-by 1928*

*South Washington Mennonite
Church near Washington, Illinois
Org. June 24, 1894; discont.
July 18, 1937*

Michael Kinsinger (1849-1912): June
24, 1894-1911
Christian Imhoff (1861-1899): Sept.
14, 1898-Sept. 17, 1899
Albert B. Cooper: d, 1908-by 1913
John Kennel (1877-1932): 1912-1932
Emil A. Sommer (b. 1884): 1934-1936
Allen Miller (1870-1950): 1936-1937

*Twenty-Sixth Street Mission
720 W. Twenty-sixth Street,
Chicago, Illinois
Org. Sept. 24, 1906 (MC); discont.
1942; (joined CC August 28, 1923)*

Amos M. Eash (1882-1952): supt.,
Sept. 24, 1906-Sept., 1909; Sept.
1909-1919, 1921-1936
Nelson Litwiller (1898-): Sept. 1920-
Sept. 1921
Vernon J. Sprunger: 1936-1937
Cleophas Harold Eash (1906-): 1937-
1939
Carl John Landes (1904-1972): Oct. 1,
1939-Jan., 1941
Victor Bendson: Feb. 16, 1941-1942

*Weston Congregation[3]
near Weston, Illinois
Org. 1866; discont. 1891*

Joseph Baechler: 1866-ca. 1871
Andrew Baechler (1798-1874): 1866-
1874
John Rupp (1824-1913): 1866-1872
Simon Baechler (1834-1921): 1866-
1891

---

3. Never an official member of the Central Conference Mennonite Church because it discontinued before the Central Conference was founded, but was part of the Stuckey Amish group from 1872 until its discontinuance.

Joseph Stuckey (1826-1902): bp*, 1870-1891

CENTRAL DISTRICT CONFERENCE (GC)

Bethel Mennonite Church
Route 2, Pekin, Illinios
Org. Aug. 6, 1905

David D. Augspurger (1853-1935): 1890-1892
Peter Schantz (1853-1925): 1892-1898*
Valentine Strubhar (1853-1941): 1892-1898*; bp* 1905-1914
Moses D. Ropp (1851-1913): 1898-1900
Peter W. Ropp (1845-1921): 1900-1907
Allen H. Miller (1870-1950): Aug. 6, 1905-1914; bp, 1914-Oct. 1, 1930
Frank R. Mitchell (1896-1972): 1924
Benjamin Esch (1887-1971): 1930-1931
Vernon Strubhar: 1930-1931
Joseph H. King (1861-1935): 1931-1932
Emil A. Sommer (1884-1957): 1933-1934
Samuel Ummel (1892-1969): Feb. 27, 1934-1946
Frank R. Mitchell (1896-1972): 1946-1947
Ernest Hostetler (1894-1968): 1947
Paul DeMuth: 1948-1949
Benno Toews: 1948-1949
Lloyd W. Gundy (1926-): 1, May 1, 1949-1954
William B. Weaver (1887-1963): 1953-1954
Roy Henry (1946-): Oct. 26, 1954-1957
Samuel T. Moyer (1893-): 1957-1967
Grant Noll (1932-): 1967-1974
Paul Dahlenburg: 1974-1979
Lawrence Reel (1944-): 1, 1979-1980
Mel Friesen (1945-): 1980-

Boynton Mennonite Church
Hopedale, Illinois
Org. Sept. 15, 1901

Peter Schantz (1853-1925): 1901-1908
John W. Litwiller (1874-1955): 1908-1922
Wilmer Shelly (1893-): June-Dec. 1920
Lester Homer Bixel (1890-1934): 1, 1921-1924
Frank R. Mitchell (1896-1972): 1924-1927
Ernest Hostetler (1894-1968): 1924-1945
Willard Wieker (d. 1967): 1945
Maynard Shelly (1925-): Sept. 15, 1946-July 10, 1950
Melvin Funk (1919-): 1, Oct. 15, 1950-Nov. 11, 1951; Nov. 11, 1951-Sept. 1, 1953
Paul Dyck (1926-): Sept. 1953-1954
Joseph W. Davis (1895-): 1954
William B. Weaver (1887-1963): 1954-1960
Louis L. Miller (1886-1981): Jan.-May, 1961
Harvey E. Nunemaker (1893-1972): 1961-1965
Samuel Ummel (1892-1969): 1965-1969
Melvin Norquist (1916-): 1969
Ivan Kauffmann (1922-): 1968
Edward Springer (1939-): 1968-1972
Herschel Thompson: 1972-1976
Donald Hochmuth (1953-): 1976-1977
Herbert Dalke (1918-): 1977-

Calvary Mennonite Church
formerly East Washington
Mennonite Church
115 East Jefferson Street,
Washington, Illinois
Org. May, 1866

Joseph Stuckey (1826-1902): bp*, 1864-1875
Peter Stuckey (1844-1929): Nov., 1868-1875; bp, 1875-Feb. 1889
Peter Guengerich (1825-1898): Nov., 1868-1880
Jacob Unzicker (1808-1893): 1869-1893
Michael Kinsinger (1849-1912): June 10, 1890-1892; bp, ca. 1892-1894
David D. Augspurger (1853-1935): June 10, 1890-1892
Valentine Strubhar (1859-1941): Jan.

Congregations and Leaders 535

10, 1893-ca. 1900; bp. ca. 1900-Apr. 14, 1935
Benjamin Esch (1887-1971): Jan. 14, 1911-July 17, 1938; e, July 17, 1938-1951
Harry Yoder (1904-): 1951-Dec. 1, 1955
William Klassen: May, 1956-Aug. 8, 1956
Heinz Janzen (1927-): Aug., 1956-1965
Ward W. Shelly (1914-): 1965-1979
Walter Dyck (1908-): 1979-1980
Gary Stenson (1934-): Aug., 1980-
Robert Sprunger (1956-): Jan. 15, 1981

Carlock Mennonite Church
217 East Washington St., P.O. Box 41, Carlock, Illinois
Org. Apr. 14, 1914

Joseph H. King (1861-1935): Apr. 14, 1914-June 6, 1920
Warren S. Shelly (1885-1956): June 6, 1920-July 1, 1927
Raymond L. Hartzler (b. 1893): Apr. 1, 1928-Dec. 20, 1931; e, Dec. 20, 1931-1941
Harry Yoder (1904-): 1941-1946
Lotus E. Troyer (1915-): 1946-1952
David Habegger (1925-): 1952-Jan. 1, 1955
Stanley Bohn (1930-): Jan.-May, 1955
Ernest Hostetler (1894-1968): 1955-1956
Paul N. Roth (1900-1979): 1956-1966
James L. Dunn (1941-): 1966-1969
Elmer Wall (1929-): 1971-
Walter Dyck (1908-):. 1971-1977
George Classen (1917-): 1979-

Community Mennonite Church
16200 South Kedzie Ave., Markham, Illinois
Org. Mar., 1957

Ronald Allan Krehbiel (1931-): 1957-1969
Lawrence Voth (1934-): 1961-1973
Edward Springer: 1973-1977
Menno Ediger (1928-): 1978-
Margaretha Ediger (1926-): 1978-

Congerville Mennonite Church
P.O. Box 96, Congerville, Illinois
Org. Jan., 1896

Lee J. Lantz (1873-1970): Apr., 1899-Jan., 1908
George Gundy (1880-1951): Oct. 4, 1909-Jan. 1, 1925
Reuben J. Zehr (1899-1972): Jan. 1, 1925-1928
Joseph H. King (1861-1935): 1928-1935
John F. Smith: 1935-1941
Robert David Sommer (1920-): June 21, 1941-Aug., 1941
Paul Tschetter: 1941-1945
Raymond Yoder (1914-): 1946-1957
Joseph Atherton (1921-): 1957-1967
David Loewen: 1967-1970
Jerry Quiring: 1970-1971
J. Leon Martin: 1971-1981
Lawrence Reel (1944-): 1, 1981
Brian Arbuckle: Dec. 1981-

First Mennonite Church[4]
(founded as a rescue mission Oct. 1, 1914)
1477 West 73rd Street, Chicago, Illinois
Org. Dec. 11, 1921

W. W. Miller (1858-1941): Mar. 5, 1914-Apr. 1919, Oct. 1, 1920-June 3, 1923
J. F. Balzer: Apr.-July, 1919; June-Oct., 1920
Warren S. Shelly (1885-1956): July, 1919-June 2, 1920
M. M. Lehmann: June 3, 1923-Aug., 1927
William Clyde Rhea: Jan. 1, 1928-Mar., 1934
Amos Hershey Leaman (1878-1950): Sept. 16, 1934-Sept. 15, 1940; Mar. 1, 1946-Nov. 13, 1949
Erwin A. Albrecht (1906-): Sept. 15, 1940-Jan. 1, 1946
Paul McElfresh: 1, Jan. 1, 1946-Mar.

---
4. Member of former Middle District Conference (GC).

1, 1946; Nov. 13, 1949-Feb. 6, 1950;
Oct. 15, 1961-June 3, 1962
Aaron J. Epp: Feb. 6, 1950-June 18,
1952
Leland D. Harder (1926-): June 18,
1952-July 1, 1957
Robert Coon (1931-): July 1, 1957-Oct.
15, 1961
Harry Spaeth: June 3, 1962-June,
1968
Arthur L. Jackson: 1968-1973
John H. Burke, Jr.: 1973-

*First Mennonite Church
918 South University Street,
Normal, Illinois
Org. March 27, 1912; discont. 1976
(merged with Bloomington
Mennonite Church to form
Mennonite Church of Normal)*

Peter Schantz (1853-1925): July,
1911-June, 1912
Lee J. Lantz (1873-1970): June, 1912-
June, 1918
LeRoy D. Hartzler (1881-1925): June,
1918-1919
Andrew S. Bechtel (1874-1968): Apr.
13, 1919-Oct., 1920
William Henry Grubb (1879-1940):
May 1, 1921-Feb. 29, 1928
Emanuel Troyer (1871-1942): May 1,
1928-May 24, 1936
Irvin R. Detweiler (1873-1946): June
1, 1936-Sept. 1941
Alvin J. Beachy (1913-): June 14,
1942-Sept., 1946
Harvey Leonard Metzker (1911-): Jan.,
1947-Dec. 1953
Henry N. Harder (1905-): Sept. 1,
1954-Oct. 1, 1963
Ernest Bohn (1894-): Jan., 1964-June,
1964
Walter Gering (1908-): Sept. 6, 1964-
Sept., 1970
J. Leon Martin: Sept., 1970-Aug., 1971
James Waltner (1931-): Sept., 1972-
Sept., 1976

*First Mennonite Church
Oak Park, Illinois
Org. 1980*

David Whitermore: 1980-1981
Ardean Goertzen: Oct. 18, 1981-

*First Mennonite Church[5]
Summerfield, Illinois
Org. Apr. 1, 1861*

Christian Detweiler (1799-1879):
1856-1858
Johannes Schmidt (1795-1870):
1858-1864
Daniel Hege (1826-1862): 1859-1862
Daniel Hirschler (1821-1888): 1861-
1864
Jacob E. Krehbiel (1829-1896): 1863-
1890
Christian Krehbiel (1832-1909):
1864-1865; bp, 1865-1879
Carl H. A. van der Smissen (1851-
1950): 1890-1911
John B. Baer (1854-1939): 1911-1918
Peter J. Boehr: 1911-1914
? Plassman: 1919-1920
Grover Soldner (1892-1981): 1920-
1923
Franz Voelker (1872-1925): ?
Andrew S. Bechtel (1874-1968): 1923-
1928
Delbert E. Welty (1896-1979): 1928-
1930
Adolph Friesen (b. 1897): 1930-1936
Elmer Basinger (1882-1958): 1936-
1948
Rollin Oswald: 1948-1949
David Habegger (1925-): 1948-1949
Andrew S. Bechtel (1874-1968): 1948-
1949
Henry B. Grimm (1921-): 1949-1955
Walter Neufeld: 1955
Donald Gross Wismer (1931-): 1956
Ernest Neufeld (1932-): 1956-1960
Harold Thiessen (1922-): 1960-1968
Carl O. Basinger (1920-1972): 1969-
1970
George C. Dick (1907-): 1971
Lotus E. Troyer (1915-) 1971-1972
George C. Dick (1907-): 1972-

---

5. Member of former Middle District Conference (GC).

*First Mennonite Church of
Champaign-Urbana*[6]
*formerly Inter-Mennonite
Fellowship (1961)*
*912 W. Springfield Road, Urbana,
Illinois*
Org. 1964

Richard Yordy (1922-): July, 1965-Aug., 1969
James L. Dunn (1941-): Jan., 1970-Dec. 31, 1979
Peter Dyck (1948-): Mar. 8, 1981-
Sheryl Dyck (1951-): Mar. 8, 1981-

*Flanagan Mennonite Church
Box 217, Flanagan, Illinois
Org. Fall, 1878*

Christian Rediger (1849-1938): 1878-1885; bp, 1885-Dec. 1885
William Egle (1860-1944): Apr. 1883-1887
Stephen Stahly (1842-1916): 1885-1887; bp, 1887-1916
Joseph B. Zehr (1853-1940): 1887-Oct., 1890; bp, Oct. 19, 1890-1934
Emanuel C. Ulrich (1890-1961): May 26, 1918-1934; bp, 1934-June 1, 1958; pastor emeritus, Sept. 4, 1958-Mar. 10, 1961.
Marvin Zehr (1936-): 1, 1958
Earl Salzman (1895-1961): Sept. 15, 1958-July 30, 1961
Robert Coon (1931-): Oct. 18, 1961-Aug. 22, 1965
Donald Nester (1936-): Dec. 19, 1965-May 21, 1972
Lotus E. Troyer (1915-): July 1, 1972-
Steven R. Estes (1956-): 1, June 1, 1980-Nov. 1980; June 1, 1982-Aug. 15, 1982

Grace Community Church[7]
*formerly The Mennonite Bible
Mission*

*4221 South Rockwell St., Chicago,
Illinois
Org. 1917*

Abram F. Wiens (1868-1937): Nov. 1917-Jan. 10, 1937
John T. Neufeld (1895-1961): Feb. 23, 1936-Apr. 9, 1961; pastor emeritus, Apr. 9, 1961-July 13, 1961
Jack D. Kressly (1919-): 1, 1958-Apr. 9, 1961; Apr. 9, 1961-July 1, 1963
Grant Noll (1932-): July 1, 1964-July 1, 1967
Alvin Voth (1904-): Oct., 1967-Mar., 1976
Lee Hochstetler (1938-): July, 1976-
Betty Hochstetler (1943-): July, 1976-
Mark Winslow (1952-): Sept., 1979-

*Meadows Mennonite Church
Route One, Chenoa, Illinois
Org. Jan. 2, 1890*

Andrew Vercler (1850-1928): Aug. 30, 1891-Oct. 23, 1897; bp, Oct. 23, 1897-1925
Joseph Kinsinger (1855-1925): Aug. 30, 1891-Oct. 23, 1897; bp, Oct. 23, 1897-1925
Aaron Roszhart (1887-1918): 1916-1918
George I. Gundy (1880-1951): 1925-1951
Frank R. Mitchell (1896-1972): 1952
Lotus E. Troyer (1915-): 1952-1965
Bruno Penner (1928-): 1966-1975
Lotus E. Troyer (1915-): 1976
Leo L. Miller (1926-): 1976-

Mennonite Church of Normal[8]
*merger of First Mennonite Church
of Normal and Bloomington
Mennonite Church
603 South Cottage Street, Normal,
Illinois
Org. 1976*

---

6. Dual conference congregation, member of Central District Conference (GC) and Illinois Mennonite Conference (MC).

7. Member of former Middle District Conference (GC).

8. Dual conference congregation, member of Central District Conference (GC) and Illinois Mennonite Conference (MC).

James Waltner (1931-): Sept., 1976-
Carl K. Newswanger (1941-): Sept., 1976-June 1979
Margaret Richer Smith (1951-): Oct., 1979-
Mary Lehman Yoder (1953-): June 22, 1981-

*Mennonite Gospel Church
formerly Mennonite Gospel Mission (CC)
1001 N.E. Adams Street, Peoria, Illinois
Org. July 19, 1914; merged with Ann Street Mennonite Church to form United Mennonite Church of Peoria, in 1971*

Jacob Sommer (1878-1953): 1914-Dec. 14, 1931; e, Dec. 14, 1931-Mar. 1, 1939
Frank McNutt: June 1, 1938-1940
Frank R. Mitchell (1896-1972): 1940-1945
Samuel Ummel (1892-1969): 1945-May 16, 1948; e, May 16, 1948-1962
Melvin Norquist (1916-): 1945-Dec. 1968
Walter Regier: 1968-1971

*North Danvers Mennonite Church
formerly Rock Creek Amish Mennonite Congregation
Box 217, Danvers, Illinois
Org. Fall, 1851*

Jonathan Yoder (1795-1869): bp, 1851-1869
Isaac Schmucker (1810-1893): bp, 1851-Aug., 1852
Michael Miller (1795-1873): d, 1851-1873
Jacob Miller (1811-1893): d, 1851-1893
Jonas Fry (1806-1872): 1853-1872
Johannes Koenig (ca. 1795-ca. 1860): 1854-ca. 1860
John Miller (1783-1859): bp, 1855-1859
Joseph Stalter (1807-1888): 1855-ca. 1875
Joseph Stuckey (1826-1902): Apr. 8, 1860-Apr. 26, 1864; bp, Apr. 26, 1864-Feb., 1902
John Strubhar (1808-1883): d, Apr. 8, 1860-1883
John Stahly (1827-1900): bp, 1864-1900
Christian Miller: by 1866-?
Michael King (1806-1872): by 1866-1872
Christian Imhoff (1838-1881): d, 1867-1881
Peter Schantz (1853-1925): Sept. 18, 1881-1892
Joash Stutzman (1853-1891): Sept. 18, 1881-Sept., 1891
Joseph H. King (1861-1935): Apr. 17, 1892-Apr. 29, 1900; bp, Apr. 29, 1900-Apr., 1914
Joseph J. Clark (b. 1861): Apr. 17, 1892-Jan., 1893
John P. Kohler (1859-1930): Apr. 30, 1899-Apr. 29, 1900; bp, Apr. 29, 1900-1921
Millard O. Rose: 1919
Lawrence B. Haigh (1881-1963): Jan., 1922-July 1, 1922
William B. Weaver (1887-1963): July 1, 1922-Sept. 11, 1927; bp, Sept. 11, 1927-June 30, 1952
Harris Waltner (1925-): 1, Oct. 12, 1952-Nov. 30, 1952
Hugo Mierau (1916-1972): Dec. 1, 1952-Dec. 1, 1955
Arnold Funk (b. 1900): Sept. 23, 1956-Jan. 14, 1962
Benjamin W. Krahn (1928-): Mar.-Apr., 1962
Frank Zacharias (1930-): May-Oct., 1962
Samuel Ummel (1892-1969): Nov.-Dec., 1962
Herbert Miller (1908-): Jan. 20, 1963-Sept. 26, 1965
Raymond L. Hartzler (1893-): Oct. 17, 1965-June, 1966
George C. Dick (1907-): June 26, 1966-June 28, 1970
Wilbur Nachtigall (1918-): Sept. 5, 1970-July 25, 1971
Elmer Wall (1929-): Aug. 8, 1971-
Walter Dyck (1908-): Sept. 19, 1971-Sept. 1, 1977
George Classen (1917-): July 1, 1979-

Plow Creek Fellowship[9]
Route 2, Tiskilwa, Illinois
Org. 1971

Conrad Wetzel (1931-): 1971-

Tiskilwa Mennonite Church
Tiskilwa, Illinois
Org. Nov. 23, 1911

Eugene Augspurger (1874-1944): June 12, 1912-Sept., 1920
Frank Mitchell (1896-1972): 1920-1921
John Wiens: 1921
P. V. Hutchins: 1922
Benjamin Esch (1887-1971): 1923
Henry Fast: 1924
E. G. Hutchinson: 1924-1925
Ernest J. Bohn (1894-): 1, Sept. 20, 1925-Aug. 15, 1926; Aug. 15, 1926-1930; e, 1930-Aug. 15, 1931
Harvey E. Nunemaker (1893-1972): Oct. 1, 1931-1941
Henry Toews: 1941-1943
L. R. Amstutz (1917-): Sept. 19, 1943-1945
Jacob Goering: 1945
Rudolph Martins: 1945-1948
Henry Grim: 1945-1948
Ernest Hostetler (1894-1968): 1945-1948
Emil A. Sommer (1884-1957): Oct. 23, 1948-Sept. 1, 1952
Benjamin Esch (1887-1971): Nov. 23, 1952-1962
James Ralph Gundy (1934-): 1966-1967
Jay M. Shelly: Dec. 1967-1969
A. E. Appelquist: Jan., 1970-Nov., 1973
Joseph Atherton (1921-): Nov., 1973-

United Mennonite Church of Peoria[10]
Merger of Ann Street Mennonite Church and Mennonite Gospel Church
2105 West Ann St., Peoria, Illinois
Org. Apr. 4, 1971

Walter Regier: 1971-1972
J. Frederick Erb (1922-): 1972-1977
Paul C. Sieber (1921-): Dec. 1977-

Woodlawn Mennonite Church
1143 E. 46 St., Chicago, Illinois
Org. Jan. 28, 1951; discont. 1972

Jesse N. Smucker (1892-): 1952-1955
Delton Franz: 1956-1967
Vincent G. Harding: Oct. 6, 1956-1958
Curtis Burrell (1932-): Jan., 1966-1972

CONSERVATIVE MENNONITE CONFERENCE

Prairie Chapel
Arthur, Illinois
Org. 1968; discont. 1977

Jesse L. Yoder (1923-): bp, 1968-1977
Levi W. Stutzman (1919-): 1968-1977

Quinn Chapel
Arthur, Illinois
Org. 1957

Henry J. Plank (1926-): Sept. 29, 1957-1968; bp, 1968-
Lyle Gross (1955-): Mar. 28, 1980-

Sunnyside Conservative Mennonite Church
Arthur, Illinois
Org. 1945

Shem Peachey (1889-1973): 1945-1947
Levi M. Miller (1913-): 1947-?
John F. Miller: 1954-?
Elmer Schwartzendruber: bp*, 1957-?
Menno H. Mast (1909-): ?
Levi W. Stutzman (1919-): 1968-1980
Jacob L. Graber: bp, July 26, 1980-
Levi A. Beachy (1943-): 1977-

---

9. Dual conference congregation, member of Central District Conference (GC) and Illinois Mennonite Conference (MC).

10. Dual conference congregation, member of Central District Conference (GC) and Illinois Mennonite Conference (MC).

EASTERN PENNSYLVANIA
MENNONITE CHURCH

Ewing Mennonite Congregation
Ewing, Illinois
Org. ca. 1971

Ministers supplied

Mt. Pleasant Mennonite Church
Anna, Illinois
Org. ca. 1960

Homer D. Bomberger (1909-): bp, 1970-1971
Isaac K. Sensenig: bp, 1970-
Phares W. Martin (1932): 1964-
David M. Weaver (1929-): d, 1964-
Jesse Neuenschwander (1933-): bp, 1980-

Orchardville Mennonite Church
Keenes, Illinois
Org. ca. 1971

Raymond F. Zimmerman, d, 1972-
Jesse Neuenschwander (1933-): bp, 1977-1980
James M. Sensenig: 1980-

EVANGELICAL MENNONITE
BRETHREN CONFERENCE

Brighton Mennonite Church
formerly Hoyne Avenue Mission
(founded Spring, 1907)
1852 W. 34th Pl., Chicago, Illinois
Org. Spring, 1907; discont. 1978

Abram F. Wiens (1868-1937): 1907-June, 1916
George P. Schultz (1880-1957): Sept. 1, 1916-1951
Edward Peters: 1951-1952
Richard Ratzlaff: 1952-1955
C. Edward Adshade: 1955-1958
Charles Miller: 1958-1963
David Brandt: May, 1964-July, 1965

Rollie Loewen: Aug. 1965-1968
James Brandt: 1968-1978

Happy Hour Mission[11]
437 State Street, Chicago, Illinois
Org. Nov. 1908; discont. Apr. 16, 1916

George P. Schultz (1880-1957): 1908-Apr. 16, 1916

EVANGELICAL MENNONITE
CHURCH

Calvary Memorial Church
formerly Salem Gospel Mission
(founded 1908)
111th Street and Roberts Road,
Palos Hills, Illinois

Joseph K. Gerig (1868-1944): 1908-1917; e, 1917-1928
Amos Oyer (1882-1931); Apr. 16, 1929-Dec. 2, 1931
Joseph K. Gerig (1868-1944): 1931-Apr. 24, 1932
C. E. Rediger (1887-1969): Apr. 24, 1932-Nov. 1934
Ivan R. Calhoun (1907-1975?): Nov. 1934-1948
C. E. Rediger (1887-1969): 1948-1949
Allen Sedgwick: 1949-1952
C. Merlin Bilhorn: 1952-1953
Richard Rupp: 1953-1955
Alan Tschiegg: 1955-1958
Clarence Fast: 1958
William T. Pauley: 1959-1963
Tillman Amstutz: 1963-1968
James Glenn: 1969-1972
Arthur Enns (1928-): 1972-

Eureka Bible Church
Eureka, Illinois
Org. 1977

Gary Hedrick: 1978-1980
John Erwin (1951-): 1981-

---

11. Joint mission sponsored by the following Mennonite groups then in Chicago: Mennonite Church, Central Conference Mennonite Church, Defenseless Mennonite Brethren, Defenseless Mennonite Conference, Krimmer Mennonite Brethren, and General Conference of Mennonites in North America.

*Grace Evangelical Mennonite
Church
1050 South Fourth Street, Morton,
Illinois
Org. June 8, 1958*

Milo Nussbaum (1924-): 1958-
Bryce Wintereg (1940-) Jan., 1973-
1976
Stephen Ford, 1976-1977
Lowell Gisel (1951-): 1977-
William C. Bennett (1912-): 1979-

*Groveland Evangelical Mennonite
Church
formerly the "Busche Gemein"
Amish Congregation
Route one, Pekin, Illinois
Org. 1837*

Michael Moseman (d. 1898): 1837-ca.
1840; bp, ca. 1840-1898
Nicholas Roth (1815-1894): by 1868-
1894
Andrew Roth (1811-1886): d.?
Peter Hochstettler (1834-1924): ca.
1870-ca. 1881; bp, ca. 1881-1924
John Detsch: ca. 1880-ca. 1881; bp,
ca. 1881-1883
Benjamin Birky (1861-1939): 1888-
1939
Joseph C. Rediger (1865-1936): 1888-
ca. 1920
Joseph Springer: ?
Christian Oyer (1862-1954): 1895-
1943
Moses D. Ropp (1851-1913): ca. 1901-
1913
Benjamin Roth: d, ca. 1911-Apr. 5,
1936
Amos Oyer (1882-1931): Apr. 11,
1920-Jan. 14, 1923
Benjamin Rupp (1862-1929): e*,
1924-1929
Emanuel Rocke (1892-1968): May 21,
1922-Sept. 9, 1934; e, Sept. 9, 1935-
Feb. 25, 1945
Daniel Ackerman (1860-1932): d,
1925-1932
David M. Zimmerman (1869-1954)
1929-Dec. 29, 1933; e, Dec. 29,
1933-1934
Elias E. Zimmerman (1891-1980): 1 d,
July 3, 1938-Nov. 14; d, Nov. 14,
1941-Aug. 1, 1973; honorary d,
Aug. 1, 1973-July 1, 1977
James Bertsche (1921-): Feb., 1945-
Sept., 1945
Paul W. Rupp (1916-): Sept., 1945-
Sept., 1954
Milo Nussbaum (1924-): Oct., 1954-
Sept., 1958
Walter McDowell: Apr., 1959-Aug.
1965
Joseph W. Davis (1895-): Aug., 1965-
Sept., 1965
Thomas Taylor: Sept., 1965-Aug.,
1972
Walter Regier: Aug. 1972-Aug. 1973
Emil J. Krahn (1929-): Aug., 1973-
1981

*Oak Grove Bible Church
Springfield Road, East Peoria,
Illinois
Org. 1955*

Paul W. Rupp (1916): Sept. 1954-

*Salem Evangelical Mennonite
Church
Route 2, Gridley, Illinois
Org. May 1866*

Joseph Rediger (1826-1904): 1866;
bp, 1866-1904
John Rediger: ca. 1866-?
Christian King: d, ?-1883; 1883-?
Christian R. Egle (1858-1926): 1883-
1893; bp, 1893-1926
Nicolas B. Stuckey (d. 1913): d, 1883-
1913
Peter Ehresman (1836-1893): d,
1883-1893
Benjamin Rupp (1862-1929): e, 1926-
1929
John Slagle (1857-1938): d, 1901-
1911
Peter P. Oyer (1850--1929): d, 1913-
1915
David N. Claudon (1867-1947): d,
1915-?
Joseph M. Gerig: d, 1915-?
Eli Oyer: 1915-1920
Christian Rediger: 1915-1920
A. C. Zimmerman: d, ?
Christian Gerig (1880-1962): d, ?

Benjamin E. Rediger (1893-1931):
   1920-Apr. 20, 1926
David W. Zimmerman (1869-1954):
   *Oct. 25, 1930-Aug. 1933
Harry E. Bertsche (1897-1971): Aug.,
   1933-Sept. 7, 1934; e, Sept. 7, 1934-1948
Ivan R. Calhoun (1907-1975): 1948-1951
Edward Enns: 1951-1955
Charles Zimmerman (1926-): 1956-1960
John Lehman: 1960-1968
Charles Rupp (1924-): 1968-1974
Earl Cecil (1946-): 1974-1975
L. R. Amstutz (1917-): Jan., 1972-
Donald Ashley: 1977-1980
Philip Watson: 1981-

ILLINOIS MENNONITE
CONFERENCE (MC)

Amity Chapel
   Claremont, Illinois
   Org. 1953; discont. 1958

Joseph I. Kauffman (1931-): 1953-1956
Kenneth G. Good (1910-): bp*, 1956-1957
J. Alton Horst (1924-): 1957-1958

Ann Street Mennonite Church
   formerly Garden Street Mission
   (founded Feb. 16, 1919)
   2105 W. Ann St., Peoria, Illinois
   Org. Oct. 29, 1922; discont. 1971
   (merged with Mennonite Gospel
   Church to form United Mennonite
   Church of Peoria)

John Roth (1884-1969):l supt., 1919
John Harnish (b. 1896): supt. 1919-1922; 1922-1925
Lloy Kniss (1897-): 1925
Earl Miller: 1925-1929
C. Warren Long (1904-1969): 1929-1949
Wilfred Ulrich (1920-): 1947-1950
Howard J. Zehr (1916-1977): 1951-1952
Jonathan J. Hostetler (1905-): 1953-1967
John Lehman (1932): 1970
Walter Regier: 1971

Arthur Mennonite Church
   710 East Park St., Arthur, Illinois
   Org. 1940

Henry J. King (1891-): Oct., 1938-Aug., 1958
Richard J. Yordy (1922-): Mar., 1948-Aug., 1950
Steve Plank (1909-): d, May 1951-ca. 1958
Theodore Wentland (1917-): Sept., 1954-1959
Richard J. Yordy (1922-): May, 1960-July, 1965
Paul Sieber (1921-): July, 1965-Nov., 1977
Glenn Richard (1916-): Aug., 1978-July, 1979
Wayne Hochstetler (1947-): Aug., 1979-

Bellevue Bible Church
   formerly Bellevue Mennonite
   Church (founded Dec., 1938),
   1943-1950.
   C.M.R. 105, Peoria, Illinois
   Org. 1943; discont. 1952 (now
   unaffiliated)

C. Warren Long (1904-1969): Dec., 1938-1940
Orie A. Miller (1908-): l, 1940-Oct. 11, 1942; Oct. 11, 1942-1952

Bethel Mennonite Church
   Chicago, Illinois
   Org. Aug., 1944

James H. Lark (1889-1978): l, Feb., 1945-Oct. 6, 1946; Oct. 6, 1946-1954; bp, 1954-1956
Paul O. King (1921-): 1953-1962
Cecil Ashley (1930-): 1960
Joseph L. Holloway: 1963-1966
Leamon Sowell (1918-): 1970-
Clarence Yutzy (1937-): 1970
Alvin Brown: 1971-1973

Bloomington Mennonite Church
1101 North Roosevelt Street,
Bloomington, Illinois
Org. 1956; 1976 merged with First Mennonite Church (Normal) to form Normal Mennonite Church

Joseph I. Kauffman (1931-): 1956-1958
Kenneth G. Good (1910-): bp*, 1956-1957
Henry J. King (1891-): 1958-1959
Harold Zehr (1903-1975): Nov. 1, 1959-1973
Carl K. Newswanger (1941-): 1973-1976

Cazenovia Mennonite Church
Cazenovia, Illinois
Org. 1949

Vernon Schertz (1925-): 1949-1955
Melvin Hamilton (1918-): 1957-1960
Wayne D. King (1931-): 1963-1966
Paul Miller (1913-): 1970-1971
Joseph Diener (1932-): 1973-1977
Valentine Swartzendruber (1909-): 1978-

(Old) Chicago Congregation
near Lincoln Park, Chicago, Illinois
Org. 1866; discont. 1871

John F. Funk (1835-1930): 1866-Apr. 6, 1867

Cullom Mennonite Church
Cullom, Illinois
Org. ca. 1860; discont. 1963

Henry Baer (1815-1870): ca. 1860-1870
Jost Bally (1795-1878): bp*, ca. 1860-Oct. 26, 1872
Abram Blosser (1842-1919): d, ca. 1865-1882
Peter Y. Lehman (1836-1925): 1870-1874
David Lehman: d, ?
John R. Snyder (1831-1920): d, 1870-1908
Emanuel M. Hartman (1849-1912): 1873-1874

Benjamin F. Hamilton: 1876-1882
Christian D. Beery (1815-1878): *1877
Peter Haun (1834-1908): d, 1908
Peter Unzicker (1859-1938): 1882-?
Peter B. Snyder (1864-1948): 1889-1894
Lewis J. Lehman: 1892-1908
Alvin K. Ropp: 1905-1908
Elias Christophel: d, 1908-1919
Samuel Honderich (1878-1971): 1909-1913
John W. McCulloh (1860-1923): Dec. 20, 1916-Jan. 3, 1923
Daniel W. Slagel (1864-1947): *1923-1926
Joseph A. Heiser (1888-1977): bp*, 1923-1951
S. Jay. Hostetler (1901-1978): Sept. 25, 1926-1928
Joseph W. Davis (1895-): 1, May, 1930-July, 1931; July, 1931-1934
Amos Hershey Leaman (1878-1950): *1934-1939; *May, 1946-Aug., 1949
Noah Roeschley (1896-1975): 1, 1939-May 1946; Aug.,. 1949-Nov. 6, 1949
Paul McElfresh: 1948
Theodore Wentland (1917-): 1, Aug. 1949-Nov. 6, 1949; Nov. 6, 1949-Jan., 1954
Arthur Reeb: 1*, 1955-1962

Dewey Mennonite Church
Box 21, Dewey, Illinois
Org. 1947

Ivan L. Birkey, (1921-): 1, 1947-Feb., 1955; Feb., 1955-

Dillon Mennonite Church
R. 2, Tremont, Illinois
Org. Sept. 14, 1952

John V. Troyer (1911-): Sept. 14, 1952-
Robert Nafziger (1951-): Jan. 6, 1980-

East Bend Mennonite Church
Box 526, Fisher, Illinois
Org. 1889

Peter Zehr (1851-1922): 1889-1893; bp, 1893-1922

Daniel Grieser (1840-1924):1890-1924
Joseph Baecher (1853-1931): 1893-1931
George Gingerich (1832-1906): bp., 1893-1906
Samuel Zehr (1870-1943): d, June, 1906-1943
Joseph A. Heiser (1888-1977): Aug. 5, 1917-May 1, 1921; bp, May 1, 1921-1951
Harold A. Zehr (1903-1975): 1931-1959
George D. Troyer (1890-1969): 1937-1944
Howard J. Zehr (1916-1977): 1952-1958
J. Alton Horst (1924-): 1958-1968
Irvin Nussbaum (1925-): 1968-1977
Wilbur Nachtigall (1918-): 1977-Sept. 1, 1980
Theodore Wentland (1917-): Sept. 1, 1980-Sept. 1, 1981
Paul King (1921-): Sept. 1, 1981-

G. Irvin Lehman: June-Sept., 1945
Earl S. Lehman (1920-): Sept., 1945-1950
John I. Byler (1881-1970): 1951-Oct., 1952
J. Otis Yoder (1914-): 1953-1954
Don Driver: June-Oct., 1954
Laurence Horst (1915-):Oct., 1954-1963
James Christophel (1932-): 1956
Wayne D. King (1931-): 1958
Stanlee D. Kauffman (1935-): 1964-1970
Lemon Sowell (1918-): 1967-1968
Maynard Brubaker: 1970
Alvin Brown: 1970-1971
Clarence Yutzy (1937-): 1971
Patrick Hunt (1948-): 1971
Ambers Wright (1922-): 1971-1979
Paul Smith: 1976-1977
Louis Hagans: 1977-
Charles Snipes: 1981-

Englewood Mennonite Church formerly Chicago Home Mission (founded 1893)/Union Avenue Mennonite Church
832 West 68th St., Chicago, Illinois
Org. 1903

Menno S. Steiner (1866-1911): 1893-1894
Samuel F. Coffman (1872-1954): 1894-Mar. 5, 1896; 1896-1897
Noah Metzler: 1897
A. I. Yoder: 1897
Amos Hershey Leaman (1878-1950): Supt., Sept., 1897-Apr. 7, 1902; Apr. 7, 1902-1920
Henry R. Schertz (1886-1954): Sept. 1920-June 1923
Simon M. Kanagy (1869-1941):1923-1932
Peter A. Friesen (1879-1967): 1932-1938
Josephus W. Shank (1881-1970): 1932-1933
Edwin Weaver (1903-): 1932-1938
Levi C. Hartzler (1909-): 1932-1933
Nelson Litwiller (1898-): 1933-1934
Raymond Yoder (1914-): Jan., 1938-June, 1945

Evanston Mennonite Church formerly Mennonite Fellowship (founded 1958)
736 Dobson Street, Evanston, Illinois
Org. Feb. 26, 1961

Ronald Goetz: Oct., 1961-June, 1963
Lawrence M. Horst (1915-): July, 1963-Aug., 1969
Albert George: Sept., 1969
LeRoy Kennel (1930): Sept. 1969
James Lehman: July, 1970-May, 1971
James A. Burkholder (1934-): Oct., 1971-Apr., 1973
Jean Hostetler (1948-): 1, 1975-1976
Janelle Landis: 1, 1977
Karen Martin: 1, 1978-1980

First Mennonite Church
111 Greenwood St., Morton, Illinois
Org. 1941 (merger of Plesant Grove and Goodfield Mennonite Church

Simon Litwiller (1880-1956): bp* 1941-1956
Jonas Litwiller (1865-1944): 1941-1944
Harold Oyer (1905-1961): 1941-1943
Leland Bachman (1907-): 1941-1947

Joseph W. Davis (1895-): 1943-1947
Noah Roeschley (1896-1975): 1948-1952
Kenneth Good (1910-): 1953-1961
Clyde Fulmer (1931-): 1961-1972
Milo Kauffman (1898-): 1973-1974
Mahlon D. Miller (1931-): 1974-1977
James Detweiler (1926-): 1978-

First Norwood Mennonite Church
6605 Jones Road, Peoria, Illinois
Org. 1959

Lester Sutter (1924-): 1959-1976
Vernon Isner (1944-): 1976-

Freeport Mennonite Church
Route 3, Freeport, Illinois
Org. ca. 1845

Martin Lapp (1801-1875): 1845-1855; 1869-1875
Samuel Lapp (1803-1877): d, 1845-Oct. 24, 1877
John Brubaker (1794-1855): 1848-1855
Matthais Eby (1809-1894): 1855-?; bp, ?-1875
Christian Snyder (1819-1872): 1864-1872
Christian Snavely (1831-1905): 1875-1905
David Ebersole (1844-1899): d, 1877-1899
Ephraim Shellenberger (1837-1919): 1878-1887; 1909-1919
Joseph S. Lehman (1847-1936): 1887-1892
Joseph S. Shoemaker (1845-1936): 1892-1902; bp, 1902-1936
John V. Fortner (1854-1946): 1899-1946
Simon Graybill (1873-1941): 1903-1941
William Pfile (b. 1885): d, 1936-1963
Howard J. Zehr (1916-1977): 1941-1950
Richard Yordy (1922-): 1950-1960
Donald Blosser (1937-): 1960-1969
Paul King (1921-): 1970-Sept. 1, 1981

Gardner Mennonite Church
Gardner, Illinois
Org. 1863; discont. 1885

John G. Bachman (1799-1870);1863-1870
Jost Bally (1795-1878): bp*, 1863-Oct. 26, 1872
John F. Funk (1835-1930): May 28, 1865-Apr., 1867
Henry L. Shelly: May 28, 1865-1885
A. Bachman: d, by 1876-ca. 1885

Germantown Mennonite Church
formerly Germantown Mission
C.M.R. 119, East Peoria, Illinois
Org. 1949; discont. ca. 1972

Wayne D. King (1931-): 1965-1970
Donald Schmidt: 1971

Gibson City Mennonite Church
Gibson City, Illinois
Org. 1949; discont. ca. 1972

Roy Ingold (1899-1967): 1958-1967

Goodfield Mennonite Church
formerly Mackinaw Meeting (ca. 1838-1872)
(Merged with Pleasant Grove Mennonite Church to form First Mennonite Church, 1941)
Near Goodfield, Illinois
Org. 1873; discont. 1941

Peter Farni (1797-1873): bp, ca. 1838-1843
Christian Farni (b. ca. 1800): ca. 1838-1843
? Barnhardt (d. 1846): bp, 1843-1846
Christian Ropp (1812-1896): 1840-1846; bp, 1846-1896
Jonathan Yoder (1795-1869): bp, 1851
Isaac Schmucker (1810-1893): bp, 1851
Daniel Zehr (1803-1855): bp, 1853-1855
Jacob Zehr (1825-1898): June 12, 1859-May 20, 1863; bp, May 20, 1863-1893
Christian Reeser, Sr. (1819-1923): 1867-1923

Peter Zehr (1851-1922): 1883-1889
Christian King (1840-1924): 1889-1924
Solomon Yoder: 1889-ca. 1890
Andrew Schrock (1863-1949): *1894-1898; bp*, 1898-1941
Daniel Zehr (1849-1942): 1895-1942
Samuel Gerber (1863-1929): bp, 1911-1929
Jacob Zehr (1875-1929): 1912-1929
Earl Miller: ?
Harold Oyer (1905-1961): 1931-1941

Harmony Mennonite Church
6 miles north of Eureka, Illinois
Started 1902; discont. 1929

Ministers same as those of Roanoke and Metamora congs.

Highway Village Mennonite Church
125 Norwood Place, East Peoria, Illinois
Org. 1935

Carl A. Magnusen (1894-1975): 1937-1945
Wilfred Ulrich (1920-): 1945-1947
Paul A. Friesen (1923-): 1947-1951
Robert A. Harnish (1925-): 1951-1973
Clarence R. Sutter (1921-): 1973-

Hopedale Mennonite Church
formerly Delavan Prairie Amish
Mennonite Congregation
Route One, Hopedale, Illinois
Org. 1854

Andrew Ropp (1807-1890): bp*, 1854-1860
John Sutter (1795-1887): 1854-1887
Christian Nafziger (1819-1899): 1855-1861; bp, 1861-1899
Andrew Baechler (1798-1874): 1855-1866
Simon Baechler (1834-1921): 1864-1866
Noah Augspurger (1817-1903): by 1866-1903
Joseph Litwiller (1800-1884): d, ?-1884
Johannes Egly: by 1872-after 1878
William Unzicker: ?

Joseph Hochstetler: ?
John Nafziger: by 1871-?
Andrew Birky: ?
Joseph Birky: ?
Joseph Springer (1837-1902): 1885-1890
Jacob Unzicker: ?
Daniel Grieser: ?
Joseph Egli (1852-1915): 1891-1915
John Egli: 1892-?
Daniel Nafziger (1860-1934): Mar. 17, 1892-Nov. 16, 1934
John C. Birky, bp, 1896-1920
Samuel Gerber (1862-1929): bp*, 1920-1925
Simon Litwiller (1880-1956): 1910-1925; bp, 1925-1956
Benjamin Springer (1881-1968): 1921-1965
Ivan J. Kauffmann (1922-): 1949-1971
Wilbur Nachtigall (1918-): 1969-1970
Lee J. Miller (1907-): 1972-1974
Aden J. Yoder (1925-): 1975-
Donald Rheinheimer (1952): 1, June 1-Aug. 31, 1980
John Schrock (1946-): 1, June 1-Aug. 31, 1981
John Wiebe (1957-): 1, June 1-Aug. 31, 1982

Iglesia Mennonita Evangélica
2628 S. Komensky Ave., Chicago, Illinois
Org. 1962

Victor M. Ovando: 1962-

Iglesia Mennonita Evangélica
1021 West 19th St., Chicago, Illinois
(incorporated as Spanish Mennonite Church, 1976)
Org. 1974

Guillermo Espinoza (1934-): 1972-
Miguel Torrejón:?

Iglesia Mennonita Hispana
1649 W. 51st St., Chicago, Illinois
Org. 1977

Guillermo Espinoza (1934-): 1977-
Lilia Espinoza (1934-): 1977-

Congregations and Leaders 547

Lake City Bible Church
Lake City, Illinois
Org. 1945; discont. 1960 (presently under Southern Baptist auspices)

Roy Arden: 1*, 1945-1948
Menno Plank: 1*, 1945-1948
? Moore: 1*, 1945-1948
Harold Oyer (1905-1961): Jan., 1948-1960
Joseph A. Heiser (1888-1977): bp*, 1948-1951

Lancaster Heights Mennonite Church
Lancaster, Illinois
Org. 1953, discont. 1970

Paul C. Sieber (1921-): 1958-1965
Floyd Sieber (1918-): 1965-1966
Melvin Hamilton (1918-): 1966-1970

Lawndale Mennonite Church
formerly known as Second Mennonite Church, Iglesia Mexicana (founded 1932), or Iglesia Evangélica Menonita
2520 S. Lawndale Ave., Chicago, Illinois
Org. 1934

Josephus W. Shank (1881-1970): 1932-1933
Nelson Litwiller (1898-): 1933-1934
David Castillo (1905-) 1934-1940
Lester T. Hershey (1912-): 1940-1947
Amos Orley Swartzentruber (1926-): 1947
D. Parke Lantz (1881-1962): 1947-1948
Frank M. Ventura (1925-): 1948
Elvin Snyder (1900-): 1948-1949
William Lauver (1896-): 1949-1950
Josephus W. Shank (1881-1970): 1950-1951
John T. N. Litwiller (1928-1971): 1951-1953
Mario Snyder (1931-): 1953-1961
Donald Brenneman (1934-): 1961-1966
Albert Landis: 1966-1967
J. Weldon Martin (1918-): 1967-1970
Neftali Torres: 1970-1972

William Hallman (1904-): 1970-1974
Ronald Collins (1939-): 1974-June, 1981
Paul Leichty: 1981-
Orlando Redekop: 1981-

Lombard Mennonite Church
formerly Western Suburb Mennonite Fellowship (founded Dec., 1952)
528 East Madison Street, Lombard, Illinois
Org. Sept., 1954

LeRoy Kennel (1930-): Oct., 1954-1966
E. Joe Richards (1929-): Sept. 1, 1968-
Emma Sommers Richards (1927-): Oct. 15, 1972-
Ryan Ahlgrim (1957-): youth minister, Sept. 1, 1979-Aug. 31, 1980
Janice Yordy (1957-): youth minister, Sept. 1, 1980-Aug. 31, 1981
David Sutter (1958-): youth minister, Jan. 1, 1981-Aug. 31, 1982

Mennonite Community Chapel
formerly part of Chicago Home Mission/Union Avenue Church (1893-1957)
1758 West 21st Street, Chicago, Illinois
Org. 1959

Howard Beltz: 1957-1958
Samuel Miller: 1960
Chester Helmick: 1961-1962
Paul L. Wenger (1938-): 1962-1966
Peter Hofer: 1965-1966
Victor Ovando: 1965
Vernice Begly: 1966-1968
Jeff Zehr: 1971-1972
Henry Wyse: 1972-1974
Guillermo Espinoza (1934-): 1972-1975
Noah Helmuth: 1976-

Metamora Mennonite Church
formerly Partridge Creek Amish Congregation
Route 1, Metamora, Illinois
Org. 1833

Christian Engel (d. 1838): bp, 1833-1838
Joseph Engel (ca. 1792-1852): bp, 1836-1852
Joseph Belsley (1812-1879): d, ca. 1836-1879
John Nafziger (1802-1856): bp, 1837-1856
Andrew Bachman (d. 1864): bp, 1839-1864
John Gingerich (d. 1845): bp, 1839-1845
George Summer (1801-1883): d, ca. 1840-1883
Peter Beller (1800-1887): bp, 1850-?
Christian Esch (1818-1882): bp, 1852-1882
Joseph Bachman (1826-1897): bp, 1852-1897
Joseph Maurer (d. 1867), bp, 1856-1867
Andrew Ebersole: (by 1877)
Peter Sommer (1843-1922): ?
Christian Garber: by 1866-?
Peter Gingerich (1825-1898): 1880-1898
Christian Naffziger: ?
Joseph D. Schertz (1850-1915): d, ?-1915
Andrew A. Schrock (1863-1949): July 8, 1894-Apr. 24, 1898; bp, Apr. 24, 1898-1941
Peter Garber (1849-1939): 1894-1939
Peter Schertz (1857-1932): 1888-1932
Christian Schertz (1832-1889): c. 1875-1889
Henry R. Schertz (1886-1954): Feb. 5, 1917-Sept., 1920, June, 1923-1941; bp, Apr. 16, 1941-1954
Edward H. Oyer (1881-1974): d, 1920-1974
LeRoy Kennel (1930-): 1954-1955
Roy Bucher (1920-): 1955-1970
Milo Kaufman (1898-):1970-1971
James Detweiler (1926-): 1971-1978
Joseph W. Davis (1895-): 1972-1975
Gail Fisher (1947-): 1976-1979
LeRoy Kennel (1930-): 1978-1979

Larry Augsburger (1948-): 1, 1979-1981; 1981-

Midway Mennonite Church
Route 3, Pekin, Illinois
Org. April, 1950

Howard D. Wittrig (1915-): 1, 1950-1955; 1955-

Milwaukee [Spanish] Mennonite Church[12] organized 1959; closed ca. 1980

Mario Bustos (1922-1975): 1958-1971
Elvin V. Snyder (1900-): 1974-1976
William H. Shumaker (1931-): 1977-

Milwaukee Mennonite Fellowship[12]
Waukesha, Wisconsin
Org. 1978

Ross Collingwood (1952-): 1976-1977
William H. Shumaker (1931-): 1977-

Morrison Mennonite Church
Route 4, Morrison, Illinois
Org. 1868

Henry Nice, Sr. (1822-1892): bp, 1868-1892
Leonard Hendricks (ca. 1821-1890): d, ca. 1870-1880s
John Kornhaus: 1871-1887
Daniel H. Deter (1852-1943): d, 1884-1892
John Nice (1858-1931): 1887-1895; bp, 1895-1931
Henry T. Nice, Jr. (1850-1927): d, 1892-1912; ca. 1914-1927
John M. McCulloh (1860-1923): Nov., 1893-Dec. 1916
Daniel H. Deter (1852-1943): 1902-?
J. Kore Zook (1894-): 1933-1937
Aaron Nice (1909-): 1938-

Newcastle Bible Church
Deer Creek, Illinois

---

12. Although located in Wisconsin, the Milwaukee Mennonite Fellowship is a member of the Illinois Mennonite Conference, as was the earlier Spanish-speaking Milwaukee Mennonite Church.
13. Date of termination of conference affiliation.

Org. 1936; discont.[13] 1952
(presently unaffiliated)

Robert E. Zehr (1914-): 1936-1952

Pleasant Grove Mennonite Church
formerly Dillon Creek Amish
Mennonite Congregation
near Tremont, Illinois
Org. 1837; discont. 1941 (merged
with Goodfield Mennonite Church
to form First Mennonite Church,
Morton, Illinois

Michael Moseman (1802-1898): 1837
Andrew Ropp (1807-1890): 1837-ca.
 1840; bp, ca. 1840-1890
Peter Ropp (1815-1893): d, ca. 1843-
 1893
Valentine Birky (1817-1856): ca.
 1847-1856
John Sutter (1795-1887): 1850-1854
John Birky: by 1866-?
Joseph Birky: by 1866-?
Andrew Birky: by 1866-?
Peter Hostetler (1834-1924): ca. 1858-
 1868
Joseph Burcky (1833-1920): 1863-
 1868
Daniel Roth (1833-1922): ca. 1866-
 1922
Peter Guth (1806-1886): d, by 1871-
 1886
Johannes Bachman (1818-1888): d,
 by 1871-1888
Peter W. Ropp (1845-1921): ca. 1890-
 1897
Joseph Litwiller (1837-1902): ?
Isaac A. Miller (1839-1903): c. 1895-c.
 1899
John Smith (1843-1906): bp, 1896-
 1906
Jonas Litwiller (1865-1944): Nov. 10,
 1904-1941
John C. Birkey (1849-1920): bp, 1906-
 1911
Samuel Gerber (1863-1929): May 2,
 1897-May 1, 1911; bp, May 1, 1911-
 1929
Simon Litwiller (1880-1956): bp,
 1929-1941
Leland Bachman (1907-): 1932-1941
Joseph W. Davis (1895-): 1935-1937

Pleasant Hill Mennonite Church
South Pleasant Hill Road, East
Peoria, Illinois
Org. 1924 (first services 1920)

John D. Conrad (1878-1958): 1, 1924-
 1935
J. Norman Kaufman (1880-1966):
 1935-1945
Roy D. Roth (1921-): 1945-1951
Roy Bucher (1920-): Sept., 1951-Apr.,
 1955
I. Richard Miller: Aug., 1956-Aug.,
 1958
Wayne King (1931-): Aug., 1958-July,
 1962
Paul King (1921-): July, 1962-July,
 1970
Stanlee Kauffman (1935-): Aug., 1970-
 1976
Wayne King (1931-): Aug., 1970-July,
 1974
Lester Zook (1949-): June, 1975-Aug.,
 1979

Reba Place Fellowship[14]
727 Reba Place, Evanston, Illinois
Org. 1955

Julius Henry Belser, Jr. (1931-):
 senior e, 1974-
John Edrei Lehman (1932-): senior e,
 1974-
Virgil Vernard Vogt (1934-): senior e,
 1974-

Rehoboth Mennonite Church
Box 294, St. Anne, Illinois
Org. Summer, 1949

James H. Lark (1888-1978): 1949-
 1952
Robert Stoltzfus: 1953
Ray Yoder: 1954
Mark N. Lehman (1930-): 1955-1973

---
14. Dual membership fellowship, as member of the Illinois Mennonite Conference (MC) and of the Church of the Brethren; joined the Illinois Mennonite Conference in 1974.

Richard Yoder (1941-): 1974-1977
Mark N. Lehman (1930-): 1978-

*Richland Valley Sunday School
sponsored by Metamora
Mennonite Church
Lowpoint, Illinois
Org. 1939; discont. 1964*

Edward H. Oyer (1881-1974); d. 1939-1964

*Roanoke Mennonite Church
grew out of Partridge Congregation
and Mackinaw Meeting
Eureka, Illinois
Org. 1873*

Peter Farni (1797-1873): bp, ca. 1838-1843
Christian Farni (b. ca. 1800): ca. 1838-1843
? Barnhardt (d. 1846): bp, 1843-1846
Christian Ropp (1812-1896): 1840-1846; bp, 1846-1896
Jonathan Yoder (1795-1869): bp, 1851
Isaac Schmucker (1810-1893): bp, 1851
Daniel Zehr (1803-1855): bp, 1853-1855
Jacob Zehr (1825-1898): June 12, 1859-May 20, 1863; bp, May 20, 1863-1893
David Schertz: 1864-?
Christian Reeser, Sr. (1819-1923): 1867-1923
Joseph Wagner (1835-1894): 1867-1894
Christian Schrock (ca. 1818-ca. 1878): d, ca. 1868-ca. 1878
Joseph Rediger (1807-1889): ca. 1868-1881
Christian Zehr (1812-1893), d, by Dec. 1876-Nov. 22, 1893
Peter Zimmerman (1842-1931): May 20, 1883-1909
John Smith (1843-1906): 1887-ca. 1892; bp, ca. 1892-1906
Christian B. Reeser, Jr. (1859-1940): 1887-ca. 1917

Christian S. Schertz (1851-1937): June, 1893-1924
Peter D. Schertz (1848-1928): June, 1893-1928
Andrew Schrock (1863-1949): bp*, 1906-1922
Clayton F. Derstine (1891-1967): 1915-1922; bp, 1922-1924
Ezra B. Yordy (1892-1980): July 9, 1916-Sept. 11, 1925; bp, Sept. 11, 1925-1952
John L. Harnish (1896-): 1922-
Wesley E. Jantz (1914-): 1957-1961
Norman Derstine (1920-): July, 1962-1969
Percy Gerig (1931-): Sept., 1969-May, 1977
Moses Slabaugh: Sept., 1975-Feb., 1976
Walter Dyck (1908-): Sept. 1, 1977-Jan., 1978
Norman E. Yutzy (1930-): Feb., 1978-1981
Kenneth Good (1910-): 1981-

*Robein Mennonite Church
506 Washington Road, East
Peoria, Illinois
Org. 1950; discont. 1975*

Stanley Eldon Kortemeier (1932-1960): 1950-1960
Norman Kauffmann (1940-): 1962-1969
Paul King (1921-): 1970
Robert Harnish (1925-): 1971
Paul Miller (1913-): 1973-1975

*Rockwell Mennonite Church
Sheffield, Illinois
Org. 1945; discont. 1950*

John Detweiler (1918-): 1945-1948
John I. Byler (1881-1970): 1948-1950

*Scales Mound Congregation[15]
Jo Daviess County, Illinois
Org. ca. 1848; discont. ca. 1878*

Johannes Baehr (1790-1863): ca. 1848-1863

---

15. Not an official member of the Illinois Mennonite Conference but served by (Old) Mennonite personnel.

Michael Musselman (b. 1829): ?-ca. 1878

Science Ridge Mennonite Church
Route 2, Sterling, Illinois
Org. ca. 1857

Abraham E. Detweiler: 1858-ca. 1875
Elias Snavely (1820-1865): d, 1859-1865
Benjamin Hershey: 1860-1870; bp, 1870-1871
Joseph Allebaugh: 1862-1863
Benjamin Lapp: 1863-1866
Jacob E. Rutt (ca. 1815-1890): d, 1865-1887
Henry Nice (1822-1892): 1865-1868; bp, 1868; bp*, 1869-1892
Henry Yother (1810-1900): bp, 1868-1869
Abraham Ebersole (1823-1892): 1869-1889
John W. Rutt: 1869-1870
John Reisner: 1881-1889
Philip Nice (1845-1914): d, May 30, 1887-1891; 1891-1902
Amos Landis: d, 1891-1894
Abram Burkhart (1857-1931): d, Feb., 1895-1922
John L. Rutt: June 14, 1897-1899
Joseph S. Shoemaker (1854-1936): bp*, 1902-1934
Christian Good (1842-1916): *Summers, 1903-1905
Samuel Heatwole Rhodes (1880-1957): *Summers, 1903-1905
Samuel Good (1878-1905): July, 1904-Aug., 1905
Aaron C. Good (1881-1978): Feb., 1906-1934; bp, 1934-1951; pastor emeritus, Feb., 1956-1978
Daniel Ebersole (1855-1922): d, 1909-1922
Amos E. Kreider (1889-1976): June, 1918-Sept., 1921
Solomon R. Good (1871-1933): d, 1923-1933
Benjamin Mellinger (1902-1968): d, 1923-1948
Gaius Horst: d, 1947-1952
Robert Keller (1926-): 1950-1954
J. Frederick Erb (1922-): 1956-1962
Edwin J. Stalter (1922-): 1963-1972

Mark N. Lehman (1930-): 1973-1978
Philip Helmuth (1953-): 1978-

South Pekin Mennonite Church
110 Second Street, Pekin, Illinois
Org. 1960

Joseph W. Davis (1895-): 1960-1973
Donald Kauffmann (1948-): 1973-1978
Jerry L. Walker (1951-): 1978-
Steven Blaum (1951-): 1980

Trinity Mennonite Church
Route One, Morton, Illinois
Org. Aug. 21, 1977

Mahlon D. Miller (1931-): Oct. 1, 1977-

Union Mennonite Church
near Washington, Illinois
Org. ca. 1847; discont. 1929

Jost Bally (1795-1878): ca. 1847-ca. 1850; bp, ca. 1850-Oct. 26, 1872
Henry Baer (1815-1870): ca. 1850-ca. 1860
Samuel Hirstein (1809-1876): Oct., 1864-1876
Joseph Kindig (d. 1862): d, ca. 1850-1862
John R. Snyder (1831-1920): d, 1869-1870s
Jacob Smith: after 1852-?
Albrecht Schiffler: Mar., 3, 1872-1878
Henry Nice (1822-1892): bp*, 1872-1876
Emanuel M. Hartman (1849-1912): 1874-Nov. 12, 1876; bp, Nov. 12, 1876-1897
Jacob Kinsinger (1846-1900): d, ca. 1892-1900
John Nice (1858-1931): bp*, 1897-1902
Joseph S. Shoemaker (1854-1936): bp*, 1902-1920
Alpha L. Buzzard (1871-1964): Sept. 2, 1906-1929
Andrew A. Schrock (1863-1949): bp*, 1920-1929
Clayton F. Derstine (1891-1967): bp*, 1922-1924
Ezra B. Yordy (1892-1980): bp*, 1925-1929

Waldo Mennonite Church
  formerly Gridley Prairie Amish
  Mennonite Congregation
  Route One, Flanagan, Illinois
  Org. 1860

Christian Ropp (1812-1896): bp*, 1860-1872
John P. Schmitt (ca. 1820-1904): 1860-1904
John Rediger: 1860-1866
Jacob Rediger (d. 1863): 1860-1863
? Oyer: 1860-after1867
John Albrecht (1833-1900): d, 1860-1900
Joseph Rediger (1826-1904): 1863-May, 1866
Christian Schlegel (1819-1884): 1863-1872; bp, 1872-1884
Jacob Wagler (1806-1872): d, by 1866-1872
Joseph Gascho (1841-1902): 1872-1878
Daniel Greiser (b. 1838): 1878-1879
C. C. Zimmerman: ?
Valentine Nehauser (1814-1899): d, ca. 1866-1899
Joseph Ackerman: ?
Joseph Unzicker: ?
Valentine Agustein (1821-1872): d, ca. 1870-1872
Daniel Steinman (1830-1916): 1872-1885; bp, 1885-Apr. 5, 1908
Daniel Orendorff (1848-1918): 1890-1918
Daniel W. Slagel (1864-1947): July 3, 1900-1940
George Summers (1871-1937): 1908-1920; bp, ?
Joseph D. Hartzler (1884-1970): Sept. 15, 1920-July 25, 1927; bp, July 25, 1927-Nov. 24, 1957
Edward A. Rediger (1876-1943): d, Nov. 1, 1925-Sept., 1941
Edwin J. Stalter (1922-): Dec. 12, 1948-1964
Earl Sears (1935-): 1964-1968
David Eschleman (1936-): 1969-1972
Robert Harnish (1925-): 1973-1978
Lester Zook (1949-): 1979-

West Sterling Mennonite Church
  formerly West Sterling Mission,
  1928-1956
  1003 Griswold Ave., Sterling, Illinois
  Org. 1956

Jonas Baer: 1928-1933
Daniel G. Lapp (1867-1951): 1941-1946
Robert Keller (1926-): Sept., 1949-1950
Paul A. Friesen (1924-): 1951-1955
Vernon Schertz (1925-): 1955-1959
Melvin Hamilton (1918-): 1960-1966
Donald Schrader (1945-): 1966-1968
Harley Stauffer (1942-): 1969-1979
Jared Yoder (1950-): Apr., 1979-Dec., 1979
John V. Troyer (1911-): 1980)

Willow Springs Mennonite Church
  formerly Bureau Creek Amish
  Mennonite Congregation
  Route One, Tiskilwa, Illinois
  Org. ca. 1835

Jacob Burkey: ca. 1835-?
Daniel Burkey: 1836-?
Joseph Albrecht (1817-1895): d, ca. 1840-1885
Daniel Holly (1816-1887): 1848-ca. 1855
John Nafziger (1802-1856). bp*, 1837-ca. 1845
John Gingerich (d. 1845): bp*, 1839-1845
Andrew Ropp (1807-1890): bp*, 1851-1869
Joseph Maurer (d. 1867): bp*, 1855-ca. 1857
Peter Naffziger (1789-1885): bp*, ca. 1855-ca. 1857
Andrew Zimmerman (1834-1893): 1855-ca. 1871
John Michael Kistler (1808-1876): *1857-1862
Joseph Stuckey (1826-1902): bp*, 1864-1871
Joseph Burkey (1833-1920): 1868-1869; bp, 1869-1920
Joseph Stauffer (1846-1903): by 1871-1903
Andrew Oesch (1848-1940): Feb. 1874-Nov., 1887

Christian Sears (1831-1891): d, 1887-1891
Jacob Ringenberg (1849-1917): 1889-1917
Henry V. Albrecht (1860-1938): d, 1892-1938
Chancy A. Hartzler (1876-1947): 1913-1914; bp, 1914-1947
Ira H. Eigsti (1895-1964): Sept. 17, 1919-Apr. 3, 1949
C. Warren Long (1904-1969): 1949-1968
Milo Kauffman (1898-): 1970
Donald Heiser (1926-): 1971-

IOWA-NEBRASKA CONFERENCE (MC)

Iglesia Evangélica Menonita
613 Third Street, Moline, Illinois
Org. 1963

Andres Gallardo: 1963-

MENNONITE BRETHREN CHURCH

Lakeview Mennonite Brethren Church
formerly the Lincoln Avenue Gospel Mission (KMB)
2812 Lincoln Avenue, Chicago, Illinois
Org. July, 1915

David M. Hofer (1869-1944): Oct. 2, 1915-1944
Joseph W. Tschetter (1876-1955): Oct. 2, 1915-1941
John S. Mendel: 1941-1970
Edward Wilms: 1970-1972
Dennis Becker: 1972-1974
George Classen (1917-): 1974-1979

MIDDLE DISTRICT CONFERENCE (GC)

Light and Hope Church[16]
formerly Light and Hope Rescue Mission (founded June 8, 1892)
414 West Harrison Street, Chicago, Illinois
Org. 1895; discont. 1898

John A. Sprunger (1852-1911): June 8, 1892-May 8, 1896, Aug. 1897-1898

Mennonite Loop Meetings[17]
33 North Clark Street, Chicago, Illinois
Org. May 7, 1944; discont. Oct., 1945

Erwin Albrecht (1906-): *1944-1945
John T. Neufeld (1895-1961): *1944-1945

OLD ORDER AMISH

Bourbon District, #10
Moultrie County, Illinois
Org. 1957; divided with District #13 in 1976

Christian N. Bontrager: 1957-
Daniel A. Miller: Apr. 20, 1958-Apr. 2, 1961; bp, Apr. 2, 1961-
Eli J. Stutzman: Oct. 6, 1957-1976
Joseph D. Yoder: d, Apr. 15, 1960-1976; Apr. 10, 1977-
Samuel D. Schrock: Apr. 10, 1977-
Lewis J. Chupp: d, Oct. 9, 1977-

Caldwell District, #1
Moultrie County, Illinois
Org. 1888; divided to form District #6 in 1906

Daniel J. Beachy (1847-1933): bp, 1888-1933
John A. Miller: 1888-1890
Christian P. Herschberger (1845-1919): d, 1888; 1888-1910

---

16. Not an official member of the Middle District Conference, but conducted under auspices of Middle District Conference ministers.
17. Inter-Mennonite Services held monthly, conducted by Middle District ministers, at Dixon Chapel on the second floor of the Methodist Temple, Chicago.

Gideon N. Kauffman (1863-1928):
  1892-1906
Eli Y. Otto (d. 1922): d, Nov. 1895-
  1922
Christian Yutzi (1830-1910): d, 1900-
  1910
Elias Brenneman (1857-1905); d,
  1903-1905
Samuel N. Beachy (1879-1958);
  1906-1920, bp, 1920-ca. 1923
Samuel D. Beachy (1884-1920): Oct.,
  1910-1920
Daniel G. Schlabach (1866-1942):
  1916-1919; bp, 1919-1942
Obed Diener: Apr. 23, 1921-Oct. 11,
  1949; bp, Oct. 11, 1949-
David A. Troyer (1881-1976): d, Oct. 9,
  1921-1965
Jacob E. Miller: 1929-?
Joni Plank (1860-1932): ?-1926
Noah A. Yoder (1905-1953): Nov. 11,
  1934-Nov. 5, 1938; bp, Nov. 5, 1938-
  1953
John C. Gingerich: 1935-1936
Noah S. Beachy: Nov. 7, 1936-
William G. Miller: Apr. 26, 1937-
Abraham C. Gingerich: Oct. 17, 1953-
  1954; bp, 1954-
Jonas J. Herschberger: d, Oct, 1965-

Chestervville District #4
Douglas County, Illinois
Org. 1921; divided to form District
#10 in 1957

Noah B. Schrock (1888-1959): Oct. 2,
  1921-Oct. 9, 1927; bp, Oct. 9, 1927-
  1959
John W. Stutzman (1882-1944): Oct.
  1, 1922-1944
Noah Bontrager: Oct. 24, 1962-1972
Jacob E. Stutzman (1893-1951): d,
  Apr. 30, 1933-1951
Roman N. Bontrager: d, Apr. 20, 1952-
John E. Herschberger: Oct. 13, 1957-
  Oct. 8, 1960; bp, Oct. 8, 1960-
David J. Stutzman: Oct. 10, 1959-Jan.,
  1970
John C. Plank: bp, after 1959-
Levi J. D. Herschberger: Mar. 29,
  1970-
Edwin D. Schrock: Apr. 9, 1972-

Cook's Mill District, #9
Douglas County, Illinois
Org. 1951

Jerry Otto (ca. 1900-1961): bp, 1951-
  1955
David J. Mast (1871-1957): 1951-
  1957
David J. Beachy: Nov. 18, 1952-Apr.
  23, 1955; bp, Apr. 23, 1955-
Joseph H. Hochstetler: May 8, 1954-
Levi J. Stutzman: Oct. 15, 1960-1975
Alvin J. Kauffman: d, Apr. 1, 1961-
Ervin J. Hochstetler: d, Oct. 9, 1977-

County Line District, #8
Douglas and Moultrie Counties,
Illinois
Org. 1934

Obed E. Diener: 1934-1949
Daniel E. Otto (1893-1971): Oct.
  1938-1969
Levi J. Chupp: May 15, 1946-
Christian E. Otto: Oct. 22, 1946-Apr.
  29, 1948; bp, Apr. 29, 1948-
Joseph S. Graber: d, Apr. 19, 1947-
  1969
Levi J. Yoder: Apr. 4, 1970-?
Levi C. Otto: d, Oct. 18, 1970-
Melvin L. Miller: Oct. 13, 1974-

East Prairie District, #5
Douglas County, Illinois
Org. 1926; divided to form District
#9 in 1951

William D. Schrock (1877-1949): d,
  1926-1949
David J. Mast (1871-1957): 1926-
  1951
Joni Plank (1860-1932): 1926
Noah M. Otto (1895-1968): Oct. 28,
  1928-1968
Jerry S. Otto (1899-1961): May 16,
  1935-May 29, 1939; bp, May 29,
  1939-1961
Henry N. Borntrager: Apr. 19, 1952-
  1960s
Joseph A. Yoder: d, Oct. 4, 1952-
Simon C. Gingerich: 1953-ca. 1957
Andrew J. Kauffman: Oct. 23, 1960-
  Apr., 1962; bp, Apr., 1962-

Menno J. Hochstetler: Apr. 19, 1961-
1963
Noah E. Herschberger: Apr. 5, 1964-
Abraham J. Yoder: Oct. 9, 1971-1973
Menno D. Miller: Nov. 3, 1974-

Fayette County Church
Brownstown, Illinois
Org. 1892; discont. 1903

Moses J. Yoder: 1893-1903
John A. Miller: 1893-1903
Samuel Bender: ca. 1895-?; bp, ?-1903
John Bontreger: ?-1903

"First Amish Church"
Moultrie and Douglas Counties,
Illinois
Org. 1865; divided into Districts #1
and #2 in 1888

Joseph N. Keim (1826-1872): 1865;
bp, 1865-1872
Jonas J. Kaufman: 1868-1873; bp,
1873-1880
Moses J. Kaufman (d. 1898): 1868-
1898
Daniel Schrock (d. 1890): 1870-1890
Joseph Yoder (d. 1882): 1877-1882
Daniel J. Beachy (1847-1933): 1881-
1885; bp, 1885-1888
John A. Miller: 1880-1888
Christian P. Herschberger (1845-
1919): d, 1885-1888

Jonathan Creek District, #11
Moultrie County, Illinois
Org. 1969

Levi G. Miller: 1969-
William A. Mast: Oct. 11, 1970-Oct. 10,
1971; bp, Oct. 10, 1971-
Eli F. Schlabach: Mar. 27, 1970-
Lester Jess (d. 1976): d, Apr. 9, 1971-
1976

Elva M. Chupp: d, Oct. 16, 1977-

North Fairbanks District, #6
Moultrie County, Illinois
Org. 1906; divided to form District
#7 in 1926

Gideon N. Kauffman (1863-1928):
1906-1928
John Helmuth: d, 1910-?
John J. E. Miller (1882-1972): 1916-
1920
Joseph L. Schrock (1885-1941): Nov.
17, 1918-1929
Samuel N. Beachy (1880-1958): bp,
1923-1958
Amzy J. Miller (1888-1958): d, Oct. 2,
1921-1929
Jeff G. Kauffman (1894-1975): Apr.
21, 1929-1929
Simon E. Brenneman (1888-1970):
Apr. 26, 1931-1970
John C. Gingerich: 1936-
Menno D. Herschberger: d, Oct. 5,
1947-
Jeff A. Miller: Apr. 19, 1957-
Edward E. Nisley: bp, 1958-1962
Steve Kauffman: Oct. 16, 1960-Oct.
28, 1962; bp, Oct. 28, 1962-
Joseph E. Kauffman: Apr. 25, 1976-

North Prairie District #2
Douglas County, Illinois
Org. 1888; divided to form District
#3 in 1902

David J. Plank (1858-1944): 1890-
1892; bp, 1892-1944
Joseph D. Schrock (1865-1938):
1890-1902
Henry J. Mast (1869-1952): Oct. 21,
1894-1902
Abraham D. Schrock (1876-1948):
Oct. 9, 1904-1948
Jacob E. Miller (1834-1972): 1916-
1919
Daniel M. Otto (1882-1953): d, Oct. 8,
1922-1953
Christian M. Bontrager: Apr. 22,
1928-1957
Jacob J. Helmuth (1889-1956): d, May
5, 1932-1956
Samuel E. Petersheim (1913-): May 4,
1946-1957
Menno S. Miller: Oct. 21, 1946-Apr.
28, 1951; bp, Apr. 28, 1951-
John A. Schrock: Apr. 20, 1947-
Levi G. Miller: Oct. 2, 1949-1969
Eli A. Miller: d, Apr. 19, 1957-
John C. Plank: bp, 1959-

William J. Schrock: Apr. 5, 1970-1972
Ervin J. Schrock: Apr. 16, 1972-
John J. Yoder: Oct. 22, 1977-Sept. 5, 1979

Shelby County Congregation
Shelby County, Illinois
Org. 1872; discont. 1883

Jacob Miller: 1872-by 1883
Christian Bontrager: after 1872-by 1883

South Fairbanks District, #7
Moultrie County, Illinois
Org. 1929

Joseph L. Schrock (1885-1941): 1929-1941
Amzy J. Miller (1888-1958): d, 1929-1958
Jeff G. Kauffman (1894-1975): 1929-1975
Eli D. Beachy (1889-1964): Oct. 13, 1935-1964
Edward E. Nisley: Oct. 11, 1947-Oct. 23, 1949; bp, Oct. 23, 1949-
Andrew A. Miller (1922-1969): d, Oct. 11, 1959-1969
John E. Otto: d, Oct. 9, 1971-
David E. Schrock: Oct. 20, 1974-

South Prairie District, #3
Moultrie and Coles County, Illinois
Org. 1902; divided to form District #5 in 1926

Joseph D. Schrock (ca. 1865-1938): 1902-1938
Henry J. Mast (ca. 1869-1952): 1902-1952
Andrew J. Mast (ca. 1873-1949): bp, 1904-1949
William D. Schrock (1877-1949): d, 1904-1926
David J. Mast (1871-1959): 1912-1926
Henry Yoder (1846-1917): 1913-1917
Jacob E. Miller (1884-1972): 1936-1972
Levi Jess (1899-1971): d, 1939-1971
Obed A. Diener: bp, after 1949-
Samuel E. Petersheim: ?-ca. 1957

John J. Hochstetler: Oct. 4, 1959-1971
David D. Schrock: Apr. 16, 1965-
Henry A. Miller: Oct. 13, 1968-Oct. 11, 1970; bp, Oct. 11, 1970-
Joni J. Plank: d, Oct. 10, 1971-

West Bourbon District, #13
Douglas County, Illinois
Org. 1976

Daniel A. Miller: bp, 1976-
Eli J. Stutzman: 1976-
Joseph D. Yoder: d, 1976-
Jacob E. Stutzman: Apr.17, 1977-
Willard Stutzman: Oct.15, 1978-

West Prairie District, #12
Douglas County, Illinois
Org. 1969

Joseph S. Graber: d, 1969-
Daniel E. Otto (1892-1971): 1969-1971
Amos D. Otto: Oct. 11, 1970-Apr. 22, 1973; bp, Apr. 22, 1973-
Amos Miller: Apr. 21, 1968-
Harvey Chupp: Apr. 12, 1970-

REFORMED MENNONITE CHURCH

Sterling Reformed Mennonite
Church
Sterling, Illinois
Org. ca. 1860

John Weaver (1806-1887): 1860-1887
John Hoover: d, ?
George Hagey: d, ?
John Weckesser: ?
Adam B. Spies: d, ?
Christian Schwenck: d, ?
William Miller (d. 1920): 1894-1920
Godfrey Horlacher: d, 1898-?
Michael Deter: d, 1898-1910; 1910-
William Schwenck: d, ?
Elmer Sedig: ?
Wilmer Schwank: ?

UNAFFILIATED AMISH MENNONITE CONGREGATIONS

Fairfield Amish Mennonite Church
Tampico, Illinois
Org. 1933

Congregations and Leaders

Levi C. Hostetler: 1933-by 1940; by 1940-1953
Herman Hostetler: by 1940-1942; bp, 1942-
Ora Hostetler: by 1940-1955; bp, 1955-1965
Ova Hostetler: by 1940-
S. Joseph Kropf: d, by 1940-
Harold Knox: d, 1962-1964
William Schrock: 1967-
Raymond Kauffman: 1975-

Linn Amish Mennonite Church
Roanoke, Illinois
Org. 1910

Peter Zimmerman (1842-1931): bp, 1910-1931
Joseph Reber (1874-1963): bp*, 1914?-1934
John Kennell (1862-1946): bp, by 1924-1934
Joseph J. Kennell (1847-1941): by 1922-1934; bp, 1934-1941
Daniel M. Hostetler (1893-1972): Dec. 31, 1934-June 9, 1946; bp, June 9, 1946-1970
Samuel E. Unzicker (1876-1963): d, 1930-1963
Levi C. Hostetler (1862-1952): *1937-1939
John E. Hostetler (1901-): 1945-1958; bp, Aug. 10, 1958-
Harold D. Hostetler (1926-): May 20, 1956-1978
David R. Ulrich (1910-): d, Dec. 15, 1959-
Ervin L. Hostetler (1933-): 1978-

Mt. Herman Amish Mennonite
Church
Shelbyville, Illinois
Org. 1907

John D. Kaufman (1847-1913): 1907-1911; bp, 1911-1913
Joseph Reber (1874-1963): 1912-1914; bp, 1914-1960
S. E. Yoder: ca. 1913-1945
Peter Neuschwander: 1917
Levi C. Hostetler: 1924-1933
Andrew Ulrich: 1924-1966
D. M. Ulrich: ca. 1935-1966
Christy Christner: 1957-1963; bp, 1963-
Frank Christner: 1965-1973

WESTERN DISTRICT AMISH MENNONITE CONFERENCE

(Note: Listed here are only those congregations which discontinued before this Amish Mennonite conference merged with the Illinois Mennonite Conference. Other congregations that began as Western District Amish Mennonite are listed under Illinois Mennonite Conference.)

Arthur Amish Mennonite Church
near Arthur, Illinois
Org. 1897; discont. 1914

Seth P. Hershberger (1860-1941): 1897-1906
John Smith (1843-1906): bp*, 1897-1906
Isaac A. Miller (1839-1904): ca. 1899-Dec., 1903
Moses J. Helmuth (1862-1908): 1906-1908
Peter Zehr (1851-1922): bp*, 1906-1914

Shelbyville Amish Mennonite
Congregation
Shelbyville, Illinois
Org. ca. 1890; discont. by 1920

John Smith (1843-1906): bp*, ca. 1890-1906

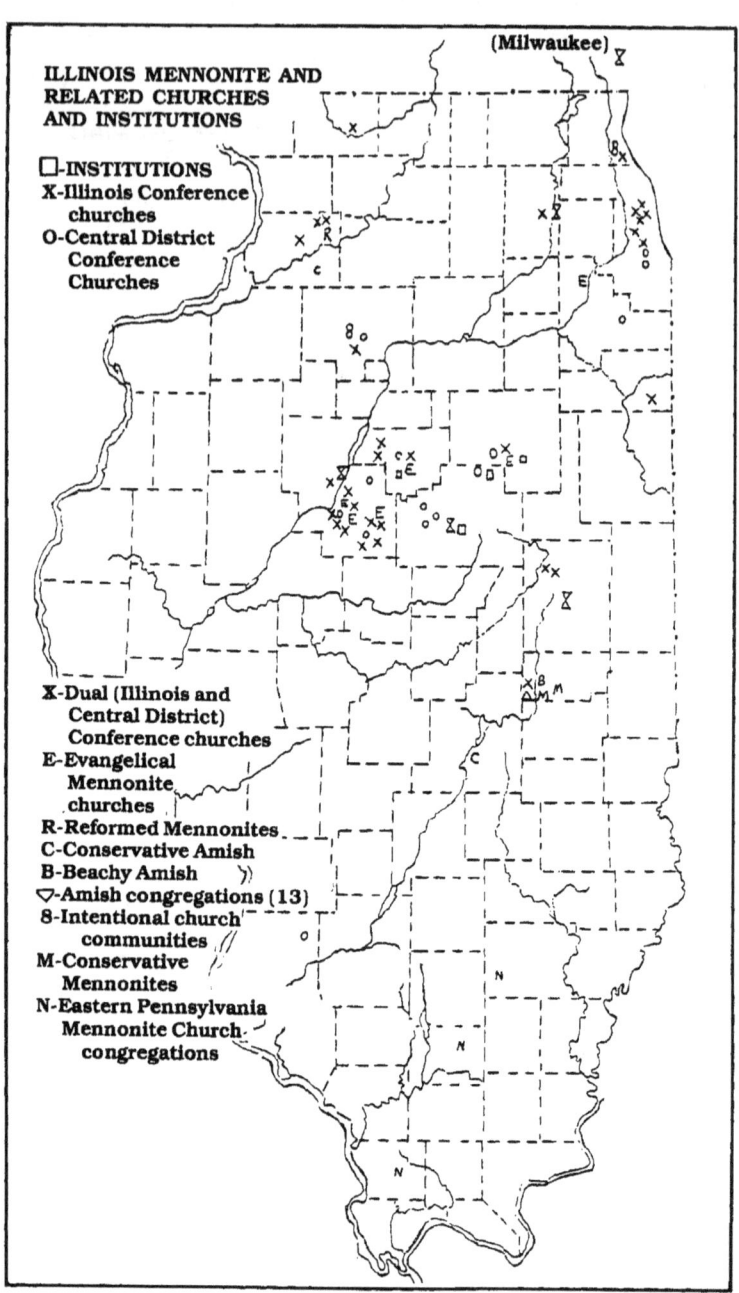

Thomas Yoder

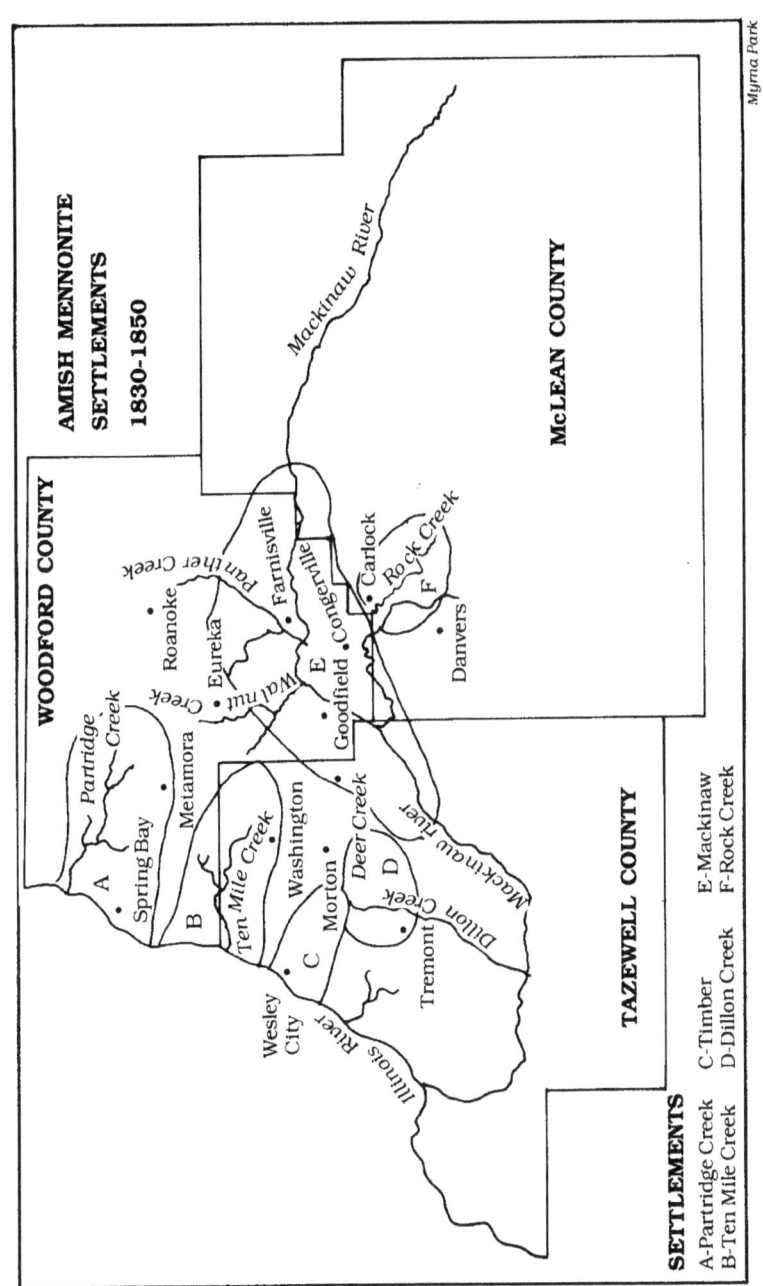

Bibliography

This bibliography includes the items cited in the footnotes, plus a few additional items that may be helpful to the inquiring reader. Although not intending to produce an annotated bibliography, I shall comment briefly on a few items.

Most of the items listed below under "Unpublished Works," "Periodicals," and "Other Published Works" can be found in the Mennonite Historical Library at Goshen College, Goshen, Indiana (MHLG).

See "Key to Abbreviations" at beginning of Notes.

Manuscript Collections

Central District Conference Archives, Mennonite Historical Library, Bluffton College (MHLB), Bluffton, Ohio. Much correspondence and other material on the various GC congregations in Illinois is located in this depository, which is the official archives of the GC Central District Conference (GC district body which includes Illinois).

Coffman, John S., papers, Archives Mennonite Church.

East Bend MC archival papers.

Erismann, Christian, unpublished diary, AMC.

Estes, Steven R., papers, in his possession, Graymont, Ill.

Evangelical Mennonite Church papers, EMC Archives, Ft. Wayne, Ind. Considerable material on the Illinois EMC churches is here.

Funk, John F., papers, AMC.

Gunden, Chris J., papers, AMC.

Hartzler, John E., papers, AMC.

Hartzler, John S., papers, AMC.

Horsch, John, papers, AMC.

Hostetler, Lester, papers, in his possession, Goshen, Ind.

Illinois Mennonite Church papers, AMC. The AMC at Goshen, Indiana, is the official archives of the Illinois Mennonite Conference. Consequently there is a vast amount of material here on the Illinois (Old) Mennonites, and some on other groups. In addition to material from the conference and its subsidiary organizations, there are also materials from many of the congregations.

Illinois Mennonite Historical and Genealogical Society Archives, at present at Normal. A growing collection of worthwhile items on the various Mennonite branches in Illinois.

Kauffman, Daniel, papers, AMC.
Kolb, A. B., papers, AMC.
Lapp, Daniel G., papers, AMC.
Loucks, Aaron, papers, AMC.
Loucks, Aaron,—Hartzler, J.S., Peace Problems Committee papers, AMC.
Nafziger, Arthur W., papers, AMC.
North Danvers Church (GC) archival papers.
Oyer, Noah, papers, AMC.
Park, Myrna, papers, in her possession, Normal, Ill.
Ropp miscellaneous papers, in possession of Edwin O. Ropp, Bloomington, Ill. Photocopies also in AMC.
Schowalter, Jacob, Oral History Project, Mennonite Historical Library and Archives, Bethel College, North Newton, Kan. Contains material on a few important Illinois draft cases in World War I, copies of which are in AMC.
Schertz, Henry R., papers, AMC.
Schertz, Henry R., papers, in possession of Mrs. Ruth Zehr, Normal, Ill.
Shoemaker, Joseph S., papers, AMC.
Shoemaker, Joseph S., papers, in possession of Robert S. Kreider, North Newton, Kan.
Smith, C. Henry, papers, MHLB. An important collection for Illinois history.
Smith, Willard H., papers, in his possession, Goshen, Ind.
Steiner, Menno S., papers, AMC.
Steiner, Menno S., papers, in possession of Esther (Mrs. J. C.) Meyer, Goshen, Ind. Used by courtesy of Mrs. Meyer.
Studer, Gerald C., papers, AMC.
Summer, Dennis, papers, AMC.
Weaver, William B., papers, AMBS library, Elkhart, Ind.
Yoder, Sanford C., papers, AMC.
Yoder, Thomas, papers, in his possession, Normal, Ill.
Zehr, Harold, papers, in possession of Mrs. Ruth Zehr, Normal, Ill.
Zehr, Howard J., papers, AMC.
Zimmerman, John S., papers, AMC.

Note: In addition to the above, some congregations have worthwhile material in their own archives, such as, for example, the GC North Danvers Church at Danvers, and the (Old) Mennonite Church at Fisher.

Unpublished Works:
Dissertations, Theses, Term Papers, Diaries, Et Cetera

Bair, Ray. "The Merger of the Mennonite and Amish Mennonite Conferences from 1911-28." Term paper, Goshen College.
Bethel Mennonite Church, Chicago. "Chicago Bethel Church Development, 1944-1953...." [Elkhart, Ind., Mennonite Board of Missions and Charities, 1953], MHLG.
Beyler, Clayton "Meaning and Relevance of the Devotional Covering: A Study in the Interpretation of 1 Corinthians 11:2-16." Master of Theology thesis, Southern Baptist Theological Seminary, 1954.
Blosser, Donald. "The Use of the Revival Meeting as an Agent for Evangelism in the Illinois Mennonite Conference." Term paper, AMBS, 1965.
Brown, Marie Diller. "An Historical Study of the Development and Growth of the Evangelical Mennonite Church Formerly Known as the Defenseless Mennonite Church." MRE thesis, Biblical Seminary of New York, 1951.
Dean, William W. "John F. Funk and the Mennonite Awakening." PhD dissertation, University of Iowa, 1965.

Ebisch, Konrad Ernst August. "The Amish Settlement of Arthur, Illinois: A Geographic Study." MS thesis, University of Illinois, Urbana-Champaign, 1940.

Egly, Henry. "Autobiography." Evangelical Mennonite Church archives, Ft. Wayne, Ind., 26 pp. (as translated from original German).

Erb, Delbert. "Index of Mennonite and Amish Mennonite Conference Resolutions." 1951, MHLG.

Espinoza, Guillermo. "A Presentation of the History of the Evangelical Mennonite Church, 1021 W. 19th St., Chicago." A short historical treatise, Chicago, 1976.

Estes, Steven R. "Bishop Peter Naffziger (1789-1885), an Amish Apostle." Unpublished, 1977, in MHLG, courtesy of Mr. Estes (also published in *Mennonite Heritage*, 1979, pp. 37, 43-45).

———. "David R. and Mary [Claudon] King: Founders of Salem Orphanage." Unpublished [1979], copy in my possession, courtesy Mr. Estes.

———. "Heaven's Temple: The Life and Religious Work of Christian Ropp, Sr." Term paper, Illinois State University, Normal, 1978.

———. "The Nebraska Brethren: The Origin and Early Development of the Flanagan Mennonite Church." Term paper, Illinois State University, Normal, 1978.

"Evangelical Mennonite Church Mission in the Congo." N.d. [late 60s], n.p. Gives names and home churches of Congo missionaries.

Fleming, Lois. "The Old Order Amish Community of Arthur, Illinois." MSEd thesis, Eastern Illinois University, 1962. Author attended school with Amish pupils in Arthur areas, resided "on the fringes of the Amish settlement," and taught Amish pupils for 11 years.

Freeney, Rosemarie. "City Planning in the Chicago Near West Side Area (with Special Reference to the Bethel Mennonite Community Church)." Social Science Seminar paper, Goshen College, 1955.

Fretz, J. Winfield. "A Study of Mennonite Religious Institutions in Chicago." BD thesis, Chicago Theological Seminary, 1940.

Gerber, Wayne Jay. "Biography of Samuel Gerber." Term paper, Goshen College, 1959.

Gingerich, James N. "*Ordnung* and the Amish Ministers Meetings of the 1860's." History Seminar paper, Goshen College, 1980.

Harmony Church "Record Book." Unpublished, in the possession of Clarence Imhoff, Roanoke, Ill., n.d. Loaned to writer courtesy Mr. Imhoff.

Hartzler, Raymond L. "A History of Mennonite Hospital." Unpublished paper, 1977, copy in writer's possession courtesy Mr. Hartzler.

[Hassan], Hazel Nice. "The History of the Morrison Red Brick Church." Term paper, Goshen College, 1952.

Hollinger, I. Wilmer. "M.S. Steiner: A Biography of His First Thirty Years." History Seminar paper, Goshen College, 1965.

Horsch, James E. "A Comparison of Past and Projected Changes in Immediate Goals and Objectives of the Congregations in the Illinois Mennonite Conference." Seminar paper, Goshen College Biblical Seminary, 1966.

Houghton, Arthur Vincent. "Community Organization in a Rural Amish Community at Arthur, Illinois." BS thesis, University of Illinois, 1926.

Kauffmann, Ivan. "Illinois Mennonite Mission Board, 1917-1957." Term paper, AMBS, 1958.

———. "The Mid-week Meeting in the Illinois Mennonite Conference," Term paper, AMBS, 1958.

Keller, Bob. "The Illinois Mennonite Conference." Term paper, Goshen College, 1947.

Kirchner, George L. "The Mennonites of McLean County, Illinois." Historical treatise, 1910. Ms. in McLean County Historical Society, Bloomington, Ill. Copy in MHLG.

Klaus, Marilyn. "'Es Giebt Ein Wunderschönes Land ...': A Story of the Gemeinschaft Evangelisch Taufgesinnter Neutaüfer, Fröhlichianer, New Amish, Evangelical Baptists and the Apostolic Christian Church of America." Term paper, AMBS, 1974.

Kortemeier, Eldon. "The Life and Growth of the Freeport Mennonite Church." Mennonite History paper, Goshen College Biblical Seminary, 1958.

Kraybill, J. Nelson. "The Birth of the Chicago Mexican Mission." History Seminar paper, Goshen College, 1978.

Lederach, Paul. "History of Religious Education in the Mennonite Church." ThD dissertation, Southwestern Baptist Theological Seminary, Dallas, Tex., 1949.

_____. "A Study of the Constitutions of the Conferences of the Mennonite Church." Term paper, Goshen College Biblical Seminary, 1946.

LeFevre, Elwin N. "Changing Concepts of Nonconformity as Seen in Illinois Mennonite Church Conference Resolutions." Term paper, Goshen College, 1953.

Liechty, Joseph. "From Yankee to Nonresistant, John F. Funk's Chicago Years, 1857-1865." Term paper, AMBS, 1979, copy in MHLG.

Maurer, Samuel E. "Life of S. E. Maurer" (autobiography). 1953. Original in the possession of Vera Root, Carlock, Ill. Copy in the possession of Steven R. Estes, Graymont, Ill.

Metz, Floyd. "Analysis of the Draft Census of the Franconia, Illinois, Indiana-Michigan, Ohio, South Central and Pacific Conferences, Jan. 1, 1952-April, 1956." Seminar paper, Goshen College, 1956.

"Minutes of Society" of Mennonite *Nähe Verein* [Sewing Circle] of the Central Conference [1906]. In the possession of Steven R. Estes, Graymont, Ill.

Moser, Arthur L. "A Brief Historical Sketch of the Apostolic Christian Church." Church History paper, Goshen College, 1949.

Musselman, Glen. "A Study of Mennonite Conference Resolutions with Reference to Young People's Activities." Mennonite History paper, Goshen College, 1952.

Nafziger, Loren. "Henry R. Schertz and Christian Education." History Seminar paper, Goshen College, 1977.

Nagata, Judith A. "Continuity and Change Among the Old Order Amish of Illinois." PhD dissertation, University of Illinois, 1968.

Nice, Hazel. See Hassan.

Oyer, Emma. Diary. Unpublished, in the possession of Edna Oyer Bachman, Goshen, Ind. By an important, longtime worker in Chicago Home Mission.

Peachey, Paul. "Seminar on a Theology of Christian Social Service." AMBS, 1963.

Plummer, Carol. "The Apostolic Christian Church as a Believers Church." Term paper, Goshen College, 1975.

Sawatsky, Rodney J. "The Influence of Fundamentalism on Mennonite Nonresistance 1908-1944." MA thesis, University of Minnesota, 1973.

Schertz, Vernon. "Local Extension Church Work in the Illinois Mennonite Conference." Term paper, Goshen College, 1956.

Schultz, Peter G. "Brighton Mennonite Church." Unpublished, 1969, ms. in the possession of Schultz, Justice, Ill., copy in MHLG.

Smith, Willard H. "The Westward Movement into Illinois." Graduate research paper, University of Michigan, 1929.

Sommer, J. J. "Sommer History 1934." Ms. in C. Henry Smith papers, MHLB.
Springer, Nelson. "Schoolteacher by Accident, Churchman Without Office." Paper read before the Illinois Mennonite Historical and Genealogical Society at Hopedale, Oct. 28, 1978, copy in MHLG.
Stevanus, Kenneth. "A Study of Trends in the Midweek Meeting of the Illinois Mennonite Conference from 1958-1964." Term paper, AMBS, 1964.
Strubhar, Valentine. "A Condensed History of the East [Washington] Mennonite Church Now Known as the Calvary Mennonite Church." Unpublished, 1940, copy in MHLG.
─────. "A Short History of the Peter Strubhar Sr. Family and His Descendants." Ms., 1933, in the possession of Mr. and Mrs. Harold D. (Claudene) Schertz, Metamora, Ill. Copy in the possession of Steven R. Estes, Graymont, Ill.
Stuckey, Harley J. "Cultural Interaction Among the Mennonites Since 1870." MA thesis, Northwestern University, 1947.
"Joseph Stuckey's Note Book." In North Danvers Mennonite Church Archives. Record of marriages, baptisms, funerals, etc.
Sutter, Earl. "Early Mennonite Settlements in Missouri." Term paper, Goshen College, 1952.
Swartz, Merlin L. "The Historical Background of the Conservative Mennonite Conference." Mennonite History paper, Goshen College, 1960.
Ulrich, Wilfred. "A Study of the Young People's Activities in the Local Congregations of the Illinois Conference." Term paper, Goshen College, 1945.
Umble, Roy H. "Mennonite Preaching, 1864-1944." PhD dissertation, Northwestern University, 1949.
Weaver, J[ohn] Denny. "Some Background to the Position of American Mennonites on Slavery." Seminar paper, Goshen Biblical Seminary, 1970. Also, résumé in *The Mennonite,* Sept. 29, 1970.
Weber, Harry F. "History of the American Mennonites of Illinois." MA thesis, Bluffton College, 1923.
Zehr, Albert and Bertha Reedy. "The Life and Family of Samuel S. Zehr." Foosland, Ill., 1976, ms. in the possession of the authors, Fisher, Ill., who are son and daughter-in-law of Samuel S. Zehr; loaned to writer courtesy of Mr. and Mrs. Zehr.
Zehr, Samuel S. "Churchbook." Unpublished personal record book in the possession of Mrs. Alva Cender, Fisher, Ill., n.d.; loaned to writer courtesy Mrs. Cender.

Periodicals

(**Note:** Where a journal's name includes the name of a town, readers may assume the town is in Illinois, unless otherwise indicated.

To locate collections of Mennonite and Mennonite-related periodicals, the reader may consult the "North America: Periodicals" section of Nelson P. Springer and A. J. Klassen, compilers, *Mennonite Bibliography, 1631-1961.* Vol. II: *North America, Indices* [Scottdale, Pa., and Kitchener, Ont.; Herald Press, 1977].)

Arcola Record Herald, 1920s.
    "Historical Sketch of Early Amish Settlers," by L. A. Miller. Clipping in Tom Yoder Papers.
Bloomington Pantagraph, Jan. 1, 1894, and about Nov. 9 or 10, 1923.
Brotherhood Beacon. Plain City, Ohio, 1971-. Succeeded *Missionary Bulletin.* Conservative Mennonite.

Bibliography 565

Central District Reporter. Goshen, Ind., later Newton, Kan., 1957-. Became insert in *The Mennonite* as of Jan. 15, 1974. GC.
Chicago Sun-Times, July 30, 1970.
Chicago Tribune, July 30, 1970.
Christian Evangel. Bloomington, Ill., 1910-1957. Very important source for history of Central Conference Mennonites. Central Conference Mennonite.
Christian Exponent. Wooster, Ohio, 1924-1928. Published by some (Old) Mennonite progressives who thought that the *Gospel Herald* was not adequately representing their position.
Christian Living. Scottdale, Pa., 1954-. Formerly *Christian Monitor* and *The Mennonite Community.* MC.
Christian Monitor. Scottdale, Pa., 1909-1953. Replaced by *Christian Living* in 1954. MC.
Christlicher Bundesbote. Newton, Kan., 1882-1947. GC.
Christliche Volksblatt. Milford Square, Pa., 1856-1866. Published by John H. Oberholtzer and his group.
Church History. Wallingford, Pa., 1932-. Stayer, James M. "The Swiss Brethren: An Exercise in Historical Definition." 47 (June 1978): 174-95.
The Commoner. Lincoln, Neb., 1917.
Congo Missionary Messenger. Berne, Ind., later Elkhart, Ind., 1929-72. Became *AIMM Messenger.* Inter-Mennonite.
CPS Bulletin. Akron, Pa., 1942-1947. Files at Mennonite Central Committee Offices, Akron, Pa.
The Eastern Mennonite Testimony. Myerstown, Pa., 1969-. Eastern Pennsylvania Mennonite Church.
El Heraldo Evangélico. Scottdale, Pa., Nov., 1942-1961. Formerly *El Heraldo Mexicano,* replaced by *El Discípulo Cristiano,* Jan., 1962. MC.
El Heraldo Mexicano. Scottdale, Pa., 1941-Oct. 1942. Changed to *El Heraldo Evangélico.* MC.
Elkhart Institute Monthly. Elkhart, Ind., 1898-May, 1903. Changed to *Goshen College Record,* Goshen, Ind. MC.
L'Essor. Schirmeck, France. Issue in MHLG.
 Jerome, Claude. "Les memorables adventures de Jean Gingrich ou du Salm aux Ameriques au siecle dernier." Special issue, 94 (March, 1977): 3-24.
Evangelical Mennonite. Berne, Ind., 1953-1968. EMC.
Evangelical Mennonite Build. Ft. Wayne, Ind., 1968-. EMC.
Family Life. Alymer, Ontario, 1968-. Old Order Amish.
Forum. Newton, Kans., 1970-. Inter-Mennonite.
The Foundation Echo. Aibonito, Puerto Rico, 1954-1959. Published by the Ulrich Foundation.
Good Tidings. Lancaster, Pa., 1922-1932. Reformed Mennonite.
Goshen College Record. Goshen, Ind., 1903-. Succeeded *Elkhart Institute Monthly* in 1903. MC.
Gospel Herald. Scottdale, Pa., 1908-. MC.
Gospel Witness. Scottdale, Pa., 1905-1908. MC.
Herold der Wahrheit. Scottdale, Pa., 1912-. Conservative Amish Mennonite.
Herald of Truth. Chicago, Ill., 1864-67, moved to Elkhart, Ind., 1867-1906. Very important, semi-official paper published by John F. Funk for Mennonites (esp. Old) and Amish Mennonites.
Journal of the Illinois State Historical Society. Custer, Milo. "Asiatic Cholera in Central Illinois 1834-1873." 23 (April, 1930): 113ff.
The Menno-light. Bloomington, Ill., 1960-. Published by Mennonite Hospital.

The Mennonite. Published variously at Philadelphia, Pa., Berne, Ind., and presently North Newton, Kan., 1885-.
The Mennonite and Christian Evangel. Hillsboro, Kan., 1934-35. These two magazines were combined in 1934-35. GC and Central Conference Mennonite.
Mennonite Church in the City. Chicago, 1956-1968.
The Mennonite Community. Scottdale, Pa., 1947-1953. Replaced by *Christian Living* in 1954. MC.
Mennonite Heritage. Normal, Ill., 1974-. Published by the Illinois Mennonite Historical and Genealogical Society.
    Albrecht, Mrs. Henry (Harriet). "The Albrecht Family of Bureau County." 4 (June 1977): 1ff.
    Brunk, Ivan W. "Mennonites in Henry County Illinois." 3 (March 1976): 3-4.
    Estes, Steven R. "History of Partridge Creek Meeting Traced." 7 (June 1980): 15ff.
    Habecker, Mrs. Albert. "The Boynton Mennonite Church." 3 (Dec. 1976): 46.
    Hassan, Hazel Nice. "The Early Mennonites of Jo Daviess County." 4 (March 1977): 3-5.
    _____. "The Hammer Cemetery." 4 (March 1977): 9-10.
    _____. "Peter Maurer, Pioneer." 6 (Sept. 1979): 29-31.
    Hassan, W. Richard. "The Fairfield Amish Mennonite Church." 4 (Sept. 1977): 27ff.
    _____. "History of the Summerfield Church." 5 (March 1978): 7-11.
    _____. "John D. Kauffman, Sleeping Preacher." 4 (Sept. 1977): 25ff.
    _____. "Rockwell Mennonite Church of Sheffield." 7 (March and June 1980): 3ff. and 17-21.
    _____. "The Sterling Reformed Mennonite Church." 6 (March 1979): 3ff.
    _____. "Valentine Strubhar and the East Washington (Calvary) Church." 2 (Sept. 1975): 27-8.
    Helmuth, Orva. "The Amish of Arthur." 2 (June 1975): 1ff.
    Helmuth, Orva and Hassan, W. Richard. "Menno Diener Talks of His Family and Church." 2 (June 1975): 15-16.
    Nafziger, Arthur, and Hassan, W. Richard. "Interview with Christian E. Martin." 1 (Dec. 1974): 7-10.
    Oyer, John S. "Life Among the Early 19th Century Amish-Mennonite Immigrants to Illinois." 3 (Dec. 1976): 40.
    Oyer, Verle. "The Oyer Family Comes to America." 3 (Sept. 1976): 25ff.
    _____. "A Short History of East Bend Church." 4 (Dec. 1977): 1ff.
    Roth, Elva Mae (Schrock). "Mennonite Work Camp: Chicago, 1938." 6 (Sept. 1979): 27ff.
    _____. "The Pleasant Grove Church." 4 (June 1977): 15-6.
    Schultz, Arnold C. "A Hershey Leaman: Pioneer Missionary." 2 (Dec. 1975): 37ff.
    Schultz, Peter G. "The Evangelical Mennonite Church in Illinois." 2 (Sept. 1975): 25ff.
    _____. "The Evangelical Mennonite Church Publications." 2 (Sept. 1975): 1ff.
    _____. "First All-Mennonite Convention." 2 (Dec. 1975): 38 ff.
    _____. "John F. Funk." 4 (Sept. 1977): 26.
    Stalter, Edwin J. "Gardner Mennonite Church." 3 (Sept. 1976): 27-8.

Yoder, Thomas. "Ezra Yordy: A Man of Many Facets." 3 (Dec. 1979): 1ff.
Mennonite Historical Bulletin. Scottdale, Pa., 1940-. MC.
    Brunk, Ivan W. "Brunk Ancestors." 37 (July 1976): 5-7.
    Gingerich, Melvin. "Sleeping Preachers." 32 (Jan., 1971): 4-6.
    _____. "Ten Leaders." 1 (Oct. 1940): 1ff.
    Helmuth, Orva. "History of the Arthur Amish Mennonite Church." 22 (Oct. 1961): 3-5.
    Hershberger, Guy F. "A Tribute to Melvin Gingerich." 36 (Oct. 1975): 2-4.
    Letter from Reuben J. Heatwole to John S. Coffman, Apr. 11, 1865. 35 (Jan. 1974): 2ff.
    Springer, Nelson P. "Mennonites in New Orleans." 15 (July 1954): 6-7.
    Yoder, Edward. "Henry Yother (1810-1900)." 5 (June 1944): 1ff.
Mennonite Life. North Newton, Kan., 1946-. Inter-Mennonite.
    Bainton, Roland H. "The Enduring Witness." 9 (April 1954): 98.
    Bender, Harold S. "Outside Influences on Mennonite Thought." 10 (Jan. 1955): 45-47.
    Byers, N. E. "The All-Mennonite Convention." 5 (July 1948): 7-8.
    _____. "C. Henry Smith as I Knew Him." 5 (April 1950): 5-8.
    _____. "The Times in Which I Lived." 7 (Jan., April, and July 1952): 44-47, 77-81, 138-41.
    Fretz, J. Winfield. "First Mennonites in Chicago." 8 (April 1953): 56-7.
    _____. "Mennonite Community: Traditional or Intentional." 30 (Dec. 1975): 5-7.
    Hostetler, John A. "Amish Problems at the *Diener-Versammlungen.*" 4 (Oct. 1949): 34-39.
    Juhnke, James C. "Mennonite Benevolence and Civic Identity: The Post-War Compromise." 25 (Jan. 1970): 34-37.
    Mendel, J. S. "Lincoln Avenue Gospel Mission." 8 (April 1953): 64-65.
    Neufeld, John T. "The Grace Mennonite Church." 8 (April 1953): 65-66.
    Smith, C. Henry. "A Pioneer Educator—N. E. Byers." 3 (Jan. 1948): 44-46.
    Yoder, Harry. "Joseph Stuckey, and Central Conference." 6 (April 1951): 16-19.
The Mennonite Quarterly Review. Goshen, Ind., 1927-. Inter-Mennonite.
    Beachy, Alvin J. "The Rise and Development of the Beachy Amish Mennonite Churches." 29 (April 1955): 118-40.
    Bender, Harold S., trans. and ed. "A Few Words About the Mennonites in America in 1841: A Contemporary Document by Jacob Krehbiel." 6 (Jan. 1932): 43-57.
    Driedger, Leo. "Native Rebellion and Mennonite Invasion: An Examination of Two Canadian River Valleys." 46 (July 1972): 290-300.
    Dyck, C. J. "The Mennonite World Conference: A Brief Introduction." 41 (July 1967): 277-87.
    Esh, Levi A. "The Amish Parochial School Movement, research notes." 51 (Jan. 1977): 69-75.
    Fretz, J. Herbert. "The Germantown Anti-Slavery Petition of 1688." 33 (Jan. 1959): 42-59.
    Gascho, Milton. "The Amish Division of 1693-1697 in Switzerland and Alsace." 11 (Oct. 1937): 235-266.
    Hershberger, Guy F. "Historical Background to the Formation of the Mennonite Central Committee." 44 (July 1970): 213-244.
    Hertzler, Silas. "Mennonite Elementary Schools, 1947-48." 23 (April 1949): 108-12.
    Hostetler, John A. "Old Order Amish Survival." 51 (Oct. 1977): 359.

Juhnke, James C. "General Conference Mennonite Missions to the American Indians in the Late Nineteenth Century." 54 (April 1980): 117-34.
Kauffman, J. Howard. "Boundary Maintenance and Cultural Assimilation of Contemporary Mennonites." 51 (July 1977): 227-40.
Keim, Albert N. "Service or Resistance? The Mennonite Response to Conscription in World War II." 52 (April 1978): 141-53.
Mennonite Central Committee Anniversary Issue. 44 (July 1970).
Ruth, Jacob Ernest. "A Journey in the Mid-Nineteenth Century." 42 (July 1968): 203-10.
Schlabach, Theron F. "Reveille for *Die Stillen Im Lande:* A Stir Among Mennonites in the Late Nineteenth Century. Awakening or Quickening? Revival or Acculturation? Anabaptist or What?" 51 (July 1977): 213-26.
Schnell, Kempis. "John F. Funk, 1835-1930, and the Mennonite Migration of 1873-1875." 24 (July 1950): 199-229.
Smith, Willard H. "C. Henry Smith, 1865-1948: A Brief Biography." 23 (Jan. 1949): 7-15.
Sprunger, Samuel F. "A Trip to Illinois and Iowa in 1872." 3 (Oct. 1929): 235-242.
Stayer, James M. "Reflections and Retractions on *Anabaptists and the Sword.*" 51 (July 1977): 197-212.
Stayer, James M.; Packull, Werner O.; and Depperman, Klaus. "From Monogenesis to Polygenesis: The Historical Discussion of Anabaptist Origins." 49 (April 1975): 83-121.
Teichroew, Allan, ed., "Military Surveillance of Mennonites in World War I." 53 (April 1979): 95-127.
Umble, John S. "John S. Coffman as an Evangelist." 23 (July 1949): 123-146.

Mennonite Reporter. Waterloo, Ontario, 1971-. Succeeded *Canadian Mennonite.* Inter-Mennonite.
Mennonite Weekly Review. Newton, Kan., 1923-. Inter-Mennonite.
The Mission Worker. Chicago, Ill. Monthly, 1906-08. MC.
Missionary Guide. Various places; quarterly, 1944-46; bimonthly, 1946-. MC.
Pekin Times. 1976.
The Peoria Journal Star. Aug. 29, 30, 31, 1961.
Post-American. Deerfield, Ill., 1972-1975. Name changed to *Sojourners* in 1976.
Rural Sociology. Provo, Utah, 1973.
Stoltzfus, Victor. "Amish Agriculture: Adaptive Strategies for Economic Survival of Community Life." 38 (Summer 1973): 196-205.
The Silver Lining. Grabill, Ind., 1943-. Apostolic Christian
Sugar Creek (Ohio) *Budget.* 1890-.
The Sword and Trumpet. Denbigh, Va., 1929-. Conservative journal oriented to MC.
Tazewell Publications. Supplement. Morton, Ill., 1978, 1979.
Washington Memo. Newsletter published from the Washington, D.C., office of the Peace Section of Mennonite Central Committee, Akron, Pa.
WHAM. [Hopedale, Ill.], 1976.
Der Wahrheitsfreund. Inman, Kan., 1915-1947. Krimmer. Mennonite Brethren.
The Weather Vane. Evanston, Ill., 1953-1960. Published by MCC 1-W and Service Units.
Your Church Library Newsletter. Morton, Ill., 1960-1966. First Mennonite (MC) Morton.

Youth's Christian Companion. Scottdale, Pa., 1920-1968. MC.

Zion's Call. Flanagan, Ill., 1898-1920. First published in interest of Salem orphanage. Official organ of the Defenseless Mennonite Conference, 1913-1920. Merged with *Good Tidings* (not the Reformed Mennonite periodical) in Sept. 1921 to form *Zion's Tidings*.

Zion's Tidings. Berne, Ind., 1921-1953. Defenseless Mennonite.

Other Published Works

Aby, Malvin Stanton, and Aby, Franklin Stanton, MD. *The Aby Family of Peoria County Illinois...,* Vol. 4. Chicago, Ill., 1924.

Annual Report and Directory of EMC Ft. Wayne, Ind. [various years].

Asbury, Herbert. *The Great Illusion.* Garden City, N.Y., 1950.

Bateman, Newton, et al., ed. *The History of McLean County, Illinois, containing* etc. Chicago, 1879.
    A subscription history with some valuable items including population statistics on page 1078.

[Baumgartner, John H.]. *The First One Hundred Years; Dec. 24, 1870-Dec. 24, 1970; Apostolic Christian Church, Bluffton, Indiana.* [Bluffton, Ind., 1970.]

Bender, Harold S. *Conrad Grebel, ca. 1498-1526: The Founder of the Swiss Brethren, Sometimes Called Anabaptists.* Goshen, Ind., 1950.

———. *Mennonite Sunday School Centennial, 1840-1940.* Scottdale, Pa., 1940. Reprinted in J[ohn] C. Wenger, *The Mennonite Church in America* (Scottdale, 1966), 144-181.

Bender, Urie. *Four Earthen Vessels.* Scottdale, 1982. C. F. Derstine is one of the four discussed in this work.

Bent, Charles, ed. *History of Whiteside County, Illinois, From Its First Settlement to the Present Time; With Numerous Biographical and Family Sketches.* Morrison, Ill., 1877.

Boggess, A. C. *Settlement of Illinois.* Chicago, Ill., 1908.

Bradsby, H. C. *History of Bureau County Illinois.* Chicago, Ill., 1885.

Browning, Clyde. *Amish in Illinois. Over One Hundred Years of the "Old Order" Sect of Central Illinois.* N.p., 1971.

Brunk, Ivan and Ann. *Lombard Mennonite Church History 1954-1974.* N.p., 1974.

Centennial Anniversary of the North Danvers House of Worship, 1872-1972. [Danvers, Ill., 1972]. Copy in MHLG.

Central Conference Year Book. N.p., various years.

Charles, Howard. "A Presentation and Evaluation of MCC Draft Status Census." In *Proceedings of the Fourth Annual Conference on Mennonite Cultural Problems.* North Newton, Kan., 1945.

Church Manual of the Defenseless Mennonite Church: 1937. Berne, Ind., 1937. Gives a bit of history of the church including start of missions. Also bylaws, articles of faith, rules of discipline, ordinances, officers, forms.

[Claassen, Frieda, ed.]. *The Woodlawn Story.* Chicago, 1958. Mostly pictures.

Clark, Olynthus. "Joseph Joder, Schoolmaster-Farmer and Poet 1797-1887." In *Transactions of the Illinois State Historical Society 1929,* Publication No. 36, pp. 150-53. Springfield, Ill., 1929.

Claudon, David N., and Claudon, Kathryn E. *Life of Bishop Henry Egly 1824-1890.* N.p. [1947].

Coffman, Barbara F. *His Name Was John: The Life Story of an Early Mennonite Leader.* Scottdale, Pa., 1964.

Coffman, John S. *Outline and Notes Used at the Bible Conference Held at*

Johnstown, Pennsylvania, from Dec. 27, 1897 to Jan. 7, 1898. Elkhart, Ind., 1898.
Cole, Arthur C. *The Era of the Civil War 1848-1870. Centennial History of Illinois*, Vol. III. Springfield, Ill., 1919.
Combined Histories of Shelby and Moultrie Counties, Illinois. Philadelphia, 1881; reprint ed., Evansville, Ind., 1974.
Commager, Henry Steele. *Documents of American History*. 7th ed. New York, 1963.
Conference Proceedings of the Western District A.M. Conference, 1890 to 1912. Scottdale, Pa. Condensed, but valuable.
Conference Report of the Conference of the Evangelical Mennonite Church. N.p., 1948-1977.
Conference Report of the Defenseless Mennonites. N.p., 1921-1947.
Cosco, Ethel Reeser. *Christian Reeser: The Story of a Centenarian*. N.p., n.d.
Custer, Milo. *Central Illinois Obituaries, 1871-1880*. Reprint edition, Normal, Ill., 1969.
Deter, Eunice. *Descendants of Ulrich Steiner*. Morrison, Ill., 1947.
Dictionary of American Biography. 20 vols. plus 5 supplements. New York, 1928-1977.
Dictionary of American History. New York, 1946, 6 vols.; revised ed., 1976, 8 vols.
Driver, Harvey A. *This Is Our Church*. Ft. Wayne, Ind. [1967].
Duis, Dr. E. *The Good Old Times in McLean County, Illinois, Containing Two Hundred and Sixty-one Sketches of Old Settlers, a Complete Sketch of the Black Hawk War . . . and All Matters of Interest Relating to McLean County*. 1st ed., 1874, 2nd ed., n.p. [Chicago], sesquicentennial issue 1968.
    An index to the above is put out by Bloomington-Normal Genealogical Society.
Dyck, Cornelius J., ed. *An Introduction to Mennonite History*. Scottdale, Pa., 1967. A revised edition came out in 1981.
_____. *The Witness of the Holy Spirit, Proceedings of the Eighth Mennonite World Conference*. Amsterdam, The Netherlands, July 23-30, 1967. Elkhart, Ind., 1967.
Eash, A. M. *After Ten Years: A Brief Report of the First Ten Years of Work of the Twenty-Sixth Street Mennonite Mission, 1900-1916*. Chicago, 1916.
    Many quotations from Chicago papers. Amply illustrated.
Echoes: A Book Containing the Report of and the Addresses Delivered at The First All-Mennonite Convention in America. Hillsboro, Kan., 1913.
Egle, Christian R. *Brief History of Salem Mennonite Church near Flanagan, Illinois as Given by Elder Christian R. Egle of Meadows, Illinois*. N.p., [1925].
Encyclopedia Americana. International ed. New York, 1974.
Erb, Ethel Estella (Cooprider). *Story of Grandmother Heatwole-Brunk-Cooprider*. Hesston, Kan., n.d.
Erb, Paul. *South Central Frontiers: A History of the South Central Mennonite Conference*. Scottdale, Pa., 1974.
Esch, Ben. "The Work of 'Father Stuckey.'" In *Year Book of the Central Conference of Mennonites 1954*, edited by R. L. Hartzler. N.p., 1954.
Estes, Steven R. *Christian Concern for Health: The Sixtieth Anniversary History of the Mennonite Hospital Association*. Bloomington, Ill., 1979.
Evangelical Mennonite Church Manual Revision. Mimeographed copy, 1979. Given to writer, courtesy EMC headquarters staff in Ft. Wayne, Ind. This *Church Manual* had been published early in the life of the group and

Bibliography 571

    revised at various times and places: 1917, 1937, 1949, 1960, 1970, and now in process of another revision.

Evidences of Modernism at Bluffton College. Compiled and published by the Board of Deacons, First Mennonite Church, Berne, Ind., 1929.

First Mennonite Church Presents Its Centennial Pageant Cherish Our Past—Share Our Future, A Historical Drama in Ten Scenes. [Morton, Ill., 1976]. At the same time the congregation published a brief history entitled *Centennial Celebration of First Mennonite Church Morton, Illinois.* [Morton, 1979]. Mrs. Ruth Gerber King and Elva Roth were largely responsible for the historical data in both of the above publications.

Fite, Emerson D. *Social and Industrial Conditions in the North During the Civil War.* New York, 1930.

Flanagan Mennonite Church Centennial Year 1876-1976, July 23-25. N.p. [1976]. Myrna Park papers. Biographies of ministers and church workers.

Fretz, Abraham James, *A Brief History of Bishop Henry Funck and Other Funk Pioneers....* Elkhart, Ind., 1899.

Funk, John F. *The Mennonite Church and Her Accusers: A Vindication of the Character of the Mennonite Church of America from Her Organization in This Country to the Present Time.* Elkhart, Ind., 1878.

Gates, Helen, et al. *Bless the Lord, O My Soul: A Biography of John Fretz Funk, 1835-1930, Creative Pioneer for Christ and Mennonite Leader.* Scottdale, Pa., 1964.

Gratz, Delbert. *Bernese Anabaptists and Their American Descendants.* Goshen, Ind., 1953.

Litwiller, Ruth, and Gerig, Viola. *History of the Salem Evangelical Mennonite Church of Gridley, Illinois.* Gridley, Ill., 1950. Prepared for its 75th anniversary. In Tom Yoder papers. Quotes Harry F. Weber, *Centennial History of the Mennonites of Illinois, 1829-1929,* on Weber's period.

_____. *Salem Evangelical Church History—100th Anniversary Aug. 29-31, 1975.* N.p., 1975.

Gingerich, Melvin. *Mennonite Attire Through Four Centuries.* Breinigsville, Pa., 1970.

_____. *Mennonites in Iowa.* Iowa City, Iowa, 1939.

_____. *Service for Peace: A History of Mennonite Civilian Public Service.* Akron, Pa., 1941.

God Hath Spoken: Twenty-five Addresses Delivered at the World Conference on Christian Fundamentals, May 25-June 1, 1919. Philadelphia [1919].

Good, Aaron C. *A Life Sketch.* Sterling, Ill., 1980.

Good, Lewis C. *A Good Tree Grew in the Valley: The Family Record of Christian Good, 1842-1916.* Baltimore, 1974.

Görz, D. *Das Weihnachtsfest der Sonntags—und Wochenschule für 1873, in Summerfield, Illinois....* N.p., 1874.

Gray, Wood, et al. *Historian's Handbook: A Key to the Study and Writing of History.* 2nd ed. Boston, 1964.

Grubb, W. H. *History of the Mennonites of Butler County, Ohio.* Trenton, Ohio, 1916.

Haab, Arthur. *The Apostolic Christian Church of America: Its Nature and Task.* N.p., n.d. (Published recently by the author, who lives at Goshen, Ind.)

Harder, Leland. *General Conference Mennonite Church Fact Book of Congregational Membership.* N.p. [probably Newton, Kan.], 1971.

_____. *Seventy-Third and Laflin.* Chicago, 1952.

Hartzler, John E. *Education among the Mennonites of America.* Danvers, Ill., 1925.

Hartzler, Jonas S. *Mennonites in the World War, or Nonresistance Under Test.* Scottdale, Pa., 1922.
Hassan, Hazel Nice. *The Nice Family History: Descendants of Henry Clemmer Nice (1822-1892).* Normal, Ill., 1965.
Heiser, Ervin William. *Sixty Years with East Bend: History and Photographic Record of East Bend Mennonite Church.* Fisher, Ill., 1949.
Helmuth, Orva S. *History of the Arthur Mennonite Church.* Arthur, Ill., 1958.
Henry, Carl F. H. *The Uneasy Conscience of Modern Fundamentalism.* Grand Rapids, 1947.
Hershberger, Guy F. *The Mennonite Church in the Second World War.* Scottdale, Pa., 1951.
───────. *War, Peace, and Nonresistance.* Scottdale, Pa., 1944.
Hiebert, P. C., and Miller, Orie O. *Feeding the Hungry: Russia Famine 1919-1925; American Mennonite Relief Operations Under the Auspices of the Mennonite Central Committee.* Scottdale, Pa., 1929.
Historical Committee. *Roanoke Mennonite Church Centennial Year 1875-1975.* [Eureka, Ill., 1975].
The History of Jo Daviess County. Chicago, 1878; reprint ed., Evansville, Ind., 1973.
History of Kankakee County. N.p., 1906.
History of Tazewell County Illinois. Chicago, 1879; reprint ed., Evansville, Ind., 1975.
Hockett, Homer C. *Political and Social Growth of the American People. 1492-1865.* 3rd ed. New York, 1940.
Hofer, David M. *Die Hungersnot in Russland und Unsere Reise in die Welt.* Chicago, 1924.
Horsch, John. *Communism: A Deadly Foe to the Christian Faith Assuming the Guise of Christianity.* Chicago [1937].
───────. *Is the Mennonite Church of America Free from Modernism?* Scottdale, Pa., 1926.
───────. *The Mennonite Church and Modernism.* Scottdale, Pa., 1924.
───────. *Mennonites in Europe.* Scottdale, Pa., 1942.
───────. *Modern Religious Liberalism: The Destructiveness and Irrationality of Modernist Theology.* Scottdale, Pa. [1924].
Hostetler, John A. *Amish Society.* 3rd revised ed. Baltimore, Md., 1980.
───────. *God Uses Ink: The Heritage and Mission of the Mennonite Publishing House after Fifty Years.* Scottdale, Pa., 1958. A good work with a good chapter on "John F. Funk and the Mennonite Publishing Company," pp. 25-64; pp. 28-40 deal with Funk in Chicago.
───────. *The Sociology of Mennonite Evangelism.* Scottdale, Pa., 1954.
Hostetler, Pius. *Life, Preaching and Labors of John D. Kauffman: A Short Sketch of the Life, Preaching and Labors of John D. Kauffman.* Shelbyville, Ill. [1916].
Illinois Mennonite [Church] Conference. *Constitution and Rules and Discipline of the Mennonite Conference of the State of Illinois.* N.p., 1922.
───────. *Constitution of the Mennonite Conference of the State of Illinois.* Cullom, Ill., 1904.
───────. *Illinois Mennonite Conference Directory.* N.p., 1947. Includes the constitutions of Illinois Mennonite Conference, Illinois. Mennonite Mission Board, Illinois Mennonite Sewing Circle, Illinois State Literary Society.
───────. *Reports 1929-1979.* (Varied wordings in title.) N.p., various years.
Illinois Ministers Meeting [Report]. N.p., 1910-[ca. 1918], annual.
In Memoriam: Dean Noah Oyer, 1891-1931. Goshen, Ind., 1931.

Irons, Frank. *An Early History of Woodford County, with Emphasis on Montgomery Township*. Congerville, Ill., 1948. Many Mennonites have resided in Montgomery Township.
Jackson, Dave. *Coming Together: All Those Communities and What They're Up To*. Minneapolis, 1978.
Juhnke, James C. *A People of Mission: A History of General Conference Mennonite Overseas Missions*. Newton, Kan., 1979.
──────. *A People of Two Kingdoms: The Political Acculturation of the Kansas Mennonites*. Newton, Kan., 1975.
Kauffman, Abraham M. *The Trouble Between A. M. Kauffman and the Amish People*. Arcola, Ill., 1915. Quite a harangue of Kauffman against Amish. He had been excommunicated.
Kauffman, Daniel, ed. *Mennonite Cyclopedic Dictionary*. Scottdale, Pa., 1937.
──────. *Fifty Years in the Mennonite Church 1890-1940*. Scottdale, Pa., 1941.
Kauffman, J. Howard, and Harder, Leland. *Anabaptists Four Centuries Later: A Profile of Five Mennonite and Brethren in Christ Denominations*. Scottdale, Pa., 1975.
Kauffman, Milo. *The Challenge of Christian Stewardship*. Scottdale, Pa., 1955.
──────. *Stewards of God*. Scottdale, Pa., 1975.
Kaufman, Edmund George. *The Development of the Missionary and Philanthropic Interest among the Mennonites of North America*. Berne, Ind., 1931.
Kenyon, Franklin L., ed. *Roanoke Centennial History . . . bridging the years, 1874-1974*. Peoria, Ill., 1974.
Kortemeier, Eldon. *The Life and the Growth of the Freeport Mennonite Church*. Goshen, Ind., 1959.
Kraybill, Paul N. *North American Inter-Mennonite Relationships*. Rosemont, Ill., 1974.
Kraus, C[lyde] Norman. *Dispensationalism in America: Its Rise and Development*. Richmond, Va., 1958.
Krehbiel, Christian. *Prairie Pioneer: The Christian Krehbiel Story*. Newton, Kan., 1961.
Krehbiel, Henry Peter. *The History of the General Conference of the Mennonite Church in North America*. [Canton, Ohio] and Newton, Kan., 1938.
Krehbiel, Jacob. *Krehbiel History and Family Records*. Compiled and mimeographed by Howard Raid. Bluffton, Ohio, 1963. Quite a bit about genealogy but also quite a bit of interesting history about conditions in Europe during the period of the French Revolution and after.
Lehman, James O. *Creative Congregationalism*. Smithville, Ohio, 1978. A history of the Oak Grove Mennonite Church in Wayne County, Ohio.
──────. *Sonnenberg: A Haven and a Heritage*. Kidron, Ohio, 1969.
Loewen, Melvin J. *Three Score: The Story of an Emerging Mennonite Church in Central Africa*. Elkhart, Ind. [1972].
Lugibihl, Walter H., and Gerig, Jared F. *The Missionary Church Association*. Berne, Ind., 1950.
Mast, John B., trans. and ed. *The Letters of the Amish Division of 1693-1711*. Oregon City, Ore., 1950. Some letters by Jacob and Ulrich Amman *et al.* upholding shunning, and letters opposing it.
Mead, Frank S. *Handbook of Denominations in the United States*. New York [1951].
[Mennonite Board of Missions and Charities]. *Chicago Bethel Church Development*. Elkhart, Ind., n.d. [1940s].

Mennonite Church Polity: A Statement of Practices in Church Government. Scottdale, Pa., 1944.

"Mennonite Church, Summerfield, Ill." In *Mennonite Yearbook and Almanac.* ... N.p., 1913.

Mennonite Church, Washington, Illinois: Our Church 1886-1960. In IMHGS Library.

The Mennonite Encyclopedia: A Comprehensive Reference Work on the Anabaptist Mennonite Movement. 4 volumes. Hillsboro, Kan., Newton, Kan., Scottdale, Pa., 1955-1959. A very valuable source of information, even for a regional history of the Mennonites.

Mennonite Home Mission, Chicago, Ill. *Report of Dedicatory Service and Missionary Conference Held at the Home Mission, Chicago, Ill., January 5th, 6th, and 7th, 1919.* Chicago, Ill., 1919.

_____. *Report of the Home Mission.* Chicago, 1894.

Mennonite Yearbook and Directory. Scottdale, Pa., various years since 1905.

Merriman, Prof., et al. *The History of McLean County, Illinois.* Chicago, 1879.

Meyer, Carl S., ed. *Sixteenth-Century Essays and Studies.* Volume I. St. Louis, 1970.

Miller, D. Paul. *The Illinois Amish.* Gordonville, Pa., 1980.

Miller, Dan A. *History of Arthur, Illinois also Records of Deaths, Marriages, and Minister Ordinations plus Extra Memo Pages for Future Records also Reports of Some of the Trying Times of the Good Old Days.* Arthur, Ill., 1975.

Miller, Levi, ed. *The Meetinghouse of God's People.* Scottdale, Pa., 1977.

Missionary Church, Inc. 1980 Directory. Ft. Wayne, Ind., 1980.

Moody, William R. *The Life of Dwight L. Moody.* New York, 1900.

Moore, Roy L. *History of Woodford County.* Eureka, Ill., 1910.

Moser, Chester C., and Moser, Helen V. *Fiftieth Anniversary Souvenir of the Salem Children's Home, Flanagan, Ill., 1896-1946.* Flanagan, Ill., 1946.

Musser, Daniel. *The Reformed Mennonite Church, Its Rise and Progress, with Its Principles and Doctrines.* Lancaster, Pa., 1873.

Nafziger, Arthur, et al. *100 Years at Hopedale.* Hopedale, Ill., 1954. Nafziger with Simon G. Birkey and Christian E. Martin were a committee which wrote this history as part of their centennial celebration. Illustrated. Above also in *Christian Living* 1 (Aug. 1954): 18-21.

Nafziger, Carolyn. *The Hopedale Story: A Historical Drama about Hopedale Mennonite Church.* Hopedale, Ill., 1976.

Neufeld, John T. and Catherine, compilers. *Mennonite Work in Chicago up to 1961.* [Chicago, 1961]. Loaned to writer, courtesy Peter G. Schultz, Justice, Ill.

Nussbaum, Stan. *You Must Be Born Again.* [Ft. Wayne, Ind.], 1980.

Oyer, Emma. *What God Hath Wrought in a Half Century at the Mennonite Home Mission.* Elkhart, Ind., 1949. Written and compiled by a veteran worker at the Mission.

Oyer, Verle and Margaret. *Jacob Zehr 1825-1898 "Mackinaw Meeting" Preacher.* Foosland, Ill., 1964.

Pannabecker, Samuel Floyd. *Faith in Ferment: A History of the Central District Conference.* Newton, Kan., 1968. Good treatment—Central District Conference of GC Mennonite Church. Includes the old Central Conference of Mennonites (Iowa, Missouri, Illinois, Indiana, Ohio, and Michigan).

_____. *Open Doors: The History of the General Conference Mennonite Church.* Newton, Kan., 1975.

_____. *Ventures of Faith: The Story of Mennonite Biblical Seminary.* Elkhart, Ind., 1975.

Parish, Arlyn J. *Kansas Mennonites During World War I.* Fort Hays, Kan., 1968.
Past and Present of Woodford County, Illinois. Chicago, 1878.
Peachey, Paul. *The Church in the City.* Newton, Kan., 1963.
―――――. *Seminar on a Theology of Christian Social Service.* Elkhart, 1963. Seminar held in Goshen at Goshen Biblical Seminary, April 5 and 6, 1963.
Pease, Theodore C. *The Frontier State 1818-1848. Centennial History of Illinois,* Vol. II. Springfield, Ill., 1918.
―――――. *The Story of Illinois.* 3rd ed. Revised by Marguerita Jenison Pease. Chicago, 1965.
Peck, J. M. *A Gazetteer of Illinois.* Philadelphia, Pa., 1837.
Pickard, Madge, and Buley, R. Carlyle. *The Midwest Pioneer: His Ills, Cures and Doctors.* Crawfordsville, Ind., 1945.
Ping, Jane Ann. *Where Past Meets Present, A History of the Arthur Amish.* Arthur, Ill., 1975.
The Portrait and Biographical Album of McLean County, Illinois. Chicago, 1887.
Proceedings of the Fourth Annual Conference on Mennonite Cultural Problems. North Newton, Kan., 1945.
Proceedings of the Eleventh Conference on Mennonite Educational and Cultural Problems. N.p., 1957.
Reba Place Fellowship. Evanston, Ill., n.d.
Report of the 22nd Annual Meeting of the Illinois District Mennonite Mission Board, Inc. N.p., 1945. These *Reports* used for various years.
Reports of the Western District A.M. Conferences for the Years 1912-1920. Scottdale, Pa. [1920].
Roanoke Mennonite Church Centennial Year 1875-1975. [Eureka, Ill., 1975].
Roeschley, Wilma, ed. and comp. *Beller, Jacob Family Record—1803-1970.* Elgin, Ill., 1970.
Ropp, Pete, comp. *Christian Ropp 1812-1896.* Normal, Ill., 1977.
Schrock, Paul M. *Four Score and Ten: The Story of Joseph Schrock, 1852-1943.* [Scottdale, Pa., 1972].
Schlabach, Theron F. *Gospel Versus Gospel: Mission and the Mennonite Church, 1863-1944.* Scottdale, Pa., 1980.
Schneider, Herbert W. *Religion in Twentieth-Century America.* Cambridge, Mass., 1952.
Schwartz, Charles P. *In the United States Court of Appeals For the Seventh Circuit ... Brief for Appellant* (Abraham Warkentin). [Chicago, 1937].
Scofield, Cyrus I. *Rightly Dividing The Word of Truth (2 Tim. ii, 15.) Being Ten Outline Studies of the More Important Divisions of Scripture.* Findlay, Ohio, 1936.
Sears, Amanda, et al., *The Albrechts 1836-1969.* N.p., 1969 ed.
75th Anniversary History, Salem Children's Home, 1971. N.p., 1971. Brochure.
Showalter, Richard A. *The Conservative Mennonite Conference; a Short History of Some Amish Mennonites, 1910-1970.* Irwin, Ohio, 1971.
[Shrock, William J.]. *A Timely Warning Or, The Midnight Cry From Heaven.* [Jerome, Mich., 1946]. On the sleeping preachers. Contains material on Kauffman and Troyer.
Sider, Harvey. *The Church in Mission.* Nappanee, Ind., 1975.
Sider, Ronald J. *Rich Christians in an Age of Hunger.* New York, 1977.
Simons, Menno. *Complete Writings.* Trans. by Leonard Verduin, ed. by J[ohn] C. Wenger. Scottdale, Pa.; 1956.
Sloneker, Elsie I. *A Brief History of the North Danvers Mennonite Church.* Danvers, Ill., 1972.

Smith, C. Henry. "The Amish in Illinois." In *Mennonite Yearbook and Directory*. [Scottdale, Pa.], 1907.
——————. *The Coming of the Russian Mennonites: An Episode in the Settling of the Last Frontier, 1874-1884.* Berne, Ind., 1927.
——————. *The Education of a Mennonite Country Boy.* Bluffton, Ohio, 1943. A small edition of 50 mimeographed copies printed for close relatives and friends—later published, with very few changes, as *Mennonite Country Boy: The Early Years of C. Henry Smith.* Newton, Kan., 1962 (the edition cited in this study).
——————. *Mennonite Country Boy.* See entry immediately above.
——————. *The Mennonite Immigration to Pennsylvania in the Eighteenth Century.* Norristown, Pa., 1929.
——————. *The Mennonites of America.* Goshen, Ind., 1909.
——————. *Metamora.* Bluffton, Ohio, 1947.
——————. *One Hundred Years Ago.* N.p., [1940]. An address at Metamora, Ill., Aug. 20, 1940.
——————. *The Story of the Mennonites.* 4th ed. Rev. and enl. by Cornelius Krahn. Newton, Kan., 1957. A fifth edition came out in 1981.
Smith, C. Henry, and Hirschler, E. J., ed. *The Story of Bluffton College.* [Bluffton, Ohio], 1925.
Smith, Willard H. *The Social and Religious Thought of William Jennings Bryan.* Lawrence, Kan., 1975.
Smucker, Carl F., and Steiner, Robert L. *A Research Study of the Aged in a Central Illinois Mennonite Community.* Newton, Kan., ca. 1961. An able study by competent authorities.
Sommer, Oscar Julius. *History of Sommer Brothers Seed Company, 1905-1955.* Pekin, Ill., 1955.
Springer, Joe, et al. *A History of Willow Springs Mennonite Church.* Tiskilwa, Ill., 1924. Nine persons helped compile this history, including the ministers (C. A. Hartzler and Ira Eigsti).
Stalter, Edwin J. *The Mennonites of Waldo 1860-1960.* N.p. [ca. 1960].
——————. *Notes on Some Early American Stalters: Joseph, John, Jacobina.* N.p., 1969.
Stalter, Edwin and Marcella. *Illinois Mennonite Conference in Mission.* Flanagan, Ill., 1980.
Steiner, Orel R., comp. *Apostolic Christian Churches and Ministers in America and Japan.* Oakville, Iowa, 1945-1977.
Stuckey, Joseph. *Eine Begebenheit, die sich in der Mennoniten-Gemeinde, in Deutschland und in der Schweiz, von 1693 bis 1700 zugetragen hat.* Elkhart, Ind., 1871. Preface trans. by Nelson Springer.
Supreme Court Reporter. Vol. 92A. St. Paul, Minn., 1974. Contains *Wisconsin vs. Yoder*, pp. 1526-1550.
Swartzendruber, Maude. *The Lamp in the West.* La Junta, Colo., 1975.
Toews, Mary Wiens. *The True Life Story of the Wiens Family.* N.p., n.d.
Trinity Mennonite Church Annual Reports. [Morton, Ill.], 1977-1978.
Trinity Mennonite Service of Dedication. Sept. 30, 1979. [Trinity Mennonite Church, Morton, Ill.].
Troyer, Noah. *Sermons Delivered by Noah Troyer, the Noted Amishman, While in an Unconscious State.* Iowa City, Iowa, 1879. Includes a brief biographical sketch of his life.
Umble, John S. *Goshen College, 1894-1954: A Venture in Christian Education.* Goshen, Ind., 1955.
Unruh, John D. *In the Name of Christ: A History of the Mennonite Central*

Bibliography 577

Committee and Its Service, 1920-1951. Scottdale, Pa., 1952.
Verhandlungen der Diener-Versammlungen der Deutschen Täufer oder Amischen Mennoniten. Lancaster, Pa., 1862-1865; 1869 at Chicago. Also published as Bericht der Verhandlungen der Diener-Versammlungen der Amischen Mennoniten(Diener und) Brüderschaft. Elkhart, Ind., 1866-67, 1870-78.
The Voters and Tax-Payers of Bureau County, Illinois. Chicago, 1877.
Warkentin, Abraham, ed. Who's Who Among the Mennonites. North Newton, Kan., 1943.
Weaver, W[illiam] B. "Biography of Joseph Stuckey." In Year Book of the Central Conference of Mennonites . . . 1954, pp. 2-4. N.p., 1954.
_____. History of the Central Conference Mennonite Church. Danvers, Ill., 1926.
_____. Thirty-Five Years in the Congo: A History of the Demonstration of Divine Power in the Congo. Chicago, 1945.
Weber, Harry F. Centennial History of the Mennonites of Illinois 1829-1929. Goshen, Ind., 1931. A detailed account from the beginning to 1920s.
Wenger, J[ohn] C. The Doctrines of the Mennonites. Scottdale, Pa., 1950.
_____. Faithfully, Geo. R.: The Life and Thought of George R. Brunk I (1871-1938). Harrisonburg, Va., 1978.
_____. The Mennonite Church in America. Scottdale, Pa., 1966.
_____. The Mennonites in Indiana and Michigan. Scottdale, Pa., 1961.
Williams, Dick, and Yoder, Elvan. The Illinois Amish and Rockhome Gardens. Evansville, Ind., n.d. [recent].
Williams, T. Harry, et al. A History of the United States to 1877. New York, 1969.
Wittlinger, Carlton O. Quest for Piety and Obedience: The Story of the Brethren in Christ. Nappanee, Ind., 1978.
The World Almanac 1966. New York, 1966.
Year Book of the General Conference of the Mennonite Church of North America. Various years. Published in several different places.
Yoder, Thomas. The Cullom Mennonite Church. Normal, Ill., 1975.
Zehr, Harold A. Constitution and Brief History of Illinois Mennonite Conference and Subsidiary Organizations. N.p., [1962]. Zehr was chairman of constitutional Revision Committee—J. J. Hostetler and Richard J. Yordy were the other members. Good statement on why it is necessary to rewrite constitutions from time to time.
Zehr, Marvin. Flanagan Illinois Mennonite Church. N.p., 1960.
Zimmerman, E. E., comp. Rinkenberger Family Record. Berne, Ind., 1949.
_____. 75th Anniversary Salem Children's Home 1896-1971. Flanagan, Ill., 1971.
Zimmerman, E. E., and Krahn, Emil J., compilers. Groveland Evangelical Mennonite Church 1878-1978. N.p., 1978.
Zimmerman, Marietta. 25th Anniversary of the Evangelical Mennonite Church in the Land Columbus Loved Best. Fort Wayne, Ind., 1971. Re EMC mission work in Dominican Republic.

Interviews (Conferences)

The names, dates, and places where the interviews or conferences were held are included in the footnotes. Many of these—especially in the Goshen-Elkhart area, but also some farther away—were by telephone. It is amazing how many people in the Goshen-Elkhart area at one time or another had important connections with the Illinois Mennonites—usually through having lived and served there. For example, upwards of forty or fifty (probably more) in the area had served in Illinois as pastors or as other kinds of church workers. Many others from Illinois have come to the Goshen-Elkhart locality for various kinds of meetings of short duration, which occasions have offered excellent opportunities for interviews. That is why the reader will observe that many of the conferences took place at Goshen. On the other hand, a good number of these conferences took place elsewhere, particularly in Illinois. As to the bibliography, it is probably more meaningful and helpful to the reader to list the home address of those interviewed, even though the conference may have occurred elsewhere. So the footnotes indicate where the interviews occurred—whether at the interviewee's home address or elsewhere—and the bibliography indicates his or her home address (or at least the home address at the time of the interview, if the present address is unknown). As the footnotes indicate, I had more than one conference with many of these.

I had interviews (conferences) with the following persons (1976-1981):

Amstutz, L. R., Flanagan, Ill.
Augsburger, Mrs. David, Goshen, Ind.
Bender, Paul, Goshen, Ind.
Bennett, Ernest, Elkhart, Ind.
Bertsche, James, Elkhart, Ind.
Birkey, Ivan, Fisher, Ill.
Blosser, Don, Goshen, Ind.
Bohn, Ernest J., Goshen, Ind.
Bohn, Stanley, Newton, Kan.
Cender, Mr. and Mrs. Alva, Fisher, Ill.
Cender, Mr. and Mrs. Emery, Gibson City, Ill.
Dahlberg, Rev., Pekin, Ill.
Dalke, Herbert, Hopedale, Ill.
Davis, Joe W., Eureka, Ill.
de Leon, Lupe, Elkhart, Ind.
Detweiler, Mrs. Alta, Fisher, Ill.
Detweiler, James, Morton, Ill.
Diener, Menno, Arthur, Ill.
Driver, Harvey A., Ft. Wayne, Ind.
Dunn, James, Champaign, Ill.
Dyck, Cornelius J., Elkhart, Ind.
Eigsti, Clayton, Morton, Ill.
Eigsti, Willis, Morton, Ill.
Estes, Steven R., Graymont, Ill.
Gingerich, Paul, Elkhart, Ind.
Glazer, Mrs., Hopedale, Ill.
Good, Mary, Goshen, Ind.
Graber, Joseph D., Goshen, Ind.
Gratz, Delbert, Bluffton, Ohio
Greaser, Lawrence, Elkhart, Ind.
Gross, Leonard, Goshen, Ind.
Harnish, John and Viola, Eureka, Ill.
Harnish, Robert, Eureka, Ill.
Hartzler, Levi and Irene, Elkhart, Ind.
Hartzler, Raymond L., Bloomington, Ill.

Hassan, Richard and Hazel, Rockford, Ill.
Heiser, Mr. and Mrs. Vernon, Fisher, Ill.
Helmuth, Orva, Arthur, Ill.
Helmuth, Phil, Sterling, Ill.
Hildebrand, Victor, Goshen, Ind.
Hirstein, Velma A, Morton, Ill.
Hochstetler, Wayne, Arthur, Ill.
Hofer, Sam and Joyce, Morton, Ill.
Hoover, Susie Snyder, Goshen, Ind.
Horst, Laurence, Goshen, Ind.
Hostetler, Debra, Cazenovia, Ill.
Hostetler, D. M., Lowpoint, Ill.
Hostetler, J. J., Goshen, Ind.
Hostetler, Lester, Goshen, Ind.
Hostetler, Ray, Cazenovia, Ill.
Hostetler, S. J., Goshen, Ind.
Janzen, Heinz, Hillsboro, Kan.
Jennings, John, Goshen, Ind.
Kauffman, Dan, Goshen, Ind.
Kauffman, J. Howard, Goshen, Ind.
Kauffman, Mike, Flanagan, Ill.
Kauffmann, Norman, Goshen, Ind.
King, Paul, Dakota, Ill.
King, Ruth, Morton, Ill.
King, Samuel M., Goshen, Ind.
Krahn, Emil, Pekin, Ill.
Lang, Eugene, Goshen, Ind.
Lapp, John A., Goshen, Ind.
Lehman, Areta and Earl, Goshen, Ind.
Lehman, Lena Gerber, Goshen, Ind.
Lehman, Mark, St. Anne, Ill.
Lind, Jerold, Elkhart, Ind.
McFadden, Dwight, Elkhart, Ind.
Mann, Lela, Goshen, Ind.

Massanari, Mr. and Mrs. Russell, Fisher, Ill.
Miller, Lee, Chenoa, Ill.
Miller, Mahlon, Morton, Ill.
Mininger, Paul, Goshen, Ind.
Nachtigall, Wilbur, Fisher, Ill. (then)
Nafziger, Anna, Goshen, Ind.
Nafziger, J. Marvin, Goshen, Ind.
Nafziger, Silas, Hopedale, Ill.
Nissley, Edward, Arthur, Ill.
Nussbaum, Milo, Morton, Ill.
Nussbaum, Stan, Lesotho, Africa.
Ortiz, José, Elkhart, Ind.
Otto, Daniel, Arthur, Ill.
Oyer, John S., Goshen, Ind.
Oyer, Verle and Margaret, Gibson City, Ill.
Pannabecker, Samuel F., Goshen, Ind.
Park, Myrna, Normal, Ill.
Petersheim, Samuel, Arthur, Ill.
Plank, George P. (et al. in a group), Arthur, Ill.
Reeb, (Mrs.) Katie Kennell, Eureka, Ill.
Reedy, Clinton, Goshen, Ind.
Roth, Mr. and Mrs. Donald, Morton, Ill.
Royer, Mary and Katherine, Goshen, Ind.
Rupp, Andrew, Fort Wayne, Ind.
Salzman, Vinora Weaver, Elkhart, Ind.
Schertz, Vernon, Goshen, Ind.
Schlabach, Theron, Goshen, Ind.
Schultz, Peter G., Justice, Ill.
Shelly, Ward, Washington, Ill.
Short, Reuben, Ft. Wayne, Ind.
Sieber, Paul, Peoria, Ill.
Smith, Arthur L., Eureka, Ill.
Smith, Tilman R., Goshen, Ind.
Smucker, Ernest and Mary, Goshen, Ind.
Smucker, Esther Meck, Goshen, Ind.
Smucker, J. N., Goshen, Ind.
Springer, Nelson, Goshen, Ind.
Stalter, Edwin, Flanagan, Ill.
Stauffer, Harley, Sterling, Ill.
Stoltzfus, Victor, Charleston, Ill.
Sutter, Mary, Flanagan, Ill.
Swartzendruber, Fred, Goshen, Ind.
Teuscher, Dan, Fisher, Ill.
Troyer, John, Delavan, Ill.
Troyer, Lotus, Gridley, Ill.
Unger, George, Morton, Ill.
Waltner, James, Normal, Ill.
Waun, G. G., Goshen, Ind.
Wenger, J. C., Goshen, Ind.
Whitermore, David, Chicago, Ill.
Whittle, Ancil, Goshen, Ind.
Wittrig, Howard, Hopedale, Ill.
Yoder, Aden, Hopedale, Ill.
Yoder, Dawn, Normal, Ill.
Yoder, Ethel Good, Goshen, Ind.
Yoder, Harry, Bluffton, Ohio
Yoder, Mathilda Schertz, Goshen, Ind.
Yoder, Raymond and Frances, Goshen, Ind.
Yoder, Robert, Eureka, Ill.
Yutzy, Norman, Eureka, Ill.
Zehr, Mr. and Mrs. Bert, Fisher, Ill.
Zehr, Edna (Mrs. Howard), Elkhart, Ind.
Zehr, Jay, Milford, Ind.
Zehr, Robert E., Upland, Ind.

Index

*By Steven R. Estes,
assisted by Jacqueline Estes, Terri Enns, and
Miriam Voran*

Abortion, 388, 409
Abrath, 134
Aby family. *See* Eby family.
Acculteration, 454, 484-487, 488-490, 491, 492
Adams County, Ind., 111
Adams County, Neb., 193
Adelphian Male Chorus, 467
Africa, missions in, 234, 235, 281-283, 294, 331. *See also* Congo Inland Mission
Africa Inland Mission, 119, 282
African Inter-Mennonite Mission, 131, 282, 462
Afro-American Mennonites, 420, 427-432; early work among, 163, 522
AIMM [Africa Inter-Mennonite Mission] *Messenger*, 235
Akron, Pa., 299
Albany, Ill., 165
Albany, N.Y., 149
Albrecht, Christian, 69
Albrecht, Elizabeth, 69
Albrecht, Ervin A., 156
Albrecht, Henry, 327-328
Albrecht, Jacob, 69
Albrecht, Joseph, 69, 91

Albrecht, Lydia H. *See* Smith, Lydia H. (Albrecht)
Albrecht, William, 251-252
Albrecht family, 48, 65, 69, 73
Alcoholism, 401-402. *See also* Temperance
Alexian Brothers Hospital, 362
Allebach, Ann Jemima, 407-408
Allebaugh family, 44
Allegheny Mountains, 26, 40
Allgyer, Samuel E., 242, 245, 288
All-Mennonite Convention, 463
Alpha, Minn., 196, 198
Alternative Service, 141, 217, 218, 351, 353, 360-366, 368, 370
Althaus family, 40
Altkirch, Alsace, 57
Alton, Ill., 30
Alton Observer, 32
American Friends Service Committee, 351, 357, 360, 361
American Legion, 359, 372
American Nativist Movement, 150

American Protective League, 354, 355
American Sunday School Union, 223
Amish, 38, 40, 41, 60, 61, 63, 64-65, 69-79, 81, 82, 85, 87, 88, 90-93, 96, 99, 100, 110-116, 120, 485; origins of, 55-56; migration of, 56-65, 67, 72-73, 75; Indians and, 59-60; worship patterns of, 64, 72, 79-81, 134, 159, 169-170; congregational organization of, 65-67; homelife of, 68, 76; unity among, 81, 86, 460-461; diversity of, 81, 91; universalism and, 86, 88-89; progressives of, 87, 157; education and, 249, 251-254. *See also* Beachy Amish Mennonites; Egly Amish; Hessian Amish; Old Order Amish; Stuckey Amish; Unaffiliated Amish Mennonites; Western District A. M. Conference
Amish Church, 62, 70,

580

Index   581

71, 79-80, 81, 91, 121, 459
Amish conferences (*Diener-Versammlungen*, 1862-1876, 1878), 71, 81-87, 101, 167, 187, 251, 478; attendance at 81-82; decisions at, 85-87; issues at, 82-83, 85-86; universalism and, 86, 88-89; Stuckey division and, 90-92; Egly division and, 111-112
Amish division, 36, 55, 459, 461, 466
Amish Mennonites. *See* Amish
Amish Mennonites, unaffiliated ("sleeping preacher" group). *See* Unaffiliated Amish Mennonites
Among Missions in the Orient and Observations by the Way, 260
Amity Chapel, 215
Ammann, Jakob, 55, 142, 460
Amstutz, L. R., 100, 343
Amstutz, Tillmann, 122
Anabaptism, 34-37, 216, 253-254, 307, 343, 367, 385, 409, 410, 415, 434, 435, 442, 456, 459, 482, 484; biblicism of, 303; women in 405, 408
Anabaptists, doctrines and beliefs of, 34-35, 36; missionary zeal of, 35, 36-37, 222; persecution of, 36-37; agriculture and, 37; education of, 248. *See also* Swiss Brethren
Anabaptists Four Centuries Later, 343, 367
Anawan, Ill., 160
Anchor, Ill., 98
Anchor Mennonite Church, 98, 322, 338; Sunday school at, 98
Angermeier, Jacobina. *See* Egle, Jacobina (Angermeier)
Angola, Ind., 275
Anna, Ill., 458
Annacker, Anna. *See* Eash, Anna (Annacker).
Anne Street Mennonite Church, 211-212, 217, 279
Apostolic Christian Church of America, 66, 145, 165, 189, 480, 503
Appalachia, 377
Appel, Lewis D., 197, 302
Archbold, Oh., 327
Archives of the Mennonite Church, 204
Arcola, Ill., 132
Argentina, Mennonite missions in, 421, 422, 423, 424
Arthur, Ill., 132-144 *passim.*, 162, 164, 212, 213, 285, 296, 301, 355, 439, 484
Arthur Amish Mennonite Church, 141, 169
Arthur Auction Company, 140
Arthur Graphic Clarion, 136
Arthur Mennonite Church, 141, 142, 157, 164, 165, 169, 212-213, 364, 437
Articles of Confederation, 26
Asbury College, 334
Ashley, Mich., 63, 194
Asiatic cholera, Mennonites and, 31, 44, 78, 147-148, 149-150
Associated Mennonite Biblical Seminaries, 407, 469
Association of Catholic Conscientious Objectors, 361-362
Atherton, Joseph C., 98, 341
Atkinson County, Ill., 52
Atlanta, Ill., 76
Auer (Oyer), Jacob. *See* Oyer, Jacob
Auer (Oyer) family, 65, 73
Augsburger, David, 411
Augsburger, Larry, 220
Augsburger, Myron, 379
Augsburger, Noah, 72
Augsburger family, 65
Augspurger, Aaron A., 98, 107, 286, 351, 463; Central Conference origin and, 103-106, 110, 282, 454-455, 462; Bluffton College and, 257-258, conservative-liberal controversy and, 315-316, 321-323, 330; John Horsch and, 321-323
Augspurger, David D., 98
Augspurger, Eugene, 100
Augstein (Eigsti) family, 65
Augusta County, Va., 39
Augustine, Daniel, 288
Australia, 61
Ava, Ill., 372
Aylmer, Ont., 136

Bachman, Andrew, 66, 78, 345
Bachman, John, 50
Bachman, Joseph, 66, 80
Bachman, Leland, 361, 364, 365
Bachman, Mrs. Leland, 361, 364
Bachman, Lizzie. *See* Schrock, Lizzie (Bachman)
Bachman family, 49, 65
Baecher, Joseph, 168
Baechler, Andrew, 61
Baechler, Barbara. *See* Claudon, Barbara (Baechler)
Baechler, Mary. *See*

Rupp, Mary (Baechler)
Baechler, Mary (Habecker), 61
Baechler family, 65
Baehr, Heinrich, 48, 49
Baehr (Bahr), Johannes, 48
Baehr, Lovina, 48
Baer, Christian, 150
Baer, Henry, 47, 147
Baer, J. B., 259
Baer, Jonas, 212
Baer, O. W., 391
Baer, Raymond, 369
Baer family, 40, 46
Bainton, Roland, 487
Baker, Newton D., 350, 351, 354, 355
Ball, Mary (Rich), 418
Bally, Jost, 41, 47, 188
Bally family, 40
Baltimore, Md., 47, 57
Ban, the, 55-56, 68, 82, 88, 104, 142, 161, 164, 170, 186
Barnes, _____, 226
Barthelhütte, Alsace, 57
Bartonville, Ill., 418
Basel, Switzerland, 57
Baughman, Samuel E., 288
Beachy, Alvin J., 100, 363
Beachy, Daniel J., 133
Beachy, Joel, 132
Beachy Amish Mennonites, 141, 164-165, 459
Bechler, _____, 359
Bechler, Andrew, 83
Bechler, LeRoy, 429
Bechler, Simon, 72
Bechtel, Andrew S., 324
Beck, Peter, 61
Becker, Mr. and Mrs. _____, 331
Beemer, Neb., 63
Beery, C. D., 195
Beher, Linda, 405-406
Beidler, Ida. See Kniss, Ida (Beidler)
Beidler, Jacob, 228
Beiler, David, 87
Beiler family, 147
Beirut, Syria, 298

Belfort, Alsace, 57
Beller, Anna (Zimmerman), 63
Beller, Jacob, 63
Beller, Peter, 66
Beller family, 65
Bellevue, Ill., 212
Bellevue Bible Church, 212, 336
Belsley, "Black" Joe, 61
Belsley, "Red" Joe, 61
Belsley family, 65
Bender, Elizabeth (Mrs. Harold S.), 498
Bender, George L., 93, 265
Bender, Harold S., 55, 203-204, 223, 229, 295, 296, 302, 363, 368, 401, 460, 468; conservative-liberal controversy and, 304, 319-320, 326, 512
Bender, Paul, 454
Berkey, E. J., 265, 305
Berlin, Ont. See Kitchener, Ont.
Bern, Switzerland, 35, 55, 56
Berne, Ind., 85, 126, 261, 290, 331, 463
Berne [Ind.] Witness Company, 118
Bert, Anna, 165
Bert, Elizabeth. See Brubaker, Elizabeth (Bert)
Bert, Sarah, 165
Bertsche, Christian, 306
Bertsche, Evan, 377
Bertsche, Harry E., 115, 127-128, 242, 362
Bertsche, James E., 115, 475
Bertsche, Mrs. James, 475
Bertsche, Purley, 446
Bertsche, Viola, 446
Bethany Biblical Seminary, 157, 220, 272, 275, 312, 419, 421, 469
Bethel College, 153, 352, 455

Bethel Mennonite Church, 98-99, 427-430
Beutler, J. A., 47
Beyler, Clayton, 209
Bible, versions of, 339-340
Bible conferences, 106, 242, 252, 309
Big Sandy River, 40
"Biography and Journal of Christian Erismann," 79
Birkey, Benjamin, 120
Birkey, Christian, 72
Birkey, Ivan, 214
Birkey, John C. (Groveland), 166
Birkey, Joseph, 72
Birkey, Levi, 352
Birky, John, 83
Birky, John C. (Hopedale), 174, 175
Bischtroff, Alsace, 62
Bixel, Lester H., 99
Bixler family, 49
Black Hawk, Chief, 40
Black Hawk War, 27, 32, 40, 59, 345
Black Partridge Creek, 61, 65, 72, 76
Blackboard Bulletin, 136
Blacks. See Afro-American Mennonites
Blaurock, George, 35, 410
Blooming Glen, Pa., 299
Bloomington, Ill., 30, 98, 100, 109, 117, 119, 131, 132, 133, 210, 216, 256, 290, 291, 437, 449
Bloomington Mennonite Church. See Mennonite Church of Normal
Bloomington-Normal School of Radiologic Technology, 450
Blosser, Abraham (Cullom), 47
Blosser, Abraham (Va.), 231

Index 583

Blosser, Don, 220
Bluffton, Ohio, 107, 252, 262, 277, 311, 330, 364
Bluffton College (formerly Central Mennonite College), 68, 109, 119, 157, 164, 252, 254, 255, 256-258, 311, 352, 374, 447, 455, 463; board of, 97, 257; difficulties at, 313, 321-322, 323, 324-325, 329-330, 332
Bluffton College and Mennonite Seminary. *See* Bluffton College
Board of Inquiry, 351
Board of Trade, 176
Bob Jones University, 310, 334
Bode, Walter, 413
Boehm, Martin, 240
Boehning, Rose. *See* Haigh, Rose (Boehning)
Boese, Glen, 391
Bohn, Ernest J., 100-101, 316
Bohn, Henry, 62
Bohn, Rosina (Zoss), 62
Bohn, Stanley, 474
Bohn family, 62
Boydson, Mr., 306
Boller, G. Z., 90
Bontrager, Obie, 212
Book family, 44
Boston, [Dr.] Gordon, 306
Bowman family, 31
Boyer, James, 53
Boyer, Susan, 53
Boynton Mennonite Church, 99-100, 407, 480
Boynton Township, Tazewell County, Ill., 99
Bremen, Germany, 299
Brenneman, Daniel (Hopedale), 72
Brenneman, Daniel (Ind.), 47, 223-230, 240

Brenneman, Don, 422
Brenneman, Henry B., 53, 243
Brenneman, Jacob, 99
Brenneman, Jacobine Iutzi (Mrs. Jacob), 99-100
Brenneman, John M., 49-50, 52, 53, 85, 224, 230, 231, 249, 347
Brenneman, Mildred, 369
Brenneman, Virgil J., 470
Brenneman, William, 427
Brenneman family (Ill.), 65, 69, 70
Brenneman family (Ohio), 422
Brethren in Christ, 145, 165, 275, 405, 459
Brethren Service Committee, 360, 361
Brighton Mennonite Church (formerly Hoyne Avenue Mission), 123, 129, 162, 163-164, 246, 267, 277-278
Brighton Mission Chapel. *See* Brighton Mennonite Church
Brighton Mission Church. *See* Brighton Mennonite Church
Brinkman, Louis C., 77
British Columbia, 61, 458
British East Africa, 119, 122, 282
Brokaw Hospital (formerly Memorial Deaconess Hospital), 290
Brooklyn, N.Y., 252
Brotherhood Aid Association of the Defenseless Mennonite Conference. *See* Brotherhood Mutual Insurance Company
Brotherhood Beacon, 235
Brotherhood Mutual Insurance Company (formerly Brotherhood Aid Association of the Defenseless Mennonite Conference), 111, 295-296
Brown, Margaret Elizabeth. *See* Kanagy, Margaret Elizabeth (Brown)
Brownfield family, 40
Brownstown, Ill., 133
Brubacher, Jacob N., 235
Brubaker, Ben, 189
Brubaker, Benjamin (Brethren in Christ), 165
Brubaker, Benjamin (Mennonite), 40
Brubaker, Elizabeth (Bert), 165
Brubaker, Elizabeth S. *See* Shoemaker, Elizabeth S. (Brubaker)
Brubaker, John, 41, 43
Brubaker, Rudolph K., 41
Brundage, Daniel, 199
Brunk, Amanda E. (Parr), 51
Brunk, George R., 52, 376
Brunk, Henry, 52
Brunk, Henry G., Jr., 52
Brunk, Ivan, 51
Brunk, Joseph, 52
Brunk, Noah, 51, 192
Brunk family, 51, 52
Bryan, William Jennings, 319, 349
Buchanan, Roy, 299, 350-351, 353
Bucher, Roy, 220, 413, 470, 476
Bucks County, Pa., 228
Buckwalter, Ruth E., 261
Buckwalter family, 49
Buerckey, Joseph. *See* Burcky, Joseph
Buffalo, Mo., 161
Buffalo, N.Y., 149
Buhler family, 147
Build, 378-379, 484
"Buildings, Buildings,

Buildings," 445
Burcky, Joseph, 70, 174, 265, 461
Bureau County, Ill., 60, 78, 160, 161
Bureau Creek, 61
Burger, Warren E., 144
Burke, John H., 389, 432
Burkey, Fred, 274
Burkey, Jacob, 69
Burkey, John, 69
Burkey, Joseph. See Burcky, Joseph
Burkey, Kenneth, 481
Burkey family, 65, 69
Burkhart, Abram, 259, 325
Burkholder, Martha E. See Good, Martha E. (Burkholder)
Burkholder Confession of Faith, 385
Burky, Andrew C., 352
Burrell, Curtis, 394-396
Bustos, Mac, 424
Bustos, Mario, 424
Butler County, Ohio, 57-74 *passim*, 87, 94, 99, 111
Buzzard, Alpha L., 187, 189
Buzzard, Joseph R., 233
Byers, Noah E., 252, 254, 256, 257, 326, 374, 441, 463; conservative-liberal controversy and, 322, 325
Byler, John I., 215, 274
Byler family, 215

Cadwell [Amish] District, 133
Cairo, Ill., 27, 29
Calhoun, Ivan R., 115, 122, 359
"Call to Unity," 472
"Calvary Hour, The," 210
Calvary Memorial Church (formerly Salem Gospel Mission), 111, 121-123, 164, 359, 364, 378

Calvary Mennonite Church (formerly East Washington Mennonite Church), 76, 92, 94-96, 98-99, 101, 110, 240, 241, 339, 340, 342, 363-364, 367, 396-397, 439, 461, 464, 468
Calvinism, 36
Camp, John, 453
Camp Association, 219
Camp Dodge, 350-351
Camp Ebenezer, 428
Camp family, 65
Camp Henry, 361, 364
Camp Menno Haven, 219, 382, 434, 476
Camp Wheeler, 351-352
Camping, 218-219
Canton, Ohio, 264
Carlock, Ill., 98, 101, 107, 241, 257, 288, 399, 418
Carlock Mennonite Church, 92, 101, 292, 359, 463
Carlson, Carl J., 165
Carroll County, Ill., 47, 49
Carstairs, Canada, 47
Carthage, Ill., 32
Cass County, Mo., 174
Castillo, Anita, 423
Castillo, David, 388, 421-422, 423
Castillo, Elsa (Shank), 388, 423
Castle Weibach, Hesse, 72
Catherine the Great, 224
Cavalier, Robert (Sieur de la Salle), 25
Cazenovia, Ill., 214
Cazenovia Mennonite Church, 214
Centennial History of the Mennonites of Illinois, 1829-1929, 60, 204, 479
Central Conference Ladies' Aid Organization, 294
Central Conference Mennonite Church

(formerly Central Illinois Conference of Mennonites), 70, 87, 88, 90, 94-98, 100, 102, 106, 109, 111, 119, 167, 187, 224, 284, 291, 292, 301, 326, 443, 453, 485; origins of, 91-92, 322, 459; Fundamentalism and, 93-94, 304, 315-316, 321-323, 326-327, 330-333, 338-341, 344; organization of, 99, 101, 102-103; annual conferences of, 99, 103, 107, 282, 304; constitutions of, 103-106, 109, 399; doctrines of, 103-106; GC and, 108, 145, 155, 166; Middle District Conference merger, 108-109, 234, 468; prosperity of 109-110; publications, 234; education and, 256-258, 329, 330, 454-455; missions of, 276-277, 281-283; inter-Mennonite cooperation and, 460, 463-466, 482-483; World War I and, 350, 352-353, 357; World War II and, 361, 362-364
Central Conference Ministerial Association, 103, 106
Central Conference Mission Board, 277
Central District Conference, 106, 369, 396, 407, 480; social concerns and, 377, 383-385, 387, 399-400; race relations and, 389, 390-397; inter-Mennonite cooperation and, 468, 470, 476-477, 479-480. *See also* Central Conference

Index

Mennonite Church;
Middle District
Conference
Central District Mission
Committee, 477
Central District Reporter,
108, 390, 432, 477
Central Illinois
Conference of
Mennonites. *See*
Central Conference
Mennonite Church
Central Illinois
Mennonite Men, 452
Central Illinois Regional
Youth Work, 482
Central Mennonite
College. *See* Bluffton
College
Chambersburg, Pa., 44
Champaign County, Ill.,
60, 167
Champaign-Urbana, Ill.,
132, 218, 470, 479
Charismatic movement,
456, 457-458
Charles, John D., 255
Chase, Stuart, 303
Chavez family, 390
Chenoa, Ill., 63
Chicago, Ill., 27, 29-51
passim, 69, 107-123
passim, 140, 150, 184,
219, 220, 235, 364,
375, 379, 398, 436,
469, 471, 479, 482,
486; missions in, 155-
157, 162-164, 165,
185, 211, 246, 260,
261-280, 290, 294,
301, 331, 326, 334-
335, 387, 405, 415,
432, 439, 453, 459;
Hispanic ministries
in, 420-427; Afro-
American ministries
in, 427-432; inter-
Mennonite ministries
in, 432-433, 476;
Mennonite witness in,
434-435, 475-476
Chicago and Alton
Railroad, 29. *See also*
Railroads

Chicago and
Northwestern
Railroad, 29. *See also*
Railroads
Chicago and Rock Island
Railroad, 29. *See also*
Railroads
Chicago Area Mennonite
Council, 435, 476
Chicago Area Steering
Committee, 476
Chicago, Burlington, and
Quincy Railroad, 29.
See also Railroads
Chicago Home Mission.
See Mennonite Home
Mission
Chicago Theological
Seminary, 164, 267,
278
Chicago World's Fair
(1893), 306
Chrisman, Bruce, 372
Christian and
Missionary Alliance,
281, 368
"Christian and Race
Relations, The," 389
Christian Business
Men's Committee, 272
Christian Century, The,
419
Christian Endeavor
Society. *See* Young
People's Society for
Christian Endeavor
Christian Endeavor
Union, 245
Christian Evangel, The,
93, 103-108 *passim,*
234, 282, 292, 316,
363, 399, 450, 462-
465 *passim*
Christian Exponent, 317,
325, 326
Christian Monitor, 310,
311, 348
Christian Witness, 163
Christian Workers Band,
117, 169
*Christliche Volksblatt,
Das,* 230, 460
Christlicher Bundesbote,
102, 228

Christophel, D. L., 412
Christophel, James, 274
Church architecture, 92,
94, 148, 168, 170, 443-
445
Church Hymnal
Committee, 192
Church of the Brethren
(Dunkards), 50, 157,
217, 359, 360, 410
Churchill, Marlborough,
354
Cincinnati, Ohio, 57
Civil rights, 375, 389,
390-391, 392
Civil War, 29, 30, 32, 52,
78, 85, 224, 297, 308,
349, 376, 386, 417;
Mennonites in, 345-
347
Civilian Public Service,
360-366, 466
Clarence Center, N.Y., 41
Classen, George, 433,
447
Claudon, Barbara
(Baechler), 62
Claudon, Daniel N., 111,
118, 234, 282, 288,
351, 463
Claudon, Joseph, 62
Claudon, Nicholas, 61-62
Clemens, Lois (Gunden),
405
Cleveland, Ohio, 261, 487
Clinton Frame
Mennonite Church
(Ind.), 91, 102, 262
Coffman, Betty, 195
Coffman, John S., 51, 53,
120, 159, 168, 185,
186, 450; Science
Ridge Mennonite
Church and, 191-192;
Cullom Mennonite
Church and, 195-198;
evangelism and, 239,
240-242, 267, 461;
education and, 250,
251, 254-255, 348;
missions and, 260,
263-264, 265; Moody
Bible Institute and,
306-307;

premillennialism and, 309
Coffman, Samuel, 196
Coffman, Samuel F., 198, 262, 263, 264, 305-306, 308-309
Coles, J. H., 50
College Mennonite Church, 255
Collins, Ronald, 422, 425
Committee on Economic and Social Relations, 402
Committee on Industrial Relations, 403
Communism (Marxist), 326-327, 358, 368, 390, 411
Community Renewal Society of the United Church of Christ, 395, 434
Compromise of 1850, 32
Confederacy (Southern), 30, 52
Confederation Congress, 26
Conference of Evangelical Mennonites, The, 127-129, 334
Conference of the Defenseless Mennonite Church of North America. *See* Evangelical Mennonite Church
Congerville, Ill., 74, 78, 98, 414, 481
Congerville Mennonite Church, 92, 98, 335, 340, 478
Congo Inland Mission (formerly United Mennonite Board of Missions), 93, 119, 123, 235, 259, 294, 462, 464-465; board of, 109, 281-283
Congo Missionary Messenger, 235
Conrad, John D., 211, 212
Conrad Grebel Lectures, 405
Conscientious objection, 345, 349-357, 360-363, 370-371, 458, 489
Conscription, 345-346, 349, 360, 364, 370-371
Conservative Amish Mennonite Conference. *See* Conservative Mennonite Conference
Conservative Mennonite Conference (formerly Conservative Amish Mennonite Conference), 142, 157-158, 162, 164, 165, 234-235, 436, 439, 459, 480; World War I and, 350
Conservative-liberal controversy, 179, 183, 202-203, 257-258, 286, 311, 315, 318, 327, 344
Constantinople, Turkey, 299, 353
Coon, Robert, 96
Councils of Defense, 354, 356
Covington, Ohio, 43
Crawford County, Ill., 53, 54
Cressman, Arnold W., 473-474
Crimea, South Russia, 162
Cullom, Ill., 46-47, 49, 195, 197, 240, 241, 281, 299, 302, 380
Cullom [Ill.] Chronicle, 195
Cullom Mennonite Church, 41, 188, 195-198, 199, 219, 221, 241, 250, 252, 256, 259-260, 364; difficulties at, 47, 196-197; close of, 48, 188, 437
Cumberland River, 27
Cumming County, Neb., 63
Dahlgren, Hans, 268
Daily [Bloomington] Pantagraph, The, 99-100, 106, 171
Daily vacation Bible school, 123, 156, 168, 210, 214, 246-247, 301, 397, 428, 479
Dakota, Ill., 204
Daley, Mayor Richard, 395
Dallas, Tex., 439
Dammerskirch, Alsace, 57
Danvers, Ill., 65, 70, 71, 72, 73, 92, 93, 94, 99, 105, 107, 241, 299
Danvers Mennonite Church (formerly South Danvers Mennonite Church), 70, 92-94, 299, 407. *See also* Hessian Amish; North Danvers Mennonite Church
Darwin, Charles, 303
Davenport, Iowa, 424
Davis, Joe W., 215
Deaconess Training School, 261-262
Deaconesses, 92, 290
Dean, William W., 225
Dearborn Street Mission, 428-429
Decater County, Kan., 63
Dechert, Marion, 401
Deer Creek, Ill., 168, 214, 384
Deere, John, 76
Defender, 310
Defenseless Mennonite Brethren of Christ in North America. *See* Evangelical Mennonite Brethren
Defenseless Mennonite Conference of North America. *See* Evangelical Mennonite Church
Delavan Prairie Church. *See* Hopedale Mennonite Church
Dellenbach, Maria, 62

Delp family, 147
Democratic Party, 386, 418, 419
Derstine, Clayton F., 174, 179-180, 183-184, 242, 351-352, 357-358, 412; pamphlets of, 184; Fundamentalism and, 310-313, 315
Derstine, Norman, 220, 382-383, 412
Derstine, William, 298
Deter, Daniel H., 193-194
Deter, Daniel S., 352
Deter, Ezra S., 298, 299, 301
Deter family, 194
Detweiler, Abraham E., 44, 45, 231-232
Detweiler, Irvin R., 107, 256, 316, 325, 402, 466
Detweiler, James, 220, 457
Detweiler, John, 214-215
Detweiler family, 44
Dewey Mennonite Church, 169, 214
Dhamtari, India, 281
Diary, The, 136
Dick, George C., 155, 437-439, 454
Dick, John R., 128-129
Diener, Dannie, 165
Diener, Menno A., 144
Diener-Versammlungen. See Amish conferences
Dillon, Ill., 215
Dillon Creek, Ill., 61, 65-66, 70, 72, 167
Dillon Creek Amish congregation. See Pleasant Grove Mennonite Church
Dillon Mennonite Church, 215, 458
Discípulo Christiano, El, 423
Dispensationalism, 309-310, 312, 333-344, 358; See also Fundamentalism

Divorce, 452, 490
Dock, Christopher, 248
Doering, Alma E., 115, 119, 281-282
Donner family, 65
Dordrecht Confession, 313
Douglas, Stephen A., 29, 32, 416
Douglas County, Ill., 132, 133
Dowie, John Alexander, 66
Dowie movement, 66
Downey, Idaho, 361
Drange, Edward R., 299, 353
Drange, Elsie. See Kaufman, Elsie (Drange)
Drescher, John, 411, 472-473
Dress, 106, 112, 113, 115-116, 134, 142, 171-172, 176-179, 182, 183, 200, 203, 207-208, 209, 216, 221, 241, 251, 264, 277, 461, 464, 485, 487, 490, 491; of young people, 240, 326; conservative-liberal controversy and, 321, 322, 324, 326, 335, 336; women and, 404-405
Driedger, Leo, 59
Driver, Don, 274
Driver, Harvey A., 123, 125, 126, 131, 334
Driver family, 52
Duerrstein (Durrstein), John Gustave, 48
Duerrstein (Durrstein), Louis, 48
Dunn, Bruce, 341
Dunn, James L., 101, 372, 470
Dunn, William E., 448
Dyck, Gordon, 477
Dyck, Paul, 99

Eash, Amos M., 107, 235, 267, 269, 275-277, 294, 316, 331; relief work and, 299, 353
Eash, Anna Annacker, 275
Eash, Cleophas Harold, 277
Eash, Joseph, 350
East Bay Camp, 470
East Bend Mennonite Church (formerly East Bend Amish Mennonite Church), 167-169, 182, 185, 212, 214, 220, 364, 442, 470; difficulties at, 307, 336-339; painted yellow, 356
East Bend Township, Champaign County, Ill., 167
East Peoria, Ill., 60, 121, 123, 212, 213, 215
East Saint Louis, Ill., 429, 438
East Washington Amish congregation. See Calvary Mennonite Church
East White Oak Bible Church. See East White Oak Mennonite Church
East White Oak Mennonite Church (presently East White Oak Bible Church), 92, 97, 100, 305, 332-333, 343, 352-353
Eastern Amish Mennonite Conference, 167
Eastern District Conference, 480
Eastern Illinois University, 138
Eastern Mennonite College, 343
Eastern Mennonite School, 310
Eastern Mennonite Seminary, 469
Eastern Mennonite Testimony, 458
Eastern Pennsylvania

Mennonite Church, 458, 459
Ebersole, Abram, 191
Ebersole, David, 43, 189
Ebersole, Esther, *See* Lapp, Esther (Ebersole)
Ebersole, Fannie E., 462
Ebersole, Frank S., 348
Ebersole, Glenn, 438
Ebersole, John R., 192
Ebersole, Solomon D., 223, 260, 262-263, 265, 306
Ebersole family, 44
Eby, Amanda. *See* Leaman, Amanda (Eby)
Eby, Clara. *See* Steiner, Clara (Eby)
Eby, Matthias, 41, 43, 189, 200
Eby (Aby) family, 495
Economics and Mennonites, 409-414
Edgar County, Ill., 53
Ediger, Margaretha, 431
Ediger, Menno, 431
Ediger, Peter, 156, 372
Edinburgh, Scotland, 260
Education, 26, 106, 109, 151, 170, 213, 236, 277, 453-454, 486, 509; English public schools and, 48, 226, 485; German private schools and, 48, 79, 226, 251, 485; among Amish, 79, 135-136, 249, 253-254; EMC and, 118-119, 126-127, 129; Moody Bible Institute and, 122, 163, 164, 197, 201, 277, 305-306; Apostolic Christians and, 166; Illinois Mennonite Conference and, 203-204, 340, 341-343; of ministries, 220, 249-250, 311-312, 329; in Great Awakening, 248-258; opposition to, 249-251, 258, 327, 329; of missionaries, 258-259; Fundamentalists and, 319, 321-323
Egle, Christian R., 111, 113, 114, 115, 116, 118, 127, 234, 242, 282, 288, 334, 354, 356, 463; Fundamentalism and, 330
Egle, Jacobina (Bena) Angermeier, 114
Egle, William, 96
Egli, Aaron D., 107
Egli family, 65, 120
Egly, Henry, 85, 86, 105-106, 111, 115, 117, 120, 129, 367, 484; life of, 111-112; ministry of, 112-115
Egly, John, 72
Egly, Joseph, 185, 453
Egly, Katherine (Goldsmith), 111
Egly Amish, 66, 111, 112-113, 187. *See also* Evangelical Mennonite Church
Ehresman, Elizabeth. *See* Zehr, Elizabeth (Ehresman)
Ehresman, Gladys (Mrs. Roy), 441
Ehrisman, Katy. *See* Litwiller, Katy (Ehrisman)
Ehrismann family, 65
Eicher, John, 346
Eicher, Michael, 149
Eigsti, Mahlon, 213
Eigsti family. *See* Augstein (Eigsti) family
Eiman, Elizabeth. *See* Ropp, Elizabeth (Eiman)
Eisenhower, Dwight D., 369, 401
Elida, Ohio, 49, 85, 230, 347
Elkhart, Ind., 31, 44-45, 49, 50, 53, 93, 117, 118, 153, 159, 169, 184, 189, 191, 192, 195, 197, 220, 232, 240, 263, 295, 297, 320, 407, 417, 451, 469
Elkhart County, Ind., 47, 82, 133, 158, 231
Elkhart Institute, 198, 223, 250, 252, 254, 255-256, 321, 348, 450. *See also* Goshen College
Elkton, Mich., 120
Emancipation Proclamation, 33
Emden, Ill., 480
Emergency Relief Committee of the General Conference, 280, 297
Engle, Christian, 40, 41
Engle, Christian (Bishop), 61, 63, 66, 345
Engle, John, 61, 345
Engle, Joseph, 66
Engle, Peter R., 78
Engle family, 65
Englewood, Ill., 424
Englewood Mennonite Church (formerly Union Avenue Mennonite Church), 274, 430. *See also* Mennonite Home Mission
English language, 71, 88, 95, 111, 118, 254, 420, 421; preaching in, 41, 46, 50, 116, 126, 159, 160, 161, 168, 189, 196; publications in, 224, 228-233; change from German to, 226-228, 327, 485-486, 489
Enns, Arthur, 122, 123
Enz, Jacob J., 513
Erb, J. Frederick, 220, 441
Erb, Paul, 52, 59-60, 321, 380, 388, 472

Index

Erie Canal, 29, 30, 57, 69
Erismann, Christian, 68, 79, 80, 85, 225-226, 235, 248, 251, 461
Erlenbach, Switzerland, 55
Esch, Benjamin F., 94, 96, 101, 107, 340, 363-364, 464
Esch, Christian, 66
Esch family, 65
Espinoza, Guillermo, 426-427
Espinoza, Lillia, 426, 453
Estes, Steven R., 290, 448, 531, 581
Eureka, Ill., 73, 125-126, 169, 182, 185, 232, 285, 286, 287, 295, 314, 356, 438, 450
Eureka Bible Church, 125-126, 130
Eureka College (formerly Walnut Grove Academy), 125, 210, 251
Eureka Hatchery, 438
Eureka Home. *See* Maple Lawn Home
Eureka Hospital, 450
Evangelical Mennonite, The, 118, 123, 129, 234, 334, 335
Evangelical Mennonite Brethren (formerly Defenseless Mennonite Brethren of Christ in North America), 118, 127-129, 163-164, 234, 246, 277, 282-283, 284, 334
Evangelical Mennonite Church (formerly Conference of the Defenseless Mennonite Church of North America), 109, 111, 113, 116, 118, 119, 123, 129, 131, 165, 200, 223-224, 245, 282, 283, 284, 294, 336; origins of, 111-116, 459; music in, 112, 118; publications of, 117-118, 234; education and, 118-119, 329, 330, 334, 443, 446, 483; inter-Mennonite cooperation and, 126-129, 286, 288, 291, 460, 464-465, 468, 475, 480, 482, 485, 487; identity of, 129-131, 484, 485; annual conferences of, 124-125, 126; missions of, 281-283; Fundamentalism and, 334, 343-344; World War I and, 351, 354, 356; World War II and, 361, 362-363, 364; peace and, 366-367; social concerns and, 377-379, 404
Evangelical Mennonite Conference (formerly Kleine Gemeinde), 283
Evangelical United Brethren Church, 214
Evangelicalism (theological), 303, 310, 333, 339
Evans, William, 310
Evanston, Ill., 216, 217-218, 397, 410, 451
Evanston Mennonite Church (formerly Mennonite Fellowship) 217-218, 474, 475
Ewing Mennonite congregation, 458
"Explo 72," 439
Exposition Gardens, 414

Fairfield Amish Mennonite Church, 160-161, 162
Faith healing, 303, 335, 337
Faith in Ferment: A History of the Central District Conference, 89, 108
Family Life, 136
Farmers Alliance, 175
Farni, Christian, 67, 83
Farni family, 65
Farniville, Ill., 67, 74, 98
Fast, Clarence, 122
Father Hillary. *See* Ledochowski, L. H.
Fauber, Laverne, 125
Fayette County, Ill., 133
Fechet, Major, 374
Federal Bureau of Investigation, 354
Federal Council of Churches. *See* National Council of Churches
Feeding the Hungry, 298
Fellowship of Hope (Ind.), 451
Filer, Idaho, 198
Finney, Charles G., 223
First Mennonite Church (Berne, Ind.), 331-332
First Mennonite Church (Chicago), 272, 391, 427, 431-432
First Mennonite Church (Morton), 213, 214, 370, 440, 441-442, 455-456
First Mennonite Church (Normal). *See* Mennonite Church of Normal
First Mennonite Church (Philadelphia, Pa.), 407
First Mennonite Church (Summerfield), 150-151, 152-155, 225, 228, 249, 257, 259, 293, 437, 439, 453, 470; Sunday school at, 238
First Mennonite Church of Champaign-Urbana, 218, 470, 477
First Norwood Mennonite Church, 217
Fisher, Ill., 167, 185, 212, 350
Flanagan, Ill., 62, 96, 105-122 *passim,* 177, 208,

589

234, 262, 283-286 passim, 299, 418, 441, 461, 483, 485
Flanagan Mennonite Church, 96, 243, 299, 384, 390, 441, 447, 469
Fleming, Lois, 137, 140, 164
Foosland, Ill., 107
Ford, Stephen, 124
Forney, Aaron, 105
Forney, Christian. See Farni, Christian
Forney, Mary B. (King), 105
Forney family, 390
Fort Clark, Ill., 40
Fort Crevecour, Ill., 25
Fort Leavenworth, Kan., 350
Fort Madison, Iowa, 150
Fort Wayne, Ind., 118, 296
Fort Wayne Bible College, 127, 334
Fosdick, Harry Emerson, 325
Fox Indians, 345
Franconia Conference, 112, 370-371, 432, 442, 473, 480
Frankfort, Ky., 40
Frankfurt, Germany, 72
Franklin and Marshall College, 255
Franklin Corners, Ill., 165
Franklin County, Pa., 45
Franz, Delton, 157, 392-394, 395, 396
Frederick, Pa., 285
Freeland Seminary. See Ursinus College
Freeman, S.D., 461
Freeport, Ill., 41, 42, 43, 165, 286, 356, 357
Freeport Mennonite Church, 41-43, 49, 185, 188, 189-191, 198, 199, 200, 220, 221, 222, 233, 251, 252, 256, 325, 364
Fremont, John C., 416

French Quarter, New Orleans, 62
French Revolutionary War, 38
Fresh-Air Program, 267-268, 269, 275, 394
Fresno, Calif., 429
Fretz, J. Winfield, 279, 296, 420, 432
Frey, Elias L., 327
Friesen, [Dr.] Florence, 274
Friesen, Paul, 212, 213
Friesen, Peter (Neb.), 306
Friesen, Peter A., 274, 387
Friessen, Jacob, 395, 407
Frohe Botschaft, Die ("Glad Tidings"), 88
Fröhlich, Samuel, 166
Fulton County, Ill., 53
Fulton County, Ohio, 85
Funck, Heinrich, 228
Fundamentalism, 179, 183, 184, 302, 303, 313; baptism of the Holy Spirit in, 121, 337; doctrines of, 121, 215, 304, 307, 309-312, 315, 316, 318-319, 320, 326, 331, 333, 334, 339; of Moody Bible Institute, 305-309; concern for orthodoxy and, 303, 307; General Conference Mennonite Church and, 314; Central Conference Mennonite Church and, 315-316, 321-323, 326-327, 330-333; Mennonite Church and, 304, 307, 313-314, 314-315, 329, 335-339, 512; continuing influence of, 340-341, 344
Fundamentalist-Modernist Controversy, 313, 315, 321
Fundamentals Conference, 313, 314

Funk, Arnold E., 94
Funk, Isaac, 30
Funk, John F., 31, 44-45, 49, 53, 153, 224, 243, 305, 347, 411; as editor, 41, 46, 49, 118, 145, 159, 184, 195, 227, 239, 254, 379, 380; as minister, 50-51, 188, 197, 199, 262; Russian Mennonites and, 153-154, 224-225; life of, 228-230, 249; Sunday schools and, 230, 235, 237, 238; revivalism and, 239-240; missions and, 260, 265; Moody Bible Institute and, 306-307; politics and, 386, 416-417
Funk, Melvin, 99
Funk, Salome Kratz, 229-230, 417
Funk family, 52, 78
Funk Seed Company, 78
"Future of the Central Illinois Conference of Mennonites, The," 104-105, 110

Galena, Ill., 29, 48
Galesburg, Ill., 252
Galveston, Tex., 277
Gamber, Salena. See Shank, Salena (Gamber)
Garber, David, 284
Garber family, 65
Garden Street Mission. See Anne Street Mennonite Church
Gardner, Ill., 46, 47, 49, 50, 184
Gardener Mennonite Church, 41, 47, 49-50, 188, 227, 232
Garrett Biblical Institute, 217
Gees, C. W., 413
General Conference Mennonite Church (formerly the General Conference of the

Index   591

Mennonite Church of North America), 63, 87, 108-109, 112, 144, 149, 151-157, 166, 194, 216, 233, 243, 246, 278, 415, 446, 484; Foreign Mission Board of, 153, 259, 282, 283, 415; Home Mission Board of, 156-157, 259, 280; orphanages of, 284; nursing homes of, 285-286, 288-290; hospitals and, 290-293; Fundamentalism and, 314, 339, 341, 343-344; Bible versions and, 339-340; World War II and, 361, 363; peace and, 368-369, 371, 372; social concerns of, 377, 383-385, 387, 404; race relations and, 389, 390-397; politics and, 418-419; evangelism in, 440-441; elderly and, 445, 446-448; origins of, 460, 473-474, 480, 482; inter-Mennonite cooperation and, 460, 468, 476, 480, 482-483; unity with MC, 472-475
General Conference Mission Board, 156
Genesco, Ill., 52
Geneva, Ind., 111
Genius of Universal Emancipation, The, 33
Gerber, Joseph, 70
Gerber, Samuel, 172, 288
Gerber family, 65
Gerig, J. F., 124
Gerig, J. M., 115
Gerig, Joseph K., 121, 122, 242, 282, 288
Gerig, Percy, 220, 341, 406
German language, 71, 79, 88, 95, 111, 118, 135, 168, 171, 269, 352; preaching in, 41, 44, 50, 116-117, 126, 159, 160, 161, 162, 164, 196, 200; publications in, 224-225, 228, 230; change to English language, 226-228, 236, 327, 355, 356, 485-486
Germantown, Ill., 214
Germantown, Pa., 37, 60, 385, 415
Germantown Mennonite Church, 214
Gibson City, Ill., 169, 214, 338
Gibson City Bible Church, 168, 214, 338, 487
Gingerich, Christian, 72, 94
Gingerich, Fidella, 214-215
Gingerich, George, 168
Gingerich, James N., 87, 498
Gingerich, John (Danvers), 94
Gingerich, John (Metamora), 66
Gingerich, Joseph, 160
Gingerich, Joseph M., 214-215
Gingerich, Melvin, 59, 172, 174, 360, 362
Gingerich, N. S., 223
Gingerich, Simon, 178
Gingerich family, 65
Gingery family, 69
Gish, Fanny, 212
"Glad Tidings." *See Die Frohe Botschaft*
Gladdin, Washington, 376
Glaubens Lieder (Songs of Faith), 118
Glenn, James, 122
Goering, Erwin C., 448
Goertz, Ron, 218
Goerz, David, 149, 154, 155, 280, 462
Goessel, Kan., 285, 290
Goldschmidt, Joseph, 59
Goldsmith, Katherine. *See* Egly, Katherine (Goldsmith)
Goldwater, Barry, 418
Good, Aaron C., 192-193, 212, 220, 242, 401, 441, 491; Fundamentalism and, 314, 328-329
Good, Christian, 192
Good, Daniel, 192
Good, DeWitt, 262
Good, Joseph C., 214
Good, Kenneth, 131, 215
Good, Mamie C., 302
Good, Martha E. (Burkholder), 192
Good, Mary, 213
Good, Samuel, 192
Good, Solomon R., 192, 328-329
Good Tidings (Defenseless Mennonite Brethren), 118
Good Tidings (Reformed Mennonite), 146, 147, 234
Goodfield, Ill., 74, 98, 167
Goodfield Mennonite Church, 67, 74, 170, 182, 213, 214, 440. *See also* Mackinaw Meeting; Roanoke Mennonite Church
Goshen, Ind., 83, 102, 107, 132, 159, 185, 189, 256, 260, 262, 349, 457
Goshen Biblical Seminary, 220, 255, 319, 393, 469; Evangelicalism and, 340, 341-342
Goshen College (formerly Elkhart Institute), 49, 68, 93, 94, 118-119, 122, 192, 202-204, 214, 216, 252, 254, 255, 256, 299, 311, 313, 323, 326, 370, 374, 383, 394, 410, 421, 427, 429, 455, 457, 460, 463, 464;

difficulties at, 255, 258, 316-317, 319, 327-329, 330, 340, 341-342
Goshen College Biblical Seminary. *See* Goshen Biblical Seminary
Goshen College Peace Society, 359
Gospel Herald, 184, 185, 186, 211, 232, 233, 235, 302, 314, 316, 318, 326, 333, 342, 369, 380-381, 388, 400, 401, 402, 411, 423, 442, 464, 466, 472, 473, 477
Gospel Tidings, 128
Gospel Witness, 185, 233
Gospel Witness Company, 233
Gothard, Bill, 341
Graber, Christian L., 172, 298
Grabill, Ind., 296
Grabill, Joseph, 166
Grabill, Noah, 195
Grace Bible Institute, 127, 334
Grace Community Church (formerly Mennonite Bible Mission), 156-157, 163, 278, 434
Grace Evangelical Mennonite Church, 121, 124-125, 130, 482
Grace Mennonite Church. *See* Grace Community Church
Grace Presbyterian Church, 340, 341
Graham, Billy, 341
Granger movement, 78, 86
Grant, Ulysses S., 48
Grantsville, Md., 132, 164
Granville, Ill., 69, 226
Graybill, Simon, 191, 220
Graybill family, 46
Greaser, Daniel, 168
Greaser, Earl, 446
Great Awakening (Mennonite), 106, 181-182, 201, 210, 486; definition of, 222-223; mission in, 223, 258-283; Protestant influences on, 223-224, 225-226; Russian Mennonites and, 224-225; deterrents to, 226; publications in, 228-235; leadership of John F. Funk, 232; Sunday schools and, 235-239, 245; revivalism and evangelism in, 239-242; young people and, 245; education in, 248-259; service aspects of, 283-301; assessment of, 302; temperance and, 398-400, 402; "second awakening," 432-433
Great Depression, 108, 122, 234, 283, 291-292, 380, 412, 420, 421, 450
Great Lakes, 57, 69
Grebel, Conrad, 34-35
Greenback movement, 78
Greenwood, Del., 158
Gridley, Ill., 113, 115, 288, 330, 377
Gridley Prairie, Ill., 285
Grieser, Daniel, 72
Groening, _____, 306
Groff, Abraham, 146
Groff, Godfrey, 41
Grove, Mary, 400
Groveland, Ill., 113, 118, 120, 130, 165
Groveland Evangelical Mennonite Church (formerly Wesley City Amish congregation), 65-66, 113, 120-121, 122, 124, 165, 283, 343, 364, 440
Groveland Missionary Church, 165
Grubb, William Henry, 100
Grundy County, Ill., 46, 49
Gsell, William, 45, 46
Guatemala, 458
Guengerich (Güngerich), Peter, 80-81, 94
Gunden, Lois. *See* Clemens, Lois (Gunden)
Gundy, George I., 97, 98, 107, 399-400
Gundy, Lloyd W., 99
Gundy, Maude, 305
Güngerich, [Peter]. *See* Guengerich, Peter
Guth, Peter, 61
Guth, Walter, 333
Guth family, 65

H. R. Schertz Memorial Scholarship Fund, 455
Habecker, Mary. *See* Baechler, Mary (Habecker)
Habegger, David, 101
Hagens, Lewis, 430
Hague Peace Conferences, 348
Haigh, Lawrence B., 282, 294
Haigh, Rose (Boehning), 282, 294
Hallman, William, 422
Halstead, Kan., 155, 284, 346
Halstead Seminary, 153
Hamilton, Benjamin F., 196
Hamilton, Melvin, 212, 214, 215, 217
Hamilton County, Ohio, 49
Hamlin, Hannibal, 417
Hammer, Catherine (Mrs. Jacob Bernhard), 48
Hammer, Howard, 210
Hammer, John Rudolph, 48
Hancock County, Ill., 51
Happy Hour Mission, 162, 164, 269, 270, 278

Index   593

Harder, Henry N., 100, 476
Harder, Leland, 130, 155-156, 343, 367, 371, 377, 402, 405, 415
Harding, Vincent G., 157, 385, 392-393, 395
Harding, Warren G., 74
Harmony Mennonite Church, 169-170, 219, 503
Harnish, Donna, 411
Harnish, James, 382, 390, 411
Harnish, John, 210, 212, 220, 278
Harnish, Robert, 213, 372, 487-488
Harnish, Viola, 278
Harper, Kan., 212
Harrisonburg, Va., 469
Harshbarger family, 46
Hartman, Emanuel M., 188, 195, 196-197, 201, 263, 264
Hartman, Peter, 40
Hartzler, Chauncey A., 174, 242
Hartzler, I. G., 178
Hartzler, Joseph D., 491-492
Hartzler, John Ellsworth, 242, 256-257, 258; conservative-liberal controversy and, 315, 322, 324, 325, 327-331
Hartzler, Jonas S., 185, 260
Hartzler, Levi C., 274, 305
Hartzler, R. J., 466
Hartzler, Raymond L., 101, 106, 107, 108-109, 110, 234, 245, 291-292, 316, 363, 364-365, 372, 389, 409, 442, 450, 460, 466, 470, 486-487
Hartzler, Mrs. Raymond L., 364
Hassan, Hazel (Nice), 194
Hassan, W. Richard, 478
Haury, Samuel S., 149, 153, 259, 280

Havre, France, 57
Haw Patch congregation (Ind.), 91
Heatwole, Reuben J., 52
Heatwole family, 52
Heckleman family, 46
Heckler family, 44
Hedrick, Gary, 126
Heer, David, 49
Heer, Henry, 48
Heer, Jacob, 48
Hege, Daniel, 149, 150-153, 249, 259
Heilsbote, Der, 115, 118, 234
Heiser, E. William, 307
Heiser [Hieser], Edward R., 350
Heiser, Joseph A., 168, 169, 174, 212, 242, 336-339
Helmuth, Moses J., 169
Helmuth, Phil, 220
Hendricks family, 44
Hennepin, Ill., 69
Henricks family, 147
Henry, Ill., 226, 361, 365
Henry, Roy W., 99
Henry County, Ill., 51, 52, 160, 161
Henry County, Ia., 147
Herald of Truth, 30-31, 41-60 *passim*, 71, 85, 88, 90, 91, 101-102, 159, 184-199 *passim*, 224, 225, 227, 239, 254, 256, 260, 321, 348, 379, 398, 409, 411, 417; start of, 228-233; Amish subscribe to, 228, 232; opposition to, 231, 249-250
Heraldo Evangélico, El, 423
Heraldo Mexicano, El, 422-423
Herner, Benjamin, 197, 198
Herner, Isaac, 47
Herner family, 46
Herold der Wahrheit (Amish), 136, 234-235
Herold der Wahrheit

(Funk's), 50, 153, 228, 232, 234. *See also Herald of Truth*
Herr, Christian, 48
Herr, Francis, 145, 146
Herr, John, 145, 146
Herrites. *See* Reformed Mennonite Church
Hershberger, Guy F., 296, 300, 346, 357, 362, 368, 420, 432
Hershberger, Lotus, 437
Hershberger, Seth H., 169
Hershey, Benjamin, 44, 45, 199
Hershey, Jacob M., 52-53
Hershey, Lester, 210, 219, 422-423, 427, 428
Hershey, [Gen.] Lewis B., 364-365
Hershey, Milton S., 147
Hershey family, 44
Hertzler, Silas, 298
Hesselein, Leonard W., 390
Hessian Amish, 70, 71-72, 94, 99-100
Hessian Amish Church. *See* Danvers Mennonite Church
Hesston, Kan., 63, 246, 299, 338, 413
Hesston Academy. *See* Hesston College
Hesston College (formerly Hesston College and Bible School), 209, 212, 246, 255, 272, 299, 309, 316-317, 343, 394
Hesston College and Bible School. *See* Hesston College
Heyworth, Ill., 368
Hiebert, P. C., 298, 465
Hieser (Heiser) family, 65
Highway Village Mennonite Church, 213, 217, 372, 487
Hillary, Father. *See* Ledochowiski, L. H.
Hillsborough, Kan., 284, 285

Hirschler, Daniel, 149, 153
Hirstein, Samuel, 236
Hirstein family, 40
Hispanic-American Mennonites, 278, 420-427
Ho Chi Minh, 369
Hochstetler, Lee, 434
Hochstetler, Wayne, 213
Hochstettler, Peter, 66, 118, 120
Hofer, David M., 162, 163, 299-300, 305, 353
Hofer, Mrs. David M., 162, 299-300, 353
Hoffman, Charles, 481
Hofmann, Melchior, 35
Hollands Grove, Ill., 40
Holloway, Joe L., 429-430
Holly, Daniel, 70
Holly (Hooley) family, 65, 69
Holmes County, Ohio, 49, 85, 112, 428
Holy kiss, 490
Holy Spirit Festival, 457
Homan, Gerlof, 437
Home and Foreign Relief Commission, 280
Honderich, Samuel, 198
Hoover, Joe, 307
Hoover, Noble O., 291
Hopedale, Ill., 62, 72, 76, 86, 93, 99, 100, 167, 177, 211, 352, 407, 478
Hopedale Amish Mennonite Church. *See* Hopedale Mennonite Church
Hopedale Mennonite Church (formerly Hopedale Amish Mennonite Church), 72, 86, 99, 159, 170, 171, 174, 178, 185, 214, 215, 226-227, 333, 356, 440, 453, 480, 485, 504; World War II and, 362, 364, 366
Horsch, John, 223, 286, 463; conservative-liberal controversy, 320-327, 331; correspondence with Aaron A. Augspurger, 321-323
Horst, Ida. *See* Troyer, Ida (Horst)
Horst, J. Alton, 168, 215, 470
Horst, John L., 243
Horst, Laurence, 218, 274, 397, 415, 475
Hospitals, 265-266, 290-293. *See also* Mennonite Hospital
Hostetler, D. M., 161
Hostetler, Ernest, 99
Hostetler, Ervin, 161
Hostetler, Harold D., 161
Hostetler, Herman, 161
Hostetler, John E., 161
Hostetler, Jonathan J., 211, 212, 305
Hostetler, Joseph, 143
Hostetler, Lester, 325, 514
Hostetler, Levi C., 160-161
Hostetler, Ova, 161
Hostetler, Pius, 158, 412
Hoyne Avenue Mission. *See* Brighton Mennonite Church
Hudson, Ill., 185, 352
Hudson River, 57, 69
Huette, Catherine, 369
Hulbert, Charles E., 282
Hull, Robert, 372
Humphrey, Hubert H., 419
Hunsberger, Ephraim, 194
Huntington College, 275
Hutter, Jacob, 37
Hutterites (Hutterian Brethren), 37, 142, 409, 459, 487

Idaho, 61, 101
Iglesia Evangélica Menonita (West Street), 426
Iglesia Menonita Evangélica (So. Komensky Ave.), 424, 426
Iglesia Menonita Hispania, 426
Illinois, 43, 103; early development of, 25-33; physical characteristics of, 26-27; diseases in, 31, 44, 60-61, 63, 78-79, 132, 133, 147-148; agriculture of Mennonites in, 30, 37, 43-44, 47-48, 60, 67-68, 71, 74, 76-78, 81, 109, 136-140, 167, 436-437, 438, 489; early Mennonite settlement in, 26-27, 30, 31, 37, 39-40, 55, 58; reasons for settlement in, 28, 32, 37, 38, 39, 52, 54, 56, 59, 62, 346; descendants of Mennonites in, 30, 51, 60, 78; migration of Mennonites from, 52, 61, 62-63, 189, 193, 197-198; scattered Mennonites in, 51-54, 232-233, 240; meeting places of Mennonites in, 40, 43, 46-51, 64-66, 70-73, 80, 92, 94, 96-101, 115, 116, 120, 127, 133, 134, 146, 148, 155, 167, 196, 443-445; prosperity of Mennonites in, 27, 33, 78, 109-110, 226, 375, 411-414, 441-443; materialism of Mennonites in, 110, 183-184, 412-413, 451, 492; spiritual problems of Mennonites in, 53-54, 110, 183-184, 226-227, 254; evangelism among Mennonites of, 46, 47, 49, 51, 53-54, 98, 106, 115, 116, 120, 124, 210, 225, 239,

Index 595

243-245, 439, 440-441, 457, 486-488, 491; occupations of Mennonites in, 52, 109-110, 436-437, 438; politics of Mennonites in, 48-49, 82, 199, 200, 201, 231, 371-372, 375, 386, 400, 416-419
Illinois and Michigan Canal, 29, 30, 150
Illinois Central Railroad, 29, 48. *See also* Railroads
"Illinois Conference: Report of the First United Mennonite Church Conference for the State of Illinois," 187
Illinois District Mission Board. *See* Illinois Mennonite Mission Board
Illinois District Women's Sewing Circle, 210
Illinois Elderly Service Program, 446
Illinois Home Mission Board. *See* Illinois Mennonite Mission Board
Illinois Mennonite Conference, 45, 93, 172, 186, 188, 193, 199, 233, 245, 371, 410, 427, 455, 456, 457, 460, 479, 480, 488; merger with Western District A. M. Conference, 185-187, 202, 221; organization of, 194, 198-199; decisions of, 199-206, 207-210, 237, 250-251, 263, 307, 311; historical interest in, 204, 439-440, 441; topics of, 205-206, 209; and Mennonite General Conference, 206-207; extension work of, 210-219, 276;

mutual aid and, 295; authority of, 303, 452, 457-458; Fundamentalism and, 305, 307, 311, 313-314, 333-334, 339-343; difficulties in, 335-339; camping in, 218-219; pastoral terms in, 219-221, 271, 272; Bible versions and, 340; war and, 347; World War I and, 350, 352, 355, 356; World War II and, 361, 364, 365, 366; peace and, 368; social concerns and, 380-389, 402, 403-404; race relations and, 385-390, 397; women's issues in, 406, 407-409, 454-455; stewardship in, 441-443; elderly and, 445, 446-447; church order in, 452-453; inter-Mennonite cooperation and, 460, 463, 470, 476-477, 480, 482-483; changes in, 470, 472, 479, 480, 488. *See also* Mennonite Church
Illinois Mennonite Conference Executive Committee, 341, 359, 408, 476
Illinois Mennonite Historical and Genealogical Society (formerly Illinois Mennonite Historical Society), 84, 86, 477-479
Illinois Mennonite Mission Board, 186, 192, 202, 204, 205, 210-213, 215, 216, 271, 275, 314, 388, 415, 416, 422, 423, 427, 428, 429, 439, 445, 477
Illinois Mennonite

Nurses Association, 466, 468
Illinois Mennonite Relief Sale, 414, 478, 480, 481
Illinois Old Order Amish Mutual Aid Plan, 296
Illinois River, 29, 57, 60, 69, 150
Illinois State Normal University, 226, 450, 479
Illinois Sunday School Conference, 186, 198, 222, 252
Illinois Territory, 26
Illinois Wesleyan University, 133, 479
Imhoff, Christ (Metamora), 453
Imhoff, Christian (North Danvers), 90
Imhoff, Ralph, 438
Imhoff family, 65
India, Mennonite missions in, 185, 211, 259, 260, 280-281, 297, 300, 355, 462
Indian Territory (Oklahoma), 153, 259, 280
Indiana, ministers from Ill., 189, 195, 196
Indiana [Mennonite] Conference, 198, 231, 295, 417
Indiana Territory, 26
Indiana-Michigan Amish Mennonite Conference, 167
Indiana-Michigan Mennonite Conference, 93-94, 206-207, 442
Indiana-Michigan Sunday School Conference, 320
Indians (American), 25, 27, 39-40, 40, 59-60, 153, 345, 377; "menace" of, 28, 31-32; Mennonite missions to, 259, 281
Ingersoll, Robert G., 310

Inglewood Mennonite Church (Los Angeles, Calif.), 429
Ingold, Roy, 487
Intentional communities, 216-217, 410-411, 439, 451-452
Intercollegiate Peace Speech Association (formerly Intercollegiate Peace Association), 255, 374
Inter-Mennonite Fellowship. *See* First Mennonite Church of Champaign-Urbana
Inter-Mennonite Ministers' Retreat, 382, 476
International Christian University, 97
International Council of Religious Education, 334
Ioder, Laura. *See* Smith Laura (Ioder)
Ioder (Yoder) family, 65, 69
Iowa, 27, 59, 82, 85, 87, 99, 132, 135; Illinois Mennonites in, 63; GC origins in, 151, 154
Iowa-Nebraska Mennonite Conference, 424
Ipava, Ill., 53
Irons, Frank, 98

Jackson, Arthur L., 431-432
Jackson, Jesse, 395, 396
Jackson, Minn., 47
James H. Lark Scholarship and Leadership Program, 429
Jansen, Cornelius, 153-154
Jantz, Wesley, 220, 341
Jantzen, D. F., 462
Janzen, Heinz, 110, 339, 367-368, 469
Janzen, Lester, 441

Jefferson, Thomas, 26, 33, 369
Jerusalem, Israel, 299
Jo Daviess County, Ill., 48, 51
Joder, Joseph, 88-89, 91
Johns, Daniel J., 91, 102, 185, 242
Johnson, Lyndon, 418
Johnson County, Iowa, 85
Johnstone, Gilbert, 305
Johnstown, Pa., 309
Joliet, Louis, 25
Jones, Emma R., 391
Jorg, Paul, 377
Juniata, Adams County, Neb., 193
Juniata County, Pa., 43
Juhnke, James, 488, 526
Jutzi family, 65

Kalona, Iowa, 160, 361
Kanagy, Elizabeth (Mrs. Simon M.), 274
Kanagy, Margaret Elizabeth (Brown), 274
Kanagy, Simon M., 272-274, 314
Kandel, Frank, 446
Kankakee, Ill., 428
Kankakee County, Ill., 50, 61
Kansas, Russian Mennonites to, 153, 155, 162, 163
Kansas City Mennonite Mission (Kan.), 174
Kansas-Nebraska Act, 32
Kauffman, A. M., 355-356
Kauffman, Abraham H., 53
Kauffman, Benjamin, 40
Kauffman, Daniel K., 184, 186-187, 388; Fundamentalism and, 304, 311, 318-319
Kauffman, Henry, 43
Kauffman, J. Howard, 130, 343, 367, 377, 402, 405, 485
Kauffman, Joe I., 215, 216

Kauffman, John D., 158-160, 161
Kauffman, Jonas J., 133
Kauffman, Milo, 338, 413, 441-442
Kauffman, Nelson, 429
Kauffman, Raymond, 161
Kauffman family, 31, 65
Kauffman Group. *See* Unaffiliated Amish Mennonites
Kauffmann, Ivan, 211, 218, 338, 433, 439, 440, 492
Kauffmann, Norman, 215, 383
Kaufman, Elsie (Drange), 198
Kaufman, J. Norman, 211, 212, 215, 383
Keenes, Ill., 458
Keim, Joseph N., 132
Keiser, Ora, Mr. and Mrs., 361
Keller, Robert, 212, 220, 441
Kelso Sanitarium, 291. *See also* Mennonite Hospital
Kennedy, John F., 389
Kennel, _____, 185
Kennel, Bertha, 294
Kennel, John, 61
Kennel, Katharina. *See* Unsicker, Katharina (Kennel)
Kennel, LeRoy, 216, 220, 381-382, 419, 476
Kennel, Peter, 78
Kennel family, 65
Kennell, John W., 161
Kennell, Joseph J., 161
"Kennel" Church. *See* Linn Township Amish Mennonite Church
Kensinger, Rev. and Mrs. William, 330
Kenwood-Oakland Community Organization, 395, 396
Key '73, 372, 486
Kickapoo Indians, 27

Index

Kindig, Benjamin, 39, 40
Kindig, David, 39, 40
Kindig family, 39, 40
King, _____, 58
King, Daniel B., 77
King, Daniel R., 284
King, Frank D., 274
King, Henry J., 212, 216
King, John, 371
King, Joseph H., 92, 101, 103, 107, 257, 282, 288, 331
King, Lois, 428, 429
King, Martin Luther, Jr., 390, 391, 395
King, Mary B. See Forney, Mary B. (King)
King, Mary (Claudon), 62, 284
King, Paul O., 220, 382, 428, 429, 454
King, Samuel M., 448
King, Wayne, 214
King family, 65
Kinsinger, John, 94
Kinsinger, Joseph, 97, 288
Kinsinger, Michael (Danvers), 72, 94
Kinsinger, Michael (Washington), 94-96
Kinsinger family, 65
Kistler, Michael, 70, 71, 100
Kistler family, 65
Kitchener, Ont. (formerly Berlin), 58
Klassen, William, 340
Kleine Gemeinde. See Evangelical Mennonite Conference
Klophenstein family, 65
Knights of Columbus, 277
Kniss, Ida Beidler (Mrs. Samuel), 189-190
Kohler, John P., 92
Kohn, Mathilda. See Stevenson, Mathilda (Kohn)
Koinonia Farms, Ga., 383
Kolb, A. B., 31
Korean War, 368

Kornhaus, John, 193
Koretemeier, Eldon, 215
Kouts, Ind., 63, 107
Kouts Mennonite Church (Ind.), 63
Krahn, Ben W., 448
Krahn, Emil J., 121, 344
Kratz, Clayton, 299, 301
Kratz, Salome. See Funk, Salome (Kratz)
Kratz family, 147
Kraybill, Paul N., 468
Krehbiel, Christian, 63, 149, 152-155, 225, 249, 346, 507, 515
Krehbiel, Henry P., 387
Krehbiel, Jacob (Palatinate), 39
Krehbiel, Jacob (Summerfield), 149, 150, 153
Krehbiel, Ronald, 430
Krehbiel, Susan (Ruth), 149, 153, 293
Krehbiel, Valentin, 346
Krehbiel family, 39
Kreider, Amos E., 235, 256, 261, 380, 441; conservative-liberal controversy, 311, 316, 325, 329
Kreider, Robert S., 369
Kreider family, 44
Krimmer Mennonite Brethren Church, 162-163, 284, 285, 299, 379. See also Mennonite Brethren Church
Kropf, Joseph, 161
Kulp, Lewis, 49, 50
Kulp, Nancy (Tinsman), 49
Kulp Hall, 49
Kurtz, Jonathan, 91, 307, 461-462

La Salle, Ill., 29
La Salle County, Ill., 51, 83
Labor concerns, 375, 376-377, 402-404, 490
Ladies' Aid Societies. See Women's Organizations

Ladies' Sewing Circle. See Women's Organizations
Lagrange County, Ind., 82, 91, 275
La Junta, Colo., 292, 388, 470
La Junta Mennonite [MC] School of Nursing, 292-293, 470
Lake City, Ill., 214
Lake City Bible Church, 169, 214
Lake Erie, 26, 149
Lake Erie and Western Railroad, 98. See also Railroads
Lake Michigan, 26, 27, 29, 30, 121, 150, 426
Lakeview Mennonite Brethren Church (formerly Lincoln Avenue Gospel Mission), 162-163, 299, 379, 433
Lambert, George, 280
Lancaster, Pa., 58, 142, 147, 235, 285
Lancaster Conference, 285, 458
Lancaster County, Pa., 40, 41, 43, 48, 142, 145, 230, 266, 267, 345
Lancaster Heights, Ill., 217
Lancaster Heights Mennonite Church, 217
Landes, Carl, 277, 301
Landis, Abraham, 146, 147
Landis, Albert, 422
Landis, Hans, 36
Landis, Jacob, 147-148
Landis, John, 147-148
Landis family, 147
Language, acculturation and, 485-486, 487. See also English language; German language
Lantz, D. Parke, 422
Lantz, Lee J., 98, 100, 107, 277;

conservative-liberal controversy and, 305, 326-327
Lantz, Milo P., 399
Lantz family, 31, 65
Lapp, D. J., 308
Lapp, Daniel G., 212
Lapp, Esther (Ebersole), 198
Lapp, Martin, 41, 43, 189
Lapp, Samuel, 41, 43
Lapp family, 44
Lark, James H., 219, 427-429
Lark, Mrs. James, 428
Lauver, William, 422
Lawndale Mennonite Church (formerly Second Mennonite Church, Iglesia Mexicana), 387-388, 422-424, 425, 427
League of Nations, 358, 359
Leaman, A. Miriam, 510
Leaman, Amanda (Eby), 266, 267
Leaman, Amos Hershey, 156, 190, 234, 242, 278, 305, 307, 510; at Mennonite Home Mission, 266-272, 274
Ledochowiski, L. H. (also called Father Hillary), 190-191
Lee County, Ill., 69
Lee County, Iowa, 149
Lehman, _____, 149
Lehman [Widow], _____, 150
Lehman, Earl S., 274
Lehman, G. Irvin, 274
Lehman, Joseph S., 189, 265
Lehman, L. J., 197, 256
Lehman, Mark N., 220, 382, 389, 429
Lehman, Pauline, 211
Lehner, Elizabeth, 274
Leisy Brewery, 397
Leisy family, 397
Leman family, 65
Leo, Ind., 185
Lexington, Ky., 40

Liberalism (theological), 303, 310-311, 313, 314, 315-316, 320, 321, 322, 326, 329, 330, 492
Liberty bonds, 355, 356-357, 362
Liechty, Joseph, 231-232
Lincoln, Abraham, 32, 369, 386, 416-417
Lincoln Avenue Gospel Mission. See Lakeview Mennonite Brethren Church
Line Lexington, Pa., 228
Linn Township Amish Mennonite Church, 158, 161-162
Little Mackinaw River, 61
Litwiller, Delton, 480
Litwiller, J., 185
Litwiller, John T. N., 422
Litwiller, John W., 99
Litwiller, Joseph, 72
Litwiller, Katherine. See Martin, Katherine (Litwiller)
Litwiller, Katy (Ehrisman), 177, 178
Litwiller, Nelson, 421
Litwiller, Simon, 177, 178, 366
Litwiller family, 65
Livingston County, Ill., 31, 72, 76, 86, 113, 122, 195, 196, 251
Lodge membership, 490
Logan County, Ohio, 158
Lombard, Ill., 215
Lombard Mennonite Church, 209, 215-216, 381, 407-408, 419, 453, 492
Lombard University, 252
Long, C. Warren, 210, 212, 216, 381, 412, 470
Long Green, Md., 82
Long Island, N.Y., 408
Long Island College (N.Y.), 252
Los Angeles, Calif., 429
Loucks, Aaron, 198, 298, 352, 354

Louisville, Ky., 40
Lovejoy, Elijah P., 32, 33
Lovejoy, Owen, 32-33
Low Point, Ill., 353
Lugibill, John C., 185
Lundy, Benjamin, 33
Luster, T. J., 31
Luther, Martin, 34
Luthy, David, 87
Lutke, Jacob, 306
Lyon [Gen.], _____, 351-352

McCloud, George, 394
McConnell, Jeffrey, 43
McCormick, Cyrus, 30
McCulloch, John W., 198
McCullough family, 31
McDowell, Walter, 120
Machen, J. Gresham, 317
MacIntyre, Carl, 343
Mackinaw, Ill., 214
Mackinaw Dells, Ill., 67
Mackinaw Meeting, 65, 66-68, 70, 72-74, 90. See also Roanoke Mennonite Church; Goodfield Mennonite Church
Mackinaw River, settlement along, 58, 61, 65, 67, 69, 73, 74, 75, 79
Mackinaw Valley, Ill., 74, 75
McLean County, Ill., 31, 59-99 passim, 238, 256, 281, 352, 371, 413, 448
McLean County Medical Society, 290
McNutt, Frank, 279
Madison County, Ill., 51
Magnuson, C. A., 213
Magnuson, Mrs. C. A., 213
Mahoning County, Ohio, 47
Malone, R. J., 354
"Malone Report," 354, 355
Manitou, Colo., 63
Manson, Iowa, 63
Mantz, Felix, 35

Index 599

Manuscripts Division of the Library of Congress, 353
Maple Lawn Home for the Aged, 284-288, 445, 446
Marion, Kan., 52
Marion College, 334
Markham Community Church, 369, 385, 408, 430-431
Markham Sheltered Care Workshop, 431
Marquette, Jacques, 25
Martensen, Ole, 268
Martin, Arthur, 143, 213
Martin, Chris E., 211
Martin, Christian, 72
Martin, J. Weldon, 422
Martin, Katherine (Litwiller), 63
Martin, Nicholas, 63, 72
Martin family, 65
Martyrs Mirror, 136
Masontown, Pa., 237, 240
Matthew, Kazadi, 283
Mattoon, Ill., 132
Maurer, Joseph, 66
Maurer, Nicholas, 60, 74
Maurer, Peter, 60
Maurer family, 65
May, Rick, 383
Mayer (Moyer), Jacob, 41
Meadows, Ill., 96-97, 107, 109, 234, 282, 283, 285, 286, 288, 289, 389, 399
Meadows Mennonite Church, 96-97, 288, 289
Meadows Mennonite Home and Retirement Center, 97, 106, 109, 111, 117, 119, 130, 284-286, 288-290, 445, 446-447, 465, 468, 469
Meadows Old People's Home. *See* Meadows Mennonite Home and Retirement Center
Meck, A. J., 357
Medaryville, Ind., 364
Medina County, Ohio, 194
Mehl, John E., 102
Mellinger family, 44
Memorial Deaconess Hospital. *See* Brokaw Hospital
Mennonite, The, 98, 108, 233, 234, 339, 340, 368, 369, 390, 392, 396, 406, 411, 419, 433, 463, 465, 472, 474, 477, 491
Mennonite Aid Plan, 295, 461
Mennonite Bible Mission. *See* Grace Community Church
Mennonite Biblical Seminary, 109, 157, 340, 363-364, 368, 392, 469, 471
Mennonite Board of Charitable Homes, 284, 286
Mennonite Board of Education, 185, 192, 203, 213, 256, 260
Mennonite Board of Missions and Charities (later, of Missions), 143, 153, 169, 185, 190, 212, 216, 240, 260-261, 271, 276, 286, 288, 355, 381, 387, 388, 421, 422, 423, 426, 429, 446
Mennonite Book and Tract Society, 263
Mennonite Brethren Church, 162-163, 297, 459, 460, 475, 483; World War II and, 361
Mennonite Brethren in Christ, 127, 223
Mennonite Central Committee, 109, 166, 271, 360, 361, 363, 365, 377, 379, 414, 442, 468, 480, 489; origin and early work of, 298-301; Mennonite cooperation and, 465, 466
Mennonite Children's Home, 284
Mennonite Church (also called [Old] Mennonite Church), 41-53 *passim*, 93-94, 98, 109, 131, 145-146, 165, 173, 178, 209, 215, 216, 436, 459, 485, 488; Reformed Mennonites and, 145-146, 209; publications of, 230-233; Great Awakening in, 222-223; revivalism and, 240-242; education and, 249-251, 454, 455; missions and, 259-276; in Chicago, 262-276; Fundamentalism and, 304, 313, 315, 317-318, 328-329; conservative-liberal controversy and, 324-325; World War I and, 354-355; World War II and, 361, 364-366; peace and, 368; social concerns and, 377, 379-383, 385-387, 404; race relations and, 385-390, 397; evangelism in, 439, 440-441; inter-Mennonite cooperation and, 186, 292-293, 463, 468, 477, 480, 482-483; unity with GC, 472-475
Mennonite Church of Normal (formerly First Mennonite Church [Normal] and Bloomington Mennonite Church), 92, 100, 216, 403, 455, 466, 470, 478, 479-480
Mennonite Community Association, 451

Mennonite Community Chapel (formerly Mennonite Home Mission), 268, 275, 424, 426. *See also* Englewood Mennonite Church
Mennonite Confession of Faith (1963), 457
Mennonite Disaster Service, 377, 468, 472
Mennonite Evangelizing and Benevolent Board. *See* Mennonite Evangelizing Board of America
Mennonite Evangelizing Board of America, 240, 260, 265, 280. *See also* Mennonite Board of Missions and Charities
Mennonite Evangelizing Committee. *See* Mennonite Evangelizing Board of America
Mennonite Fellowship. *See* Evanston Mennonite Church
Mennonite General Assembly, 408, 433, 452, 488. *See also* Mennonite General Conference
Mennonite General Board, 216, 433, 442
Mennonite General Conference, 181, 186, 206-207, 233, 349; Fundamentalism and, 313, 314-315, 316
Mennonite Gospel Church (formerly Mennonite Gospel Mission), 270. *See also* United Mennonite Church of Peoria
Mennonite Gospel Mission (formerly Mennonite Home Chapel), 277, 333
Mennonite Gospel Mission (MC). *See* Twenty-sixth Street Mission
Mennonite Great Awakening. *See* Great Awakening (Mennonite)
Mennonite Historical Bulletin, 172
Mennonite Home Chapel. *See* Mennonite Gospel Mission
Mennonite Home Mission (also called Chicago Home Mission), 98, 156, 164, 165, 185, 190, 192, 201, 216, 234, 250-251, 261-275, 305, 307, 309, 347, 359, 380, 387-388, 411, 465; fresh air program of, 267-268, 269; difficulties of, 275-276; training of others at, 277, 278; Hispanics in, 420-422, 424; opposition to, 263; Afro-Americans in, 427-428. *See also* Englewood Mennonite Church
Mennonite Hospital (formerly Mennonite Sanitarium), 106, 109, 111, 119, 131, 166, 290-293, 445, 448-450, 465, 469, 470, 523; board of, 97
Mennonite Hospital Association (formerly Mennonite Sanitarium Association), 291, 448, 450
Mennonite Hospital School of Nursing, 166, 310, 450, 455, 479
Mennonite Messianic Mission Board, 458
Mennonite Mexican Church. *See* Lawndale Mennonite Church
Mennonite Mutual Aid, 295, 472
Mennonite Nurses Training School. *See* Mennonite Hospital School of Nursing
Mennonite Old People's Home (Ohio), 79
Mennonite Publication Board, 185, 190, 233
Mennonite Publishing Company, 118, 189, 233. *See also* John F. Funk; *Herald of Truth*
Mennonite Publishing House, 233, 246, 309, 320
Mennonite Quarterly Review, 299, 353
Mennonite Relief Commission for War Sufferers, 297
Mennonite Research Foundation, 352, 436
Mennonite Sanitarium. *See* Mennonite Hospital
Mennonite Sanitarium Association. *See* Mennonite Hospital Association
Mennonite Student Services Committee, 470
Mennonite Voluntary Service. *See* Voluntary Service
Mennonite World Conference, 216, 393, 472
Mennonite Youth Fellowship, 168, 205, 210, 242
Mennonites, Anabaptist origins of, 34, 37, 130; as "quiet in the land," 22, 33, 248, 386, 393, 486; benevolence of, 488-489; migration of, 29, 49-73 *passim*; persecution of, 248, 249; modes of transportation and, 29, 43-80 *passim*, 238;

Index

place in history of, 253; publications of, 30-31, 93, 106-118 *passim*, 117-118, 136, 163, 228-235; relations with Indians, 59-60; religious changes of, 39, 112, 115-116, 129-131, 191-192, 206, 454, 470, 472; schisms among, 459; cooperation among, 41, 109, 119, 185-187, 255, 257-258, 267, 269, 272, 280-286, 291, 297, 328-330, 460-463, 466, 470-472; unity among, 41, 85, 108, 126-129, 151, 181, 185-187, 189, 251, 325, 460-463; beliefs and practices of, 39, 44, 46, 55-56, 62, 66, 68, 70, 89, 100, 103-106, 112, 161, 164, 170, 175-181, 199, 210, 215, 223, 241, 264, 317-318, 328-329, 336, 337, 486-487, 489-490, 491. *See also* Missions
Mennonites and social concerns, ch. 14, *passim*
Mennonitism, 36
Metamora, Ill., 61, 65, 66, 78, 86, 116, 181, 185, 204, 214, 255, 256, 272, 286, 298, 300, 308, 327, 353, 389, 461-462, 478
Metamora High School, 327
Metamora Mennonite Church (formerly Metamora Amish Mennonite Church), 63, 73, 169, 174, 182, 185, 213-214, 220, 246, 252, 254, 356, 364, 419, 440, 450-453, 455, 457, 467,

478; Partridge Creek congregation of, 63-64, 66, 80-81, 86, 345, 440; Partridge Creek meetinghouse of, 46, 64-65, 116, 399; Union Church joins, 48, 189, 219
Metz, Floyd, 370
Metzler, Abraham, Jr., 264
Metzler, Leonard, 100
Meyer, Esther (Mrs. Jacob C.), 510
Meyers, Abram, 165
Meyers, F. B., 305
Meyers, Thomas J., 501
Middle District Conference, 108-109, 153, 249, 468
Middlebury, Ind., 107, 265, 275
Midway, Ill., 215
Midway Mennonite Church, 215
Mifflin County, Pa., 65, 83, 85
Milford, Neb., 63, 181
Milford Square, Pa., 228
Military Branch, War Department, 355
Military Intelligence Division [MID] of the War Department, 354, 355
Military service (Mennonite), 38-39, 204, 308, 393, 458, 488-489. *See also* Peace
Miller, A. J., 301
Miller, Allen H., 99
Miller, D. Paul, 133, 139, 140
Miller, Daniel, 132
Miller, Daniel D., 170-171, 185, 242, 288
Miller, Dorothy, 456
Miller, Earl, 212
Miller, Isaac A., 169
Miller, John, 216
Miller, John H., 352, 353
Miller, L. A., 136, 300
Miller, Levi M., 158

Miller, Mahlon, 456
Miller, Milo, 99
Miller, Orie A., 212, 219, 335, 336
Miller, Orie O., 298, 299
Miller, Richard D., 476
Miller, S. B., 185
Miller, S. J., 333-334
Miller, Vern, 487
Miller, W. W., 155
Millersville State Normal, 267
Millhouse family, 44
Milwaukee, Wis., Spanish work in, 424
Milwaukee Mennonite Church (Wis.), 424, 426
Minier, Ill., 185
Mininger, J. D., 350
Mininger, Paul, 204
Ministerial Association of the Central Conference Mennonite Church, 359
Ministerial Committee of the Illinois Mennonite Conference, 206
Ministry, 204-205; supported, 219-221; attire of, 207-208, 335, 336, 490; changes in, 208, 335, 428, 453; education of, 249-250, 251, 311-312, 329, 453; cooperation among, 468, 469, 470
Mireau, Hugo J., 94
Mission Worker, The, 234
Missionary Bulletin, 235
Missionary Church (formerly Missionary Church Association), 119, 127, 129, 145; origins of, 120-121, 165-166
Missionary Guide, 218, 293, 335, 389, 413, 439, 470, 477
Missions, 39, 106, 108, 171, 198, 210; Anabaptists and, 35,

36-37; early Mennonite interest in, 258-260; home, 121, 123, 201, 260-280; foreign, 201; EMC and, 111, 115, 116, 117, 118, 121, 129; Central conference and, 101, 109; GC and, 153, 155-157; MC and, 259-276; Salem (EMC) Church and, 119; Sunday schools and, 229, 235
Missions Society. *See* Ladies Aid Society
Mississippi River, 25, 26, 27, 29, 30, 48, 57, 59, 62, 346
Mississippi Valley, 25, 27, 28, 30
Missouri Compromise of 1820, 32
Mitchell, A. N., 401
Mitchell, Franklin R., 99, 279
Model-Cities Planning Council, 395
Modernism (theological), 93-94, 303-334 *passim*, 492
Moline, Ill., 424
Molotschna Colony, Russia, 299-300
Monmouth, Ill., 52
Monroe, James, 26, 33, 73
Montgomery County, Pa., 43, 194
Moody, Dwight L., 223, 229, 235, 240, 305, 306, 307, 308, 310, 398
Moody Bible Institute, 122, 163, 164, 197, 201, 251, 267, 272, 277, 278, 308, 310, 311-312, 321, 331, 334-335, 341, 342, 428; influence on Mennonites, 305-309, 332, 333
Moody Memorial Church, 51, 229, 307
Moody Monthly, 310

Morgan, G. Campbell, 310
Morgan County, Ill., 51
Mormons, 32, 52, 246
Morrison, Ill., 45, 46, 49, 165, 298, 352
Morrison Brethren in Christ Church, 165
Morrison Mennonite Church (formerly "Red Brick Church"), 45-46, 188, 193-194, 198, 199, 219, 221, 357
Morton, Ill., 120, 121, 124, 125, 126, 130, 131, 212, 213, 236, 456
Morton Apostolic Christian Church, 480
Morton Bible Church, 124
Mosbach, Germany, 48
Moscow, Russia, 299, 326
Mosiman, Samuel K., 275, 332
Mosimann, Michael, 65, 66, 82, 113
Mosimann family, 65
"Mother Church." *See* North Danvers Mennonite Church
Moultrie County, Ill., 132, 133
Mount Carmel Home and Orphanage, 165
Mount Hermon Amish Mennonite Church, 160, 161
Mount Olive Missionary Church, 166
Mount Pleasant Mennonite Church, 458
Mountain Lake, Minn., 278
Moyer family, 44
Muncie, Ind., 74
Münsterites, 36
Musical instruments, 92, 99-100, 112, 116, 179-180, 200, 208, 452, 487, 489, 490
Musselman, Henry, 48

Musselman, Michael, 48-49
Musser, Daniel, 145-146
Mutual aid, 294-297
Mutual Security Life Insurance Company, 296
Myers family, 44

Nachtigall, Wilbur, 168
Naffziger, Barbara. *See* Springer, Barbara (Naffziger)
Naffziger, Peter, "The Apostle," 59, 70, 71, 94
Nafziger, Arthur W., 204, 218, 366, 447
Nafziger, Carolyn, 440
Nafziger, Christian, 72, 83
Nafziger, Daniel, 453
Nafziger, John, 66
Nafziger, Peter, 72
Nafziger family, 65, 69
Nafzinger, _____ (Kan.), 185
Nagata, Judith A., 137, 139, 140, 141
Nancy, Lorraine, 61
Napoleonic Wars, 38, 39, 56, 58
Nappanee, Ind., 93, 185, 461-462
Nashville, Ark., 161
National Association of Evangelicals, 334, 341, 343, 482
National Council of Churches, 334, 341, 378, 388
National League of Nursing, 450
National Service Board for Religious Objectors, 361
Nauvoo, Ill., 32
Near East Relief, 297
Neff, Peter, 50-51, 188
Nelson, Boyd, 215
Nester, Donald, 96, 482
Neuenschwander, Albert, 296
Neuenschwander, Jesse, 458

Index 603

Neuenschwander (Neuschwanger), Peter, 48
Neufeld, Elmer, 392
Neufeld, John T., 156, 165, 278
Neuhauser, Christian, 182
Neuhauser family, 65
Neuschwanger, John, 49
New Albany, Ind., 40
New Deal, 400, 402
New Mennonites. *See* Reformed Mennonite Church
New Orleans, La., 25, 57, 59, 62, 71, 74; Amish church in, 62
New Paris, Ind., 424
New Wilmington, Pa., 214
New York City, N.Y., 27, 47, 57, 69, 149
Newcastle Bible Church, 214, 336
Newswanger, Carl, 216, 439, 480
Newswanger, Louise, 406
Nice, Hazel. *See* Hassan, Hazel (Nice)
Nice, Henry, Jr., 193
Nice, Henry, Sr., 45, 46, 188, 193; and GC, 194; and Illinois Mennonite Conference, 194, 198
Nice, John, 193, 265, 267, 346, 357
Nice, Philip, 265
Nice family, 193, 194
Nissley, Peter K., 230
Nixon, Richard M., 369, 419
Noffziger, Peter, 61
Nonconformity, 202-203, 206, 207, 212-213, 221, 223, 452; conservative-liberal controversy and, 303, 313, 316, 321, 326, 328, 335, 337, 464, 486, 488, 489-490, 490-491
Normal, Ill., 97, 100, 107, 109, 226, 290, 291, 480, 482

North Central Association, 256
North Danvers Mennonite Church, 70-71, 90, 92-93, 94, 103, 108, 110, 238, 243-244, 258, 283, 304, 330, 413, 447, 454, 461; churches from, 94-98, 101; as Rock Creek (or Yoder) Congregation, 65, 67, 70-71, 81, 82, 88-90; Rock Creek Meetinghouse of, 65, 70, 71, 73, 74, 83, 94, 116
North Fork, Calif., 361
North Newton, Kan., 352
Northern Baptist Seminary, 122, 164, 278
Northern Bible Society, 359-360
Northwest Ordinance. *See* Ordinance of 1787
Northwest Territory, 26, 32
Northwestern University, 217, 255, 262, 328
Norwood, Ill., 217
"Note on the Mennonites," 354
Nunemaker, Harvey E., 94, 100, 107, 316, 325, 441, 464
Nussbaum, Irvin, 168
Nussbaum, Milo, 120, 121, 124-125, 482
Nussbaum, Stanley, 111, 112, 120-121, 129, 130, 131, 343, 367, 378, 482, 484, 500
Nyce, Dorothy, 406

Oak Grove Bible Church, 121, 123-124, 130
Oberholtzer, John H., 112, 151, 152, 225, 228, 230, 235, 237, 460, 473-474
Oberholtzer congregation (Ohio).

See Wadsworth First Mennonite Church
Oberholtzer division. *See* General Conference Mennonite Church
O'Fallon, Ill., 149
Ohio Mennonite Conference, 442
Ohio River, 26, 27, 40, 57, 59, 60
Ohio State University, 256
Oklahoma, 153, 259
(Old) Chicago congregation, 51, 188, 267
Old Colony Mennonites, 140, 485, 486, 491
(Old) Mennonite Church. *See* Mennonite Church
Old Order Amish, 55, 68, 86, 87, 132, 147, 157, 158, 164, 167, 169, 187, 212, 459, 480, 484, 485, 486; agriculture and, 132, 136-139, 140-141; districts of, 133; practices of, 134; education and, 135-136; changes among, 137, 138-139, 140, 142-143, 484; non-farming occupations of, 139-140, 300-301; transportation and, 141; publications of, 136, 234-235; World War I and, 355-356; acculteration and, 484
Old Order Mennonites (Wislerites). *See* Wislerite Mennonites
Old Order River Brethren, 459
Oliver, James, 76
Omaha, Neb., 127
Ontario Conference, 243
Orchardville Mennonite Church, 458
Ordinance of 1785, 26
Ordinance of 1787 (Northwest

604   Mennonites in Illinois

Ordinance), 26, 28, 32
Orendorff, Daniel, 174, 185
Orendorff family, 31, 65
Orientals, 432
Orphanages, early Mennonite, 283-284
Orrville, Ohio, 45, 284
Oswald, Christian, 62
Oswald, Sadie, 268, 275, 424
Oswald family, 25, 62
Ottawa, Ill., 51, 192
Otto, Daniel (pioneer), 132
Otto, Daniel (contemporary), 140, 439
Otto, Milton, 162, 439
Ovando, Victor, 424, 426
Overholt Distillery, 397
Oyer, Amos, 115, 118, 119, 120, 122, 306
Oyer, Christian, 120
Oyer, Daniel S., 305
Oyer, Edward H., 213-214
Oyer, Eli J., 115
Oyer, Emma, 268, 269, 274, 308
Oyer, Harold, 335, 336
Oyer, Jacob, 61
Oyer, Julia, 115, 119
Oyer, Noah, 203-204, 246, 255, 256, 258; conservative-liberal controversy and, 316-318
Oyer, Verle, 338-339
Oyer family. *See* Ayer family

Page, Alice Thut, 280
Page, [Dr.] William B., 262, 280, 306
Palos Hills, Ill., 122, 123
Pana, Ill., 132
Pandora, Ohio, 263
Pannabecker, Samuel F., 88, 89, 98, 102, 108, 236, 246, 392, 482, 508
Panola, Ill., 107
Paradise, Pa., 293

Paris, France, 57, 106
Park, Myrna, 559
Parr, Amanda E. *See* Brunk, Amanda E. (Parr)
Parret family, 52
Partridge Creek. *See* Black Partridge Creek
Partridge Creek Congregation. *See* Metamora Mennonite Church
Pathway Publishing Company, 136
Patton, Edna, 305
Pauley, William T., 122, 377
Peace, 130, 176, 180, 202, 370-371, 457, 458, 487, 491; as part of Great Awakening, 223-225, 229, 259; evangelism and, 372; witness for, 357-360, 365, 366-369; Fundamentalism and, 309, 311-312, 313, 326-327, 337, 358; in time of war, 345-346, 349-357; teaching of, 346-347, 366, 368; labor movement and, 403; C. Henry Smith and, 358-359, 373-374; politics and, 416-419; Mennonite cooperation and, 466, 482
Peace Committee of the Central Conference Mennonite Church, 359
Peace [Problems] Committee of the Mennonite General Conference, 359, 368, 436
Peachey, Shem, 158
Peck, J. M., 28
Pekin, Ill., 82, 98, 109, 110, 179, 188, 215
Penn, William, 37, 38
Pennsylvania, Mennonites in, 37-38;

GC origins in, 151, 460; Puerto Ricans in, 424; Afro-American missions in, 427
Pensacola (ship), 298
Peoria, Ill., 25, 40, 57, 65, 76, 98, 107, 109, 132, 133, 150, 166, 214, 217, 219, 341, 398, 437, 477, 479; missions in, 211-212, 278-279
Peoria County, Ill., 60
Peters, _____, 306
Petersheim, Sam, 165
Pfrimmerhof, Germany, 39
Philadelphia, Pa., 43, 47, 57, 58, 304, 407
Philadelphia First Mennonite Church (Pa.), 243
Philips, Dirk, 35
Philips, Obbe, 35
Piatt County, Ill., 53
Pierson, _____, 306
Pigeon, Mich., 157, 333
Pittsburgh, Pa., 57
Plank, Daniel J., 133
Plank, David E., 315, 358, 400-401, 402
Plank, Solomon K., 283
Plank family, 65
Pleasant Grove Mennonite Church (formerly Dillon Creek Amish congregation), 65, 66, 170-171, 172, 182, 185, 213, 214, 440
Pleasant Hill Mennonite Church, 212, 213, 217
Pleasant View Church, 141, 164-165
Plow Creek Fellowship, 410-411, 451
Polk, James K., 417
Polo, Ill., 165
Populist movement, 78, 175-176
Portsmouth, N.H., 27
Portsmouth, Va., 27
Prairie Chapel, 502
Prairie Farmer, 136
Prairie Street Mennonite

Church (Ind.), 93, 159, 240, 297
Prayer meetings, 117
Premillennialism, 121, 215, 390-312, 315, 333, 458. *See also* Fundamentalism
Princeton Theological Seminary, 255, 317
Progress of civilization, 348, 450-451
Prohibition, 400-401. *See also* Temperance
Prophecy, 310
Protestantism, influence on Mennonites, 223, 302, 303, 305
Provident Bookstore, 210
Puerto Rico, 169, 380, 423, 424
Pulaski, Iowa, 155
Putnam County, Ill., 33, 60, 225-226

Quakers (Society of Friends), 33, 254, 297, 308, 359, 360, 373, 374, 385, 443
Quakertown, Pa., 237, 428
Quiet Place, The, 394
Quickening. *See* Great Awakening (Mennonite)
Quinn Chapel, 158, 213
Quiring, Jacob, 324, 332

R. L. Hartzler Health Complex, 450
Race relations, 375, 377, 384-397
Railroads, 29, 30, 44, 57, 69, 72-73, 76-77, 98
Ramírez, John, 424
Ramseyer, Joseph E., 120-121, 165, 367
Ramseyer, Lloyd L., 256, 352-353
Randolph County, Ind.,
Rauschenbusch, Walter, 376, 391
Reading, Ill., 50
Reba Place Fellowship,
216-217, 410, 451-452
Reber, Joseph, 160
"Red Brick Church." *See* Morrison Mennonite Church
Red Cross, 354-355. *See also* World War I
Reddick, Ill., 197
Rediger, B. E., 115
Rediger, C. E., 122
Rediger, Chris, 115
Rediger, Christian, 96
Rediger, Jacob, 73
Rediger, Joseph (Roanoke), 73
Rediger, Joseph (Salem), 73, 113-114, 115, 118, 290
Rediger, Joseph C., 120
Rediger, Mary, 121
Rediger, Milo A., 334
Rediger family, 65, 73
Reeser, Barbara (Zimmerman), 74
Reeser, Christian, 59, 73-74, 417
Reeser, John, 74
Reform movement, 375
Reformation, 34
Reformed Mennonite Church, 43, 44, 145-149, 459
Regier, David A., 306
Regier, H. H., 462
Regier, Marie J., 384-385, 393
Rehoboth Mennonite Church, 382, 389, 427, 429
Reimer, Keith, 369
Reimer, Vic, 389, 433, 434-435
Reinhart family, 147
Reitzel family, 44
Relief Commission of the Central Conference Mennonite Church, 297
Relief work, 106, 161, 171, 205, 296-300, 365, 465, 488-489; in France, 351, 353; in Syria, 353; in Russia, 297-300, 353
Religiöser Botschafter, Der, 228
Reno County, Kan., 133
Republican Party, 386, 416, 418, 419
Ressler, Jacob A., 280
Revival meetings, 106, 116, 117, 229, 239-242; opposition to, 240-241
Revolutionary War, 224
Rhea, William C., 155-156
Rich, Joseph, 288
Rich, Mary. *See* Ball, Mary (Rich)
Richards, E. Joe, 216
Richards, Emma (Sommers), 216, 407
Richland, Ill., 213
Richland County, Ohio, 40, 41
Richland Valley Sunday School, 213-214
Richmond, Tex., 277
Richmond, Va., 27, 40
Riddick, Ed, 375, 394
Ringenberg, Norman, 418
Ringenberg (Rinkenberger) family, 65
Risser (Reeser) family, 65
Rittman, Ohio, 79, 286
Roanoke, Ill., 41, 73, 86, 158, 161, 213, 380
Roanoke Mennonite Church (formerly Roanoke Amish Mennonite Church), 63, 67, 73-74, 158, 159, 161, 169-170, 172, 174, 179, 182, 183, 185, 215, 220, 261, 310, 315, 341, 343, 356, 358, 405, 406, 409, 440, 468; architecture of, 443, 444-445. *See also* Mackinaw Meeting; Goodfield Mennonite Church
Roanoke Township,

Woodford County, Ill., 73
Robein, Ill., 215
Robein Mennonite Church, 215, 340
Roberts, Oral, 341
Rock Creek, Ill., 61, 65, 70, 71
Rock Creek Amish congregation. *See* North Danvers Mennonite Church
Rock Island, Ill., 424
Rock Island Railroad, 69. *See also* Railroads
Rocke, E. M., 115, 120, 130-131, 242
Rocke family, 65
Rockford, Ill., 27, 41, 147
Rockingham County, Va., 51
Rockome Gardens, Ill., 143, 213
Rockwell Mennonite Church, 214-215
Rodgers family, 52
Roeschley, Noah, 305, 336
Roeschley family, 390
Roggi, Christian, 61
Roggy (Rocke) family, 65
Roosevelt, Franklin D., 400
Roosevelt University, 164
Ropp, Alvin, 198
Ropp, Andreas, 57
Ropp, Andrew (bishop), 58, 65, 66, 70, 82-83
Ropp, Andrew (Dowie), 66
Ropp, Christian, Jr., 68, 76, 251
Ropp, Christian, Sr., 57-58, 59, 65, 67-68, 71, 73, 74, 81, 185, 397, 406; participation at Amish conferences, 82-83; relationship with Joseph Stuckey, 89-90
Ropp, Edwin O., 57, 67, 68
Ropp, Elizabeth (Eiman), 57
Ropp, Jacob, 58
Ropp, John, 68, 256-257, 397, 399
Ropp, Magdalena (Schertz), 67
Ropp, Mary (Rupp), 256, 257, 397
Ropp, Moses, 120
Ropp, Peter, 397
Ropp, Peter A., 406
Ropp, Peter W., 66
Ropp (Rupp) family, 58, 65, 257
Ropp Hall, 68, 257
Roseland, Neb., 194, 212
Ross, I. Mark, 215
Roszhart, Aaron, 97
Roth, Barbara. *See* Stuckey, Barbara (Roth)
Roth, Donald F., 480
Roth, Donald W., 115, 406
Roth, Elva May, 171, 370, 480
Roth, John, 211, 212, 280, 414, 480
Roth, Moses, 288
Roth, Nicholas, 113
Roth, Oscar, 208
Roth, Paul N., 101, 340
Roth, Roy, 212, 256
Roth, Ruth C., 210
Roth family, 65
Rowe, Edmund T., 277
Rupp, Andrew W., 484
Rupp, Benjamin, 111, 115, 282, 291
Rupp, Elmer, 306
Rupp, Jerald, 123
Rupp, John, 62, 277
Rupp, Mary (Baechler), 62, 256, 257, 277
Rupp, Paul W., 120, 123
Rupp, Richard, 122
Rural missions, 420, 432
Rusche, Joseph, 61
Russia, relief work in, 297-301, 353
Russian Mennonites, 59, 153-155, 199, 224-225, 229, 230, 248, 295, 296-297, 402, 486
Russian Relief Commission, 301
Ruth, David, 346
Ruth, Jacob Ernest, 150
Ruth, Susan. *See* Krehbiel, Susan (Ruth)
Ruth family, 149
Rutt, Albert B., 106, 234, 257, 267, 277, 294, 316, 331, 463
Rutt family, 44

Saales, Alsace, 63
Sac Indians, 343
Saginaw, Mich., 429
Saint Anne, Ill., 429
Saint Clair County, Ill., 149
Saint Johns, Mich., 308
St. Louis, Mo., 30, 140, 149, 150, 394, 429, 438
Salem Children's Home (formerly Salem Orphanage), 111, 117, 118, 119, 234, 281, 284, 377, 445-446
Salem Evangelical Mennonite Church (formerly Salem Defenseless Mennonite Church), 76, 111, 113-117, 118, 120, 122, 245-246, 284, 290, 330, 343, 354-355, 362, 469; mission interest of, 119, 121, 262; painted yellow, 356
Salem Gospel Mission. *See* Calvary Memorial Church
Salem Home, 285
Salem Orphanage Association, 284
Salisbury, Pa., 164
Salvation Army, 376
Salzman, Earl L., 93, 96, 97, 299
Salzman, Jacob, 285
Salzman, Vinora (Weaver), 93, 299, 407
Salzman, Warren R., 368
San Francisco, Calif., 61

Index 607

Sangamon County, Ill., 51
Sangamon River, 167
Sankey, Ira D., 229
Santa Fe Trail, 52
Sarreburg, Lorraine, 61, 62, 63
Saybrook, Ill., 104, 107, 315, 321, 330, 454
Scales Mound, Ill., 48
Scales Mound congregation, 48-49, 188
Schantz, Peter, 90, 92, 97, 99, 100, 282, 332
Schantz family, 65
Schertz, Andrew, 63
Schertz, Arthur, 467
Schertz, Ben, 453
Schertz, Christian (Hopedale), 72
Schertz, Christian (McLean County), 31
Schertz Christian S., 73, 295
Schertz, David (East Peoria), 61
Schertz, David (Roanoke), 73
Schertz, Henry R., 174, 203, 211, 214, 220, 272, 305, 380, 454; Fundamentalism and, 305, 308, 333
Schertz, John, 285
Schertz, Magdalena. *See* Ropp, Magdalena (Schertz)
Schertz, Peter D., 174
Schertz, Vernon, 212, 214, 219
Schertz, family, 65
Schlabach, Theron, 223, 265, 308, 526
Schlegel, Joseph, 181
Schleitheim, Switzerland, 36
Schleitheim Confession, 36, 55, 397
Schmidt (Smith), Christian, 31, 78, 346
Schmidt (Smith), Magdalena (Schrock), 31, 78, 346

Schmitt, John P., 73, 80, 174
Schmitt family, 73
Schowalter Oral History Project, 352
Schraeder, Don, 413
Schraeder, Ron, 212
Schrag, Conrad, 149
Schrag, David D., 446-447
Schrock, Adam, 158
Schrock, Andrew, 174, 327, 354
Schrock, Christian, 63
Schrock, Elizabeth, 278
Schrock, Elizabeth (Zentner), 63
Schrock, Mrs. Elmer, 337
Schrock, Jonathan, 82
Schrock, Joseph, 62-63, 73
Schrock, Lizzie (Bachman), 62-63
Schrock, Magdalena. *See* Schmidt (Smith), Magdalena (Schrock)
Schrock, Mildred, 442
Schrock, William, 161
Schrock family, 65
Schultz, Arnold C., 164, 242, 269, 305, 334
Schultz, David, 306
Schultz, George P., 118, 120, 123, 127, 162, 163-164, 242, 245-246, 267, 269, 278, 288, 305, 306, 334
Schultz, Peter G., 123, 418
Schuyler County, Ill., 51
Schwank, Wilmer, 149
Schwartzentruber, Hubert, 394
Science Hall, 328
Science Ridge, Ill., 44, 45
Science Ridge Mennonite Church, 43-44, 188, 191-193, 198, 199, 212, 220, 221, 238, 240, 254, 259, 293, 325, 326, 441
Science Ridge "Sisters' Meeting Day," 293

Scofield, C. I., 307, 309, 312, 513
Scofield Bible, 308, 309-310, 312
Scoggin, Aaron, 49
Scoggin, Anna (Weaver), 49
Scopes, John T., 319
Scottdale, Pa., 233, 246, 309, 320, 354, 423
Second Mennonite Church. *See* Lawndale Mennonite Church
Sedig, Elmer, 149
Selective Service Act (1948), 371
Selective Training and Service Act (1940), 360
Selma, Ala., 391
Sensenig, Isaac K., 458
Seward, William Henry, 416
Seward County, Neb., 175
Sewing Circles. *See* Ladies' Aid Society
Shalom Covenant, 452
Shank, E. C., 307
Shank, Elsa. *See* Castillo, Elsa (Shank)
Shank, Emma, 423
Shank, Joseph W., 274, 421, 422, 423
Shank, Salena (Gamber), 274
Shannon, Ill., 43
Shantz, Daniel, 46-47
Shantz, Elizabeth (Snyder), 46
Shantz, Isaac, 46-47, 49
Shantz family, 46
Shearer, Samuel, 241
Sheffield, Ill., 214
Shelby, Mich., 149
Shelby County, Ill., 133
Shelbyville, Ill., 158, 160, 161, 350
Sheldon, Charles M., 376, 379
Shellenberger, Ephraim M., 189
Shellenberger, Joseph, 43

Shellenberger, Veronica. *See* Shoemaker, Veronica (Shellenberger)
Shelley, Ward W., 384, 439
Shelly, Henry, 50, 197
Shelly, Maynard, 99, 233, 393, 419, 474-475
Shelly, Warren S., 101, 290, 359
Shelly family, 49
Shenandoah Valley, Va., 51-52
Shenk, John, 265
Shetler family, 69
Shipshewana, Ind., 93
Shoemaker, Benjamin, 43
Shoemaker, C. B., 233
Shoemaker, C. C., 233
Shoemaker, Elizabeth S. (Brubaker), 190
Shoemaker, Joseph S., 43, 186, 189-191, 192, 198, 204, 220, 233, 240, 242, 256, 260-261, 263, 265, 271, 286, 288, 347, 355, 358, 402, 405, 409-410, 417-418, 463; Fundamentalism and, 315, 325-326, 329
Shoemaker, Veronica (Shellenberger), 43
Short, Rubin D., 124, 126, 127, 130, 334
Showalter family, 49
Shultz family, 147
Shumaker, Eleanore, 424
Shumaker, William, 424
Sieber, Floyd, 217
Sieber, Paul, 213, 217
Silver Street Mennonite Church (Ind.), 102
Simons, Menno, 35, 136, 145, 253, 296, 367, 397, 491; motto of, 199
Sinsheim, Germany, 41
Sixty-second Street Mission. *See* Mennonite Gospel Mission
Slabtown, Ill., 67, 74, 98

Slagel, Arthur W., 299, 353
Slagel, Christian, 72, 73
Slagel, Vesta (Zook), 299
Slagel family, 65, 73
Slagle, Emanuel, 242
Slavery, 26, 32-33, 385-386
"Sleeping Preacher" Group. *See* Unaffiliated Amish Mennonites
Sloan, Dr. Edwin P., 291
Sloan Clinic, 291
Smith, C. Henry, 44, 46, 80, 256, 257, 348, 440, 450-451, 453, 463, 484; education of, 173, 252-254, 255; conservative-liberal controversy and, 309, 322-325, 331; peace and, 358-359, 373-374
Smith, Christian, 61
Smith, Christian (Civil War), 346
Smith, Christian H., 232
Smith, Hyrum, 32
Smith, Jacob B., 310
Smith, John, 159, 169, 174, 181, 182, 185, 186, 204, 345, 347, 374, 398, 462; education and, 172-173, 253, 256
Smith, Joseph, 32
Smith, Joseph D., 256, 288, 446
Smith, Laura (Ioder), 374
Smith, Lulu, 401
Smith, Lydia H. (Albrecht), 169, 210, 293, 405
Smith (Schmidt), Peter, 78
Smith, Tilman, 256, 446
Smith, Walter H., 299, 353
Smith family, 65
Smucker, Carl F., 447
Smucker, Don, 360
Smucker, Donovan, 486
Smucker, Ernest, 217
Smucker, J. N., 157

Smucker, Jonathan P., 185, 462
Smucker, Mary, 217
Smucker, Vernon, 311
Snavely, Abram, 147
Snavely, Christian, 43, 189
Snavely family, 44
Snyder, Christian, 41, 43, 189
Snyder, Elizabeth. *See* Shantz, Elizabeth (Snyder)
Snyder, Elvin, 422, 424
Snyder, Mario, 422
Snyder, Peter B., 196-197, 305
Social gospel, 375-385
Sommer, Adam W., 306
Sommer, Albert J., 299, 300, 353
Sommer, Emil A., 99, 100, 107
Sommer, George, 76
Sommer, George I., 189
Sommer, I. A., 463
Sommer, Jacob, 107, 270
Sommer, Oscar J., 110
Sommer (Summer) family, 65
Sommers, Emma. *See* Richards, Emma (Sommers)
Sommers, Theodore, 109
South Central Mennonite Conference, 480, 488
South Danvers Mennonite Church. *See* Danvers Mennonite Church
South Pekin, Ill., 215
South Pekin Mennonite Church, 215
South Union Mennonite Church (Ohio), 237
South Washington Mennonite Church, 95, 96, 294
South Washington Mennonite *Nähe Verein*, 294
Southwest Gospel Tabernacle. *See*

Index 609

Calvary Mennonite Church Southwestern Pennsylvania Mennonite Conference, 361
Sowell, Leaman, 430
Spaeth, Henry, 391, 431
Spanish language, 420-421
Spanish-American War, 297, 347-348, 516
Spencer, Jerry, 126
Spencer congregation (Ohio), 432
Spring Bay, Ill., 61, 65, 213
Springer, Barbara (Naffziger), 113
Springer, Benjamin, 366, 453
Springer, David, 72
Springer, Ed, 408-409, 431
Springer, George O., 299, 353
Springer, Homer, 481
Springer, Joseph, 120
Springer, William H., 110
Springer family, 65
Springfield, Ill., 31, 40, 345, 372
Springs, Pa., 158
Sprunger, Keith, 470
Sprunger, John A., 261-262, 280, 290
Sprunger, Katharine, 261
Sprunger, Milton, 368
Spurgeon, Charles, 262
Stahly, John, 90
Stahly, Stephen, 96
Stalter, Edwin J., 115, 205, 211, 220, 341, 426, 460, 480, 491-492
Stalter, Marcella, 426
Stalter family, 73
Stanford Grain Company, 110
Stanford State Bank, 110
Stauffer, Benjamin, 43
Stauffer, Harley R., 212, 340, 457
Stauffer, John L., 310

Steiner, Adam, 45
Steiner, Clara (Eby), 263, 264, 267
Steiner, E. G., 334, 362
Steiner, Menno S., 185, 186, 226-227, 240, 242, 249-250, 260, 262-264, 265, 271, 286, 305-306, 309, 347-348, 509
Steiner, Robert L., 447-448
Steinmann family, 73
Stephenson County, Ill., 41
Sterling, Ill., 43-46 *passim*, 145-147 *passim*, 193, 211, 238, 254, 260, 325, 438, 441, 459, 482
Sterling congregation. *See* Science Ridge Mennonite Church
Sterling Reformed Mennonite Church, 147-149, 377
Stevens, Thaddeus, 345
Stevenson, Alvin J., 282
Stevenson, Mathilda (Kohn), 115, 119, 281
Stewardship, 110, 413-414, 441
Stewart, R. J., 355
Stillen im Lande. See Mennonites, as quiet in the land
Stivers, Isa, 214
Stoltzfus, Amos J., 144
Stoltzfus, Edward, 488
Stoltzfus, Frank, 298
Stoltzfus, Victor, 138
Stork, David, 268
Stormer, Charles, 168
Strachan, Harry L., 308
Strasbourg, Alsace, 62
Strassburg, Pa., 145
Streid, Elizabeth, 243
Struhbar, _____, 241
Strubhar [Struphar], John, 60, 70, 85
Strubhar, Valentine, 94-96, 240, 282, 463
Stuckey, Barbara (Roth), 71

Stuckey, Joseph ("Father" Stuckey), 59, 70, 71, 81, 90-92, 96-97, 98, 100, 101-103, 105, 108, 112, 167, 232, 240, 304, 315, 331, 397; Amish conferences and 82-83, 85-87, 88-89; relationship with Christian Ropp, 89-90; inter-Mennonite cooperation and, 460, 461
Stuckey, Nicholas, 184
Stuckey, Peter, 94, 232, 240, 331
Stuckey Amish, 66, 90, 91, 96, 98, 100, 106, 108, 112, 167, 187, 241. *See also* Central Conference Mennonite Church
Stuckey Church. *See* North Danvers Mennonite Church; Stuckey Amish
Stuckey division, 86, 88-90, 91-92. *See also* Stuckey Amish
Stuckey family, 65, 120
Stutzman, Joash H., 92
Stutzman, John C., 418
Suderman, Dale, 434
Sugar Creek [Ohio] *Budget*, 136
Summer, George H., 398
Summer, J. J., 189
Summer, Joseph, 61
Summer, Peter, 185
Summerfield, Ill., 346; Mennonite settlement at, 87, 149-150
Summerfield Mennonite Church. *See* First Mennonite Church Summerfield
Summers family, 31
Summit Mills, Pa., 132
Sumner, Ill., 215
Sunday, Billy, 400
Sunday school, early Mennonite organizations, 155,

238; early advocates for, 226, 229, 230, 235, 238; benefits of, 235-236; opposition to, 44, 117, 194, 231, 235, 236-237; as start of congregations, 96, 97, 98, 100, 123, 236; extension work of, 210-215
Sunday School conferences, 106, 117, 238-239, 242, 262
Sunnyside Conservative Mennonite Church (formerly Sunnyside Conservative Amish Mennonite Church), 135, 141, 158, 213
Sutter, Christian, 72, 84, 86
Sutter, Clarence, 213
Sutter, Clayton, 446
Sutter, Lester, 217
Sutter, John, 72, 76
Sutter family, 67
Swartzendruber, Maude, 292, 293
Swartzentruber, Eli, 158
Swartzentruber, Orley, 422
Sweet, William W., 376
Sweitzer, John, 61
Sweitzer family, 65
Swiss Brethren, 34-35
Sword and Trumpet, 310
Syria, relief work in, 276
Syrian Orphanage, 299

Tampico, Ill., 160
Taylor, Thomas, 120, 379
Taylor University, 334
Tazewell County, Ill., 39, 40, 51, 60, 62, 63, 65, 67, 73, 76, 83, 96, 99
Teichroew, Allan, 353, 354
Temperance, 158, 176, 225, 375, 397, 402, 417-418
Ten Mile Creek, 61, 65
Teuscher, Daniel B., 350
Thiessen, George, 306

Thiessen, Renette, 391
Thomas, Jesse B., 32
Thomas, W. H. Griffith, 310
Thurman, Colo., 63
Tinsman, Nancy. See Kulp, Nancy (Tinsman)
Tinsman family, 49
Tiskilwa, Ill., 66, 69, 70, 91, 100-101, 107, 170, 174, 184, 210, 214, 238, 251, 327, 352, 410-411, 451
Tiskilwa Mennonite Church, 70, 100-101, 437, 451
Tobacco, 402
Toews, Henry, 100
Toews, J. S., 301
Tokyo, Japan, 97
Toledo, Ohio, 149-150, 432
Topeka, Ind., 461
Toronto, Canada, 272
Torres, Neftali, 422
Torrey, Reuben A., 305, 310
Tremont, Ill., 185, 350
Tremont Mennonite Church. *See* Pleasant Grove Mennonite Church
Trenton, Ill., 390
Trinity Mennonite Church, 455-457
Trinity United Church of Christ, 430
Tri-State University, 275
Troyer, Emanuel, 27, 100, 107, 272, 257, 292, 305, 332, 351, 407, 463
Troyer, [Dr.] George, 168, 381
Troyer, Mrs. George, 169
Troyer, Ida (Horst), 97
Troyer, John, 215, 458
Troyer, Lotus E., 96, 97, 101, 109, 389, 447, 468
Troyer, Maurice, 97, 305
Troyer, Noah, 159-160
Troyer family, 65

Tschantz, Daniel. *See* Johns, Daniel J.
Tschetter, Joseph W., 162, 163, 305
Tschetter, Mrs. Joseph W., 162
Tschetter, Paul, 98
Tuleta, Tex., 197
Turner, Frederick Jackson, 81
Twenty-sixth Street Mission (also called Mennonite Gospel Mission), 109, 269, 275, 275-277, 331

Ulrich, Emanuel C., 96, 107
Ulrich family, 65, 390
Ulrich Foundation, 381
Ulrich, Ray, 380
Ulrich, Shirley (Mrs. Wilton), 368
Ulrich, Wilfred, 213, 336
Ummel, Samuel, 99
Unaffiliated Amish Mennonites ("sleeping preacher" group), 66, 158, 160-162
Union Avenue Mennonite Church. *See* Mennonite Home Mission; Englewood Mennonite Church
Union Cemetery, 40, 41, 189
Union Mennonite Church, 40, 41, 47, 188-189, 198, 199, 221, 241, 467; Sunday school at, 41, 189, 238; close of, 48, 109, 170, 219
United Mennonite Board of Missions. *See* Congo Inland Mission
United Mennonite Church of Peoria, 279, 336
United Missionary Church, 129
United Presbyterian Church, Carlock, 101
Universalism, 51, 68, 70,

Index

86, 88-89, 91, 105
University of Chicago, 252, 253
University of Illinois, 110, 373, 470
Unrah, John D., 298-299
Unsicker, Johannes, 95
Unsicker, Katharina (Kennel), 95
Unsicker family, 65
Unzicker, Jacob, 82-83
Unzicker, Peter, 196, 197, 241
Unzicker, Roy, 107
Unzicker, William, 72
Upland, Ind., 336
Urbana-Champaign, Ill. *See* Champaign-Urbana, Ill.
Urbanism, 415-416, 432-435; Mennonites distinctives and, 433-435; rural Mennonites and, 436-437
"Urban-Racial Concerns," 389
Ursinus College, 228

Van der Smissen, Carl Heinrich Anton, 155
Vandalia, Ill., 40, 133
Varennes, France, 299
Ventura, Frank, 422
Vercler, Andrew, 97
Vercler, Ralph, 480
Verkler, John, 61
Verkler, Joseph, 61
Vietnam War, 368-369, 371, 418-419, 489
Villa Park, Ill., 405
Vincennes, Ind., 40
Virginia Mennonite Conference, 236, 237, 261
Virkler (Verkler), Peter, 166
Virkler family, 65
Vogt, Gerhard, 257
Vogt, Virgil, 216, 410
Voluntary Service, 216, 301, 372, 377, 427, 431, 489
Voth, Lawrence, 385, 430, 431

Voz Menonita, La, 423

Wabash River, 27, 40
Wadsworth, Ohio, 151, 152, 194
Wadsworth First Mennonite Church, 194
Wadsworth Institute. *See* Wadsworth Mennonite School
Wadsworth Mennonite School, 79, 152-153, 226, 249, 251, 259
Wagler (Wagner), 65, 73
Wagner, Joseph, 73
Wahreitsfreund, Der, 163, 299
Waldo Amish Mennonite Church. *See* Waldo Mennonite Church
Waldo Cemetery, 115
Waldo Mennonite Church (formerly Waldo Amish Mennonite Church), 31, 67, 72-73, 86, 96, 113, 115, 168, 174, 182, 185, 343, 383, 437, 469, 483
Waldo Township, Livingston County, Ill., 73
Wall, Jacob E., 306
Wall, James, 419
Wall, John N., 306
Walnut Grove Academy. *See* Eureka college
Waltner, Erland, 109
Waltner, James, 455, 480
War of 1812, 26, 27, 28, 37
Warkentin, Abraham, 157, 373
Warkentin, Bernhard, 149, 154, 155
Warm Springs, Va., 40
Warren County, Ill., 48, 52
Washburn, Ill., 169
Washington, D.C., 40, 47
Washington, Ill., 40, 41, 47, 65, 92, 94, 101, 107, 110, 169, 188,

611

196, 197, 215, 238, 241, 243, 283, 288, 367, 482
Watchful Pilgrim, 231
Waterloo, Ind., 118
Waterloo, Ont., 314
Waterloo County, Ont., 46, 47, 237
Watson family, 147
Watson Gailey Foundation-Mennonite Hospital Eye Bank, 292
"Way of Christian Love and Race Relations, The," 389
Wayland, Iowa, 99, 424
Wayne County, Ohio, 82; 83, 90, 184
Weaver, Anna. *See* Scoggin, Anna (Weaver)
Weaver, Edwin, 274, 387-388, 422
Weaver, Irene, 274
Weaver, Vinora. *See* Salzman, Vinora (Weaver)
Weaver, William B., 91, 92, 97, 98, 101, 102, 107, 233, 236, 245; education and, 258; Fundamentalism and, 316, 330-331; ministry of, 92-94, 99; writing and editing of, 234, 465-466
Weaver family, 44
Weber, A. I., 305
Weber, Harry F., 44, 60, 65, 98, 185, 186-187, 204, 441, 444, 478
Weekly [Bloomington] *Pantagraph, The*, 71
Weierhof, Germany, 39
Wenger, A. D., 242, 305, 309
Wenger, John Christian, 35, 159, 305
Wentland, Theodore, 212, 427
Wesley City, Ill., 60, 61, 82
Wesley City Amish congregation. *See* Groveland Evangelical

Mennonite Church
West Clyde Schoolhouse, 46
West Liberty, Ohio, 85, 237, 245, 285
West Point, Iowa, 150, 151, 194
West Sterling Mennonite Church, 212, 213, 340, 457-458
West Swamp Mennonite Church (Pa.), 237
Western Amish Mennonite Sunday School Conference, 405
Western District Amish Mennonite Conference, 45, 87, 109, 141, 159, 170, 405, 417; Fundamentalism and, 313; extent of, 167, 172; annual sessions of, 171-174, 182; leaders of, 172-175; merger with Illinois Mennonite conference 172, 174, 185-187, 221; organization of, 174, relation to congregations, 175; decisions of, 175-181, 237, 243, 313; Illinois ministers meeting of, 175, 186; education and, 251; mutual aid in, 295; temperance and, 398
Western District Conference (GC), 153, 480
Western Suburban Mennonite Fellowship. *See* Lombard Mennonite Church
Weston, Ill., 92, 96
Weston congregation, 96
Wetzel, Conrad, 411
Weyeneth, Benedict, 166
Wheaton College, 334
White Sulphur Springs, Va., 40
Whiten, Bennie, 434

Whitermore, David M., 415, 432-433, 434, 435, 522
Whiteside County, Ill., 43, 45, 145, 161, 193
Whitmer, Paul E., 253; conservative-liberal controversy and, 311, 322, 325
Whitmore, Willy, 252
Whitmore family, 49
Wichita, Kan., 429
Widmer, Gladys, 424
Wiebe, Frank, 306
Wiebe, Jacob A., 163
Wiens, Abraham F., 156, 163, 267, 277-278
Wiens, Katherine, 163, 277
Willard, Frances E., 397-398
Willow Springs Amish Mennonite Church. *See* Willow Springs Mennonite Church
Willow Springs Mennonite Church (formerly Willow Springs Amish Mennonite Church), 69-70, 91, 100, 169, 174, 182, 184-185, 210, 214, 238, 381, 413, 437, 451
Wilson, Woodrow, 349, 350, 354, 355, 516
Winger, Adam, 53, 54
Winona Lake School of Theology, 164, 340
Winter, Conrad, 48
Winteregg, Bryce, 124
"Wisconsin vs. Yoder" (1972), 135, 143-144
Wisler Mennonites, 223
Witmarsum Theological Seminary, 109, 119, 157, 255, 257, 258, 464; start of, 328-329; difficulties at, 321, 322, 323, 324, 325, 327-329, 330-332
Wittmer, John, 149
Wittrig, Mrs., 99
Wittrig, Howard, 215

WMBI (radio station), 305, 308
Woman Liberated, 405
Women, 112, 116, 200, 208-209, 213, 216, 221, 365; ordinations of, 216, 407-408, 452-453; Sunday schools and, 238; at Moody Bible Institute, 305; conservative-liberal controversy and, 324, 325, 326; rights of, 375, 400, 404-409, 415; dress of, 490; church membership of, 151, 429-430; education of, 74, 305
Women in the Church, 408
Women's Christian Temperance Society, 397
Women's District Missionary Society, 186, 293
Women's organizations, 92, 106, 117, 155, 168, 198, 293-294
Wood, Jethro, 76
Woodburn, Ind., 121
Woodford County, Ill., 41, 46, 58-83 *passim*
Woodlawn Mennonite Church, 157, 369, 384, 385, 392-396, 401, 471
World Council of Churches, 341
World Court, 358, 359
World Missionary Conference, 260
World Peace Conference, 306
World War I, 108, 116, 171, 227-228, 293, 297, 299, 308, 373, 387, 400, 420, 451, 465, 485-486; peace activities after, 357-360; surveillance of Mennonites during, 353-356; Mennonites and, 348-358, 360,

Index 613

362, 364
World War II, 108, 140, 301, 367, 451, 453; alternative service in, 141, 360-366, 466; Mennonites and, 360-366, 370; peace activities before, 357-360. *See also* Civilian Public Service; alternative service
World's Christian Fundamentals Association, 303-304
Wrangel, General, 299
Wright, Ambers, 430

Yake, Clayton F., 246
Yellow Creek Mennonite Church (Ind.), 44, 231-232
Yoder, A. G., 178
Yoder, Aden, 382, 440
Yoder, Allen, 107
Yoder, D. S., 264
Yoder, D. Z., 184
Yoder, Mr. and Mrs. Elvan, 143, 501
Yoder, Frances, 274
Yoder, Harry, 94, 101, 258
Yoder, J. Otis, 274
Yoder, Jared, 457-458
Yoder, John Howard, 343
Yoder, John K., 82, 90
Yoder, Jonathan, 65, 70-71, 82-83, 85, 88, 91, 97
Yoder, Moses, 132
Yoder, Raymond M., 98, 272, 274, 316, 335, 336
Yoder, Robert, 413
Yoder, Sanford C., 172, 258, 288, 317, 388, 421
Yoder, Simon S., 107
Yoder, Solomon, 82
Yoder, Thomas, 195-196, 218, 437, 453-454, 527, 558
Yoder, Walter E., 326, 467
Yoder Amish congregation. *See* North Danvers Mennonite Church
Yoder family, 65
Yordy, Anna, 274, 308
Yordy, Clarence, 481
Yordy, Ezra, 174, 178, 179-180, 220
Yordy, Richard J., 211, 213, 220, 415, 439, 445, 470, 472, 477
Yordy, Walter, 427, 428
Yordy family, 65, 390
Yother, Henry, 53
Young, Andrew, 391
Young, Brigham, 32
Young Companion, 136
Young People, 116, 243-245, 246, 395, 397, 468, 469-470, 476, 487
Young People's Christian Association of Goshen College, 301
Young People's Organizations, 92, 106, 117, 155, 242-246, 301, 468, 482; conventions of, 245-246, 254; opposition to, 198, 203
Young People's Paper, 263
Young People's Problems Committee, 203
Yutzy, Norman, 220

Zehr, Christian, 74
Zehr, Elizabeth (Ehresman), 74
Zehr, George, 72
Zehr, Harold A., 168, 215, 216, 293, 337-339, 381, 389, 470, 477
Zehr, Howard J., 168, 210, 212, 220-221, 336, 338, 340
Zehr, Jacob, 71, 73-75, 78, 90
Zehr, Joseph B., 96
Zehr, Peter, 74, 79
Zehr, Peter (Fisher), 168, 169, 356
Zehr, Reuben J., 97, 98, 332-333
Zehr, Robert E., 214, 335, 336
Zehr, Samuel S., 168
Zehr family, 31, 65, 74
Zenst, John, 47
Zentner, Elizabeth. *See* Schrock, Elizabeth (Zentner)
Zierlein family, 69
Zimmerman, Andrew, 83
Zimmerman, Anna. *See* Beller, Anna (Zimmerman)
Zimmerman, Anna F., 115, 119
Zimmerman, Barbara. *See* Reeser, Barbara (Zimmerman)
Zimmerman, Charles, 378
Zimmerman, D. M., 115
Zimmerman, David, 298
Zimmerman, Elias E., 115, 120, 130, 445, 526
Zimmerman, Gordon, 256
Zimmerman, Joseph, 178
Zimmerman, Peter, 158, 160, 161
Zimmerman family, 65
Zimmerman Ford, Ill., 75
Zion Chapel (Goshen, Ind.), 457
Zion Mennonite Church (Ohio), 262
Zion's Call, 118, 234
Zion's Tidings, 118, 128, 234, 334, 362
Zook, A. R., 264
Zook, J. Kore, 194
Zook, John R., 160
Zook, Vesta. *See* Slagel, Vesta (Zook)
Zook, Walter A., 261
Zook family, 65, 194
Zoss, Rosina. *See* Bohn, Rosina (Zoss)
Zuck, Mr., 58
Zur Heimath, 225, 228
Zurich, Switzerland, 34, 35, 36
Zwingli, Ulrich, 34

Willard Harvey Smith, professor emeritus of history at Goshen College, Goshen, Indiana, since 1972, was born to John J. and Catherine E. Smith on October 15, 1900, at Eureka, Illinois. He was married to Verna Graber at Wayland, Iowa, on September 3, 1930.

He received his formal education at Goshen College (BA), University of Michigan (MA), University of Chicago (postgraduate work), and Indiana University (PhD).

At Goshen College he was instructor in history (1929-35), dean of men (1932-35), and professor of history (1937-72). He headed the department of history and chaired the division of social sciences from 1949-68.

Smith was director of the Mennonite Central Committee work in Paraguay (1944-45) and in Mexico (1955). He led student groups to Europe (1953) and to Mexico and Central America (1955-57, 1961, 1964, 1972).

He is author of *Paraguayan Interlude* (Herald Press, 1950); *Schuyler Colfax—The Changing Fortunes of a Political Idol*, Indiana Historical Bureau (1952); *William Jennings Bryan, Christian Reformer* (Bryan College, 1969); and *The Social and Religious Thought of William Jennings Bryan* (Coronado Press, 1975). He has contributed to *Indiana Magazine of History, Mississippi Valley Historical Review, Proceedings of Indiana Academy of Social Sciences, Mennonite Quarterly Review, Journal of American History,* and *Journal of Negro History.*

Smith's professional affiliations include Mennonite Historical

Society (board of directors and consulting editor, 1940-); American Historical Association; Organization of American Historians; and Indiana Academy of Social Sciences (board of directors, 1963-65). He is a former member of the Indiana History Teachers Association (president 1954).

A member of College Mennonite Church at Goshen, he enjoys music and travel.

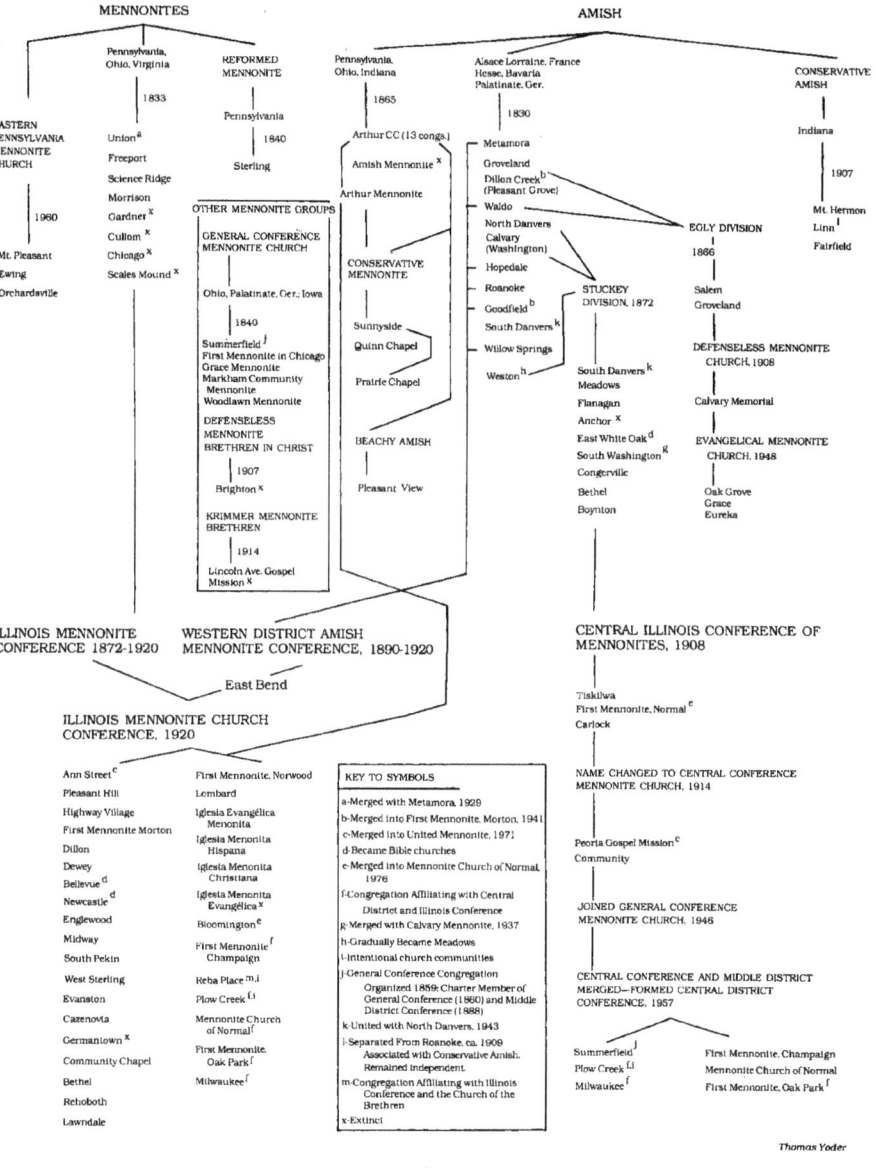

ORIGINS OF ILLINOIS AMISH AND MENNONITES

Thomas Yoder

www.ingramcontent.com/pod-product-compliance
Lightning Source LLC
Chambersburg PA
CBHW052041290426
44111CB00011B/1579